"Adrian Pabst presents here an extraordinary survey of Western metaphysical doctrine from a political-theological perspective. He narrates how reality as participation was lost as the result of specific turnings in the history of ontology. In doing so Pabst takes the current debate about theology and metaphysics to a new level, while exploring how conceptions of relationality and individuation impact on how we conceive the political. No scholar or student of theology, philosophy, or politics could fail to benefit from reading this book. It is a brilliant contribution."

— WAYNE HUDSON
University of Tasmania

"Pabst's *Metaphysics* challenges both metaphysicians and theologians to find a more effective way of working together in a revivification of some Trinitarian religious life in the world, under what it calls a new imperative of relationality, to counteract the absolutization of individuality. . . . This is a book that should interest not only metaphysicians and theologians but also all those who find themselves cut off from any need to transcend their human condition as isolated individuals caught in a struggle for survival."

— OLIVA BLANCHETTE
Boston College

"This bold new study argues for the pivotal importance of both the Christian doctrine of *creatio ex nihilo* and the theology of participation in the development of Western metaphysics and political thought. Pabst explores their subsequent degeneration and decline when, in modernity, these teachings were forgotten or discarded. A clarion call to recover the economy of love, grounded in the gift — and a welcome new voice in political philosophy."

— JANET SOSKICE
Jesus College,
University of Cambridge

D1546280

INTERVENTIONS

Conor Cunningham and Peter Candler

GENERAL EDITORS

It's not a question of whether one believes in God or not. Rather, it's a question of if, in the absence of God, we can have belief, any belief.

"If you live today," wrote Flannery O'Connor, "you breathe in nihilism." Whether "religious" or "secular," it is "the very gas you breathe." Both within and without the academy, there is an air common to both deconstruction and scientism — both might be described as species of *reductionism.* The dominance of these modes of knowledge in popular and professional discourse is quite incontestable, perhaps no more so where questions of theological import are often subjugated to the margins of intellectual respectability. Yet it is precisely the proponents and defenders of religious belief in an age of nihilism that are often — unwittingly or not — among those most complicit in this very reduction. In these latter cases, one frequently spies an accommodationist impulse, whereby our concepts must be first submitted to a prior philosophical court of appeal in order for them to render any intellectual value. To cite one particularly salient example, debates over the origins, nature, and ends of human life are routinely partitioned off into categories of "evolutionism" and "creationism," often with little nuance. Where attempts to mediate these arguments are to be found, frequently the strategy is that of a kind of accommodation: How can we adapt our belief in creation to an already established evolutionary metaphysic, or, how can we have our evolutionary cake and eat it too? It is sadly the case that, despite the best intentions of such "intellectual ecumenism," the distinctive voice of theology is the first one to succumb to aphonia — either from impetuous overuse or from a deliberate silencing.

The books in this unique new series propose no such simple accommodation. They rather seek and perform tactical interventions in such debates in a manner that problematizes the accepted terms of such debates. They propose something altogether more demanding: through a kind of refusal of the disciplinary isolation now standard in modern universities, a genuinely interdisciplinary series of mediations of crucial concepts and key figures in contemporary thought. These volumes will attempt to discuss these topics as they are articulated within their own field, including their historical emergence and cultural significance, which will provide a way into seemingly abstract discussions. At the same time, they aim to analyze what consequences such thinking may have for theology, both positive and negative, and, in light of these new perspectives, to develop an effective response — one that will better situate students of theology and professional theologians alike within the most vital debates informing Western society, and so increase their understanding of, participation in, and contribution to these.

To a generation brought up on a diet of deconstruction, on the one hand, and scientism, on the other, Interventions offers an alternative that is *otherwise than nihilistic* — doing so by approaching well-worn questions and topics, as well as historical and contemporary figures, from an original and interdisciplinary angle, and so avoiding having to steer a course between the aforementioned Scylla and Charybdis.

This series will also seek to navigate not just through these twin dangers, but also through the dangerous "and" that joins them. That is to say, it will attempt to be genuinely interdisciplinary in avoiding the conjunctive approach to such topics that takes as paradigmatic a relationship of "theology and phenomenology" or "religion and science." Instead, the volumes in this series will, in general, attempt to treat such discourses not as discrete disciplines unto themselves, but as moments within a distended theological performance. Above all, they will hopefully contribute to a renewed atmosphere shared by theologians and philosophers (not to mention those in other disciplines) — an air that is not nothing.

CENTRE OF THEOLOGY AND PHILOSOPHY

(www.theologyphilosophycentre.co.uk)

Every doctrine which does not reach the one thing necessary, every separated philosophy, will remain deceived by false appearances. It will be a doctrine, it will not be Philosophy.

Maurice Blondel, 1861-1949

This book series is the product of the work carried out at the Centre of Theology and Philosophy (COTP), at the University of Nottingham.

The COTP is a research-led institution organized at the interstices of theology and philosophy. It is founded on the conviction that these two disciplines cannot be adequately understood or further developed, save with reference to each other. This is true in historical terms, since we cannot comprehend our Western cultural legacy unless we acknowledge the interaction of the Hebraic and Hellenic traditions. It is also true conceptually, since reasoning is not fully separable from faith and hope, or conceptual reflection from revelatory disclosure. The reverse also holds, in either case.

The Centre is concerned with:

- the historical interaction between theology and philosophy.
- the current relation between the two disciplines.
- attempts to overcome the analytic/continental divide in philosophy.
- the question of the status of "metaphysics": Is the term used equivocally? Is it now at an end? Or have twentieth-century attempts to have a postmetaphysical philosophy themselves come to an end?
- the construction of a rich Catholic humanism.

I am very glad to be associated with the endeavors of this extremely important Centre that helps to further work of enormous importance. Among its concerns is the question whether modernity is more an interim than a completion — an interim between a premodernity in which the porosity between theology and philosophy was granted, perhaps taken for granted, and a postmodernity where their porosity must be unclogged and enacted anew. Through the work of leading theologians of international stature and philosophers whose writings bear on this porosity, the Centre offers an exciting forum to advance in diverse ways this challenging, entirely needful, and cutting-edge work.

Professor William Desmond, Leuven

METAPHYSICS

The Creation of Hierarchy

Adrian Pabst

WILLIAM B. EERDMANS PUBLISHING COMPANY

GRAND RAPIDS, MICHIGAN / CAMBRIDGE, U.K.

Published 2012 by

Wm. B. Eerdmans Publishing Co.

2140 Oak Industrial Drive N.E., Grand Rapids, Michigan 49505 /
P.O. Box 163, Cambridge CB3 9PU U.K.

Printed in the United States of America

17 16 15 14 13 12   7 6 5 4 3 2 1

Library of Congress Cataloging-in-Publication Data

Pabst, Adrian.
Metaphysics: the creation of hierarchy / Adrian Pabst.
p.   cm. — (Interventions)
Includes bibliographical references (p.   ) and index.
ISBN 978-0-8028-6451-2 (pbk.: alk. paper)
1. Metaphysics — History. 2. Individuation (Philosophy) — History.
3. Philosophical theology.   I. Title.

BD111.P28   2012

110 — dc23

2011041671

www.eerdmans.com

In memoriam

Ruth L. Pabst

11 May 1917–21 February 2006

Contents

CONTENTS

CONTENTS

Contents

Foreword

John Milbank

This is a remarkable work that breaks new ground in both philosophical and political theology. In his book Adrian Pabst achieves two things. First of all, he successfully recasts the terms in which the history of the metaphysics of individuation has been written. Second, he outlines more precisely than hitherto the links between ontological individuation, on the one hand, and the political understanding of the human individual, on the other hand.

The first achievement is the most extensively realized. Broadly speaking, philosophical treatments of individuation, while they may gesture towards the Platonic theory of forms, tend to deal with it in strictly immanentist terms. How and why things occur always in an individual mode is seen as a strictly this-worldly problem. Pabst, however, carefully delineates the genealogy of this approach, from Avicenna and Gilbert Porreta in the eleventh and the twelfth centuries through the late scholasticism of John Duns Scotus and William of Ockham to Suárez, Spinoza, Kant, and even some contemporary thinkers such as Husserl and Heidegger. Correspondingly, he argues that the main axis of division within the treatment of this topic has lain historically between those who treat it theologically and those who effectively bracket God out of the picture — even if they do so for paradoxically theological reasons.

He first of all sets up this division through a contrast of Aristotle with Plato. In Aristotle one has the germs of the immanentist approach. Individuation concerns the coming together of form with matter (and here Pabst rightly eschews over-simplistic readings of this in terms of matter alone as the individuating factor) within an individual concrete substance. The first mover is relatively removed from this scenario because, while it is the final lure of actualization, it is not the generative source of temporal actuality or form. In consequence, individuation is a kind of 'autonomous' achievement rather than being defined relationally. On the latter conception, by contrast, the 'individuality' of a thing is essentially its positioning in relation to other things. It is this model that Plato embraces, *just because* he understands the transcendent realm governed by the Good as 'giving itself' ecstatically to finitude in an original relation whose reverse face is the 'participation' of temporal things in the realm of the forms which alone brings about their particular existence.

This account is as simple and original as it is scholarly, careful, and nuanced. Pabst is also quick to do justice to Aristotle: Plato cannot really explain the role of matter in individuation, and here Aristotle's language of potency and act is indispensable. But he is surely right to argue that the Christian and pagan Neo-Platonist synthesis of Plato with Aristotle conserved the Platonic priority of relation over substance. Linked to this is the notion of the first principle as generative and self-giving. Pabst stresses other metaphysical nuances that survive all the way from Plato to Aquinas. For example, 'individuality' is linked to transcendental unity, such that God himself is hyper-individual and therefore it is not so much that something general is problematically converted into something specific as rather that a supreme mode of united 'definiteness' (*yliatim* for Aquinas in his commentary on the *Liber de Causis*) is channeled into a more limited mode of the same thing. Thus, the Neo-Platonist metaphysics of individuation shows how the unique individuality of each and every particular human being really is the image and likeness of God in which we are all created. The hierarchy of Creator and creation fuses the ontological difference with radical equality amongst creatures and their — supernaturally infused — natural desire for the supernatural good in God of which they partake.

Here he rightly speaks against both monism and 'postmodern' pluralism in the name of a certain mediation between the one and the many. This is already present in Plato as the aesthetic interplay between the One and the Dyad or as the 'horizontal' participation amongst the forms themselves, which constitutes their mutual positioning or 'individuation.' Pabst brings out the way in which, already for Plato, this 'relational positioning' belongs in the transcendent realm of the forms and constitutes the precondition for participation, which can be understood as an asymmetrical one-way pure relationship of dependence.

Perhaps more than any other previous author, Pabst argues that this priority of relation within Platonism is the most fundamental reason why the Neo-Platonist (Platonic-Aristotelian) legacy is a constitutive aspect of Christianity — as Pope Benedict XVI has repeatedly suggested. For clearly the doctrine of the Trinity tends to accentuate just this priority, as Pabst recounts in his reading of Augustine and Boethius. Augustine shows that creation *ex nihilo* newly brings matter itself within the scope of originating asymmetrical relationality, while the supremacy of relation over substance in the case of the Godhead itself is affirmed by Boethius.

Pabst's choice of authors and texts over a long historical stretch is exemplary. Clearly Augustine had to be dealt with, but Boethius also proves crucial for two reasons. First of all, he newly reintegrated Aristotle within Augustine's vision, in terms of the priority of act and the notion that the creative relation with finite particularity is most of all a giving of a share in being or actuality itself. But second, while Aquinas stressed this 'existential' aspect of Boethius, he was read in an opposite sense (deemed by Pabst to be wrong) by the influential Gilbert Porreta, who argued in his commentary on the Roman author for a priority of essence over existence.

The book shows that Gilbert's 'Mathematical Platonism' or 'Platonism of essence' (after Porphyry), rather than of transcendental being or unity, helped to shape both a turn to the primacy of logic and semantics over metaphysics and a more immanentist construal of individuation. Instead of the latter being seen as a limited 'share' of divine unity, it is now seen either as a transcendentally necessary logical category or as a state of affairs simply willed by God and telling us nothing of the inner divine reality at all. Here there are striking parallels with some aspects of key Islamic philosophers and theologians, as Pabst shows more clearly than most other scholars.

Essentially he contends that a long line of thinkers elaborated variations on these twin themes — from Duns Scotus and the nominalists such as Ockham via Baroque scholastics like Suárez and early modern figures such as Descartes and Spinoza to Wolff and Kant, and also virtually all of their contemporary disciples (including Deleuze and Derrida). Once creation is no longer seen as participation, it is gradually reduced to efficient causality, which means that particularity is regarded as either a simple result of a divine *fiat* or as something brought about by an individual thing itself under a transcendental compulsion (or both at the same time). So, on the one hand, individuation retreats into fideistic mystery, but, on the other hand, it ceases to be something that requires explanation at all, because 'being individual' is now seen as the transcendental condition for existing or making sense in any fashion whatsoever. Thus by the time one reaches Suárez in the late sixteenth and early seventeenth centuries, individuality has an absolute ontological priority and all things 'are' in themselves before they enter into relation with each other. This also means that an individual thing, even though it is caused by God as existing, is not thought of as created with especial respect to its individual nature. For this is no longer seen as a participation in divine unity but instead as a state of affairs that makes complete sense in finite terms alone, bracketing God out of the picture.

Pabst therefore argues that the more 'secular,' immanentist approach to individuation was itself the paradoxical result both of a 'Platonism of essence' in a line from Porphyry through Gilbert, and of a fideistic and voluntarist theology — which can be found in both Christian and Muslim thinkers, as chapter 4 documents. At many points in his monograph he ably points out the metaphysical arbitrariness of such an approach and hence its questionability on objective philosophical grounds.

At the center of the book lies the exposition of Aquinas, who is seen here as elaborating Boethius. Pabst clearly demonstrates that individuation for Aquinas is not simply carried out by matter alone or even by the matter/form complex alone, as for Aristotle, but rather by the act of participation in being which realizes form. Hence Aquinas's account is entirely relational and theological, and it restores Neo-Platonist metaphysics to the heart of Christian theology against the logicized 'Platonism of essence' — an argument that has perhaps never been made so clearly hitherto.

By contrast, the tradition that stretches from Gilbert via Scotus and Ockham to Suárez eschews metaphysics in favor of ontology, which is essentially a transcendental science of what can be known about univocal being. This includes Spinoza, who is seen as developing some late scholastic problematics and as representing the emergence of a 'secular' treatment of the problem now within an avowedly immanentist metaphysics. Here Pabst adroitly shows that, without transcendence, particularity cannot really be explained relationally, and therefore that finitude must here remain a surd mystery. This verdict then falls back upon the earlier writers since Scotus: viewed nonrelationally, individuation lacks any ultimate causal ground accessible to human reason in any measure whatsoever and is grounded in a blind belief that foregrounds a narrow natural rationality cut off from any infusion of supernatural faith. Paradoxically, both rationalism and fideism are from the outset wedded to the nominalist and voluntarist ontology that displaced the realist and intellectualist metaphysics of Christian Neo-Platonism.

The book's second achievement is to indicate some of the political corollaries of all this. Pabst's main political argument concerns the removal of God from the political sphere, and he wishes to show that this is itself grounded in the metaphysical removal of God from individuation as such. Thus from Aristotle through to Suárez, he shows how the individual prior to relation will generate a politics of either individual or collective autonomy, deficient in any true sense of a sharing in a common good and the primacy of a specific set of relations and reciprocal duties over individual rights — which can only be abstract and empty when not referred to such a context. A polity not acknowledging its relation to God (in receptivity and gratitude) will prove to be a polity without true human relations — bound either to disintegrate or else to submit to an enforced tyrannical unity. Pabst successfully shows how, even in the case of Spinoza, advocated democracy is but a desperate and second-best device designed to make the competitions of ignorant individuals balance each other out. (This claim runs strongly against the dominant consensus of Spinoza scholarship.)

This is an incredibly ambitious undertaking for a first monograph. But the astonishing thing is that Pabst has brought it off and in a relatively short compass. His scholarship is exemplary and on the whole cautious; his mastery of many languages evident. The very original main argument emerges as it were organically, almost by stealth and entirely without swagger — namely, that the Christian Neo-Platonist theory of individuation is 'relational and positional' only because it is theological. This got abandoned for a logicized (and de-Platonized Aristotelian) theory that posits a substantive 'self-individuation' because it brackets God, even though it did so for initially theological reasons.

This is the philosophical novelty of this book. But it also possesses a theological one: with extraordinary simplicity and directness Pabst shows here, more clearly I think than anyone else hitherto, just how Trinitarian theology and a theology of creation as participation hang together under the category of relation. An awful lot has been written in recent years about the primacy of relation by Christian theologians. Pabst confirms their intuition yet also exposes their attempt to explicate it for the paltry stuff it mostly is: especially in terms of the dismissal of Plato, Augustine, and Aquinas, who are perhaps the main heroes of his account.

Pabst's arguments are equally significant for contemporary political theology, particularly with respect to the post-Schmittian theory of sovereignty and the debate between Jürgen Habermas and Joseph Cardinal Ratzinger (now Pope Benedict XVI) regarding the foundations of the democratic state and the place of religion therein.[1] He has been exploring the thesis common to both the latter — that we are now in a 'postsecular' phase where religious and other ideological bodies should be able to express themselves directly in their own terms within the public square. However, for Habermas the norms to regulate this debate remain procedural and majoritarian. For Ratzinger, by contrast, there must be a plural search for a shared common good, which notably he does not say is merely pregiven in a readily known natural law. Thus in the latter case a reinvention of constitutional corporatism in a more pluralist guise against modern liberalism is linked to an insistence on fundamental metaphysical relationality and basic social units above the level of the individual — such as communities, groups, and associations that constitute the realm of civil society, which should embed both the central state and the free market.

Equally it is linked to a stress, encouraged by other Catholic thinkers like Robert Spaemann, Luigi Giussanni, and Alasdair MacIntyre, that education as the transmission and exploration of the truth is as fundamental a dimension of politics as the will of a democratic majority. The modern political right has always focused on the absolute power of the one and the arbitrary right to decide on the state of exception, while the modern left has insisted on an equally absolute right of the many to found and withdraw legitimacy. Thus both can be taken to ignore the primacy of natural and cultural relation, and of the mediating role of 'the few' concerned with truth and virtue. A politics focused on the latter would be a more theological politics, which would define the secular realm as concerned with things in time and with necessary coercion, only through its ultimate outlook towards transcendent norms that alone supply ultimate standards beyond the will either of the one or of the many.

By investigating these new proposals, Pabst is asking nothing less

---

1. See Adrian Pabst, "Modern Sovereignty in Question: Theology, Democracy and Capitalism," *Modern Theology* 26, no. 4 (October 2010): 570-602.

than "whether our politics of 'right and left' remains caught within shared secular, liberal axioms — axioms that are *also* those of theocratic fundamentalisms since they too deal in a politics of the indifferent will, inherited — as is ultimately the case for liberalism — from the theological voluntarism of the late Middle Ages." Further, he continues:

> This is not at all to search for a new political center; on the contrary, it is to search for a way that cannot be charted on our current conceptual map. It is to investigate again notions of fundamental relationality, of the common good and economic reciprocity, and of principles that can determine appropriate 'mixtures' of government as between the one, the few, and the many; the center and localities; political government and prepolitical society; international community and nations; education in time and government in space; absolute right and free decision; economic freedom and just distribution; and finally, secular and religious authorities. In short, it is to investigate whether we might enter into a new sort of postsecular politics beyond modern liberal norms. (Conclusion, p. 449)

This enterprise is of the greatest possible relevance for questions of the relationship of faith to politics and encourages thinking that refuses both religious fundamentalism and secular dogmatism. Pabst is endeavoring to explore ways in which some degree of shared metaphysics and religious vision across faiths can help to shape a new political agenda, while also trying to work out both the possibilities and limits of areas of valid autonomy for different religious groups. Like the current patriarchs of Rome, Moscow, and Canterbury, he tends to see 'pluralism of sovereignty' as both a political position shared by different faith groupings and one that will allow a certain social play to their differences.

This book does nothing less than to set new standards in combining philosophical with political theology. Pabst's argument about relationality has the potential to change debates in theology, philosophy, and politics.

Acknowledgments

This book draws on my doctoral dissertation at Cambridge which I wrote between 2002 and 2006 under the guidance of Dr. Catherine Pickstock. I revised and expanded my Ph.D. thesis during my time at the Centre of Theology and Philosophy at the University of Nottingham from 2007 to 2009 with the encouragement and help of Professor John Milbank. The manuscript was finally completed after I moved to the University of Kent at Canterbury with the support of Professor Richard Sakwa.

I am indebted to Conor Cunningham and Peter M. Candler Jr. for including my monograph in the Interventions series at Wm. B. Eerdmans. I would also like to thank SCM for granting me permission to reproduce in chapter 4 material from a previously published essay: 'Sovereign Reason Unbound: The Proto-modern Legacy of Avicenna and Gilbert Porreta,' in *The Grandeur of Reason: Religion, Tradition and Universalism,* ed. Peter M. Chandler Jr. and Conor Cunningham (London: SCM, 2010), pp. 135-66.

First of all, I wish to acknowledge various sources of financial assistance: Bourse Formation-Recherche (Ministère de la Culture, de l'Enseignement supérieur et de la Recherche du Grand-Duché de Luxembourg), a Burney Studentship and the Gregg Bury Fund (Faculty of Divinity, University of Cambridge), a bursary from the Cambridge European Trust, as well as an early Career Fellowship from the Leverhulme Trust.

My special thanks go to Dr. Armand Clesse, Director of the Luxembourg Institute for European and International Studies, whose generosity has enabled me to pursue my research while working as a Research Fellow for ten years. I am immensely grateful to him for his continual support. I would also like to acknowledge the help of my colleagues at the Institute, in particular Ms. Denise Schauls and Mrs. Anemone Thomas.

I would like to thank Anthony Baker, Phillip Blond, Matthew Bullimore, Pete Candler, Conor Cunningham, Andrew Davison, Erik Friedel, Alessandra Gerolin, Karl Hefty, John Hughes, Samuel Kimbriel, Didier Mineur, James Noyes, Simon Oliver, Quentin Perret, Aaron Riches, Christoph Schneider, and Olivier-Thomas Venard, OP. To all I wish to convey my deep appreciation for their friendship, conversation, and encouragement.

I also wish to thank all those whom I have studied under or learned from during my studies of theology, philosophy, and political thought. At the London School of Economics and Political Science, I benefited greatly from Professor John Gray's teaching on liberalism and its late modern critics as well as from Professor Paul Kelly's lectures on modern political philosophy. I owe a special debt of gratitude to Professor Jean-Marie Donegani from the Institut d'Études Politiques de Paris, who directed me towards political theology. I also had the privilege of working with some of the best minds at the Institut Catholique de Paris, including Professor Olivier Boulnois, Professor Philippe Capelle, Professor Henri-Jérôme Gagey, Professor Jean Greisch, Professor Emmanuel Falque, and Gilles Berceville, OP.

At Cambridge, I would like to acknowledge all those in the Faculty of Divinity and at Peterhouse who supported my research, notably Dr. Timothy Jenkins, Dr. Philip Pattenden, Professor Janet Martin Soskice, and Dr. Tony Street. At the Centre for Research in the Arts, Social Sciences and Humanities (CRASSH), I had the chance to work with Professor Ludmilla Jordanova and Professor Roberto Scazzieri, and I am very grateful for their manifold contributions and helpful advice. The late Emile Perreau-Saussine was an outstanding teacher and fine mind, and he is greatly missed.

My Ph.D. examiner, Fergus Kerr, OP, has been a constant source of support. I am very grateful for his incisive comments on my doctoral dissertation and his generous help in relation to my postdoctoral research.

I owe the greatest debt of gratitude to Dr. Catherine Pickstock, for her imagination, rigor, and ceaseless encouragement, and to Professor John Milbank for his boundless generosity, support, and wisdom.

Above all, I would like to thank my family, in particular my parents, Reinhart and Brigitte, for their lifelong love and faith in me, and my sister

ACKNOWLEDGMENTS

Stephanie for her continual care and help. To my wife Elena, I give thanks for unconditional love and unfailing loyalty. I am especially grateful to my dear grandmother Ruth, an exceptionally courageous woman and accomplished painter whose presence and radiance sustained the whole family. This book is dedicated to her memory.

From Individuality to Relationality

This essay seeks to retrieve metaphysics and reveal its theological nature. It shows how ancient and modern conceptions of being in terms of individual substance fail to account for the irreducible, ontological relations that bind immanent, finite beings to each other and to their transcendent, infinite source in God. Instead of some abstract 'individuality' that begs the question, the essay suggests that a thing's unique form is both existentially and essentially its metaphysical positioning in relation to other things. In turn, the relational ordering of all things suggests a priority of relation over substance, which intimates a first principle and final end that is itself relational — the creative relationality of the three divine persons that brings everything out of nothing into actuality and gives all beings a share of Trinitarian being in which the created order participates. Based on a genealogical account of rival theories of creation and individuation from Plato to 'postmodernism,' the essay argues that the Christian Neo-Platonic fusion of biblical revelation with Greco-Roman philosophy developed Hellenic Judaism in the direction of a theological metaphysic that fulfills and surpasses ancient, modern, and contemporary ontologies and conceptions of individuality.

The essay attempts to radicalize the theological turn of philosophy by extending the 'rehellenization' of theology in a metaphysical sense. Its chosen focus is the dual question of individuation in metaphysics and individuality in politics. My argument is that the individuation of substances in general and of persons in particular cannot be explained in secular, immanentist terms as some autonomous achievement owing to substantiality but is best construed as the imperfect reception and return of God's originating gift of relationality. The tradition from which this argument hopes to derive its logic is that of patristic and medieval Christian Neo-Platonism, a tradition that preserved and expanded the original hellenization of Christianity.

The primacy of relation over substance within Platonism is the most fundamental reason why the Neo-Platonic legacy is a constitutive aspect of Christendom in both East and West. The notion that theology can dispense with metaphysics is just as misguided as the notion that metaphysics is not *also* theological. It is similarly erroneous to claim that metaphysics ever ended (each critique or deconstruction of metaphysics is always in the end another metaphysic) or that it cannot be restored to the heart of the arts, humanities, and the sciences. My contention is that the renewed visibility of religion and the greater presence of theology in academic as well as public debate will help sustain the resurgence of a Christian metaphysic that never ceased to be at the center of creedal Christianity.

Why metaphysics and why hierarchy? By linking the relational positioning of all individual substances to their shared source in God, my argument is that only a theological metaphysic can position being in the intermediary realm of 'the between' (Plato's *metaxu*). In this realm, the original relation among the divine persons and the participatory relation between creation and creator intersect without however collapsing into one another. As such, 'the between' reflects the double hierarchy in creation and the creator. The created order of being fuses 'monarchic' with 'egalitarian' elements in such a way that the hierarchy of substances according to their degrees of being and goodness is coextensive with the equality of all finite things — compared with the perfection of infinite, divine being. In Dionysius who coined the term *hierarchia* (ἱεραρχία), receiving divine illumination and the sacraments marks the perfection of our God-given unique form and the elevation *(anagōgē)* to union with the Trinitarian *monarchia*. Hierarchy and anagogy describe the ascending movement whose original, reverse movement is *kenosis* in the divine humanity of Jesus Christ. In this manner, 'the between' of Christian metaphysics can perhaps be depicted as a spiral paradox whereby individual substances are individuated relationally by participating in the substantive relationality of the triune God.

Since being so construed upholds both *analogia entis* and the 'ontological difference,' the account advanced here refuses the dominant modern solutions of monism, dualism, or pluralism, for all three refuse any mediation between the infinite one and the finite many. It will also be suggested that relationality cuts across other perennial binaries characterizing philosophy both past and present: the actual and the virtual; the process of individuation and the event of the individual as representable *res;* absolute, immaterial reason and unreasoning, material reality. Thus, the theological metaphysic which this essay describes outflanks the modern science of transcendental ontology and various late (or post)modern attempts to construct ontologies of pure immanence.

My account draws on two specific strands of Christian theology. First, the Neo-Platonic conception of the infinite Good or One which 'gives itself' ecstatically to finitude in a primary relation whose *volte-face* is the participation of immanent things in the transcendent source of universal being — in God — which alone brings about their particular existence. Second, the biblical idea — developed by the Church Fathers and Doctors — of a personal creator who actualizes everything out of nothing and in so doing imparts particular shares of universal being. The latter can be understood as part of the divine unity of transcendentals in which finite, immanent things participate by way of an asymmetric relation that encompasses matter and not just form. Under the 'meta-form' or 'meta-category' of relation, it will be argued that the Christian Neo-Platonic theology of creation *ex nihilo* and the Trinity offers an account of individuation that avoids both Aristotle's theo-ontology and the idolatry of onto-theology inaugurated by John Duns Scotus.

In terms that will become clearer as the analysis unfolds, the essay traces a series of shifts from a metaphysics of creation and individuation to an ontology of generation and individuality. The main traits of these shifts and their implications for the twin thematic of *what* it is that *makes* an individual an individual constitute the primary object of this research. As such, the essay is not a historical survey of rival, metaphysical theories of individuality[1] and selfhood[2] (or individualism[3]). Nor is it a

1. E.g., Jorge J. E. Gracia, *Individuality: An Essay on the Foundations of Metaphysics* (Albany: State University of New York Press, 1988).

2. Recent examples include Charles Taylor, *Sources of the Self: The Making of Modern Identity* (Cambridge, MA: Harvard University Press, 1989); and Jerrold E. Seigel, *The Idea of the Self: Thought and Experience in Western Europe Since the Seventeenth Century* (Cambridge: Cambridge University Press, 2005).

3. Cf. Alan Macfarlane, *The Origins of English Individualism: The Family, Property and Social Transition* (Oxford: Blackwell, 1978); Louis Dumont, *Essais sur l'individualisme. Une perspective anthropologique sur l'idéologie moderne* (Paris: Éditions du Seuil, 1983).

speculative treatise on a new principle of individuation.[4] Rather, it combines a genealogical inquiry into the formation of two rival accounts with a theological critique of ancient and modern philosophy as well as a wider argument in favor of a theological metaphysic that overcomes the unresolved tension between the one and the many bequeathed by both antiquity and modernity.

Why the chosen problem of individuation? Traditionally, the one and the many have been held in opposition, at least since the Greek philosopher Parmenides elevated the unity of essence over the multiplicity of appearance. Variations of this duality between unity and diversity are recurrent in the history of philosophy and theology — the universal and the particular, the intelligible and the sensible, the substantial and the accidental, the cosmic and the psychic, the first cause and secondary effects, the collective and the individual, the realm of transcendence and that of immanence. The opposition of the one and the many seems perennial and perhaps even indelible. However, to oppose them is simply to assert that they represent contrary principles and that as such they are incompatible, producing conflict and violence. This opposition is based upon the undemonstrated and unwarranted assumption that substance is prior to relation and that individuality is absolute. So configured, every individual is indeterminately and indiscernibly equivalent to every other individual. To subordinate reciprocal relation to individual substance is to elevate the self-identity of individuals over above the commonality of being in which all things seem to share. And to conceive individuality in this manner is to ignore particular specificities that are only manifest in the positioning of individuals in mutual relations with each other and their shared source of being.

Moreover, the primacy of substance over relation shifts the onus of individuation onto the individual entity itself, as transcendent causality is excluded from the actualization of individual substances. The first cause acts either as the ultimate *telos* to which individuals are drawn or as the transcendental warrant for their unity. But causality so construed cannot explain *how* particular sensible things are individuated or *why* the pure actuality of the one would wish to be allied to the pure potency

---

4. See, among many others, Gilbert Simondon, *L'individu et sa genèse physico-biologique (l'individuation à la lumière des notions de forme et d'information)* (Paris: Presses Universitaires de France, 1964); and Carl G. Jung's analytic psychology in his *Memories, Dreams, Reflections*, ed. C. Winston, trans. R. Winston (New York: Random House, 1989).

of matter. This essay shows that only the concept of a Trinitarian Creator God can account for the individuation of things in ways that uphold both the absolute unity of their shared source of being and the diverse multiplicity of their particular instantiation.

Content and Structure

The first part of the essay traces the original shift between metaphysics and ontology. The key locus will be identified with Plato and Aristotle. Chapter 1 begins with Aristotle, for it is he who introduces a wedge between theology and ontology. By sundering the actuality of the First Mover or God (*Metaphysics* Λ 7) from the generation and evolution of individual substances and also from the abstraction and predication of individual substantial form, the Stagirite separates the divine from temporal being and knowing. Since the First Mover only acts as final cause and is not the generative source of temporal actuality or form, the ultimate 'cause' of individuation is immanent, and individuality is equated with the autonomous sovereignty of the sublunary world and all things therein. At the same time, the genetic and epistemic modalities of individuation are over-determined by a dependency on the self-contemplation of the divine First Mover who is "thought thinking itself" and as such acts exclusively as the final cause that all intelligent substances endeavor to emulate. (In this sense, Aristotle foregrounds a theo-ontology whose reverse face is the onto-theology inaugurated by John Duns Scotus, as I shall argue in chapter 6.)

By contrast, Plato links the constitutive relation between the Good and all the other (numerically indeterminate) forms to the participatory relation among eternal forms as well as between them and temporal things. There is thus in his metaphysics the priority of the relational 'giving' of presence over participation wherein the Good infuses all things with goodness. It is this generative presence in immanent things that enables them to participate in the universal forms and perfect their given goodness. Human beings do so by partaking of the good life within the republic governed by laws and virtues.

Chapter 2 describes how patristic theology fuses Greco-Roman philosophy with biblical revelation to produce an integral account of being that mirrors the Trinitarian economy of the divine mind. Both Gregory of Nyssa and Augustine reconfigure Plato's Good and Plotinus's One in the direction of the Creator God and Trinitarian relationality. The Christian Neo-Platonist synthesis of Plato and Aristotle conserves the Platonic priority of relation over the Aristotelian category of substance. The doctrine of creation *ex nihilo* and the Trinity tends to accentuate this priority, as divine creation of everything out of nothing brings matter itself within the scope of the originating asymmetrical relationality between creator and creatures — brilliantly described by Augustine in his subtle commentary on the Book of Genesis.

Likewise, the primacy of relation over substance in the case of the triune Godhead itself is affirmed by Augustine and further developed Boethius, who shows that divine substantiality is unreservedly relational, as chapter 3 argues. Beyond the Nicene language of substance, Augustine and Boethius argue that individuation marks the positioning of particular things in relation to other particular things, the whole cosmos, and their shared source of being in God. For this reason, individuation is not concerned with the generation of individuals within the confines of pure immanence but rather the actualization of particulars who always already participate in the transcendent actuality of God's goodness. Being created in the image and likeness of God describes our share in the relationality of the Trinitarian economy. In the work of Dionysius the Areopagite briefly discussed at the end of chapter 3, creation and individuation are construed as our elevation to union with God and our ever-greater participation in the relational hierarchy of infinite being.

Part II of the essay is an inquiry into a series of medieval shifts from the Neo-Platonic metaphysics of creation and individuation to an Aristotelianized ontology of generation and individuality. The work of Boethius discussed in chapter 3 is pivotal. Chapter 4 shows how as early as the tenth and eleventh centuries, various Muslim philosophers and Christian theologians argued for the priority of essence over existence. Building on Porphyry's logicized Aristotelianism, Avicenna was first to elevate possibility over actuality and to introduce an onto-logic of necessity into the doctrine of free creation. Likewise, the influential twelfth-century theologian Gilbert Porreta (Gilbert of Poitiers) defended in his commentary on Boethius' theological tractates the primacy of essence vis-à-vis existence rather than the idea of transcendental being or unity. Crucially, Porreta's 'Mathematical Platonism' or 'Platonism of essence' (after Porphyry) engenders a turn to the supremacy of logic and semantics and also a more immanentist construal of individuation. Instead of the latter being seen as a limited 'share' of divine unity, it is now seen either as a transcendentally necessary logical category or as a state of affairs simply willed by God and telling us nothing of the inner divine reality.

By contrast, Thomas Aquinas restores the Boethian primacy of act over potency and further develops early scholastic theology in the direction of a Neo-Platonic metaphysic of creation and individuation, as chapter 5 explores. Individuation for Aquinas is neither simply the result of *materia designata* nor the form/matter complex, as for Aristotle. Instead, the first and final 'reason' for individuation is the divine act of pure *esse* and the creative act of participating in being which realizes form in matter. In this manner, Aquinas blends the Neo-Platonist metaphysics of the Fathers with Aristotle's language of act and potency in order to defend the primacy of divine act against not just Porreta's and Avicenna's shared Platonism of essence but also against the priority of philosophy over theology in twelfth- and early-thirteenth-century radical Aristotelianism (increasingly influential at the universities of Oxford and Paris). For Thomas, just as the intra-Trinitarian relations individuate the substances of the three divine persons and draw in the whole of creation, so too God's creative act of being is the ultimate cause of individuation (and created matter its principle). Likewise, the self-diffusive, supernatural Good in God constitutes the source for the interconnectedness of all beings throughout the *cosmos,* channeling divine hyper-individuality into more limited shares of the same modes (rather than somehow converting universality into particularity). The divine act makes all beings good and enables them to perfect their given goodness by participating in God through the practice of relations with other beings. The common good that all beings can share in provides the link between Aquinas's metaphysics and his conception of politics.

Chapter 6 explores how John Duns Scotus, William of Ockham, and Jean Buridan intensify the twelfth-century separation of theology from philosophy and the importance of logic and semantics as the foundation of metaphysics. In spite of some significant differences, Scotus, Ockham, and Buridan share the idea that individuality is more real than universality and that material substances are in the final instance self-individuating. The elimination of God from actuality entails the exclusion of divine creative action from the actualization and individuation of particular sensible things. This marks a fundamental rupture from the metaphysics of creation, relationality, and participation — the vision of individuating relations is abandoned in favor of the primacy of

God's absolute power *(potentia Dei absoluta)*. At the same time, the universe and the polity become autonomous from God's creative action, a shift largely internal to theology that foreshadows the transition from scholasticism to modernity.

The third part of the essay charts some key early modern moments in the shift from metaphysics to ontology. In chapter 7, it is argued that Francisco Suárez consecrates general metaphysics as an all-encompassing system that replaces the theological metaphysics of the Fathers and the Doctors. Metaphysically, the individuality of substances holds sway over mutual relations with other substances or their common source in God. Politically, inalienable individual rights and human sovereignty are elevated over and above communal discernment and the pursuit of the common good in accordance with the mediate presence of God's transcendence. This shift eschews the idea of individuating relations between a transcendent God and his immanent creation in favor of an alternative theory of individuation that revolves around two tenets of early modern metaphysics: first, the transcendental dependence of effects upon their cause and the self-individuation of entities (Suárez); second, the immanent generation of individual beings and their individuation in a perpetual rivalry with other individual beings (Spinoza). In this sense, Suárez's transcendentalism and Spinoza's immanentism represent two sides of modern philosophy and politics.

Chapter 8 traces Spinoza's invention of pure immanence and his theory of individuation. The mark of Spinoza's ontology is that he rejects the idea of creation *ex nihilo* altogether and invents a realm of pure immanence where the oneness of the substance determines the diversity of finite modes. In the natural order all finite modes are equal and there is no hierarchy. But both his ontology of single substance and his politics of plural democracy are defined along essentially negative lines. The single substance is infinite and auto-productive, but this begs the question of why it would choose to express itself in finite modes. Likewise, democracy is a necessary consequence of the nature of individual knowledge — the limits on human understanding according to which individuals ignore their own particular station in the communal order and fail to grasp the universal fixed laws of the eternal universe. The result is that individuals confound their own self-interest with the common sharing in the substance. As such, democracy is constitutively incapable of resolving the conflict between clusters of individual finite modes. All of which underscores the absence of mediation in early modern philosophy.

Chapter 9 concludes this essay by way of a thematic inquiry into the modern conception and institution of metaphysics as a transcendental science of ontology and the concomitant substitution of immanent individual generation for transcendent individuating creation. Key to this process is the invention of a new science of the individual that replaces a metaphysics of the relation between universals and particulars. Several strands can be distinguished: the rationalist mechanism of Descartes and Leibniz; the materialism and atomism of Hobbes and Locke; the transcendental immanence of Wolff and Kant. What binds them all together is the modern science of ontology which collapses either into transcendentalism or into positivism or into both at once, trapped as it is in a binary dialectic of the one and the many. The alternative, which chapter 9 briefly outlines, is a theological metaphysic of creation and individuation that locates being in the 'between' that is produced in the divine act of creation and its eternal unfolding — the fusion of the divine with the human elevating the entire cosmos to union with God, as revealed and renewed by the unique event of the Incarnation of the relational *Logos* (John 1:1).

Beyond the modern and contemporary opposition between the one and the many, I argue that individuals are constituted relationally by the transcendent universal Good in the pure relationality of the one triune God. By focusing on the reception and transformation of Greek metaphysics by Christian Neo-Platonism, I aim to show that some premodern accounts of the link between the one and the many blend self-identity, differentiation, and relationality. These conceptions reject absolute dualism, arbitrary monism, and indiscriminate pluralism. Instead, they argue for a mediating relation between unity and diversity. As a result, they surpass modern and contemporary theories and provide the only coherent conceptual alternative to current ontologies of pure immanence.

PART I

Substance and Relation

The belief upon which our science rests remains a metaphysical belief. We seekers after knowledge today, we godless ones and anti-metaphysicians, we too continue to take our flame from that fire ignited by a belief which is millennia old, that Christian belief, which was also Plato's belief, that God is the truth, that the truth is divine. . . .

Friedrich Nietzsche[1]

From its inception, Plato's metaphysics came under attack for essentially the same reason: an unresolved ontological and epistemological dualism between the visible realm of things and the invisible realm of ideas. Beginning with Aristotle, philosophers and theologians from Tatian and Tertullian to Heidegger and Derrida wrongly contended that in Plato the transcendence of the Good is divorced from the immanence of the world. Linked to this is the unwarranted claim that Platonist forms are unintelligible to the human mind, except if we hold to the blind belief in the immortality of the soul. It was of course Nietzsche who derided Christianity for being little more than popular Platonism — a desperate worship of otherworldliness for fear of real change and revolutionary transformation. By importing Plato's eternal forms, so Nietzsche's argument goes, Christian theology took a fatal metaphysical turn that led to an idolatry of abstract concepts and a hatred of the becoming of be-

---

1. Friedrich Nietzsche, *On the Genealogy of Morals,* trans. Douglas Smith (Oxford: Oxford University Press, 1996), Essay III, para. 24, p. 127 (original italics).

ing.[2] In consequence, Christianity is nihilistic because it embraces the Platonist priority of the timeless ideal vis-à-vis the changing real and as such inverts the primacy of life over death. To praise God's eternity and the divine source of life is for Nietzsche to celebrate the stasis of nature and the human will to nothingness.[3] As such, Christianity's Platonist metaphysics marks the death of God and the end of religion.

In the first part of this essay, I seek to rehabilitate Plato's metaphysics as a prolegomenon to Christian theology. Prior to Aristotle, Plato had already outlined a metaphysics of relationality and participation that avoids an ontological dualism, pluralism, or atomism without lapsing into monism. The Platonist distinction of the world of things and the world of ideas is qualified by the higher unity of the Good and the participation of immanent particulars in transcendent universal forms. As the form of all forms, the Good is best understood as a relational absolute that orders the other universals. Matter-form compounds are best described as relational beings that are endowed with existence and essence by the Good. Moreover, against the pre-Socratic poets and philosophers Aristotle followed Plato's cosmological argument in favor of the existence of a single immaterial first cause: just as Plato's Good is the Form of all forms that orders everything in the world of things (*The Republic* VI 505 A 1-10; 509 B 6), so Aristotle's Prime Mover is the final end of all substances in the sublunary world (*Metaphysics* Λ 7). But both Aristotelian metaphysics and politics shift away from the Platonist synthesis towards a more dualistic system. The separation of the primary cause from all secondary effects removes the actuality of the Unmoved Mover from the heavens and the sublunary world and devalues particular beings therein. For the sole *telos* of everything is to emulate the self-reflexivity of the Prime Mover. On the contrary, Plato views particulars as unique and irreplaceable instantiations of the universal Good.

2. Friedrich Nietzsche, *The Twilight of the Idols,* trans. Duncan Large (Oxford: Oxford University Press, 1998), "Reason in Philosophy," para. 1-2, pp. 16-17.

3. In the *Antichrist,* Nietzsche famously writes that "The Christian concept of God . . . is one of the most corrupt concepts of God ever arrived at on earth: it probably touches low-water mark in the ebbing evolution of the God-type. God degenerated into the *contradiction of life.* Instead of being its transfiguration and eternal Yea! In him war is declared on life, on nature, on the will to live! God becomes the formula for every slander upon the 'here and now,' and for every lie about the 'beyond'! In him nothingness is deified, and the will to nothingness is made holy." Friedrich Nietzsche, *The Antichrist,* trans. Thomas Common (Mineola, NY: Dover Publications, 2004), para. 18, p. 88 (translation modified).

For Plato, forms are relational in the sense that they are ordered by the Good, the form of all forms. Likewise, individual composites are relational in the sense that they depend for their essence, their existence, and their continuous being on the Good. The presence of the Good in particulars makes them relational and enables them to participate in the universal forms and in goodness itself. Individuals are actualized and individuated by relations with other individuals and their orientation towards the Good. They can perfect their individual form through the highest instance of relation, the praxis of justice in the *polis*.

My argument is that Plato's individuals are not 'bare and basic units' (Marilyn McCabe). Nor are they simply given and self-evident. Rather, things are generated as individuals by other individuals and further individuated not only by their proximate causes but also by the action of the first principle and final end of all, which is the Good. In Plato's metaphysics and politics, the ecstatic plenitude and the self-diffusion of the Good can explain why there are a diverse reality and a multiplicity of individual composites. I conclude that Plato's Good provides a richer metaphysical account of relationality than Aristotle's Prime Mover. However, Plato excludes matter from the essence of concrete composites and is thus unable to explain how and why materiality matters to their individuation.

In chapters 2 and 3, I explore the work of St. Augustine, St. Gregory of Nyssa, Boethius, and Dionysius the Areopagite on creation and individuation. The crucial points of divergence with both Plato and Aristotle include the ontological difference between the Creator and creation, the idea of *creatio ex nihilo,* and the real relation of the world to God (though not of God to the world, as nothing is or possibly could be outside the divine orbit). At the same time, these (and other) patristic figures produced the first systematic synthesis of biblical revelation with ancient philosophy that gave rise to the tradition of Christian Neo-Platonism. Metaphysically, creation *ex nihilo* is amenable to natural reason and fuses the Christian idea of the Trinitarian *donum* of life with the Platonist notion of the Good as 'giving itself' ecstatically to finitude in an original relationality whose reverse face is the 'participation' of temporal things in the realm of the forms which alone brings about their particular existence.

For this reason, the 'real ideal' of creation — as revealed in the complex interplay of the Book of Nature, the Book of Scripture, and the Book of History — leads Augustine and Boethius to reconfigure substance and relation and to develop an account of composite substances created in the image and likeness of God's relational substance. I also argue that the ecstatic plenitude of divine relationality can explain not only *how* and *why* composite substances are individual but also *to what end* they are individuated. In this sense, the patristic (onto)-logic of creation builds on Plato's metaphysics of the Good and Aristotle's indispensable language of act and potency in order to surpass the ancient (heno)-logic of the one over the many in the direction of Trinitarian relationality.

CHAPTER I

The Primacy of Relation over Substance

1. Introduction: The Legacy of
Pre-Socratic Poetry and Philosophy

The opposition of the one and the many is the hallmark of pre-Socratic poetry and philosophy. None of the dominant schools or thinkers could reconcile the apparent contradiction of unity and diversity in the world of material things and immaterial ideas. For instance, Hesiod's poem *Theogony* describes how out of the infinite nothingness of chaos emerges a single divine cosmos, generated and maintained by the omnipotent Zeus. Even though it acts as the first cause and final end of the natural order, the power of the gods is wholly unintelligible to the human mind and a matter of blind belief.[1] (This myth is invoked by Plotinus to describe the eternal procession of the many from the One, as we shall see in chapter 2.) In Hesiod, as in Homer's *Odyssey*, the presence of gods is absolute and divine intervention in the world is arbitrary.[2]

Early pre-Socratic philosophers, by contrast, contended that the perceptible world of nature can be cognized and explained in terms of its own inherent principles. This argument eschews cosmic fatalism in favor of rational knowledge and human agency. However, it leaves the problem of the opposition between the one and the many unresolved.[3]

1. Hesiod, *Theogony,* trans. S. Lombardo (Indianapolis: Hackett, 1993).
2. Homer, *The Odyssey,* rev. ed., trans. E. V. Rieu (London: Penguin Classics, 2003).
3. Michael C. Stokes, *One and Many in Pre-Socratic Philosophy* (Cambridge, MA: Harvard University Press, 1972).

Faced with the simultaneous occurrence of being and nonbeing, the physicists, for example, searched for some fundamental principle (ἀρχή) that could explain the multiplicity of things within the overarching cosmos — water in Thales, air in Anaximenes, or the indefinite/borderless *(to apeiron)* in Anaximander.[4] But they could not solve the paradox of stability and change over time and across space that characterizes the single enduring material stuff which was thought to be both the origin of all things and the cause of their continuing existence. By positing some basic constituent of materiality that is itself eternal and underlies all change (one or several of the four elements), they reduced the whole of reality to a single substratum and advocated a form of material monism. The problem with this sort of monism is that it fails to explain how a multiplicity of things can emerge out of the oneness of the underlying principle and how the immaterial mind can know the material world in both its diversity and unity. As such, material monism is unable to account for the unity of matter itself.

Later pre-Socratic philosophers like Xenophanes, Heraclitus, and Parmenides defended an immaterial monism, arguing that there is something like a first principle which is unitary and permanent and which contrasts with the multiple and transitory nature of the living cosmos. Xenophanes writes that "[o]ne god is greatest among gods and men, not at all like mortals in body or in thought."[5] Likewise, Heraclitus refers in the opening lines of his book to the "*logos* which holds forever,"[6] a law-like principle that embodies the divine order and rules all things within the universe and therefore can be known by the human mind. And since nothing comes from nothing, as Parmenides held, that which *is* either is necessary or is contingent. Necessary being is necessarily "ungenerated and imperishable; Whole, single-limbed, steadfast and complete; nor was [it] once, nor will [it] be, since it is, now, all together, One, continuous."[7] For Parmenides, as for Xenophanes and Heraclitus,

4. W. K. C. Guthrie, *A History of Greek Philosophy* (Cambridge: Cambridge University Press, 1965), vol. 1; Jonathan Barnes, *The Presocratic Philosophers,* 2nd ed. (London: Routledge & Kegan Paul, 1982).

5. James H. Lesher, *Xenophanes of Colophon: Fragments* (Toronto: University of Toronto Press, 1992), fragment 23, p. 31.

6. T. M. Robinson, *Heraclitus: Fragments* (Toronto: University of Toronto Press, 1991), fragment 1, p. 11.

7. David Galop, *Parmenides of Elea: Fragments* (Toronto: University of Toronto Press, 1991), fragment 8, p. 63.

the unity of the primary principle subsumes the diversity of the second-ary reality that comes into being and passes away. The problem with this kind of immaterial monism is that it cannot demonstrate how the mind alone can have access to being without the import of the senses. Nor can it give a reason why the oneness of true reality (that which is) would be allied to the void (that which is not) in order to produce the multiplicity of the universe (κόσμος) that hovers between being and nonbeing.[8]

Neither pluralism nor atomism resolved the opposition between the one and the many bequeathed by the physicists and left unresolved by Parmenides' Eleatic monism. Anaxagoras and Empedocles replaced a single immaterial substratum as the source of being with a plurality of material elements, but both had to appeal to the operation of the mind or intellect (νοῦς) — a unitary, separate, cosmic, intelligent force that brings the mixture of elements into rotation and holds the universe to-gether. As a result, the pluralism of Anaxagoras and Empedocles comple-ments Parmenides' emphasis on the absolute unity of being with an irre-ducible multiplicity of material stuffs. The (pre-)Socratic atomists Leucippus and Democritus went further than the pluralists by arguing that all forms of union are illusory and that every whole is reducible to its parts. Yet at the same time, all atoms are made of the same founda-tional matter and (unlike in Parmenides) true reality is not limited to be-ing but extends to the void, defined as that which individuates atoms and distinguishes them from one another. Thus, both the pluralist and the atomist schools maintained a strict division of unity and diversity by positing a cause or principle of individuation that is separate from plural material elements or bare atoms.

8. Here I do not follow W. K. C. Guthrie's reading of Parmenides as a strict monist (see, *supra*, note 4). Nor do I accept Bertrand Russell's and G. E. L. Owen's logical-dialectical interpretation or Patricia Curd's characterization of Parmenidean metaphys-ics in terms of "predicational monism," which combines Jonathan Barnes's claim of a nu-merical plurality of "Parmenidean Beings" with the assertion that each thing that is can only be one thing. Rather, my argument is that Parmenides' metaphysics is beset by an ir-reducible dualism between that which is and cannot-not-be and that which may be but could not be. As such, Parmenides did *not* anticipate Plato's metaphysics. Instead, Plato's concept of relationality and participation corrected Parmenides' ontological monism, as this chapter will show. Cf. Bertrand Russell, *A History of Western Philosophy* (London: Routledge, 2004; orig. pub. 1945), pp. 55-59; G. E. L. Owen, "Eleatic Questions," *The Classical Quarterly*, n.s. 10 (1960): 84-102; Barnes, *The Presocratic Philosophers*, pp. 122-81; Patricia Curd, *The Legacy of Parmenides: Eleatic Monism and Later Presocratic Thought* (Princeton: Princeton University Press, 1998).

In short, material and immaterial monism is unable to account for the unity of matter and the plurality of finite things, whereas pluralism and atomism need to appeal to a unitary force that secures the oneness of the cosmos. As such, they all mask an ontological and epistemological dualism between the one and the many. The reason is metaphysical and theological: the link between the universe and its source remains hidden, since pre-Socratic poetry and philosophy view the gods as external to the world and divinity as unintelligible to the human mind. Fundamentally, the infinite incomprehensible origin of being and the finite perceptible world of beings are coterminous not consubstantial: being and beings do not belong to separate realms, nor do they share in the same substance. Rather, they are like two parallel galaxies linked by the arbitrary and absolute power of the divine. This is equally true for the material substratum in the physicists, the νοῦς in Anaxagoras and Empedocles, the greatest god in Xenophanes, reason (λόγος) in Heraclitus, and true reality (or the "What Is") in Parmenides. In consequence, the relation between form and materiality is unresolved, since matter is finite but eternal, whereas form is infinite but immanent. Moreover, there is no real, discernible relation between the sensible and the intelligible realm. The implication is that infinite being and finite beings are divorced from each other, leaving the unique individuality of each material thing unexplained. Are different particular beings merely copies of one and the same universal form, differentiated by accidental properties rather than substantial essences? If each individual being has its own unique form, is form particular or universal? If form is universal, is it individuated by eternal general matter? Or is eternal general matter particularized by substantial form?

Socrates, Plato, and Aristotle agreed with their forebears that pure materiality approximates nonbeing and lacks order. Beyond pre-Socratic poetry and philosophy, they sought to show that transcendent universal form gives being to matter (rather than some immanent material principle), that the divine is unitary (rather than multiple), and that the oneness of immaterial form is paradoxically embodied in the plurality of material things (rather than corrupted and destroyed). For Plato, material things are imperfect copies of immaterial forms and only exist by participation. Similarly, for Aristotle the being or actuality of form — essence — brings the nonbeing or potency of matter into existence. As a result of the relation between form and matter, concrete things constitute individual form-matter compounds and are intelligible to the mind via the senses. However, Aristotle rejected Plato's theory of forms because, according to the Stagirite, it is confused and fails to overcome the pre-Socratic dualism between the empirical and the ideal. Aristotle was the first to assert that Plato's separation of timeless forms from preexistent matter can neither solve the problem of motion and rest nor explain the unity of body and soul. Moreover, Plato was unable — so Aristotle's argument goes — to demonstrate how and why the human mind can cognize the presence of transcendent eternal structures in immanent ephemeral phenomena. Aristotle's critique of Plato's metaphysics led him to abandon the concept of participation and to theorize the relation between particulars and universals in terms of the union of singular essence with material substrate, in an attempt to tie matter more closely to form. The material component of composite substances stands in potency to the actuality of individual substantial form. Similarly, all composites stand in potency to the pure actuality of the Prime Mover. As such, the unity of the first cause constitutes the final end of the multiplicity of substances in the sublunary world. By arguing that forms do not stand above and beyond things but that instead being inheres in beings, it was apparently Aristotle — not Plato — who first resolved the metaphysical dualism between the one and the many, the universal and the particular, and the singular and the collective.[9]

2. The Preeminence of Substance

A. Separating Theology from Ontology

In what follows, I contest this interpretation of Plato and Aristotle. My argument is that Aristotle's priority of substance (οὐσία) over being (τὸ ὄν) privileges essentiality over existentiality and drives a wedge between the science of being *qua* being (ontology) and the science of the divine (theology). This in turn entails a metaphysical dualism between particular beings in the sublunary world and the universal Prime Mover (or

9. In part, this sort of reading explains why much of late modern and contemporary philosophy, in particular French phenomenology and certain strands of the analytic tradition, look back to Aristotle in order to challenge the dualism bequeathed by both Descartes and Kant. The reinvention of ontology that characterizes contemporary philosophy and theology is to a significant extent grounded in a rejection of Plato's metaphysics and a reinterpretation of Aristotle's ontology and theology. See, *infra,* chapter 9.

God), in the sense that the latter produces the motion of the heavens and the world of nature but does not bring particular beings into being. As the pure unreserved actuality of thought and life, the Prime Mover imparts intelligibility to both simple and complex substances and is desired as the ultimate end or finality (τέλος) of all that exists, but equally it is "separate from sensible things" and does not bestow actuality upon them.[10]

In consequence, the actualization of material things is severed from the actuality of the Prime Mover, and individuation is reduced to the generation of individuals by individuals.[11] Contrary to Plato's metaphysics of the universal Good as the author of all things (*The Republic* VI 508 E, 511 B, VII 516 B) which positions all particulars relationally in virtue of its ecstatic overflow, the Prime Mover as the supreme primary substance whose actuality is thought thinking itself neither brings composite substances into being nor thinks their complex essence of form and matter (since the noetic activity of Aristotle's Prime Mover encompasses individual substantial form but does not extend to the idea of matter). As a result, Aristotle's Prime Mover is ultimately indifferent to material beings in the sublunary world. Unlike the Platonist Good, which endows all things with goodness and thereby acts as efficient and

10. Aristotle, *Metaphysics* Λ 7, 1072^{b}10-31 (henceforth *Met.*) and *Met.* Λ 7, 1073^{a}5, in *The Complete Works of Aristotle*, revised Oxford translation in two volumes, ed. Jonathan Barnes (Princeton: Princeton University Press, 1984), vol. 2, p. 1695.

11. Past debates on Aristotle's theory of individuation have wrongly focused on whether the principle of individuation is either purely material or exclusively formal. On matter, see, *inter alia*, Elisabeth Anscombe, "Symposium: The Principle of Individuation II," *Aristotelian Society* suppl. 27 (1953): 83-96; Antony C. Lloyd, "Aristotle's Principle of Individuation," *Mind* 79, no. 316 (October 1970): 519-29. On form, see, *inter alia*, Jan Lukasiewicz, "Symposium: The Principle of Individuation I," *Aristotelian Society* suppl. 27 (1953): 69-82; William Charlton, "Aristotle and the Principle of Individuation," *Phronesis* 17 (1973): 239-49; Jennifer E. Whiting, "Form and Individuation in Aristotle," *History of Philosophy Quarterly* 3, no. 4 (October 1986): 359-77. Richard Rorty and Mary Gill are right that, for Aristotle, individuation is neither simply formal nor entirely material but instead marks the union of individual substantial form and proximate matter. See Richard Rorty, "Genus as Matter: A Reading of *Metaphysics* Z-H," *Phronesis* suppl. 1 (1973): 393-420; Mary L. Gill, *Aristotle on Substance: The Paradox of Unity* (Princeton: Princeton University Press, 1989); Mary L. Gill, "Individuals and Individuation," in *Unity, Identity, and Explanation in Aristotle's Metaphysics*, ed. Theodore Scaltsas, David Charles, Mary L. Gill (Oxford: Clarendon Press, 1994), pp. 55-71. Beyond Rorty and Gill, I argue in this chapter that Aristotle's primacy of substance tends to privilege essence over existence and to separate the being of beings from the actuality of the Prime Mover.

final cause that is perfective of form, the actuality of the Prime Mover does not inhere in individual substances that exist in the sublunary world but instead is a distant τέλος that merely acts as final causality.

Moreover, it is not clear in Aristotle's ontology and theology whether the actuality of individual substantial form is at all related to the pure actuality of the Prime Mover. The latter is but a remote cause that imparts motion to composite substances exclusively by final causality and not by efficient causality. Once the first cause is limited to final causality, the actualization and perfection of composites are cut off from the Prime Mover. Joseph Owens rightly argues that "he [Aristotle] does not seem to have any means of explaining how the actual contact is made between separate substance and material substance."[12] My critique of Aristotle's philosophy, and particularly his theory of individuation, must therefore begin with his account of substance.

Aristotle's distinction between being and substance is absolutely central to his conception of ontology and theology. First of all, the notion of being has multiple meanings and the reality of being is different in diverse things (just like the good and the one).[13] In consequence, being is not synonymous and univocal, as advocates of analytical univocalism like Bertrand Russell, W. V. O. Quine, Morton White, and more recently Peter van Inwagen have wrongly claimed.[14] Second, even though there is not a single type of 'being' that can be predicated of everything that is (τὸ ἐστίν), it does not follow for Aristotle that being is homonymous and equivocal. For being is that which is "common to all things" (*Met.* Γ 3, 1005ᵃ27), yet at the same time particular and distinct in each single substance (whether simple or composite).[15] Third, the commonality of being in all that exists cannot be conceived exclusively in terms of unity in analogical difference or unity through foundation in an immutable essence. For Aristotle subordinates the analogy of being to the categories

12. Joseph Owens, "The Relation of God to the World in the *Metaphysics*," in *Études sur la Métaphysique d'Aristote,* ed. Pierre Aubenque (Paris: Vrin, 1979), p. 217, note 18. Cf. Julia Annas, "Forms and First Principles," *Phronesis* 19 (1974): 257-83.

13. Aristotle, *Categories* I 1ᵃ1 (henceforth *Cat.*); *Eudemian Ethics* I 8, 1217ᵇ20-26 (henceforth *Eud. Eth.*); *Topics* I 15, 106ᵃ9 (henceforth *Top.*).

14. For an overview and critique of analytical univocalism, see Enrico Berti, "Multiplicity and Unity of Being in Aristotle," *Proceedings of the Aristotelian Society* 101 (2000): 185-207, esp. pp. 185-89.

15. *Met.* Γ 2. Cf. *Cat.* VII 17ᵃ40-ᵇ1; *Parts of Animals* 644ᵃ24-25 (henceforth *Pa. An.*); *Met.* Z 8, 1034ᵃ5-8; Z 11, 1036ᵃ26-28; Z 13, 1038ᵇ10-12.

and views substance as the substrate for all beings, though the categorial term of substance implies substantial change and cannot be seen as static or foundationalist in a proto-modern transcendentalist manner (as Frege, Husserl, Heidegger, and others rightly argue).

Fourth, Aristotle restricts the link between the primary substance of the Unmoved Mover and being to final causality (whereas for Plato the Good also acts as efficient and formal cause). Just as the divine first mover is a special purely intelligible substance separate from the general category of substance, so theology is a special science of one kind of being (the divine) cut off from the universal science of being as such (or ontology). As such, Aristotle inaugurates not so much 'onto-theology' as 'theo-ontology' and divides the study of being *qua* being from the study of the Prime Mover. In this way, he lays down the main conceptual foundations for Porphyry's logicized Neo-Platonist ontology and the later scholastic distinction of *metaphysica specialis* and *metaphysica generalis* that mutated into the modern supremacy of ontology over theology.[16]

B. Elevating Substance over Being

For now let us return to Aristotle's account of the preeminence of substance relative to being. Being *qua* being (ὂν ὡς ὄν) is not generic and does not constitute an immutable substance that could serve as the universal essence to all things that are: "Being does not act as essence to any existing thing, for what it is is not a genus."[17] Since "the genera of the beings are different," it follows for Aristotle that "none of the [principles] common [to all beings] is such that from them everything can be proved."[18] In other words, there is no universal science of being *qua* be-

16. Very briefly: what is common to the three breaks in medieval theology that gave rise to modern philosophy (i.e., first, the primacy of essence vis-à-vis existence in Avicenna and Gilbert Porreta; second, the shift from analogy and the real distinction to univocity and the formal distinction in John Duns Scotus; third, the denial of the presence of universals in things in William of Ockham) is the — predominantly Franciscan — focus on Aristotelian substance at the expense of Neo-Platonist relationality and the subsumption of theology under ontology, a development resisted by Aquinas and other Dominicans (as I shall argue in chapters 4-6).

17. "τὸ δ' εἶναι οὐκ οὐσία οὐδενί," *Posterior Analytics* II 7, 92ᵇ13-14 (henceforth *Post. An.*), in *The Complete Works of Aristotle*, vol. 1, p. 152.

18. *Post. An.* I 32, 88ᵃ36-ᵇ2, in *The Complete Works of Aristotle*, vol. 1, p. 145 (translation modified). Cf. *Top.* VI 12, 149ᵇ18-23.

ing that includes both the Prime Mover and secondary substances. And since the Prime Mover is not prior in theoretical knowledge to all existing things, theology is not synonymous with 'first philosophy' or metaphysics. Thus there is no single science that encompasses each and every kind of being, including the divine first mover — just as the latter is not the real good in virtue of which all other goods exist by participation, a solution that Aristotle famously dismissed as a Platonic myth.[19] That is why Aristotle contrasts Platonic forms with his system of categories of beings — an alternative that Kant in his *Critique of Pure Reason* §10 no less famously dismissed as a rhapsody. From the outset of post-Socratic philosophy, there is a crucial point of contrast between Plato's theological metaphysics of the Good and other forms, on the one hand, and Aristotle's meta-logical ontology of substance and the rest of the categories, on the other hand.

It is true that Aristotle ties the logical terms of species, genera, and differentia to the higher ontological unity of substance and the other categorial terms. The analogy of being is the ontological correlate of the unity of epistemological theorems in universal science, as all things are governed by analogical units such as the three elements (matter, form, privation) and the four analogically related causes (material, formal, final, and efficient).[20] As such, different kinds of existing beings are united by analogy: "[T]hings that are not all in one genus are one by analogy" (*Met.* V 6, 1017^{a}2-3). In this way, analogy describes how things exist under the different categories and how the categorial terms relate to one another. However, to say that being is analogous cannot explain why anything exists in the first place and why there would be a definitive number of categorial terms. Nor does the analogy of being account for the paradoxical and ultimately aporetic grounding (πρὸς ἕν) of a multiplicity of categories in the unity of groundless being, as Pierre Aubenque has ex-

19. "If a number of things are in accord with a single [Platonic] idea, there is also a single science of them; hence [if there were a Platonic idea of good], there would be a single science of all goods. But in fact there are many sciences even of the goods under one category," *Nicomachean Ethics* I 6, 1096^{a}29-32 [henceforth *Nic. Eth.*], in *The Complete Works of Aristotle*, vol. 2, p. 1732 (translation modified). Cf. *Eud. Eth.* I 8, 1217^{b}33-^{a}2.

20. ". . . they [the first principles] are all like chance associations, since they are coincidental, but appropriate to one another, and one by analogy. For in each category of being there is the analogous thing; as the straight line is in length, so is the plane in surface, the odd perhaps in number, and the white in color," *Met.* XIV 6, 1093^{b}16-20, in *The Complete Works of Aristotle*, vol. 2, p. 1728 (translation modified).

tensively documented.[21] Perhaps most importantly of all, the analogical ordering of being does not provide answers to the question of why things come into being and why they are directed towards the final cause in the divine first mover.

Aristotle sidesteps this aporia by saying that analogical being has a focal meaning and a nuclear realization in substance, as G. E. L. Owen and Donald MacKinnon indicate. Owen writes that "all the senses of *on* must be defined in terms of *ousia,* substance."[22] Drawing upon Aristotle's notorious example of the link between the multiple meanings of being healthy and health itself in *Metaphysics* Γ 2, MacKinnon explains that "it is this relation of other manifestations to the nuclear realization of health that gives to those other manifestations what I have called their relativity. So it is with being in relation to substance."[23] According to Owen and MacKinnon, Aristotle posits an asymmetric relation between substance and being: substance exists *per se,* whereas everything else is relative to substance. Aristotle also suggests that substance inheres in all beings that actually exist and makes them what they are. In relation to individuation, the question is whether universal substance or essence is particularized by concrete being, as he appears to suggest in the *Categories,* or whether individual substance or essence individuates general being, as he seems to argue in the *Metaphysics.*

In fact, it is neither. Aristotle's account of individual substance is notoriously complex and controversial, and it is best understood in the context of his critique of Plato's theory of forms. As C. D. C. Reeves notes, Aristotle's objection to Plato's metaphysics is less concerned with the relation between the one form and the many things or the 'third man' problem of the infinite regress of ideas. Instead, the main thrust of his critique can be expressed in terms of the following two, closely related questions. First, how can a single thing be both ontologically particular (a particular 'this') and noetically universal (a universal 'such'), for other-

21. Pierre Aubenque, *Le problème de l'être chez Aristote. Essai sur la problématique aristotélicienne* (Paris: Presses Universitaires de France, 1997; orig. pub. 1962), pp. 134-250.

22. G. E. L. Owen, "Logic and Metaphysics in Some Early Works of Aristotle," in *Aristotle and Plato in the Mid-Fourth Century: Papers of the Symposium Aristotelicum Held at Oxford in August 1957,* ed. Ingemar Düring and G. E. L. Owen (Göttingen-Stockholm-Uppsala: Elanders, 1960), pp. 162-90 (184 note 16).

23. Donald MacKinnon, "Aristotle's Conception of Substance," in *New Essays on Plato and Aristotle,* ed. Renford Bambrough (London: Routledge & Kegan Paul, 1965), pp. 97-119 (98).

wise "any proposed definition will fragment the unitary *definiendum* into all the different particulars [if man or animal is seen as a particular 'this'] that appear in the *definiens*"?[24] Second, how can both an individual substance and its essence be ontologically and epistemologically primary, for otherwise either the unity of the thing is threatened or — if substance and essence are detached from one another — substance is unknowable and essence does not exist?[25] In other words, Aristotle claims that Plato's metaphysics of the Good as the form of all forms cannot explain how one and the same thing — individual substance — is both universal and particular. As we shall see, his own solution is to say that beyond the Platonic fallacy of particular things participating in the universal forms, real substantive things are composed of individual universal form and proximate matter. In virtue of their universal formal aspect, they desire the ultimate actuality of the Prime Mover's unique primary substance. By contrast, Plato views things as instantiations of the universal forms and forms as "themselves 'things' in the most eminent possible sense."[26]

How does Aristotle arrive at his proposed solution of individual substances that are both universal and particular? In the *Categories,* he maintains that substance is the first in the hierarchy of categories of being and that as such it is universal and general, not particular and individual. By the time he writes the later books of the *Metaphysics* (especially Z and H, but also Λ),[27] he has modified this position and replaced universal substance with primary substance, which (at least in matter-form compounds) is individual essence. This shift is the result of his investigation of substantial change in the *Physics* and his analysis of physical objects in terms of matter and form. So what is primary substance? In *Metaphysics* Z 1, substance is defined as the 'what-ness' of being, "that which is primarily and *is* simply (not is something)."[28] Primary sub-

24. *Met.* III 6, 1003^{a}7-17. Cf. C. D. C. Reeve, *Substantial Knowledge: Aristotle's Metaphysics* (Indianapolis: Hackett, 2000), pp. 13-15 (15).

25. *Met.* VII, 6, 1031^{a}25-^{b}14. Cf. Reeve, *Substantial Knowledge,* pp. 15-17; A. R. Lacey, "Οὐσία and Form in Aristotle," *Phronesis* 10 (1965): 54-69.

26. John Milbank, "Only Theology Saves Metaphysics: On the Modalities of Terror," in *Belief and Metaphysics,* ed. Conor Cunningham and Peter M. Candler Jr. (London: SCM, 2007), pp. 452-500 (465).

27. On the chronology of *Met.* Λ, see Günther Patzig, "Theology and Ontology in Aristotle's Metaphysics," in *Articles on Aristotle,* ed. Jonathan Barnes, Malcolm Schofield, and Richard Sorabji (London: Duckworth, 1979), vol. 3, pp. 33-49.

28. *Met.* Z 1, 1028^{a}30, in *The Complete Works of Aristotle,* vol. 2, p. 1623.

stance is self-subsistent and provides the formal, ontological substratum for all other categories to exist. Against Plato, who is said to posit three types of substance (the Forms, the objects of mathematics, and the substance of sensible bodies), Aristotle insists that substance is one and individual (*Met.* Z 2, 1028^{b}19-21) and that it is a thing's essence because otherwise an infinite regress would ensue (*Met.* Z 6, 1032^{a}4; Λ 3, 1070^{a}1-3). Since the primary substance that underpins all things is individual, each and every thing is generated as an individual and entertains links with other things and also with the Prime Mover, links that are purely categorial — not metaphysical. In other words, the existence of things is individual, not relational. Likewise, the ties that pertain among things and between things and the divine first mover are predicated on the individuality of the substance to which all other categories are subordinated. Relation is just another categorial term that describes how a thing exists, not a metaphysically constitutive principle that helps explain why something is in the first place and why it might be generated by the Prime Mover.

C. The Priority of Essence over Existence

This primacy of substance over relation in Aristotle's ontology entails a division of essence and existence within composites and a separation of the first mover's actuality from the being of beings. In this way, substances are generated by other substances, and not ultimately by the Prime Mover. As such, substances self-individuate (as I will explain). There are at least three reasons for this. First of all, in *Metaphysics* Z 13 the argument that essence or substance is prior to universals prompts Aristotle to reject Plato's metaphysics of participation. The Stagirite defines Platonist universals as "a this" (τόδε τι) or a quality (ποιόν). So conceived, universals are predicable of things that participate in them, yet at the same time universals are definite and actual entities that are prior to and separate from their participants — forms that exist. The reason why Aristotle repudiates Plato's universals is that they threaten the unity of primary substances. Universals or qualities (ποιά) are viewed as components of substance and therefore prior to substance. But for Aristotle nothing can be prior to substance, for without substance there is nothing and nothing is apart from or outside substance (*Met.* Z 1, 1028^{a}32-35; Z 6, 1031^{a}28-1031^{b}21; 1032^{a}4-5). If this is so, then, as

Aristotle himself concludes, "[N]o universal attribute is a substance, and this is also plain from the fact that no common predicate indicates a 'this,' but rather a 'such.'"[29] So, contrary to Plato (and Christian Neo-Platonists like Augustine, Boethius, Dionysius, and Aquinas), universals are not transcendentally convertible in Aristotle's philosophy. They are properties *of* substance that 'owe' their existence *to* substance. In other words, Aristotle drives a wedge between substance, universals, and particulars by making the latter two unilaterally dependent on the former. Aristotle's Prime Mover is not present in other substances but instead acts as their final cause. Plato's Good, on the other hand, is relational vis-à-vis other forms and things in the sense that it is present in them, so that they may participate in it — though the participants can of course never exhaust the range of the participable Good and the other participable forms.

The second reason is that the Prime Mover only acts as final cause and not as efficient cause, as I have repeatedly hinted at.[30] Aristotle writes in *Metaphysics* Λ that the Prime Mover produces "the primary eternal and single movement" (*Met.* Λ 8, $1073^a25\text{-}26$), and in the same paragraph he explains that this movement is the end of all other kinds of movement in the heavens and in the sublunary world. Likewise, the Prime Mover as the pure actuality of thought and life is the end that all things desire. Again in *Metaphysics* Λ where Aristotle likens the link between the Prime Mover and the sublunary world to the relation between a general and his army, he states that things are connected with one another, "for all are ordered together to one end" (*Met.* Λ 10, $1075^a17\text{-}18$). There is kinetic movement in the heavens and in the world of nature, and

---

29. *Met.* Z 13, $1038^b35\text{-}1039^a2$, in *The Complete Works of Aristotle,* vol. 2, p. 1640.

30. Whether the causative power of Aristotle's Prime Mover is exclusively final or also efficient has been the subject of an intense controversy. On the former, see Owens, "The Relation of God to the World in the *Metaphysics,*" pp. 207-28; and Lloyd P. Gerson, *God and Greek Philosophy: Studies in the Early History of Natural Theology* (London: Routledge, 1990), pp. 120-41. On the latter, see W. J. Verdenius, "Traditional and Personal Elements in Aristotle's Religion," *Phronesis* 5 (1960): 56-70; Thomas De Koninck, "La 'Pensée de la Pensée' chez Aristote," in *La question de Dieu chez Aristote et Hegel,* ed. Thomas De Koninck (Paris: P.U.F., 1991), pp. 69-151; Sarah Broadie, "Que fait le premier moteur d'Aristote?" *Revue philosophique* 183 (1993): 375-411; David Bradshaw, *Aristotle East and West: Metaphysics and the Division of Christendom* (Cambridge: Cambridge University Press, 2004), pp. 24-44. For an overview of earlier rival accounts, see Leo Elders, *Aristotle's Theology: A Commentary on Book Λ of the Metaphysics* (Assen: Van Gorcum, 1972), pp. 1-43. Cf. H. J. Easterling, "The Unmoved Mover in Early Aristotle," *Phronesis* 21 (1976): 252-65.

there is also noetic activity among intelligent substances because all things are ordered to the supreme τέλος in the Prime Mover whose actuality somehow elicits the desire of everything that exists.[31] In consequence, the actuality of the Prime Mover is severed from the actuality of primary substance or essence. This raises the question of why form would at all 'wish' to be allied to matter and how the pure potency of matter can be 'lured' to the unreserved actuality of form — a question I will return to in the following sections.

Third, primary substance is always already individual and singular, as I have already indicated. For this reason, universals such as the good and the beautiful do not individuate things. They are properties that act as nonessential qualities in things. Moreover, as the following section shows, the individuation of composites marks the unity between individual substantial form and proximate matter. If, as Aristotle also holds, form makes a thing what it is, then this raises the question of whether matter is part of the complex form of a composite or whether matter merely differentiates the essentially identical members of a species.

3. Can Substances Self-Individuate?

Coupled with the primacy of substance, the critique of Plato's metaphysics of participation leads Aristotle to develop an alternative account of the relation between universal immaterial essences and particular material things in terms of the unity of individual substantial form and proximate matter.[32] From the outset of the *Metaphysics,* he emphasizes the oneness of composites, for each matter-form compound is constituted by the unity of substantial form and proximate matter. Substantial form is defined as a 'this' (τόδε τι), not a 'such' (τοιόνδε), and it is thus individ-

---

31. David Bradshaw is right to point out that in *Met.* Λ 7-10, the actuality of Prime Mover is not limited to producing kinetic movement but in fact encompasses thought thinking itself and as such extends to noetic activity. See Bradshaw, *Aristotle East and West,* pp. 30-32, 38-44. However, it simply does *not* follow that Aristotle's Unmoved Mover acts as formal and efficient cause. Aristotle repeatedly refers to the latter as the *end* of all motion and thought. Substances in the sublunary world are lured forward by the Unmoved Mover and thereby perfect their unique form through ever more actualization of their material potency, but neither their coming-into-being nor their continuous existence is caused by the Prime Mover.

32. Rorty, "Genus as Matter: A Reading of *Metaphysics* Z-H," p. 402.

ual, not general.[33] Proximate matter is defined as "that which, not being a 'this' actually, is potentially a 'this,'"[34] and it is therefore in potency to the actuality of form. The unity between individual substantial form and proximate matter is real (rather than merely conceptual), and it constitutes the actuality (ἐντελεχεία) of the composite as a whole (not just of the formal aspect). This alternative model is grounded in Aristotle's ontology of actuality and potentiality, as detailed in *Metaphysics* Δ 2, 4, 7, and 12. In *Metaphysics* H (and elsewhere),[35] Aristotle connects act and potency to the question of unity of a composite at a given moment and over time. The interplay of act (ἐνέργεια) and potency (δύναμις) at the heart of each and every material composite can account for synchronic as well as diachronic individuation.[36] In the case of composites, form and matter constitute a compound that is both individual and complex. Form and matter do not represent separate parts but are distinct aspects of one single entity. Individual substantial form is in actuality what proximate matter is in potency: ". . . the proximate matter and the form are one and the same thing, the one potentially, the other actually."[37] For instance, in the case of man, individual substantial form is the unique soul of a certain body, which is the proximate matter of *that form*.[38]

Aristotle's key argument is that form and matter are not separate from one another. Rather, they are two necessary constituents of the same one individual composite — proximate matter is potentially what the substantial individual form is in actuality because the potential and

33. *Met.* Δ 8, 1017ᵇ25; H 1, 1042ᵃ29; Θ 7, 1049ᵃ28-29; Λ 5, 1071ᵃ27-29; *On Generation and Corruption* 318ᵇ32 (henceforth *De Gen. et Corr.*). Already in the *Categories*, Aristotle views substances as irreducibly individual, e.g., *Cat.* 2ᵇ1-3ᵃ33. Cf. Rogers Albritton, "Forms of Particular Substances in Aristotle's *Metaphysics*," *Journal of Philosophy* 54 (1957): 699-708; Michael Frede, "Individuals in Aristotle," in Michael Frede, *Essays in Ancient Philosophy* (Oxford: Clarendon Press, 1987), pp. 49-63.

34. *Met.* H 1, 1041ᵃ27-28, in *The Complete Works of Aristotle*, vol. 2, p. 1645.

35. Ellen Stone Haring, "Substantial Form in Aristotle's *Metaphysics* Z," *Review of Metaphysics* 10 (1956-57): 308-32, 482-501, 698-713.

36. For this as well as other reasons, Aristotle's ontology does account for synchronic and diachronic individuation, contrary to critics such as Karl Popper and Marc Cohen. See Karl Popper, "Symposium: The Principle of Individuation III," *Aristotelian Society* suppl. 27 (1953): 97-120, esp. pp. 98-101, 112; S. Marc Cohen, "Aristotle and Individuation," in *New Essays on Aristotle*, ed. Francis J. Pelletier and John King-Farlow (Calgary, AB: University of Calgary Press, 1984), pp. 41-65, esp. 41-44.

37. *Met.* H 6, 1045ᵇ17-19, in *The Complete Works of Aristotle*, vol. 2, p. 1651.

38. *De Anima* II 1, 412ᵇ1-11; II 2, 414ᵃ27; II 4, 415ᵇ10-11 (henceforth *De An.*); *Met.* Z 11, 1037ᵃ5-9.

the actual constitute a unity (*Met.* H 6, 1045^{b}21) and the primary meaning of unity is actuality (*De An.* II 1, 412^{b}8-9). The actuality (ἐντελεχεία) of individual composites is the unity of an individual form with determinate matter. In the case of man, form is the act of a body of a definite kind that has the potency to be an individuated complex: "[T]he soul is an actuality or account of something that possesses a potentiality of being such."[39] Form is an actuality or a 'this,' and matter is a potentiality or a 'such.' Composites are form-matter compounds that have two parts, one which is actual and the other which is potential. Form-matter compounds are individual precisely because they are the real actual unity of the power of the individual substantial form that actualizes the capacity of proximate matter to be *this* rather than *that*.

Before I can give a full account of Aristotle's theory of individuation, I need to explain his conception of the unity of individual substantial form and proximate matter. In *Metaphysics* H, he defines this unity as follows:

> . . . to ask the cause of their [proximate matter and form] being one is like asking the cause of unity in general; for each thing is a unity, and the potential and the actual are somehow one. Therefore there is no other cause here unless there is something which caused the movement from potentiality into actuality.[40]

However, to say that unity is determined not only by individual substantial form but also by proximate matter is not to suggest that form and matter are identical or equivalent. Form is preeminent because it is universal and actual and as such can realize the potency of matter. As such, individuality follows from matter when conjoined with form: the universal is only actual as individuated by matter, for the form of composites does not exist in actuality without matter. Just as actualization is primarily formal but requires potency in order to bring something into actuality, so individuation is primarily material but requires form in order to make real the potentiality of matter to be *this* rather than *that*.

As such, Aristotle's account of individuation does not entirely rule out the 'reality' of universals. Universality is reconfigured as the particu-

---

39. *De An.* II 2, 414^{a}28, in *The Complete Works of Aristotle,* vol. 1, p. 659.

40. *Met.* H 6, 1045^{b}19-23, in *The Complete Works of Aristotle,* vol. 2, p. 1651. Cf. *GA* II 1, 734^{a}30-32.

larity of forms that are common to many individuals.[41] Man is now conceived as a body-soul compound, as an "ensouled body" (*De An.* I 1, 403ᵃ3-25) — the ensouled body *is* the individual man (*De An.* II 1, 413ᵃ2-3). As such, man is both particular (*this* ensouled body rather than *that*), yet at the same time universal because "ensouled body" can be predicated of more than one composite. Aristotle relates particularity and universality in terms of his understanding of analogy: "If he [Socrates] is simply this particular soul and this particular body, the individual is analogous to the universal."[42] Concrete composites are individual because they are the particular analogue of the universal matter-form compound (the "ensouled body" in general) that is individual. The individuation of composite substances marks the particularization of universality. In other words, individuation is the particular manifestation of a universal that is common to a multiplicity of beings.

The trouble with this conception is that the singularity of individual substantial form reduces individuation to generation: "The universal causes . . . do not exist. For the individual is the source of the individuals. For while man is the cause of man universally, there is no universal man; but Peleus is the cause of Achilles, and your father of you."[43] In other words, the origin of individuality is the indwelling of individual substantial form in proximate matter, both of which have immediate causes but neither of which originates in the first and final cause of the Prime Mover, as I show in the following section.

4. Aristotle's 'Indifferent God'

The primacy of substance implies that an infinite regress in the order of causes is ontologically impossible. If there is an individual primary substance that exists and is the condition of possibility for everything else, then there must be a Prime Mover whose actuality is the final cause. That is how Aristotle describes the divine or God (θέος) in *Metaphysics* Λ 7. The first heaven is defined as eternal and set in motion by a superior movement which does not undergo any change but instead imparts mo-

---

41. This contrasts with an alternative conception that emphasizes the generality of species and genera and views individuation in terms of primary matter, which limits species form.

42. *Met.* Z 11, 1037ᵃ8-9, in *The Complete Works of Aristotle*, vol. 2, p. 1637.

43. *Met.* Λ 5, 1071ᵃ20-22, in *The Complete Works of Aristotle*, vol. 2, p. 1692.

tion as an object of desire and through the movement of the first heaven moves the rest of things.[44] He goes on to say that "the primary objects of desire and thought are the same . . . [in thought] substance is first, and in substance, that which is simple and exists actually."[45] Substances in the heavens and in the sublunary world love and desire the Prime Mover as ultimate first cause. Therefore Aristotle infers that "[o]n such a principle, then, depend the heavens and the world of nature."[46]

But it is not clear how in Aristotle's metaphysics the actuality of substantial form is related to that of the Prime Mover. The latter is but a remote first cause that imparts motion exclusively by final causality, not by efficient causality. The Prime Mover cannot act as efficient cause on the heavens and the sublunary world because, as Joseph Owens explains, Aristotle's conception of efficient causality prohibits this:

> The action of an efficient cause is not regarded as a further intrinsic perfection, but rather as a perfection that is always present and that produces its effect upon contact with the *passum* and the removal of hindrances [*Physics* VIII 4, 255^{a}1-^{b}24]. The new actuality brought about by its activity lies therefore outside itself as cause. If separate substances were an efficient cause, then it would be in potentiality to something else.[47]

Moreover, in the *Metaphysics* Aristotle describes the pure actuality and activity of the Prime Mover as the end which all things desire and to which they are ordered, as I have already suggested in the previous sections.

Once the first cause is denied efficient and formal causality and limited to final causality, the individuation of composites is severed from the Prime Mover. For this reason, Owens — to quote his remark again — is right to conclude: "[H]e [Aristotle] does not seem to have any means of explaining how the actual contact is made between separate substance and material substance."[48] Notably, in his commentary on Aristotle's *Metaphysics,* St. Thomas Aquinas argues that the finite existence of composites is caused efficiently by the subsistent existence of God and that

44. Owens, "The Relation of God to the World in the *Metaphysics*," pp. 210-15.

45. *Met.* Λ 7, 1072^{a}27-32, in *The Complete Works of Aristotle*, vol. 2, p. 1694.

46. *Met.* Λ 7, 1072^{b}13-14, in *The Complete Works of Aristotle*, vol. 2, p. 1695.

47. Owens, "The Relation of God to the World in the *Metaphysics*," p. 216.

48. Owens, "The Relation of God to the World in the *Metaphysics*," p. 217, note 18.

therefore God's actuality is more than simply the final cause of the actuality of creation.[49] As a result of limiting God to final causality, Aristotle's theology severs the individuation of concrete composites from the causative action of the Unmoved Mover. Individuality is thus grounded in the individuals themselves. Aristotle's God is desired and loved as the ultimate final cause but this God is utterly indifferent to the sublunary world — "thought thinking itself," a purely self-directed energy. Moreover, the eternity of matter does not in any way intimate God's existence and essence, the pure actuality of form itself. Individuation is immanentized and reduced to generation, as I have already indicated.

Likewise, individuation is exclusively a function of immediate immanent proximate causes: proximate matter is the material cause and substantial form is the efficient and formal cause. The matter and form of composites are presupposed rather than brought into existence by the first cause: "The natural things which (like some artificial objects) can be produced spontaneously are those whose matter can be moved even by itself in the way in which the seed usually moves it; but those things which have not such matter cannot be produced except by parents."[50] Indeed, Aristotle writes that ". . . neither the matter nor the form comes to be — i.e. the proximate matter and form. For everything that changes is something and is changed by something and into something."[51]

In summary, for Aristotle the individuality of concrete composites is self-grounded and individuation is a function of other individual composites. Therefore, he cannot account for why composites are ultimately individual and how and why they are individuated. Ultimately, this is because the Greek form-matter dualism lingers in his work: prime matter and universal form are simply presupposed and in no way related to the Prime Mover (*Met.* Λ 9, 1074^{b}15-1075^{a}10). As I argue in the remainder of this chapter, the difference with Plato is that Aristotle lacks any account of the Prime Mover as the efficient and formal cause which brings everything into being and makes it what it is. Aristotle cannot explain why God would wish to actualize or individuate anything at all because he does not envision the Good as that which 'eminently' moves matter and form into place and infuses everything with the form of goodness. As I

---

49. St. Thomas Aquinas, *In duodecim libros Metaphysicorum Aristotelis expositio,* 2nd ed. (Rome: Marietti, 1971), lectura 1, no. 1164.

50. *Met.* Z 9, 1034^{b}3-7, in *The Complete Works of Aristotle,* vol. 2, p. 1633.

51. *Met.* Λ 3, 1069^{a}35-1070^{a}1, in *The Complete Works of Aristotle,* vol. 2, p. 1690.

show in the following two sections, this ontology and theology commit him to separate human activity within the household (οἶκος) and the city-state (πόλις) from the wider operation of the universe (κόσμος) and therefore introduce an unwarranted dualism between practical and intellectual activity.

5. Ontology, Theology, and Politics

At the end of the section in the *Metaphysics* on the Prime Unmoved Mover, Aristotle defends the primacy of the first principle and ultimate end to which everything is ordered. He goes on to quote from the *Iliad* II, 204: "The rule of many is not good; let there be one ruler."[52] This passage is indicative not only of the importance of hierarchy but also of the link between his account of being and his vision of the polity. In this section, I argue that Aristotle's ontological and theological theory of individuation has a political correlate. Just as the individuation of beings is the actualization and perfection of individual form in proximate matter, so the individuation of 'political animals' is the actualization and perfection of personal and collective civic virtue. Since God's causative action is absent from the operation of the sublunary world, Aristotle's vision of politics and ethics restricts divine presence in the polity by separating the actuality of God as the final cause from the actuality of the natural and human realm. In turn, this separation underpins Aristotle's celebration of self-sufficiency and sovereignty at the level of the individual, the οἶκος, the πόλις, and the κόσμος. This also entails a reconfiguration of action, defined as the prime mode of actualizing and perfecting form and of attaining the goods that are proper and internal to each activity. For Aristotle, activity is divided into theoretical and practical activity, and this division poses problems for the unity and universality of the good and the particularity and perfection of personal and collective civic virtue.

Plato and Aristotle challenge the dualism in pre-Socratic metaphysics between the ideal and the real, the intelligible and the sensible, and the universal and the particular, as I indicated at the beginning of this chapter. For both, there is a more fundamental unity of being that is manifest in material beings and, as such, it can be perceived by the

---

52. *Met.* Λ 10, 1076ª4, in *The Complete Works of Aristotle*, vol. 2, p. 1700.

physical senses and grasped by the immaterial mind. According to Aristotle, this unity encompasses the *cosmos* and the *polis* and also extends to individuals and their activities, for effects resemble their cause and everything has a final cause that is unitary. Unity is essential, not accidental, because essence is one, not many. In consequence, unity is teleological and dynamic because a thing's finality corresponds to *that* thing's particular essence and orders its movement and specific activities to the highest good which is particular and internal to each and every activity. To achieve one's τέλος is to be free from any sort of dependency or need: "[T]he final cause and end of a thing is the best, and to be self-sufficing is the end and the best."[53] The supreme goal of all beings is unitary because it is to attain autarchy. Likewise, the activity that secures autarchy is also unitary — the contemplative understanding of the divine. For Aristotle, this is the highest intellectual virtue (*Nic. Eth.* X 7, 1177^{a}11-1178^{a}8).

In pursuing this *telos,* beings fulfill their nature and are oriented towards the supreme good, for nature determines what is right for each and every thing: "[T]hat which is proper to each thing is by nature best and most pleasant for each thing."[54] Nature (φύσις) is both ethical and political because it is structured by a hierarchy of goods and virtues.[55] So conceived, nature propels all beings to pursue and fulfill their potency to be as autarchic as possible and to secure the autonomy of the *polis* (*Pol.* I 2, 1253^{a}29; VII 3, 1325^{b}14-32). Just as human nature is always already good insofar as it is oriented towards the highest good, so human nature is also always already political insofar as individual self-sufficiency can only be achieved within the collective polity.[56] (This contrasts sharply with the modern idea of a prepolitical or apolitical state of nature, whether Hobbes's unmediated violence in the state of nature, Locke's peaceable order, or Rousseau's original freedom, as I explore in chapter 9.) In the words of Aristotle, "The proof that the state is a creation of nature and

---

53. *Politics* I 2, 1252^{a}1 (henceforth *Pol.*), in *The Complete Works of Aristotle,* vol. 2, p. 1987.

54. *Nic. Eth.* X 7, 1178^{a}5-6, in *The Complete Works of Aristotle,* vol. 2, p. 1862. Cf. *Pol.* I 2, 1253^{a}2-25.

55. *Nic. Eth.* I 7, 1097^{b}12; IX 9, 1169^{b}20; *Pol.* III 6, 1278^{b}19.

56. However, there are two exceptions: first, those who are human without being in the *polis* and those who are in the *polis* without being properly human. On the latter case, see John M. Rist, *The Mind of Aristotle: A Study in Philosophical Growth* (Toronto: University of Toronto Press, 1989), esp. pp. 249-52.

prior to the individual is that the individual, when isolated, is not self-sufficing; and therefore he is like a part in relation to the whole."[57]

The tension governing Aristotle's ethics and politics is then between the *telos* of individual self-sufficiency based on the individual contemplation of the divine on the one hand, and the dependency of individuals on the *polis* as a result of the political nature of man, on the other hand. The resulting complex reciprocal relation between nature and politics has far-reaching implications for the question of individuation. To pursue the highest good — the virtue of autarchy — is to perfect one's form and be individuated, because the highest good is both that which all things desire and that which actualizes their potency.[58] Politics is ultimately at the service of individual self-sufficiency and collective autonomy within the *oikos* and the *polis*. This, in essence, is how Aristotle envisions the political and ethical correlate of his ontological account of individuation.

Theologically and ontologically, individuation and perfection in the sublunary world take the form of actualizing potentiality. Composite substances stand in potency to the higher actuality of separate substances and ultimately to the pure act of the Prime Mover. However, there is no link between the Prime Mover and the sublunary world other than by way of final causality, as I argued in previous sections. Aristotle's divinity is loved and desired as the final cause (*Met.* Λ 7, 1072^{a}26-1072^{b}31), but God does not impart motion to matter-form compounds. Efficient causation is restricted to individual composites themselves and to other composites that generate them. Material causation is limited to proximate matter and formal causation to individual substantial form. Given the connection between metaphysics, politics, and ethics (especially in terms of act and potency), what are the consequences of Aristotle's causal account for the individuation of composites in the *polis?* Aristotle's God is the *telos* of all things, but not the source of their activity, such that the origin of being remains unexplained.[59] For the Stagirite, to love and desire God is to

---

57. *Pol.* I 2, 1252^{a}25-27, in *The Complete Works of Aristotle,* vol. 2, p. 1988.

58. On the link between the ontological and the political dimension of actualization, see Alasdair MacIntyre, *Whose Justice? Which Rationality?* (London: Duckworth, 1988), p. 101. *Contra* MacIntyre, who argues that Aristotle develops and corrects Platonism, I contend that Aristotle abandons the transcendence of the Good and embraces an account of God that severs human activity in the sublunary world from divine activity in the Prime Mover. See, *infra,* main text (sections 7-9).

59. This *aporia* in Aristotle's theology was instrumental to Neo-Platonic reflections on the One as generative. See, *infra,* chapter 2, esp. sections 1 and 2.

approximate as much as possible God's autarchy and sovereignty by way of contemplation. All activities (practical and theoretical) and all virtues (moral and intellectual) are ordered toward this single end, but they are not sustained by the actuality of Aristotle's God.

Politically, this vision implies that the operation of the *polis* and the actions of individuals are self-grounded. The *telos* of politics and ethics is the pursuit of the highest human good that is inscribed in nature and common to all individuals, autarchy and sovereignty. The good is dynamic because it marks the actualization of form or essence. Therefore autarchy and sovereignty are not static but instead teleological. Activity provides the link between Aristotle's theological, ontological, and political account of individuation in particular, as I argued at the beginning of this section.[60] This is because activity (ἐνέργεια) produces actuality (ἐντελεχεία), which is its own end or finality (*Met.* Θ 8, 1050ᵃ21-23). In the *Poetics,* Aristotle writes that the quest for the good is a certain kind of activity, not a quality. In the *Nicomachean Ethics* and the *Politics,* he argues that in the case of human beings, activity takes the form of work. Activity in general (and work in the case of man) is the principal mode of actualizing and perfecting individual form: "[W]hile making has an end other than itself, action cannot; for good action itself is its end."[61] This conception of activity severs the link between the operation of the *polis* and the actuality of God and foregrounds Aristotle's celebration of autarchy and sovereignty.

6. Virtue, Autarchy, and Sovereignty

Aristotle divides activity (πράξις) into two separate types. First, purely practical action that is governed by moral virtue. Second, exclusively in-

---

60. For a detailed exposition of activity in relation to politics and ethics, see Martha Nussbaum, "Nature, Function, and Capability: Aristotle on Political Distribution," *OSAP* Supplementary Volume (1988): 144-84; Martha Nussbaum, "Human Functioning and Social Justice: In Defense of Aristotelian Essentialism," *Political Theory* 20 (1992): 202-46; Jill Frank, *A Democracy of Distinction: Aristotle and the Work of Politics* (Chicago: University of Chicago Press, 2005), pp. 32-53. *Contra* Nussbaum, I agree with Frank that Aristotle's account of nature does not warrant an essentialist and objectivist reading of his vision of politics. In contrast with Frank, I argue that Aristotle fails to relate activity in the *polis* to the actuality of the Prime Mover, which is the final cause of the sublunary world and all composites therein. This failure undermines Aristotle's ontology and his theory of individuation.

61. *Nic. Eth.* VI 5, 1140ᵇ5-7, in *The Complete Works of Aristotle,* vol. 2, p. 1800.

tellectual contemplation that is governed by intellectual virtue. Even though both types are linked via knowledge of first principles (ἀρχαί), only contemplative activity leads to genuine blessedness (εὐδαιμονία). For intellection is the only activity that is both self-sufficing and also in accordance with the highest excellence. By contrast, practical activity lacks the completeness of intellection, and the virtues that praxis embodies do not attain the excellence of contemplation (θεωρία).[62] *Praxis* calls forth contemplation and cannot be grasped without knowledge of first principles, but it does not mediate divine transcendence nor is it upheld by the actuality of Aristotle's God. Only the intellectual virtue of contemplative understanding has Aristotle's divinity as its object. The entire range of practical activity, from farming to handicraft, architecture, poetry, and music, and from warfare to statesmanship, is organized by a hierarchy of goods and standards of excellence. However, the happiness that the pursuit and perfection of this hierarchy generate is exclusively human and neither intimates nor requires God's actuality. As Alasdair MacIntyre remarks, "The happiness achieved in political life is purely human; the happiness of contemplative activity moves to a higher level, 'divine in comparison with human life' [*Nic. Eth.* X 7, 1177[b]32]."[63] The separation of human practical from divine contemplative activity is the result of denying God's transcendence any presence in the immanence of the world. This is because the self-sufficiency of the Prime Mover is such that "the gods and the universe . . . have no external actions over and above their own energies."[64] Aristotle's divinity is self-directed and utterly indifferent to the sublunary world and all things therein.

To the extent that the human mind contemplates the divine, it itself becomes self-sufficient and self-directed: "thoughts and contemplations . . . are independent and complete in themselves."[65] The principle, virtue, and excellence of autarchy and sovereignty are not limited to theology, ontology, and epistemology but extend to politics. Because the highest good is defined in terms of self-sufficiency,[66] Aristotle envisages the possibility of fully autarchic states "which are cut off from others and choose to live alone."[67] While autarchy is not the only desirable condition, Aris-

---

62. On intellection, see *Nic. Eth.* X 7, 1177[a]11-18. On praxis, see *Pol.* VII 3, 1325[b]14-32.
63. MacIntyre, *Whose Justice? Which Rationality?* p. 108.
64. *Pol.* VII 3, 1325[b]29-30, in *The Complete Works of Aristotle*, vol. 2, p. 2104.
65. *Pol.* VII 3, 1325[b]19-20, in *The Complete Works of Aristotle*, vol. 2, p. 2104.
66. See, *supra*, note 53.
67. *Pol.* VII 3, 1325[b]22-24, in *The Complete Works of Aristotle*, vol. 2, p. 2104.

totle's defense of it implies that the relations between *politai* are not essential to their individual welfare. For each *polis* is a whole composed of parts, and mirrors the completeness of the *cosmos*. As such, even relatively small city-states can approximate autarchy — just as in the case of individual souls it is practical wisdom or prudence (φρόνησις) that seeks to balance the passions by using reason but without producing any relational activity with other intelligent substances. This is the result of Aristotle's claim that individuality is self-grounded in substances rather than generated by a relational Prime Mover, as I have already shown. For this reason, individuation is a function of self-actualization and self-perfection. Indeed, immediately following his point about autarchic states he writes that

> . . . activity, as well as other things, may take place by sections; there are many ways in which the sections of a state act upon one another. *The same thing is equally true of every individual.* If this were otherwise, the gods and the universe, who have no external actions over and above their own energies, would be far enough from perfection. Hence it is evident that the same life is best for each individual, and for states and for mankind collectively.[68]

However, my argument seems to meet easy refutation. Does not Aristotle's rejection of dualism and his emphasis on the unity of the *cosmos* guard against self-individuating substances and the autarchy of self-activity? Does not the idea of justice as a quest for personal and collective excellence suggest an overcoming of the false dichotomy of the individual and the communal? For Aristotle, the *cosmos* is the ultimate order of things and frames the operation of each and every *polis*. As such, there is a cosmic counterweight to autarchy and sovereignty, not least because heavenly bodies impart motion to the world and therefore constitute the efficient causes of all sublunary movement.[69] But Aristotle presupposes the existence of heavenly bodies and therefore does not explain why they exist and why they cause movement in the sublunary world. By contrast with Plato's idea of the Good as the ordering principle of the universe, within Aristotle's theology and politics it is not clear what the cosmic dimension of justice might be. In fact, he seems to locate the exercise of

---

68. *Pol.* VII 3, 1325ᵇ24-32, in *The Complete Works of Aristotle*, vol. 2, p. 2104 (my italics).
69. Owens, "The Relation of God to the World in the *Metaphysics*," pp. 215-19.

justice exclusively at the level of the *polis*. Within the polity, justice is transcendent and inclusive, in that it involves judgment and praxis beyond ethnic, social, and economic division.[70] In this sense, justice is individuating because it binds together a multiplicity of diverse individuals and strengthens their moral and intellectual virtues (*Pol.* III 2, 1277^{b}12-21). For justice is a virtuous activity that aims at actualizing the potency of all individuals and the *polis* as a whole in order to attain the highest good. Only a shared polity that is not ruled by arbitrary force based on absolute power or by a social contract based on individual volition but instead governed by the exercise of virtues can hope to achieve the highest good — a contemplative understanding of God as the final cause of all that is.

To practice the virtue of justice (δικαιοσύνη) is to promote corrective and distributive justice in relation with other citizens. This consists in restoring and extending a harmonious order as well as fostering obedience to the principle of distribution that governs the just order secured by corrective justice.[71] As such, justice is relational because it is both individual and communal and directs the relations between particular citizens and the entire community, structuring the *polis* towards unity: "[J]ustice is the bond of men in states; for the administration of justice, which is the determination of what is just, is the principle of order in political society."[72] The faculty of judgment involved in practical wisdom or prudence (φρόνησις) — an intellectual virtue cutting across the divide between theory and praxis — is indispensable to the exercise of justice. Aristotle defines justice as the proper application of right reason (κατὰ τν ὀρθὸν λόγον [*Nic. Eth.* VI 1, 1038^{b}25]). Thus, justice is the ordering norm of ethics in politics — the deployment of justice is impossible outside relations within the *polis*.

However, the virtues that a good life in a just polity embodies are purely human and secondary to the ultimate *telos* — the contemplation of an impersonal unchanging divinity which, as MacIntyre argues, "can itself take no interest in the merely human . . . [and] is nothing other than thought timelessly thinking itself and conscious of nothing but itself."[73]

---

70. For a defense of Aristotle concerning the status of slaves and foreigners in the *polis*, see Frank, *A Democracy of Distinction*, pp. 26-32.

71. MacIntyre, *Whose Justice? Which Rationality?* pp. 103-23.

72. *Pol.* I 2, 1253^{a}37-40, in *The Complete Works of Aristotle*, vol. 2, p. 1988.

73. Alasdair MacIntyre, *After Virtue: A Study in Moral Theory*, 2nd ed. (London: Duckworth, 1985), p. 158.

To the extent that human beings approximate this *telos,* they become both self-sufficing and sovereign. In so doing, they turn away from practical activity and embrace abstract contemplation. Just as at the metaphysical level the supreme *telos* is the autarchy and sovereignty of the individual (within the *oikos* and the *polis*) by a sort of disjunctive echo that paradoxically cuts humans off from the divine exactly to the extent that they imitate it, so at the political level the highest good is also the autarchy and sovereignty of the polity by a similar sort of disjunctive echo that paradoxically separates polities from each other and the rest of the universe to the extent that each excels in different activities and all would benefit from mutual cooperation and solidarity.

At both levels, it is clear for Aristotle that individuals cannot be fully self-sufficing because they require practical activities within the *oikos* and the *polis* to secure basic needs. However, these and other needs are covered by the *oikos* and the *polis,* which are structured according to the secondary goods of the purely human sphere. This is why MacIntyre is right to conclude that "[t]he household and the city-state make the metaphysical human project possible; but the goods which they provide are, although necessary, and although themselves part of that whole human life, subordinate from the metaphysical standpoint."[74] Precisely because of the *oikos* and the *polis* and their self-sufficiency and sovereignty, certain individuals discard this purely human realm and focus exclusively on the divine. In so doing, they become like God and turn away from the activity of the city-state. Aristotle's celebration of self-sufficiency and sovereignty separates the operation of the *polis* from the movement of the *cosmos* and ultimately from the pure actuality of God. As such, Aristotle's divinity as the final cause makes no difference to the ordering relations of justice within the city-state. Everything in the household and the city-state is at the service of abstract contemplation, but contemplative understanding of the timeless λόγος does not transform the polity or the dispensation of justice. Aristotle's vision of metaphysics and politics thus marks a departure from Plato's ideal of philosopher-king (even though at the end of the *Politics* Aristotle talks about the ideal rule of a single supremely good man). It is therefore to Plato that I finally turn in the remainder of this chapter.

74. MacIntyre, *After Virtue*, p. 158.

7. The Primacy of Relation

It was Plato who first argued that the universe marks the ordering of chaotic matter by perfect form. The Socratic and Platonist revolution was to discern the presence of perennial structures in ephemeral phenomena and to theorize this presence in terms of the participation of particular things in universal forms.[75] Prior to Aristotle, Plato had already challenged the dualism between the empirical and the ideal.[76] Indeed, he sought to demonstrate that all binaries are qualified by a more fundamental unity which is phenomenally visible. As such, it can be perceived by the senses and grasped by the mind. Even though this unity is neither fully manifest nor comprehensively intelligible, it is disclosed in all those things that are individually beautiful and collectively form a harmonious whole, for beauty is the first visible effect of the Good in the world.[77] Thus the Good is present in forms and things, positioning them in mutual, real relations.

Key to Plato's metaphysics is his account of 'relationality' (μετά-σχεσις) and participation (μέθεξις) because it explains how and why universal forms are present in particular things. Why relationality and not just participation? The reason is *not* that Plato fails to provide a single definition of the concept of participation, prompting Aristotle's unwarranted charge of "empty talk" and "poetic metaphor."[78] Much rather, Plato deploys other notions such as presence (παρουσία) and communion (κοινωνία), which exceed the notion of particulars participating in uni-

75. *Pace* Joseph Owens, who writes: "He [Plato] saw that the Idea had to be both immanent and transcendent.... Because its nature involved being, it could not be immanent and transcendent at the same time. The difficulty was frankly acknowledged, but no solution was ever offered by Plato." Owens, "The Relation of God to the World in the *Metaphysics*," p. 221.

76. The charge of dualism tends to be based on Plato's account of the body and the soul in the *Phaedo*, especially the idea that the soul seeks to liberate itself from the constricting shackles of the body in order to dwell in the realm of timeless forms (*Phaedo* 78 B 4–84 B 8 [henceforth *Phaed.*]). This sort of selective reading ignores the wider argument in the *Phaedo* and elsewhere in the Platonic corpus, as I will argue below.

77. *Phaedrus* 250 C-D (henceforth *Phaedr.*).

78. *Met.* A 9, 991^{a}20-23, in *The Complete Works of Aristotle*, vol. 2, p. 1566. Cf. *Met.* A 9, 992^{a}26-29; M 5, 1079^{b}24-26. See Gail Fine, "Relational Entities," *Archiv für Geschichte der Philosophie* 65 (1983): 235; Gail Fine, "Forms as Causes: Plato and Aristotle," in *Mathematics and Metaphysics in Aristotle/Mathematik und Metaphysik bei Aristoteles*, ed. Andreas Graeser (Bern: Haupt, 1987), p. 85.

versals because they suggest that forms are somehow present in things. The relation that brings on form is inextricably intertwined with the participation in forms that things receive and that makes them what they are. This raises two questions. First, how can immanent particulars participate in transcendent universals? Second, why would forms 'wish' to be participated in? Plato's answer to both questions is that the Good as the "form of forms" and the "author of all things" *is* in all other forms and in all particulars.[79] Even though Plato does not deploy these exact terms, there is in his metaphysics the priority of the relational giving of presence over participation: the Good 'gives' itself ecstatically in such a way that it infuses all things with goodness, and it is this generative presence in immanent things that enables them to participate in the universal forms and thus perfect their given goodness. As such, Plato distinguishes the relationality of forms to other forms and the Good (the participation of forms in the Dyad, e.g., *Phaed.* 101C) from the relation that brings on form and imparts being in which things participate (e.g., *Phaed.* 100D; cf. *The Republic* IV, 437E; *The Sophist* 247A, 248C, and 248E). In this way, he positions being in the intermediary realm of 'the between' (μεταξύ, e.g., *Symposium* 202B5) where the original relation among the Good and all the forms and the participatory relation between things and forms intersect without, however, collapsing into one another.

This account is analogous to the argument that for Plato, form acquisition in some important sense precedes and enables form possession.[80] Both relationality (μετάσχεσις) and participation (μέθεξις) derive from the same root 'to participate' (μετέχειν). The grammatical difference is that the former indicates acquisition while the latter connotes possession. If, as Plato believed, forms are present in things, then the presence of forms includes both dimensions — acquisition and possession, 'relationality' and participation. In response to possible misunderstandings arising from the notion of participation, Plato opts in the *Parmenides* and the *Philebus* for the language of likeness of particulars to forms. Likeness indicates that particulars are reflections of originals. As such, likeness is the 'form' of the presence of universals in particulars. Particulars are relational because they depend on universal forms for their existence, essence, and continuous being. Instead of being self-generating and self-

---

79. *Euthydemus* 281 E (henceforth *Euthyd.*); *The Republic* VI 508 E, 511 B, VII 516 B (henceforth *Rep.*); *Philebus* 64 E, 65 A 3-5, 66 A-B (henceforth *Phileb.*).

80. *Inter alia, Phaed.* 101 C 2-4. Cf. Fine, "Forms as Causes: Plato and Aristotle," p. 93.

subsistent substances, they are caused and sustained by forms (*Phaed.* 100 C-D). There is an asymmetric relation between immanent particulars and transcendent universals. Universals are not self-sufficient either because they are coextensive with other universals — being, beauty, unity are all coterminous. There is thus a symmetric relation amongst forms. Moreover, universals are themselves relational because they all proceed in some sense from the Good, the form of forms. Finally, there is an asymmetric relation between the forms and the Good. So particulars are relational because the forms that are present in particulars and in which the particulars participate are constituted relationally by the Good which is transcendent and infuses everything with goodness. For Plato, individuation marks the preservation and perfection of relationality through knowledge of the Good and the praxis of justice in the *polis*. In this sense, individuation is both metaphysical and political.

At first, it would appear that my reading meets easy refutation. According to David Armstrong, Plato's theory of universals is relational and therefore open to Aristotle's critique of the 'third man' and infinite regress.[81] On this view, Aristotle's alternative is superior because in his metaphysics "although particularity and universality are inseparable aspects of all existence, they are neither reducible to each other, nor are they related. Though distinct, their union is closer than relation."[82] If this is true, then Plato's conception of particulars and universals (and the relation that pertains between them) suffers from the problem of the 'third man' and from the fallacy of the infinite regress. Moreover, the inferiority of Plato's conception of universals is often thought to be the result of separating transcendent forms from immanent particulars. As Gareth Matthews and Marc Cohen maintain in an influential article, this sepa-

---

81. On the controversy surrounding the 'third man' argument and the critique of an infinite regress in Plato, see Gregory Vlastos, "The Third Man Argument in the Parmenides," *Philosophical Review* 63 (1954): 319-49; Wilfrid Sellars, "Vlastos and the Third Man," *Philosophical Review* 64 (1955): 405-37; Gregory Vlastos, "Addenda to the TMA: Reply to Professor Sellars," *Philosophical Review* 64 (1955): 438-48; Peter T. Geach, "The Third Man Again," *Philosophical Review* 65 (1956): 72-82; G. Vlastos, "Postscript to the TMA: Reply to Professor Geach," *Philosophical Review* 65 (1956): 83-94; A. L. Peck, "Plato versus Parmenides," *Philosophical Review* 71 (1962): 159-84; John M. Rist, "The Immanence and Transcendence of the Platonic Form," *Philologus* 108 (1964): 217-32; Gail Fine, *On Ideas: Aristotle's Criticism of Plato's Theory of Forms* (Oxford: Clarendon, 1993), pp. 203-41; Mary M. McCabe, *Plato's Individuals* (Princeton: Princeton University Press, 1994), pp. 83-90.

82. David M. Armstrong, *Universals and Scientific Realism* (Cambridge: Cambridge University Press, 1978), vol. 2, p. 3.

ration has the effect that Plato is left either with 'bare particulars' that stand apart from forms or with 'mere relational entities' that depend on other entities for their existence and their essence.[83]

The problem with this sort of argument is that it asserts rather than demonstrates an absolute gulf between immaterial intelligible forms and material sensible particulars in Plato's metaphysics. Mary McCabe rightly contends that concrete individual compounds are basic units that are individuated by relations with other such compounds. As she has documented, individuality is central to Plato's metaphysics not only because both universal forms and concrete particulars are individual, but also and above all because for Plato, to be is to be one and being one is being an individual.[84] Since nothing in the sensible world is in or by itself, individual sensible particulars call forth an explanation in terms of universal causes or forms. McCabe goes on to show that the *aporiai* of the theory of forms (as exposed most clearly in the *Parmenides, Theaetetus, Timaeus,* and the first part of *The Sophist*) lead Plato (in the remainder of *The Sophist, Philebus,* and *Politicus*) to envision the *cosmos* and all therein as a collection of "basic items, their properties and the relations between them." In consequence, sensible particulars are individuated by being individuals in their own right, having relations with other individuals and being differentiated from other individuals, a process that McCabe terms a "context-relative account of individuation."[85]

However, my reading differs from hers insofar as I maintain that for Plato individuation concerns the very nature of beings and is therefore not simply a matter of 'context' (even though the *polis* is a kind of context). Compared with the pre-Socratic physicists, Plato's innovation is to demonstrate that individuality and relationality are inextricably linked because neither substance nor accidents can account for identity over time and across space. Rather than merely showing that individuals are "bare and basic units" (McCabe) that entertain nonessential relations with other such units, Plato's metaphysics attempts to explain why things are individual and what the finality of individuation might be.[86]

83. Gareth B. Matthews and Marc S. Cohen, "The One and the Many," *Review of Metaphysics* 21 (1967-68): 630-55, esp. pp. 634-35, 643-44.

84. McCabe, *Plato's Individuals,* pp. 3-5. The convertibility of being and oneness foreshadowed the Neo-Platonic emphasis on the generative One, as I shall argue in the next chapter. See, *infra,* chapter 2, section 5.

85. McCabe, *Plato's Individuals,* p. 5.

86. Cf. McCabe, *Plato's Individuals,* pp. 3-21, 221-62, 301-8.

The relations that individual particulars participate in are essential, not accidental or contextual, because the essential properties of particulars are fully relational, as has been argued independently by Héctor-Neri Castañeda and Gail Fine.[87] According to Castañeda's reading of the *Phaedo,* Plato, instead of positing "bare particulars,"[88] defends the idea that particulars are relational in two distinct yet connected ways. First, particulars can participate in universal forms because the latter can be participated in. Second, particulars are related to one another because they participate in forms that are interconnected with each other. In consequence, the relation between particulars reflects — albeit imperfectly — the relation amongst forms.[89] Fine rightly argues that Plato rules out the existence of "bare particulars" because material things in the world are more than passive receptacles, for each particular has essential properties by being connected to form. As such, all particulars have essential properties relationally.

But Fine wrongly concludes that this account is similar to Aristotle's theory in the sense that concrete compounds are what they are in virtue of being related to form or substance: "Platonic particulars are copies of model forms; but they are also roughly independently identifiable spatio-temporal continuants. In just the same way, Aristotelian primary substances are roughly independently identifiable spatio-temporal continuants — even if they bear essential connection to other things, and so do not exist independently of everything else."[90] Leaving aside Fine's point about the convergence of Plato and Aristotle, her reading does not as yet explain why forms are participable and why particulars are participatory. Nor does it account for why particulars can be relational vis-à-vis other particulars. Beyond Castañeda and Fine, I contend that individual particulars are relational not only in the sense of having 'essential properties relationally,' but also and above all in the sense of having individual forms which are themselves relational because they are ultimately brought into existence and sustained in being by the Good — the form of all forms. Before I set out the implications of the self-emanating Good for

87. Héctor-Neri Castañeda, "Plato's Phaedo Theory of Relations," *Journal of Philosophical Logic* 1 (1972): 467-80; Fine, "Relational Entities," pp. 225-49.

88. On "bare particulars," see Robert Stalnaker, "Anti-Essentialism," *Midwest Studies in Philosophy* 4 (1979): 343-55; Michael J. Loux, *Substance and Attribute: A Study in Ontology* (Dordrecht: Reidel, 1978), pp. 140-52.

89. Castañeda, "Plato's Phaedo Theory of Relations," pp. 470-71.

90. Fine, "Relational Entities," p. 248.

the individuation of concrete particulars, I examine particulars and 're-lational forms' in the following section.

8. Relational Form

For Socrates and Plato, the realm of all things visible and invisible discloses at once the unity of the cosmos and the diversity of its constituents. As such, our experience of reality raises the problem of the relation between the one and the many. Both reject the idea that the perceptible world and everything therein is either illusory or self-evident. Instead, there are causes that explain the being and the becoming of all that is, seen and unseen (e.g., *Phaed.* 95 E 9–96 A 1). In discerning intelligible structures at the heart of sensible phenomena, Socrates and Plato seek to identify universal explanatory factors that can account for the oneness of reality and the plurality of particulars. In the *Euthyphro,* Socrates wonders about the holy and searches for "the general idea which makes all pious things to be pious."[91] Likewise, in the *Theaetetus,* Socrates' objection to his interlocutor's numerous examples reflects this same quest: "When I asked you for one thing you have given me many; when I asked you for something simple, you gave me what is complex."[92]

These and other passages indicate that Plato is no less concerned with the overarching unity of the universe and everything therein than is Aristotle, but his solution to the question of how individual things can (be said to) be both universal and particular differs significantly from his pupil's. Contrary to Aristotle's definite list of categories, principles, and causes, Plato's meditations on the exact number of forms and on the presence of multiple forms in particular things remain inconclusive, as John Milbank has remarked.[93] This reflects a more fundamental difference between Aristotle's focus on the generation and evolution of things, on the one hand, and Plato's concentration on the derivation and origination of things, on the other hand. While Aristotle separates God's primary substance from the being of beings and describes *how* individuals

91. *Euthyphro* 6 D (henceforth *Euthy.*), in *The Dialogues of Plato,* trans. B. Jowett in two volumes (New York: Random House, 1937), vol. 1, p. 387.

92. *Theaetetus* 146 D (henceforth *Theaet.*), in *The Dialogues of Plato,* vol. 2, p. 147. Cf. *Hippias Major* 289 D (henceforth *Hipp. Maj.*) 292 C-D; *Meno* 72 A-B, 74 D-E, 97 A (henceforth *Men.*).

93. Milbank, "Only Theology Saves Metaphysics," pp. 464-66.

are generated by other individuals, Plato views the Good as the source and author of all things and shows *why* the existence of everything can be traced to the ecstatic outflow and relational self-giving of the Good in which all participate. (This is developed significantly by the [Christian] Neo-Platonist synthesis of Plato and Aristotle, as I will suggest in subsequent chapters.) Arguably then, Plato provides a more compelling account of how things are actualized and individuated precisely because he insists on the priority of the 'why' of relationality and participation over the 'how' of substance and form-matter union. It is only because the Good positions all things relationally that things are ordered to the transcendent final cause they always already desire (though Aristotle's theory of causation and the concept of act and potency is indispensable for a proper understanding of exactly how things undergo substantial change without losing their unique station in the order of being).

On this basis I wish to make a number of points about Plato's theological metaphysics and metaphysical epistemology. First of all, Plato does not advocate a turn away from sensible ephemeral particulars in the perceptible world of things towards transcendent timeless forms in the invisible world of ideas. Even though forms are themselves 'things' in "the most eminent way" (a conception that Christian Neo-Platonists developed in the direction of divine ideas in God's intellect),[94] nothing in reality is except by participation in the self-giving relational Good and the other forms.[95] Second, Plato locates the unity of particulars in the particulars themselves, even though the ultimate source of this unity transcends each particular. Already in the *Phaedo,* when he objects to Anaxagoras' explanation of generation and corruption (*Phaed.* 97 C–99 B), Plato puts forward the alternative of particulars participating in forms (*Phaed.* 100 C 4-6, 101 C 2-4) by pointing to the communion or presence of forms in particulars: "[N]othing makes a thing beautiful but the presence or the communion of beauty (or whatever the manner and nature of the relation may be); as I do not go so far as to affirm that, but only that it is by the beautiful that all beautiful things are beautiful."[96]

Third, in the *Phaedo* 101 C 2-4 Plato uses the verb 'to participate' but draws the distinction between the present and the aorist in order to em-

---

94. Milbank, "Only Theology Saves Metaphysics," p. 465.

95. On the question of separation and the immanence of forms in Plato, see Gail Fine, "Separation," *OSAP* 2 (1984): 31-87; Gail Fine, "Immanence," *OSAP* 4 (1986): 71-97.

96. *Phaed.* 100 D 4–E 3, in *The Dialogues of Plato,* vol. 1, p. 484.

phasize the difference between form possession and form acquisition. For example, something is hot because fire is in it and brings on the form of heat.[97] In other words, particulars can participate in forms precisely because forms are always already present in particulars, as I have previously indicated. For this reason, my fourth point is that there is within the Platonic corpus a priority of metaphysics over epistemology. The actual, real presence of forms in things explains why things exist in the first place and how the hyper-substantive Good engenders formalized material beings. To grasp universal forms in particular things is therefore to know a thing's essence and existence.

I will delay addressing the key question of how Plato theorizes knowledge of forms in things. For now, a fifth point needs to be made about Plato's realist metaphysics. Why and how can universal immaterial form be in particular material things? The starting point of the theory of forms and the metaphysics of relationality is the shape of particulars. For Plato, the shape of particulars intimates the presence of universals. This presence is manifest in the beauty of sensible particulars, which is mediated via the senses. Beauty is "shining in clearness through the clearest aperture of sense. For sight is the most piercing of our bodily senses . . . this is the privilege of beauty, that being the loveliest she is also the most palpable to sight."[98] But in itself, the appeal to beauty does not explain how universal forms might be present in particular things. That is why Plato's enquiry is not limited to separate causes that explain the existence of discrete things but extends to the reality of particulars and to that which constitutes particulars *qua* particulars. It is this enquiry that leads him to embark upon his "second voyage" (*Phaed.* 99 D 1-2)[99] — the quest for a different conception of causation that binds together efficient, formal, and final causes (αἰτίαι) and relates everything to the ultimate first principle and final end, the Good.

In this quest, Plato confronts the problem of one essential form and multiple accidental forms in particulars. He begins by arguing that each particular is constituted by a single form: "[i]f a man . . . does away with ideas of things and will not admit that every individual thing has its own determinate idea which is always one and the same, he will have nothing

---

97. Fine, "Forms as Causes: Plato and Aristotle," p. 89, note 41.

98. *Phaed.* 250 D, in *The Dialogues of Plato*, vol. 1, pp. 254-55.

99. Cf. Seth Bernadete, *Socrates' Second Sailing: On Plato's Republic* (Chicago: University of Chicago Press, 1989).

on which his mind can rest; and so he will utterly destroy the power of reasoning."[100] Only a single form which is proper to a particular being can explain *that* being's identity in difference and the stable unique identity over time and across space (e.g., *Phaed.* 103 B). Single form, Plato continues, is not a product of the mind in the mind for the mind but instead is manifest in each and every particular. As such it is perceptible to the senses and intelligible to the mind. Why? Just as the eyes of the body can glimpse the beauty of single unified forms (*Phaedr.* 250 A), so the eyes of the mind can grasp the forms themselves which are mediated in sensible particulars (*Rep.* VI 510 B 4-9, 511 B 3–C 2; VII 532 D).

At this juncture, I need to say something about Plato's epistemology, which avoids both proto-Cartesian innate ideas and hyper-Aristotelian mental abstraction from sense perception. In fact, these two extreme positions put the emphasis on human intellectual agency at the expense of divine illumination and the natural desire for knowledge of the supernatural Good in God. Since sensory experience of the physical world awakens the soul to the presence of intelligible forms in sensible things, Platonic knowledge of ideas exceeds mere recollection (ἀνάμνησις) of what the soul had contemplated before its descent from heavenly heights of eternity to the earthly embodiment in temporality, as Jean-Louis Chrétien has documented.[101] In fact, the process of ἀνάμνησις is best described as a gradual awakening that does not consist in remembering innate ideas and enabling the soul to overcome bodily entrapment through abstract contemplation but rather encompasses the natural desire to know, the senses that mediate perceptions, and an intellect that has the capacity to receive species forms. Even the formation of concepts to theorize the inherence of forms in things can be traced to the creative and self-diffusive Good.[102] Thus Plato describes a double movement whereby the presence of infinite *logos* in finite reason enables and reinforces the participation of finite reason in the infinite *logos* — a realist-idealist paradox beyond materialist dialectics and nihilist rationalism.

100. *Parmenides* 135 B 5–C 2 (henceforth *Parm.*), in *The Dialogues of Plato,* vol. 2, p. 96.

101. Jean-Louis Chrétien, *L'inoubliable et l'inespéré* (Paris: Desclée de Brouwer 1991), pp. 15-64. Cf. Rémi Brague, *Du temps chez Platon et Aristote. Quatre études* (Paris: Presses Universitaires de France, 1982).

102. Cf. Christoph Helmig, "What Is the Systematic Place of Abstraction and Concept Formation in Plato's Philosophy? Ancient and Modern Readings of *Phaedrus* 249 b-c," in *Platonic Ideas and Concept Formation in Ancient and Medieval Thought,* ed. Gerd Van Riel and Caroline Macé (Leuven: Leuven University Press, 2004), pp. 83-97.

Taken together, Plato's realist metaphysics and his metaphysical epistemology help explain why and how forms are relational and can be known as such. What is it that the senses perceive and the mind cognizes when they are directed by beauty towards particular things? It is the relationality of material particulars to immaterial forms. Just as the thought or concept of beauty points to the Form of Beauty, so the sensible particular intimates the universal form. But *why* is the form, which is proper to a particular, relational? *How* can it be so without undermining the unity and identity of itself and of *that* same particular? Julia Annas disputes that Plato's theory in the *Phaedo* (and thereafter) is teleological and causal. She argues that "goodness does not enter into it [Plato's theory]" and that "it is not a causal explanation." Instead, "what is being explained, is why a thing has a quality F; the Form explains this with no reference to any particular processes or events of a thing's coming or ceasing to be F. Plato, in fact, has changed the subject."[103] Gail Fine contends that Plato views forms as constituents rather than causes. The link between forms and particulars in terms of bringing on the form in the particular can (but does not necessarily) involve efficient causality, in the sense that forms are constituents of events and states of affairs that cause change.[104] I agree with Fine that forms cannot be equated with efficient causes because they exceed efficient causality and all types of causation, since forms account for the constitution of particulars and the entire *cosmos*. I also share her analysis of Plato's teleology of the Good. First, she is right in her critique of Gregory Vlastos, who wrongly claims that final causes are confined to the actions of minds and souls, when in fact for Plato they extend to material things.[105] Second, she is right in her argument that the form of the Good acts as a final cause not only in the 'realm' of the physical (as the ordering principle of the Demiurge's creative activity in the *Timaeus* and the form of life in the *Phaedo* 106 D 5-7) but also in the 'realm' of the ethical and the political (as the ordering principle of all virtues in *The Republic*, the *Symposium*, and the *Phaedrus*).[106] As such, Plato's account of the causation of forms can

103. Julia Annas, "Aristotle on Inefficient Causes," *Philosophical Quarterly* 32 (1982): 318.

104. Fine, "Forms as Cause: Plato and Aristotle," p. 102.

105. Gregory Vlastos, "Plato's 'Third Man' Argument (*Parm.* 132A1-B2): Text and Logic," *Philosophical Quarterly* 19 (1969): 289-301.

106. Fine, "Forms as Cause: Plato and Aristotle," pp. 108-12. On the absolute goodness of the Demiurgos and the way in which his activities may be described as "overflowing,"

only be understood in relation to the Good, which as the final cause brings everything into being and orders it to its proper finality.

Beyond Fine, my contention is that for Plato forms in particulars are not universal forms but instead particular reflections of universals — the *real* presence of universal forms in particular things. The 'meta-logic' of Plato's metaphysics is not a relation between the one whole and its many parts but instead — I would argue — the idea of relationality, which follows from the transcendence and radiance of the Good throughout the *cosmos*. So configured, the Good enables the participation of diverse particulars in the one and only universal (I delay until the following section my discussion of Plato's vision of the Good). Unlike Fine, who restricts relationality to some essential properties, I argue that the essence of a particular as a whole is relational because it cannot exist independently of the universal form, which is *in* each particular and imparts to all particulars their proper singular form. The presence of universal forms in particulars also explains how and why particulars are one and individual. They are so because universals are one and individual and preserve their oneness and individuality in particulars (though not their simplicity). So the difference between universals and particulars is not oneness or individuality but simplicity and complexity (or compound-ness).

If this is accurate, then how does Plato understand the relationality of particulars in connection with forms? If not in terms of many parts to the one whole, which idea best describes the link between sensible particulars and universal forms? As R. E. Allen has argued, already in the 'middle dialogues' Plato's theory of forms rests on the metaphysical difference between forms and particulars and the analogy of "relation-to-standard," for forms function as paradigms that particulars imitate.[107] The crux is the exact meaning and metaphysical status of "paradigm" and "imitation." Plato does not say that particulars resemble forms and that their *telos* is to become like them in the sense of absolute identity. He views particulars as manifold diverse reflections of universal forms. This is important, as the link between an original and its reflections is not the same as the connection between a model and its copies or a

---

see John M. Rist, *Eros and Psyche: Studies in Plato, Plotinus, and Origen* (Toronto: University of Toronto Press, 1964), pp. 16-55. On the centrality of Ἔρως in relation to creative activity, see also, *infra*, section 9.

107. R. E. Allen, "Participation and Predication in Plato's Middle Dialogues," *Philosophical Review* 69 (1960): 147-64.

whole and its parts. Rather, the 'being' of a reflection is wholly relational because it is utterly dependent upon the 'being' of the original. Yet at the same time, the 'being' of the original is totally other than the 'being' of its reflection (*Tim.* 50 D). The particular exists only as a resemblance, like a shadow or an image in the mirror (though not, of course, a mirror image). Put differently, particulars do not entertain symmetric relations with universals, for this would introduce an intermediary instance between binary terms. Instead, particulars are constituted by universals and as such are relational entities. Allen puts this well:

> The reflection does not *resemble* the original; rather, it is a *resemblance of* the original. This is its nature, and the whole of its nature. "Resemblances of" are quasi-substantial; relational entities, not relations. They stand to their originals as the dependent to the independent, as the less real to the more real. Plato's metaphor of imitation brilliantly expresses a community between different orders of objects, different levels of reality; it does not, as his recent critics have maintained, collapse that order.[108]

In consequence, forms are not commutative universals, in the sense of attributes that can be instantiated in material substrates. Rather, forms refract across the *cosmos,* and particulars are 'refractions of forms' that stand in analogous relation to the original source. Particulars mark unique manifestations of universals in materiality.

This account implies that there is no relation between particulars and forms, since an infinite regress would ensue. Instead, particulars as exemplifications are irreducibly relational to forms as exemplars (*Tim.* 29 B). Particulars only imitate universals insofar as they share in them, which is why particulars cannot be autonomous and universals do not stand apart from their diverse reflections. As such, there can be neither shared attributes nor a univocal community of being between sensible particulars and universal forms. For particulars only exist to the extent that they are in universals which are present in them, both existentially and essentially (so to speak). Here we can go further than R. E. Allen. To

---

108. Allen, "Participation and Predication in Plato's Middle Dialogues," p. 155 (original italics). Cf. E. N. Lee, "On the Metaphysics of the Image in Plato's *Timaeus*," *The Monist* 49 (1966): 341-68; Seth Bernadete, "On Plato's Timaeus and Timaeus' Science Fiction," *Interpretation* 2 (1971): 21-63.

recognize that each and every particular is relational is to know that all particulars are only in relation to the universal forms they participate in. Universal forms are themselves relational, in the sense that they depend on a first principle and final end — the Good — which (as I shall argue) constitutes them *qua* forms and which also constitutes particulars *qua* particulars. To cognize the Good is to know that the Good is "the first principle of the whole."[109] If this is true, then two further questions can be raised which I address in the following section. First, why and how is the Good self-exteriorizing? Second, is the Good purely teleological or does it also act as the efficient cause of concrete particulars?

9. The Individuating Power of Plato's Good

Aristotle claims that Plato's idea of a self-subsistent form of the Good which acts as a formal cause is untenable and must be abandoned in favor of a conception of the Good in terms of ultimate end (τέλος) that is the final cause of all things. Aristotle's understanding of cause is "that which is sought as an end" (τὸ δ᾽ οὗ ἕνεκα ὡς τέλος).[110] Consequently, the Good is "that at which all things aim."[111] As I argued in sections 4 and 5 of the present chapter, the Good so configured by Aristotle does not impart actuality to the sublunary world and all things therein. As a result, it cannot account for the preservation and perfection of individual substantial form. Likewise, the separation of the Prime Mover from the world and the emphasis on the self-sufficiency of the supreme *telos* shapes Aristotle's account of politics, leading him to privilege the autarchy of the city-state, champion the sovereignty of individuals, and focus on the goods that are purely human.

By contrast, Plato's form of Good is "the good itself" (αὐτὸ τὸ ἀγαθόν), a universal which is coextensive with all forms because all forms are in virtue of the ecstatic self-exteriorizing 'being' of the Good. The idea that the Good is "beyond being" (ἐπ᾽ ἐκεῖνα τῆς οὐσίας) expresses its superabundance and plenitude, not its separation from being. As such, the Good governs all forms and actualizes all particulars. By analogy with the sun, the Good is "not only the author of visibility in all

---

109. *Rep.* VI 511 B 6-7, in *The Dialogues of Plato*, vol. 1, p. 772.
110. *Eud. Eth.* I 8, 1218ᵇ10, in *The Complete Works of Aristotle*, vol. 2, p. 1929.
111. *Nic. Eth.* I 1, 1094ᵃ3, in *The Complete Works of Aristotle*, vol. 2, p. 1729.

visible things, but of generation and nourishment and growth."[112] Unlike Aristotle's Prime Mover, Plato's Good acts as formal and final cause and co-acts as efficient cause because it is the source whence all forms derive and all particulars are generated. It is also the *telos* to which all forms refer and all particulars are ordered. The power of the Good to individuate particulars operates both at the ontological and the epistemological level. Just as the sun illuminates all things, so the Good enables the mind to know particulars as relational. The Good does so by instilling the desire to know the ultimate origin of all that is via the presence of beauty in the physical world — an argument of Plato's to which I alluded above and which I discuss in greater detail below. For Plato, knowledge of the Good is knowledge that the Good is in all and all is in the Good. To cognize the Good as "the first principle of the whole" is to know that everything is relational to the Good and that particulars are connected to one another by sharing in the interrelation of forms. I first examine the implications of relationality for the individuation of particulars before turning to the interrelation of forms.

Already in the *Phaedo* Plato looks to the form of the Good (*Phaed.* 99 B-C) as he embarks upon his "second voyage in quest of the ultimate causes" (*Phaed.* 99 D 1-2). To say that the Good is the form of forms is to say that the Good makes all entities good (e.g., *Rep.* VII 533 C 9). In the *Timaeus,* he characterizes the Demiurge as good, free from jealousy, seeking to order materiality as beautifully as possible in accordance with the highest Good (*Tim.* 28 A–47 D, esp. 29 E). In the words of Plato, "God desired that all things should be good."[113] For the Good refracts across the *cosmos* (*Rep.* VI 505 A 1-10; 509 B 6) and in so doing orders matter to form. How can this be? According to Plato, the (relative) nonbeing and privation of matter, which is the opposite of unity (*Soph.* 251 C–253 C), serves as a passive receptacle for the reception of universal forms in particulars (*Tim.* 49 A, 51 A). This would seem to suggest that matter individuates form, as the 'this-ness' of the material substrate imposes limits on the 'such-ness' of form (*Tim.* 49 C–50 A). Yet at the same time, matter is described as "formless, and free from the impress of any of those shapes which it is hereafter to receive from without."[114] To define matter as being "devoid of any particular form" (*Tim.* 51 A) would appear to suggest

---

112. *Rep.* VI 509 B, in *The Dialogues of Plato*, vol. 1, p. 770.
113. *Tim.* 30 A, in *The Dialogues of Plato*, vol. 2, p. 14.
114. *Tim.* 50 C, in *The Dialogues of Plato*, vol. 2, p. 31.

that form individuates matter. But since matter limits form on account of its relative nonbeing or privation, matter 'acts' as an ultimate ungenerated substrate and must exist if forms are to be reflected at all.[115] Plato views matter as irrational because it is neither sensible nor intelligible and can only be apprehended by "a kind of spurious reason" (*Tim.* 52 B). As such, matter remains unexplained because its necessary existence is presupposed, not demonstrated. This conception of matter shifts the onus of individuality and individuation onto form. That which makes composites particular and secures their identity over time is their form, not the composition of matter-form (as Aristotle argued). Matter only matters to individuation insofar as it has been ordered by form and thus dimly reflects the being and goodness of the Good.

However, Plato's account of individuation is not fatally undermined by his claim that matter is unintelligible and inexplicable. Here the *Philebus* is crucial because it makes clear that universal forms are not opposed to particular things. Instead, forms introduce limits into the unlimited and thus constitute individuals (*Phileb.* 26 D 9-10). Referring to *Philebus* 25 A 8–B 1, Kenneth Sayre argues that forms do so by providing "'proportions of numbers and measures' by which Limit is imposed upon the Unlimited. To put it summarily, Forms are the numbers and measures by which the Great and (the) Small is made definite and determinate."[116] Limits consist of that which relates as number to number or measure to measure. Opposites in the Unlimited are made intelligible and harmonious by the introduction of numbers and measures (*Phileb.* 25 B 1–E 2). For Plato, individuals are constituted and individuated by the interaction of the unity of forms with the divisions of matter. What individuates concrete compounds is the diverse particular refraction of the universal Good in particular entities composed of both form and matter.

This underlines the importance of beauty in the phenomenal unfolding of the Good. In the *Timaeus,* Plato also describes beauty as the standard for the Good (*Tim.* 87 C 4-5). As the *Phaedrus* makes clear, beauty is the prime medium through which the mind via the senses is alerted to the presence of the Good in the physical world. For beauty

---

115. For a more detailed discussion of matter in Plato's metaphysics, see Leonard J. Eslick, "The Material Substrate," in *The Concept of Matter in Greek and Medieval Philosophy,* ed. Ernan McMullin (Notre Dame: University of Notre Dame Press, 1963), pp. 39-54.

116. Kenneth M. Sayre, *Plato's Late Ontology: A Riddle Resolved* (Princeton: Princeton University Press, 1983), p. 164.

shines forth within the visibility of the material and thus stirs up love for the Good (*Phaedr.* 250 C).[117] This love moves the soul away from the passions for the merely physical and uplifts the mind towards knowledge of beauty and goodness. It also induces the praxis of justice, which preserves the Good and operates its extension in the *polis*. The Good does not merely manifest itself locally but is the very appearance and visibility of phenomena (*Phaedr.* 250 D). Therefore, the Good is analogous to the sun, which does not simply shed light onto things but is itself light and luminosity. Such is the ecstatic plenitude of the Good that it is not by itself but acts "in that in which it exists and which it affects."[118] As Hans-Georg Gadamer remarks, Plato described in the *Philebus* how the Good via the beautiful constitutes and individuates the entire cosmic order, which is

> raised out of the limitless flowing away of mere genesis and raised up into *ousia* (being). Its having been raised to *ousia* constitutes the intelligibility *(nous)*, or dis-concealedness *(alētheia)*, of the cosmic order. In all these instances the eidetic-ideal can be discerned, picked out, because it is contained in them (*heurēsein gar enousan* [for (it is) to be found existing therein]) (*Phileb.* 16 D). . . . To this extent the beautiful is the same as the good, which provides everything that is with its true being — with the being, namely, that we have called here eidetic-ideal.[119]

In summary, all particulars are relational because they depend for their essence, their existence, and their continuous being on the Good. Likewise, forms are relational because they are united by the Good and the Good is coextensive with each and every form, for all the forms intimate the Good and the Good unifies all the forms.

For Plato, it is beauty in the physical world that propels us to seek the Good which we desire. He describes the ascent of the mind from the per-

---

117. Hans-Georg Gadamer, *Die Idee des Guten zwischen Plato und Aristoteles* (Heidelberg: Winter, 1978), English translation: *The Idea of the Good in Platonic-Aristotelian Philosophy,* trans. and intro. P. Christopher Smith (New Haven: Yale University Press, 1986), pp. 116-18; Catherine Pickstock, "The Soul in Plato," in *Explorations in Contemporary Continental Philosophy of Religion,* ed. Deane-Peter Baker and Patrick Maxwell (Amsterdam and New York: Editions Rodopi B. V., 2003), pp. 115-26.

118. *Rep.* V 477 C-D, in *The Dialogues of Plato,* vol. 1, pp. 740-41.

119. Gadamer, *The Idea of the Good in Platonic-Aristotelian Philosophy,* p. 117. On the Good in the *Philebus,* see also Sayre, *Plato's Late Ontology,* pp. 118-86.

ception (αἴσθησις) of sensible particulars via knowledge of forms by way of concepts (νόημα) towards the cognition (νόησις) of the Good (*Rep.* VI 510 B 4-9; 511 B 3–C 2). Following this ascent (*Symp.* 210 A), the mind sees first of all the relationality of each and every particular because nothing comes from nothing and nothing can sustain itself in being. The mind also discerns that particulars are ultimately constituted by the Good and shaped by diverse forms that are interrelated (*Soph.* 252 D–254 B). Knowledge of particulars and forms as relational and of the Good as the 'first principle of the whole' individuates the knower insofar as the *telos* of human beings is to fulfill their desire to know. Likewise, knowledge in some sense individuates the things known because the *telos* of all things is to reflect the plenitude of the Good. So being is coextensive with knowing and knowledge perfects being.

Already in *The Republic* but also in later dialogues like the *Theaetetus* and *The Sophist*, Plato emphasizes the interrelation of forms.[120] This idea implies not only that individuals participate in a variety of forms when they participate in one form, but also that there is a reflection of the interrelation of forms in the physical world — the interrelation of particulars. Relations amongst individuals in the *polis* individuate each and every participant, especially in the communal discernment and exercise of justice. The power of the Good generates and sustains the individuating effects of relations between individuals. The love of beauty, which is elicited by the beautiful forms of particulars in the physical world, awakens the desire to know the forms and their ultimate source. The philosopher who knows forms seeks to preserve forms in the sensible world and to defend and extend the goodness present in all particulars. As John Rist notes, in the *Symposium*

> [h]is [the philosopher's] object of love is Beauty itself, and, since he knows the Forms, he cannot but create and beget true virtue. Love of Beauty must make the philosopher creative. His creativity is the outcome of his vision of the world of Forms; it is not *desired* for any ulterior motive of obtaining immortality. Is it then unreasonable to call such activity 'overflowing,' and is not such overflowing the culmination and effect of Ἔρως? There can be no reasonable doubt that the

120. *Rep.* VI 510 B, 511 B, VII 517 B-C, 519 C-D, 526 E; *Theaet.* 206 C–208 B; *Soph.* 259 E, 263 E–264 A. Cf. Alexander Nehamas, "Participation and Predication in Plato's Late Dialogues," *Review of Metaphysics* 32 (1982): 343-74.

Ἔρως of the philosopher 'overflows' into creation in a way that cannot possibly be dismissed as simply appetitive.[121]

The recognition of goodness in the beauty of the physical world leads the philosopher to search for the form of justice and to make it real in the *polis*, by helping to create order out of chaos upon the return to the Cave (*Rep.* VII 520 C). He does so by modeling institutions and practices according to the form of justice and the virtues embodying them.[122] The unity of the *polis* and of a virtuous good life is secured by the unity of the Good which informs the knowledge of forms and sustains the action to make the ideal of the Good real in the *cosmos*. This for Plato is what it is to be a more fully individuated particular being.

10. Conclusion: Matter Matters

Plato's metaphysics surpasses Aristotle's ontology by refusing any separation between the divine first principle which is also the final end and all the immanent beings that are oriented towards their transcendent source. However, the Good as the form of all forms orders chaotic matter; it does not create it.[123] Plato presumes rather than demonstrates the preexistence of matter. In consequence, Plato's metaphysics fails to explain how matter comes into being and why it would 'desire' to be formed. Aristotle's account of matter is more philosophically developed but no less theologically problematic. To identify form or essence with substance is to run into an impasse, as Richard Rorty remarks, because concrete substances are generated out of matter and contain matter, but as pure potency matter *is not* (*Met.* Z 7, 1032^{a}15-23). The problem is that form is the sole cause of substances, yet at the same time form requires

121. Rist, *Eros and Psyche,* p. 36 (original italics).

122. A longer exposition of Plato's metaphysical politics is beyond the scope of this chapter. See Zdravko Planinc, *Plato's Political Philosophy: Prudence in the* Republic *and the* Laws (Columbia: University of Missouri Press, 1991); Lloyd P. Gerson, *Knowing Persons: A Study in Plato* (Oxford: Oxford University Press, 2003), pp. 148-275; Dominic O'Meara, *Platonopolis: Platonic Political Philosophy in Late Antiquity* (Oxford: Clarendon Press, 2003); Catherine Pickstock, "Justice and Prudence: Principles of Order in the Platonic City," *Telos* 119 (Spring 2001): 3-17; Catherine Pickstock, *Theory, Religion and Idiom in Platonic Philosophy* (Oxford: Blackwell, forthcoming).

123. Eslick, "The Material Substrate," pp. 39-54.

matter, which is purely passive. This is compounded by Aristotle's use of two different meanings of substance in the *Metaphysics* — substance as essence and substance as a form-matter compound. Moreover, matter is part of the formula (λόγος) of composite substances (*Met.* Z 7, 1033ᵃ6).[124] This raises two questions. First, how can the pure potency of matter be capable of being actualized? Second, how can matter be part of a thing's essence and definition? Aristotle addresses both questions by rejecting the idea of form and matter as separate parts of a unified whole in favor of the idea that matter and form are one and the same thing, the former potentially and the latter actually:

> [T]he proximate matter and the form are one and the same thing, the one potentially, the other actually. Therefore to ask the cause of their being one is like asking the cause of unity in general; for each thing is a unity, and the potential and the actual are somehow one.[125]

Matter and form are unified by the efficient cause, defined as that which actualizes the potency of matter to be *this* rather than *that*. So configured, matter is a proximate material cause. As such, matter can act as a material cause for other composites, yet at the same time it can be particular to a single substance: "[T]here is a matter proper to each [thing]."[126] Aristotle maintains that matter is integral to the essence of individual unified composites by arguing that proximate matter is potentially what individual substantial form is actually. In consequence, individual substantial form and proximate matter constitute a unity which is one and individual.

But to say that matter acts as material cause whereas form acts as formal and efficient cause and to say that conjointly they produce individual composites raises a second set of problems, in particular the metaphysical status of matter as potency.[127] Aristotle's understanding

124. Rorty, "Genus as Matter: A Reading of *Metaphysics* Z-H," esp. p. 404.

125. *Met.* H 6, 1045ᵇ17-21, in *The Complete Works of Aristotle*, vol. 2, p. 1651.

126. *Met.* H 4, 1044ᵃ17, in *The Complete Works of Aristotle*, vol. 2, p. 1648.

127. On Aristotle's account of matter in relation to form, see Harold F. Cherniss, *Aristotle's Criticism of Plato and the Academy* (Baltimore: Johns Hopkins University Press, 1944), pp. 83-173, 376-479; John J. FitzGerald, "'Matter' in Nature and Knowledge of Nature: Aristotle and the Aristotelian Tradition," in McMullin, ed., *The Concept of Matter in Greek and Medieval Philosophy*, pp. 59-78, esp. pp. 69-74; Norbert Luyten, "Matter as Potency," in *The Concept of Matter in Greek and Medieval Philosophy*, pp. 102-23, esp. pp. 105-10; Joseph

of matter in relation to the problem of individuation seems to be ambivalent at best and contradictory at worst. Matter is variably conceived as either prior to form because it is the subject for form and exists before and after substantial change (e.g., *Phys.* I 7, 191ª8-12) or posterior to form because nothing can be in actuality without the act of form (e.g., *Met.* Z 8, 1033ª24–1033ᵇ19). Aristotle attempts to solve this conundrum with the following two arguments. First, proximate matter is coextensive with individual substantial form in the sense that form and matter are somehow both in being — both constitute equally the matter-form complex that determines what a thing is. Second, proximate matter cannot exist or be what it is independently of the form of the object — the material composite is fully determined what it is by its form. However, this solution solves nothing because it fails to specify the genesis of proximate matter and the reasons for its capacity to be *this* particular composite rather than *that* particular composite. For Aristotle, the origin and change of proximate matter is a function of other instances of proximate matter that act as agents. For example, man engenders man and all plants are generated from seeds.[128] In order to guard against an infinite regress, Aristotle needs to posit the existence of matter as pure potency which is eternal and the existence of substantial form which ultimately derives from the pure actuality of an indifferent God.

My critique of Aristotle's ontology and theology centers on his undemonstrated presupposition that matter is the formless ground of material reality (*Phys.* I 7, 191ª8-12). Matter thus conceived is neither individual nor universal but rather void of all determinations. Therefore, matter does not come from nothing, but it tends towards nothing. It persists throughout substantial change and remains after all forms have been removed. As such, it is the substrate for generation and corruption (*GC* I 4, 320ª2-5). Matter is defined in the *Metaphysics* as "that which in itself is neither a particular thing nor of a certain quantity nor assigned to any other of the categories by which being is determined."[129] But the eternity

---

Owens, "Matter and Predication in Aristotle," in *The Concept of Matter in Greek and Medieval Philosophy*, pp. 79-101, esp. pp. 79-93; Rorty, "Genus as Matter: A Reading of *Metaphysics* Z-H," pp. 397-420; Mary L. Gill, "Perceptible Substances in Metaphysics H 1-5," in *Aristoteles, Metaphysik, die Substanzbücher* ([*Zeta*], [*Eta*], [*Theta*]), ed. Christof Rapp (Berlin: Akademie Verlag, 1996), pp. 209-28.

128. See, *inter alia, Phys.* I 7, 190ᵇ1-4; *Met.* Z 8, 1033ᵇ29-33.

129. *Met.* Z 3, 1029ª20-22, in *The Complete Works of Aristotle*, vol. 2, p. 1625. Cf. Jean Ma-

and formlessness of matter deprive Aristotle's ontology of an account of material capacity to receive form and be actualized. If all that is stands in potency to the Prime Mover as the final cause and if there is no formal mediation of actuality, then Aristotle cannot explain how the realm of form-matter compounds comes into existence and is sustained in being. He can only presuppose a kind of drive of material potentiality towards the final *telos* for which his idea of matter as pure potency gives no warrant. Indeed, the actuality of the first mover does not act as efficient cause for the sublunary world and thus cannot explain how and why individual composites are actualized and individuated. From the pure passivity of matter it follows that Aristotle shifts the onus of individuation onto individual substantial form because the actuality of substantial form is the efficient and formal cause of concrete composites. In short, Aristotle's account of matter as pure potency is philosophically superior to Plato's idea of matter as formless chaos, but Aristotle's indifferent God is theologically regressive compared with Plato's vision of an ecstatic Good that infuses all things with goodness.

To recapitulate: I have shown that in Aristotle's first philosophy the exclusively causal link that pertains between the Prime Mover and the sublunary world rules out any cosmic transcendence of the Good and privileges the justice of certain 'aristocratic' virtues. The result is that the divine is eliminated from 'lower' practical activities and thereby from the individuation of human beings who actualize and perfect their form by engaging in such activities. Thus, the individuality and individuation of concrete composites is ultimately severed from the pure actuality of Aristotle's divinity. By contrast, for Plato the individuation of composites is the relationality of particulars to forms and ultimately the Good. I have also shown that only the Good so configured can account for the relationality of particulars. This is because particulars depend for their existence, their essence, and their continuous being on forms and the Good as the form of forms which constitutes them relationally. For Plato, what individuates individual compounds is the participation in the relations amongst forms and the praxis of relations with other individual compounds. Unlike Aristotle's Prime Mover, Plato's Good constitutes the

---

rie Le Blond, *Logique et méthode chez Aristote: Étude sur la recherche des principes dans la physique aristotélicienne* (Paris: Vrin, 1939); William Norris Clarke, "The Limitation of Act by Potency in St. Thomas: Aristotelianism or Neo-Platonism," *New Scholasticism* 26 (1952): 167-94, esp. pp. 178-83.

final, formal, and efficient cause of all that is; yet at the same time, the Good is beyond causality because it constitutes the *cosmos* as a whole and sustains everything within it in being. As a result, the Good is in all things and all things are in the Good. Only the ecstatic plenitude and self-exteriorization of the Good across the entire *cosmos* explain why particulars and forms are relational.

Plato's argument in the *Philebus* about forms providing limits in terms of numbers and measures is significant for three reasons. First of all, it implies that matter (conceived as a receptacle) does not individuate universal form because form is always already individuated and exists in particulars. As such, individual beings reflect in particulars and diverse ways the manifold mediation of universal forms and the form of forms. Accordingly, matter merely accounts for the numerical diversity of particulars which share in the same form, but materiality is excluded from the essence of matter-form compounds. Second, Plato's conception of unintelligible matter which functions as a receptacle does not explain how and why in particular sensible things matter is part of essence and can be known as such. Aristotle's definition of matter as pure potency marks an improvement but also fails to explain why there is any materiality in the first place. By contrast, Christian theology provides an account of matter in terms of creation *ex nihilo* and explains why matter is part of the essence of compounds, as I will suggest throughout this essay. Third, this account is based on Plato's idea of forms as numbers and measures and as thoughts in the divine mind.[130] This vision is later retrieved and transformed by patristic and medieval theologians such as Gregory of Nyssa, Augustine, Boethius, and Aquinas in their account of the individuation of concrete composites. By fusing the biblical idea of creation *ex nihilo* with Plato's metaphysics of the Good and Aristotle's ontology of act and potency, Christian Neo-Platonism ties the divine to the cosmic and the human and thus overcomes the dualism between the one and the many left unresolved by pre-Socratic poetry and philosophy. That is what I argue in the following chapters.

---

130. *Rep.* VI 510 B 4-9, 511 B 3–C 2; *Tim.* 29 E 1-3, 30 C 2–31 A 1.

CHAPTER 2

Trinitarian God and Triadic Cosmos

1. Introduction: Ancient Philosophy and Biblical Revelation

In the autumn of 1947, Albert Camus wrote the following entry in his notebook: "If, to outgrow nihilism, one must return to Christianity, one may well follow the impulse and outgrow Christianity in Hellenism."[1] A few years later, Camus restated his belief that Greek philosophy is the only genuine alternative to both Christianity and modernity: "Go back to the passage from Hellenism to Christianity, the true and only turning point in history."[2] Camus's claim that the Christian tradition usurps and diminishes the universality of Greek philosophy is at odds with an earlier work of his titled *Christian Metaphysics and Neoplatonism*, where he (rightly) argues that "Greece is continued in Christianity. And Christianity is prefigured in Hellenic thought."[3] This brings into sharp focus the nature of the link between ancient philosophy and biblical revelation.

The recent and current debate on this link is commonly associated with the work of Adolf von Harnack (1851-1930), in particular his assertion that the encounter between Hellenic thought and the Christian faith led to a distortion of Jesus' "plain and simple teaching"[4] and of Paul's Christocentric theology: "The decisive thing was the conversion of the

1. Albert Camus, *Notebooks 1942-1951*, trans. Justin O'Brien (New York: Paragon House, 1991), p. 183.

2. Camus, *Notebooks 1942-1951*, p. 267.

3. Albert Camus, *Christian Metaphysics and Neoplatonism*, trans. Ronald D. Srigley (Columbia: University of Missouri Press, 2007), p. 43.

4. Adolf von Harnack, *History of Dogma*, 3rd ed., trans. Neil Buchanan (London: Williams & Norgate, 1897), vol. 1, p. 61.

Gospel into a doctrine, into an absolute philosophy of religion."[5] More recently, Pope Benedict XVI in his controversial Regensburg lecture on the hellenization and de-hellenization of Christianity has provided a powerful and compelling refutation of Harnack's view. Benedict's argument is that there is a profound harmony between Greek enquiry and biblical faith, and that the rapprochement between the two was not a matter of chance but instead responded to an intrinsic necessity to explore the dual meaning of *Logos* as both reason and word.[6] Far from reactionary nostalgia, the Pope's intervention seeks to recover and extend the shared Hebraic and Hellenic emphasis on the rational intelligibility of the divinely created cosmos. This ancient legacy was accomplished by the biblical revelation that God is the incarnate *Logos* and that faith intensifies reason through universal divine grace and love — a revelation mediated in and through the complex interplay of the Book of Scripture, the Book of Nature, and the Book of History, as the Church Fathers and Doctors in both East and West demonstrated.[7]

Notably, Benedict contends that the premodern tradition of theological intellectualism and metaphysical realism was aborted by the (predominantly Franciscan) conception and institution of voluntarism and nominalism. In turn, advocates of a voluntarist and nominalist theology in the late Middle Ages such as John Duns Scotus (c. 1265/66-1308) and William of Ockham (c. 1288/89-1349) inaugurated the modern secular separation of nature from the supernatural and the concomitant divorce of philosophy, physics, and ethics from theology that was reinforced by influential early modern figures such as Francisco Suárez

---

5. Harnack, *History of Dogma*, vol. 1, p. 252. For a useful account of Harnack's position, see William V. Rowe, "Adolf von Harnack and the Concept of Hellenization," in *Hellenization Revisited,* ed. Wendy Hellman (Lanham, MD: University Press of America, 1994), pp. 69-98.

6. Pope Benedict XVI, "Glaube, Vernunft und Universität. Erinnerungen und Reflexionen," lecture at the University of Regensburg on 12 September 2006, published as *Glaube und Vernunft. Die Regensburger Vorlesung* (Freiburg: Herder, 2006); *The Regensburg Lecture,* trans. James V. Schall, SJ (Chicago: St. Augustine's Press, 2007).

7. Henri de Lubac, *Exégèse Médiévale: Les Quatre sens de L'Écriture,* 4 vols. (Paris: Aubier-Montaigne, 1959-1961), première partie, chs. 1, 2 and 5, pp. 56-74, 100-118; ch. 3, pp. 171-220; ch. 5, pp. 305-72. Cf. Dom Gregory Dix, *The 'Hellenization' of the Gospel* (Uppsala: Almqvist & Wiksell, 1953); Alois Grillmeier, "Hellenisierung-Judaisierung des Christentums als Deuteprinzipien der Geschichte des kirchlichen Dogmas," in Grillmeier, *Mit ihm und in ihm. Christologische Forschungen und Perspektiven* (Freiburg: Herder, 1975), pp. 423-88.

(1548-1616), as I will discuss in chapters 6 and 7. This legacy is fiercely guarded and faithfully perpetuated by the Pope's neo-scholastic (and theo-conservative/neo-liberal) critics, including George Weigel, Michael Novak, Ralph McInerny, and Romano Cesario, OP, who pour scorn on Benedict's defense of *nouvelle théologie* against neo-scholasticism and advance modern readings of patristic and medieval theology.[8] What these and other papal despisers ignore is the Pope's point about the equation of de-hellenization and secularization: in the long and nonlinear passage to modernity, faith was sundered from reason and reason was gradually reduced to the narrow rationality of logical deduction, mathematical calculation, and scientific experimentation.[9] As a result, the patristic and medieval account of human reason in terms of illumined cognition of the presence of the Creator God in all created things was abandoned in favor of innate ideas of the divine. Such a conception is entirely compatible with both theism and deism, as the history of modernity attests.

By contrast, catholic orthodox Christianity always viewed reason itself as a gift of God that is elevated by revelation and faith. As I shall argue in the present chapter, St. Augustine of Hippo argued against the Skeptics that the proper exercise of reason involves a kind of prerational trust or faith *(pistis)* in the senses, the imagination, and the intellect precisely because even after the Fall the created mind is always already attuned to the Good in all things. For many, this will be cause for dismissing Augustine's theology as little more than a partially Christianized variant of Neo-Platonist idealism. But Augustine outflanks all his critics by developing the Platonic account of beauty as the first effect of the Good in the world (*Phaedrus* 250 C-D) in a Trinitarian direction. He does so by showing that the triadic structures of self and the world — high-

---

8. For example, see Ralph McInerny, *Being and Predication: Thomistic Interpretations* (Washington, DC: Catholic University of America Press, 1986) and *Aquinas and Analogy* (Washington, DC: Catholic University of America Press, 1996).

9. For detailed accounts that corroborate the Pope's distinction between the premodern hellenization of Christianity and its modern de-hellenization, see, *inter alia,* Romano Guardini, *Das End der Neuzeit* (Würzburg: Werkbund-Verlag, 1950); Hans Blumenberg, *Die Legitimität der Neuzeit* (Frankfurt am Main: Suhrkamp, 1996 [1966]); Amos Funkenstein, *Theology and the Scientific Imagination from the Middle Ages to the Seventeenth Century* (Princeton: Princeton University Press, 1986); Louis Dupré, *Passage to Modernity: An Essay in the Hermeneutics of Nature and Culture* (New Haven, CT: Yale University Press, 1993); Catherine Pickstock, *After Writing: On the Liturgical Consummation of Philosophy* (Oxford: Blackwell, 1998), pp. 121-66.

lighted in the Neo-Platonism of Plotinus (c. 204/5-270) and Iamblichus (c. 240-325) — mirror the triune nature of God. Knowledge of the Trinitarian vestiges in the world is available to fallen man precisely because Christ's unique nature and personhood discloses the filial relation with the Father and the workings of the Spirit.[10] Through an awakening (ἀνάμνησις) of the intellect to the presence of God's wisdom, which orders all things according to the triadic structure of measure, number, and weight (as Scripture alerts us to in the Book of Wisdom 11:20-21), Christ restored mediate cognition of God in the human mind through divine illumination, an account that differs fundamentally from Cartesian innate ideas (as I have already hinted).[11]

This chapter also suggests that for Augustine, faith habituates reason to see the effects of God in all things, just as reason helps 'faith seeking understanding' (*De Trin.* XV.li [prayer]) by relating the natural desire for the supernatural Good in God to the whole of creation, which reflects the Creator in diverse ways that no single finite mind can ever be equal to. Hence faith upholds reason and broadens its scope while reason binds faith to cognition and thereby ties together perception and imagination ('lower reason') with intellectual vision ('higher reason') so that knowledge of the world *(scientia)* and knowledge of God *(sapientia)* converge and prepare man for the beatific vision in the life to come.

My argument in this chapter is therefore twofold. First, Augustine's synthesis of Neo-Platonist metaphysics and the biblical doctrine of creation *ex nihilo* does not compromise the autonomy of philosophy or distort the integrity of theology. To the contrary, it fulfills the insights of Neo-Platonism and elucidates the truth of scriptural revelation. Just as only Trinitarian theology can explain why the whole of reality is ordered in triadic ways, so too only the sacred triads of Neo-Platonism can explain how the vestiges of the Trinity are mediated in this world. Second, Augustine's account of creation and individuation is neither a proto-Cartesian antecedent of the modern obsession with the subjectivity of the self nor a regressive return to the dualism of Plato, which in any case is a distortion of Plato (as I suggested in the previous chapter). Much rather, Augustine's

10. St. Augustine, *De Trinitate* XIII.xi.15; XII.x.14 (henceforth *De Trin.*).

11. On Augustine's theological epistemology, see Lydia Schumacher, *Divine Illumination: The History and Future of Augustine's Theory of Knowledge* (Oxford: Wiley-Blackwell, 2011). Cf. Adrian Pabst, "Wisdom and the Art of Politics," in *Encounter between Eastern Orthodoxy and Radical Orthodoxy: Transfiguring the World Through the Word,* ed. Adrian Pabst and Christoph Schneider (Aldershot, UK: Ashgate, 2009), pp. 109-37.

Trinitarian theology accentuates the priority of 'relational positioning' that is already intimated in the horizontal participation amongst the forms themselves in Plato, the aesthetic interplay of the One and the Dyad in Plotinus, and the hierarchical, triadic groupings in Iamblichus (and later Proclus). By relating the individuation of creation to the triune Creator, Augustine brings matter itself within the scope of the vertical asymmetrical relationality that forms the precondition for the participation of all that exists in the original source of being in God. As such, the theological metaphysics of Christian Neo-Platonists like Augustine, which informs the Pope's narrative in the Regensburg address, offers a rich and as yet unrealized potential for an alternative modernity where both the rationalism of militant secularists and the fideism of religious fundamentalists are abandoned in favor of the 'grandeur of reason' and a new kind of engagement between all faiths and cultures.

In what follows, I begin by arguing that the early Christian fusion of ancient philosophy with biblical revelation surpasses both the Hellenic and the Hebraic account of the link between the one and the many and provides an account of individuation in terms of a theological metaphysics of creation *ex nihilo.* This synthesis can be traced to the Apostolic Fathers, the Apologists, and the Cappadocians, especially Gregory of Nyssa (sections 2-4). It finds its first full expression in the work of Augustine (sections 5-10). Gregory's and Augustine's contributions to patristic reflections on the paradox of divine unity and diversity and the participation of creation in the Trinitarian relationality of the Godhead were complementary and critical to the development of pre- and post-Nicene Christian theology in both East and West. Building upon the scholarship of Rowan Williams and Lewis Ayres, one of my arguments is that the opposition between 'western' Latin monistic and 'eastern' Greek pluralistic conceptions of the Trinity is misleading and fails to recognize the shared theological-philosophical framework that underpinned Roman and Byzantine Christendom.

2. (Neo-)Platonism and Christian Metaphysics

A. The Hellenization of Christianity

From the dawn of the Church, Christian thinkers in both East and West debated the status of philosophy in relation to theology. The encounter between biblical revelation and ancient philosophy did of course not date from the times of the earliest Christians but can be traced to those Jewish communities in whose midst emerged Hellenized Judaism. This is perhaps most of all true for Philo of Alexandria (20 BC–AD 50), who was a contemporary of Jesus and argued for an allegorical interpretation of Scripture that drew on ancient mythology and philosophy — an experience that foreshadowed the 'inculturation' of Christianity in pagan societies.[12] Indeed, both Jesus himself and the Apostles were rooted in the Hellenic tradition of Judaism, as were the Apostolic Fathers and the Apologists who viewed Greek and Roman thought as *preparatio evangelica*. But among the Jewish people there were those like the Maccabees and the Zealots who opposed any rapprochement with Hellenism. Likewise, among Christians there were those like Tatian (c. 110-180) and Tertullian (c. 160-220) who equated ancient philosophy with unbelief and heresy: "What has Athens to do with Jerusalem?" Tertullian asked provocatively.[13] "Wretched Aristotle," he proclaimed, "God has spoken to us: it is no longer necessary for us to philosophize. Revelation is all that is required. He who merely believes in the word of God knows more than the greatest philosophers have ever known concerning the only matter of vital importance."[14]

Instead of such a binary opposition, the Fathers and Doctors of the Church who integrated both Hellenized Judaism and the Greco-Roman tradition into Christianity developed a symbiotic relation: just as Christian theology fulfills ancient philosophy, so ancient philosophy assists Christian 'faith seeking understanding' — exploring the paradox of Christ's full divinity and humanity and making the unknowable mystery of the Incarnation and the Resurrection rationally intelligible.[15] Nowhere

12. On Philo, see Matthew J. Bullimore, "Government by Transcendence: The Analogy of the Soul, the City and the Cosmos in Plato, Philo and St Paul" (University of Cambridge Ph.D. thesis, 2007). Cf. Martin Hengel, *Juden, Griechen und Barbaren. Aspekte der Hellenisierung des Judentums in vorchristlicher Zeit,* Stuttgarter Bibelstudien 76 (Stuttgart: Katholisches Bibelwerk, 1976), English translation: *Jews, Greeks and Barbarians: Aspects of the Hellenization of Judaism in the Pre-Christian Period,* trans. John Bowden (Philadelphia: Fortress, 1980); Martin Hengel, *The 'Hellenization' of Judea in the First Century after Christ,* trans. John Bowden (Philadelphia: Trinity, 1989).

13. Tertullian, *De praescriptione haereticorum,* in *The Ante-Nicene Fathers,* ed. Alexander Robertson, James Donaldson, and Arthur Cleveland Coxe (New York: Cosimo, 2007; orig. pub. 1885), vol. 3: *Latin Christianity,* p. 246.

14. Tertullian, *De praescriptione haereticorum,* p. 246 (translation modified).

15. On the status of ancient philosophy in Christian theology, see, *inter alia,* A. H. Armstrong and R. A. Markus, *Christian Faith and Greek Philosophy* (London: Darton,

was this synthesis more decisive in the formative period of Christian theology than in the process leading to the Council of Nicaea in 325 and the formation of a post-Nicene 'theological culture' composed of a diversity of strands binding together different accounts of metaphysics, cosmology, epistemology, anthropology, and exegesis, as Lewis Ayres has comprehensively documented.[16] In this complex and nonlinear development, a wide range of theologians in both East and West transformed (Neo-)Platonism and other traditions of ancient philosophy into Christian metaphysics, which helped address some of the Christological and Trinitarian disputes and thereby made a critical contribution to the emergence of an orthodox catholic Christian theology.[17] The Christianized (Neo-)Platonism of Church Fathers such as Justin, Clement, Origen, Gregory, and Augustine did not simply correct the philosophical and theological errors of Plato (the preexistence of chaotic matter; the creation of formal order out of material chaos, etc.) and Plotinus (equating matter with absolute evil; the tension between the absolute unity of the One and the plurality of its products; the relation between the One and the metaphysical hierarchy of the world, etc.). Much rather, Christian (Neo-)Platonists modified ancient philosophy precisely in order to develop the theology of Creation and Incarnation. As such, the Platonist metaphysics of relational participation and the Neo-Platonist theology of sacred triads helped elucidate the nature of Christ's hypostatic union, the relations within the triune Godhead, and the participation of creation in Trinitarian self-giving. In the next subsection, I briefly show just how instrumental Plato's metaphysics was for the hellenization of early patristic theology and Christian theology in the run-up to, and after, the Nicene Council.

B. St. Justin Martyr and Clement of Alexandria

Following St. Paul, it was St. Justin Martyr (c. 100-165) who first showed how the theology of the New Testament fulfills the promise of the Old

---

Longman & Todd, 1960); R. A. Markus, *Christianity in the Roman World* (London: Thames & Hudson, 1974), esp. pp. 13-48; Jean Daniélou, *Message Evangélique et Culture Hellénistique* (Tournai: Desclée & Cie, 1961), esp. pp. 11-128.

16. Lewis Ayres, *Nicaea and Its Legacy: An Approach to Fourth-Century Trinitarian Theology* (Oxford: Oxford University Press, 2004), pp. 11-84.

17. Harry A. Wolfson, *The Philosophy of the Church Fathers*, 3rd ed. (Cambridge, MA: Harvard University Press, 1970), esp. part II.

Testament and the ancient philosophy of the *Logos*. For Justin, paganism produces a partial knowledge of the *Logos* or Divine Person of the Word, the highest truth of God in God through God. By contrast, Christian theology has received in Christ the *Logos* itself. In the *Second Apology,* Justin suggests that Socrates knew Christ partially because Christ was and is the omnipresent Word (*II Apol.* X.8).[18] Likewise, the Stoics established an ethics on the basis of just and universal principles because the seed of the Word is innate in the whole of mankind. But only in Christ is the Word fully revealed and only through Christ can the Word be known. This idea of a partial knowledge of God and the seed of the Word goes back to Justin's theory of *logos spermatikos* (the seed of the *Logos*), "seeds of truth, sent down to humanity" (*Dial.* II.1; *I Apol.* XLIV; *II Apol.* VIII). Reinforced by the supernatural gift of faith, human reason itself participates in the divine Word incarnate in Christ and as such can have approximate knowledge of God.[19]

Justin's theory of *logos spermatikos* draws on two distinct yet complementary philosophical traditions. First, the Platonist framework of participation in the Good and the natural desire to know truth, beauty, and unity, described as "not radically different from Christianity but not quite the same" (*II Apol.* XIII). Second, the Stoic theory that knowledge of truth is indispensable to a just and virtuous life and the idea that there is one set of universal natural laws. Justin develops these two philosophical traditions in a distinctly Christian direction by arguing that it is the Word made flesh which acts in us and, analogically speaking, plants the seeds of the divine *Logos* in our mind. Contrary to Descartes, Justin does not suggest that the human intellect achieves cognition of God based on innate ideas. Instead, it is the action of the Word within each intelligent creature that enables us to know God. For this reason, the truths already known by Socrates, Plato, and the Stoics are indebted to divine Revelation. The philosophers' quest for truth, beauty, and goodness follows natural principles that are encapsulated by the prophets and embodied in Christ, leading Justin to speak of "Christians before Christ." In this

18. St. Justin Martyr, *Second Apology,* in *The Ante-Nicene Fathers,* ed. Alexander Robertson, James Donaldson, and Arthur Cleveland Coxe (New York: Cosimo, 2007; orig. pub. 1885), vol. 1: *The Apostolic Fathers with Justin Martyr and Irenaeus,* pp. 188-93. The *First Apology (I Apol.)* and the *Dialogue with Trypho (Dial.)* are also published in this volume of *ANF.*

19. Ragner Holte, "Logos Spermatikos: Christianity and Ancient Philosophy according to St. Justin's Apologies," *Studia Theologica* 12 (1958): 109-68.

sense, philosophy was and is never independent or self-sufficient but always already linked to theology (*I Apol.* XLIV.9). Moreover, Justin's knowledge of the Platonist metaphysics of relationality and participation reinforces his conviction that the difference or 'otherness' of the incarnate *Logos* as distinct from God the Father does not involve either a transference or a loss of divinity from Father to Son because the principle of 'undiminished giving' implies an equivalence of God the Father and God the Son (*Dial.* 61.2; 128.4). As we shall see, the logic of gift-giving and gift-exchange that underpins Justin's theology will be critical to the development of pre- and post-Nicene Christology and Trinitarianism.

Like Justin in the Latin 'West,' Clement of Alexandria (c. 153-220) and Origen of Alexandria (c. 185-254) in the Greek 'East' also viewed philosophy as a preparation for the truth of the gospel. In the *Stromata,* Clement sketches a pyramidal ordering of the sciences wherein philosophy is the handmaid to theology, the queen of wisdom and of all sciences: "But as encyclical branches of study [rhetoric, grammar, music, and geometry] contribute to philosophy, which is their mistress; so also philosophy itself cooperates for the acquisition of wisdom. For philosophy is the study of wisdom, and wisdom is the knowledge of things divine and human; and their causes."[20] Since knowledge of causes points to the ultimate source of all that is, philosophy's love of wisdom and pursuit of universal truth points to God's *Logos,* revealed in the Book of Nature and the Book of Scripture. As such, philosophy has the noble task of serving as handmaid to theology. Clement bequeathed this theological ordering of sciences to Boethius and Aquinas, who both integrated important Aristotelian elements within this wider Christian Platonist framework, as I will suggest in chapters 3 and 5.

C. Origen of Alexandria and Nicaea

For his part, Origen's unique contribution to the formation of Christian metaphysics was precisely to fuse Aristotle with Plato. Endowed with an extensive knowledge of Greek philosophy (Platonist, Aristotelian, Stoic, and Epicurean), Origen adopted the basic elements of Plato's cosmology

---

20. Clement of Alexandria, *Stromata* I, V, in *The Ante-Nicene Fathers,* ed. Alexander Robertson, James Donaldson, and Arthur Cleveland Coxe (New York: Cosimo, 2007; orig. pub. 1885), vol. 2: *Fathers of the Second Century,* p. 306.

and psychology while borrowing terminology and definitions from the work of Aristotle. St. Gregory Thaumaturgus (c. 210-260), one of his students, said of him:

> He deemed those worthy to philosophize who with every energy had read all the writings of the ancient philosophers and poets, neither excluding nor disdaining (since not yet able to discriminate), except those which belong to the atheists who, since they have abandoned common human beliefs, say that there is no God or providence. . . . But [he did think it worthwhile] to take up and become conversant with all the rest, neither biased in favor of one nation or philosophic doctrine, nor yet prejudiced against it, whether Hellenic or barbarian, but listening to all. . . . He gathered and presented to us everything which was useful and was true from each of the philosophers but excluded what was false.[21]

Beyond Justin and others before him, Origen argues that *Logos* and *Sophia* are not just agents of God's creation and providence within the divine *oikonomia* but eternal and intrinsic to the triune Godhead. And since it is in the nature of God to be Trinitarian (and not only in his economy), human knowledge of the divine cannot be confined to an abstract belief in the Trinity as an article of faith but in fact extends to experience of God's eternal triune being in his temporal creation, as Mark Edwards has demonstrated.[22] But here one can go beyond Edwards and suggest that Origen combines Plato with Aristotle to demonstrate that the created world dimly reflects the triune Creator and that temporality mediates eternity.

Far from importing pagan philosophy into Christian theology, Origen bases this account on the scriptural injunction that the word and wisdom of God are essential to his nature (*Peri Archōn* I.2.3). As the *Logos,* God is the Word or Idea, and the substance of the Godhead is the mind. For this reason, God's creative activity is to think ideas or *logikoi,*

---

21. Gregory Thaumaturgus, *In Origenem oratio,* in *St. Gregory Thaumaturgus, Life and Works,* trans. Michael Slusser, The Fathers of the Church (Washington, DC: Catholic University of America Press, 1998), pp. 91-126 (116-17, 120).

22. Mark J. Edwards, "Christ or Plato? Origen on Revelation and Anthropology," in *Christian Origins: Theology, Rhetoric and Community,* ed. Lewis Ayres and Gareth Jones (London: Routledge, 1998), pp. 11-25; cf. M. J. Edwards, *Origen against Plato* (Aldershot, UK: Ashgate, 2002).

intelligible paradigms that govern all things at every station in the order of being, such that knowledge of any given concrete individual thing requires and presupposes the ability to comprehend *logikoi*. There is thus an analogy between created human minds and God's uncreated mind. As such, cognition of the ultimate origin and end of all things is rationally intelligible. Even the Trinity, as I have already indicated, is for Origen not simply an article of faith but can in some sense be discerned in creation — albeit partially and imperfectly. Indeed, he draws a further analogy between the structure of rational creatures and the Trinitarian being of their Creator: God is mind (ideas), soul *(Logos)*, and matter (Spirit), disclosing his creative presence in the created order. Drawing on Plato's theological metaphysics and St. Paul's philosophical theology, Origen affirms that man is a triadic unity of body, soul, and mind that dimly reflects the triune nature of the Godhead.

Unlike earlier theologians including Tertullian (c. 160-220) and St. Hippolytus of Rome (c. 170-236), for whom the three divine persons are only manifest in God's created temporal economy, Origen also insists that the Son and the Holy Spirit are divine persons from all eternity. Since personhood serves to differentiate each of the three persons from each other and their equally shared divine substance, the term 'person' *(hypostasis)* is of greater metaphysical importance than the term 'essence' *(ousia)* in describing the triune Godhead who surpasses human understanding. Notably, Origen ascribes to *hypostasis* individual subsistence. So if a person is an individual existent, then the Son is 'other in subsistence than the Father', that is to say, a distinct person which is a real existent from all eternity who nevertheless shares the same essence as the Father. All of which was critical in the emergence of pro-Nicene Christology and Trinitarianism, in particular the Nicene Creed which was of course first to codify the church's teaching that Christ is begotten, not made, and that he is 'of one being' *(homo-ousion)* with the Father.[23] As a result, the Council of Nicaea affirmed the eternal procession of the Son from the Father and the full divinity of Christ.

However, Nicaea raised a number of metaphysical problems and

---

23. Henry Chadwick, *The Early Church* (London: Hodder & Stoughton, 1967), pp. 125-32; J. N. D. Kelly, *Early Christian Doctrines*, 4th ed. (London: Adam & Charles Black, 1968), pp. 127-37; Stuart G. Hall, *Doctrine and Practice in the Early Church* (London: SPCK, 1991), pp. 121-36; Basil Studer, *Trinity and Incarnation: The Faith of the Early Church* (Edinburgh: T. & T. Clark, 1993), pp. 77-87; Gerald O'Collins, *Christology: A Biblical, Historical and Systematic Study of Jesus Christ* (Oxford: Oxford University Press, 1995), pp. 1-121.

questions. First of all, an overreliance on (the predominantly Aristotelian language of) substance, which emphasizes the different natures of Christ in terms that could be misconstrued as inversely related. Second, a failure to specify the Son in terms of the filial relation (rather than substantiality) and the converse union of the finitude of creation and the infinity of the Creator. For these reasons, the grammar of Nicaea centered on substance was unable to specify that the unity of Christ's filiation is the metaphysical ground of difference because the *maior dissimilitudo* is constituted in the oneness of his relation to the Father, such that union is the first term of difference. As Aaron Riches has shown, it was Cyril of Alexandria (c. 378-444) who first clarified these issues and framed the 'normative standard' of Christological doctrine at the Council of Ephesus (431).[24] Moreover, the Council of Chalcedon (451) must be read as being organically rooted in Ephesus and as anticipating the specifications and supplementations of the Councils of Constantinople I (553) and Constantinople II (680-81). In this sense, the Definition of Faith codified at Chalcedon was not a synthesis between the School of Alexandria and the School of Antioch — a misguided interpretation that has given credence to a quasi-Nestorian reading of the *Definitio fidei*. Rather, the Cyrilline account puts the emphasis firmly on the eternal personhood of the Son and the synergistic mode of the unity between his fully divine and his fully human nature. At the heart of these complex doctrinal developments were controversies over the status of divine substance or essence in connection with the triple bond of divine person, filial relation, and Trinitarian relationality.

In the following two sections, I will suggest that within the context of 'Cappadocian theology' Gregory of Nyssa is instrumental in transforming pagan Neo-Platonist metaphysics in the direction of Trinitarianism by making an important contribution to the early patristic understanding of personhood that foreshadows some of the achievements at Ephesus, Chalcedon, and Constantinople. Fusing the biblical revelation of a God who creates everything *ex nihilo* with Plato's metaphysics of relational positioning and Iamblichus' Neo-Platonist metaphysics of hierarchical and triadic structures, Gregory challenges the Aristotelian categorial primacy

---

24. Aaron Riches, "After Chalcedon: The Oneness of Christ and the Dyothelite Mediation of His Theandric Unity," *Modern Theology* 24 (April 2008): 199-224. See also Aaron Riches, *Christ: The End of Humanism* (Grand Rapids: Eerdmans, forthcoming). I am indebted to the author for arguments in this paragraph.

of substance over relation and the Nicene overemphasis on the unity of the divine essence at the expense of the distinctness of each divine person. He also proposes an analogy between the individuating relations within the Trinity and the individuation of human persons. As such, he offers a Trinitarian theology that outwits in advance the misleading opposition between the social, pluralistic Trinitarianism of the Greek East and the psychological, unitary Trinitarianism of the Latin West.

3. The Priority of Person over Essence according to Gregory of Nyssa

In this and the following section, I offer a close analysis of *Ad Petrum: On the difference between substance and person* (or *Epistula* XXXVIII [*Ep.* 38]).[25] Wrongly attributed to Basil of Caesarea (c. 329-379), this letter was in reality composed by Basil's brother Gregory of Nyssa (c. 335-395) in 369 or 370.[26] Ever since Gregory's authorship of his letter was established beyond any reasonable doubt, scholars like Reinhard Hübner, Lewis Ayres, Lucian Turcescu, and Johannes Zachhuber have debated whether his account of substance and person is shaped either by the Aristotelian distinction between individual and species or by the Stoic distinction between individual or common qualification or indeed by both. Aristotelian and Stoic elements are certainly present in Gregory's theology, but my contention is that such and similar interpretations fail to acknowledge the influence of Platonism and Neo-Platonism on his argument that the Christian conception of divine person avoids the tension between universal essence and individual particularity that is characteristic of Aristotle's ontology and Stoic philosophy alike.

25. Gregory of Nyssa, "Ad Petrum," in *Saint Basil: The Letters,* trans. Roy J. Deferrari, Loeb Classical Library (London: Heinemann, 1961), pp. 197-227. Henceforth references to this text will be in parentheses in the main text.

26. On the authorship and the dating of *Ad Petrum,* see Reinhard Hübner, "Gregor von Nyssa als Verfasser des Sog. Ep. 38 des Basilius," in *Epektasis: Mélanges patristiques offerts au Cardinal Daniélou,* ed. Jacques Fontaine and Charles Kannengiesser (Paris: Beauchesne, 1972), pp. 463-90; Lucian Turcescu, "The Concept of Divine Persons in Gregory of Nyssa's Epistle to His Brother Peter, On the Difference between Ousia and Hypostasis," *Greek Orthodox Theological Review* 42 (1997): 63-82; Johannes Zachhuber, *Human Nature in Gregory of Nyssa: Philosophical Background and Theological Significance* (Leiden: E. J. Brill, 2000), p. 63 *passim;* Lucian Turcescu, *Gregory of Nyssa and the Concept of Divine Persons* (Oxford: Oxford University Press, 2005), pp. 47-60.

Moreover, contrary to the assertion in much of modern biblical and patristic scholarship that essence/substance *(ousia)* and person *(hypostasis)* are grammatically synonymous and ontologically coextensive, Gregory's fusion of Platonist metaphysics with Pauline theology shifts the emphasis away from substance towards person and crucially towards the filial relation of the Son with the Father. As such, this more orthodox Christology (and Trinitarianism) enables Gregory to show how the "mysterious doctrine of the Trinity" blends the substantial real unity of the divine substance or essence with the irreducible diversity and distinctness of each divine person or hypostasis. This also leads him to develop a more theological and philosophical account of the link between the triunity of the Creator God and the triadic ordering of creation.

Gregory begins his reflections by drawing a distinction between substance and person. Substance is a thing's essence, that which makes it participate in a certain genus or species. As such, substance does not differentiate between different members of the same genus or species. By contrast, person is the nature or subsistence that is present in a given being. So Paul is Paul on account of 'Paulness' — that which makes him Paul rather than Peter. According to Gregory, individuality or particularity is not on account of properties or accidents but instead in virtue of a unique given form (197-203). Notably, Gregory does not follow either the Aristotelian concept of individual substantial form (and proximate matter) or the Stoic distinction between general essence and individuating characteristics (or bundles of properties). Instead, he edges in a more distinctly Platonist direction by ascribing individuality neither to formal essence nor to material accidents but rather to the individuating relations that exist among individual forms and between created forms and their divine warrant. Properly construed, form is relational vis-à-vis other forms because each unique thing entertains individuating relations with other things and its creative source. As such, individuation cannot be attributed to substance but instead is linked to personhood.

By analogy, this argument — Gregory suggests — also applies to the Godhead: "Accordingly, if you transfer to divine dogmas the principle of differentiation which you recognize as applying to substance and person in human affairs, you will not go astray" (203). Although God is "beyond all conception," the same conception of Being can be attributed to God the Father and to the Son and to the Holy Spirit because all three are equally divine. Here Gregory makes the important point that not even divine being can be said to be univocal, as the Father "proceeds from no other principle" (207) and is the ultimate source whence both the Son and the Holy Spirit proceed. Moreover, the second and the third person of the Trinity are also ontologically differentiated insofar as the Son "shines forth as the only begotten from the unbegotten light," whereas the Holy Spirit "is produced after the Son and with Him and He has His subsistence from the Father" (207). There is thus an intra-Trinitarian differentiation within the unity of the divine substance or essence. In fact, Gregory goes beyond the (Aristotelian) language of substance and cause by speaking of "a certain continuous and uninterrupted community [which] appears in [the three divine persons]" and an "inner harmony of the divine essence" that excludes any "interposition of some outside thing" and any "void, in the form of an interspace in which there is no subsistence, between the three Persons" (209). Only the Trinity, Gregory concludes, blends unity and diversity, oneness and plurality, communion and unicity. And since the Trinitarian persons are not somehow confined to God's *oikonomia* but are in reality intrinsic to the eternal Godhead (as Justin Martyr and Origen had already suggested), the Holy Trinity is the ultimate origin and end of unity and diversity within divine creation.

Far from "general speculation," this theological metaphysics of relationality outlined by Gregory is grounded both in the Book of Scripture and the Book of Nature. Scripture, he suggests, alerts us to the divine power of grace that orders all things (1 Cor. 12:11) and teaches us that all things were made by God and in him cohere (John 1:3):

> Then when we have been lifted up to that conception, we are again led on by the divinely-inspired guidance and taught that through this power all things are brought into being from not-being; not, however, even by this power without a beginning; nay, there is a power which exists without generation or beginning, and this is the cause of all things that exist. For the Son, by whom all things are, and with whom the Holy Spirit must always be conceived as inseparably associated, is of the Father. (205-7)

Since all three have their unique "distinguishing notes" (207), Gregory argues that God always already makes himself known to us both in terms of each individuated divine person and the community of the single unified divine substance: ". . . the individuality of the persons of the Godhead, as they have been handed down in our faith, is made known to us, for each is apprehended separately by means of its own particular distinguishing notes" (207-9). At the same time, Gregory insists that the faith-inspired conception of the Father, the Son, and the Holy Spirit points to the Trinitarian communion they form:

> But he who has conceived the Father, and conceived of Him apart by Himself, has at the same time mentally accepted the Son also; and he who lays hold of the Son does not dismember the Spirit from the Son, but in due sequence, so far as their order is concerned, yet unitedly [*sic*], as regards their natures, forms within himself an image of the faith that is a blending of the three in the same way . . . there is apprehended among these three a certain ineffable and inconceivable communion and at the same time distinction, with neither the difference between the persons disintegrating the continuity of their nature, nor this community of substance confounding the individual character of their distinguishing notes . . . we devise a strange and paradoxical sort of united separation and disunited connection. Indeed, unless you are listening to what I say in a contentious and spiteful spirit, even among things perceptible to the senses a similar phenomenon may be found. (209-13)

In other words, Gregory argues that scriptural revelation itself points to God's self-manifestation in nature. There is no dualism opposing the Book of Scripture to the Book of Nature, as both are complementary modes of human cognition and in this sense mutually reinforcing.

Gregory also contends that we can infer the ontological coincidence of unity and distinction "by analogy from things which appear to our sense-perception" (213). Here his indebtedness to Platonist metaphysics is critical. In the well-known Myth of the Cave (*Rep.* VII, 514 A–520 A), Plato describes the Good as the sun that is both light itself and illuminates everything that is. Thus, the Good infuses all things with goodness and in so doing individuates each being relationally — as I argued in the previous chapter. Similarly, Gregory depicts the Holy Trinity in analogical terms as a rainbow that manifests all the different colors in their individual distinctness and in their inseparable unity. Like Plato's allegory that emphasizes the natural desire for knowledge of the supernatural Good, Gregory's analogy focuses not just on what Trinitarian unity-in-difference is but also on how and why we come to know it. Arguably, he chooses the image of the rainbow in order to suggest that we can apprehend the Trinity not because there might be possibilities of a 'social' analogy but because there is a 'natural' ontological and epistemological analogy through which the triune God makes himself known to the mind via the senses within the divine economy of creation.

The image of the rainbow serves as an analogical approximation of the Holy Trinity. Indeed, the formation of a rainbow involves a paradoxical bending of the light and its return upon itself, as sunbeams refract across the mixture of moisture and air and are thrown back upon themselves. By analogy then, we can know the Trinity not itself and as such, but rather we can catch a glimpse of it — so to speak — on its way back to itself. In Augustine's and Aquinas's words, we know God on his return *(reditus)* to himself, as I will discuss in the present chapter and also in chapter 5.

Reverting for the moment to Gregory, it is clear from his depiction that when we see a rainbow we do not see light itself and as such. Nor do we discern any intervening space between all the different, separate colors. Rather, what we discover is the unity of all the colors as well as their individual distinctness — an 'appropriate' natural analogy of the incomprehensible supernatural Holy Trinity:

> Just as, therefore, in the illustration we distinguish clearly the different colours and yet cannot perceive by our senses any interval that separates the one from the other, conclude, I pray, that you may in the same way draw inferences from analogy regarding the divine dogmas. You may thus reason: that the individual traits of the Person, which may be compared with a particular hue of the colours of the rainbow, flash their light upon each of those whom we believe to constitute the Holy Trinity; that, however, no difference can be perceived in the individual character of the nature of one as compared with another, although together with their community of substance the distinguishing characteristic traits of each shine forth. (217)

Of course Gregory does not suggest that rainbows themselves represent natural traces of the supernatural Holy Trinity, for that would be a form of pagan pantheism. Instead, just as the natural phenomenon of a rainbow elucidates the nature of light which nevertheless we cannot fully grasp, so too supernatural faith illuminates the apostolic teaching on the unity of the three divine persons which nonetheless remains incomprehensible by reason alone. In Gregory's words, for just as in the case of things which appear to our eyes experience seems better than a theory of causation, so too in the case of dogmas which transcend our comprehension faith is better than apprehension through processes of reasoning, for faith teaches us to understand that which is separated in person but at the same time united in substance. (217)

Since divine substance is both one and three and can be known as such by the fusion of faith with reason, Gregory has already subverted the Aristotelian terminology of substance and causation in the direction of Trinitarian relationality and eternal gift-exchange — a theological transformation that is more fully developed in the work of Augustine, as I will suggest.

4. After Nicaea: Gregory's Trinitarianism

Nor is Gregory's insistence on the limits of reason some form of premodern fideism. His insight that we have to believe — beyond demonstrable proof — in divine Incarnation and its disclosure of the infinite reasonableness of God, suggests that a rational affirmation of truth can only be upheld by faith. Far from supplanting reason, faith itself must be reasonable in the sense of making beliefs rationally intelligible. As a result, the exercise of reason itself requires a super-rational trust (*pistis* or faith) in its very possibility. Faith in the Holy Trinity is then a reasoned belief that God is both one and three and that we cannot understand either the triune Godhead or the three individual divine persons separately and in or by themselves but only in relation to God as a whole and to each of the persons. In turn, the fusion of reason and faith elucidates scriptural revelation and helps us grasp the true meaning of the apostolic witness handed down within the living tradition of the Church. The example Gregory chooses is Hebrews 1:3, where the writer uses the word hypostasis in order "to establish the true sonship, the indivisibility, and the intimacy of the relationship of the Son to the Father . . . he [the writer] defines the glory of the Only-begotten as 'the brightness of the glory' of the Father, causing the Son to be associated inseparably with the Father in our thoughts by making use of the light by way of illustration" (221).

Once more, the influence of Plato on Gregory is striking. By conceiving the Good as the Form of all forms which endows all things with goodness, Plato outlines a metaphysics of relationality and participation that avoids in advance any crass dualism between the world of things and the world of ideas. Moreover, Plato anticipates Aristotle's theory of analogy by attribution, as goodness in things is the result of endowment by the Good itself — as expressed by the allegory of the sun that illuminates all things and renders them visible — all of which I showed in the previous chapter. Taken together, Plato's metaphysics and the Platonist-Aristotelian principle of analogy provide the foundation for patristic (and subsequently medieval) accounts of the relation between Creator and creation. Like Plato before him, Gregory uses the image of the light to suggest that God is always already present in the world and that the world reflects and describes its divine origin and end. God 'enfolds' the entire spectrum of creative possibilities, which 'unfold' in the history of creation. We can know this not because we are created with innate a priori ideas or because we are endowed with a mind that reflects on a posteriori sense impressions. Rather, we can know the Creator because God has made himself known to us in and through his incarnate Son: "[H]e who gazes intently with his soul's eyes upon the 'figure' of the Only-begotten at the same time becomes keenly aware of the 'hypostasis' or person of the Father" (223). This passage strongly resonates with John 14:9, where it is said that "[h]e who has seen me has seen the Father."

That is why Gregory plays on the dual meaning of the term 'imprint' (χαρακτήρ) in the concluding part of Ad Petrum. On one level, 'imprint' means 'figure' or 'exterior form,' and in this case Gregory's argument is that the Son is "the figure of His (that is, the Father's) person" (225). This applies not just to John 14:9 but also to Colossians 1:15 and Wisdom 7:26 where the writer speaks of the Son as the image of the invisible God and as the image of His goodness. On another level, 'imprint' refers to 'image,' which means that the Son does not merely disclose the Father but is in reality the image of the Father. With this dual use Gregory underscores both the distinctness of each divine person and the unity of Father and Son through the filial relation that individuates both, "for all the attributes of the Father are beheld in the Son, and all the attributes of the Son belong to the Father, in so much as the Son abides wholly in the Father and in turn has the Father wholly in Himself" (227) — an argument that echoes and elucidates John 14:10 where Jesus responds to his disciples' incredulity: "Do you not believe that I am in the Father, and the Father in me? The words I speak to you, I speak not of myself. But the Father who abides in me, he does the works."

In the final instance then, Gregory combines the Platonist metaphysics of relationality and participation (and the Platonist-Aristotelian theory of analogy) with the biblical revelation of creation *ex nihilo* and God's Incarnation in order to argue that the whole of creation intimates the triune Creator, as creaturely goodness is the product of the inflowing of divine creative grace by the self-diffusive Good of God in which we can all participate.[27] Conversely, Gregory's reasoning about intra-Trinitarian relations of individuation suggests that creation itself dimly discloses the ontological coextensionality of unity and diversity, as no single creature alone can reflect God's goodness or be equal to God's revelation. The link between the triune Creator and his creation is divine goodness 'giving itself' ecstatically to finitude in an original relation whose reverse face is the 'participation' of temporal things in God, who alone brings about their particular existence unchanged.

In conclusion of the previous section and this one, I want to suggest that Gregory's account of relational personhood overcomes the overemphasis on substance at Nicaea and the tendency to specify the unity of Christ's two natures in terms of dual, separate substances held together by the divine hypostasis of the Son caused by the Father. By conceiving the unity of Christ's dual nature in terms of the irreducible union of personhood and the filial relation with the Father, Gregory moves beyond the limits of Nicaea and contributes to the formation of the 'theological culture' (Lewis Ayres) that paved the way for the discussions leading to the First Council of Constantinople (381), the Council of Ephesus (431), and the Council of Chalcedon (453).[28] Specifically, Gregory eschews the Aristotelian primacy of substance in favor of personhood, thereby shifting the emphasis away from individuation by individual substantial form towards the individuating relationality of the three divine persons. The crucial theological implication is that the Son and the Holy Spirit proceed eternally from the Father within the triune Godhead,

---

27. Commentators like Cornelius Plantinga neglect the theological metaphysics at the heart of Gregory's Trinitarianism. See Cornelius Plantinga, "Gregory of Nyssa and the Social Analogy of the Trinity," *The Thomist* 50 (1986): 325-52.

28. On Gregory's contribution to post-Nicene Trinitarian theology, see Ayres, *Nicaea and Its Legacy*, pp. 344-63; Michel René Barnes, *The Power of God: Dunamis in Gregory of Nyssa's Trinitarian Theology* (Washington, DC: Catholic University of America Press, 2001), pp. 260-307.

which blends the uniqueness of each divine person with their Trinitarian communion. Since human beings are created in the image and likeness of God, Gregory concludes that we can infer analogically from the infinite relationality within the Trinity to the relational nature of the human person.

In the remainder of this chapter, I argue that the theological metaphysics of relationality and the philosophical theology of the Trinity outlined by Gregory are more fully developed in the work of Augustine. Against Porphyry's more Aristotelianized Neo-Platonism, Augustine retrieved and extended the Plotinian focus on the creative activity of the One and the hierarchical ordering of the many. Beyond the misleading opposition between a psychological, unitary, and typically 'western' Trinitarianism on the one hand and a social, pluralistic, and typically 'eastern' Trinitarianism on the other hand, Augustine's Trinitarian theology combines reasoned faith in infinite Trinitarian relationality with a discovery of the triadic ordering of creation.

5. Augustine's Neo-Platonist Theology

A. The Errors of Augustine's Critics

The philosophy and the theology of Augustine (354-430) have come under attack for essentially the same reason. The charge is that his Neo-Platonist ideas led him to embrace a metaphysics that privileges the one at the expense of the many, and to develop a theology that prioritizes God's unity over the Holy Trinity. The prominence of Neo-Platonism in patristic thought in general and in the Latin Church Fathers in particular also seems to preclude any significant knowledge of Aristotle prior to Boethius (c. 480-524).[29] Coupled with the conviction that reflections on the nature of individuality and on the cause of individuation are simply absent from Augustine's works,[30] the claim is that Augustine does not engage with Aristotelian logic and metaphysics. Even after his conversion to Christianity, the Neo-Platonist legacy is thought to hold Augus-

---

29. Vernon J. Bourke, *Augustine's View of Reality* (Villanova, PA: Villanova University Press, 1964), pp. 98, 131.
30. Jorge J. E. Gracia, *Introduction to the Problem of Individuation in the Early Middle Ages* (Munich: Philosophia Verlag, 1984), p. 13.

tine hostage to philosophical ideas that are contrary to his new theological commitments. For instance, due to his fixation upon Plotinian oneness, Augustine's philosophy stands accused of favoring abstract form and neglecting plurality, particularity, and materiality.[31]

Moreover, Augustine is said simply to assert the truth of the doctrine of creation *ex nihilo* rather than attempting to give a rationally intelligible account of it. Equally, as a result of his alleged obsession with divine simplicity, Augustine's theology has been questioned, especially his alleged modalism and his insufficiently Trinitarian understanding of God.[32] Others who do not brand him a modalist nevertheless argue that his depiction of the Trinity prioritizes divine and human inwardness at the expense of God's creative and salvific activity and man's communal and transformative response.[33] Yet others have seen in Augustine's conception of the ego the prototype for Descartes's *cogito*. Thus, Augustine is held responsible for the turn to subjectivism in western philosophy and the fascination with self-reflexivity and solipsism.[34]

In what follows, I argue that such and similar interpretations of Augustine are mistaken because they contain a number of undemonstrated and untenable presuppositions and assertions — chief of all the claim that his Neo-Platonism commits him to the substantiality of God and the purification of the immaterial inner self from outer material reality. This

---

31. Stephen C. Layman, "Tritheism and the Trinity," *Faith and Philosophy* 5 (1988): 291-98.

32. Colin E. Gunton, *Enlightenment and Alienation: An Essay towards a Trinitarian Theology* (Basingstoke, UK: Marshall, Morgan & Scott, 1985); John D. Zizioulas, *Being as Communion: Studies in Personhood and the Church* (Crestwood, NY: St. Vladimir's Seminary Press, 1985); Cornelius Plantinga, "Social Trinity and Tritheism," in *Trinity, Incarnation and Atonement: Philosophical and Theological Essays,* ed. Cornelius Plantinga and Ronald Feenstra (Notre Dame: University of Notre Dame Press, 1989), pp. 21-47; Colin E. Gunton, *The Promise of Trinitarian Theology* (Edinburgh: T. & T. Clark, 1991); Richard Swinburne, *The Christian God* (Oxford: Oxford University Press, 1994).

33. David Brown, "Trinitarian Personhood and Individuality," in Plantinga and Feenstra, eds., *Trinity, Incarnation and Atonement,* pp. 48-78; Catherine M. LaCugna, *God for Us: The Trinity and Christian Life* (San Francisco: HarperSanFrancisco, 1991).

34. Stephen P. Menn, *Descartes and Augustine* (Cambridge: Cambridge University Press, 1998); Charles Taylor, *Sources of the Self: The Making of Modern Identity* (Cambridge, MA: Harvard University Press, 1989); Gareth B. Matthews, *Thought's Ego in Augustine and Descartes* (Ithaca, NY, and London: Cornell University Press, 1992); Phillip Carey, *Augustine's Invention of the Inner Self: The Legacy of a Christian Platonist* (Oxford: Oxford University Press, 2000); Wayne J. Hankey, "Between and Beyond Augustine and Descartes: More Than a Source of the Self," *Augustinian Studies* 32 (2001): 65-88.

claim relies on a misreading of Platonist metaphysics and Augustine's transformation of Neo-Platonic ideas (a point I will elaborate on later in the present section). Since there is no ontological or epistemological dualism between the world of things and the world of ideas, Augustine insists that individual material forms *(formae corporeae)* exhibit beauty in themselves and harmony with other forms. Contrary to Aristotle's autonomous individual substances, Augustine develops Plato's relational forms in the direction of Trinitarian theology by suggesting that all things are governed by the numbers and ratios of God's wisdom. Reality as a whole is numerically and proportionally ordered. As such, material forms are both individual and relational, and the entire *cosmos* is constituted by relations among beings and between beings and Being (*De Mus.* VI.vii.19; VI.xi.29). This is the fundamental context in which to understand his account of human selfhood.

I also argue that there is an analogy between true knowledge of the world and true knowledge of the self. For both are ultimately grounded in God's creative activity. Knowledge of the world reveals a relational triadic ordering of all things, which paradoxically intimates the triune Creator who is unlike his creation. Likewise, self-knowledge discloses a relational soul that originates from God and seeks an ever-closer union with him. To know the self is therefore to know that it is created and that the soul is sustained by God's wisdom because this is how God communicates himself to himself and to his creation. To know that the self stands in irreducible relations with its Creator in whose image and likeness it is created is also to know that the triune God is both infinite divine substantiality and unreserved Trinitarian relationality — precisely because God is wholly unlike our immaterial mind and soul.

However, I do not rehearse all the arguments in favor of Augustine's Trinitarian theology.[35] Nor do I revisit the debate about the difference

---

35. In defense of Augustine's Trinitarianism, it has been argued that his account blends divine unity with divine plurality. See Sarah Heaner Lancaster, "Three-Personed Substance: The Relational Essence of the Triune God in Augustine's *De Trinitate*," *The Thomist* 60 (1996): 123-39; Michel René Barnes, "Augustine in Contemporary Trinitarian Theology," *Theological Studies* 56 (1995): 237-50; M. R. Barnes, "De Régnon Reconsidered," *Augustinian Studies* 26 (1995): 51-79; M. R. Barnes, "Rereading Augustine's Theology of the Trinity," in *The Trinity: An Interdisciplinary Symposium on the Trinity*, ed. Stephen T. Davis, David Kendall, and Gerald O'Collins (Oxford: Oxford University Press, 1999), pp. 145-76; Lewis Ayres, "'Remember That You Are Catholic' (serm. 52.2): Augustine on the Unity of the Triune God," *Journal of Early Christian Studies* 8 (2000): 39-82; M. R. Barnes, "The Visi-

between Augustine's account of the *ego* and Descartes's conception of the *cogito*.[36] Nor does my account of relationality start either with the Holy Trinity and proceed to the Trinitarian image in the soul,[37] or move from the outward orientation of the self to the relational nature of divine substance.[38] Instead, I begin with Augustine's redescription of the world as a relational order that manifests God's creative activity which sustains all beings. This vision, which is already to some extent articulated in his early writings, distinguishes Augustine's Christian metaphysics from ancient skepticism and from the Aristotelian emphasis on substance and cause in Neo-Platonism.[39] Augustine's experience of the world as relational was instrumental in the process of his conversion and led him to discern that the universe and everything therein is created (*Conf.* VII.xvii.23). Only creation can explain how and why all things have a particular station within the relational order and thus are individuated in and by relations with God and within the universe. Before I can make this case, I need to say something about individuation in Augustine and also about his reception and transformation of Neo-Platonism.

---

ble Christ and the Invisible Trinity: Mt. 5:8 in Augustine's Trinitarian Theology of 400," *Modern Theology* 19 (2003): 329-55; Ayres, *Nicaea and Its Legacy*, pp. 364-83.

36. A number of scholars have argued emphatically and demonstrated beyond any reasonable doubt that Augustine's thought does not foreshadow Descartes's *cogito*. See Rowan Williams, "The Paradoxes of Self-Knowledge in the *De Trinitate*," in *Augustine: Presbyter Factus Sum*, ed. Joseph T. Lienhard, Earl C. Muller, and Roland J. Teske, Collectanea Augustiniana 2 (New York: Peter Lang, 1993), pp. 121-34; Denys Turner, *The Darkness of God: Negativity in Christian Mysticism* (Cambridge: Cambridge University Press, 1995), esp. p. 69; Catherine Pickstock, "Music: Soul, City and Cosmos after Augustine," in *Radical Orthodoxy: A New Theology*, ed. John Milbank, Catherine Pickstock, and Graham Ward (London: Routledge, 1999), pp. 243-77; Michael Ward, "Desire: Augustine beyond Western Subjectivity," in Milbank, Pickstock, and Ward, eds., *Radical Orthodoxy*, pp. 109-26; M. Hanby, "Augustine and Descartes: An Overlooked Chapter in the Story of Modern Origins," *Modern Theology* 19 (October 2003): 455-82; M. Hanby, *Augustine and Modernity* (London and New York: Routledge, 2003), esp. pp. 6-26, 134-79.

37. John Milbank, "Sacred Triads: Augustine and the Indo-European Soul," *Modern Theology* 13 (October 1997): 451-74.

38. Rowan Williams, "*Sapientia* and the Trinity: Reflections on the *De Trinitate*," in *Collectanea Augustiniana: Mélanges T. J. von Bavel*, ed. Bernard Brunning, Mathijs Lamberigts, and Jozef van Houtem (Leuven: Leuven University Press, 1990), pp. 317-32.

39. Goulven Madec, *Saint Augustin et la Philosophie* (Paris: Institut d'Études Augustiniennes, 1996).

B. The Problem of Individuation in Augustine

Jorge Gracia claims that prior to Boethius (c. 480-525) individuation was not central to patristic philosophy and theology. The reason seems to be that knowledge of Aristotle was limited to the Categories and did not extend to the metaphysical conceptuality of act and potency. It was only after substantial parts of the *Organon* had been translated and transmitted to the Latin world in the late fifth and the early sixth century that Christian theology turned to this question. Since he introduced Aristotle's metaphysics into Christian theology, "medieval discussions of the problem of individuation began with Boethius,"[40] so Gracia's argument goes. However, to assert — as Gracia does — that Augustine was not concerned with the nature of individuality and the cause of individuation is to make one of the following unwarranted assumptions. Either the assumption is that Augustine's knowledge of Aristotle was insignificant and did not encompass the metaphysical aspects of the *Categories* or elements of his metaphysics, in particular, the primacy of substance or essence over relation and the interaction of the actuality of form and the potency of matter. Or the assumption is that Augustine embraced Plato's theory of universal forms in which particular things participate and thus sided with Plato's metaphysics of the one (the Good as the form of forms) against Aristotle's metaphysics of the many (individual substantial forms). Or else again the assumption is that Augustine wrote a nonphilosophical theology that altogether failed to address questions about the nature of individuality or the principle of individuation.

None of these assumptions stand up to serious scrutiny. Augustine had knowledge of Aristotle's *Categories* but rejected the primacy of substance over relation on philosophical and theological grounds. He was also familiar with other concepts of Aristotelian metaphysics like act and potency, and in his commentaries on the Book of Genesis he reconfigured them in order to produce a rationally intelligible account of creation *ex nihilo* in terms of how the potency of seminal reasons *(rationes seminales)* is activated by the concurrence of the primary causality of God and the secondary causality of the natural order. Moreover, he out-

---

40. Jorge J. E. Gracia, "The Legacy of the Early Middle Ages," in *Individuation in Scholasticism: The Later Middle Ages and the Counter-Reformation, 1150-1650*, ed. J. J. E. Gracia (Albany: State University of New York Press, 1994), pp. 21-38 (21). Cf. Gracia, *Introduction to the Problem of Individuation in the Early Middle Ages*, esp. pp. 11-16.

lined an alternative 'first philosophy' that blends the substantiality of essences with the relationality of persons. In so doing, he recast Plato's idea of the transcendence and creativity of the Good which constitutes all things relationally. This alternative, which is indebted to Neo-Platonism yet constitutes a properly Christian account, lies at the center of his Trinitarian theology. To say this raises the question of the influence of Neo-Platonism on Augustine's account of individuation, to which I now turn.

C. Augustine's Neo-Platonism

Between Plato and Augustine stand not only Aristotle and his successors but also the so-called Middle Platonists, early Christian Platonists like Clement and Origen, as well as members of the Neo-Platonist school such as Plotinus (c. 204/5-270) and Porphyry (c. 234-305).[41] It has been claimed that Augustine was significantly influenced by Porphyry, who shifted the focus from Platonic metaphysics to Aristotelian logic. Porphyry's logicized Neo-Platonism was transmitted to Augustine through a variety of different channels, including the works of another Christian convert, Marius Victorinus (c. 280-365). However, as John Rist notes, "Much of what has been proposed as Porphyrian material in the early Augustine is indeed Porphyrian but equally Plotinian and often more generally 'Platonic.'"[42]

For this reason, one way to distinguish different strands of (Chris-

41. On the complex interaction of Christian theology and the Platonist tradition in the fourth century, see John Rist, "Basil's 'Neoplatonism': Its Background and Nature," in *Basil of Caesarea: Christian, Humanist, Ascetic. A Sixteen-Hundredth Anniversary Symposium*, ed. Paul J. Fedwick (Toronto: Pontifical Institute of Mediaeval Studies, 1981), pp. 137-220, reprinted in John Rist, *Platonism and Its Christian Heritage* (London: Variorum, 1985), ch. 12. On Plotinus and patristic theology, see J. Rist, "Plotinus and Christian Philosophy," in *The Cambridge Companion to Plotinus*, ed. Lloyd P. Gerson (Cambridge: Cambridge University Press, 1996), pp. 386-413. On Augustine's Neo-Platonism, see John J. O'Meara, "The Neoplatonism of Saint Augustine," in *Neoplatonism and Christian Thought*, ed. Dominic O'Meara (Albany: State University of New York Press, 1982), pp. 34-41; Scott MacDonald, "Augustine's Christian-Platonist Account of Goodness," *The New Scholasticism* 63 (1989): 485-509; Robert Crouse, "*Paucis Mutatis Verbis*: St. Augustine's Neoplatonism," in *Augustine and His Critics: Essays in Honour of Gerald Bonner*, ed. Robert Dodaro and George Lawless (London: Routledge, 2000), pp. 37-50.

42. John Rist, "Basil's 'Neoplatonism': Its Background and Nature," p. 148.

tian) Neo-Platonism is according to whether they are more Platonist or more Aristotelian. Since he tends to follow Plotinus rather than Porphyry, Augustine's Neo-Platonism is — broadly speaking — more Platonist than it is Aristotelian. In the *Contra Academicos,* Plotinus is described as "Plato born again" (*Cont. Acad.* III.xviii.41). The prominence of Plotinian Neo-Platonism is true for his 'philosophical theology' in general and his thinking on individuality in particular, including in his early works (386-91).[43] I will now briefly discuss a number of Plotinus's concepts which Augustine adapts and integrates into his philosophy before I turn to the influence of Platonism on his account of individuation.

Augustine shares with Plotinus a critique of Aristotle's claim that the self-thinking mind is the first principle of the cosmos.[44] For Plotinus, the One is both 'interiorizing' and 'exteriorizing.' Because the One is the universal source of existence, all things at lower levels in the hierarchy of being can be like it — even though the One is of course never like them. Just as the One exceeds the self-thinking νοῦς, so too souls can exceed themselves and reach beyond the forms of things to Form itself. Augustine, like Plotinus, argues against Aristotle that the activity of thinking is not limited to self-reflexivity. To think is to think of something other than of the self in itself and as such. For this reason, there is a difference between the thinking subject and the object that is thought. Following Plotinus, Augustine emphasizes the unlikeness of the human and the divine mind (*De Trin.* XIV.iv.15): the human self is not confined to self-awareness but can go beyond itself, precisely as a result of the ecstatic self-exteriorization of God's intellect that upholds our natural desire to know the truth and directs our mind to its supernatural end in God. Perhaps most importantly, Augustine associates with the highest principle not only the unity of divine substance or essence

43. O'Connell rejects the thesis that Augustine follows Porphyry in his thinking on the nature of man and makes a case for the centrality of Platonism in Augustine. See Robert O'Connell, *St. Augustine's Early Theory of Man, AD 386-391* (Cambridge, MA: Belknap Press of Harvard University Press, 1968), p. 20 *passim,* and R. O'Connell, *Saint Augustine's Platonism* (Villanova, PA: Villanova University Press, 1984). On Plotinus's Platonic understanding of particularity, see John Rist, *Plotinus: The Road to Reality* (Cambridge: Cambridge University Press, 1967), pp. 103-11.

44. On Plotinus's critique of Aristotle, see John Rist, "The One of Plotinus and the God of Aristotle," *Review of Metaphysics* 27 (1973): 75-87. I am indebted to Professor Rist's work for some arguments in this paragraph. Cf. A. Hilary Armstrong, *The Architecture of the Intelligible Universe in the Philosophy of Plotinus: An Analytical and Historical Study* (Cambridge: Cambridge University Press, 1940).

but also the source of material existence in all its diversity. Instead of Aristotle's indifferent God, the creative activity of Augustine's highest being *(summe est)* resembles the ecstatic overflow of Plotinus's One which generates all existents and sustains them in being.[45] It is Plotinus's conception of the One as both inward-looking and out-flowing that helps bring Augustine closer to the radiance of Plato's Good than to the self-directed energy of Aristotle's Prime Mover.

Moreover, Christian Neo-Platonism retrieves and extends two other ideas that are central in Plotinus: first of all, the infinity of the highest principle and, second, the participation of particulars in universals, as William Norris Clarke has indicated.[46] This also applies to Augustine. Beyond the materialism and the dualism of the Manicheans, Augustine finds in Neo-Platonism the intellectual resources in order to grasp the ultimate reality as transcending all material categories. This enables him during the process of his conversion to conceptualize ultimate reality as Being itself: *idipsum, ipsum esse* or supreme being.[47] So conceived, Being is beyond space, time, and change — it is infinite yet perfect, for its infinity is not of defect but of excess, giving being and goodness to everything that it brings from the nothingness of potency into the plenitude of actuality.[48] The infinity and ecstatic overflow of the Creator *is* the ontological difference with his creation. Contrary to the chasm between Aristotle's Prime Mover and the sublunary world, Augustine combines the Plotinian Neo-Platonist focus on participation and on degrees of being/goodness with the biblical emphasis upon creation *ex nihilo* and the natural striving for an ever-closer union with the supernatural Good in God (e.g., *Conf.* VII.xi.17). And since in God infinite Being and the perfection of the Good are coextensive, to be created is to share in the goodness of Being which

---

45. *Ver. Relig.* XIII.26. Even Edward Booth, who attributes more Aristotelian elements to Augustine's account of self-knowledge than do most interpretations, recognizes the indifference of Aristotle's prime mover vis-à-vis the world. See Edward Booth, "St. Augustine's 'notitia sui' Related to Aristotle and the Early Neo-Platonists," *Augustiniana* 27 (1977): 70-132, 364-401, esp. p. 324. Cf. E. Booth, *Saint Augustine and the Western Tradition of Self-Knowing: The St. Augustine Lecture 1986* (Villanova, PA: Villanova University Press, 1989).

46. William Norris Clarke, "The Limitation of Act by Potency in St. Thomas: Aristotelianism or Neo-Platonism," *New Scholasticism* 26 (1952): 167-94, esp. 184-88.

47. On *idipsum*, see *Conf.* IX.x.24; XII.vii.7; XII.xv.20; XIII.xi.12. On *ipsum esse*, see *En. Ps.* 135 (134) and *Ion. Ev.* XXXVIII.8-9. On supreme being, see *Ver. Relig.* XIII.26 and *Civ. Dei* XII.2.

48. Étienne Gilson, *Introduction à l'Étude de Saint Augustin* (Paris: Vrin, 1941), pp. 26-30.

'gives itself' ecstatically and in so doing positions all things relationally.[49] The biblical and Neo-Platonic conceptual framework is key to Augustine's account of creation and individuation, as I show below.

Two further parallels between Plotinian Neo-Platonism and Augustine's 'philosophical theology' are relevant to the question of individuation: first, the presence of triadic structures in material and immaterial things; second, the centrality of conversion to the divine and the process of deification or divinization. For example, Augustine deploys the Plotinian triad in the νοῦς (existence, living, and thinking)[50] in order to refute the Skeptics' dyad of doubt and the doubting mind. This is central to his account of self-knowledge, which is not confined to self-awareness but issues forth into knowledge of the self as relational, as I will suggest. Likewise, Augustine draws on Plotinus for the idea of conversion,[51] in the sense of turning to the presence of the divine in oneself and in created things (*Conf.* VII.xvii.23). The emphasis on knowledge of God and conversion also brings Augustine into engagement with the question of deification. The self can become like God, even though God could of course never become like the self. In Augustine, the paradox of likeness and unlikeness takes the form of an asymmetrical relation between God and creation, which is partly analogous to the relation between the One and the soul in Plotinus. To know God through the confluence of faith and reason is always already to become deified, as contemplation of God directs the soul to its divine origin and end and also orders relations within creation according to divine intentionality.

Nor is deification purely theoretical and abstract, as is the case of contemplation of the Prime Mover in Aristotle. Like Plato and Iamblichus (whose works, however, he did not know directly), Augustine associates deification with transformative action that is both doxological and political — worship and civic virtue, in particular the dispensation of justice, are indispensable to a godly life. As such, Augustine's synthesis of ancient philosophy and biblical revelation seeks to combine contemplative knowledge and deifying practices. On this crucial point Augustine is much closer to the theurgical Platonism of Iamblichus which em-

---

49. *Lib. Arb.* III.ii.4; *Ver. Relig.* XI.21 and XLIII.81; *Gen. ad Lit. Imp.* XVI.57; *Nat. Bon.* III.

50. For an overview of triadic structures in Augustine's theory of self-knowledge, see Edward Booth, "St. Augustine's 'notitia sui' Related to Aristotle and the Early Neo-Platonists," *Augustiniana* 29 (1979): 97-124. On Plotinus, see A. Hilary Armstrong, "Form, Individual and Person in Plotinus," *Dionysius* 1 (1977): 49-68.

51. O'Meara, "The Neoplatonism of Saint Augustine," p. 38.

phasizes the soul's creative mirroring of, and engagement with, the cosmos than he is to the contemplative Platonism of Porphyry which advocates the soul's disengagement and retrenchment from the created world.[52]

However, the most fundamental difference between (Plotinian) Neo-Platonism and Augustine's theology is a rejection of the idea that chaotic matter preexists the harmony of the cosmos which was formed by the Demiurge or emanated from the One. Only creation *ex nihilo*, Augustine maintains, can explain not just how but also why we are brought into being and what temporality, materiality, and mortality might signify. Moreover, Augustine eschews the theory of subordinationism in favor of the alternative conception codified at Nicaea of the Son's dual nature within a unified person and crucially the Son's filial relation with the Father. Like Gregory of Nyssa's Trinitarianism, Augustine's Trinitarian theology is wrongly portrayed as psychological, unitary, or 'western.' Rather, it develops an account that relates triads in the soul and in the cosmos to infinite relationality within the triune Godhead. Neo-Platonist concepts such as creative activity, infinity, participation, and triads as well as degrees of being and goodness are central to his vision of the Trinity and his theory of individuation, as I argue in the following section.

6. 'Musical Metaphysics' and Divine Illumination

A. The Beauty and Harmony of Material Forms

Already in his early writings, including the dialogues composed at Cassiciacum in 386-87, Augustine offers a description of the world that differs markedly from Greek and Roman philosophy and foreshadows a properly Christian metaphysics. In the *Confessions*, he recalls how his love for material things sparked reflections on the nature of beauty and harmony and gave rise to his first treatise, *On the Beautiful and the Harmonious*, which is lost.[53] Fortunately, some of Augustine's seminal

---

52. Gregory Shaw, *Theurgy and the Soul: The Neoplatonism of Iamblichus* (University Park: Pennsylvania State University Press, 1995).

53. Augustine's first treatise, *De pulchro et apto* (c. 380-81), was already lost at the time when he wrote the *Confessions* (c. 397-400). Cf. Takeshi Katô, "Melodia interior — Sur le traité *De pulchro et apto*," *Revue des études augustiniennes* 12 (1966): 229-40.

works such as *Confessiones* and *De Musica* preserve and extend these reflections:

> To my friends I would say "Do we love anything but the beautiful? What then is the beautiful? And what is beauty? What is it that entices and unites us to the things we love? For unless there were a grace and beauty in them, they could not possibly attract us to them." And I reflected on this and saw that in material objects themselves there is a kind of beauty which comes from their forming a whole and another kind of beauty that comes from mutual fittingness — as the harmony of one part of the body with its whole, or a shoe with a foot, and so on.[54]

As Augustine notes in this passage, material things are not passive entities that are merely 'there' in and by themselves. Rather, they exert an attraction upon us in virtue of the beauty of their own individual form and the harmony of their fitting ties with other forms. Beauty manifests the unity of a composite, whereas harmony describes the agreement (or 'mutual fittingness') with other composites. For this reason, material things can be said to be both beautiful in themselves and to stand in harmonious relations with other things — they are individual *and* relational. From this and other texts on beauty, it emerges that a thing's individuality and relationality are not merely logical properties that the mind conceives by abstracting form from matter but rather pertain to a thing's essence. Since the beauty and harmony of form is translucent and 'shines forth,' it has a phenomenal visibility and discloses itself in a thing's appearance. As such, the individuality and the relationality of form are real

---

54. "*. . . dicebam amicis meis. Num amamus aliquid nisi pulchrum? Quid est ergo pulchrum? Et quid est pulchritudo? Quid est quod nos allicit et conciliat rebus, quas amamus? Nisi enim esset in eis decus et species, nullo modo nos ad se mouerent. Et animadvertebam et videbam in ipsis corporibus aliud esse quasi totum et ideo pulchrum, aliud autem, quod ideo deceret, quoniam apte accommodaretur alicui, sicut pars corporis ad universum suum aut calciamentum ad pedem et similia*" (*Conf.* IV.xiii.20 [p. 65, translation modified]). This citation continues as follows: "This realization welled up in my mind from my innermost heart, and I wrote some books entitled *The Beautiful and the Harmonious*, two or three books I think — you know, O God, but it escapes me, for I no longer have them; they have somehow been lost" (*"Et ista consideratio scaturivit in animo meo ex intimo corde meo, et scripsi libros* De Pulchro et Apto, *puto, duos aut tres; tu scis, Deus nam excidit mihi. Non enim habemus eos, sed aberraverunt a nobis nescio quo modo*" [*Conf.* IV.xiii.20 (p. 65); cf. *Conf.* IV.xiv.23; IV.xv.24]).

embodied essential characteristics that the senses can somehow perceive and the mind can cognize.

Like Plato, Augustine argues that forms do not stand apart from the things that embody them but are present in the very materiality of things. As such, form is not primarily a concept *of* the mind *in* the mind but has a visibility that the senses mediate to the intellect: "My mind scanned material forms, and I defined and distinguished what was beautiful in itself from what was harmonious because fittingly adapted to something else, supporting my distinction with material examples."[55] So to say that a thing is beautiful in itself and harmonious with other things in virtue of its material form *(forma corporea)* is to say that a thing's material form is both individual and relational and can be discerned and known as such.

In the *De Musica* (c. 387-391), Augustine suggests that the beauty and harmony of things is a function of their 'numberliness' *(numerositas)*. In fact, the whole of material and immaterial reality alike is governed by numbers and ratios which constitute the individual forms and the relations that pertain between them. But how do we know that this might be so? By contrast with Aristotle's 'mathematical ontology' and his epistemology of formal abstraction, Augustine's 'musical metaphysics' is linked to his theory of divine illumination. It is precisely because the triune Godhead illumines human cognition and directs the created intellect to its creative source that we can discern the relational ordering of material creation and the image of the Trinitarian God in ourselves and in our neighbors. Here Augustine's 'incarnational' philosophy shifts the Aristotelian emphasis away from individual substantial form towards universal form instantiated in particular materiality. Theologically and philosophically, the reality of Creation and Incarnation binds together form and matter in such a way that a particular material thing uniquely reflects the universal form it embodies.

This specifically Augustinian focus on the link between form and matter is not confined to the content of cognition but encompasses the initial source of cognitive capacity and the process of cognition. Impressed with divinely ordered numbers and ratios, physical organs like the senses can mediate the presence of immaterial structures in mate-

---

55. "*ibat animus per formas corporeas et pulchrum, quod per se ipsum, aptum autem, quod ad aliquid accommodatum deceret, definiebam et distinguebam et exemplis corporeis astruebam*" (*Conf.* IV.xv.24 [p. 67]).

rial things to the intellect, thus directing our natural desire for knowledge to forms embodied in matter and to their ultimate origin in God. What sustains this cognitive dynamic is the free gift of divine wisdom to all persons so that they may discover the image of the Trinitarian God in them.

I will now explore the link between Augustine's 'musical metaphysics' and his account of divine illumination in greater detail. Since the senses themselves are infused with numbers and ratios (*De Mus.* VI.iii.4–VI.iv.5), they can delight in the beauty and harmony of 'material form':

> [T]he very sense of delight could not have been favourable to equal intervals and rejected perturbed ones, unless it itself were imbued with numbers; then too, the reason laid upon this delight cannot at all judge of the numbers it has under it, without more powerful numbers.[56]

In other words, numbers and ratios are not only in objects of knowledge but also in the senses and in reason. As such, it is not the human mind that projects categorial structures onto the world. Instead, the senses and the intellect discern a numerical structure at the heart of reality because they are endowed with the capacity of recognizing it. But how can the physical senses delight in something intangible which they do not themselves fully grasp? How can the immaterial mind rejoice in something material that it does not as yet know? Why do humans desire that which they as yet ignore?

Augustine's proposed solution to this paradox mirrors and develops Plato's theory in the *Meno* where he accounts for our natural desire to know the unknown in terms of the presence of the Good in us. In his early works, we can find a theological resolution of the *Meno* paradox which frames Augustine's account of individuation and creation. Far from advocating a "flight from the physical world,"[57] his argument is that we come to love material things and to desire the beauty and harmony of material form because the numbers and ratios in objects alert us to the numbers and ratios in our senses, in our judgment, and ultimately in our soul. Blending Plato's metaphysics of relationality and participation with

---

56. "*nisi quibusdam numeris esset ipse delectationis sensus imbutus, nullo modo eum potuisse annuere paribus intervallis, et perturbata respuere: recte etiam videri potest ratio, quae huic delectationi superimponitur, nullo modo sine quibusdam numeris vivacioribus, de numeris quos infra se habet posse iudicare*" (*De Mus.* VI.ix.24 [p. 350]).

57. Menn, *Descartes and Augustine*, pp. 395-400.

Aristotle's ontology of act and potency, Augustine shows how only sensory experience of actual physical beauty and harmony can activate our sense of beautiful and harmonic proportions in material things and thus actualize our potency to know beauty and harmony in themselves and as such (*De Mus.* VI.ii.2-3).

Augustine's theological epistemology also operates important modifications of Plato's theory of ἀνάμνησις and Aristotle's language of act and potency. Like Plato in the later dialogues, Augustine maintains that knowledge of forms exceeds mental recollection because sensory experience awakens the soul to the presence of intelligible forms in sensible things.[58] Beyond Plato, Augustine denies that the soul itself effects bodily sensation and the memory. Both sensation and the memory are activated by the numbers and ratios in objects that kindle our desire for beauty and harmony (*De Mus.* VI.iii.4–VI.iv.5). With Aristotle (and against Plato), Augustine holds that the coming into being of finite material things is not the product of a Demiurge which uses form to create order out of chaotic matter but rather the outcome of a formal act of being which actualizes the potency of matter. Since the senses mediate species form to the mind, sense perception — not mental abstraction — is at the origin of knowledge of forms that inhere in matter: "... among our senses also, which the mind uses in acting through the body, there is nothing more valuable than the eyes, and so in the Holy Scriptures all the objects of sense are spoken of as visible things."[59] The senses, in particular vision, are central to Augustine's account of knowledge because there are according to him "traces of reason in sensations *(vestigia rationis in sensibus)*" (*De Ord.* II.xi.33). Since both Creation and the Incarnation mark the instantiation of the intelligible in the sensible, Augustine concludes that to perceive anything sensible is to discern the intelligible that activates our cognition (*Retrac.* I.i.1).

Beyond Aristotle, he also contends that matter is not purely passive but instead always already contains a capacity to receive form, akin to a seed whose form unfolds in the presence of active forces (*De Mus.* VI.xvii.57). Likewise, judgment of beauty and harmony is a capacity that, like sensation and memory, is triggered by the numbers and ratios in ob-

---

58. Jean-Louis Chrétien, *L'inoubliable et l'inespéré* (Paris: Desclée de Brouwer, 1991), pp. 15-64.

59. "... *quia et ipsis sensibus nostris, quibus anima per corpus utitur, nihil est oculis praeferendum; et ideo in Scripturis sanctis visibilium nomine sensibilia cuncta denotantur*" (*Mor. Eccl. Cath.* XX.37 [p. 85]).

jects. By contrast with Descartes's transcendentalist rationalism or Locke's immanentist empiricism, Augustine's 'musical metaphysics' and his theory of divine illumination combines the priority of being over knowledge (e.g., "the knowables beget knowledge," *De Trin.* XIV.iii.13) with the Neo-Platonist idea that knowing a thing perfects both the knowing subject and the known object, as I will suggest below.

B. The Modulations of Measure, Number, and Weight (Wis. 11:20-21)

Returning for now to the numerical and proportional ordering of reality, Augustine's innovation is the idea that the presence of numbers and ratios in objects, sensation, the senses, the memory, and judgment intimates a hierarchy of forms (numbers) that is governed by ordering relations (ratios) of equality.

> These beautiful things, then, please by number, where we have shown equality is sought. For this is found not only in that beauty belonging to the ears or in the motion of bodies, but also in the very visible forms where beauty is more usually said to be. . . . For there's not one of these sensibles [which] does not please us from equality or likeness. But where equality and likeness, there numberliness. In fact, nothing is so equal or like as one and one.[60]

For Augustine, 'numberliness' is the ordering principle of all that is. The mind is enticed by beautiful and harmonious things because they embody varying degrees of likeness with the One. Individual things are beautiful and harmonious insofar as they reflect the unity of oneness. The hierarchy of numbers and ratios is coextensive with the equality of all things compared with the perfection of the One. This conjunction of hierarchy and equality suggests an irreducible link between metaphysics and politics in Augustine's cosmology, as Rowan Williams has shown.[61]

---

60. *"Haec igitur pulchra numero placent, in quo iam ostendimus aequalitatem appeti. Non enim hoc tantum in ea pulchritudine quae ad aures pertinet, atque in motu corporum est, invenitur, sed in ipsis etiam visibilibus formis, in quibus iam usitatius dicitur pulchritudo . . . nihil enim est horum sensibilium, quod nobis non aequalitate aut similitudine placeat. Ubi autem aequalitas aut similitudo, ibi numerositas; nihil est quippe tam aequale aut simile quam unum et unum"* (*De Mus.* VI.xiii.38 [pp. 363-64]).

61. On this link between hierarchy and equality in Augustine's politics, see Rowan

The theme of 'numberliness' and the preeminence of oneness in Augustine's description of the cosmos can be traced to the Pythagorean variant of Neo-Platonism, bequeathed by Plotinus and transmitted to Christian theology by Porphyry and Philolaus.[62] Against Aristotle's causal cosmology and immanentist ontology, Augustine fuses the self-exteriorization of the Good in Plato and the One in Plotinus with the biblical doctrine of creation *ex nihilo* and the hierarchical and triadic groupings in the theurgic metaphysics of Iamblichus (transmitted via Porphyry).[63] On that basis, he offers a redescription of the world. Each and every thing is what it is in virtue of a unique number and a unique set of ratios between lower and higher numbers. Such numerical structures are manifest in the beauty of individual material forms and the harmonious relations that pertain between them, as I have already indicated. The number and ratios, which individuate a thing formally and materially, express not only *that* thing's unique location in space but also its unique occurrence in time (*De Mus.* VI.xvii.57). Hence, the individuality and unicity of material form is both temporal and spatial. Since time and space are coextensive and correlated, material form is individuated by the particular interaction of universal temporality and spatiality, here mirroring the 'horizontal' participation amongst the forms themselves in Plato.

How can this be so? In the *De Musica,* numbers and ratios are defined as measurements or modulations *(modulationes)* over time and across space. Modulations describe motion, rest, and the transition between them (*De Mus.* VI.ii.3; VI.vii.18). As such, they are neither part of a perpetual succession of anterior and posterior moments without any teleology nor determined by fixed proportions that confine them to a static existence. Instead, modulations are particular discrete 'moments' within the universal passage of time in space. Each 'moment' comes into

---

Williams, "Politics and the Soul: A Reading of the *City of God,*" *Milltown Studies* 19/20 (1987): 55-72.

62. For fragments from Porphyry and Philolaus, see Andrew Barker, *Greek Musical Writings,* Volume II: *Harmonic and Acoustic Theory* (Cambridge: Cambridge University Press, 1989), I.1 and I.11, pp. 30, 36.

63. On triads in Iamblichus, see Shaw, *Theurgy and the Soul,* pp. 129-42, 199-215. On the proximity of Iamblichus and Augustine in relation to triads, see Milbank, "Sacred Triads: Augustine and the Indo-European Soul," pp. 451-74, and John Dillon, "Iamblichus' Defence of Theurgy: Some Reflections," *The International Journal of the Platonic Tradition* 1 (2007): 30-41.

existence and passes into nothingness. Material form is therefore individuated by the relations that pertain between higher and lower numbers over time and across space. Here Augustine makes the point that each particular modulation, within a wider movement of time reflecting eternity, intimates a higher number which has a greater equality and likeness with the One. The One is the source of all existence and a higher act of being but — *pace* Plato and Plotinus — it cannot be impersonal, for why would an anonymous cause bring anything into actuality and sustain things in being? For this reason, Augustine operates a profound transformation of Platonist metaphysics and its Neo-Platonist developments, arguing that the creative formation of order out of chaos in Plato or the generative power of the One in Plotinus cannot account for the relational ordering of the world. Only a triune Creator can explain why and how everything is brought out of the vacuity of nothingness into the plenitude of being.

Augustine's redescription of reality resonates with the Iamblichean emphasis on hierarchical and triadic structures. All things, corporeal and incorporeal, share three common features. In *De Vera Religione,* he writes that "every being, substance, essence or nature, or whatever better word there may be, possesses at once these three qualities: it is a particular thing; it is distinguished from other things by its own proper form; and it does not transgress the order of nature."[64] These three features — 'measure' (or limit), 'form,' and 'order' (echoing the Book of Wisdom 11:20-21) — depict the metaphysical structure of the world.[65] They are universal principles that govern all particular beings. What emerges from his redescription is a world brought into being, sustained, and perfected by God's creative activity which directs all things to their divinely given *telos*. Form embodied in matter denotes a thing's individuality, singularity, or unicity. It is that "by which a thing is what it is" (*Civ. Dei* VIII.6). Order is a thing's station in the hierarchy of all beings. As such, it marks a thing's relationality and its finality — forming harmonious relations with other things, which perfects individual form and that of the order as a whole. *Telos* so configured is dynamic, not static, because it is

---

64. *"Omnis enim res, vel substantia, vel essentia, vel natura, vel si quo alio verbo melius enuntiatur, simul haec tria habet; ut et unum aliquid sit, et specie propria discernatur a ceteris, et rerum ordinem non excedat"* (*Ver. Relig.* VII.13 [pp. 43-44]).

65. See W. J. Roche, "Measure, Number and Weight in Saint Augustine," *The New Scholasticism* 15 (1941): 350-76, and C. Harrison, "Measure, Number and Weight in Saint Augustine's Aesthetics," *Augustinianum* 28 (1988): 591-602.

coextensive and coeval with time itself. Unlike Aristotle's indifferent God, there is in Augustine a metaphysical link between the unity of the world and the oneness of its Creator, neither of which the human mind can ever fully grasp or comprehend. Von Balthasar puts this well:

> It would be a mistake to take the harmony of the world, which is built on fixed numerical relationships in space and time, as an ultimate, static entity, from the passive contemplation of which the contemplating mind receives aesthetic sensations. On the contrary, for Augustine, this beauty itself is only a dynamic striving towards a unity that can never be attained.[66]

Conjointly, form and order express the beauty that is specific to each and every thing and the beauty of harmonious relations between things. Composite things are beautiful because individually and collectively they form compounds and tend towards a kind of equality and proportionality that blends unity with diversity — a dim reflection of Trinitarian relationality. As such, composites are both individual and relational, and they perfect their singularity and relationality by forming relations with other composites. In so doing, they also help perfect the beauty of the *cosmos* as a whole: "Such is the force and power of completeness and unity that many things, all good in themselves, are only found satisfying when they come together and fit into one universal whole."[67]

But why do composite things strive towards unity and why does cosmic beauty reveal a creative transcending ordering of all things? Augustine's response is that both form and order require measure or limit — the third metaphysical principle that governs all things. Without limits in space and time, nothing can be formed or ordered in itself and as such. Form and order require a natural temporal and spatial limit. In the case of corporeal things, this is matter, which is repeatedly described in the three commentaries on the Book of Genesis as "basic material, unsorted and unformed" (*Gen. C. Man.* I.v.9). This is not to say that Augustine endorses Plato's *kora* or Aristotle's hylomorphism. To the contrary, he defines matter as that which *per se* lacks form but has the disposition

---

66. Hans Urs von Balthasar, *The Glory of the Lord: A Theological Aesthetics*, trans. and ed. Joseph Fessio and John Kenneth Riches (Edinburgh: T. & T. Clark, 1989), p. 129.

67. *"Tanta est vis et potentia integritatis et unitatis, ut etiam quae multa sunt bona tunc placeant, cum in universum aliquid conveniunt atque concurrunt. Universum autem ab unitate nomen accepit"* (*Gen. C. Man.*, I.xxi.32 [I-13: 60]).

to be given a form because it is neither totally chaotic (as for Plato) nor purely passive (as for Aristotle), as I have already indicated:

> By "hyle" I mean matter completely without form and quality, out of which are formed the qualities we perceive. . . . It ["hyle"] has no form by which we can perceive it. Indeed, it can hardly be conceived because it is so utterly without form. But it has the capacity to receive form.[68]

Since matter stands in potency to the actuality of form, matter is for Augustine an integral part of actual formation. Like Plato and Aristotle, he knows that "nothing could by itself come into being" (*Immort. An.* VIII.14) and that "nothing can form itself because nothing can give itself that which it does not have" (*Lib. Arb.* II.xvii.46). So both matter and form are caused by something other and higher than themselves. But unlike Plato and Aristotle, Augustine maintains that material potency is neither totally chaotic nor purely passive but is instead directed to formal actuality. I explore Augustine's transformation of the (Neo-)Platonist account of matter and actualization in the following section.

7. Matter, Causality, and the Gift of Creation

For Augustine, the capacity of matter to receive form calls forth actualization. Even utterly formless unsorted matter in some sense does not 'wish' to remain what it is but seeks a higher level in the hierarchical gradation of being that is characteristic of Plotinian and Iamblichean Neo-Platonist metaphysics. Matter requires not only form and order so as to be what it is and to perfect its potential. It also requires a power of being *(virtus essendi)* in order to be brought into being and to abide, for that is according to Augustine the finality of all things (*Gen. ad Lit.* I.viii.14). To be brought into being and to abide in being is to reveal the utter plenitude of the creative source of being which inhabits all things and which all things inhabit insofar as they are: "[B]y his immutable and surpassing

---

68. *"Sed hylen dico quamdam penitus informem et sine qualitate materiem, unde istae quas sentimus qualitates formantur . . . Nec ista ergo hyle malum dicenda est, quae non per aliquam speciem sentiri, sed per omnimodam speciei privationem cogitari vix potest. Habet enim et ipsa capacitatem formarum"* (*Nat. Boni* XVIII [p. 46]; cf. *Ver. Relig.* XVIII.36).

power, not in any local sense or spatial sense, he is both interior to every single thing, because in him are all things [Rom. 11:36], and exterior to every single thing because he is above all things."[69]

Contra Aristotle, final causation — however configured — cannot explain why the eternal prime cause would sustain finite beings and draw them into a plenitudinous relational order that is more than the sum of its parts (*Conf.* XIII.ii.2; XIII.iv.5). And yet this ecstatic plenitude is inscribed in finite existence and the numerical structure of the world. In his unfinished literal commentary on the Book of Genesis, Augustine writes that "every nature, whether it is perceived by merely sentient or fully rational observers, preserves, in its parts being like one another, the effigy of the whole universe."[70] So in perceiving material composite beings, we grasp their singularity, relationality, and the overarching order in which they share as beings. The phenomenally visible triadic structure of finite things (limit, form, and order) intimates an infinite creative source, which can only be God. All that exists intimates "traces of certain numbers without any matter, for it is there where the highest kind of unity is" (*Ver. Relig.* XLII.79).

Augustine's focus on the unity of the highest being and the highest good does not compromise his emphasis on the material mediation of God. Quite the reverse, Augustine's innovative blending of Plotinian and Iamblichean Neo-Platonist metaphysics with his 'incarnational' philosophy and Trinitarian theology leads him to make a very good, if controversial, case for saying that absolute immanence *is* absolute transcendence: "I call the whole that contains and sustains us, whatever it is, the 'world' — the whole, I say, that appears before my eyes, which I perceive to include the heavens and the earth."[71] If in the *De Trinitate* Augustine exhorts "faith in temporal things,"[72] it is precisely because the very limit of material things mediates God's ecstatic and creative activity. In the *Confessions,* he describes his intellectual conversion in terms of a theo-

69. *"cum sit ipse, nullo locorum vel intervallo vel spatio, incommutabili excellentique potentia et interior omni re, quia in ipso sunt omnia, et exterior omni re, quia ipse est super omnia"* (*Gen. ad. Lit.* VIII.xxvi.48 [I-13: 374]).

70. *"omnem naturam, sive quae sentientibus, sive quae ratiocinantibus occurrit, similibus inter se partibus servare universitatis effigiem"* (*Gen. ad Lit. Imp.* XVI.59 [I-13: 148]).

71. *"Ego itaque hoc totum, qualecumque est quod nos continet, atque alit; hoc, inquam, quod oculis meis apparet, a meque sentitur habere terram et coelum, aut quasi terram, et quasi coelum, mundum voco"* (*Cont. Acad.* III.xi.24 [p. 152]).

72. *De Trin.* XIV.i.3 [p. 371]. Cf. *De Trin.* IV.iv.24; XIII.ii.5; XIV.i.1.

logical vision that transcends the false division between contemplative and mystical experience: "[M]y mind attained to That Which Is [*id quod est*], in the flash of one tremulous glance. Then indeed *did I perceive your invisible reality through created things*."[73] Hence Augustine insists that all material things, which "the eternal artist has formed . . . in limit, form and order,"[74] exhibit a desire for ever more intense actualization and union with their Creator.

For this reason, Augustine develops both Platonism and Neo-Platonism in a Christological and a Trinitarian direction. But there is ample confusion about the precise nature of Augustine's account of matter and causation. In his book *Augustine's View of Reality*, Vernon Bourke asserts that "it is vain . . . to attempt to relate the Augustinian treatment of causality to the Aristotelian theory of the four causes (agent [or efficient], final, formal and material). St. Augustine does not think as Aristotle does."[75] The assumption is that Augustine has replaced Aristotle's sophisticated account of causality with a more simplistic mono-causal explanation centered on Plato's Good, Plotinus's One, and the Trinitarian God of Christianity. Likewise, it has been argued that Augustine's Neo-Platonism is the ultimate source of 'occasionalism,' which holds that all things (and all actions between things) are the product of God's direct, unmediated intervention in this world. The idea is that each and every event is but an 'occasion' for God to intervene in the world so that his will be done. Nicolas Malebranche, the French seventeenth-century Oratorian priest and philosopher, drew on Augustine, William of Ockham, and Descartes to systematize this conception of divine cause and effect into the doctrine of 'occasionalism.'[76] As such, Augustine is widely held to be the patristic precursor of modern philosophy of science.

However, in this section I argue that Augustine profoundly transformed ancient accounts of causation and that his own conception of causality is diametrically opposed to 'occasionalism.' My contention is that, first of all, Augustine remodeled the Platonist idea of formal and material causation and the Aristotelian teaching of the immanent

---

73. "*pervenit ad id, quod est in ictu trepidantis aspectus. Tunc vero invisibilia tua per ea quae facta sunt intellecta conspexi*" (*Conf.* VII.xvii.23; my italics [p. 138]).

74. *Enchir.*, quoted in von Balthasar, *The Glory of the Lord*, p. 138, n. 3.

75. Bourke, *Augustine's View of Reality*, p. 131.

76. Michael Buckley, *At the Origins of Modern Atheism* (New Haven and London: Yale University Press, 1987), pp. 145-65: Funkenstein, *Theology and the Scientific Imagination*, pp. 80-89.

causes and effects. Second, he developed a theory that overcomes the *aporiai* of Platonist and Aristotelian causality, in particular Plato's presupposition that matter is eternal and Aristotle's failure to explain *why* the primary cause would wish to bring about secondary effects. Finally, Augustine's understanding of causality allows for secondary causality on the part of creatures. Thus it secures freedom and values human agency, while also grounding divine causality in God's love and goodness.[77]

Augustine shares with Greek and Stoic philosophy the argument that no sensible material thing can ever be self-generated, self-sufficient, or self-contained. All things require a cause for their being. Consider the following three quotes: "nothing can be generated without a cause" (*De Ord.* I.iv.11); "nothing makes or begets itself" (*Immort. An.* VIII.14); "there's absolutely no thing whatsoever that brings itself into being" (*De Trin.* I.i.1). To come into existence is always already to have a cause that is irreducible to its effect. Things also require a cause for their form and their operation: "nothing can give itself that which it does not have" (*Lib. Arb.* II.xvii.45). Finally, things have not one but a set of causes: "nothing can be generated without . . . a determined order of causes" (*De Ord.* I.iv.11). *Pace* Bourke, the similarity between Aristotle's and Augustine's account of causality is apparent from the following passage:

> For everything that exists, that whereby it is established, that whereby it is distinguished, and that whereby it is in agreement are different. Therefore, the created universe, if it exists in some way and is far from being utterly nothing and yet is in agreement with itself and its parts, there must be a threefold cause, by which it is, by which it is this, by which it is in agreement with itself.[78]

Transposed into Aristotelian idiom, the last sentence can be restated as follows: there must be a threefold cause — efficient, formal, and final. These concepts are analogous to the triadic structure of all individual things, 'limit,' 'form,' and 'order,' which I outlined in the previous section.

77. On this point, I have benefited from Montague Brown, "Augustine and Aristotle on Causality," in Lienhard, Muller, and Teske, eds., *Augustine: Presbyter Factus Sum*, pp. 465-76.

78. *"Omne quod est, aliud est quo constat, aliud quo discernitur, aliud quo congruit. Universa igitur creatura si et est quoquo modo, et ab eo quod omnino nihil est plurimum distat, et suis partibus sibimet congruit, causam quoque eius trinam esse oportet: qua sit, qua hoc sit, qua sibi amica sit"* (*Div. Quest.* XVIII [p. 86]).

However, the missing element is material causation. Bourke offers the following explanation for this lacuna: "There is no theory of potency and act in Augustine's thought, so matter simply means the original stuff that God created out of nothing."[79] It is correct that Augustine speaks of matter as formless. For instance, commenting on Genesis 1:2 ("the earth was without form and void"), he writes "so then the first thing to be made was basic material, unsorted and unformed, out of which all the things would be made which have been sorted out and formed" (*De Gen. C. Man.* I.v.9). But it is equally clear — as I have already indicated — that for Augustine matter is not purely passive (as it was for Aristotle). If there is mutability, which means that there is temporality, there must be something that is capable of being acted upon. If there is any matter at all, then it must be mutable and therefore exist in time, in which case it cannot be utterly formless, for how else to account for change in time? It follows that no individual material thing is ever utterly formless, but has the potency to be formed: "For the mutability of mutable things is itself capable of all those forms into which mutable things are changed" (*Conf.* V.vi.6). For this reason, Augustine's conception of matter emphasizes the capacity to receive form.[80]

How are we to understand this idea of capacity to receive form? Developing the insight of St. Justin Martyr, Augustine explains the material capacity to be formed in terms of 'seminal reasons' *(rationes seminales)*, which he defines as primordial seeds that can be activated. He writes that things unfold and come forth

> in manifest forms and natures from the secret formulae that are causally latent in creation. . . . [They] carry within them a repetition, so to say, of their very selves, invisible in some hidden power of reproduction, derived from those primordial causes of theirs, in which they were inserted into the world that was created "when the day was made," before they ever burgeoned into the visible manifestations of their specific natures.[81]

79. Bourke, *Augustine's View of Reality,* p. 98.
80. See, *supra,* note 68.
81. ". . . *ex occultis atque invisibilibus rationibus, quae in creatura causaliter latent, in manifestas formas naturasque prodierunt . . . quodammodo inchoata sunt ea ipsa quae consequentibus evolvenda temporibus primitus Deus omnia simul creavit, cum faceret mundum: consummata quidem quia nihil habent illa in naturis propriis, quibus suorum temporum cursus agunt, quod non in istis causaliter factum sit; inchoata vero, quoniam quaedam erant quasi semina futurorum*" (*De Gen. ad Lit.* VI.x.17–VI.xi.18 [I-13: 310-11]).

In other words, Augustine conceives of matter as always already infused with a certain shape that is inscribed in its potency and can be actualized. But against the Stagirite, the Bishop of Hippo insists that the individuality of material things is not the product of an immanent substantial form but linked to the transcendent actualization by God's creative power. In order to develop this alternative account, Augustine deploys the Aristotelian language of act and potency to explain *how* an individual material thing comes into being: "It was in the seed that all the rest was originally to be found, not in the mass of full material growth, but in the *potentiality of its causative virtue*."[82] By contrast with Aristotle's indifferent God, divine actualization explains *why* things are brought from the nothingness of nonexistence into the plenitude of actuality. Nor does the primary causality of God diminish the secondary causality of the natural order. To the contrary, Augustine makes a further distinction between God's original act of creation and his concurrent creative act:

> It is one thing, after all, to establish and administer creation from the inmost and supreme pivot of all causes, and the one who does that is God the sole creator; it is another matter to apply activity from outside, in virtue of power and capacities distributed by him, so that the thing being created turns out to be like this or like that. All these things around us have been seminally and primordially created in the very fabric, as it were, or texture of the elements; but they require the right occasion actually to emerge into being.[83]

This distinction allows Augustine to explain why matter has the potency and the desire to be actualized and individuated and how God's creative activity encompasses first- and second-order causation, that is to say, bringing into existence the universal *cosmos* and actualizing particulars therein. In other words, divine activity sustains even the individuating actualization of things in this world. There can therefore be no separation of the supernatural grace of God from the natural operation of the universe. As such, Augustine's theological account of causation eschews

---

82. *"in semine ergo illa omnia fuerunt primitus, non mole corporeae magnitudinis, sed vi potentiaque causali"* (*De Gen. ad Lit.* V.xxiii.44, my italics [I-13: 299]).

83. *"Aliud est enim ex intimo ac summo causarum cardine condere atque administrare creaturam, quod qui facit solus Creator est Deus, aliud autem pro distributis ab illo viribus et facultatibus aliquam operationem forinsecus admovere ut tunc vel tunc sic vel sic exeat quod creatur"* (*De Trin.* III.ii.16 [I-5: 136]).

the modern dualism between nature and the supernatural and also various modern attempts like 'providential occasionalism' to bridge a gap that according to orthodox theology simply does not exist.

Based on this conceptuality of act and potency, Augustine also attributes 'meta-causality' to God, that is to say, the action which preserves and perfects actuality in matter which has received it. The crucial difference with both Plato and Aristotle is that Augustine reconfigures materiality as the active capacity to receive form, which together with God's continuous creative action constitutes human agency. In *De Civitate Dei*, Augustine speaks of the 'power of the seeds' (*Civ. Dei* VII.30) and of the efficient cause in things as 'productive energy' (*Civ. Dei* XII.25). Each and every individual material thing displays at once formal, material, efficient, and final causation: formal and material, since no matter can ever be formless (otherwise it would be infinite in space and could therefore not exist in time); efficient and final, since no material thing is immutable but changes over time and moves to a *telos* which transcends it (otherwise it would be capable of giving itself that which it does not have).

However, Augustine's theory of 'seminal reasons' is not confined to a reformulation of Greek theories of causality. Aristotle's Prime Mover cannot explain why individual things are engendered and Plato's Demiurge cannot account for why particulars are material, as I showed in the previous chapter. Thus, Augustine seeks to reach beyond two forms of causation. First, the cause that brings about single-act subsistent existence and, second, the cause that generates the effective operation of more intense existing. Neither cause, according to Augustine, can account for why a 'first-order' cause would wish to bring into being and sustain 'second-order' effects; causality cannot explain why a unique, simple, indivisible, immaterial 'first-order' cause would generate a multiplicity of individual, composite, divisible, material things.

As a result of these limitations, Augustine not only recasts Aristotelian causation but also emphasizes the ecstatic plenitude of God and his love as the ultimate cause of creation. The cause *qua* cause encompasses its effects and effects are more than themselves because in their unfolding they manifest their continuous cause. Effects only *are* in virtue of being in the cause (and are therefore always already more than themselves). Likewise, the cause only *is* cause of something in virtue of being utterly ecstatic (*Lib. Arb.* I.vii; *De Trin.* XIV.xiii; *Civ. Dei* XI.26). For Augustine, to say this is to say that all things intimate not only *that* they are and *what* they are (effects of a cause that exceeds them), but also, most importantly, *why* they are — in order to be and to testify to the utter plenitude of the creative source which inhabits all things and which all things inhabit insofar as they are:

> This force and incorporeal nature which effected the whole body, however, preserves the whole by its ever-present power. For, after the making, it did not vanish and did not desert the thing made. . . . *For, what does not exist through itself will certainly not exist if deserted by that through which it exists.* We cannot say, however, that when the body was made it received also the gift of being self-sufficient and self-supporting, in case it should be deserted by its creator. . . . *A form is present in the whole body, because a more excellent nature supplies and conserves the thing it has made.* This change, naturally, does not deprive the body of being a body, but lets it pass from one form to another by a well-ordered movement. For no single part of the whole can be reduced to nothing, because that effecting force comprises the whole and, through its power, that neither works nor is inactive, gives existence to everything that exists through it insofar as it does exist.[84]

In short, Augustine argues that in each individual thing there is at work some creating power that exhibits three features: first of all, it is a 'power' of a 'more excellent nature'; second, it 'supplies and conserves the thing it has made,' 'gives existence,' and 'preserves the whole'; and finally, this power ensures change 'from one form to another by a well-ordered movement.' In the following section, I show how Augustine's account of creation *ex nihilo* frames his theory of individuation.

---

84. "*Haec autem vis et natura incorporea effectrix corporis universi praesente potentia tenet universum. Non enim fecit, atque discessit effectumque deseruit. . . . Quod enim per se non est, si destituatur ab eo per quod est, profecto non erit: et non possumus dicere id accepisse corpus cum factum est, ut seipso iam contentum esse posset, etiamsi a conditore desereretur. . . . Adest igitur species universo corpori, meliore natura sufficiente atque obtinente quae fecit: quare illa mutabilitas non adimit corpori Corpus esse, sed de specie in speciem transire facit motu ordinatissimo. Non enim quaepiam eius pars ad nihilum redigi sinitur, cum totum capessat vis illa effectoria nec laborante nec deside potentia, dans ut sit omne quod per illam est, in quantum est*" (*Immort. An.* VIII.14-15; my italics [p. 78]).

8. Self, Cosmos, and God

A. Knowledge, Wisdom, and Love

According to Augustine, there is an analogy between knowledge of the world and knowledge of the self. Just as knowledge of the world reveals a relational ordering of all things that intimates God, so too knowledge of the self discloses a self in relation. Indeed, the self is of course no monolithic substance but rather a complex compound that consists of being, willing, and knowing, as well as memory, love, and understanding. For Augustine, these mental triads reflect the image of the Holy Trinity in us. Here Augustine's fusion of (Neo-)Platonism with Trinitarianism is critical. The triadic structures of all material and immaterial things reveal that everything is actualized and individuated by God's loving wisdom. For this reason, Augustine exhorts us not to focus exclusively on the internal 'self' or the external 'other' but instead to discern that which brings them both into actuality and sustains them in being. That is why true love is indispensable to knowledge of the truth. For true love always already involves the lover, the loved, and love itself — none of which can be reduced to each other, as Rowan Williams notes.[85] Since love for the self and love for the other (or the neighbor) is *love for love*, Augustine insists that love itself is relational and ecstatic, disclosing a transcendent source that overflows into immanence. Thus he concludes that "[t]his trinity of the mind is not really the image of God because the mind remembers and understands and loves itself, but because it is also able to remember and understand and love him by whom it was made."[86]

The love that is involved in knowing the real ordering of the world and the real constitution of the self is God's loving wisdom, for that is how God communicates himself to creatures. To discover divine *sapientia* at the heart of the *cosmos* and the self is to discover the integral and ecstatic openness and direction of all that is to God. For Augustine, this is to discover our creatureliness and the createdness of the whole universe, which is hierarchically and triadically ordered to reflect the diverse degrees of being and goodness. Rowan Williams puts this well:

---

85. Williams, "The Paradoxes of Self-Knowledge in the *De Trinitate*," pp. 121-34.

86. *"Haec igitur trinitas mentis non propterea Dei est imago, quia sui meminit mens, et intellegit ac diligit se: sed quia potest etiam meminisse, et intellegere, et amare a quo facta est"* (*De Trin.* XIV.iv.15 [I-5: 383]).

> Its [the mind's] knowing and loving of God in this context is also a knowing of its proper place in creation's hierarchy, its freedom from temporal and material conditioning in its deepest orientation. It is possible for human minds to be set free for God, because there is nothing in the order of creation that intrudes between the mind and God's self-communication.[87]

To know that we are created is to know that we are good in virtue of proceeding from the supreme Good itself. Our emanation from the One God constitutes an ontological relation that was broken by the Fall and restored by the Resurrection of Jesus Christ and the full revelation of the Trinitarian God — Word and Wisdom, *Logos* and *Sapientia,* Christ and *Sophia.* The divine free gift of creation grants us both freedom from and freedom for the Creator. What we discover at the heart of being is that "God is more interior to me than I to myself."[88] That is why for Augustine we need to keep God firmly as the object of our being, willing, and knowing (here surely echoing Plotinus and Iamblichus). To do so is to share in his loving wisdom and to transform ourselves and the world according to the highest Good, so that we may preserve the goodness that we have by participation and perfect the justice that we attain (here resonating with Plato). We can do so by acting in accordance with God's intentionality, which is mediated to us in and through the triple bond of the Book of Scripture, the Book of Nature, and the Book of History.

As such, Augustine's (Neo-)Platonist Trinitarian theology rules out any interpretation that imputes to him some form of idealist anti-materialism. Since in this world matter and form do not stand apart from one another but instead constitute material form *(forma corporea),* the material reality we encounter mediates the form of the highest being and good in God. Likewise, our soul cannot flee the body it inhabits but through its embodiment can come to know why and how matter itself was created by the Creator. However, Augustine also agrees with the Aristotelian imperative to abstract from sense impressions and to separate form from matter in order to attain the truth of immaterial ultimate form that is the cause of all that is (*De Trin.* VIII.i.2-3). Here it is important to note that abstraction in Augustine's theological epistemology

---

87. Williams, "*Sapientia* and the Trinity: Reflections on the *De Trinitate,*" pp. 317-32 (320).

88. "*Deus interior intimo meo*" (*Conf.* III.vi.11).

must be understood in the context of his theory of divine illumination, as I indicated in the previous section. It is precisely openness to the reception of the free gift of divine wisdom that enables the human mind to cognize the image of the triune Godhead in the self and in the other. This also allows us to understand that God is not just the initial origin of cognitive capacity but also the continued source of the process and the content of cognition.

Nor does this reduce ordinary knowledge to a product of proto-Cartesian innate ideas that devalue the cognitive input of sense impressions or the outcome of proto-Kantian noumenal structures that reverse the priority of being over knowledge. To the contrary, Augustine outwits in advance such and similar epistemological alternatives by equating higher reason with the capacity to identify the supreme good of God in created things by abstraction. By contrast with Aristotelian abstraction that promotes contemplative retreat from the sublunary world, Augustinian abstraction encourages a deeper immersion in the self and a closer engagement with one's inner embodied soul precisely in order to find that we are created and individuated by relations with other 'selves' and with the relational God.

B. Self-Knowledge and Relationality

In this section, I will develop the point made at the end of the previous section about self-knowledge and relationality. In *Contra Academicos* (written after his conversion and before his baptism on Easter Day 387), Augustine describes the self as a relational and dynamic entity that is constituted by an outward and an inward movement, towards the multiplicity of the external world and back to its own original unity and wholeness (*Cont. Acad.* II.i.2). His Neo-Platonist language of *exitus* and *reditus* does not involve a "flight from the physical world"[89] but instead links intellectual contemplation to sensory experience. Knowledge of the self starts with the things that the senses mediate to the mind. The self, far from being private and solipsistic, is oriented towards the *cosmos*. In the process leading to self-knowledge, the soul discovers that it is both substantial and relational — the self is some kind of substance that entertains relations with the body, the world, and God.

89. See, *supra,* note 57.

In *De Trinitate,* the key to Augustine's account of self-knowledge in Book X is in fact to be found in Book VIII, as Rowan Williams has conclusively shown.[90] Having concluded that we have no direct grasp of the truth by way of abstraction because our minds cannot sustain the excessive light of God, Augustine insists that true knowledge of the self has ultimately and essentially God's loving wisdom for its object. For that is what creates, sustains, and upholds the movement of our mind. True self-knowledge is knowledge of the self as created because to posit a self-sufficient mind or self-generating reflexivity cannot explain why we desire that which we do not as yet know — truth, being, the good, beauty, unity, etc. If we can make judgments about things in the world (and, *contra* the Skeptics, doubt for Augustine is a kind of judgment to withhold assent), then we must already have some sense of the form of that which we desire without knowing it in itself and as such (*De Trin.* VIII.ii.5).

The natural desire to know oneself leads to the discovery that the human mind is neither endowed with innate ideas and/or purely noumenal structures nor a fixed object of static contemplation. Moreover, abstraction from the 'internal mind' always terminates in self-reflection, which is a movement caused and directed by desire (*De Trin.* VIII.iii.7-8). However, if this is an accurate depiction of Augustine's account, then it seems to end in an impasse. Innate desire for self-knowledge causes mental activity, which we come to recognize as self-reflection. In turn, self-reflection is the product of innate desire. It would seem as if Augustine's epistemology is circular at best or a priori at worst.

However, Augustine's emphasis on desire makes the point that it is not exclusively by abstraction that one knows the truth but predominantly by judgment. This is why in Book VIII he leaves the question of truth open and turns instead to knowledge of beauty and the good, which involves judgment. The senses are alerted to the presence of species forms in things and mediate them to the mind, which abstracts from materiality. In *De Civitate Dei,* Augustine states that "mind and reason . . . [are] quite rightly called a kind of sense because it involves judgement [*sententiae*], a word which is derived from *sensus*" (*Civ. Dei* XI.3). Judgment, however, involves and exceeds both sense perception and mental abstraction by relating individual form to pure form and also back to its material instantiation. Judgment is a synthetic faculty in that it concerns

90. Williams, "The Paradoxes of Self-Knowledge in the *De Trinitate*," esp. pp. 121-22.

the 'horizontal' participation amongst forms as reflected in things which make themselves known to the mind via the senses in virtue of the beauty and harmony of their material form, whose 'numberliness' appeals to the numbers and ratios in our cognitive faculties — as I suggested in the previous section. For Augustine, we can make true judgments because we are directed towards the good which is coextensive with being, beauty, unity, and truth. Since the world of material forms is characterized by degrees of being and goodness reflecting the extent to which the actuality of form realizes the potency of matter (as both Plotinus and Iamblichus held), there is among the vertical participation of things in forms a hierarchical ordering. At the top of the pyramid of being stands the supreme being and supreme good in God, and it is the self-communicating nature of God's good that infuses all things with goodness and endows intelligent beings with the capacity to judge:

> This is good and that is good. Take away this and that and see the good itself if you can. In this way you will see God, not good with some other good but the good of every good. For surely among all these good things I have listed and whatever others can be observed or thought of, we would not say that one is better than another when we make a true judgement unless we had impressed on us some notion of good itself by which we both approve of a thing, and also prefer one thing to another. That is how we should love God, not this or that good but good itself, and we should seek the good of the soul, not the good it can hover over in judgement but the good it can cleave to in love, and what is this but God?[91]

Thus, the self is relational in two ways that are coextensive with one another. The self stands in 'horizontal' relation to God and in 'vertical' relation to all other beings. True self-knowledge is knowledge of our creatureliness and the createdness of all that is, seen and unseen. Since there is no neutral interspace between the mind and self-reflection, we

---

91. *"Bonum hoc et bonum illud. Tolle hoc et illud, et vide ipsum bonum, si potes; ita Deum videbis, non alio bono bonum, sed Bonum omnis boni. Neque enim in his omnibus bonis, vel quae commemoravi, vel quae alia cernuntur sive cogitantur, diceremus aliud alio melius cum vere iudicamus, nisi esset nobis impressa notio ipsius boni, secundum quod et probaremus aliquid, et aliud alii praeponeremus. Sic amandus est Deus, non hoc et illud bonum, sed ipsum bonum. Quaerendum enim bonum animae, non cui supervolitet iudicando, sed cui haereat amando; et quid hoc, nisi Deus?"* (*De Trin.* VIII.ii.4 [I-5: 244]).

are always already in contact with our created nature. Augustine's critical point here is to show that it is cognition of the relational ordering of the world that alerts to our own creatureliness. That is why he concludes this passage of Book VIII of *De Trinitate* by relating the Platonist conception of the self-communicating Good and the Neo-Platonist account of hierarchical triads to Acts 17:27-28, where it is said that the good "is not situated far from any one of us, for in it we live, and move and are."

Self-knowledge is knowledge of that which brings the self into being and makes it what it is — the Creator God who imparts being and situates everything in the good. For it is the nature of the ecstatic and self-exteriorizing Good to communicate itself to us. It makes itself known to us, and *that is how* we come to know ourselves. A precondition for the purification of the mind from confusing sense impressions and misleading concepts is our realization that we have judgment, which indicates that we have knowledge of the good. Unlike Descartes's innate ideas or Kant's absolute volition, our natural knowledge of the supernatural good is *in* us but not *of* us, as Michael Hanby has definitively demonstrated.[92] In this way, we grasp that we are constituted by the self-communicating good. Self-knowledge is ultimately the recognition of our creatureliness, as I have already suggested. To know that we are created is to know that we are good in virtue of proceeding from the good itself. However, our natural goodness does not make us just. That is why we need to keep God firmly as the 'object' of thinking, which is to share in his creative wisdom and to actualize his creative activity — in ourselves, in others, and in the world. To do so is to govern the self, the household, and the city in accordance with God's wisdom. To be ordered in this way is for Augustine to overcome the narrow confines of inwardness and to 'spend' ourselves ecstatically in the world. It is to embrace the world, to discern at the heart of its materiality the infinite divine creative activity, and through human agency to perfect our God-given form in an ever-closer union with the Creator.

At this juncture, my reading of Augustine appears to meet easy refutation. Surely Augustine himself argues for the purification of the soul from all external sensations and internal images. Does he not reject the outer world and seek to flee to the sanctum of the pure inner self (*De*

---

92. Hanby, "Desire: Augustine beyond Western Subjectivity," p. 113; Hanby, "Augustine and Descartes: An Overlooked Chapter in the Story of Modern Origins," 455-82; Hanby, *Augustine and Modernity*, esp. pp. 72-105.

Trin. XIV.iii.13)? Does not Augustine's invocation of the Delphic motto constitute a clear injunction against self-exteriorization: "Do not wish to go out; go back into yourself. Truth dwells in the inner man"?[93] So it would appear as if self-knowledge for Augustine amounts to little more than self-reflexivity. Indeed, he recognizes that as long as memory, understanding, and love are directed at the mind itself, the mind is treated as a self-contained object and a self-sufficient agent, more akin to Aristotle's thought thinking nothing but itself (*Met.* Λ 9, 1074^{b}34-35). If so, self-knowledge would seem to be not knowledge of our createdness and of God's creative activity, but instead knowledge *of* the self, *by* the self, and *in* the self. Aren't the modern and contemporary commentators right after all to link Augustine's focus on self-knowledge to Descartes's *cogito* and therefore to see the Bishop of Hippo (as well as Plato) as the founding fathers of western modern subjectivism?

Well no, not at all. Augustine's key argument in the *De Trinitate* is that true self-knowledge is the recognition that nothing can cause itself or sustain itself in being: "There is absolutely no thing whatsoever that brings itself into existence" (*De Trin.* I.i.1). Much rather, life itself is a gift, and true knowledge of the self and the world involves a recognition that we can participate in the utter plenitude of being and the good because the highest being and good in God is 'giving itself' ecstatically to creation in an original relation whose reverse face is the participation of reality in the Creator, who alone brings about their particular existence. So just as the beauty and harmony of material form and the relational ordering of the world manifest the givenness of being and alert us to God's creative activity at the heart of materiality, so too the being and operation of the mind intimate a higher power of being at work. The self is relational because it is brought into being by something other than itself and because it desires to know what it is that upholds it. True self-knowledge is individuating because only true self-knowledge reveals our createdness and our particular station in the relational order of creation. That is why Rowan Williams is right to state that for Augustine, "Its [the mind's] knowing and loving of God in this context is also a knowing of its proper place in creation's hierarchy, its freedom from temporal and material conditioning in its deepest orientation."[94]

---

93. *"Noli foras ire, in teipsum redi; in interiore homine habitat veritas"* (*Ver. Relig.* XXXIX.72 [p. 130]).

94. Williams, "*Sapientia* and the Trinity: Reflections on the *De Trinitate*," p. 320.

9. The Triune God and the Triadic Cosmos

At this juncture it is important to stress that Augustine's theology avoids two problems that are associated with much of ancient philosophy: first, the sort of ontological dualism between the Good and the world often wrongly ascribed to Platonist metaphysics and, second, the kind of pantheistic conflation of the divine and the human frequently attributed to pagan Neo-Platonism. Indeed, Augustine rules out the possibility that true self-knowledge equals discovering the image of the Trinity in the inner recess of the soul. To the contrary, the 'mental' triad formed by memory, love, and understanding is wholly *unlike* the triune God. To quote again the key passage from Book XIV of *De Trinitate*, Augustine writes that "[t]his trinity of the mind is not really the image of God because the mind remembers and understands and loves itself, but because it is also able to remember and understand and love him by whom it was made."[95] Rather than seeing God's image directly and identically in ourselves, we come to know our createdness, for the numerical structure of reality bears an analogical resemblance with the highest number of the one and triune God, as the triadic structure of love intimates a triune God.[96] Whereas our mind and the world lack the perfect unity of simple essence and the perfect triunity of Trinitarian relations, only God combines pure substantiality and pure relationality. This is how Augustine overcomes the Aristotelian priority of substance over relation in the direction of a fully Trinitarian theology that blends the biblical revelation of a relational God (John 1:1) with the self-communicating Good of Plato and the hierarchical triads of Plotinus (and Iamblichus).

This account however seems to be in conflict with Augustine's own argument in the *De Trinitate* where in Book V he considers the category of relation in order to conceptualize the unity of God's threeness, only to abandon relation in favor of substance in Book VII in order to secure the simplicity of God's essence.[97] But long before Descartes,[98] Augustine al-

---

95. *"Haec igitur trinitas mentis non propterea Dei est imago, quia sui meminit mens, et intelligit ac diligit se: sed quia potest etiam meminisse, et intellegere, et amare a quo facta est"* (*De Trin.* XIV.iv.15 [I-5: 383]).

96. Williams, *"Sapientia* and the Trinity: Reflections on the *De Trinitate,"* esp. pp. 319-26.

97. Emmanuel Falque, "Saint Augustin ou comment Dieu entre en théologie. Lecture critique des Livres V-VII du 'De Trinitate,'" *Nouvelle Revue Théologique* 117 (1995): 84-111, esp. pp. 99-107.

98. Jean-Luc Marion has wrongly claimed that Descartes was the first in the history

ready reconfigured Aristotle's primacy of substance in the direction of relationality. The key to Augustine's account is that in God substantiality and relationality are in fact coextensive. There can be little doubt that Augustine was familiar with Aristotle's logic and some elements of his metaphysics (*De Trin.* V, prol., 2). Nor does Augustine deny that some of Aristotle's categories can be applied to theology, namely that God is substance. Or, as the Bishop of Hippo immediately adds, "perhaps a better word would be being [*essentia*]," which derives from being *(esse).*[99] In a double rebuff of the Aristotelian supremacy of substance and the Arian charge that the Father's substance differs from the Son's as a result of the latter's 'begotten-ness,' Augustine argues that even if God's immutable substance does not allow for change, this does not imply that everything said of God is said 'substance-wise' *(secundum substantiam).* Indeed, "some things are said in relation to something else, like Father with reference to Son and Son with reference to Father, which is not an accident because the one is always Father and the other always Son."[100] Hence some 'things' are predicated of God relationally, because they are neither essential nor accidental properties of the substance, for in either case they would be subordinate to substance. As such, relation belongs to a distinct order (*De Trin.* V.ii.9).

Yet at the same time, Augustine objects in Book VII to the application of relation to God: "[I]f being is predicated by way of relationship, then being is not being."[101] He goes on to argue that relation depends on substance and that the Father is the Father in virtue of his substance, not in virtue of any relation. Therefore, Father and Son are both substances. Each is one substance and they are one being, not a relation (*De Trin.* VII.i.2-3). The reason for Augustine's insistence on substantial unity seems to be that any relation between Father and Son would posit some interspace between two poles tied together by a bi-

---

of philosophy to invert the primacy of substance over all other categories. See Jean-Luc Marion, *Dieu sans l'être*, 2nd ed. (Paris: Presses Universitaires de France, 1991), pp. 80-155.

99. *"substantia vel si melius hoc appellatur essentia, quam graeci ousian vocant. Sicut enim ab eo quod est sapere dicta est sapientia et ab eo quod est scire dicta est scientia, ita ab eo quod est esse dicta est essentia"* (*De Trin.* V.i.3).

100. *"Dicitur enim ad aliquid sicut pater ad filium et filius ad patrem, quod non est accidens quia et ille semper pater et ille semper filius"* (*De Trin.* V.i.6 [I-5: 192, translation modified]).

101. *"si essentia ipsa relative dicitur, essentia ipsa non est essentia"* (*De Trin.* VII.i.2 [I-5: 219]).

nary link. (Neo-)Platonism notwithstanding, substance appears to wield supreme sway, bringing Augustine's theology closer to Aristotle's metaphysics after all.

But for Augustine God is always Father, Son, and Holy Spirit. The *Logos* is already with God (John 1:1), and the image of God in us is the image of a Creator who is both one and triune. Augustine's God is always already relational and creative, not by necessity but in virtue of the self-imparting communication of his loving wisdom. Hence the Bishop of Hippo operates a radical transformation of Aristotelian categories that is in accordance with orthodox theology and with the shared legacy of Plato, Plotinus, and Iamblichus. God is both substance and relation, substantial insofar as the three persons share a single divine essence yet precisely for this reason always already relational. Here one cannot emphasize enough the difference between Aristotle and Augustine. It is not the case for the latter that God is a relational substance, for this would merely qualify the primacy of substance. Since God transcends all categories of being and knowledge, neither infinite substance nor the pure actuality of essence can capture the mysterious paradox of perfect unity and unreserved triunity. Trinitarian relationality is perhaps the closest we can come to describe in a single concept God's absolute oneness and the unique distinctness of each of the three divine persons. Since for the whole of creation existence, essence, and continued being are received and the desire of intelligent beings can be diverted from *caritas* and *dilectio* to *voluptas,* nothing other than God is either purely substantial or fully relational.

Here it is notable that Augustine proposes an analogy between a thing's triadic structure (form, measure, and order) and its transcendent cause — a higher power which brings everything into being, makes things what they are, and orders them according to their divine warrant. Since there is no regression *ad infinitum* for Augustine, there must be some primary cause. This cause is neither Plato's Good, nor Aristotle's Prime Mover, nor Plotinus's One. It is instead the highest being *(esse),* which is at once Beauty, Goodness, and Truth and which makes all other beings:

> In this order, then, it is understood that a form is given by the highest Being through the soul to the body — the form whereby the latter exists, in so far as it exists. Hence the body subsists through the soul and exists by the very fact that it is animated, whether universally, as is the

world, or individually, as is each and every thing that has life within the world.[102]

Augustine does not use 'essence' *(essentia)* in contradistinction to 'existence' *(existentia)*. Despite some inconsistencies, it is clear from his texts that Augustine posits the absolute primacy of being or, perhaps more accurately, 'to be' *(esse)*. Unlike Boethius and later Aquinas, Augustine does not draw systematic distinctions between *esse* and *essentia*, but this does not render him an 'essentialist.'[103] In *De Trinitate* and elsewhere, Augustine insists that both *essentia* and *existentia* derive from *esse*: "[J]ust as we get the word 'wisdom' [*sapientia*] from 'wise' [*sapere*], and 'knowledge' [*scientia*] from 'know' [*scire*], so we have the word 'being' [*essentia*] from 'be' [*esse*]" (*De Trin.* V.i.3; cf. *Lib. Arb.* II.xvii.46; *Gen. ad Lit.* V.xvi.34; *Civ. Dei* VIII.6; XI.2).

The primacy of 'to be' has three important implications. First, to say that 'to be' is the highest, truest, and most real station in the order of beings is to posit an ontological difference between the 'to be' that makes and sustains beings and all other things that are made and sustained (*Conf.* VII.xx.26; cf. IX.x.25; X.vi.9; XI.iv.6). Second, within the hierarchy of all that is, there are degrees of being among the things that are made and sustained: "All other things which he made received existence from him, each in its own degree" (*Nat. Bon.* XIX; cf. *Ver. Relig.* XVI.30). Finally, 'to be' preserves and enhances being by situating individuals according to their particular station within the universal order. To refuse hierarchical ordering is to negate the very being that is given and to lapse into nothingness: "For to defect from that which supremely is, to that which has a less perfect degree of being: that is what it is to begin to have an evil will" (*Civ. Dei* XII.7).

But why are individual things created and why are they created as individuals? If nothing is by or for itself but instead is made and sustained in being, it follows that all which has being was made from nothing and in the beginning (*ex nihilo* and *in principio*). To have being and to retain

---

102. "*Hoc autem ordine intellegitur a summa essentia speciem corpori per animam tribui, qua est in quantumcumque est. Per animam ergo corpus subsistit, et eo ipso est quo animatur, sive universaliter, ut mundus; sive particulariter, ut unumquodque animal intra mundum*" (*Immort. An.* XV.24 [p. 96]). Cf. *Immort. An.* XII.19; *Gen. ad Lit.* I.xvii.34-35; III.xii.18; *Ver. Relig.* XI.22.

103. Dominique Dubarle, *Dieu avec l'être. Traité d'ontologie théologale* (Paris: Éditions Cerf, 1986).

existence is itself the purpose of creation. The whole of creation, insofar as it is, is brought into being "in order that it should be, and in order that it should abide" (*Gen. ad Lit.* I.8.14). In a move that binds together *apophasis* and *cataphasis,* Augustine argues that all which has being testifies to its transcendent creative source which is individual in the unity of its essence and the triunity of its three persons. The Creator is in himself incomprehensible but discernible through the traces *(vestigia)* imprinted upon creation. All things that have being bear the mark of their creator or being itself or *idipsum* (*Conf.* IX.x.24; XII.vii.7; XII.xv.20; XIII.xi.12; *De Trin.* III.iii.8).

The creative cause is in the effect and all effects are in the cause. The cause is always already more than itself. It is ecstatic creativity which is manifest in all that is created: to discern being itself which is 'to be,' the mind comes to have a glimpse of the utter transcendence and plenitude of the creating cause:

> *Solely by your plenteous goodness has your creation come to be and stood firm,* for you did not want so good a thing to be missing. It could be of no profit to you, nor equal to yourself as though proceeding from your own substance, yet there was the possibility of its existing as your creation. . . . It was no indigence on your part that drove you to make them. *Out of the plenitude of your goodness, you upheld them and converted them to their form;* it was not as though your own blessedness stood in need of accomplishment and completion by them.[104]

There is thus no sense in which Augustine defends a foundationalist metaphysics that combines the alleged ontological dualism of Plato's distinction between the world of ideas and the world of things with the purported essentialism of Aristotle's account of individual substance. Instead, Augustine stresses the ecstatic overflow of God's being and goodness — an emphasis that underscores the proximity with Boethius and Dionysius, whose theology is the subject of the next chapter.

---

104. "*Ex plenitudine quippe bonitatis tuae creatura tua substitit, ut bonum, quod tibi nihil prodesset nec de te aequale tibi esset, tamen quia ex te fieri potuit, non deesset . . . quae non ex indigentia fecisti, sed ex plenitudine bonitatis tuae cohibens atque convertens ad formam, non ut tamquam tuum gaudium compleatur ex eis*" (*Conf.* XIII.ii.2; XIII.iv.5; my italics [pp. 309, 311]).

10. Conclusion: Christian Universalism

I began this chapter by mentioning that Pope Benedict's defense of Christianity's hellenization at Regensburg has earned him the scorn of many neo-scholastic critics who defend the neo-scholastic separation of sacred doctrine from philosophy in Scotus, Ockham, and Suárez against the papal championing of *nouvelle théologie*. What underpins in large part Benedict's compelling narrative is the 'integral' metaphysical theology of Christian Neo-Platonism. As I hope to have shown, both Gregory and Augustine made decisive contributions to the patristic synthesis of ancient philosophy and biblical revelation by fusing Plato's metaphysics of 'relational' participation, Plotinus's self-ecstatic creative One, and Iamblichus' sacred triads with the scriptural (and natural) disclosure of a God who is always already triune and who creates everything out of nothing.

In calling for the rehellenization of Christianity, Pope Benedict renews not just the synthesis of the Fathers and the Doctors of the Church but also the Hellenic Jewish tradition in which both Jesus and the Apostles were rooted. The encounter between biblical revelation and ancient philosophy marks the advent of universalism beyond divine election and the law, as Alain Badiou has convincingly argued in relation to the writings of St. Paul.[105] Benedict's retrieval and extension of *nouvelle théologie* is perhaps the most significant attempt since nineteenth-century Russian sophiology to blend Pauline theology with Neo-Platonist metaphysics and thus to conceptualize the universality of the Christian narrative, a theme I will continue to explore in the following chapters focusing on Boethius and Dionysius the Areopagite.

---

105. Alain Badiou, *Saint Paul: La Fondation de l'Universalisme* (Paris: Presses Universitaires de France, 1998).

CHAPTER 3

Relational Substance and Cosmic Hierarchy

1. Introduction: Between Antiquity and the Middle Ages

In the previous chapter, I argued that Gregory of Nyssa and Augustine —
albeit in different ways — combined Platonist relationality and participation and Neo-Platonist conceptions of the One and sacred triads with the
biblical revelation of a relational God who creates everything out of nothing. The world and all that it encompasses is created and receives both its
existence and its essence from God. In him, existence and essence coincide and he alone is substance and relation, one and triune. In this chapter, I argue that Boethius (c. 480-525) and Dionysius the Areopagite
(c. 470-525) systematize and extend Gregory's and Augustine's Trinitarian
theology by incorporating elements of Aristotle (Boethius) and pagan
Neo-Platonism (Dionysius). In so doing, they deepen and broaden a
Christian metaphysics that theorizes individuation in terms of an ever-
greater participation in the relational order of divine creation.

Compared with Augustine, Boethius's synthesis of ancient philosophy and Christian theology provides a more systematic treatment of the
'ontological difference' between God and creation and a more radically
philosophical conception of God's utter ecstatic plenitude. In particular,
Boethius emphasizes the relationality of the Godhead by developing an
account of God as being beyond substance *(deus ultra substantiam)*,
which had been foreshadowed by Augustine (Boethius, *De Trinitate* IV.2,
15-16, 18, 23 [17/19]).[1] By retrieving and transforming the legacy of both

---

1. Throughout this chapter, references in either square brackets or parentheses refer
to the page numbers of Boethius' works in the Loeb edition.

113

Plato and Aristotle, Boethius does not just in some sense fulfill patristic theology but also inaugurates medieval philosophy. As such, he was indeed "the last Roman and the first scholastic," a Christian thinker in his own right whose original thought made a decisive contribution to the emergence of the scholastic method and had a lasting influence on some of the most eminent medieval figures, from Alcuin (c. 735-804) and John Scotus Eriugena (c. 800-877), via Abelard (1079-1142), Gilbert of Poitiers (c. 1085-1154), and some members of the School of Chartres, to Albert the Great (c. 1206-1280), St. Thomas Aquinas (c. 1225-1274), and John Duns Scotus (c. 1265/66-1308).[2]

There is an ongoing debate on the importance of metaphysics and the status of *esse* in Boethius' commentaries on logic and also in his theological writings, the *Opuscula sacra*. Some commentators maintain that Boethius' ontology is grounded in the primacy of essence over existence.[3] In an influential book, Brosch argues that Boethius confines his treatise to the essence of God and beings, but that he fails to grasp the distinction between *esse essentiae* and *esse existentiae*.[4] Others, like Pi-

---

2. Marie-Dominique Chenu speaks of the twelfth century as the *aetas boetiana* ('Boethian age'). See Marie-Dominique Chenu, *La théologie au douzième siècle,* 3rd ed. (Paris: Vrin, 1976), pp. 142-58. On the influence of Boethius, see also Martin Grabmann, *Die Geschichte der scholastischen Methode* (Freiburg im Breisgau: Herdersche Verlagshandlung, 1911), vol. 2, p. 148 *passim;* Henry Chadwick, *Boethius: The Consolations of Music, Logic, Theology, and Philosophy* (Oxford: Oxford University Press, 1981), pp. 108-253; Margaret Gibson, "The *Opuscula Sacra* in the Middle Ages," in *Boethius: His Life, Thought and Influence,* ed. M. Gibson (Oxford: Blackwell, 1981), pp. 214-34; Osmund Lewry, "Boethian Logic in the Medieval West," in Gibson, ed., *Boethius: His Life, Thought and Influence,* pp. 90-135; John Marenbon, *From the Circle of Alcuin to the School of Auxerre: Logic, Theology and Philosophy in the Early Middle Ages* (Cambridge: Cambridge University Press, 1981), pp. 18-19; J. Marenbon, "Boethius: From Antiquity to the Middle Ages," in *Medieval History: Routledge History of Philosophy* (London: Routledge, 1998), vol. 3, ch. 1, pp. 11-28; J. Marenbon, *Boethius* (Oxford: Oxford University Press, 2003), pp. 164-82.

3. This has been argued by Lambertus M. de Rijk, who emphasizes the centrality of quiddity in Boethius' translation and commentaries on Aristotelian logic. See Lambertus M. De Rijk, "Boèce logicien et philosophe. Ses positions sémantiques et sa métaphysique de l'être," in *Atti di Congresso Internazionale di Studi Boeziani,* ed. Luca Obertello (Rome: Herder, 1981), pp. 141-56; L. M. de Rijk, "On Boethius' Notion of Being — A Chapter on Boethian Semantics," in *Meaning and Inference in Medieval Philosophy,* ed. Norman Kretzmann (Amsterdam: Kluwer, 1988), pp. 1-29.

4. Herman J. Brosch, *Der Seinsbegriff bei Boethius. Mit besonderer Berücksichtigung der Beziehung von Sosein und Dasein* (Innsbruck: Verlag von Felizian Rauch, 1931), pp. 7-73, 95-120.

erre Hadot, have contended that Boethius draws on Porphyry's and Marius Victorinus's Neo-Platonism in order to give an account of *esse* as supreme Being, synonymous with the One and pure act of Existing *(l'acte pur d'Exister)* that is beyond essence and existence and prior to both being *(l'être)* and *ens (l'étant)*.[5] This debate is significant for the question of individuation, as the metaphysical status of essence or existence determines the mode of actualization of particular individual things. My argument is that Boethius focuses on finite existence more than finite essence because this configuration allows him to combine the primacy of act over potency with the potentiality of finite essences vis-à-vis God's infinite act of being. Coupled with his demonstration that divine substance is relational, he argues that God creates everything *ex nihilo* and actualizes universal being in all particulars. The relationality of beings enables the participation and perfection of the Good. As "the last Roman," Boethius provides a unique synthesis and transformation of Plato's and Aristotle's legacy. As "the first scholastic," he extends Augustine's works and prefigures Aquinas's vision. Above all, he systematizes the 'ontological difference' and develops a Trinitarian theology that is amenable to natural reason.

2. Boethius' Philosophical Ordering of the Sciences

For Augustine knowledge *(scientia)* is ultimately ordered by God's wisdom *(sapientia)*, as I showed in the previous chapter. For this reason, knowledge of the self is sustained by divine self-communication. By retrieving and transforming Plato's and Aristotle's legacy, Boethius systematizes and extends Augustine's conception of Christian metaphysics and Trinitarian theology. Drawing on Porphyry's *Isagoge* (the standard commentary on Aristotle at his time), he follows Aristotle's distinction between speculative and practical knowledge.[6] Philosophy or speculative

5. Pierre Hadot, "Fragments d'un commentaire de Porphyre sur le Parménide," *Revue des Études Grecques* 74 (1961): 410-38; P. Hadot, "La distinction de l'être et de l'étant dans le *'De hebdomadibus' de Boèce*," in *Die Metaphysik im Mittelalter. Ihr Ursprung und ihre Bedeutung*, ed. Peter Wilpert (Berlin: De Gruyter, 1963), pp. 147-53; P. Hadot, *"Forma essendi:* Interprétation philologique et interprétation philosophique d'une formule de Boèce," *Les Études Classiques* 38 (1970): 143-56; P. Hadot, "L'être et l'étant dans le néoplatonisme," *Études néoplatoniciennes* (1973): 27-41.

6. *Met.* E 1, 1026a6-33, in *The Complete Works of Aristotle,* vol. 2, p. 1620. Cf. P. Merlan,

science *(scientia speculativa)* is concerned with speculative knowledge, which can be divided into three branches: physics, mathematics, and theology *(De Trinitate* II.5-16). Theology is a proper science because like physics and mathematics, it deploys rational concepts and combines reason with faith. It is the highest science since it operates intellectually *(intellectualiter)* in order to "apprehend that form which is pure form and no image, which is very being and the source of being."[7] Since Boethius rejects the possibility that being itself is univocal and Creator and creation fall under one and the same category of being, his definition of metaphysics differs radically from that of later medieval scholastic theologians such as John Duns Scotus. Indeed, Boethius' identification of theology with 'first philosophy' lays the metaphysical foundations of what long after him would come to be known as the 'ontological difference' and the concept of 'analogy of being.'

First I discuss Boethius' philosophical ordering of the sciences in some detail. Since all things that exist in this world and can be known via the senses and the mind are matter-form compounds, the first speculative science is physics, which investigates "the form of bodies together with their constituent matter" *(De Trinitate* II.8). Matter-form compounds, though forming an individual entity, manifest to the mind their dual aspect. The distinction or separation between the formal and the material is performed by the intellect and gives rise to the second speculative science, mathematics. The human mind is not limited to the cognition of form in relation to matter but can attain vision of pure form, for "all being is dependent on form"[8] and this dependence is intelligible in actual beings. The natural light of reason mediates the simplicity and unity of form, in which all material things participate. In the *Consolatio,* the particular is described as "the specific form itself, which is present in single individuals."[9] Moreover, all particulars point to universal form it-

---

From Platonism to Neoplatonism, 3rd ed. (The Hague: Nijhoff, 1968), pp. 59-87; Marenbon, *Boethius,* p. 82 n. 25; Sten Ebbesen, "Boethius as an Aristotelian Commentator," in *Aristotle Transformed: The Ancient Commentators and Their Influence,* ed. Richard Sorabji (London: Duckworth, 1990), pp. 373-91.

7. "*. . . inspicere formam quae vere forma neque imago est et quae esse ipsum est et ex qua esse est*" *(De Trinitate* II.19-21 [9/8-10]). On the three sciences and their respective methods, see James A. Weisheipl, "Classification of the Sciences in Medieval Thought," *Mediaeval Studies* 27 (1965): 54-90, esp. pp. 58-62.

8. "*Omne namque esse ex forma est*" *(De Trinitate* II.21 [10/11]).

9. "*. . . speciem[que] ipsam quae singularibus inest . . .*" *(De Consol.* V.iv.87-88 [410/411]).

self. Nothing that is in act is immutable, everything is subject to change, and so there is an ontological discrepancy between what a thing actually is and what it potentially could be. Actual being is in act, but not wholly so because otherwise how would it change, and why? There is then in actual being the act of form and the potency of matter. Here Boethius goes beyond Aristotle's account of individuation in terms of the union between proximate matter and individual substantial form by relating all particular matter-form compounds to form itself (or Plato's Good). For matter and form do not exist by themselves. Instead, there is something that brings them into actuality and makes them what they are. Crucially, Boethius links the individuation of particular things to the actualization of beings.

In what sense does this account of Christian metaphysics differ from Greek philosophy? Vision of pure form is for Boethius nothing less than vision of God, who creates all forms *ex nihilo*. Since the senses are attuned to individual particular things and mediate sensible species to the mind, the first object of the intellect is that which is *(id quod est)*. In perceiving that which is, sense perception discerns more than an isolated self-contained entity. The very actuality of that which is discloses its transcendent source. For the potency of particular sensible things requires a higher act in order to be brought into actuality. Concrete things are particular, yet at the same time instantiate a universal essence and also have a universal source of being. Like Plato's Good and Plotinus's One, this source or power of being *(virtus essendi)* must be ecstatic and self-communicating, otherwise how would it impart actuality to beings? There is such a first cause, which is being itself *(ipsum esse)*. Only God is being itself, for only God's goodness and love can explain why he wishes to create beings that bear his trace and depend on him for their existence, their essence, and their continuous being. To be created is to be made in his image and likeness, to stand in analogous relation to the one and only power of being. All this foreshadows Aquinas's concept of the pure act of self-subsistent being, as I will show in chapter 5.

How do actual things themselves intimate a creative transcendent source of being and how can the mind cognize it as such? Boethius takes from Augustine not only the principle of divine illumination but also and above all the argument that illumination operates through reason in *De Trinitate* Book X, as I suggested in the previous chapter. Boethius' innovation is to deploy Plato's account of relationality and Aristotle's concepts of act and potency in order to show that knowledge of actual things is knowledge of the transcendent source which brings them into being and makes them what they are. Knowledge of a thing-in-act leads the knower to cognize being itself or God, for "all being is dependent on form." Since there is no absolute unbridgeable gulf that separates reason from faith and philosophy from theology, forms in things disclose form itself or God. Just as there is no pure faith that is transcendentally imposed, there can be no pure self-sufficient reason that operates alone within the immanent realm. Instead, Boethius radicalizes Augustine's principle that intellection points to, and calls forth, belief in God, while faith seeks and upholds understanding.

This is not to say for Boethius that the natural order is inherently defective and requires the supernatural correction of divine grace. Nor does he imply that faith and illumination are transcendental data that devalue sense perception and empirical evidence. Instead, reason always already involves a prerational trust (*pistis* or faith), and belief can — indeed must — be rationally mediated and elaborated. This is why Boethius writes in the prologue of his treatise on the Trinity that "[w]e should of course press our inquiry only so far as the insight of man's reason is allowed to climb the height of heavenly knowledge."[10] In this quest, he hopes to be faithful to Augustine's vision. Indeed, Boethius exhorts Symmachus, to whom the *De Trinitate* is dedicated, to "examine whether the seeds of argument sown in my mind by St. Augustine's writings have borne fruit."[11] In the following sections, I argue that Boethius prolongs and radicalizes Augustine's Trinitarian metaphysics, in particular the idea that creation is a hierarchical relational order and that each and every being is made in the image of a fully relational God who is beyond substance *(ultra substantiam)*.

3. Perception of Particulars and Cognition of Universals

In this section, I examine the relation between Boethius' ontology and his epistemology in his commentaries on Aristotle. Boethius focuses on the ontological foundation of Aristotelian, Stoic, and Neo-Platonist logic

10. *"Sane tantum a nobis quaeri oportet quantum humanae rationis intuitus ad divinitatis valet celsa conscendere"* (*De Trinitate*, prol., 22-24 [5/4]).

11. *"an ex beati Augustini scriptis semina rationum aliquos in nos venientia fructus extulerint"* (*De Trinitate*, prol., 31-33 [4/5]). Cf. Robert Crouse, *"Semina Rationum:* St. Augustine and Boethius," *Dionysius* 4 (December 1980): 75-86.

and epistemology. This is most apparent in his 'solution' to the problem of the universals. Like Plato and Aristotle, Boethius insists that universals are not separate entities that the mind produces by abstracting from concrete particulars. Rather, universals are *in* the mind but not *of* the mind, for they are present in actual particulars that exist by participating in them. For this reason, individuality marks the constitutive presence of universals in particulars, and individuation describes the actualization of universality in particularity — as I now show.

A. Metaphysical Realism

In his commentary on Aristotle's *Categories,* Boethius draws on Porphyry's *Isagoge,* the standard Neo-Platonic introduction to the *Categories* in those late patristic times.[12] The core insight that Boethius retains from Aristotle (and Porphyry) is that universal categories are real in the sense that they are present in particular sensible things. The relation of universals and particulars is neither posited a priori nor induced a posteriori but is real and intelligible. As such, it can be perceived by the senses and cognized by the mind. The priority of particulars (*In Cat.* 183 C–184 B) is indispensable to a proper understanding of Boethius' theological epistemology: both words and concepts refer primarily to particular sensible things, not to mental structures or products of intellectual activity. In other words, knowledge of particulars is knowledge of how and why particulars exist and of what constitutes them *qua* particulars.

Paradoxically, to know what constitutes something as *this* particular rather than *that* particular involves knowing universals. For particulars are differentiated from one another not just quantitatively but also qualitatively. Here Boethius combines Aristotle's theory of abstraction with Augustine's account of divine illumination. Knowledge of qualitative differentiation requires knowledge of genus and species. Such knowledge is obtained through speculative abstraction.[13] Since the mind encounters all material things through the senses, abstraction is based on sensorial perception and on concepts of the mind (*mentis*

12. Jorge J. E. Gracia, "Boethius and the Problem of Individuation in the *Commentaries on the 'Isagoge,'*" in Obertello, ed., *Atti di Congresso Internazionale di Studi Boeziani,* pp. 169-82.

13. *"prima est quaestio, utrum genera ipsa et species vere sint an in solis intellectibus nuda inaniaque fingantur"* (*1 In Isag.* I. c. 10 [24]).

ratione concepta, In Cat. 183 C). Like Aristotle's epistemology, the process of cognition in Boethius can be described as a virtuous, upward cycle or spiral whereby the senses activate the mind by mediating sensible species, just as intellection informs judgment and the imagination. Knowledge of the relation between particulars and universals constitutes a movement from the sensible via the intelligible to an ever more intense grasp of the sensible. Here there is a striking similarity with Plato's 'second voyage' in the middle and later dialogues and the idea of fashioning the real in the light of the ideal, as I discussed in chapter 1. In developing this account, Boethius makes three related arguments. First, universals in some sense exist. Second, they are neither purely corporeal nor exclusively incorporeal. Third, they entertain an irreducible link with particular sensible things.

Before I can examine each argument, I need to make a wider point about Boethius' metaphysical realism. The opposition between Platonism and Aristotelianism still haunts contemporary interpretations of Boethius' 'solution' of the problem of universals. According to Henry Chadwick, Boethius' position oscillates ambiguously between Aristotle and Plato. The Aristotelian argument (taken from Alexander of Aphrodisias) is, as Chadwick understands it, that universals exist as mental concepts in the mind but have some basis in the reality of particulars. The Platonist argument is that universals can only be formed by speculative abstraction from all corporeality until the mind attains pure form.[14] Similarly, it has been asserted that Boethius rejects naïve realism and skeptical idealism in favor of a mediating position, which Alain de Libera terms 'abstractionist, conceptual realism.' On his account, Boethius sides with Aristotle against Plato. Universals are the result of abstracting from particulars, and knowledge of universals entails a fuller grasp of particulars.[15] Albeit in different ways, both Chadwick and de Libera claim that Plato's and Aristotle's accounts of the metaphysical status of universals are incompatible and that Boethius failed to grasp and resolve this incompatibility.

However, the Platonist and the Peripatetic positions on universals share the conviction that universals are real, not nominal or conceptual.[16]

14. Chadwick, *Boethius*, pp. 124-33.

15. Alain de Libera, *L'art des généralités. Théories de l'abstraction* (Paris: Aubier, 1999), pp. 205-24.

16. Gail Fine, *On Ideas: Aristotle's Criticism of Plato's Theory of Forms* (Oxford: Clarendon, 1993), pp. 24-29. See, *supra*, chapter 1.

Against Chadwick and de Libera, I contend that it was Boethius' ambition to illustrate this fundamental agreement. His works go some way towards demonstrating Plato's and Aristotle's shared realism (*2 In Isag.* I. c. 11 [167:7-20]). Boethius' account of universals consists of four closely connected ideas: first, particulars stand in a 'vertical' relational participation to universals; second, the mind can grasp this relationality; third, knowledge of this relationality is knowledge of a thing's actuality (*id quod est*), its potentiality (*esse*), and the power of being (*virtus essendi*) which actualizes it and makes it what it is; fourth, such knowledge is ontological in the sense that in making itself known to the mind through the senses, a thing actualizes not only its cognoscibility but also the knower's potency to know (*potestas rationis*). Let me now discuss these four ideas in turn.

Boethius describes Plato's and Aristotle's shared realism in terms of the idea that the universal and the particular do not pertain to separate independent realms but that particular material form is a reflection of universal immaterial form. Knowledge of the relational participation of particulars to universals is based upon actual material things, not innate ideas. Here Boethius fuses Augustine's theory of divine illumination with Aristotle's emphasis on abstraction from sense perception, as I have already indicated: "For individuals stand out to the highest degree if either, leaving the name unmentioned, they are pointed out to the eye or shown by touch."[17] The mind does not abstract universal immaterial form from particular sensible matter. Rather, cognition of the essence of particular sensible things is cognition of a complex matter-form compound, not cognition of pure form (*2 In Isag.* I. c. 11 [165:3-7]). That is why mathematics, the second in the order of sciences, investigates forms *of* bodies.

According to de Libera, the mark of Boethius' metaphysics and epistemology is the metaphysical coincidence of the universal and the particular in actual beings, which is paralleled by the noetic coincidence of the senses and the intellect. As a result, the particularity which the senses perceive in a thing is the universality which the mind cognizes in all things that pertain to a certain species or genus.[18] De Libera also argues that this 'solution' is indebted to Alexander of Aphrodisias' Neo-Platonist argument, according to which existence is not confined to either purely mental constructs or exclusively material realities but also

---

17. *"Individua enim maxime ostendi queunt, si vel tacito nomine sensui ipsi oculorum digito tactuue monstrentur"* (*2 In Isag.* III, c. 10 [233-34]).

18. De Libera, *L'art des généralités,* pp. 187-93.

includes "notions of things," that is to say, mental constructs that have a real correlate (as opposed to signifying notions of nonexistent things such as chimerae or centaurs).[19] In support of his interpretation, he refers to the concept of resemblance and quotes from Boethius' second commentary on the *Isagoge:*

> [A] species should be considered as nothing other than a thought collected from the substantial likeness of many individuals which differ by number, whilst a genus is a thought collected from the likeness of species. . . . [T]his likeness becomes sensible when it is in singulars and in universals it becomes intelligible, and in the same way when it is sensible it remains in singulars, when it is grasped by the intellect, it becomes universal.[20]

So conceived, *similitudo* is not purely nominal or conceptual but real. As such, universality is not a function of ratiocination, but instead marks the presence of forms in things. Universals entertain an irreducible link with the reality of particulars. The substantial likeness of individual things gives rise to universal categories. This likeness and the objects that share in it are somehow simultaneously particular and universal. John Marenbon writes that "an object is both singular and universal [and quoting Boethius], 'universal when it is considered in thought, single when it is perceived sensibly in those things in which it has its being.'"[21] On this account, Boethius' epistemology can be described as constructivist-realist abstraction, in the sense that genera and species are mental constructs that enable a better grasp of things than sense perception because particulars reflect universals in diverse ways.[22]

---

19. De Libera, *L'art des généralités,* pp. 209-10. John Marenbon's reading relativizes the influence of Alexander of Aphrodisias on Boethius. See Marenbon, *Boethius,* pp. 26-32.

20. Marenbon, *Boethius,* pp. 29-30. This quote from Boethius is in *2 In Isag.* I. c. 11 (166: 16-21): *"nihil aliud species esse putanda est nisi cogitatio collecta ex individuorum dissimilum numero substantiali similitudine, genus vero cogitatio collecta ex specierum similitudine . . . haec similitudo cum in singularibus est, fit sensibilis, cum in universalibus, fit intellegibilis, eodemque modo cum sensibilis est, in singularibus permanet, cum intellegitur, fit universalis."*

21. Marenbon, *Boethius,* pp. 30-31. The quote from Boethius is in *2 In Isag.* I. c. 11 (167: 4-7): *"universale est, cum cogitatur, alio singulare, cum sentitur in rebus his in quibus esse suum habet."*

22. De Libera, *L'art des généralités,* pp. 224-49, 267-80. Cf. Marenbon, *Boethius,* pp. 26-32.

B. Theological Epistemology

What does the mind know about a thing when it cognizes universality? According to de Libera, knowledge of things is for Boethius knowledge of their essence. Knowledge is the abstraction of species and genera from matter and the contemplation of essence by the intellection of species and genera. To cognize species and genera requires some kind of resemblance *(similitudo)* between individual sensible things. Boethius' epistemology is therefore not limited to deduction, but also includes induction. For de Libera, Boethius' innovation is the idea of abstraction as cognition by collection *(cogitatio collecta)*, as opposed to cognition by the senses or the imagination. Abstraction so configured produces a representation in the mind of essential likeness *(similitudo substantialis)*, which oscillates between the unity of essence of an individual thing and the concept of this unity.

However, this interpretation posits an undemonstrated priority of essence over existence, grounded in the equally undemonstrated primacy of the mind over that which is and makes itself known. Abstraction is taken to be the "condition of possibility"[23] of *cogitatio collecta*, which, as the mental representation of *similitudo substantialis*, is the "apperception of the common traits"[24] of individual sensible things. On this point, de Libera's language can barely disguise his proto-Kantian reading of Boethius, notably the assertion that universals are exclusively in the mind and that essence is prior to existence. Moreover, he wrongly attributes to Boethius the claim that intellection wields supreme sway over actual things,[25] a position that is in complete contradiction with Boethius' insistence on the metaphysical primacy of being over knowing, which he takes from both Plato and Aristotle. This primacy implies that particulars are the first object of intellect (*In Cat.* 182 C) and that the mind first encounters composites, rather than simple substances (*In Cat.* 184 A-B). The priority of existent particulars is the cornerstone of Boethius' metaphysical realism. He also shares with Aristotle the argument that the essence of composites is not form abstracted from matter, but form in relation to matter. This is also true for Plato, insofar as universal forms require matter in order to be reflected

23. De Libera, *L'art des généralités*, p. 279.
24. De Libera, *L'art des généralités*, p. 228.
25. De Libera, *L'art des généralités*, pp. 274-79.

in diverse ways, as I argued in chapter 1. There is thus a distinction, but no separation, of form from matter and essence from existence. As Boethius clearly holds, just as there is no naïve idealism in Plato, there is no brute materialism in Aristotle. According to Plato's and Aristotle's shared realism of universals, all material reality is a reflection of ideal form. In the 'sublunary world of things,' universals are not and cannot be outside or apart from particulars. The relational participation of particulars in universals can be glimpsed by sense perception and grasped by intellectual cognition.

The claim that Plato's and Aristotle's accounts of universals are diametrically opposed and that Boethius posits the primacy of essence over existence also dictates interpretations of his theory of semantics and mental language. According to Lambertus de Rijk, Boethius argues that language is the product of the mind that conceives things *(res)* as notions *(intellectus)* signified by words *(voces)*. Since notions are always true notions of the true nature (or 'quiddity') of things, words refer principally *(principaliter)* to the essence of things and only indirectly to the actual things (2 *In Periherm.* 24.12-13). For de Rijk, the quiddity of things signified by words is Aristotle's *passiones animae,* not Plato's transcendent Forms.[26] Curiously, de Rijk quotes the *Cratylus* in support of his reading, but it is precisely in this dialogue that Plato equates the notion of power (δύναμις) not simply with the action of 'words' upon the mind but also with a wider psychological sense and crucially a cosmic principle that orders reality and holds all nature (*Crat.* 399 E–400 B). As such, de Rijk wrongly privileges the semantic-epistemic function of power over the cosmic-metaphysical dimension that is more prominent in Plato's philosophy.[27] This misreading explains why Boethius' mention of quiddity is likened to the priority of formal essence over material instantiation in Aristotle rather than the real actuality of transcendent forms in immanent things in Plato.

Against such and similar essentialist interpretations, John Magee rightly contends that the mark of Boethius' epistemology and semantics is a double mediation and a double movement. The double mediation is

26. L. M. de Rijk, "Boèce logicien et philosophe: Ses positions sémantiques et sa métaphysique de l'être," pp. 141-56; de Rijk, "On Boethius' Notion of Being: A Chapter on Boethian Semantics," pp. 1-29.

27. Michel René Barnes, "The Role of Δύναμις in Plato's Philosophy," in *The Power of God: Dunamis in Gregory of Nyssa's Trinitarian Theology* (Washington, DC: Catholic University of America Press, 2001), pp. 54-93, esp. pp. 70-76.

performed by sense perception and the mind. The double movement goes from actual things *(res)* via the senses *(sensus)* and thoughts (*intellectus* or *passiones animae*) to written letters *(litterae)* and/or words *(voces)*, and from the letters or words via *intellectus* and *sensus* back to the senses.[28] The point is that Boethius combines Aristotle's emphasis on sensible things as the first object of the intellect with Plato's argument that the intelligible is not a realm in itself but reflected in the sensible (*1 In Periherm.* 37.4; *2 In Periherm.* 20.17) — the material only *is* by virtue of partaking in the ideal, so that in perceiving materiality we always already discern its participation in ideality (*2 In Periherm.* 21.8). Just as the universal requires the particular to be reflected in diverse ways, so the particular requires the universal in order to be. This parallelism is echoed at the level of knowledge. Cognition of particulars does not stop either at particulars themselves or at universals but involves an exit from, and a return to, materiality in order to grasp how the universal constitutes the particular that reflects it.[29] Here the theological epistemology of Boethius is already apparent.

4. Individuation and the Metaphysics of Act and Potency

In this section I will suggest that Boethius' metaphysical realism and his theological epistemology are linked to his transformation of Aristotle's language of act and potency. The common assumption in de Libera and de Rijk is that Boethius follows Aristotle and develops a theory of knowledge of essences based on abstraction. But the double movement from the sensible via the intelligible back to the sensible and the double mediation by sense perception and intellectual cognition highlight Boethius' attempt to relate the existence of material particular things to the essence of immaterial universal forms. His fusion of epistemology with ontology has important implications for his theory of individuation. At first, it would seem as though he simply attempts to synthesize Plato and

---

28. John Magee, *Boethius on Signification and Mind* (Leiden: E. J. Brill, 1989), pp. 49-92.

29. Both de Libera and de Rijk would object that there are notions which are at once nonexistent and signifying like chimerae or centaurs and therefore that knowledge is noumenal rather than phenomenal. However, as Magee suggests, such notions are for Boethius matters of opinion *(opinabile)*. As such, they are not strictly speaking knowable *(scibile)*, and the sole truth about them is that they do not exist (*1 In Periherm.* 166.6; *2 In Periherm.* 375.23–376.23). Cf. Magee, *Boethius on Signification and Mind*, pp. 83-84.

Aristotle, arguing that matter is brought from potency into actuality by form, which does not exist outside embodiment. Thus, individuation describes the ordering of particular concrete matter by universal immaterial form.

A. *Ipsum Esse* or *Act of Being*

However, already in his commentaries on Aristotelian logic, Boethius' account surpasses Greek metaphysics and develops Augustine's theology. Beyond Aristotle (and in some sense Plato), Boethius argues that particulars as form-matter compounds intimate being itself *(ipsum esse)*. For the actuality of particulars stands in potency to that which brings them into actual existence and makes them what they are. A thing's actuality mediates both *that* thing's potentiality and the act that actualizes it. Therefore actualization individuates things by aligning forms in particulars more closely with the first principle and final end of all beings — that which is being *(id quod est esse)* or God (*De Hebdom.* reg. VI), a clear contrast with Aristotle's indifferent God.

To know a thing is to cognize the ontological coincidence of universal form in particular matter. Thus to know a thing is to cognize *that* thing's 'vertical' relationality to *esse ipsum,* which brings beings from potency into actuality and makes them what they are. So configured, knowledge actualizes both a thing's cognoscibility *(scibilitas)* and the mind's capacity to know *(potestas rationis)*. For this reason, knowledge is ontological. Boethius' account prolongs and radicalizes Plato's and Augustine's idea that being and knowing are coextensive. His innovation is to demonstrate that knowledge of form is not only ontological but also teleological, for the *telos* of knowable objects is to be known and that of capable minds is to know. As a result, knowledge of form individuates both the knowing mind and the known object.

In the process of developing this account, Boethius transforms both Aristotelian and Neo-Platonist metaphysics, in particular Aristotle's tendency to privilege substance over relation. Before showing why for Boethius relation is not subordinate to substance and how relationality precedes participation, I explore his understanding of act and potency. The logical and metaphysical priority of actuality of being over potency to know, which Boethius takes from Aristotle, implies that actual things *(res)* can subsist without being cognized, whereas thoughts *(intellectus)* cannot ultimately exist without actual things. All effective knowledge is ultimately grounded in actualized reality. Yet at the same time, things that have been brought from potency into actuality may not actually be known — things are cognoscible *(scibilia)* without being effectively cognized *(scita)*. Here two questions can be raised. First, why would things be 'knowables'? Second, how might 'knowables' *(scibilia)* become 'knowns' *(scita)?*

Concerning the first question, Boethius argues that all things have a potency to be and to be known. The *telos* of all things is to actualize their ontic and epistemic potency. This twofold potentiality is inscribed into the nature of all created things and the whole of creation. God's creative activity brings things into being and makes them what they are.[30] In the unfolding of reality, it actualizes their potency and in turn is manifest in their actualization. So in coming into being things disclose God's active creativity. In coming to know their being we come to know their createdness (or creatureliness) and God's continuous creative action which upholds all beings. Through corporeal things that appear to the senses and the mind, God manifests himself because his love and goodness communicate themselves. This conception foreshadows the idea of *bonum diffusivum sui* in Aquinas, as I will show in chapter 5. For Boethius, the communicability of universals is an indication that a higher actuality is at work in particulars.[31]

With respect to the second question, Boethius suggests that things pass from cognoscibility to cognition because they make themselves known to the mind through the senses. There only is sense perception because the senses perceive something actual. In virtue of the senses the mind is always already in contact with reality. Magee puts this succinctly: "*sensus* is activated by the presence of a *res*."[32] As such, sense perception is the origin of knowledge — *sensus* is the *origo intellectus*.[33]

---

30. Here Boethius is influenced by the Neo-Platonist emphasis on *theosis* and theurgy. See Pierre Courcelle, *La Consolation de Philosophie dans la tradition littéraire. Antécédents et postérité de Boèce* (Paris: Études Augustiniennes, 1967), pp. 163-64; P. Courcelle, *Late Latin Writers and Their Greek Sources* (Cambridge, MA: Harvard University Press, 1969), pp. 301-2; Robert Crouse, "The Doctrine of Creation in Boethius: The *'De hebdomadibus'* and the *Consolatio*," in *Studia Patristica: Eighth International Conference on Patristic Studies,* ed. E. A. Livingstone (Oxford: Pergamon Press, 1979), Part 1, pp. 417-21.

31. *2 In Periherm.* 2.7 (136: 20–137: 13).

32. Magee, *Boethius on Signification and Mind,* p. 104.

33. Magee, *Boethius on Signification and Mind,* p. 99.

Sense perception is at once passive and active, an intellective faculty and a content of intellection. It is itself cognitive because it induces both a physical change in sense organs and a mental (or spiritual) change in the mind (a point that was later developed by Aquinas, as we will see in chapter 5).

What is it that we perceive when we see a particular sensible thing? According to Boethius, we perceive a compact composed of matter and form. But unlike the intellect, sense perception does not divide and compose form and matter or abstract form from matter. Instead, it apprehends the unity of things, form instantiated in matter or, more accurately, 'material form': "For sense examines the shape set in the underlying matter."[34] As such, sense perception gives access to a thing's existence as well as its essence. That which the senses perceive and mediate to the mind is a thing's singularity, its unique composition of universal form particularized in matter. Knowledge and understanding of universals belong to intellectual cognition, but a certain apprehension of particulars belongs to sensory cognition.[35]

In perceiving particulars and cognizing the universals which are present in them, the mind passes from the potency of understanding *(potestas rationis)* to the act of knowing *(actus intelligentiae)*. In knowing the being of things, the knower ascends in the hierarchy of being. For nonrational beings, to be is to have the disposition to be known. Likewise for rational beings, to be is to have the disposition to know. For human beings, to know is to enhance their actuality and therefore to perfect their form. Both knowledge and being require a higher act to come into actuality (2 *In Periherm.* 238.20-27). So knowledge of things implies some knowledge of being itself because to know is to know that a thing passes from potential 'knowability' to actual 'known-ness' in virtue of a higher actuality — God's creative act of being.

B. 'Modal' Metaphysics

This conclusion is not based on a blind belief in the existence of God but emerges from Boethius' modification of Greek and Roman philosophy.

---

34. *"sensus enim figuram in subiecta materia constitutam . . . perpendit"* (*De Consol.* V.iv.84-85 [411/410]).

35. 2 *In Periherm.* 29.6; 55.17; 1 *In Isag.* 24.14; 84.7; 136.7.

Notably, he reconfigures the relation between logic and metaphysics and argues that modality is ultimately grounded in reality rather than being a product *of* the mind *in* the mind. Quoting from Boethius' commentary on Aristotle's *Peri Hermeneias,* Simo Knuuttila writes that

> the absence of unqualified possibility suggests that all modalities are real rather than logical, i.e. the truth of modal axioms is evaluated from the point of view of the actual world and its history. I think this is taken for granted in Boethius' description: "The Stoics have postulated as possible that which is susceptible of true affirmation, when things that are external to it but happen together with it do not in any way prevent it. The impossible is that which never admits of truth, other external things preventing it [2 *In Periherm.* 234.27–235.1]."[36]

In order to tie possibility to potency and exclude both accident and fate as ultimate causes of the actuality of things, Boethius situates modality in being, not in the mind. For instance, he challenged Alexander of Aphrodisias' idea of possibilities that will never be actualized.[37] To believe in nonactualizable possibilities is to believe in a nondemonstrable a priori, since such possibilities are by definition without any relation to actual beings and thus wholly unintelligible (2 *In Periherm.* 197.11–198.3).

At the same time, Boethius goes beyond Aristotle's account of act and potency and formulates an account of nature that balances the substance of being with the relation between actuality and potentiality. Nature is actuality that stands in potency to the act that brings it into being and makes it what it is. As such, nature and all things therein exhibit a disposition to be: "[W]e know that nature regularly develops no property in vain" (2 *In Periherm.* 236.16-17). Everything that has potency can be brought into actuality. As a result, potencies that will never be actualized cannot be because they would be contrary to nature and therefore contrary to God's creation. To say this is to say that nonactualizable potencies are false — the only truth about such potencies is that they *are not.* What determines the truth or falsehood of any given proposition is whether it describes the world, both actual and potential.

---

36. Simo Knuuttila, *Modalities in Medieval Philosophy* (London and New York: Routledge, 1993), pp. 17-18.

37. Alexander of Aphrodisias, *De fato* (176.15-16), quoted in Knuuttila, *Modalities in Medieval Philosophy,* p. 18.

If all potencies are actualizable, then it also follows that all actualities have the potency to be. Act and potency are not circular but hierarchical because in order to be actual, a potency requires a higher act that actualizes it (*1 In Periherm.* 120.24–121.16; *2 In Periherm.* 237.1-5). In actual things, we can discern the power that brings them from their potency to be into the actuality of being because the coming-into-being (and passing-away) of individual substances involves a change in the substance which is irreducible to the substance itself, since nothing can be its own cause of generation (as Plato, Aristotle, Plotinus, and other ancient philosophers insisted). As a result, substance alone cannot account for the substantial change in the process of actualization.

Here Boethius' metaphysics of act and potency differs significantly from Aristotle's. First of all, the latter denies that substantial change as such is actual because he excludes any state between nonbeing and being (*Phys.* VI 5, 235^{b}6-32). By contrast, Boethius draws on Augustine (*Civ. Dei* XII.2) to argue that actualization, though instantaneous, takes place in time and not in eternity. Since prior to existence there is nothing (though *nothing is not* because it lacks any ontological station), the 'ontologic' underpinning the process of actualization is best described by the idea of creation *ex nihilo*.

The second difference between Aristotle and Boethius concerns the alternation of motion and rest in individual substances, which raises questions about whether the passage from motion to rest and from rest to motion constitutes substantial or kinetic change. As Simo Knuuttila indicates, Aristotle envisages the possibility that individual motion is a change in the substance itself but tends to associate all changes with kinetic energy — modifications in the state of a substance, not substantial change itself.[38] This ambivalence in Aristotle prompts Boethius to explore the temporal inscription of all that is finite. Actuality is modal as well as temporal — it is a matter of *when,* not only of *whether.* The temporal and ontological nature of actualized potencies leads Boethius to chart a middle way between the relative possibility of accidentalism and the absolute necessity of fatalism. He argues that *when* things are actual they are so necessarily, in the sense that their actualization owes nothing to accident or fortune (*1 In Periherm.* 110.28–111.1). Yet at the same time, actual things are contingent because neither their actualization nor their actuality is in itself necessary. For nothing can actualize itself or

---

38. Knuuttila, *Modalities in Medieval Philosophy,* pp. 21-22.

preserve itself in being by itself alone. The contingency of things that are actual hovers between necessity and possibility, as it were independently of any kind of fate or probability.[39] There is thus a stark contrast between Aristotle's actualism and Boethius' idea of a kind of actual necessity: everything that is in act poses its own necessity, which is nevertheless always contingent on the act that brings it into existence and sustains it in being.[40]

Boethius also holds that the temporality of motion and rest and the finitude of beings-in-act intimate a power of being that not only brings things into being and makes them what they are, but also sustains them in being and perfects their singularity. The mark of Boethius' metaphysics is his emphasis on the temporality of actualization and the temporal unfolding of potentiality into actuality. The rejection of accident and fate as causes of actuality leads him to develop an alternative account of causation that preserves the radical contingency of all that is and the priority of act over potency. Both existence and essence are in potentiality to being itself *(ipsum esse)*. Particular things stand in potency to the supreme actuality of being and thus manifest the 'ontological difference,' as I will discuss in the following section. This difference, though absolute, is qualified by the 'vertical' relationality of particular form to universal form. To be individuated is to reflect the universal diversely in particular ways.

5. Individual Substance and the 'Ontological Difference'

In the following three sections of this chapter, I investigate Boethius' metaphysics and his account of substance, relation, and participation in his theological tractates — the *Opuscula sacra*. Boethius configures the difference and relation between the Creator and creation in terms of the difference and relation between being itself *(esse ipsum)* and that which is *(id quod est)*. Following (and perhaps surpassing) Augustine, he describes God as fully relational and the divine persons as being beyond substance *(ultra substantiam)*. The relationality of the 'ecstatically self-

---

39. It is in terms of temporal, qualified necessity of actual things that Boethius reads Aristotle's balancing act of combining the principle of bivalence with the idea of radical contingency in Book 9 of the *Peri Hermeneias*. Cf. Gail Fine, "Truth and Necessity in *De interpretatione* 9," *History of Philosophy Quarterly* 1 (1984): 23-47.

40. Cf. Zev Bechler, *Aristotle's Theory of Actuality* (Albany: State University of New York Press, 1995).

giving' Godhead is the reason why creation exists and can participate in the Trinity. To say that beings are relational is to say that they are always already good, not in and of themselves but by virtue of the universal Good which communicates itself and is present in particulars. Likewise, to say that beings are participatory is to say that they preserve and perfect their goodness by exercising virtue and ordering their life according to God's intentionality.

Already in *De Fide Catholica,* Boethius highlights the difference between existence and *esse.* In the opening lines, the divine substance is said to have existed *(exsistere)* since eternity *(De Fide* 13 [52]). Similarly, the verb 'to exist' is used to describe how the world was created *ex nihilo,* not made from divine substance or fashioned according to "the existence of some independent nature."[41] *'Exsistere'* contrasts with *'esse,'* which is deployed in connection with the divine persons *(De Fide* 17 [52], 21-48 [54]) and with the coming into being of the world *(De Fide* 58 [56]). The use of *exsistere* and *esse* is not in any way systematic. However, Boethius does emphasize their difference, insisting that *exsistere* in some sense depends on *esse.* For instance, creation exists by virtue of having been brought into being *(De Fide* 55-63 [56]). *Esse* exceeds *exsistere* because all that exists has been brought into being *(esse)* in order to be *(ut esset).* And if that which exists only *is* because it has received *esse* and if what it is *is to be,* then *esse* binds together both existence and essence.

In the *Contra Eutychen et Nestorium,* essence, existence, and *esse* are analyzed in greater detail and with more rigor. Before refuting the two heresies in question, Boethius defines a metaphysical framework that underpins his theological writings. This framework conceptualizes the difference between God's *esse* and the *esse* of all nondivine substances on the basis of the predicative difference in respect of 'nature' and 'person.' Nature is predicable of all things that are *(esse)* and as such can be cognized in some manner *(quoquo modo)* by the human mind *(Contra Eut.* I.8-12 [78]). Nature so defined extends to God, for "God and matter . . . are apprehended in some way through the removal of things."[42] But nature cannot be predicated univocally of material things and God. Divine substance is simple; as such, it only acts and cannot be acted upon. By contrast, nondivine substances are complex; as such, they can be

---

41. *". . . existentia propriae naturae . . ." (De Fide:* 61 [56]).

42. *"deus et materia . . . aliquo tamen modo ceterarum rerum privatione capiuntur" (Contra Eut.* I.14-15 [79/78]).

acted upon as well as act. Similarly, if "nature is the specific *differentia* that informs a thing,"[43] then it can be predicated of both God and men. But predication is not univocal, for Christ has two natures, divine and human. Here Boethius' fusion of metaphysics with theology is crucial: the simplicity of divine substance and Christ's twofold nature highlights the predicative difference between God and man.

Boethius then goes on to show how this predicative difference also holds in the case of 'person' and how predicative differences are not nominal but real. Since 'nature' is either a substance or an accident and since "nature is a substrate of person and . . . person cannot be predicated apart from nature,"[44] it follows that 'person' can only be predicated of substances, corporeal or incorporeal, because 'person' cannot consist exclusively of accidents. So 'person' is predicable of God in the sense that he is a rational substance, though of course not in the same way as man. For God alone is an incorporeal substance, which is immutable and impassible. Likewise, both God and man are persons because substance only is in individuals:

> [I]f person belongs to substances alone, and these [are] rational, and if every substance is a nature, and is not in universals but in individuals, we have found the definition of person: 'the individual substance of a rational nature.'[45]

In contemporary theology, there is an ongoing debate on whether this definition privileges a more substantialist account of the human person or whether we already find in Boethius a fully relational metaphysics and anthropology. In a number of important interventions and programmatic contributions, Joseph Ratzinger has questioned the insufficiently anthropological basis of Boethius' account.[46] However, it can be contended that the 'last Roman and first scholastic' provides a radical fusion

43. *"natura est unam quamque rem informans specifica differentia"* (*Contra Eut.* I.57-58 [80]).

44. *". . . personae subiectam esse naturam nec praeter naturam personam posse praedicari"* (*Contra Eut.* II.10-11 [83/82]).

45. *"si persona in solis substantiis est atque in his rationabilibus substantiaque omnis natura est nec in universalibus sed in individuis constat, reperta personae est definitio: 'naturae rationabilis individua substantia'"* (*Contra Eut.* III.1-5 [85/84]).

46. Joseph Ratzinger, *Introduction to Christianity* (New York: Herder & Herder, 1970), pp. 102-3; J. Ratzinger, "Concerning the Person in Theology," *Communio* 17 (1990): 438-54.

of Greek concepts with biblical elements, a contribution to the 'hellenization' of Christian theology of which Pope Benedict XVI spoke so eloquently in his controversial Regensburg address. Indeed, individual substance is not predicated univocally of God and man because this definition of person derives from the Greek ὑπόστασις, which denotes individual subsistence *(individua subsistentia)*, and the divine persons are the only self-subsistent substances:

> Man has . . . οὐσία or essence because he is, οὐσίωσις or subsistence because he is not any subject, ὑπόστασις or substance because he is subject to other things which are not subsistences or οὐσίωσεις, while he is πρόσωπον or person because he is a rational individual. Next, God is οὐσία or essence, for He is and is especially that from which proceeds the being of all things. He is οὐσίωσις, i.e. subsistence, for He subsists in absolute independence; and ὑφίστασθαι, for He is substance. Whence we go on to say that there is . . . one essence and subsistence but three ὑποστάσεις, that is, three substances. And indeed, following this use, men have spoken of One essence of the Trinity, three substances and three persons. For did not the language of the Church forbid us to say that there are three substances in God, substance might seem for this reason to be predicated of God, not because he is set under other things like a substrate, but because, just as he is before all things, so He is as it were the principle beneath all things, supplying them with οὐσιώσθαι or subsistence.[47]

In this passage, Boethius clearly argues that the difference between God and man is both predicative and real. God's essence is not identical with man's essence, since God is the source of all being, whereas man is the re-

---

47. *"Est . . . hominis quidem essentia, id est* οὐσία *quidem atque essentia quoniam est,* οὐσίωσις *vero atque subsistentia quoniam in nullo subiecto est,* ὑπόστασις *vero atque substantia, quoniam subset ceteris quae subsistentiae non sunt, id est* οὐσίωσεις; *est* πρόσωπον *atque persona, quoniam est rationabile individuum. Deus quoque est et* οὐσία *est et essentia, est enim et maxime ipse est a quo omnium esse proficiscitur. Est* οὐσίωσις, *id est subsistentia (subsistit enim nullo indigens); et* ὑφίστασθαι: *substat enim. Unde et etiam dicimus unam esse . . . essentiam vel subsistentiam deitatis, sed tres* ὑποστάσεις, *id est tres substantias. Et quidem secundum hunc modum dixere unam trinitatis essentiam, tres substantias tresque personas. Nisi enim tres in deo substantias ecclesiasticus loquendi usus excluderet, videretur idcirco de deo dici substantia, non quod ipse ceteris rebus quasi subiectum supponeretur, sed quod idem omnibus uti praesset ita etiam quasi principium subesset rebus, dum eis omnibus* οὐσιώσθαι *vel subsistere subministrat"* (Contra Eut. III.79-101 [91-93/90-92]).

cipient of being. God's subsistence is not identical with man's subsistence, since God is absolutely independent, whereas man is dependent on God in order to be brought into being. God's substance is not identical with man's substance, since God is never subject to anything, whereas man is a substrate for the existence of accidents. And God is three substances in one, whereas man is of one substance only. Finally, God is not a person in the same way as man, since God is not only an individual substance of a nature endowed with reason, but a relational substance, three persons in one. I now turn to the three remaining *Opuscula sacra,* which set out Boethius' metaphysical account of individuation in terms of man's 'vertical' participation in God's infinite relationality.

6. *Deus Ultra Substantiam*

In the *Utrum Pater,* Boethius examines the claim first formulated in the *Contra Eutychen et Nestorium* that the three persons of the Trinity can be predicated substantially of the divinity. All three persons are individual substances. Yet at the same time, they are also — taken together — one single substance, noncomposite and indivisible, simply one. What is predicated substantially of the deity must be common to all three substances (*Utrum Pater* 5-17 [32/34]). The name of God is an exemplary case, but so are other divine names such as truth, goodness, immutability, justice, and omnipotence. If so, can the individual persons also be predicated of the common substances, precisely because each is a substance? In other words, are Father, Son, and Holy Spirit also substantially predicated of the divinity? Boethius denies this, as the Father does not transmit His name to the Son or the Holy Spirit. The three are "not predicated substantially [of the divinity] but in some other way"[48] — not accidentally, because no divine attribute is accidental, but relatively *(ad aliquid).* Since predication refers to real things, 'relative' predication points to the relational nature of the Godhead.

According to Boethius, 'relative' predication means that the predicable applies not to one substance only, but to the relations that the substances entertain with one another. This applies to the three persons of the Trinity and the Trinity itself, as the Father only is a Father

---

48. *"non substantialiter praedicari sed alio modo"* (*Utrum Pater* 34 [35/34]).

with respect to a Son and the Trinity cannot be equated with any of the three persons. Boethius takes this solution from Augustine, who in Book V of the *De Trinitate* argues that the Arian dualism of substantial and accidental predication fails to take into account the Aristotelian category of relation, as I argued in the previous chapter.[49] Since it concerns the predicative difference with respect to the category of substance, this point has a direct bearing on the 'ontological difference' between God and creation. In Boethius' *De Trinitate,* substance is reconfigured in terms of relationality. God is three persons in one subsistent substance precisely because divine substantiality is constituted by Trinitarian relations (*De Trinitate* IV.11, 15-16, 18, 23). By contrast, man is not a subsistent substance because he depends on God's substance. Likewise, man is not fully relational because man only exists by participating in God's relationality (*De Trinitate* II.51-56). I now detail this argument.

Boethius demonstrates the relationality of substance on the basis of nondivine substances, which stand in potency to the actuality of God; as such, the finite essence of such substances does not coincide with the infinite act of being (*De Trinitate* II.31-37 [11/10]). Since divine substance is pure form without matter and everything else has being by virtue of substantial form, there is only one true form, God. All other forms are not genuine forms but images of the one true form: "For from these forms which are outside matter have come those forms which are in matter and produce a body. We misname the entities that reside in bodies when we call them forms, since they are images; for they only resemble those forms which are not incorporate in matter."[50] The difference of pure form and 'material form' leads Boethius to argue that substantial form cannot be predicated univocally of God and man. Strictly speaking, neither God nor man is a genuine substance, though for very different reasons:

> When we name a substance, as man or God, it seems as though that of
> which the predication is made were itself substance, as [if] man or

---

49. Cf. Stephen Gersh, *Middle Platonism and Neoplatonism: The Latin Tradition* (Notre Dame: University of Notre Dame Press, 1986), vol. 2, pp. 705-7; Marenbon, *Boethius,* pp. 77-78.

50. *"Ex his formis quae praeter materiam sunt, istae formae venerunt quae sunt in materia et corpus efficiunt. Nam ceteras quae in corporibus sunt abutimur formas vocantes, dum imagines sint. Adsimulantur enim formis his quae non sunt in materia constitutae"* (*De Trinitate* II.51-56 [13/12]). Cf. Marenbon, *Boethius,* pp. 80-82.

God were substance. But there is a difference: since man is not simply and entirely man, and therefore is not substance after all. For what man is he owes to other things which are not man.[51]

The claim that man is not a true substance follows from the metaphysical argument that man is a matter-form compound and therefore stands in potency to a higher actuality. Man *is not* substance; man has substance by virtue of participating in God's *esse*.

If man has substance by participating in God, God must be substance. However, Boethius repeatedly states that God is *ultra substantiam* — beyond substance.[52] For God exceeds substantial predication. Following the *Utrum Pater,* Boethius extends Augustine's teaching on 'relative' predication in the direction of relationality. Only substantial predication in conjunction with relative predication respects the predicative and 'ontological difference' that pertains between God and man. Substantial predication alone establishes the sameness of the divine substance in the three Trinitarian Persons, but it does not express the 'otherness of the divine persons' (*De Trinitate* IV).

Since no relation can be related to itself, inasmuch as one which makes a predicate by itself is a predication which lacks relation, the manifoldness of the Trinity is produced in the fact that it is predication of a relation, and the unity is preserved through the fact that there is no difference of substance or operation. . . . So then, the substance preserves the unity, the relation makes up the Trinity . . . the relation in the Trinity of Father to Son, and of both to Holy Spirit is like a relation of identicals. But if a relation of this kind cannot be found in all other things, this is because of the otherness natural to all perishable, transitory objects.[53]

---

51. "*cum dicimus 'substantia' (ut homo vel deus), ita dicitur quasi illud de quo praedicatur ipsum sit substantia, ut substantia homo vel deus. Sed distat, quoniam homo non integre ipsum homo est ac per hoc nec substantia; quod enim est, aliis debet quae non sunt homo*" (*De Trinitate* IV.29-34 [19/18]).

52. *De Trinitate* IV.11, 15-16, 18, 23 (16/18).

53. "*Sed quoniam nulla relatio ad se ipsum referri potest, idcirco quod ea secundum se ipsum est praedicatio quae relatione caret, facta quidem est trinitatis numerositas in eo quod est praedicatio relationis, servata vero unitas in eo quod est indifferentia vel substantiae vel operationis. . . . Ita igitur substantia continet unitatem, relatio multiplicat trinitatem quod est idem ad id quod est idem . . . et similis est relatio in trinitate patris ad filium et utriusque ad*

137

Crucially, 'relative' predication neither refers to a binary relation between two terms nor denotes a single identity that is reducible to substance. Instead, "the relation in the Trinity" describes the 'horizontal', infinite, and unreserved participation of the Trinitarian persons in each
other without any *tertium quid* or univocal foundation in substance. It is
the original 'ecstatic self-giving' of this relationality beyond substance
that brings everything out of nothing into actuality and enables the
whole of creation to perfect its unique form by participating ever more
intensely in God's relational being. In the *De Hebdomadibus*, to which I
now turn, this emphasis on relationality is supplemented by the argument that participation enables man to attain an ever-greater likeness
with God by preserving and enhancing the goodness that is bestowed
upon particulars by the divine act of being. Man is individuated by sharing in the economy of the Trinitarian God and by the exercise of virtue,
chief of all the virtue of justice.

7. Relationality and Participation

The *De Hebdomadibus* concerns the sense in which substances can be
said to be good. The main question is the nature of the relationship between being *(esse)* and goodness *(bonum),* on the one hand, and that
which is *(id quod est),* on the other hand. The paradox that Boethius explores is how composite finite substances can be said to be good without, however, being identical with the good. The treatise is divided into
two parts: first, an exposition of nine rules and, second, their application
to the question of whether substances can be (said to be) good. The key
to Boethius' solution of this *aporia* is the 'ontological difference' between
being and that which is. Rule two reads as follows: "[B]eing and that
which is [*id quod est*] are different: being itself is not yet, but that which
is, having taken the form of being, is and consists."[54] How are we to inter-
pret *esse?* In the *De Hebdomadibus*, Boethius distinguishes between the
being *(esse)* of that which is and being itself *(esse ipsum).* The former is
the immanent form, "which [in the *De Trinitate*] Boethius had said

---

spiritum sanctum ut eius quod est idem ad id quod est idem. Quod si id in cunctis aliis rebus
non potest inveniri, facit hoc cognata caducis rebus alteritas" (De Trinitate VI.1-24 [29-31/28-
30]).

54. *"diversum est esse et id quod est; ipsum enim esse nondum est, at vero quod est
accepta essendi formam est atque consistit"* (De Hebdom. 28-30 [41/40]).

should really be considered an image (for instance the form humanity that makes Socrates a man)."[55] As immanent form, *esse* is not self-generated but derives from being itself *(ipsum esse)*: "[T]hey [all non-divine things] take that which they are from that which is being."[56] Boethius defines *ipsum esse* as that which 'is not yet,' 'does not participate in any way in anything,' is not anything but itself, can be participated in by that which is and thus gives it being (*De Hebdom.* 29, 31-32, 36-37, 41-42). In chapter 5, I show how Aquinas extends this framework by introducing the distinctions between *ens, esse commune,* and *ipsum esse subsistens.*

For now reverting to Boethius, the following question can be raised: If there is a difference between *esse* and *id quod est,* how can that which is be good? First, Boethius distinguishes goodness by substance from goodness by participation. Both modes are inadequate to explain goodness in composite substances. Goodness by substance means that substances are intrinsically good, which implies that "they are like the first good, and thereby they will be that good itself; for nothing is like it save itself. Hence all things that are, are God — an impious assertion."[57] Goodness by participation means that substances are in no way good in themselves. But "the common opinion of the learned . . . that everything that is tends to the good and everything tends to its like."[58] So if substances cannot be good either by substance or by participation, in what sense can they be good at all? Boethius' proposed solution to this *aporia* is to say that all nondivine substances are actually good insofar as they flow from being itself, which is the first good. Yet at the same time, they are potentially good insofar as they stand in potency to the actuality of being itself, which is the highest good.

> For the first good, since it is, is good in virtue of its being; but the secondary good, since it has flown from that whose very being is good, is itself also good. But the very being of all things has flown from that which is the first good and which is such a good that it is rightly said

55. Marenbon, *Boethius,* p. 89.

56. *"id quod sunt autem habent ex eo quod est esse"* (*De Hebdom.* 70 [45/44]).

57. *"primo sint bono similia ac per hoc ipsum bonum erunt; nihil enim illi praeter se ipsum simile est. Ex quo fit ut omnia quae sunt deus sint, quod dictu nefas est"* (*De Hebdom.* 77-80 [45/44]).

58. *"tenet enim communis sententia doctorum omne quod est ad bonum tendere, omne autem tendit ad simile"* (*De Hebdom.* 58-59 [43/42]).

to be good in virtue of its being. Therefore the being of these things is good; for then it is in the first good.[59]

In this passage, Boethius argues that the 'ontological difference' entails a distinction between the good itself and that which is good by virtue of emanating from it. In order to substantiate this argument, Boethius configures the good itself to be coextensive with being itself: "[T]hat very first good is being itself and is the good itself and good being itself."[60] So that which is always already *is* good because it is relational to being itself which is the good itself. The ecstatic plenitude of being itself and the good itself communicates being and goodness to all beings that are brought into existence. All that is has a share in the actuality of being itself and thus in the good itself. The Good is not beyond being in the sense of being separate from it.[61] Instead, being and goodness are coterminous. Boethius' idea of the coextension of the good and being prefigures the medieval conception of the convertibility of the transcendentals.

This is significant for individuation because the difference between the actual and the potential goodness of nondivine substances paves the way for the exercise of justice as the highest individuating activity. Boethius argues that all that exists is always already good but not just, for only God's absolute goodness is justice. To do justice is to preserve and extend the goodness that is given by God and received by nondivine substances: "[B]eing good refers to essence, being just to action."[62] To do justice is to be individuated and to individuate those things to which action imparts justice because it is to pursue the God-given *telos* of tending to the good (*De Hebdom.* 58-59). To pursue this *telos* is to perfect our individual form and to perfect the form of things

---

59. *"Primum enim bonum, quoniam est, in eo quod est bonum est; secundum vero bonum, quoniam ex eo fluxit cuius ipsum esse bonum est, ipsum quoque bonum est. Sed ipsum esse omnium rerum ex eo fluxit quod est primum bonum et quod bonum tale est ut recte dicatur in eo quod est esse bonum. Ipsum igitur eorum esse bonum est; tunc enim in eo"* (*De Hebdom.* 121-27 [47-49/46-48]).

60. *"illud ipsum bonum primum est et ipsum esse sit et ipsum bonum et ipsum esse bonum"* (*De Hebdom.* 149-50 [49/48]).

61. This has been argued extensively by Jean-Luc Marion, who wrongly attributes this position to Dionysius the Areopagite and Thomas Aquinas, as I will argue in this chapter and also in chapter 5. See Jean-Luc Marion, *L'idole et la distance. Cinq études*, 3rd ed. (Paris: Biblio-Essais, 1991 [1977]), esp. pp. 190-201; Marion, *Dieu sans l'être* (Paris: Presses Universitaires de France, 1991), pp. 81-155.

62. *"bonum esse essentiam, iustum vero esse actum respicit"* (*De Hebdom.* 165-66 [51/50]).

which are drawn into the just order. So Boethius' solution to the '*aporia of the good*' is that composite finite substances are good by participation, not by substance, because the Good is coextensive with being (not above being) and thus communicates itself to all substances that have being by virtue of God's creation *ex nihilo*. The relationality of the Godhead imparts relational being to all that is, and participation in the Trinity marks the preservation and perfection of goodness thus given and received.

8. The Coextension of Being and the Good according to Dionysius

Like Boethius, Dionysius the Areopagite views Christian theology as the continuation and accomplishment of a long tradition reaching back to Plato — a shared understanding that correlates with that of Augustine and Gregory of Nyssa. Broadly speaking, there is thus no opposition between some of the main Church Fathers in the Greek East and the Latin West on the centrality of Neo-Platonism and the fusion of the biblical idea of creation *ex nihilo* with Plato's self-diffusive Good. As I will suggest in the final two sections of the present chapter, Dionysius' specific contribution to this 'hellenization' of Christian theology is at least threefold: first of all, binding together the Platonist emphasis on goodness and the Aristotelian accentuation of being *qua* being; second, relating divine illumination to deification *(theosis)* and union with God (with and beyond Augustine); third, developing a kind of 'mystagogical metaphysics' that brings together the mystical theology of elevation (anagogy) with the twin (ecclesiastical and celestial) hierarchy as well as the double *theoria* of Scripture and the sacraments (as in Origen). It is this theological metaphysics of the Christian Neo-Platonist tradition that Aquinas defends and develops in the face of both radical Aristotelianism and Avicennian Augustinianism at the universities of Paris and Oxford in the mid-thirteenth century, as I will suggest in different ways in chapters 4-6.

For now let me return to Dionysius, who argues that individuation marks the participation of the angelic and human intelligences in the hierarchical ordering of the cosmos which is created by, and describes to us, the infinite beauty and goodness of the divine thearchy. Hierarchy, a term coined by the Areopagite, is central to his theological metaphysics of individuation:

... hierarchy is a sacred order, a state of understanding and an activity approximating as closely as possible to the divine. And it is uplifted to the imitation of God in proportion to the illuminations divinely given to it. The beauty of God ... reaches out to grant every being, according to merit, a share of light and then through a divine sacrament, in harmony and in peace, it bestows on each of those being perfected its own form.[63]

As such, individuation for Dionysius is closely connected with the triadic links between the sacred order created by God, the divine activity that sustains all things in being, and the science or *theoria* through which we are deified — an account that combines elements of both Christian and pagan Neo-Platonism (above all Proclus), as I will suggest in greater detail below.[64]

For all these reasons, it is somewhat baffling that scholars like Vladimir Lossky and Jean-Luc Marion have repeatedly dismissed and denied the import of Neo-Platonist metaphysics in the theology of Dionysius.[65] In making this dubious claim, they do not just ignore Nicholas of Cusa's recognition of the prominence of Proclean elements in Dionysius' metaphysics and all the nineteenth-century scholarship attesting to this, as Wayne Hankey has documented.[66] Perhaps more importantly, both Lossky and Marion provide a distorted reading of Dionysius' thought and his influential legacy in East and West. Since Hankey has conclusively refuted Lossky's interpretation and devotes less attention to Marion, in what follows I shall focus on the latter.

63. Dionysius the Areopagite, *Celestial Hierarchy,* 164D, in *Pseudo-Dionysius: The Complete Works,* trans. Colm Luibhéid (Mahwah, NJ: Paulist Press, 1987), pp. 153-54 (translation modified). Henceforth *CH.*

64. See, *inter alia,* Istvân Perczel, "Pseudo-Dionysius and the Platonic Theology: A Preliminary Study," in *Proclus et la Théologie Platonicienne,* ed. A. Ph. Segonds and C. Steel (Leuven: Leuven University Press, 2000), pp. 492-530; Eric D. Perl, *Theophany: The Neoplatonic Philosophy of Dionysius the Areopagite* (Albany: State University of New York Press, 2007).

65. Vladimir Lossky, *Essai sur la Théologie Mystique de L'Église d'Orient* (Paris: Éditions Cerf, 2005; orig. pub. 1944); English translation: *The Mystical Theology of the Eastern Church* (Crestwood, NY: St. Vladimir's Seminary Press, 1997; orig. trans. and pub. 1957). For biographical references to Marion's work on Dionysius, see Marion, *L'idole et la distance* (cited in note 61, above).

66. Wayne J. Hankey, "Misrepresenting Neoplatonism in Contemporary Christian Dionysian Polemic: Eriugena and Nicholas of Cusa versus Vladimir Lossky and Jean-Luc Marion," *American Catholic Philosophical Quarterly* 82 (2008): 683-703.

For Marion, the metaphysical oscillation between presence and absence must be abandoned in favor of the phenomenological concept of distance, which alone liberates God from being confined to some foundational substance and from the language of 'object.' Both represent an ontic approach to the ontological difference and are therefore 'idolatrous.' Marion's concept of distance is based on his reading of Αἰτία in the Dionysian corpus. Αἰτία suspends the predicative language of metaphysics and 'ab-solves' God from any idolatrous naming. Only when we conceive of God as Αἰτία can we attain "the point of view of the absolute . . . : freed from all relation, therefore also from all thinkable relation which would tie [God as the absolute] to an absurd 'other than Himself.'"[67] Here Marion is right to argue that Dionysius configures Αἰτία as gift rather than cause and that he substitutes liturgy for predication.

Paradoxically, Marion's spectacular blindness to Dionysius' Neo-Platonist metaphysics masks the true meaning: just as Marion restricts the excess of donation over reception to saturated phenomena (instead of phenomenality as a whole), so too he suggests that Dionysius confines liturgical praise to eminence (instead of extending it to cataphasis and apophasis). However, it is clear from the text of the *Mystical Theology* that divine excess, which "surpasses all being" (1000B), transforms all language in a liturgical direction, so that affirmation and negations dimly reflect God's eminent nature. For Dionysius, we discern God's excess in all that is (*Divine Names* [henceforth *DN*] 593D). Indeed, in the *Celestial Hierarchy,* even the human body is described as a locus that manifests the transcendent in the immanent. Each bodily sense not only registers sense impressions passively, but relates these back to their source (*CH* 332A–333C). This source must be transcendent, for all finite bodies share in it yet never exhaust it.

If all things immanent intimate their transcendent cause, then it is also analogically the case that all divine names point to something more than themselves — God's excess over all names: "Realizing all this, the theologians praise it [the Cause of all] by every name — and as the

---

67. Marion, *L'idole et la distance*, pp. 179-201, 226-27 (179). According to Marion, what elevates ordinary discourse to the*ology* — discourse on God — is the intervention of Αἰτία (Cause), which is the advent of absolute transcendence within immanence (or Heidegger's *Ereignis*). As such, immanence is in excess of donation over reception and in excess of reception over being. Put differently, the immanent is for Marion given before it is received and is received before it *is*.

Nameless One" (*DN* 596A). Naming the 'Nameless' God ceases to be mere predication and, by liturgical subversion, becomes itself a form of praise of absolute divine transcendence, in the very act of expressing its constitutive indigence. Cataphasis always already implies apophasis, and conjointly cataphasis and apophasis imply 'eminence.' Contrary to Marion's assertion, Dionysius does not conceive the passage from cataphasis and apophasis to 'eminence' as a rupture. Here the term ὑπέρ (beyond) is key. It does not mean 'above' (in the sense of wholly superposed), 'apart from' (in the sense of without), or let alone 'outside' (in the sense of absolutely separate). Rather, ὑπέρ expresses some analogical resemblance between all that is and Αἰτία.[68] Precisely because God does *not* resemble the world but rather the world describes God as revealed in Christ's works (*Ecclesiastical Hierarchy* [henceforth *EH*] 432B), we can say that the triadic structures of the created order intimate the Trinitarian nature of the Creator. And *contra* Gilson, who wrongly ascribes a form of Porphyrian essentialism to Dionysius,[69] one can argue that the Areopagite fuses the Proclean emphasis on theurgy and triadic schemes in the world with the Platonist idea of a self-diffusive Good whose ecstatic outflow endows all things with goodness and draws them into the twin hierarchy which proceeds from and returns to God (*EH* 424B–445C).

For Dionysius, this has been disclosed by the divine works of Jesus Christ, which are described as the "consummation of the divine words" (*EH* 432B) and which are transmitted to us by Scripture and by the unspoken traditions of liturgical symbols and gestures. All acts and language are ultimately liturgically ordered.[70] Theology and theurgy conjoin in calling forth divine songs of praise, as the whole Dionysian corpus attests (e.g., *DN* 637C; *EH* 441C-D, 444A, 485A-B). So while Marion correctly shows that Dionysius' account of causation is couched in terms of donation and excess, he wrongly suggests that it implies God's absolute distance vis-à-vis creation, beyond the metaphysical presence-absence

68. René Roques, *L'univers dionysien. Structure hiérarchique du monde selon le Pseudo-Denys* (Paris: Éditions Cerf, 1983), pp. 53-59.

69. Étienne Gilson, *Being and Some Philosophers* (Toronto: Pontifical Institute of Mediaeval Studies, 1949), ch. 1, esp. pp. 30-34.

70. Andrew Louth, *Denys the Areopagite* (Wilton, CT: Morehouse-Barlow, 1989), pp. 17-32; Denys Turner, *Eros and Allegory* (Kalamazoo, MI: Cistercian Publications, 1995), pp. 47-70; D. Turner, *The Darkness of God* (Cambridge: Cambridge University Press, 1999), pp. 19-49.

divide. In turn, this argument is based on the primacy of Goodness *(Bonté)* over Being which Marion wrongly ascribed to the Areopagite, as I will now argue.

Marion's reading that divine goodness can only be given and received in virtue of the ontological distance discussed earlier appears at first unassailable. Indeed, in the *Divine Names* Dionysius appears to trace the first principle to God's goodness beyond being: "And we may be so bold as to claim also that the Cause of all things loves all things in the superabundance of his goodness, that because of his goodness he makes all things, brings all things to perfection, holds all things together, returns all things" (*DN* 708A-B). However, Marion's prioritizing of chapter four of the *Divine Names* over chapter five and other texts is misguided. His interpretation leads him to gloss over some key Neo-Platonic concepts in Dionysius' metaphysics, starting with the coextension of the Good, the Beautiful, and the One. This is borne out by the following two passages, the first taken from chapter four of the *Divine Names* itself and the second from chapter one:

> The Beautiful is therefore the same as the Good, for everything looks to the Beautiful and the Good as the cause of being, and there is nothing in the world without a share of the Beautiful and the Good. (*DN* 704B)

> Indeed, the inscrutable One is out of the reach of every rational process. Nor can any words come up to the inexpressible Good, this One, this source of all unity, this supra-existent Being. (*DN* 588B)

If the Good, the Beautiful, and the One are coextensive, it is hard to see why Goodness would assume absolute primacy over Being. What would it mean to say that Goodness is somehow prior to Being, which after all is coterminous with the Good, as we shall presently see? Marion's insistence on the primacy of the Good over Being arises from the fact that he throws out the Neo-Platonist baby with the Porphyrian bathwater, so to speak. Of course he is right to distance Dionysius from Porphyry's essentialism of the One: in the *Mystical Theology,* it is said that Αἰτία "is neither one nor oneness" (1048A). But it does not follow that the Areopagite views the first principle and final end as being entirely outside the orbit of Being. On the contrary, all beings proceed from and return to their source of being in God. Indeed, Dionysius describes God in book five of the *Divine Names* as the source and the giver of being:

> The first gift therefore of the absolutely transcendent Goodness is the gift of being, and that Goodness is praised from those that first and principally have a share of being. From it and in it are Being itself, the source of all beings, all beings and whatever else has a portion of existence. This characteristic is in it as an irrepressible, comprehensive and singular feature. (*DN* 820C-D)

Moreover, all reverts ultimately to the One and the Perfect — in an *epistrophe* that mirrors Proclus, as Wayne Hankey has rightly remarked. For this reason, the *henosis* of the *Mystical Theology* is not a Porphyrian fusion with the One beyond difference but rather a union with God that preserves the ontological difference through analogical relation. Indeed, God is equally participant in all beings, and beings participate differently in God as a function of their capacity to receive the gift of the excess of Being (*CH* 121C; *DN* 644B; *Epistles* 1092B).[71] Here Dionysius is much closer to the Proclean strand of Neo-Platonism, which emphasizes the ecstatic overflow of God, as I have already indicated.

For the Areopagite, God is both supra-existential and supra-essential (*DN* 956B; *MT* 1000A) prior even to the cause of Being — pure plenitude whose ecstatic overflow is both without and within the existence and essence of all that is. In the words of Fran O'Rourke, Dionysius conceives of divine being as "the plenary presence of the perfection of all reality."[72] The sheer excess of divine transcendence is such that God manifests himself in all that he brings into being out of nothingness. As a result, our apophatic ascent to the supreme Cause depends on its prior cataphatic descent in a dialectic of eminence that surpasses both modes. This is what the analogical relation between creative and created Goodness (ὁμοάγαθον) and Being (τὸ εἶναι) means for Dionysius.[73] God's love for his creation is manifested in the cataphatic

---

71. Roques, *L'univers dionysien*, pp. 59-67; Vladimir Lossky, "Le sens des 'analogies' chez Denys le Pseudo-Aréopagite," *Archives d'histoire doctrinale et littéraire du Moyen Âge* 5 (1930): 279-309.

72. Fran O'Rourke, *Pseudo-Dionysius and the Metaphysics of Aquinas* (Leiden: E. J. Brill, 1992), p. 69.

73. Cf. Walther Völker, *Kontemplation und Ekstase bei Pseudo-Dionysius Areopagita* (Wiesbaden: Steiner, 1958).

kenosis of the Incarnation: "[T]hough himself beyond being, he [Jesus] took upon himself the being of humans. Yet he is not less overflowing with transcendence. He is the ever-transcendent, and so superabundantly so" (*Epistles* 1072B). In the Letters, the Areopagite relates once more both cataphasis and apophasis to eminence in such a way that his theological metaphysics outflanks the ancient and modern dualism between presence and absence:

> Someone beholding God and understanding what he saw has not actually seen God himself but rather something of his which has being and which is knowable. For he himself solidly transcends mind and being. He is completely unknown and non-existent. He exists beyond being and he is known beyond the mind. And this quite positively complete unknowing is knowledge of him who is above everything that is known. (*Ep.* 1065A-B)

In different ways, both Lossky and Marion view Christian Neo-Platonism through the prism of modern philosophy. For this reason, they ignore the theological metaphysics that underpins the Dionysian corpus and transforms the account of being. As the gift of God, being is always already analogical and hierarchical. It is precisely the Platonist emphasis on the self-diffusive Good and the relational positioning of all things that separates the Areopagite's theology from the Porphyrian focus on unity with the One.

9. Individuation and Hierarchy

Like Augustine, Gregory, and Boethius, Dionysius eschews the Aristotelian language of individual substance and efficient causality in favor of a more Platonist vision of relational beings that participate in the creative activity of the first principle and final end in God. As such, both being and knowing are given rather than self-generated. According to the Areopagite, to receive and return the gift of being is to enter the (asymmetrical) movement of perfective elevation — the movement from and to God (not unlike *exitus* and *reditus* in Augustine). This also applies to how we come to know the supreme Cause. We are elevated to knowledge of God through the confluence of self-purification and divine illumination. To be purified is to abandon the contemplation of the self and the fixation on all things immanent. Likewise, illumination is the reception of the light that directs human sight to the threshold of the transcendent. Conjointly, purification and illumination uplift the mind beyond all there is to transcendence itself: "By an undivided and absolute abandonment of yourself and everything, shedding all and freed from all, you will be uplifted to the ray of the divine shadow which is above everything that is" (*MT* 997B–1000A).

This metaphysics of anagogy or elevation has a theological correlate, which is the doctrine of *creatio ex nihilo* — the gratuitous, free, and continuous divine gift of being that brings everything out of nothing into actuality. The Incarnation manifests God's kenotic descent and calls on the whole of creation to receive and return it liturgically in an asymmetrical gift-exchange that perfects the degrees of being of each creature standing in an analogical relation to its creator. Divine creativity issues forth in a sacred order wherein individuation is neither purely internal nor purely external to beings but instead marks God's gift of goodness that actualizes all things relationally. This sacred order is both hierarchical and participatory in the sense that the cosmos is characterized by degrees of being and perfection and things are positioned relationally at different stations in the hierarchy of creation.

Not unlike the other Church Fathers discussed in this essay, the immanent discloses for Dionysius the transcendent at the heart of the material world. As shown above, the doxological nature and dynamic of his theology exhorts beings to "turn to all of creation" (*DN* 593D) and discern the resemblance and analogical relation of all that is to the supreme Cause in God (*MT* 1000D–1001A) through purification and illumination. In this manner, we come to know the harmonious sacred order that underpins and upholds the whole of reality. This hierarchy of creation is intimated in the 'perceptible symbols' of natural and social life:

> . . . because of this inspired, hierarchical harmony each one is able to have as great as possible a share in him who is truly beautiful, wise and good. . . . We see our human hierarchy . . . as our nature allows, pluralized in a great variety of perceptible symbols lifting us upward hierarchically until we are brought as far as we can be into the unity of deification. . . . For us . . . it is by way of the perceptible images that we are uplifted as far as we can be to the contemplation of what is divine. Actually, it is the same one whom all one-like beings desire. . . . (*EH* 373A-B; translation modified)

Here as elsewhere in the Dionysian corpus, individuation is described in terms of the gift of goodness and being which enables us to participate in the creation of hierarchy.[74]

Like the whole of his theology, the notion of hierarchy has a profoundly doxological meaning; it denotes the sacred order of the celestial and the ecclesiastical hierarchy, which are triadically arranged (the three orders of the three angels) and express heavenly and earthly praise of God. Dionysius transforms the Proclean idea of polytheistic divine energies and different rituals for the simple and the wise in the direction of a doxological metaphysics where the whole world speaks of God and in praise of Creator and his creation. Conjointly all the forces constitute a cosmic liturgy and form a hierarchical symphony that reflects the beauty of God and extends from the seraphim, the archangels, and angels to man and the whole of the natural world. As such, the doxological is neither invented by humans to contain religious experience nor is it limited to the ecclesia. On the contrary, liturgy is at the heart of divine creativity and of God's gift of being and goodness. The Creator reveals himself as one and triune through the praise of his work as expressed through the Son and the Holy Spirit, who bind together the all of creation in hymns of praise — an elevating of *hymnein* to God with songs of praise that are reflected and embodied in sacramental rites and divine works. As such, liturgy is also always theurgic and theurgy is also always liturgical. Likewise, deification is elevating and elevation is deifying.

The mystery of divine Creation and Incarnation is not confined to the sacramental rites within the ecclesiastical hierarchy but extends to the entire cosmos. The Areopagite, following Proclus's harmony of the celestial choirs, complements in some important way Augustine's 'musical metaphysics' with a stronger emphasis on liturgical theurgy and anagogical *theosis*. Since this cosmic praise encompasses each individual, unique path back to the Creator, it is also the case that God is not just intelligible to the few wise who cognize him through abstract concepts. Rather, divine disclosure is dispersed throughout the cosmos and perceptible for all in simple images as much as in apophatic contemplation — if not more so. For the light of truth and love shines forth in the world and illuminates our mind to see divine beauty in all created things as

---

74. Ronald F. Hathaway, *Hierarchy and the Definition of Order in the Letters of Pseudo-Dionysius: A Study in the Form and Meaning of the Pseudo-Dionysian Writings* (The Hague: Nijhoff, 1969).

mediated through our senses. The supernaturally infused gifts of faith and grace direct our natural desire to know the first cause and final end, towards an encounter with God in Christ.

10. Conclusion: Analogical Hierarchy

In this chapter, I have argued that Boethius deploys both Platonist and Aristotelian concepts in order to give a more systematic exposition of Augustine's Trinitarian theology. Beyond Greek metaphysics, he argues that only God's love and goodness can explain why particular sensible things are brought out of nothing into existence. Beyond Augustine's theory of illumination, he provides an epistemology centered upon Plato's account of universals and Aristotle's metaphysics of act and potency. What constitutes individuals *qua* individuals is the relation of universal form to particular matter. And what perfects individual form is the ever more intense actualization of universal form in particular things, above all the exercise of justice, which preserves and enhances the goodness of all nondivine substances.

More specifically, to know a thing is for Boethius to cognize the ontological coincidence of universal form instantiated in particular matter. Thus to know a thing is to cognize *that* thing's relation with *esse,* which brings beings from potency into actuality and makes them what they are. For Boethius, universals only exist in particulars, and the logic that governs the link between particulars and universals is relation, which is in some sense prior to participation because participation alone cannot explain why universals are present in particulars. By contrast, the (onto-) logic of creation and the relation between *ipsum esse* and *id quod est* can account for the ontological and noetic coincidence of particulars and universals. Participation describes how a particular thing further actualizes its potency and thereby perfects its universal form in particular diverse ways. So while relation explains why created things can be said to be good, participation shows how something that is good can also be just. This is how Boethius connects the metaphysical dimension of individuation to his conception of politics.

Whereas Boethius emphasizes participation and analogy, Dionysius the Areopagite accentuates hierarchy and anagogy. Transforming the pagan Neo-Platonism of Proclus, he links sacred triad and the cosmic movement of all things towards union with the first principles to Trinitarian traces in the world and union with God the Creator. In so doing, the Areopagite combines Plato's focus on the Good with Aristotle's emphasis on the unity of existence and essence in substances. Moreover, Dionysius ties Augustinian divine illumination to deification and develops a cosmic and doxological theology that blends liturgy and theurgy.

In this manner, individuation is neither intrinsic nor extrinsic to things but instead marks God's gift of being and goodness, which are received and returned in an asymmetrical gift-exchange within the twin ecclesiastical and celestial hierarchy of the divinely sustained order of creation. As such, Dionysius' focus on cosmic praise and mystical ascent outwits in advance the false early modern divide between the purely rational and the purely affective, as chapter 9 will also suggest. Before that, Part II of this book will examine how the shared patristic legacy of Augustine, Gregory, Boethius, and Dionysius was received and transformed by medieval theology and in what ways the theological metaphysics of creation and individuation evolved.

Matter and Form

In his Regensburg lecture of 2006, Pope Benedict XVI firmly ties metaphysics to politics by linking violence in religion to the absoluteness of divine volition in Islam. Controversially, his argument is that in the dominant Islamic traditions of Sunnism and Shi'ism, God's will is inscrutable and therefore unintelligible to the human mind. As a result, divine injunctions cannot be fully understood and must instead be blindly obeyed. In other words, the Pope's charge is that the gulf between God and human categories in much of Islam diminishes the 'grandeur of reason' by sundering rationality from faith. Taken to its extreme, this paved the way for the secretly collusive complicity of fideism and rationalism in such a way that absolute divine power is disjoined from divine intellect and becomes the overriding category. What underpins all this is a series of metaphysical positions that Benedict calls into question: first of all, an incipient dualism between essence and existence; second, a separation of human agency from divine creativity; third, the rise to power of both militant secularism and religious fundamentalism, which are mirror images of each other insofar as both combine a blind transcendentalism of the will with an empty positivism of power.

As I will argue in the second part of this essay, the origins of the modern separation of reason from faith can in fact be traced to the confluence of certain developments in both Islamic and Christian theology as early as the late eleventh and the twelfth century. Indeed, there are key elements in the works of Avicenna (Ibn Sīnā) and Gilbert Porreta that gave rise to a whole series of modern dualisms. By contrast, influential thirteenth-century figures such as Aquinas and Al-Arabī opposed this strand of medieval thinking by appealing to a richer and more complex synthesis of theology, philosophy, and mysticism that puts a greater emphasis on participation and mediation. This theological resistance to the proto-secular tendencies has important implications for present and future efforts to restore the 'grandeur of reason' and envision a proper engagement among the faiths and also between religious and other ideological bodies around a debate on universals such as the nature of the divine, the relation between peace and justice, and the irreducible link between ethics, politics, and economics.

The next three chapters turn to medieval accounts of creation and individuation, in particular the work of Gilbert Porreta (c. 1085-1154), St. Thomas Aquinas (c. 1225-1274), John Duns Scotus (1265/66-1308), William of Ockham (1288/89-1349), and Jean Buridan (c. 1300-1361). In chapters 4 and 5, I examine two rival interpretations of Boethius, that of Porreta and that of Aquinas. My argument is that Gilbert inherited a tradition that was no longer primarily metaphysical but instead tended to privilege logic and grammar. Within this strand of Platonism and Neo-Platonism, the primacy of mathematics over physics or natural philosophy led to an increasing formalization of theology and prioritized unity and individuality over against diversity and relationality. In chapter 5, I explore how Aquinas drew not only on Aristotelian 'first philosophy' but also on Platonist metaphysics in order to reconfigure *divina scientia*. My contention is that he developed a metaphysics of creation and individuation that blends the universality of the act of being with the particularity of beings in act. By extending and transforming Augustine's and Boethius' metaphysics, Aquinas showed that relations individuate substances and that the act of being is the ultimate cause of individuation.

Finally, I investigate in chapter 6 how Scotus, Ockham, and Buridan radicalized the twelfth-century separation of theology and philosophy and the importance of logic and semantics as the foundation of metaphysics. In spite of some significant differences, Scotus, Ockham, and Buridan share the idea that individuality is more real than universality and that material substances are self-individuating. The elimination of God from actuality entails the exclusion of divine creative action from the actualization and individuation of particular sensible things. This marks a fundamental rupture from the metaphysics of relationality and participation, for the individuating relation of creation becomes unhinged and is progressively replaced by the idea of individuality as a decree of God's absolute power.

CHAPTER 4

The Priority of Essence over Existence

1. Introduction: Islam, Christianity, and the Medieval Roots of Modernity

In his groundbreaking Regensburg address, Pope Benedict XVI links a postsecular politics to a presecular metaphysics.[1] The metaphysics underpinning the Pope's narrative offers a rich and as yet unrealized potential for an alternative modernity where both the rationalism of militant secularists and the fideism of religious fundamentalists are abandoned in favor of the 'grandeur of reason' and a new kind of engagement between all faiths and cultures — above all the world's largest religions, Christianity and Islam. For Benedict, it is now equally clear that the modern divorce of religion from politics reinforces the absolutism of secular reason and the "dictatorship of relativism which does not recognize anything as definitive and whose ultimate goal consists solely of one's own ego and desires."[2]

1. Pope Benedict XVI, "Glaube, Vernunft und Universität. Erinnerungen und Reflexionen," lecture at the University of Regensburg on 12 September 2006, available online at http://www.vatican.va/holy_father/benedict_xvi/speeches/2006/september/documents/hf_ben-xvi_spe_20060912_university-regensburg_ge.html. Published as *Glaube und Vernunft. Die Regensburger Vorlesung* (Freiburg: Herder, 2006); *The Regensburg Lecture,* trans. James V. Schall, SJ (Chicago: St. Augustine's Press, 2007).

2. Joseph Cardinal Ratzinger, "Homily during the Mass *pro eligendo romano pontifice,*" 18 April 2005, online at http://www.vatican.va/gpII/documents/homily-pro-eligendo-pontifice_20050418_en.html.

Benedict's political critique of value-free democracy (in his dialogue with Jürgen Habermas) and his social and cultural critique of the 'dictatorship of relativism' are of a piece with his theological defense of the Hellenic metaphysics of relationality and the biblical doctrine of creation *ex nihilo*. By making these and other complex links in the Regensburg address (which were clearly lost on most commentators), the Pope was asking nothing less than whether the modern poles of the individual and the collective (and cognate ideas such as freedom and justice, rights and responsibility, etc.) are caught within shared secular, liberal axioms. These axioms are *also* those of theocratic fundamentalisms since they equally deal in a politics of the indifferent will, inherited — as is also the case in the end for liberalism — from the nominalism and voluntarism of the late Middle Ages, as André de Muralt has documented.[3] Benedict's paradoxical argument is that a postsecular politics requires a presecular metaphysics. The theological origins of secular modernity will be one of the main arguments in this part of the essay.

In calling for the 'rehellenization' of Christianity, Benedict renews not just the synthesis of the Fathers and the Doctors of the Church but also the Hellenic Jewish tradition in which both Jesus and the Apostles were rooted. The encounter between biblical revelation and ancient philosophy marked the advent of universalism beyond divine election and the law, as Alain Badiou and others have convincingly argued. This encounter also gave rise to the pan-European civilization that is now under threat from both modern militant secularism and modern religious extremism. In this light, a fundamental question raised by the Regensburg address is how Christianity, which as a result of shifts within Christian theology was so deeply implicated in the genesis of secular modernity, can offer a postsecular alternative. This is linked to the contemporary resurgence of religion in international relations and the growing importance of Islam in global politics.[4] It was of course in the same Regensburg lecture that Pope Benedict linked violence in religion to the absoluteness of divine volition in Islam, as I suggested in the introduction to Part II of this book. All this raises questions about the origins and nature of modernity.

3. Alain de Muralt, *L'unité de la philosophie politique. De Scot, Occam et Suárez au libéralisme contemporain* (Paris: Vrin, 2002).

4. See, *inter alia*, Pavlos Hatzopoulos and Fabio Petito, eds., *Religion in International Relations: The Return from Exile* (London: Palgrave Macmillan, 2003); Scott M. Thomas, *The Global Resurgence of Religion and the Transformation of International Relations: The Struggle for the Soul of the Twenty-First Century* (London: Palgrave Macmillan, 2005).

In this chapter, I will argue that the original modern separation of reason from faith can in fact be traced to the confluence of certain developments in both Islamic and Christian theology as early as the late eleventh and the twelfth century, in particular key elements in the works of Avicenna (Ibn Sīnā) and Gilbert Porreta such as the priority of essence over existence, the separation of philosophy from theology, and the primacy of individual substance over relational particulars.[5] By contrast, influential thirteenth-century figures such as Aquinas and Al-Arabī opposed these dualisms. Instead, they retrieved and extended a more mediated tradition that shifts the emphasis back on the participation of the whole of creation in divine creativity. Before I can outline this tradition, I will explore how the twin questions of creation and individuation were articulated in the eleventh and the twelfth centuries in both Islamic and Christian theology.

2. The Division of Ontology and Theology in Early Islamic Philosophy

A. Al-Kindī and Al-Fārābī

The relationship between philosophy and theology has arguably been the main determinant in the history of ideas since the encounter of biblical revelation and ancient reason. There can be little doubt that it has decisively shaped the evolution of both Christianity and Islam. From the dawn of the church to the end of the Middle Ages, ancient philosophy was integral to Christian theology, commencing with St. Paul, the Apostolic Fathers, and the Apologists, as I argued in chapter 2. Though early patristic figures such as Tatian and Tertullian accused pagan thought of engendering heresy, the Fathers and Doctors of the Church spoke of *philosophia christiana* (Augustine) and *divina scientia* (Aquinas). By contrast, Plato and Aristotle were absent from the formative period of Islam and marginal during the first two centuries until a concerted translation movement centered in Baghdad made the philosophic inheritance of the Greeks available in Arabic — with the help of many Syriac Christians such as Hunayn ibn Ishāq and his son Ishāq ibn Hunayn in the ninth cen-

---

5. Cf. Edward Booth, *Aristotelian Aporetic Ontology in Islamic and Christian Thinkers* (Cambridge: Cambridge University Press, 1983).

tury.[6] Based on translated manuscripts of Aristotle and Neo-Platonist thinkers from Plotinus to Proclus, it was Al-Kindī (d. 870) — the founder of Islamic philosophy — who stated that metaphysics is theological. For 'first philosophy' studies the truth that is one, and only God is pure oneness *(wahda faqat mahd):*

> Indeed, the human art which is highest in degree and most noble in rank is the art of philosophy, the definition of which is knowledge of the true nature of things, insofar as is possible for man. The aim of the philosopher is, as regards his knowledge, to attain the truth, and as regards his action, to act truthfully. . . . We do not find the truth we are seeking without finding a cause; the cause of the existence and continuance of everything is the True One, in that each thing which has being has truth. The True One exists necessarily, and therefore beings exist. . . . The noblest part of philosophy and the highest in degree is first philosophy, by which I mean the science of the First Truth, Who is the cause of all truth.[7]

Following Al-Kindī, Al-Fārābī (c. 870-950) argues that both reason and revelation share the same first principles and final ends. Since they enable proper perception and intellectual vision, the theoretical virtues of 'true philosophy' are indispensable to knowledge of the truth and supreme happiness *(sa'adah),*[8] a concept that provides the link between his reflections on ontology and his foundational contribution to Islamic political philosophy.[9] Influenced by Ammonius (c. 435/445-517/526), who harmonized Aristotle with Plato by (wrongly) claiming that the Prime

6. On Hunayn's role, see A. Z. Iskandar, "Hunayn Ibn Ishāq," in *The Dictionary of Scientific Biography,* ed. Charles Coulston Gillispie (New York: Charles Scribner's Sons, 1978), vol. 15 (suppl. 1), pp. 230-49. On the dissemination of Greek philosophy and theology in the Arabic world via Syriac translations beginning in the fifth century, see Cristina D'Ancona, "Greek into Arabic: Neoplatonism in Translation," in *The Cambridge Companion to Arabic Philosophy,* ed. Peter Adamson and Richard C. Taylor (Cambridge: Cambridge University Press, 2005), pp. 10-31.

7. Al-Kindī, "On First Philosophy," in Alfred L. Ivry, *Al-Kindī's Metaphysics* (Albany: State University of New York Press, 1974), pp. 55, 98.

8. Al-Fārābī, "Part I: The Attainment of Happiness," in Al-Fārābī, *Philosophy of Plato and Aristotle,* trans. Mushin Mahdi, rev. ed. (Ithaca, NY: Cornell University Press, 2001), iv.55-56, pp. 44-45.

9. Muhsin S. Mahdi, *Alfarabi and the Foundation of Islamic Political Philosophy: Essays in Interpretation* (Chicago: University of Chicago Press, 2001).

Mover is not just the final but also the efficient cause which brings the sublunary world into being,[10] Al-Fārābī contends that the work of Plato and that of Aristotle are identical: "Let it be clear to you that, in what they presented, their purpose is the same, and that they intended to offer one and the same philosophy." Since "the true philosophy" (according to which "the idea of Imam, Philosopher and Legislator is a single idea") "was handed down to us by the Greeks from Plato and Aristotle only," Al-Fārābī rejects the idea of a diametric opposition between ancient reason and religious revelation. Instead, he insists that the true philosopher "should have sound conviction about the opinions of the religion in which he is reared, hold fast to the virtuous acts in his religion and not forsake all or most of them."[11]

In line with the strongly Aristotelianized strand of Neo-Platonism stretching from Porphyry to Ammonius that grounds the study of being in logic, Al-Fārābī was the first Islamic philosopher to posit a real distinction between existence and essence in created beings. The concept of a form-matter compound does not imply that a thing exists, and knowledge of a thing's essence does not require that thing's existence. Just as existence is ordered as a predicate to essence in the order of logic, so existence is ordered merely as an accident to essence in the order of being. In God existence and essence coincide because according to Neo-Platonist cosmology there is a hierarchical gradation of being, and the highest being is the One whose simplicity and indivisibility rule out any real distinction between existence and essence.

However, there is in Al-Fārābī's work an incipient split between ontology and theology that betrays his logicized and Aristotelianized Neo-Platonism. Ontologically, there must be a first cause and a final end of all that is because causation and generation cannot have an infinite regress. Even though in the Neo-Platonist scheme the cause is superior to its effects, both are inscribed within the same horizon of being as a result of the 'onto-theo-logic' of emanation. As such, God as the Active Intellect that causes the existence of nature and natural things through self-reflection falls under the same concept of being as beings that emanate

---

10. On the opposition between Plato and Aristotle in relation to efficient causality and the creative activity of God, see, *supra*, chapter 1. On the different strands of Neo-Platonism (Porphyrian-Ammonian vs. Iamblichean-Proclean) that shaped Christian and Islamic philosophy and theology, see below main text and also chapters 3 and 5.

11. Al-Fārābī, "Part I: The Attainment of Happiness," iv.63-64, pp. 49-50; iv.57, p. 46; iv.60, p. 48.

from it.[12] This leads Al-Fārābī to claim that first philosophy is primarily the study of being *qua* being and only incidentally of God. In part, the division between ontology and theology is the result of Al-Fārābī's failure to recognize Plato's conception of ideas or forms as the metaphysical relation between the immaterial Good and all material things. For this and other reasons, he concludes his commentary on Aristotle by stating that "we do not possess metaphysical science."[13]

Theologically, Al-Fārābī appeals to the Plotinian scheme of emanation whereby the First Cause (in thinking itself) emanates the immaterial being of the first intellect, which in turn thinks of the First Cause and of itself. Thus a multiplicity of being and thought ensues. But in the absence of a transcendent Good that brings all things into being and makes them what they are, Al-Fārābī's reliance on the Aristotelian logic of causality leads him to restrict rational knowledge of the highest being to an anonymous first cause that is the source of all being — about which he says that "one should believe that it is God."[14] This division of ontology from theology foreshadows a proto-modern separation of reason from faith and the contours of Islamic rationalism and fideism that can in part be traced to Avicenna or Ibn Sīnā (c. 980-1037), who together with Averroes or Ibn Rushd (c. 1126-1198)[15] was the most influential Islamic philosopher and theologian in the Middle Ages.

B. Avicenna

Avicenna is notorious for having read Aristotle's *Metaphysics* forty times and knowing it off by heart without, however, grasping the meaning of first philosophy. It was only after consulting Al-Fārābī's commentary on the Stagirite that Avicenna understood why metaphysics is first and foremost the study of being *qua* being and not principally of God. Even though he describes metaphysics as 'divine science' and 'absolute wis-

---

12. Al-Fārābī, "Part III: The Philosophy of Aristotle," in *Philosophy of Plato and Aristotle*, xix.129-30, pp. 128-29.

13. Al-Fārābī, "Part III: The Philosophy of Aristotle," xix.133, p. 130.

14. Quoted in David C. Reisman, "Al-Fārābī and the Philosophical Curriculum," in *The Cambridge Companion to Arabic Philosophy*, pp. 52-71 (57).

15. Jan A. Aertsen and Gerhard Endress, eds., *Averroes and the Aristotelian Tradition: Sources, Constitution and Reception of the Philosophy of Ibn Rushd (1126-1198). Proceedings of the Fourth Symposium Averroicum* (Leiden: E. J. Brill, 1999).

dom,' he also clearly states that the subject-matter of metaphysics is the existent *(al-mawjūd)* insofar as it exists "rather than the more specific existence of God, which is 'sought' rather than 'postulated' in that science [i.e., metaphysics]."[16] Unlike Al-Kindī, who associates first philosophy with the highest truth in God, Islamic thought after Al-Fārābī and Avicenna tends to redefine metaphysics as the study of being *qua* being or ontology.[17]

Moreover, Avicenna reconfigures not just the subject-matter of metaphysics but also the object of the new science of ontology, replacing the Neo-Platonist emphasis upon God's power of being *(virtus essendi)*, which brings everything into actuality and makes it what it is, with a more logicized Aristotelian stress on divine essence, which causes nondivine essences. Reading the work of Aristotle and the Neo-Platonists through the prism of Al-Fārābī's real distinction between existence and essence, he agrees with his forebear that a thing's existence is extrinsic to its essence and that 'thing' is the supreme genus, divisible into the species 'existent' and the species 'nonexistent.'[18] Coupled with the abstraction of 'existence' *(wujūd)* from 'existent' *(mawjūd)* and of 'thingness' *(shay'iyya)* from 'thing' *(shay)*, Avicenna subsequently replaced 'thingness' with the Aristotelian-Fārābian notion of essence or quiddity *(māhiyya)* — an early indication of his onto-logical essentialism.

Indeed, Avicenna's variant of the distinction between existence and nonexistence further devalues a thing's actual existentiality in favor of its abstract essentiality because the cause and principle of individuation does not encompass the coming into being of particular things but is instead confined to a being's 'thingness,' which is independent of that thing's actualization.[19] As Robert Wisnovsky has convincingly argued,

16. Avicenna, *Metaphysics,* trans. P. Morewedge (Chicago: University of Chicago Press, 1973), I.6.

17. For references to the scholarship of Dimitri Gutas and Amos Bertolacci documenting the shift in the Islamic tradition from a theological to an ontological conception of metaphysics, see Thérèse-Anne Druart, "Metaphysics," in *The Cambridge Companion to Arabic Philosophy,* pp. 327-48, esp. p. 328.

18. The priority of thing over existent and nonexistent in Al-Fārābī derives from the Mu'tazilī *mutakallimūm,* who formed the first school of Islamic doctrinal theology and argued that 'thing' *(shay')* is the most universal category applicable to reality, which can be subdivided into 'existent' *(mawjūd)* and 'nonexistent' *(ma'dūm)*.

19. Avicenna, *Metaphysics* VII.1; cf. David Burrell, "Essence and Existence: Avicenna and Greek Philosophy," *Mélanges de l'Institut Dominicain des Études Orientales* 17 (1986): 53-66.

what underpins Avicenna's ontology is the logical primacy of a thing's 'what-ness' (or essence) over above that thing's 'that-ness' (or existence): "Even if we permit Avicenna to deny having advocated an ontological scheme — analogous to the Mu'tazilī's and Al-Fārābī's views — in which 'thing' is extensionally broader than existent, 'thing' will at least be seen now to enjoy a logical priority over existent, that is, be viewed as more basic than existent."[20] Therefore, Avicenna's ontology can perhaps be described as a 'meta-logic' of essences.

It is hard to overstate the preeminence of logic vis-à-vis ontology and theology in Avicenna. Beyond Aristotle, he develops the logical distinction between the first object of the intellect and the second object which is human knowledge of the real in an ontological and epistemological direction by claiming that the categories of logic precede both universality and particularity and that universal created essences are prior to their particular embodiment.[21] For Avicenna, 'horseness' is the essence of horse, and, like all other created essences, this essence exists and can be known independently of whether it refers to the horse in general or to a living horse in particular.[22] That is why Avicenna coins a dictum that was frequently quoted in the Middle Ages: *equinitas est equinitas tantum.*[23] Since created essences are indifferent to the singularity of particulars and the universality of being, it is logic that grounds and governs physics, mathematics, and first philosophy (or theology) — Aristotle's tripartite division of the sciences. For Avicenna, the object of logic is the totality of universal categories. By contrast, the object of physics is individual existent things, that of ontology is the general realm of being *qua* being, and that of theology is the more specific coincidence of existence and essence in God. Avicenna's meta-logical ontology of abstract disembodied essences severs the metaphysical relation between particular created beings and the universal being of the Creator God, which is

20. Robert Wisnovsky, "Avicenna and the Avicennian Tradition," in *The Cambridge Companion to Arabic Philosophy,* pp. 105-13 (109).

21. Conor Cunningham, *Genealogy of Nihilism: Philosophies of Nothing and the Difference of Theology* (London: Routledge, 2002), esp. pp. 9-13.

22. Avicenna Latinus, *Liber de philosophia prima sive scientia divina,* ed. S. Van Riet, 2 vols. (Louvain: E. Peeters, 1980), p. 233, line 36–p. 234, line 44. Cf. Avicenna, *Opera,* trans. Dominic Gundissalinus (Venice: Bonetus Locatellus for Octavianus Scotus, 1508), folio 87ra.

23. Étienne Gilson, *La philosophie au Moyen Âge. Des origines patristiques à la fin du XIVe siècle,* 2nd rev. ed. (Paris: Éditions Payot & Rivages, 1999 [1922]), p. 352.

central to the vision of the ecstatic, plenitudinous, self-diffusive Good in the Boethian-Dionysian and Iamblichean-Proclean strands of Neo-Platonism.

Moreover, Avicenna also posits an absolute essence beyond material embodiment and mental existence, which is "possible of existence in itself" *(mumkin al-wujūd bi-dhātihi).*[24] As such, essence is not just logically prior to existence but it is also extensionally broader than existence — with the implication that there are essences in the divine mind that are never actualized. But since for Avicenna all actual essences necessarily emanate from the first cause whose essence *is* existence, there is a tension between the monism of the uncreated cause and the dualism of a created being whose existence is extrinsic to the essence that must somehow preexist in God.[25] Although he seems to distance himself from this sort of 'meta-logic' of essences in other passages of the *Metaphysics* in the *Shifā*, the ambiguity in relation to the philosophical status of essence and existence has shaped the entire Islamic philosophical tradition (perhaps with the exception of certain mystics like Al-Arabī). This influence is evinced, for example, by the false opposition between the essentialism of Suhrawardī (d. 1191), who equates existence with products of the mind *(i'tibārī),* and the existentialism of Mullā Sadrā (d. 1640), who reduces essences to mere mental constructs. In either case, created beings entertain a merely causal link with uncreated being, and the real ontological difference between existence and essence is replaced by simply conceptual distinctions.

Even those theologians *(mutakallimūm)* such as Al-Rāzī (d. 1210) and Al-Tūsī (d. 1274) who attempt to chart a middle ground tend to start on the basis of Avicenna's logicized ontology and the introduction of abstract essentiality into theology.[26] In this setting, both Shī'ī and Sunnī *mutakallimūm* disseminate the Avicennian tradition even when they reject certain aspects of it such as the idea of necessity in creation, which many opposed on the grounds of absolute divine power and volition.

24. Avicenna, *Isagoge,* in *Treatise on Logic,* trans. F. Zabeeh (The Hague: Martinus Nijhoff, 1974), I.2.

25. Amélie-Marie Goichon, *La distinction de l'essence et de l'existence d'après Ibn Sīnā (Avicenne)* (Paris: Desclée de Brouwer, 1937), pp. 3-148.

26. Among many others, see Amélie-Marie Goichon, *La philosophie d'Avicenne et son influence en Europe médiévale,* 2nd rev. ed. (Paris: Adrien-Maisonneuve, 1951), pp. 89-133; Robert Wisnovsky, *Avicenna's Metaphysics in Context* (Ithaca, NY: Cornell University Press, 2003).

Avicenna's fusion of Arabic Aristotelianized Neo-Platonist philosophy *(falsafa)* with Islamic doctrinal theology *(kalām)* predetermined the conceptual space within which Islamic thought evolved. Crucially, this underscores a profound consensus in Islamic philosophy and theology centered on the Avicennian onto-theological priority of essence vis-à-vis existence (and God's act of being) and the concomitant primacy of possibility over actuality.

Taken together, Avicenna's essentialism and his possibilism introduce necessity in creation and drive a wedge between reason and faith. Indeed, Avicenna's idea of essence 'possible of existence in itself' *(mumkin al-wujūd bi-dhātihi)* is linked to his conception of God as that which is "[the] necessary of existence in itself" *(wājib al-wujūd bi-dhātihi).*[27] Beyond the Ammonian fusion of Aristotle with Plato, Avicenna's variant of Islamic Neo-Platonism makes two claims: first, that this sort of necessity implies divine qualities such as simplicity, immutability, and eternality, to which all other types of necessity ultimately refer; second, that this necessity is the productive source of all other necessities. Avicenna's God is both a final and efficient cause whose effects are 'necessary of existence through another' *(wājib al-wujūd bi-ghayrihi).* In *Metaphysics* I.6, Avicenna insists that essence determines existence: a thing whose essence is insufficient to bring it into existence is caused, whereas a thing whose essence is sufficient to bring it into existence is uncaused.

Avicenna's emphasis on the unity of being in virtue of essence is the philosophical parallel of the Mu'tazilī *mutakallimūm,* who viewed really distinct divine attributes as a violation of Islam's cardinal tenet of God's indivisible oneness *(tawhīd).* As the only being in which existence is the same as essence, God is the sufficient condition of possibility for the necessary existence of possible essences. That is why in Avicenna's theology (according to the Latin translation) God is *necesse esse (wājib al-wujūd bi-dhātihi),* whereas everything else is possible and actualized through God's absolute necessity. But the implication is that the actuality of particular beings discloses nothing other than the dependence of their essence on a higher cause. Since their existence is extrinsic to their essence, knowledge of what actually existent things are does not require or involve knowledge of why *that* thing exists or what it is that

27. Goichon, *La distinction de l'essence et de l'existence d'après Ibn Sīnā (Avicenne),* pp. 156-200.

brought *that* thing into actuality. So just as at the metaphysical level essence precedes existence by a sort of disjunctive echo that paradoxically cuts off actual existents from the divine exactly to the extent that they depend on it for their existence, so at the theological level the primacy of necessity and possibility over actuality diminishes divine intellection of beings in favor of divine volition that wills essences into an existence that remains purely extrinsic, accidental, and thus arbitrary from a human perspective.

That is how Avicenna introduces a radical rupture in Neo-Platonist theology between Creator and creation. In consequence, human reason can only infer the necessary existence of a first cause that is the source of all possible essences. But faith alone confirms that the God of Aristotle is in fact the God of the Qur'an. By contrast with other Neo-Platonists before Avicenna such as Boethius and Al-Kindī, who argued that reason can have a certain approximate knowledge of God as the highest being beyond being, Avicenna tends to separate reason from faith and to restrict knowledge of the divine as the first principle and final end of all that is to the 'holy intellect' *(intellectus sanctus)* of the Prophet Mohammed. Avicenna's ontology of essences serves to reinforce the emphasis in Islamic theology on the priority of divine volition over divine intellection — a voluntarism that is prominent in the orthodox Sunnī tradition but absent from many strands of Shī'ī and Sufi mysticism.

As I have already indicated, Avicenna's synthesis of Aristotelianized Neo-Platonist philosophy *(falsafa)* and Islamic doctrinal theology *(kalām)* shaped Islamic thought throughout the Middle Ages and the early modern era in the Arab world and beyond. However, it would be historically inaccurate and theologically simplistic to attribute knowledge of Aristotle in Christian Europe to the rapid expansion of Islam or to blame Islamic philosophy for the rise of radical Aristotelianism at Christian universities in the twelfth century. Rather, there is growing evidence to suggest that already at the time of St. Anselm, medieval Christian theologians had access to key elements of Aristotelian and Neo-Platonist metaphysics via the Latin translations of Greek patristic works in the monastic and cathedral libraries of England and Normandy.[28] Moreover, Sylvain Gouguenheim has shown that Aristotle in the original Greek was known at Gall and Mont Saint-Michel prior to the arrival of

---

28. For example, see Giles E. M. Gasper, *Anselm of Canterbury and His Theological Inheritance* (Aldershot, UK: Ashgate, 2004), esp. pp. 107-73 and 201-6.

Arabic translations.[29] Coupled with the transmission of Christian Neo-Platonism by the Latin Church Fathers, medieval Christian theology was in fact permeated by Greek philosophy based on original sources in a variety of places. For precisely this reason, the acceptance of radical Aristotelianism by Christian theologians cannot be blamed on the advent of Islam in Europe. Instead, it was a shift internal to Christian theology in the late eleventh and the twelfth century that paved the way for the reception and integration of Aristotelian-Avicennian essentialism into the Christian tradition. The key figure in this process was Gilbert Porreta (c. 1085-1154) and the Porretan School he inspired, as I will argue in the following sections.

3. The Turn from Being to Essence in Medieval Christian Theology

Not unlike later Islamic Neo-Platonists like Al-Kindī, early Christian Neo-Platonists such as Boethius followed Aristotle's distinction of theoretical and practical science and his tripartite division of theoretical science into physics, mathematics, and first philosophy (or theology) — as I showed in the previous chapter. Accordingly, theology is a properly philosophical discipline because like physics and mathematics, it deploys rational concepts and does not operate on the basis of supernatural faith alone. As the science that investigates the "very being and the source of being,"[30] theology orders all sciences because all sensible particular things intimate being itself *(esse ipsum)*, which brings them into existence and makes them what they are. Only knowledge of being itself enables a proper grasp of universals in particulars. Both mathematics and physics are indispensable to the process of abstraction and to knowledge of the actual world, but they are framed by the primacy of being over knowing and of theology over ontology.

By contrast, Gilbert Porreta who commented extensively on Boethius inherited a tradition that was no longer primarily concerned with the metaphysical reality of the self-diffusive Good of God but instead focused on dialectical and grammatical questions like the philo-

---

29. Sylvain Gouguenheim, *Aristote au Mont Saint-Michel. Les racines grecques de l'Europe chrétienne* (Paris: Éditions du Seuil, 2008).

30. Boethius, *De Trinitate*, II.19-21 (8-10).

sophical status of mental language. He was influenced by twelfth-century theology, in particular the metaphysically impoverished Platonism of Roscelin de Compiègne (c. 1050-1120), who claimed that words signify things literally and that there is a proper substance that corresponds to each noun.[31] Coupled with the geometrical method based on Euclidean a priori assumptions, this 'grammatical Platonism' (Jean Jolivet)[32] tends to privilege discursive mediation over above sensory mediation and the imagination. It maintains that linguistic conventions and rules of language determine knowledge and the human understanding of God's unity and triunity. Knowledge of the individuality of universal substances is thus grounded in the singularity of names and not in the actuality of actual particular things known through perception, the imagination, and abstraction, as for Christian Neo-Platonists in East and West such as Gregory of Nyssa, Augustine, Dionysius the Areopagite, and Boethius — as I have shown in chapters 2 and 3.

First I will put Gilbert Porreta's work in context before discussing its impact on Christian theology from the mid-twelfth century to the early fourteenth century. Unlike Boethius before him and Aquinas after him, Porreta did not bequeath to philosophy and theology the same range of seminal works as the *Opuscula sacra* or the *Summa Theologiae*. There are only three writings that can be attributed unequivocally to him, all of which are commentaries: on Boethius' *Opuscula sacra*, on the Psalms, and on the Pauline epistles. However, Gilbert's influence was significant because his works made a decisive contribution to the very terms of philosophical and theological debates that were to prevail from the second half of the twelfth to the early fourteenth century. Chief of all was his reconceptualization of two methods of demonstration: dialectical *quaestiones* and 'mathematical' reasoning *(more geometrico)*, to which I will return.

What is more contentious is the nature of Porreta's influence on medieval philosophy and theology. His distinction between *quod est* and

31. Marie-Dominique Chenu, "Un essai de méthode théologique au XIIe siècle," *Revue des Sciences Philosophiques et Théologiques* 24 (1935): 258-67; Chenu, *La théologie au douzième siècle*, 3rd ed. (Paris: Vrin, 1976), esp. pp. 109-58, 309-22; Constant J. Mews, "Nominalism and Theology before Abaelard: New Light on Roscelin of Compiègne," *Vivarium* 30 (1992): 4-33.

32. Jean Jolivet, *Aspects de la pensée médiévale: Abélard. Doctrines du langage* (Paris: Vrin, 1987); J. Jolivet, "Rhétorique et théologie dans une page de Gilbert de Poitiers," in *Gilbert de Poitiers et ses contemporains. Aux origines de la logica modernorum*, ed. Jean Jolivet and Alain de Libera (Naples: Bibliopolis, 1987), pp. 183-97.

quo est, which he developed in his commentary on Boethius' *De hebdomadibus,* is widely accepted as the most important contribution of his work. There are however two competing interpretations of Gilbert's works, particularly regarding this distinction. The first interpretation is similar to the reading of Boethius, according to which this distinction is best understood in terms of existence and essence. Since Berthaud devoted the first monograph to Porreta's philosophy in 1892,[33] in which he argued that this distinction is real, a large number of works have addressed the nature of this distinction (real, formal, causal, or objective) and its philosophical and theological ramifications, in particular the status of essence with respect to *esse.*[34] By contrast, the second interpretation contends that Gilbert's distinction can only be understood in the light of his division of the sciences and the classification of natural and theological rules or modes of reasoning *(rationes).* This interpretation, which was pioneered by Grabmann and systematized by Schmidt,[35] raises two sets of questions. First, is Porreta's method predominantly shaped by semantics, grammar, or rhetoric? Second, do his philosophical positions determine his theology or does his theology frame his philosophical enquiry?[36]

33. Auguste Berthaud, *Gilbert de la Porrée, évêque de Poitiers, et sa philosophie (1077-1154)* (Frankfurt am Main: Minerva Verlag, 1985 [1892]), pp. 191-230, esp. pp. 213-17.

34. François Vernet, "Gilbert de Poitiers," in *Dictionnaire de théologie catholique* (Paris: Librarie Letouzey et Ané, 1915), vol. 6, col. 1350-58, esp. 1352-53; Maurice de Wulf, *Histoire de la philosophie médiévale,* 6th ed. (Louvain: Institut Supérieur de Philosophie, 1924), vol. 1, pp. 156-59; Aimé Forest, "Le réalisme de Gilbert de la Porrée dans le commentaire du 'De Hebdomadibus,'" *Revue Néoscolastique de Philosophie* 36 (1934): 101-10; André Hayen, "Le Concile de Reims et l'Erreur Théologique de Gilbert de la Porrée," *Archives d'histoire doctrinale et littéraire au Moyen-Âge* 10 (1935): 29-102; M. H. Vicaire, "Les Porrétains et l'avicennisme avant 1215," *Revue des Sciences Philosophiques et Théologiques* 26 (1937): 449-82; Nikolaus M. Häring, "The Case of Gilbert de la Porrée Bishop of Poitiers (1142-1154)," *Mediaeval Studies* 13 (1951): 1-40; Michael E. Williams, "The Teaching of Gilbert Porreta on the Trinity as Found in His Commentaries on Boethius," *Analecta Gregoriana* 41 (1955), section B, pp. 1-130, esp. 11-41.

35. Martin Grabmann, *Die Geschichte der scholastischen Methode* (Freiburg im Breisgau: Herder, 1909), pp. 420-30; Martin A. Schmidt, *Gottheit und Trinität nach dem Kommentar des Gilbert Porreta zu Boethius De Trinitate* (Basel: Philosophische Gesellschaft, 1956), pp. 24-49.

36. Nikolaus M. Häring, "Sprachlogische und philosophische Voraussetzungen zum Verständnis der Christologie Gilberts von Poitiers," *Scholastik* 32 (1957): 373-98; Lauge Olaf Nielsen, "On the Doctrine of Logic and Language of Gilbert Porreta and His Followers," *Cahiers de l'Institut du Moyen Âge Grec et Latin* 17 (1976): 40-69; L. O. Nielsen, *Phi-*

What is common to both interpretations is the claim that Porreta defends a variant of metaphysical realism. He is credited with a realist account of universals that centers upon the substantial conformity of native forms *(formae nativae)* that are common to diverse, subsistent substances.[37] As a result, he seems to offer an alternative to Roscelin of Compiègne, who was famously indicted by Anselm for equating universal substances with "the puff of an utterance" *(flatum vocis)*.[38] Likewise, Gilbert does not appear to embrace Aristotle's substantialist metaphysics, which would threaten the personal and relational nature of the Trinitarian persons. Rather, his metaphysical realism seems consonant with his Trinitarian theology. Moreover, it has been argued that he develops a non-univocal account of person. Thus, he preserves the 'ontological difference' between Creator and creation and the limits of human language and knowledge.[39]

losophy and Theology in the Twelfth Century: A Study of Gilbert Porreta's Thinking and the Theological Expositions of the Doctrine of the Incarnation during the Period 1130-1180 (Leiden: E. J. Brill, 1982), pp. 87-189; L. O. Nielsen, "Peter Abelard and Gilbert of Poitiers," in *The Medieval Theologians: An Introduction to Theology in the Medieval Period,* ed. Gillian R. Evans (Oxford: Blackwell, 2001), pp. 102-28, esp. pp. 116-20; John Marenbon, "Gilbert of Poitiers," in *A History of Twelfth-Century Western Philosophy,* ed. Peter Dronke (Cambridge: Cambridge University Press, 1988), pp. 328-52; J. Marenbon, "Gilbert of Poitiers and the Porretans on Mathematics in the Division of Sciences," in *"Scientia" and "Disciplina." Wissenstheorie und Wissenschaftspraxis im 12. und 13. Jahrhundert,* ed. R. Berndt, M. Lutz-Bachmann, and R. M. W. Stammberger (Berlin: Akademie Verlag, 2002), pp. 37-69; Lambertus M. de Rijk, "Gilbert de Poitiers, ses vues métaphysiques et sémantiques," in Jolivet and de Libera, eds., *Gilbert de Poitiers et ses contemporains. Aux origins de la logica modernorum,* pp. 141-71; L. M. de Rijk, "Semantics and Metaphysics in Gilbert of Poitiers: A Chapter of Twelfth-Century Platonism (1) and (2)," *Vivarium* 26 (1988): 73-122 and *Vivarium* 27 (1989): 1-35; J. Jolivet, "Rhétorique et théologie dans une page de Gilbert de Poitiers," pp. 183-97; Klaus Jacobi, "Natürliches Sprechen — Theoriesprache — Theologische Rede. Die Wissenschaftslehre des Gilbert von Poitiers (ca. 1085-1154)," *Zeitschrift für Philosophische Forschung* 49 (1995): 511-28; K. Jacobi, "Philosophische und theologische Weisheit. Gilbert von Poitiers' Interpretation der 'Regeln' des Boethius *(De hebdomadibus)*," in Berndt, Lutz-Bachmann, and Stammberger, eds., *"Scientia" and "Disciplina,"* pp. 71-77.

37. Forest, "Le réalisme de Gilbert de la Porrée dans le commentaire du 'De Hebdomadibus,'" pp. 101-10.

38. St. Anselm, *De incarnatione verbi* (ed. Schmitt [1938-68]), VI.ii.9:20–10:1.

39. Joke Spruyt, "Gilbert of Poitiers on the Application of Language to the Transcendent and Sublunary Domains," in *The Winged Chariot: Collected Essays on Plato and Platonism in Honour of L. M. de Rijk,* ed. Maria Kardaun and Joke Spruyt (Leiden: E. J. Brill, 2000), pp. 205-35.

In the following sections, I argue that Gilbert privileges mathematics over natural philosophy (or physics) and thus formalizes metaphysics by importing 'mathematical' reasoning into the transcendent domain. The primacy of mathematics also leads to the priority of abstraction vis-à-vis sense perception. As a result, reflections on the Trinity and God the Creator become disjoined from any inquiry into the created world, which henceforth is thought to manifest nothing but its own existence. Thus, the link between creation and its transcendent author is no longer a matter of rational discernment but tends to be fideistic. My account of Porreta qualifies his realism and highlights the formalist character of his metaphysics, which (as I will show in chapter 6) was later amplified by Scotus, Ockham, and Buridan. This is significant for the question of individuation, as the onus of individuation shifts from transcendent causes to immanent principles. I begin with a brief analysis of *more geometrico* and the division of the sciences. I then outline his distinction of singularity, dividuality, and individuality and his conception of subsistent substances. Finally, I examine his account of creation and concretion.

4. *More geometrico:* A Mathematical Ordering of the Sciences

By contrast with Boethius' metaphysical realism and his theological ordering of the sciences, Porreta combines 'grammatical Platonism' with a hierarchy of disciplines that is grounded in the nominalist method of 'mathematical' reasoning. To say this is not to say that Anselm's indictment of twelfth-century theology was correct. His charge that Roscelin's universal substances are nothing but a *flatum vocis* is misguided because the universality of substances is based upon the general structures of mental language, a position shared by Gilbert. In this sense, Porreta (like Roscelin) is no ontological nominalist. But since Gilbert denies that the mind acquires true knowledge of forms via sense perception, his is a position of metaphysical formalism. Indeed, 'grammatical Platonism' commits him to the idea that knowledge of composite substances is governed by grammatical categories and framed by logic and mathematics, in particular a priori definitions, axioms, postulates, and theorems. At first, it would seem as if mathematics, on the basis of abstraction from actual things, merely aims to identify the forms that inhere in material things and act as their causes. However, as Porreta understood it, mathematics is derived from the idea of *mathēsis,* which he translates as *disciplina*[40] and which represents an a priori mapping of forms according to the similarity with other forms. Mathematical abstraction yields forms at their most general and most abstract, neither particular forms (like Aristotle's substantial individual form) nor universal forms (like Plato's form of beauty or justice).

This configuration of mathematics has far-reaching implications for Porreta's division of the sciences. First, whereas natural philosophy (or physics) concerns the mode of being of forms in things, mathematics abstracts not only from matter but also from any determinants such as genus, species, and differentia. Second, insofar as it aims at forms outside any determination, mathematics does not have its own proper objects because it can be applied to all things and all forms. As such, matter is "coextensive with natural philosophy . . . [and] 'constitutes an epistemological precondition for natural philosophy.'"[41] The mapping of form according to some meta-formal content or similarity entails a 'mathematicization' of knowledge because form is identified with *notio* or concept, not with the real presence of universals in particulars. This is why Gillian Evans is right to argue that "Gilbert considers mathematics a 'higher study' precisely because it is not restricted by the limited nature of real things: 'it [mathematics] is a higher discipline — which the Greek called *mathēsis* — that abstracts from concrete things.'"[42]

Given the monopoly of mathematics over form, the third implication is that natural philosophy is restricted to the study of secondary forms (*'quo ests'*), which inhere in concretized things (*'quod ests'*).[43] By itself, natural philosophy cannot obtain knowledge of the link between the form of a thing and its transcendent cause. Any such link is either purely abstract and a matter of mathematicized knowledge, or else it is exclusively supernatural and a matter of knowledge based on

40. *In de Trin.* I.ii.39 (86: 25-30).

41. Nielsen, *Philosophy and Theology in the Twelfth Century*, p. 95.

42. Gillian R. Evans, "*More geometrico:* The Place of the Axiomatic Method in the Twelfth-Century Commentaries on Boethius' *Opuscula sacra*," *Archives internationales d'histoire des sciences* 27 (1977): 207-21 (214). The reference to the quote from Gilbert is as follows: "*ea, quae a concretionibus alterior disciplina — quae Graece dicitur 'mathesis'? abstrahit*" (*In de Hebdom.* 6 prol. [184: 28-29]).

43. In what follows, I use the term *'quo ests'* in order to emphasize that Porreta tends to view it as a plurality. For a discussion of this as well as the notion of *formae nativae* (which was coined by members of the Porretan school in the later twelfth century), see, *infra*, main text. Cf. Gilson, *La philosophie au Moyen Âge*, pp. 262-68.

faith alone. However, this does not imply that theology is an autonomous science. Since mathematics enables knowledge of forms which are inaccessible in natural philosophy, mathematics is not so much a propaedeutic tool but instead acts as a corrective of natural philosophy and makes knowledge of forms possible for theology.[44] Based on mathematics, theology discloses true form or what is simple *(simplex)*, independently of all matter and according to *rationes* which are both shared with mathematics and specific to theology (*In de Trin.* I.2.41 [86: 38–87: 45]).

So configured, mathematics induces theology to abandon the actuality of particular sensible things in the quest for pure form. The turn away from actual things is reinforced by the intervention of supernatural faith, which operates outside natural reason — a conception that is diametrically opposed to the Christian Neo-Platonist injunction of 'faith seeking understanding.' For Gilbert, faith enables human cognition to engage in total abstraction *(remotio, rationis abstractio)* from all material instantiation.[45] As such, reason knows some natural principles, but only faith can provide knowledge of God and pure form which is inaccessible to reason.[46] According to Porreta, knowledge of God is more certain than knowledge of mutable things because it rests on the "most certain and firmest foundation" *(certissimum atque firmissimum fundamentum)* of faith. The operation of faith pushes mathematical abstraction to its logical conclusion, to the point where matter is absolutely discarded as a medium of form. This differs markedly from the patristic and early medieval insistence that the presence of the Creator is mediated in and through material things (Rom. 1:20) and that theology orders all other sciences on account of the primacy of God's act of being over all things, as I have argued with respect to the work of Gregory, Augustine, Boethius, and Dionysius in chapters 2 and 3. By contrast with this preeminence of theology, Porreta posits the priority of 'mathematical' reasoning over sense perception and judgment, and views *'more geometrico'* as the most universal method of enquiry. As such, the only difference between theology and the other sciences is that in theology supernatural faith not only produces a perception of pure form but also commands as-

44. For a summary of different interpretations of mathematics in Porreta's works, see Marenbon, "Gilbert of Poitiers and the Porretans on Mathematics in the Division of Sciences," pp. 42-43.

45. *"remotio, rationis abstraction"* (*In Contra Eut.* I.25 [247: 33]).

46. *In de Trin.* II.i.7, 9-11 (164: 34-38, 42-40; 165: 50-57).

sent to this perception.[47] While this is not wrong in itself, the separation of faith from reason foregrounds the division of ontology from theology — precisely the legacy of Avicenna, as I have already indicated. In the concluding section of this chapter, I will suggest that this, coupled with the priority of essence over existence, explains the compatibility and confluence of Avicenna's and Porreta's metaphysically impoverished theology. For now I will proceed with a critical reading of Gilbert's application of *'more geometrico'* to the question of creation and individuation.

5. Singularity, Dividuality, and Individuality

In this section I analyze Porreta's ontology and his account of particulars and universals. Commenting on Boethius' distinctions between universality, particularity, and personality in the theological tractates, Gilbert also contrasts the singular, the individual, and the personal.[48] But these terms have markedly different meanings in his work compared with those in Boethius' *Opuscula sacra*. First, he defines the notion of singularity as that which specifies both the commonality and the difference between that by which *(id quo)* something is and that which it is *(id quod):*

> The property [of a person] is called 'singular' for one reason, 'individual' for another, and 'personal' for another. For, although whatever is individual is [also] a singular — and whatever is a person is [also] a singular and individual — nevertheless, not every singular is an individual. Nor is every singular or individual a person. For, in natural [things], whatever is, is something by what is other than itself. And since that by which it is something is singular, that also which is something by it is singular. . . . And so by the singularity of that by which it is, that which is something by it is singular.[49]

47. *"in religione prima est fides que quidem generaliter est veritatis cuiuslibet rei cum assensione perceptio"* (*In de Trin.* I.1.3 [71: 11-12]).

48. Klaus Jacobi, "Einzelnes — Individuum — Person. Gilbert von Poitiers' Philosophie des Individuellen," in *Individuum und Individualität im Mittelalter*, ed. Jan A. Aertsen and Andreas Speer (Berlin and New York: De Gruyter, 1996), pp. 3-22.

49. *"alicuius proprietas alia ratione 'singularis,' alia 'indiuidua,' alia 'personalis' uocatur. Quamuis enim quicquid est indiuiduum, est singulare — et quicquid est persona, est singulare et indiuiduum — non tamen omne singulare est indiuiduum. Nec omne singulare uel indiuiduum est persona. In naturalibus enim quicquid est, alio, quam ipsum sit, aliquid*

In this passage, he argues that actual particular sensible things *(naturalibus)* are best described as singular and that their singularity is a function of the singularity of their *quo est* (that by which they are some-thing). The reason why particular sensible things are not individuals is that they differ only numerically from other particulars (not qualita-tively). If they share the same *'quo ests,'* then they conform with one an-other and also with the *'quo ests'* that make them similar: "[T]herefore, not only those [things] which they are, but also those by which they con-form, are one dividual [*sic*]."[50]

Porreta deploys the notion of 'dividual' in order to mark the differ-ence between singularity and individuality. Not all singulars are individ-uals, and not all individuals are persons. By contrast, all individuals are singular and all persons are both singular and individual. Put differently, the extension of individuality is more limited than that of singularity, and the extension of personality is more limited yet. That which explains the similarity of certain singulars (for example, the similarity between men — their humanity and rationality) cannot be individual, otherwise it would make singulars not merely numerically distinct but also qualita-tively different. Thus, that by which singulars conform to one another is a 'dividual' *(diuiduum)*. 'Dividuals' are universal because they are com-mon to more than one singular.

Unlike Augustine's and Boethius' universals, which are really present in particular things, Porreta's 'dividuals' are exclusively mental entities: "Some substances are universal by the substantial similarity of the form [i.e., dividuality], others are particulars, that is to say individuals by the dissimilarity of their complete properties."[51] Since the similarity between singular instances of humanity or rationality is the result of a mental operation[52] and has no correlate in beings (or no correlate that can be

---

est. Et quoniam id, quo est aliquid, singulare est, id quoque, quod eo est aliquid, singulare est. . . . Itaque singularitate eius, quo est, singulare est etiam id quod eo aliquid est" (In de Trin. I.v.22-23 [143: 53–144: 60]).

50. *"ideoque non modo illa, quae sunt, uerum etiam, illa, quibus conformia sunt, unum diuiduum sunt"* (In de Trin. I.v.24 [144: 64-65]).

51. *"RURSUS SUBSTANTIARUM ALIAE SUNT UNIUERSALES substantialis forme simili-tudine: ALIAE SUNT PARTICULARES, i.e. indiuiduae plenarum proprietatum dissimilitudine"* (In Contra Eut. II.22; Boethius' text in capital letters [269: 36-38]).

52. Richard J. Westley, "A Philosophy of the Concreted and the Concrete: The Con-struction of the Creatures according to Gilbert de la Porrée," *The Modern Schoolman* 37 (1960): 257-86.

discerned as such), it follows that the metaphysical status of 'dividuals' is purely formal. It is true that Gilbert speaks of the intellect as that which "on the basis of whatever particulars grasps universal things."[53] But it is far from clear what in particular sensible things can account for the existence of universals. The term similarity *(conformitas)* is too vague to serve as an adequate concept in order to explain the reality of universals. Even if universals were not only mental constructs but also real entities, there would be no instance of verification other than the mind itself. As I argued in the previous sections, Gilbert denies sense perception any genuine cognitive import.

In addition to 'dividuals,' Porreta's other conceptual innovation is the already mentioned distinction between that which is something *(id quod est)* and that by which it is something *(quo est)*. The latter is not a transcendent cause which makes the thing what it is. Instead, *quo est* refers both to substantial properties like humanity and to accidental characteristics such as tallness. Since each *id quod est* is constituted by a collection of substantial properties and accidental characteristics, Porreta speaks of *'quo ests.'* The question that arises is whether the singularity of the *id quod est* is due to the singularity of one *quo est* or several *'quo ests'* or all of them. It seems that the totality of substantial properties and accidental characteristics constitutes particulars as individuals. Conjointly, substantial properties and accidental characteristics form what he calls "the total property" *(tota proprietas,* e.g., *In Contra Eut.* II.29). The essence of things is therefore composed of a multiplicity of properties or forms. As such, it differs fundamentally from unitary essence in Gregory, Augustine, Boethius, and Dionysius, as I have shown in chapters 2 and 3. Moreover, Gilbert's thesis on multiple forms in many respects foreshadows the late medieval separation of individuation in the immanent realm from transcendent divine creative activity, as I will suggest in chapter 6, and also modern conceptions of ontology such as Leibniz's monads and Hume's atomism, as I will argue in chapter 9.

For now let me return to Porreta's account of individuation in terms of 'the total property' which makes a singular an individual rather than a 'dividual' by differentiating *that* singular from otherwise similar singulars which together form a 'dividual':

---

53. The full quote is as follows: *"Res universales intellectus ex quibuslibet particularibus sumit"* (*In Contra Euty.* III.31 [278: 1-2]).

For things are said [to be] 'individual' because each of them is constituted from such properties, the whole collection of which, having
been produced in thought, will never be the same in any other of the
numerically particular [things] by a natural conformity. For this reason the total form of Plato — which conforms to no one in act and nature [i.e., potency] — is truly individual. But every part of it is indeed
singular, although not individual since it conforms to many at least by
nature. And so his soul, the total form of which is part of the form of
Plato, is not truly called 'individual' by name.[54]

The key point in this passage is that things are not individuated by the
act of being that brings form-matter compounds into actuality and
makes them what they are. Instead, that which constitutes particular
things *qua* individuals is the totality of '*quo ests.*' As I show in the following section, '*quo ests*' are not transcendent causes. Nor do they depend
on transcendent causes in order to individuate things. Instead, they represent immanent principles that explain how actualized substances are
individuated. The implication of all this is that Porreta does not address
the question as to why things are unique individuals in the first place
and why they tend towards ever-greater individuation.

6. The Generation and Subsistence of Singular Substances

Porreta's theory of individuation can only be fully understood by examining the metaphysical status of *id quod est* and *quo est*. Since things are
one yet at the same time exhibit a plurality of attributes, he draws a distinction between that which is *(id quod est)* and that by which *(quo est)* it
is what it is.[55] This distinction is not merely logical but in fact extends to
the metaphysical structure of the world. It describes the causal relationship between the plurality of attributes or forms and the dual aspect of

---

54. *"Nam 'indiuidua' dicuntur huiusmodi quoniam unumquodque eorum ex talibus
consistit proprietatibus quarum omnium cogitatione facta collectio nunquam in alio quolibet
alterutrius numero particularium naturali conformitate eadem erit. Hac igitur ratione
Platonis tota forma — nulli neque actu neque natura conformis — uere est indiuidua. Omnis
uero pars eius singularis quidem est: non autem uere indiuidua quoniam multis est saltem
natura conformis. Itaque anima eius, cuius tota forma pars est forme Platonis, non uero
nomine dicitur 'indiuidua'"* (*In Contra Eut.* III.14-15 [274: 85-93]).

55. *In de Hebdom.* I.67 [202: 86].

each thing, material and formal. Crucially, Gilbert views both matter and form as purely immanent. As Nielsen remarks, "Every object is itself matter, and as such formed by the thing's own form: *'... quod unumquodque subsistentium aliquid est, est ex propria forma, que inest materia.'*"[56] Porreta's construal of the subsistence of matter-form compounds locates actualization and individuation exclusively in particular sensible things themselves. The Good, which emanates *(defluxit)* from God's absolute power (*In de Hebdom.* II.150 [220: 59-64]), provides the condition of possibility for the generation and corruption of things but does not make any difference to the actuality of particulars or the perfection of their own substantial form. Instead of individuation being seen as a limited 'share' of divine unity, it is now seen either as a transcendentally necessary meta-logical category or as a state of affairs simply willed by God and telling us nothing of the inner divine reality in which the whole of creation participates.

Let me substantiate this claim. For Gilbert, a material thing is absolutely dependent upon its formal principle, just as form cannot be without being in the actual thing (*In Contra Eut.* III.33 [278: 8]). This metaphysical dependence follows from the relationship of causality: the *id quo* which serves as the cause determines the *id quod* which is its effect. Since the cause precedes and surpasses its effect, the *id quo* or *esse* (or form or essence) is prior to the *id quod* (actuality): "Everything which is being is naturally prior to that which is."[57] What distinguishes Porreta's 'grammatical Platonism' from the metaphysical realism of patristic Christian Neo-Platonists is the status of essence. By equating *esse* with form, Porreta abandons the metaphysical link between God's transcendent power of being and the actuality of material things in favor of the immanent subsistence of individual substances and the priority of formal essence over real existence.

This is significant for individuation because the cause of actualization is now exclusively immanent. First, the *id quo* is that which is in matter *(forma, que inest materia).*[58] The concepts of participation *(participatio)* and inherence *(inesse)* are used to describe the mode of presence of form in matter and the connection between *id quod est* and

---

56. Nielsen, *Philosophy and Theology in the Twelfth Century,* p. 47. The reference for the quote from Porreta is *In de Trin.* I.ii.52 (89: 10-11).

57. *"omne vero esse eo, quod est, naturaliter prius est"* (*In Contra Eut.* I.1 [242: 5-6]).

58. See *supra,* note 56.

id quo est or *esse:* "Everything which is participates in that which is be-ing."[59] As Nielsen explains, Gilbert's description of this causal relation-ship in terms of *habitus* shows that the human mind can cognize this link as it is found in things. He posits a purely causal connection between essence and existence which the mind can know because this connec-tion is not only in each thing but also lacks any transcendent cause. The transcendence of *esse* (the power of being or *virtus essendi*) in Augustine and Boethius contrasts with the immanence of *esse* (essence or *essentia*) in Porreta.

Second, a particular thing is what it is by virtue of having both sub-stantial properties and accidental features. This distinction requires a substrate in which both can be present. Substantial properties require a substance *(substantia)* in order to inhere in a thing. However, for Porreta substance is neither Aristotle's category nor Boethius' matter-form com-pound. Instead, substance is substantial form, which gives beings 'some-thing' (this-ness or essence). The reason for emphasizing this-ness or es-sence is that ultimately all substantial forms depend on divine essence (*In de Hebdom.* I.27-28 [93: 54-65]). The difference with Augustine and Boethius is that Gilbert's account focuses on the essential link of the Cre-ator and creation and excludes any existential link. As I will suggest in the following chapter, Aquinas sought to shift the focus away from the essentialism of both Avicennian and Porretan theology to the metaphys-ical realism of God's pure act of being.

Third, substance denotes not only substantial form but also that which subsists (*In de Trin.* I.iv.99 [135: 95-101]). So configured, subsistence *(subsistentia)* is the substantial form of a particular thing that subsists *(subsistens).* This conceptuality departs from the primacy of person over substance in Gregory, Augustine, Boethius, and Dionysius, as I will now show. Porreta stipulates a hierarchy of subsistences, beginning with the most general subsistence *(subsistentia generalissima)* which is created, yet not subject to generation and corruption and therefore eternal (*In de Hebdom.* I.98 [208-9: 64-70]). This subsistence gives rise to two different forms, both eternal *(perpetue):* corporeal form, which is the eternal sub-sistence of all bodies, and spiritual form, which is the eternal subsistence of all immaterial beings. As Nielsen concludes, "One consequence of this is that Gilbert, no more than he advocates a substantial-existential form,

59. *"omne quo est participat eo quod est esse"* (*In de Hebdom.* I.96 [208: 60]). Cf. *In de Hebdom.* I.100 [209: 84].

propounds an essential form which is common to all that is created."[60] Thus Porreta puts the emphasis on essence rather than existence and divides created essence into two elements, corporeal and incorporeal. As a result, God's creative action does not encompass the actualization of all beings. Likewise, matter oscillates ambiguously between primary matter (i.e., unformed matter which is created first and acts as the *prima subsistentia* for substantial form)[61] and corporeality (i.e., matter which is always already formed and only exists in virtue of a form).

Coupled with the overarching priority of essence over existence, the unresolved relation between matter and form at the level of the most general subsistence impacts upon the relation of matter and form at the subsequent levels in the hierarchy of subsistences. The eternal subsistences are followed by a series of 'differences' *(differentiae)* that give rise to genera and species, e.g., the composite genus animal with the simple *differentia* rationality yields the species man.[62] The actual form, humanity, is found in every human being and can therefore be said to be universal. Yet at the same time, this and other universals are not real because they are the result of a mental operation that is based on a similarity that is not substantial (unlike Boethius' *similitudo substantialis*).

At the bottom of the hierarchy of subsistences are particular sensible things, also called subsistent *(subsistens)*. Gilbert views particulars as subsisting substances because they provide the 'material' for substantial forms (*In Contra Eut.* III.36 [279: 24-28]). The key problem in his line of argument is that there is no account of what brings this material into existence. For substantial forms act as the causes that make the concrete thing (as effect) capable of receiving further forms (both substantial and accidental). What remains unexplained is the generation and individuation of particulars, which are so configured that they can be further formed. To say that particular things continue to receive new substantial forms could imply that the essence of particulars changes. Conjointly with the idea of a plurality of substantial forms, both the identity and the unity of particular sensible things are threatened. This raises fundamental questions about the nature of individuality and the cause of individuation in Porreta's metaphysics.

---

60. Nielsen, *Philosophy and Theology in the Twelfth Century,* p. 51.

61. On Porreta's account of primary matter and the relation with Platonism, see Étienne Gilson, "Note sur les noms de la matière chez Gilbert de la Porrée," *Revue du moyen âge latin* 2 (1946): 173-76.

62. *In de Trin.* I.ii.65 [92: 96-100]; *In de Hebdom.* I.99-100 [209: 71-85].

The primacy of essence over existence entails a focus on form at the expense of matter. That is in part why Aquinas reintegrates matter into his account of individuation, as I will argue in the following chapter. By contrast with the Neo-Platonist emphasis on triadic relationality, Gilbert's 'grammatical Platonism' posits that everything is by itself something *(per se aliquid est)* and is one *(per se una est)* by virtue of having a substantial form.[63] As such, that which subsists does so in virtue of the formality of *'quo ests':* "[E]ach subsistent subsists by the agglomeration of a multiplicity of *quo ests:* genus, differentia and accident."[64] The actual materiality of composites does not make a difference to a thing's actuality. Since a thing's essence is composed of a plurality of substantial forms, they cannot be the source of unity and individuation. Likewise, since a thing can be formed by further substantial forms over time, they cannot be the source of identity either. This leaves matter, but matter is subject to corruption and therefore cannot be the principle of diachronic individuation. The plurality of immanent substantial forms requires a higher cause that can secure its unity and identity. As a result, Porreta is compelled to locate the unity of particular sensible things exclusively in the only subsistence that is perfectly immaterial and absolutely one — the divine essence. In the absence of any existential link, the divine essence acts as a transcendental guarantee of unity and identity. This contrasts markedly with the Neo-Platonist idea of the transcendent Good, which is the source of both existence and essence and infuses all things with goodness. In the following section, I show how Gilbert's conception of divine essence provides the necessary transcendental securing of the unity of composites that subsist by themselves.

7. Creation, Concretion, and the Transcendental Securing of Unity

In his discussion of Porreta's account of universals and individuals, Jean Jolivet argues that universality is synonymous with the conformity among singulars in terms of certain common *'quo ests'* that co-constitute them.[65]

---

63. *In de Trin.* I.v.29 [145: 95-100]; cf. *In de Trin.* I.ii.57, 61; I.iii.48; I.iv.6; I.iv.99; *In de Hebdom.* I.35; *In Contra Eut.* I.89; II.12; III.43.

64. *"omne subsistens multorum quibus est, i.e. generis et differentiae et accidentis, concretione subsistit"* (*In de Trin.* I.v.26 [144: 79-81]; cf. *In de Trin.* I.ii.6 prol.).

65. Jean Jolivet, "Trois variations médiévales sur l'universel et l'individu: Roscelin,

Accordingly, the totality of 'quo ests' differentiates *this* singular from *that* singular and makes it an individual rather than a 'dividual.' Porreta also posits the participation of every 'subsistent' *(subsistens)* in a hierarchy of forms, commencing with secondary forms (later called *formae nativae* by his disciples, who formed the Porretan school)[66] and extending to the most general subsistence.[67] As Jolivet points out, the noetic upward movement from the singular via the conformity with other singulars to the universal is mirrored by the ontological downward movement from the most general to the specific subsistence.[68]

However, this reading begs the question as to how the intellect is able to know universals on the basis of singulars. There is nothing in the actuality of particular things that intimates the presence of common forms that inhere in them. Gilbert's response is that the actualization of particular sensible things involves not just secondary but also primary forms: "[A]ll natural things are not only created but also concretized."[69] How are we to understand the distinction between creation and concretion? According to Porreta, creation marks the reception of the substantial form and the coming into existence of a subsistent. As such, creation is identical with generation, and both are immanent in the sense that they are unrelated to transcendent forms. By contrast, concretion represents the specification of general forms. Indeed, it is only when he speaks of concretion that a link between the secondary forms in particular things and the primary forms emerges. As Nielsen puts it, "'[C]oncretion' . . . describes not only the ordering of the accidental forms, but also the linking together of secondary natures to the primary form, i.e., *differentiae* to *genus generalissimum* or, as Gilbert calls the two general forms, corporeality and spirituality, the *perpetuae subsistentiae*."[70] Nielsen goes on to argue that particular things come to exist by virtue of one subsis-

---

Abélard, Gilbert de la Porrée," *Revue de métaphysique et de morale* 97 (1992): 111-55, esp. pp. 141-55.

66. Gilson, *La philosophie au Moyen Âge,* esp. pp. 262-68; Vicaire, "Les Porrétains et l'avicennisme avant 1215," pp. 449-82.

67. *"generalissima subsistentia"* (*In de Hebdom.* I.98 [208-9: 64-70]). See Forest, "Le réalisme de Gilbert de la Porrée dans le commentaire du 'De Hebdomadibus,'" esp. p. 107.

68. Jolivet, "Trois variations médiévales sur l'universel et l'individu: Roscelin, Abélard, Gilbert de la Porrée," pp. 144-45.

69. *"omnia naturalia non modo creata, sed etiam concreta sunt"* (*In de Hebdom.* I.57 [199: 19-20]).

70. Nielsen, *Philosophy and Theology in the Twelfth Century,* p. 70.

tence or substantial form through creation before they can be formed by virtue of several subsistences through concretion.

But this conception of generation (creation) and formation (concretion) is based upon the priority of form and essence to the detriment of matter and existence. Since he simply presupposes that the recipient material exists and that it has the capacity to receive form, Porreta does not elucidate how substantial form can be received. In this sense, singularity is part of the determination of actual particular things, but remains unexplained. Not only are we left wondering how matter can receive substantial form; we also ignore why substantial form would want to inhere in matter. Like Aristotle, Porreta's focus on essence does not account for the existence of the realm of singular matter-form compounds. Divine immaterial essence somehow issues forth into nondivine material substances that are created as subsistents and concretized as individuals. This requires a brief discussion of divine essence with respect to form and matter.

All particular composite substances are generated and formed according to certain eternal ideas. These ideas act as archetypes, models, or exemplars. Copies of ideas include both immanent substantial forms and actual things themselves which have essences from such forms.[71] Even though created forms are derived from their exemplars by deduction *(deductio),* the resemblance between them is extrinsic.[72] Thus, immanent forms represent but a very remote imitation *(imitatio).* This differs significantly from Plato's idea of forms in the world that are diverse *reflections of* the one source (rather than copies), as I showed in chapter 1. If something is a reflection, then it is relational to that of which it is a reflection. By contrast, to speak of copies is either to posit a relation that threatens the 'ontological difference' or to impose a distance that undermines the possibility of participation. Moreover, as Nielsen explains, the only reason why the mind can effectively ascertain the presence of immaterial created (i.e., derived or deduced) ideas in material things and the participation of such things in such ideas is the transference or transmutation of names from the theological realm of pure form without matter to the natural realm of form in connection with matter.[73] Only faith, not reason, can provide knowledge of the link between things

71. *In de Trin.* I.ii.17 (82: 98); I.ii.97 (99-100: 11-20).
72. *"secundum extrinseca"* (*In de Hebdom.* I.76 [204: 37-47]).
73. Nielsen, *Philosophy and Theology in the Twelfth Century,* p. 73.

and their ultimate origins. As I have already indicated in section 2 of the present chapter, this incipient fideism can also be found in some strands of Islamic theology.

Likewise, matter is also created according to ideas in the divine mind. In his commentary on the Pauline epistles, Porreta describes these ideas in Augustinian terms as *ars divina* or *Verbum*.[74] Coupled with the two eternal subsistences (corporeality and spirituality) and the theory of archetypes or models, matter as a divine idea is an exemplar of corporeality, from which singular bodies can be derived. However, Gilbert departs from the Augustinian vision in two crucial respects. First, there is nothing in singular material beings that would intimate their relation with the eternal subsistence of corporeality, let alone with the divine idea of matter. This is because, according to Porreta, the mathematical structure of nature does not manifest God's creative activity in the world. By contrast, Augustine's reconfiguration of the Stoic and Neo-Platonist scheme of numbers and ratios is a model that describes the world in terms of relational individuals. Second, matter remains unexplained, above all the capacity of matter to receive form and of material form to be perfected. Neither creation nor concretion can account for the reception and perfection of form. This is because matter is created formless.[75] Likewise, secondary forms embodied in concrete matter are concretized by being related back to the primary forms, but it is not clear *why* primary forms would want to inhere in matter or *how* the mind can cognize such transcendent forms based on its immanent self.

Gilbert addresses these two objections by referring to the divine essence and supernatural faith. The mind seeks universal forms only if supernatural faith produces a perception of pure form and commands assent to this perception.[76] This is why, as Jolivet observes, the mind transcends the plurality of *'quo ests'* and cognizes that which secures the unity of all *'quod ests'*: "[T]here could not be in a single being such a plurality [of *'quo ests'*] if a unique principle had not bound them together."[77] The principle that binds together the plurality of *'quo ests'* is "the will of the Good whence derives the being of each of the subsistents, i.e., not

---

74. For a textual reference to Porreta's commentary on the Pauline Epistles, see Nielsen, *Philosophy and Theology in the Twelfth Century*, p. 73, n. 192.

75. Nielsen, *Philosophy and Theology in the Twelfth Century*, p. 76, n. 213.

76. See, *supra*, note 47.

77. "*Neque uero in uno tanta multitudo . . . esse posset nisi unum principium haec in illo iunxisset*" (*In De Hebdom.* II.148 [219: 49-51]).

only that which is and that which is something and that by which it is and by which it is something, but also being and being something."[78] Even though this might seem to be close to Augustine's and Boethius' Neo-Platonist account, the crucial difference is that Porreta restricts the link to abstract essence, not actual existence. There is nothing in a thing's actuality that would intimate its createdness. Moreover, Porreta differs from Augustine and Boethius in that both his division of the sciences and his theory of knowledge privilege the immanence of secondary forms. The only participation that the mind can know rationally is the participation of a thing in its own form, which inheres in it. The link with higher forms is purely essential and as such not perceptible to the senses. Only faith can propel the mind to seek remote traces of the divine essence in subsistent substances.

Therefore, the actuality of things does not in any way intimate the presence of God. Instead, knowledge of the principle that guarantees the unity of subsistent substances is grounded in an a priori assumption that God is that "essence out of which is whatever is."[79] The divine essence is such that from the will of the Good emanates a unitary principle that secures transcendentally the unity of all immanent forms that inhere in material things. On this point, Gilbert wrongly equates Neo-Platonism with an unmediated primacy of the One, ignoring the generative activity as a result of the One's ecstatic overflow. For Porreta, that which upholds both the unity and the identity of particular sensible things is the oneness and immutability of God's *essentia,* not his existence.

8. Towards *Potentia Dei Absoluta* and Formal Modality

In the previous section, I showed that Gilbert develops a Platonism of essential derivation, which contrasts with the Christian Neo-Platonist metaphysics of existential creation. Porreta stresses the link between forms and the divine essence but fails to explain how God might be related to the creation and concretion of matter and the generation of material particulars. The downward movement of form from the most ab-

---

78. ". . . *esse eorum, i.e. non modo id quod est et aliquid est itemque id quo est uel quo aliquid est uerum etiam illud et esse et aliquid esse A BONI UOLUNTATE DEFLUXIT"* (*In de Hebdom.* II.150 [220: 58-61]).

79. "*esse, ex quo est quicquid est"* (*In de Trin.* I.i.7 [71: 35-36]).

stract and general eternal subsistence to the concrete 'subsistents' is explained in terms of the 'outflow' *(deflux)* of the will of the Good. But this conception cannot account for the desire of the mind to know the highest form and conform to it as best as possible. In this section, I argue that Gilbert's metaphysics of essential derivation devalues actuality. The metaphysical status of actuality has implications for both theology and metaphysics. Theology is governed by the absolute power of God and metaphysics is structured by formal modality. So configured, theology and metaphysics combine to produce a formalist synthesis that stands in stark contrast to the metaphysical realism of Christian Neo-Platonism.

According to Porreta, the world's metaphysical structure is composed of three elements — subsistence, singularity, and plurality of forms. Subsistence is that which is by itself.[80] Knowledge of the dependence of concrete composite substances on a transcendental instance arises from the following logical and semantic consideration: strictly speaking, things are not because only God is and therefore "the existential sense of 'is' can be used properly only in theology."[81] Therefore, *esse* (transferred or 'transumed' from theology into natural philosophy) describes a thing's essences, rather than its actuality. As I argued in previous sections, Gilbert's redefinition of *esse* has the effect of shifting the focus from the actuality of particular sensible things to their essence: "[B]eing is indeed naturally prior to all which is."[82] The primacy of essence over existence is a mark of Porreta's metaphysics (*In de Hebdom.* I.27-35 [193: 55–194: 92]) and reduces the relation between the world and God to essential likeness, independently of their actuality. The link between God and creation is purely formal and does not extend to efficient causality.

However, does not Porreta's concept of conformity *(conformitas)* among particular sensible things indicate a substantial likeness that provides a basis for the reality of universals?[83] If so, do not particulars partake of the real being of God by participating in forms that are ideas in the divine mind? The problem with this sort of reading is that it ignores the logic underpinning Porreta's account. The latter begins with

---

80. Schmidt, *Gottheit und Trinität nach dem Kommentar des Gilbert Porreta zu Boethius De Trinitate,* pp. 31-35, 59.

81. Marenbon, "Gilbert of Poitiers," p. 337.

82. See, *supra,* note 57.

83. *In de Trin.* I.v.24-25 (144: 63-78); *In Contra Eut.* II.22-24, 28 (269: 34-50; 270: 73-77).

God and traces the inherence of uncreated ideas in particular sensible things by deduction. Universals are in particulars because the will of the Good gives rise to a derivation that makes everything good by metonymy, i.e., by contiguity, not by actual similarity. Likewise, forms that descend along the hierarchy of being until they reach embodiment confer subsistences that can only be mathematically identified and analyzed. Gilbert's approach is therefore exclusively formal and centered around logic and language.

Moreover, the mathematical method of abstraction and induction from particular things is based upon the a priori assumption that forms can only be apprehended by the mind, not the senses. Therefore, demonstration by *more geometrico,* which consists in mapping forms according to the highest generality and abstraction, commits Porreta to discarding the actuality of particular sensible things in favor of logical possibility. This contrasts with Boethius, for whom all things are at once singular and universal. The relationality of particulars to God is phenomenally discernible because a thing's actuality intimates both its own potency and the power of being *(virtus essendi)* which actualizes it and thereby perfects its form. The principal difference is that Boethius focuses on metaphysical potentiality, not logical possibility.

The divergence between Boethius' and Porreta's development of the shared metaphysical tradition could hardly be more marked. Boethius follows Augustine in arguing that God's choice among an infinite set of possibilities reveals his goodness and love and that actualization and individuation mark the perfection of divinely given form, so that everything may be and may abide and in so doing testifies to God's plenitudinous reality. Under the influence of eleventh-century theology, in particular the concept of divine omnipotence in Petrus Damianus (c. 1007-1072), Gilbert argues that God's choice among an infinite set of possibilities reveals nothing other than his absolute power.[84] This theological — or perhaps fideistic — approach implies that in Porreta's 'grammatical Platonism' there is no rational demonstration of a thing's pro-

---

84. For a detailed account of the shift from Augustine and Boethius to Porreta, see Simo Knuuttila, "Possibility and Necessity in Gilbert of Poitiers," in Jolivet and de Libera, eds., *Gilbert de Poitiers et ses contemporains,* pp. 199-217; Knuuttila, *Modalities in Medieval Philosophy,* (London: Routledge, 1993), pp. 81-82; Knuuttila, "On the History of Theory of Modality as Alternativeness," in *Potentialität und Possibilität. Modalaussagen in der Geschichte der Metaphysik,* ed. Thomas Buchheim, Corneille H. Kneepkens, and Kuno Lorenz (Stuttgart: Frommann-Holzboog, 2001), pp. 219-36, esp. pp. 230-36.

cession from God and its reversion to him because that which the human mind perceives has been emptied of all cognitive content in such a way that faith alone leads human cognition from things to God.

This approach is evinced by Porreta's commentary on the Pauline epistles, in particular the following extract:

> It says that philosophy is knowledge about natural things and that it is deduced from rational principles, but the necessity which belongs to them is the customary one. One divine power is the source of the motion and substance of all things and of the connection of the causes of those things which are said to belong to them. Some people, who don't understand what is said, when hearing that some things are called necessary, not considering the reasons for saying so, deprive them of God's power, thinking that what is called necessary on the basis of custom of nature cannot be not the case absolutely. This is why they deny that a virgin could have given birth to a child and other similar things called impossible in the sense just mentioned.[85]

In other words, natural regularities depend for their operation on God's will. Revealed truths about God's essence, namely his absolute power, have a corrective function in that they can highlight which natural phenomena are erroneously taken to be absolute necessities by natural philosophy and natural reason. However, Porreta goes further than this and argues that the very actuality of particular things is misleading because their changeability induces a wrong sense of necessity: "Because no temporal things are free from mutability, the whole customary necessity belonging to them is shaky."[86]

That which is *(id quod est)* entertains no rationally intelligible rela-

---

85. *"Philosophiam vocat scientiam naturaliam deductam ex principiis rationum, quorum tamen est consuetudini accommodata necessitas. Sed divina ex una potestate omnium motus est atque substantia et earum, quae ad se dicuntur, causarum conexio. Quidam autem imperiti ea, quae dicuntur, ex dicendi rationibus minime iudicantes cum audiunt quaedam esse necessaria, divinae derogant potestati putantes id, quod iuxta naturae consuetudinem dicitur, necessarium absolute non posse non esse. Ideoque negant virginem peperisse et huiusmodi alia, quae predicto modo dicuntur impossibilia"* (quoted in Nielsen, *Philosophy and Theology in the Twelfth Century,* p. 136, n. 82; translation in Knuuttila, *Modalities in Medieval Philosophy,* pp. 75-76).

86. *"Et quoniam in temporalibus nihil est quod mutabilitati non sit obnoxium, tota illorum consuetudini accommodata necessitas nutat"* (*In de Trin.* II.i.7 [164: 36-8]).

tion with transcendent forms, nor is it relational to God. For divine creative and 'concretive' activity produces copies that bear but a weak resemblance to their exemplar *(secundum extrinsica)*;[87] a resemblance that can only be ascertained by mathematical abstraction in the mind and is absent from the phenomenal manifestation of material forms (as for Plato and Augustine). That which exists merely represents one possibility in an infinite set of equally probable possibilities. As Simo Knuuttila has documented, Gilbert, "inspired by Peter Damian's more pious than philosophical ideas,"[88] asserted that the actual world and its history are no more compelling than any other possible set of alternative providential projects:

> All things are similarly subject to His power, so that as those, which have not been existent can have been existent, and those which do not exist or will not exist, can exist, in the same way those which have been existent can have been non-existent, and those which are or will be, can be non-existent.[89]

In this passage, Porreta claims that divine power is absolute and can alter the past, the present, and the future. The actuality of particular beings is not only radically contingent. More importantly, it does not disclose anything about God's creative and concretive activity other than his absolute will. Since both the actuality of particular things and the perfection of form can retrospectively be undone, neither actualization nor individuation nor perfection matters metaphysically.

---

87. Nielsen, *Philosophy and Theology in the Twelfth Century*, p. 73.

88. Knuuttila, "Possibility and Necessity in Gilbert of Poitiers," p. 199. For Petrus Damiani's *Letter on Divine Omnipotence*, see *Pierre Damien. Disputatio super quaestione qua quaeritur, si deus omnipotens est, quomodo potest agere ut quae facta sunt facta non fuerint* (c. 1067), trans. and ed. A. Cantin (Paris: Éditions Cerf, collec. "Sources chrétiennes" no. 191, 1972). On Damiani's conception of *potentia Dei absoluta*, see William Courtenay, *Capacity and Volition: A History of the Distinction of Absolute and Ordained Power* (Bergamo: Pierluigi Lubrina Editore, 1990), esp. pp. 25-28. See also Teresa Antonelli, "Elementi della metafisica di Pier Damiani — Il problema del possibile nel medio evo," in *Die Metaphysik im Mittelalter*, ed. Peter Wilpert (Berlin: De Gruyter, 1963), pp. 161-64.

89. *"Aeque etenim uniuersa eius subiecta sunt potestati ut silicet sicut, quaecumque non fuerunt, possunt fuisse et, quaecumque non sunt uel non erunt, possunt esse ita etiam, quaecumque fuerunt, possunt non fuisse et, quaecumque sunt uel erunt, possunt non esse"* (*In De Trin.* I.iv.72 [129: 25-28]; translation in Knuuttila, *Modalities in Medieval Philosophy*, p. 78). Cf. *In Contra Eut.* II.16 (267: 94–268: 98).

The reason for this devaluation of actuality is *not* Porreta's argument that relation is extrinsic to God, which is true because God lacks nothing at all and nothing can be added to him. Instead, actuality is abandoned in favor of possibility in order to emphasize God's absolute power. All we can know about God is the absoluteness of his will. The goodness that derives from divine volition has no objective basis other than the mind and its faculty to abstract forms from particulars and to relate them to their transcendental source based on the belief in a Creator God, not by intellectual cognition based on induction (*In Contra Eut.* I.32-33 [248: 73–249: 83]). As Nielsen puts it, "in faith and theology, where one does not restrict oneself merely to considering the created world, knowledge of true necessity is achieved by experiencing the divine will, which is truly immutable."[90] This account of actuality and possibility marks a radical break with that of patristic Christian Neo-Platonism, according to which things, *when* they are actual, are so necessarily, in the sense that their actualization owes nothing to accident or fortune.[91] So configured, actuality testifies to God's power of being and the love and goodness by which he imparts being to everything that is, seen and unseen.

Coupled with the nonactual likeness or similarity *(conformitas)* among particular sensible things, the primacy of essence reinforces the focus on logical possibility rather than metaphysical actuality. Contrary to Boethius' metaphysical understanding of potency as dispositions of real powers to be, Gilbert's understanding is theological or, more accurately, fideistic because *this* world is but one in an infinite number of equally probable possibilities that God can bring into actuality for no reasons other than his absolute will. Likewise the natural operation of *this* world and the underlying natural laws can be suspended or abrogated:

> When it is said that man cannot be dissolved or that man cannot be not dissolved, it is not because God could not do it, but because God ordained that the condition of man is such before the fall or after the fall or after the resurrection. In the same way it is said that the sun cannot be not moving, although divine power could stop it from moving. There is an infinity of similar cases.[92]

---

90. Nielsen, *Philosophy and Theology in the Twelfth Century,* p. 137.

91. For example, Boethius, *1 In Periherm.* 110.28–111.1. See, *supra,* chapter 3.

92. *"Non enim iccirco dicitur non posse uel dissolui uel non dissolui quod Deus haec facere non possit sed quod, ut ita se haberet uel ante peccatum uel post peccatum uel post*

For Porreta, God's power and God's will are not coextensive. While divine executive power is immutable and absolute, divine choice determines which of the alternative providential programs will be realized and which of the hitherto unrealized potentialities will be actualized in the real world. In other words, there is a difference between God's absolute power and God's power *in actu*. This difference was later called the distinction between *potentia Dei absoluta* and *potentia Dei ordinata*.[93] Even though his conceptuality is clearer than Damian's, Porreta also privileges *potentia Dei absoluta* and stresses God's arbitrary will.[94] As such, God's rationally unintelligible will replaces the transcendence and radiance of divine goodness in the patristic Christian Neo-Platonism of Gregory, Augustine, Boethius, and Dionysius.

This is significant for the question of individuation because it raises the problem of the uniqueness of the world and all individuals therein. As I argued in section 5 of this chapter, Gilbert distinguishes between singularity, individuality, and personality. Singular things are individuated by possible properties, and it is the modal element that determines individuality:

> The property of something, which is naturally dissimilar to everything else that actually or potentially was or is or will be, is truly called and truly is, not only singular or particular, but individual. . . . For this reason Plato's whole form, which is neither in act nor by nature similar to anything else, is truly individual.[95]

In his commentary on *De Trinitate*, Porreta highlights the modal character of his theory of individuality: "Platonity collected from all things

---

resurrectionem homo, diuina uoluntas statuit. Secundum hoc dicitur sol non posse non moueri cum tamen diuina potestas eum, ut non moueatur, sistere possit. Et huiusmodi sunt infinita" (*In Contra Eut.* V.42 [322: 43-49]). Translation in Knuuttila, *Modalities in Medieval Philosophy*, p. 77 (translation modified).

93. Courtenay, *Capacity and Volition*, esp. pp. 25-36, 65-79; Knuuttila, *Modalities in Medieval Philosophy*, esp. pp. 100-102.

94. Grzegorz Stolarski, *La possibilité et l'être. Un essai sur la détermination du fondement ontologique de la possibilité dans la pensée de Thomas d'Aquin* (Fribourg: Éditions Universitaires, 2001), pp. 204-5.

95. *"Illa uero cuiuslibet proprietas, quae naturali dissimilitudine ab omnibus — quae actu uel potestate fuerunt uel sunt uel futura sunt — differt, non modo 'singularis' aut 'particularis' sed etiam 'indiuidua uere et vocatur et est.'. . . . Hac igitur ratione Platonis tota forma — nulli neque actu neque natura conformis — uere est indiuidua"* (*In Contra Eut.* III.13, 15 [274: 81-90]).

which, in act and by nature [potency], have been, are or will be Plato's." The term 'by nature' indicates that which could be without ever being actually, i.e., an abstract possibility that may or may not be concretized and depends for its concretion on divine will alone. Knuuttila summarizes Gilbert's modal metaphysics as follows: "Necessities and possibilities are not considered primarily as types of events or individuals, instantiated in various degrees in actual history. Modal terms basically refer to things and structures in various conceivable states of affairs which, as the intentional correlates of divine choice and power, are in principle realizable."[96]

God's absolute power tends to undermine human agency and overrides nature rather than accomplishing it. Unlike the Church Fathers and Doctors who (albeit in different ways) connect actualization with the Neo-Platonist concept of perfectibility, Gilbert severs individuation from action. This move is mirrored by his claim that the first good can only be participated in extrinsically and externally (*In De Trinitate* I.2.10).[97] Thus, the link between the Good and the existence and actuality of particulars becomes unhinged; relationality is abandoned in favor of an absolute dependency of created being on God, which undermines the capacity of particulars to perfect their form by participating in the Trinitarian relationality.

9. Islam, Christianity, and the Passage to Modernity

In this final section, I will connect my earlier discussion of Islamic theology and Avicenna to my reading of Gilbert Porreta. By driving a wedge between creation and Creator, Ibn Sīnā and Porreta paved the way for the long and nonlinear transition from the Middle Ages to modernity. Both reduced divine creative activity to a causal link between the uncreated essence of the first being or God and the created essences of particular beings. As such, they elevated essence over above existence and also redefined metaphysics as the science of being *qua* being rather than the divine source of being, thereby subordinating God to the general category of being and privileging ontology vis-à-vis theology. There is thus a clear lineage from Avicenna and Porreta via Duns Scotus and

---

96. Knuuttila, *Modalities in Medieval Philosophy*, p. 82.
97. Nielsen, *Philosophy and Theology in the Twelfth Century*, esp. pp. 77-81.

William of Ockham to Descartes, Spinoza, and Kant, as I will indicate at the end of this section and develop in greater detail in chapters 6-9.

In section 2 of the present chapter, I already mentioned the lasting impact of Avicenna on Islamic philosophy and theology. Though undoubtedly less renowned, Porreta was a key figure in medieval thought. Through the influence of the Porretan school, Gilbert's ontology shaped Christian theology from the late eleventh to the early fourteenth century. Porreta's *De sex principiis* was commented on by Albert the Great, Robert Kilwardby, and Walter Burleigh. More importantly, the main disciples of Gilbert who endorsed and developed his thinking included influential figures like Thierry of Chartres, Alain of Lille, Simon of Tournai, and Nicholas of Amiens. Each of them made a decisive contribution to the terms of philosophical and theological debate that prevailed from the second half of the twelfth to the early fourteenth century and beyond, notably the two methods of demonstration — dialectical *quaestiones* and 'mathematical' reasoning *(more geometrico)*.[98]

Avicenna's and Porreta's shared emphasis on the abstraction of general essences at the expense of the embodiment of universal being in particular beings influenced the reception of Aristotle's ontology and theology into medieval Christian and Islamic thought. That is why Gilson is right to say that Gilbert's teaching "favored the diffusion of that form of Platonism which one might term the realism of essences and which Avicenna's philosophy was soon to reinforce so powerfully."[99] The variant of Platonism referred to by Gilson is precisely the strand that we can trace to Porphyry and Ammonius, a strongly logicized and Aristotelianized synthesis of Aristotle and Plato that Avicenna and Porreta supplemented with Aristotelian logic, grammar, and ontology — notably Aristotle's substitution of the concept of individual substantial essence for Plato's account of transcendent forms in things (as shown in chapter 1).

Indeed, the priority of essence and possibility over existence and actuality entered Christian theology through Gilbert's legacy. This legacy was reinforced by the translation of Avicenna's *Shifā* (including the

---

98. On the influence of Gilbert, see Chenu, "Un essai de méthode théologique au XIIe siècle," pp. 258-67; Chenu, *La théologie au douzième siècle*, pp. 98-106, 124-28, 142-48, 308-14, 379-85; Henri de Lubac, *Exégèse Médiévale*, 4 vols. (Paris: Aubier-Montaigne, 1959-61), II.1, p. 232; Marc Ozilou, "Introduction générale," in *Saint Bonaventure. Les Sentences, Questions sur Dieu, Commentaire du premier livre des sentences de Pierre Lombard,* ed. M. Ozilou (Paris: Presses Universitaires de France, 2002), pp. 11-13.

99. Gilson, *La philosophie au Moyen Âge,* p. 268 (my translation).

Metaphysics) and also by a Porphyrian-Ammonian (rather than an Iamblichean-Proclean) reading of major books such as the *Liber de causis,* whose historical importance has been established beyond reasonable doubt: "[T]he main interest of this *opus,* from a historical point of view, is to provide a testimony of the insertion of Avicenna's *Metaphysics* into Western philosophy."[100] Building on Gilson's pioneering research in relation to the impact of Avicenna on Christian theology,[101] Marie-Thérèse d'Alverny has traced Latin translations of Avicenna's works to the second half of the twelfth century in Toledo, where Ibn Daūd (Avendauth) and Dominicus Gundissalinus completed the Latin version of Avicenna's *Shifā,* including the *Metaphysics,* and made it available to the emerging network of European universities.[102] Whether or not Gundissalinus was himself in contact with Gilbert's disciples of the Chartrean School, there is sufficient historical evidence to suggest that

> the milieu of Gilbert of Poitiers' disciples ... was particularly well prepared to receive Avicenna's *Metaphysics* insofar as the latter drew on Plotinus much more than its Aristotelian parts. It is among them [Gilbert's disciples] that one can sense the syntheses of Saint Augustine, of the great mystic Dionysius the Areopagite and of Avicenna. These syntheses characterize what Étienne Gilson has termed 'Latin Avicennism' [*avicennisme latin*].[103]

This analysis is confirmed by M. H. Vicaire, who has documented the crucial impact of Avicenna's position on Gilbert's disciples, and this already before 1215.[104]

Coupled with Avicenna's essentialism and possibilism, Gilbert's formalism endorsed and developed the Porphyrian scheme of emanation

100. Marie-Thérèse d'Alverny, *Avicenne en Occident* (Paris: Vrin, 1993), ch. 11, p. 173 (my translation).

101. Étienne Gilson, "Les sources gréco-arabes de l'augustianisme avicennisant," *Archives d'histoire doctrinale et littéraire du Moyen Âge* 4 (1929): 5-107; É. Gilson, "Avicenne en Occident au Moyen Âge," *Archives d'histoire doctrinale et littéraire du Moyen Âge* 39 (1969): 89-121.

102. Alverny, *Avicenne en Occident,* ch. 3, pp. 64, 69; ch. 5, pp. 71-75.

103. Alverny, *Avicenne en Occident,* ch. 2, p. 15 (my translation). Though Alverny's reading of the Aristotelian and Neo-Platonist traditions needs to be qualified (see, *supra,* section 2), I agree with her point about the integration of Avicenna into Christian theology by Porreta's disciples.

104. Vicaire, "Les Porrétains et l'avicennisme avant 1215," pp. 449-82.

rather than the Boethian and Dionysian conception of divine plenitude and self-diffusion. He thereby reinforced the stress on causation and multiplicity of forms rather than the rival concept of relation and form-matter union, all of which is apparent in the interpretation of the aforementioned *Liber de causis* that was dominant in the twelfth and early thirteenth century,[105] until Aquinas rightly attributed the book to Proclus. As M.-T. d'Alverny remarks, the *Liber* is not an isolated instance of Avicenna's influence on Christian theology. Others include an *Epistola de causa et causato* and two anonymous texts that go back to the beginning of the thirteenth century.[106] A prime example of this confluence and mutual reinforcement are the later works by some members of the School of Chartres. In these writings, individual substantial form contains and determines a thing's essence, supplanting the divine act of being which brings that thing into existence.[107] The implication is that the actuality of created beings is severed from God's pure act and that the perfection of created beings is separate from the synergic fusion of human and divine work (or theurgy) that is central to the Neo-Platonism of Iamblichus and Proclus (as well as Aquinas, as I will suggest in the following chapter).[108]

Porreta's 'Latin Avicennism' was not confined to individual members of the School of Chartres but extended to leading Franciscans — here I anticipate some of the arguments that I develop in greater detail in chapter 6 — notably John Duns Scotus (c. 1265/66-1308) and William of Ockham (c. 1289/90-1349). In a groundbreaking article of 1927, Étienne Gilson showed how Avicenna's ontology and theology constituted the basis for Scotus's early modern alternative to Aquinas's synthesis of biblical revelation and ancient philosophy.[109] As Gilson notes, the link between Avicenna and Porreta and Scotus and Ockham is Henry of Ghent (d. 1293), a contemporary of St. Thomas Aquinas (c. 1225-1274). Under the

---

105. Alverny, *Avicenne en Occident,* ch. 5, p. 81; ch. 11, pp. 170-81.

106. Alverny, *Avicenne en Occident,* ch. 11, p. 178.

107. For instance, an anonymous *Commentary of Boethius' De Trinitate,* attributed to the Chartrean School, says that *"actus enim possibilitatis perfectio, perfectio vero omnis ex forma est. Actus igitur forma"* (quoted in Chenu, *La théologie au douzième siècle,* p. 312).

108. On Iamblichus and Proclus, see Gregory Shaw, *Theurgy and the Soul: The Neoplatonism of Iamblichus* (University Park: Pennsylvania State University Press, 1995), pp. 21-27, 59-106, 199-228, and John Milbank, "Sophiology and Theurgy: The New Theological Horizon," in Adrian Pabst and Christoph Schneider, eds., *Encounter between Eastern Orthodoxy and Radical Orthodoxy* (Aldershot, UK: Ashgate, 2009), pp. 45-85.

109. Étienne Gilson, "Avicenne et le point de départ de Duns Scot," *Archives d'histoire doctrinale et littéraire du Moyen Âge* 2 (1927): 89-149.

influence of Avicenna, Henry of Ghent introduced into Christian theology the separation of divine essence from divine ideas *(ideae)* and that which they produce *(ideatae)*. In line with Gilbert, Ghent conceptualizes the link between *ideae* and *ideatae* in merely causal terms, as a relation of producer to product.[110]

Even though he (rightly) rejects Avicenna's claim that creation is necessary, Ghent nonetheless agrees with him — and here I paraphrase Heidegger — that "logical possibility stands higher than real actuality" (at least for created beings).[111] Since God does not create out of necessity but rather in an act of supreme freedom, it follows for Ghent that essences are possible unless and until they are actualized. In his idiom, possible essences have *esse essentiae* before they are given *esse existentiae*. So configured, possibility is an intermediary instance between pure divine imagination and full actuality.[112] As possibles, these essences or *ideatae* have their own independent being. The being of essence *(esse essentiae)* must be different from the radical simplicity and unity of divine essence. Yet precisely because only God's essence is existence, the being of created essence cannot be the same as the actuality of existence. Since Ghent does not follow Aquinas's account of actualization in terms of God's pure act of being *(actus purus)*, he tends to devalue *esse existentiae* to the point where it expresses nothing but God's free will that a thing may be and may abide. As such, Ghent's account of God's free creation is little more than the mirror image of Avicenna's conception of God's necessary creation whereby God's volition which causes things to exist cannot be rationally known as divine but must be fideistically believed.

Moreover, Ghent separates the actuality of created things from the Creator's pure being by claiming that the difference between *esse existentiae* and *esse essentiae* is not real but instead purely formal. The implication is that the general category of *esse* is now the first object of

---

110. Henry of Ghent, *Summa*, q. 2 a. 5, 7-14, cited in Cunningham, *Genealogy of Nihilism*, p. 15.

111. In chapter 9, I briefly argue that Heidegger's attempted deconstruction of metaphysics in terms of onto-theology is historically and conceptually flawed because it is grounded in the modern (and residually transcendentalist) primacy of possibility over actuality. However, the confusion of the highest being and the most general being that is expressed by the concept of onto-theology is an important hermeneutical key to unlock the key difference between the medieval account of analogous being and the modern theory of univocal being.

112. Cunningham, *Genealogy of Nihilism*, pp. 13-16.

human intellection and that as such it is thinkable apart from and outside God.[113] Since *esse* now provides both the highest and most general ground for being *qua* being, Ghent can be said to be the co-founder (together with Avicenna) of onto-theology.[114]

Building on Ghent, Duns Scotus establishes the absolute priority of possibility over actuality by positing as the object of metaphysics univocal being *(ens univocum)*, an account consonant with Avicenna's conception of common nature in his *Metaphysics* V.1-2. So construed, being can only be cognized if we can somehow have prior knowledge of what can be, in order to avoid reducing ontology either to physics or to logic. As Catherine Pickstock has shown, the univocity of being and the formal distinction between essence and existence imply that the link between actuality and potentiality is now no longer ontological and as such making itself known to the human intellect. Rather, it is epistemological and thus constructed by the mind and projected onto the world.[115] After Scotus, being as an actuality is not just thinkable apart from or outside of God before it is actualized by God's free will (as in Ghent). But, more fundamentally, being as a logically possible existence has its own reality: in the words of Scotus, "a logical possibility could remain separately in power by its own nature, even when there were, *per impossibile,* no omnipotence to which it could be an object."[116] Here the threefold influence of Avicenna is palpable. First, *ens* is the object of metaphysics and the first object of the intellect. Second, human experience of reality involves general categories rather than singular beings or universal being. Third, the cause of knowledge is separate from the object known. Taken together, these three claims amount to axiological primacy of abstraction over the senses and the imagination and an epistemological dualism between subject and object. As for Porreta, knowledge of the cause is different from knowledge of its effect, which means that

113. Henry of Ghent, *S. Qu. Ordin.,* a. 24, q. 7, ad 1 and ad 2; q. 8, q. 9, in *Henry of Ghent's Summa: The Questions on God's Existence and Essence (Articles 21-24),* trans. J. Decorte and R. J. Teske, SJ (Leuven: Peeters, 2005), pp. 243-73.

114. For a reading of Ghent in this sense, see Édouard-Henri Wéber, "Eckhart et l'ontothéologisme: Histoire et conditions d'une rupture," in *Maître Eckhart à Paris. Une critique médiévale de l'ontothéologie,* ed. Emile Zum Brunn et al. (Paris: Presses Universitaires de France, 1984), pp. 13-83.

115. Catherine Pickstock, *After Writing: On the Liturgical Consummation of Philosophy* (Oxford: Blackwell, 1998), pp. 121-31.

116. Duns Scotus, *Ordinatio* I, d. 36, q. 60-61, in *Opera Omnia* (Civitas Vaticana: Vatican, 1982), vol. 6, n. 296.

any form of 'adequation' *(convenientia)* between the knowing subject and the known object no longer pertains (as for the Christian Neo-Platonism of Aquinas, as I will suggest in the following chapter).

Finally, Ockham radicalizes Scotus's position by arguing that possible being is somehow present before being is intelligible and that "possible being is something a creature has of itself . . . [and that] a creature is possible, not because anything pertains to it, but because it can exist in reality."[117] For Ockham, any form of community of being is void of any reality. As Cunningham has pointed out, the ontological real difference of essence and existence is reduced to factuality.[118] In consequence, being as a logical possibility is of itself, and a thing's actual existence does not alter its potency in any way. In other words, for Ockham, actuality loses all ontological importance and is nothing but an expression of God's unknowable (and, in this sense, arbitrary) *potentia absoluta*. After Ockham, actual being ceases to entertain any phenomenally perceptible or ontologically intelligible relation with potential being, a move that reduces ontological potency to a priori possibility.

Thus, possibility is granted not only its independent ontological station, but becomes the absolute precondition of knowing actuality. It is the absolute primacy of possibility over actuality that constitutes the mark of modern metaphysics. In this sense, modern metaphysics is secular because the primacy of possibility, far from respecting God's free will and absolute initiative, is ultimately complicit with a form of necessitarianism that is at odds with orthodox Jewish, Christian, and Muslim teachings on divine creation. By inverting the patristic and medieval primacy of real actuality over modal possibility, Ghent, Scotus, and Ockham build on Avicenna and Porreta's shared legacy and inaugurate a new era in theology: "[U]ntil the early fourteenth century possibilities were treated as having a foundation in God; in the modern theory they were dissociated from this ontological backing."[119] Moreover, possi-

---

117. William of Ockham, *I Sent.* d. 43, q. 2, in Guillelmi de Ockham, *Opera Philosophica et Theologica,* ed. G. I. Etzekorn and F. E. Kelley (St. Bonaventure, NY: St. Bonaventure University, 1979), vol. 4, pp. 640-50.

118. Cunningham, *Genealogy of Nihilism,* p. 19. I am indebted to Cunningham's work for arguments in this paragraph.

119. S. Knuuttila and L. Alanen, "The Foundations of Modality and Conceivability in Descartes and His Predecessors," in *Modern Modalities: Studies of the History of Modal Theories from Medieval Nominalism to Logical Positivism,* ed. S. Knuuttila (Dordrecht: Kluwer, 1988), pp. 1-69 (41).

bilities are not only removed from actuality, but actuality itself is drained of all relation to its divine source: "[D]ivine actuality disappears behind the infinite variety of what is possible."[120]

Following Avicenna and Porreta, it was Ghent, Scotus, and Ockham who developed the primacy of essence over existence. As such, they were instrumental in the birth and rise of modern ontology and theology. Coupled with the univocity of being and the formal distinction between existence and essence, the primacy of possibility over actuality provides the basis for a universal *mathēsis* whereby reality is reduced to abstract and spatialized relations among things and between the knowing subject and the known object. This formalization of being underpins modern philosophy from Descartes via Suárez, Wolff, and Leibniz to Kant and Peirce.[121] Indeed, the binary account of being in terms of the possible and the necessary, which Christian theology inherited from both Gilbert and Avicenna, stretches in different ways via Leibniz's equation of God with *possibilitas* and Kant's claim that being "is not a real predicate," since "the real contains no more than the merely possible,"[122] to Hegel's logic of necessity. In the West at least, late scholastic theology established the hegemony of the possible over the actual, a hegemony perpetuated by modern philosophy.

10. Conclusion: Faith and Reason

Modernity unfolded in different ways in the Latin West and in the Byzantine East or in the Islamic world. It is therefore dangerous to apply

120. Harry R. Klocker, *William of Ockham and the Divine Freedom* (Milwaukee: Marquette University Press, 1992), p. 114.

121. See, *inter alia*, Étienne Gilson, *Jean Duns Scot. Introduction à Ses Positions Fondamentales* (Paris: Vrin, 1922), pp. 595-640; Gilson, *La philosophie au Moyen Âge*, pp. 591-620, 638-86; Ludwig Honnefelder, *Ens inquantum ens. Der Begriff des Seiendes als solchen als Gegenstand der Metaphysik nach der Lehre des Johannes Duns Scotus* (Münster: Aschendorff, 1979); L. Honnefelder, *Scientia transcendens. Die formale Bestimmung der Seiendheit und Realität in der Metaphysik des Mittelalters und der Neuzeit (Duns Scot, Suarez, Kant, Peirce)* (Hamburg: F. Meiner, 1990); L. Honnefelder, "Der zweite Anfang der Metaphysik. Voraussetzungen, Ansätze und Folgen der Wiederbegründung der Metaphysik im 13/14. Jahrhundert," in *Philosophie im Mittelalter. Entwicklungslinien und Paradigmen*, ed. J.-P. Beckmann et al. (Hamburg: F. Meiner, 1987), pp. 165-86; Jean-François Courtine, *Suarez et le système de la métaphysique* (Paris: Presses Universitaires de France, 1990).

122. Immanuel Kant, *Critique of Pure Reason*, A599/B627.

the same methods, assumptions, and historical templates. But to recapitulate the argument of this chapter, it is clear that in the passage to the modern era theology was separated from philosophy and reason sundered from faith. The origins of modern rationalism and fideism can be traced to influential figures such as Avicenna and Gilbert Porreta who redefined metaphysics as the study of being *qua* being and restricted rational cognition to the causal dependence of particular beings on the universal being of God. By focusing on essence at the expense of existence, both abandoned the Neo-Platonic vision of God's creative act of being and human union with the divine through both contemplation and theurgic practices framed by the doxologic of praising and giving thanks to the divine through prayer, worship, and works.

Moreover, the emphasis on essence in both high medieval Islamic and Christian thought introduced a split between Creator and creation, as the link pertaining between them was now increasingly viewed in purely causal terms. Taken together, Avicenna's and Scotus's shared formal distinction between existence and essence and Ockham's denial of the reality of divine universals in created particulars favored the emergence of ontological nominalism and theological voluntarism, which characterize modernity in both the Christian and the Islamic world. Reinforced by the growing separation of reason from faith and the rise of rationalism and fideism, the modern settlement has promoted the kind of secular extremism and religious fundamentalism which have sidelined traditional religion and which the Pope's Regensburg address condemned.

In this chapter, I have also examined Porreta's twelfth-century theory of individuation. Gilbert's account of universals is not nominalist but his position tends to be formalist, in the sense that there is no objective basis for the presence of universals in particulars other than what the mind establishes independently of perceiving actually existing things (by contrast, for Augustine and Boethius, actuality discloses God's creative and concurrent activity). Particular composites are individuated by the confluence of a thing's 'total property' (i.e., the collection of all *'quo ests'* that constitute an individual) and the derivation of the Good from divine volition. Based on the separation of theology from natural philosophy and the primacy of the mathematical method (demonstration by *more geometrico*), Porreta focuses on the descent of forms into materiality as a result of the will of God whence everything derives. However, this derivation is not amenable to human reason. Only faith can give us access to the ultimate cause that actualizes and individuates particular material things.

One of the main differences with Plato, Aristotle, and Boethius is that Porreta reasons from abstract possibility to concrete actuality. As a result, particular sensible things neither mediate nor intimate the creative and concretive action of God that individuates them. Creation, concretion, and individuation are not manifest in the actuality of things and thus cannot be cognized rationally by the mind. According to Gilbert, only faith gives access to the presence of transcendent forms in immanent things. The centrality of divine absolute power and modal possibility marks a radical departure from the Platonist framework of relationality and participation and the Aristotelian metaphysics of act and potency. Porreta's emphasis on abstraction and demonstration by *more geometrico* leads him to separate theology from natural philosophy and to make Trinitarian relationality an object of pure faith that is not intelligible to natural reason. As a result, participation in the Trinity is extrinsic and does not affect the existence and actuality of created beings. Gilbert thus severs the real existential link between the Good and particular beings and thus undermined the vision that Augustine and Boethius had inherited from the Platonist tradition and extended towards a metaphysics of relationality. It was Aquinas who provided a compelling critique of 'grammatical Platonism,' radical Aristotelianism, and the essentialism of both Porreta and Avicenna — as I show in the following chapter.

CHAPTER 5

Participation in the Act of Being

1. Introduction: Aquinas's Retrieval of Neo-Platonist Realism

In the previous chapter, I examined Gilbert Porreta's theory of individuation and drew some comparisons with Boethius' work upon which he commented. Gilbert's realism can be questioned because his metaphysics and epistemology begin with forms or essences, not the actual existence of particulars. Contrary to Boethius' metaphysics, which emphasizes the difference between existence and essence and the relational orientation of individual composite substances, Porreta privileges modal metaphysics and *more geometrico,* which moves from abstract possibility to concrete actuality. This devaluation of actuality means that particular things disclose little more than their own immanent forms, a collection of *'quo ests'* that constitute a thing's 'total property' and make it an individual. Particulars neither mediate nor intimate God's universal creative and concretive action, which is the first cause of actualization and individuation.

In this chapter, I argue that St. Thomas Aquinas (c. 1225-1274) retrieves and extends the metaphysical tradition of Christian Neo-Platonism that he inherited from figures such as Gregory, Augustine, Boethius, and Dionysius. Unlike Porreta's 'grammatical Platonism' centered upon abstraction and demonstration by *more geometrico,* Aquinas reconfigures the relation between 'natural philosophy' and 'revealed theology' along Neo-Platonist lines. In this manner, he reverses the formalist priority of essence over existence and develops an account of individuation that can (perhaps anachronistically but nonetheless validly) be described as both realist and idealist, in the sense that God's universal act of being (which is also an infinite intelligence always in act) actualizes all particular beings in virtue of divine self-diffusive goodness and love. Thomas's emphasis on God's love and goodness as well as on ideas in the divine mind is evidence that his theology is neither proto-rationalist nor purely natural; instead it blends God's cataphatic kenosis as well as the unity of the divine and the human in Christ (following the Cappadocians) with our apophatic ascent to union with the Creator (following Dionysius). Far from emphasizing reason alone, Aquinas fuses rationality with the supernaturally infused habit of faith and argues that our bodily sensing is at once physical *and* spiritual (as I will show in sections 4 and 5). As such, our mind and body are elevated to union with God through spiritual sensing, the intellect, and the imagination. In this way, particulars are constituted and individuated by God's continuous gift of being.

I also argue that Thomas draws a distinction between the cause of individuation and the principle of individuation. The cause is the act of being which brings everything into actuality and makes it what it is. The principle is designated matter *(materia signata)*, which receives this act and thus explains diversity amongst specifically or formally identical beings. The act of being acts as a primary cause, which sustains the principle that functions as secondary causality. Knowledge of God's act of being enables composites to be further actualized and individuated by perfecting their own divinely given form. Such action also enhances the relational orientation of other beings and helps perfect the hierarchical cosmos as a whole.

2. *Subalternatio:* A Theological Ordering of the Sciences

The question of individuation is absolutely central to the work of the Angelic Doctor, and his account has generated scholarly controversies since the reception of his oeuvre.[1] According to Aquinas, the individuation of

1. For example, see Ingbert Klinger, *Das Prinzip der Individuation bei Thomas von Aquin: Versuch einer Interpretation und Vergleich mit zwei umstrittenen Opuscula* (Münster-schwarzach: Vier-Türme-Verlag, 1964). The most significant recent debate is between Joseph Owens and John F. Wippel. See Joseph Owens, "Thomas Aquinas: Dimensive Quantity as Individuating Principle," *Mediaeval Studies* 50 (1988): 279-310, and John F. Wippel, *The Metaphysical Thought of Thomas Aquinas: From Finite Being to Uncreated Being* (Washington, DC: Catholic University of America Press, 2000).

composites is both a philosophical and a theological problem. Philosophically, individuality concerns the Porphyrian logical tree in which the predicates descend from the most universal down to the most specific in connection with the individual subject of which they are affirmed or denied. Likewise, individuality pertains to natural philosophy, which describes how substantial form is received into matter and diversified by embodiment. Finally, individuality is metaphysical in the sense that it encompasses both the unity of particulars and their differentiation from other particulars, as unity is a transcendental that is convertible with being. Theologically, the individuation of composites raises questions about why the immaterial God would create not only immaterial substances composed of being and form (e.g., angels) but also material composite substances composed of being, form, and matter. How might such material composites partake of God's self-subsistent being and his absolute goodness and plenitude? This description of the problem of individuation emphasizes the inextricable link with the idea of creation and ties revealed theology *(sacra doctrina)* to metaphysics or natural theology *(divina scientia)*. The conjunction of both and their joint subordination to *Scientia Dei* is the mark of Aquinas's account of the sciences and constitutes the cornerstone of his theory of subalternation *(subalternatio)*.[2] Thomas elaborates this theory in his commentaries on Boethius, which differ significantly from those of Porreta, in particular concerning the relation between metaphysics and theology.[3] The main difference is that for Aquinas all human beings share the quest for the knowledge of truth *(veritas rerum)* and to know the truth is to know that everything is created *ex nihilo* (*In de Caelo* I 10, lec. 22, no. 8; *In II Met.* lec. 1, no. 275).

2. This is the basis for Aquinas's hierarchy of the sciences, which is ultimately governed by God's ordering wisdom. See Mark D. Jordan, *Ordering Wisdom: The Hierarchy of Philosophical Discourses in Aquinas* (Notre Dame: University of Notre Dame Press, 1986).

3. Martin Grabmann, *Die theologische Erkenntnis- und Einleitungslehre des heiligen Thomas von Aquin auf Grund seiner Schrift "In Boethium de Trinitate" im Zusammenhang der Scholastik des 13. und beginnenden 14. Jahrhunderts dargestellt* (Freiburg in der Schweiz: Paulusverlag, 1948); Siegfried Neumann, *Gegenstand und Methode der theoretischen Wissenschaften nach Thomas von Aquin aufgrund der* Expositio super librum Boethii De Trinitate (Münster and Westfalen: Aschendorfsche Verlagsbuchhandlung, 1965); Matthias Lutz-Bachmann, "Die Einteilung der Wissenschaften bei Thomas von Aquin. Ein Beitrag zur Rekonstruktion der Epistemologie in Quaestio 5, Artikel 1 des 'Kommentars' von Thomas zum Trinitätstraktat des Boethius," in *"Scientia" and "Disciplina." Wissenstheorie und Wissenschaftspraxis im 12. und 13. Jahrhundert,* ed. R. Berndt, M. Lutz-Bachmann, and R. M. W. Stammberger (Berlin: Akademie Verlag, 2002), pp. 235-47.

First I will spell out Thomas's theological ordering of the sciences in terms of his theory of subalternation. Compared with Gilbert's twelfth-century method, the nature of theological enquiry at the time of Aquinas displays both fundamental continuities and discontinuities. The *quaestio*-technique has become the dominant form of theological debate and writing, perhaps first and foremost in Peter Lombard's *Liber sententiarum*. Under the influence of a number of key figures such as Alain of Lille (d. 1203), William of Auxerre (d. 1231), Alexander of Hales (c. 1170-1245), William of Auvergne (c. 1180-1249), and Albert the Great (c. 1206-1280), the *quaestio*-approach is by now vastly extended in three different directions. First, the scope of application extends to all theological matters, except for exegesis. Second, the mode of operation includes the techniques of grammar, rhetoric, and dialectic. Third, the format consists of a meticulous subdivision in articles, each divided in questions, answers, objections, and responses to objections, as well as an increasing part devoted to free commentary — the *expositio textus*.[4] The main change relative to Gilbert's time is the increasing use of new philosophical concepts within theology. For this reason, the subject matter of theology has expanded to include speculative questions.[5] In part, this is the result of a growing influence of Aristotelian metaphysics mediated by Islamic theologians such as Averroes and Avicenna but also by Anselm and other medieval Christian theologians, as Sylvain Gouguenheim and others have shown.[6] In the specific case of Aquinas, the Neo-Platonist metaphysics of relational participation is the main conceptual framework that he uses in his critique of both 'grammatical Platonism' and radical Aristotelianism,[7] as I will suggest in this chapter.

Indeed, Aquinas's critical adaptation of Aristotelian metaphysics into Christian Neo-Platonist theology (which of course is itself already

---

4. Marie-Dominique Chenu, "Un essai de méthode théologique au XIIe siècle," *Revue des Sciences Philosophiques et Théologiques* 24 (1935): 258-67; André Hayen, "La théologie aux XIIe, XIIIe et XXe siècles," *Nouvelle Revue Théologique* 79 (1957): 1009-28, and 80 (1958): 113-32; M.-D. Chenu, *La théologie comme science au XIIIe siècle*, 3rd ed. (Paris: Vrin, 1969), pp. 15-57; M.-D. Chenu, *Introduction à l'étude de Saint Thomas d'Aquin* (Paris: Vrin, 1993), pp. 230-32; Jan A. Aertsen, *Nature and Creature: Thomas Aquinas's Way of Thought*, trans. Herbert D. Morton (Leiden: E. J. Brill, 1988).

5. Chenu, *La théologie comme science au XIIIe siècle*, pp. 22-26.

6. See, *supra*, chapter 4, notes 28 and 29.

7. Cf. Fernand van Steenberghen, *Thomas Aquinas and Radical Aristotelianism* (Washington, DC: Catholic University of America Press, 1980).

Aristotelian) is evident in his early works, the first commentary on the Sentences *(In Sent.)* and the treatise *De ente et essentia (De ente).* By the time Aquinas composes the former in 1252-56, one of the central disputes concerns the nature of theology and, more widely, the relation between philosophy and theology and between reason and faith. Thomas rethinks the status and operation of theology *(sacra doctrina)* by sketching a synthesis of the established theory of literary modes of interpreting Scripture with new metaphysical and epistemological considerations derived from the Neo-Platonism of Aristotle mediated by both patristic Christian Neo-Platonism and the early Islamic theology of Averroes and Avicenna. Indeed, Aquinas combines the shared Platonist and Aristotelian metaphysical priority of being over knowledge[8] with the Christian theological emphasis on divine self-revelation in order to develop a new account of divine illumination, as I will suggest in this and the following section.[9]

This synthesis charts a middle ground beyond the (false) opposition between the philosophical fideism of Petrus Damiani and Gilbert Porreta, on the one hand, and the theological rationalism of Alain de Lille (c. 1128-1202/03) and William of Auvergne (d. 1249), on the other hand.[10] Contrary to Gilbert's separation of faith and reason, Aquinas insists on the difference and analogy that apply to the light of faith *(lumen fidei)* and the rational intellection of principles *(intellectus principiorum).* By extension, this analogical difference also pertains to the first theological principles and the first principle of the νοῦς or agent intellect *(In I Sent.* prol. art. 3, sol. 2, ad. 2; *In I Sent.* prol. art. 3, sol. 3, ad. 3). According to Aquinas, this analogical difference or 'differential analogy' signifies that knowledge in faith and in reason deals with the same objects from different yet somehow continuous perspectives, for the *habitus* of sci-

---

8. Chenu, *La théologie comme science au XIIIe siècle,* p. 42.

9. Étienne Gilson, "Pourquoi saint Thomas a critiqué saint Augustin," *Archives d'histoire doctrinale et littéraire au Moyen-Âge* 2 (1926): 5-127.

10. Alain de Lille fused Aristotle with Pythagorean elements and claimed that all religious truths (including the mysteries of faith) derive from first principles that are self-evident to human reason without the aid of revelation. William of Auvergne defended a similar variant of rationalism. Among other texts, he wrote *De immortalitate animae,* a rescript of a book by Dominicus Gundissalinus who translated some of Avicenna's work into Latin and helped the diffusion of Avicennian essentialism, as I argued in the previous chapter. There is thus a certain genealogical link stretching from Gilbert Porreta and Avicenna via Gundissalinus to Lille and Auvergne.

ence and the *habitus* of faith both draw on the *habitus* of principles.[11] The analogy between the light of reason and the light of faith means that God is the object of both philosophy and theology. Concomitantly, cognition of God is given to the mind not only through faith but also through reason via sense perception and intellection (*In II Sent.* d. 14, q. 1, a. 2). This stands in contrast with Porreta's claim that pure form pertains exclusively to theology and that natural philosophy can only know immanent form. It is also markedly different from Gilbert's separation of faith from reason and the division of the sciences based on *more geometrico.*

Here I need to say more about the science of theology. The scientific status of *sacra doctrina,* as Thomas sees it, is grounded in the distinction between theology and faith. The former operates in virtue of the naturally acquired *habitus* of reason. By contrast, the latter is a supernaturally infused *habitus.*[12] Whereas theology draws on natural principles, faith is by supernatural grace alone and — *pace* Alain de Lille — cannot be inferred from first principles. This conception underpins Aquinas's later theory of *subalternatio,* with both *divina scientia* and *sacra doctrina* subordinated and directed to *Scientia Dei.*[13] The emphasis on natural principles and reason, which are nevertheless supernaturally oriented, entails a focus on immanent actual things and knowledge of the transcendent causes that bring them into actuality. Contrary to the 'natural' priority of essence over that which is, Aquinas accentuates actual being *(ens)* and God's act of being *(actus essendi).* By relating the particular individuality of created things to the divine universal unitary pure act of being, Thomas reverses the severing of actualization from individuation in the shared legacy of Avicenna and Gilbert and overcomes the protomodern separation of nature from the supernatural good in God.

This difference with Avicennian and Porretan essentialism is central

11. For example, *". . . habitus scientiae inclinat ad scibilia per modum rationis . . . sed habitus fidei, cum non rationi innitatur, inclinat per modum naturae, sicut habitus principiorum"* (*In III Sent.* d. 23, q. 3, art. 3, sol. 2, ad. 2) and *"praeterea lumen fidei se habet ad articulos sicut lumen naturale ad principia naturaliter cognita. Sed lumen naturale facit videre principia per se nota. Ergo et lumen fidei facit videre articulos"* (*In III Sent.* d. 24, q. 1, art. 1, sol. 1).

12. *"sicut habitus principiorum non acquiritur per alias scientias, sed habetur a natura, sed acquiritur habitus conclusionum a primis principiis deductarum — ita etiam in hac doctrina non acquiritur habitus fidei, qui est quasi habitus principiorum, sed acquiritur habitus eorum quae ex eis deducuntur et quae ad eorum defensionem valent"* (*In I Sent.* prol., q. 1, art. 3, sol. 2, ad. 3).

13. Chenu, *La théologie comme science au XIIIe siècle,* pp. 67-92.

to the question of individuation. Paradoxically, knowledge of God's existence is knowledge of how and why composites are individuated. For Aquinas, only the ecstatic goodness of God's self-subsistent being can ultimately explain why the universal act of being is present in every particular being and secures both its unity and differentiation from other beings. Likewise, only the divine idea of materiality can account for the reception of substantial form in designated matter *(materia signata)* and the essential relation *(habitudo essentialis)* between them that individuates matter-form compounds. As Rudi te Velde has argued *contra* Norman Kretzmann,[14] God's existence is neither a working hypothesis in Aquinas's 'natural' theology nor the search for an epistemic justification of the theistic belief that God exists. Rather, in the opening chapters of the *Summa contra Gentiles,* Thomas already seeks to demonstrate God's existence as a "necessary foundation of the whole undertaking [*quasi totius operis necessarium fundamentum*]" (*SCG* I.9.8), which is to develop a rationally intelligible account of God's being and attributes. For Aquinas, to know that God exists is to know that the truth of his existence is metaphysically founded in God's actual being. True knowledge of God follows from his being which is and makes itself known as such. Knowledge of God is amenable to the light of reason and therefore the subject-matter of metaphysics. God's actuality frames not only *sacra doctrina* but also and equally *divina scientia.*

The theory of subalternation entails a different division of sciences compared with that of Boethius and Gilbert. *Contra* Boethius, Thomas does not classify the sciences according to ascending degrees of abstraction.[15] Metaphysics or 'first philosophy' is not restricted to pure form but instead encompasses all things, including individual material beings in motion, "according to the common ratio of being,"[16] i.e., according to that which is common to material and immaterial substances alike. *Con-*

14. Rudi te Velde, "'The First Thing to Know about God': Kretzmann and Aquinas on the Meaning and Necessity of Arguments for the Existence of God," *Religious Studies* 39 (2003): 251-67, esp. pp. 253-59.

15. Louis-Bertrand Geiger, "Abstraction et séparation d'après s. Thomas *In De Trinitate,* q. 5, a. 3," *Revue des Sciences Philosophiques et Théologiques* 31 (1947): 3-40. Cf. C. J. Kelly, "Abstraction and Existence: A Study on St. Thomas, *In Boethii De Trinitate* q.5, a. 3," *Laval théologique et philosophique* 21 (1965): 17-42; P. Merlan, "Abstraction and Metaphysics in St. Thomas' Summa," *Journal of the History of Ideas* 14 (1953): 284-91.

16. *"secundum communem rationem entis"* (*In Boeth. de Trin.* q. 5, a. 4, ad 6). Cf. *In VII Met.* lec. 11, no. 1526, and *In XII Met.* lec. 2, no. 2427.

tra Gilbert, Aquinas argues that mathematics does not provide a better understanding of natural phenomena than natural philosophy (or physics). Rather than viewing mathematics as a meta-logical corrective to natural philosophy and a necessary basis for knowledge of forms in theology, Thomas agrees with Augustine and Boethius that mathematical principles are grounded in the metaphysical structures of creation.

Most importantly, none of the mathematical sciences can demonstrate *propter quid* or why natural phenomena occur because they all abstract from natural matter, motion, and efficient and final causes (*In I Post. An.* lect. 25, no. 6).[17] Even though each science is autonomous and has a proper subject-matter and method, all the mathematical sciences are subordinate to natural philosophy or physics, which provides the starting point for first philosophy or metaphysics. Following Plato and Augustine, Aquinas maintains that cognition of pure form and its ultimate source — God — occurs in relation to the material world, not by fleeing from it. In developing his theory of subalternation and his classification of the sciences, he argues against the natural priority of essence over that which is (as for Porreta). The first object of the senses and the intellect is a being *(ens),* and all particular sensible things *(entia)* disclose both an essence and an act of being which brings them into existence. As I show in the following sections, Thomas's theory of individuation is inextricably linked to the metaphysical question of the link between the one and the many and to the Christian Neo-Platonist theological epistemology which centers on illumined abstraction and supernaturally infused 'natural' reason.

3. Metaphysics beyond the One and the Many

Aquinas traces the problematic of unity and diversity back to Parmenides, whose works he knows primarily via Aristotle (*In I Phys.* lec. 2; *In I Met.* lec. 9, 137-39). Against Parmenides' double claim that the absolute unity of being excludes nonbeing and that the concept of being must be univocal, Thomas opposes an account of being that stresses a hierarchical and relational ordering of analogical being flowing from God's creative pure act of being *(actus purus).* As such, individuation is not added

17. James A. Weisheipl, "Classification of the Sciences in Medieval Thought," *Mediaeval Studies* 27 (1965): 54-90, esp. pp. 81-90.

extrinsically to actualized, immanent beings. Nor can individuation be reduced to the generation of secondary effects by a primary cause. Rather, individuation is inscribed into the very structure of being and concerns the actualization of all things: "Each being possesses its act of existing and its individuation in accordance with the same factor."[18] The reality of being encompasses the unity and the diversity of all that is and could be. Likewise, the concept of being is analogical, not univocal or equivocal. The act of being which actualizes and individuates all things is anagogical (perfective and elevating), not causal or indifferent.

What accounts for the concurrent unity and unicity of each thing and the transcendent hierarchical order of all beings is the power of being (*potestas* or *virtus essendi*), which is the nature and operation of God's pure act of being (*SCG* I.28; *De potentia* q. 7, a. 2, ad 9; *In de causis*, prop. 4). The power of being is the first cause of all beings, and common being *(esse commune)* is the first effect of the power of being — a conception that combines Plato's idea of relationality with Plotinus's argument about the creative nature of the One. The following two passages make this point: "The first of all effects is being itself, which is presupposed to all other effects, and does not presuppose any other effect"; "Being is the most common first effect and more intimate than all other effects: wherefore it is an effect which belongs to God alone to produce by His own power."[19] For this reason, common being marks the actuality that stands in potency to God's self-subsistent being *(ipsum esse subsistens)*. As such, it does not have existence or essence in itself but exists by participating in God's relational being, an account that echoes Plato's metaphysics.[20]

Common being is not some secular station that is interposed between God and beings. Nor does it describe a flat and simple ontological plane that assembles all things identically. Instead, common being is that which binds together all beings *qua* beings and relates the whole of creation to its Creator in a real relation that reveals God to be both

---

18. *". . . unumquodque secundum idem habet esse et individuationem"* (*Sent. de Anima* q. 1, ad 2m).

19. *"primus autem effectus est ipsum esse, quod omnibus aliis effectibus praesupponitur, et ipsum non praesupponit aliquem alium effectum"* and *"ipsum esse enim est communissimus effectus primus et intimior omnibus aliis effectibus; et ideo soli Deo competit secundum virtutem propriam talis effectus"* (*De potentia* q. 3, a. 4, resp., and a. 7, resp.).

20. Cf. Joseph Owens, "Thomistic Common Nature and Platonic Idea," *Mediaeval Studies* 21 (1959): 211-23.

wholly transcendent and immanent.[21] This complex structuring combines both horizontal and vertical participation:

> All created causes communicate in one common effect which is being, although each one has its peculiar effect whereby they are all differentiated. . . . Accordingly, they have this in common that they cause being, but they differ in that fire causes fire, and a builder causes a house. There must therefore be some cause higher than all others by virtue of which they all cause being and whose proper cause is being: and this cause is God.[22]

Paradoxically, Aquinas's distinction between the power of being and common being secures the unity of the transcendent primary cause and the diversity of its immanent secondary effects by fusing a hierarchical, analogical relation with an asymmetrical, relational participation. Since he posits a real difference between Creator and creation which nevertheless is in God (for nothing can be outside the orbit of divine being), Thomas traces all individual things to one and the same unique divine source. As such, the individuality of creation mirrors the singularity of its Creator.

In this way, Aquinas refutes Porreta's thesis of a plurality of substantial forms and outwits in advance Duns Scotus's univocity of being as well as Suárez's formalist difference within a real unity. All things have a unique form that is created by God's pure act and participates in common being. *Esse commune* does not encompass the Creator but is instead enfolded by divine creative power. Fran O'Rourke puts this well: "*esse commune* rather is itself contained under the power of God, *sicut*

21. Cf. Michael J. Dodds, "Ultimacy and Intimacy: Aquinas on the Relation between God and the World," in *Ordo Sapientiae et Amoris: Image et message de saint Thomas d'Aquin à travers les récentes études historiques, herméneutiques et doctrinales. Hommage au Professeur Jean-Pierre Torrell, OP,* ed. Carlos-Josaphat Pinto de Oliveira (Fribourg: Éditions Universitaires, 1993), pp. 211-27; Thomas Weinandy, *Does God Change?* (Still River, MA: St. Bede's Publications, 1985) and *Does God Suffer?* (Notre Dame: University of Notre Dame Press, 2000).

22. *"Omnes autem causae creatae communicant in uno effectu qui est esse, licet singulae proprios effectus habeant, in quibus distinguuntur. . . . Conveniunt ergo in hoc quod causant esse, sed differunt in hoc quod ignis causat ignem, et aedificator causat domum. Oportet ergo esse aliquam causam superiorem omnibus cuius virtute omnia causent esse, et eius esse sit proprius effectus. Et haec causa est Deus"* (*De potentia* q. 7, a. 2, resp.; cf. *De potentia* q. 3, a. 5, resp.; a. 6, resp.; a. 7, resp.; *SCG* I.65.4; II.15.4).

contentum in continente, since his divine power extends beyond created being."[23] Moreover, the ontological relation between the simplicity of God's self-subsistent being and the unicity of each substantial form is such that the latter receives the divine act of being according to its own mode and in order to be:

> [E]very thing exists because it has being. A thing whose essence is not its being, consequently, is not through its essence but by participation in something, namely being itself. But that which is through participation in something cannot be the first being, because prior to it is the being in which it participates *in order to be.*[24]

On this account, individuation marks the confluence of the particular mode of being according to which each and every composite receives and operates the universal act of being. The first principle and the final end of individuality is (the act of) being.

In developing his metaphysical account of individuation that encompasses composites and separate substances (angelic individuation) as well as the doctrine of divine simplicity, Aquinas begins with composite substances. Just as we know the prior on the basis of the posterior (the cause on the basis of effects), so we know separate substances (and ultimately divine simplicity) on the basis of composite substances (*De ente* c. 1, 1). My focus is therefore first on the individuation of composite substances and only then on angelic individuation and the doctrine of divine simplicity. Each and every being that is in act *(ens in actu)* is so in virtue of receiving common being: "[B]eing is common to everything that is."[25] The nature of the mode of receiving common being varies according to whether things are separate substances or composites, i.e., simple or matter-form compounds. Separate substances are void of any

---

23. Fran O'Rourke, *Pseudo-Dionysius and the Metaphysics of Aquinas* (Leiden: E. J. Brill, 1992), p. 142. See also Josef de Vries, "Das *'esse commune'* bei Thomas von Aquin," *Scholastik* 39 (1964): 163-77, and Rudi A. te Velde, *Participation and Substantiality in Thomas Aquinas* (Leiden: E. J. Brill, 1995), pp. 184-206.

24. "*Omnis res est per hoc quod habet esse. Nulla igitur res cuius essentia non est suum esse, est per essentiam suam, sed participatione alicuius, scilicet ipsius esse. Quod autem est per participationem alicuius, non potest esse primum ens: quia id quod aliquid participat ad hoc quod sit, est eo prius. Deus autem est primum ens, quo nihil est prius. Dei igitur essentia est suum esse*" (*SCG* I.22.9).

25. "*Omnibus autem commune est esse*" (*SCG* II.15.4).

unrealized material potentiality, but their form or essence stands in potency to their own act of being (*De spir. creat.* q. 1, a. 1, ad. 5). In this sense, they are composed of substance and of the act of being. Composite substances, i.e., matter-form compounds, are composed of prime matter that stands in potency to its corresponding substantial form (which is the act of matter), and of an essence that is composed of matter and form and as such stands in potency to its act of being (*De prin.* I.3; *De spir. creat.* q. 1, a. 1, resp.; *SCG* II.54.1-3; *De sub. sep.* c. 6, 8).

More specifically, composite substances are made of prime matter and substantial form, and prime matter is brought into being by substantial form, which is its act. The nature or essence of composites is neither form alone nor matter alone but the composition of form and matter (*De ente* c. 2, 1). The form of the whole *(forma totius)* is that which makes the composite what it is. As such, form is that which makes a particular being *(ens) this* rather than *that.* By contrast, the act of being brings a composite into actuality *(ens in actu).* For this reason, the individuation of composite beings-in-act marks a twofold actualization: first, the actualization of prime matter *(materia prima)* that stands in potency to substantial form; second, the actualization of matter-form compounds that stand in potency to the act of being (*esse* or *actus essendi*). This is why Aquinas shifts the emphasis away from formal essence towards the partial actuality of particular beings *(entia)* and the pure act of being.

Moreover, the primacy of actual being translates into the priority of metaphysics over epistemology: "[K]nowledge has only being for its object."[26] To know a thing's individuality is not only to know the unity of *that* particular thing and to be able to differentiate it from other things but also to know the first principle and final end of individuation — the creative act of self-giving by which the act of being brings everything from nothingness into actuality and makes things what they are. In knowing a thing, the mind knows *that* thing's particularity, which is also *that* thing's unique station within the common order of universal being. So knowledge of particularity is in some fundamental sense knowledge of commonality: "[B]eing is found to be common to all things, which are by themselves distinct from one another."[27] Here Aquinas draws on

---

26. *"cognitio non sit nisi entis"* (*De veritate* q. 2, a. 3, ad 12).

27. *"esse inveniatur omnibus rebus commune, quae secundum illud quod sunt, ad invicem distinctae sunt"* (*De potentia* q. 3, a. 5, resp.).

Boethius to suggest that the metaphysical (nonidentical) coincidence of individual and common being is reflected in the noetic coincidence of the perception of particulars and the intellection of universals.[28] Beyond Boethius, Aquinas argues that to know the presence of universal being in particular beings is to know first principles:

> [S]ince nature is always directed to one thing, of one power there must naturally be one object. . . . Hence, the intellect, being one power, has one natural object, of which it has knowledge, essentially and naturally. And this object must be one under which are included all things known by the intellect. . . . Now this is none other than being. Our intellect, therefore, knows being naturally and whatever essentially belongs to being as such; and upon this knowledge is founded the knowledge of first principles.[29]

Epistemologically, since God is the source of first principles, it follows for Thomas that the divine science of metaphysics *(divina scientia)* is subordinate to the Science of God *(Scientia Dei),* as I indicated in the previous section. Ontologically, since "all beings, inasmuch as they share in being, have certain principles that are principles of all beings," as Aquinas remarks in his commentary on Boethius' *De Trinitate,*[30] common being binds together all actual particular things. And since "a principle expresses relationship to that which proceeds from it,"[31] the principles of being intimate that which brings all things into being and makes them what they are — the self-subsistent pure act of being or God. Ultimately, knowledge of a thing's individuality is knowledge of the relation between the unity of God's power of being and the multiplicity of beings. By accentuating the asymmetrical relationality of Creator to creation and the 'vertical' participation of beings in being, Thomas outflanks both the re-

---

28. See, *supra,* chapter 3, section 3.

29. *"Cum natura semper ordinetur ad unum, unius virtutis oportet esse naturaliter unum obiectum. . . . Intellectus igitur cum sit una vis, est eius unum naturale obiectum, cuius per se et naturaliter cognitionem habet. Hoc autem oportet esse id sub quo comprehenduntur omnia ab intellectu cognita . . . Quod non est aliud quam ens. Naturaliter igitur intellectus noster cognoscit ens, et ea quae sunt per se entis inquantum huiusmodi; in qua cognitione fundatur primorum principiorum notitia"* (SCG II.83.29).

30. *"omnia entia, secundum quod in ente communicant, habent quaedam principia quae sunt principia omnium entium"* (*In Boeth. de Trin.* q. 5, a. 4, co. 2).

31. *"principium autem relative ad principiatum dicitur"* (SCG II.11.1).

sidual dualism of the one and the many in ancient philosophy and the priority of essence over existence in earlier medieval theology.

In the remainder of this chapter, I explore Aquinas's theological account of individuation centering on God's act of being. Far from threatening divine unity or simplicity, Thomas shows how individuation in the created order mirrors divine singularity within the Trinitarian Godhead. Aquinas's innovation is to fuse the Neo-Platonic emphasis on the self-diffusive Good with Aristotle's conceptuality of act and potency and to blend divine substantiality with a hierarchy of different kinds of relationality. To be individuated is to preserve and perfect God's image and likeness. And to know how and why a thing is *this* rather than *that* individual is to be able to help fashion it according to its God-given unique *telos,* so that all may be elevated to their proper station within the relational order of creation: "[M]an's perfection consists in our union with God."[32]

4. Can Created Minds Know Singulars?

The question of individuation is pivotal in Aquinas's metaphysical theology of creation. For Thomas, each actual individual thing reflects in a unique and particular way the universal, transcendent, and hierarchical order of being which makes itself known to the mind via the senses and which the mind comes to know by forming universal concepts. In seeing individual things in act, the mind comes to know the divine act of being which brings them into being and makes them what they are. And to cognize the act of being is to glimpse God's creative activity, for only the onto-logic of creation can explain how and why being *(esse)* encompasses both the particularity of individual beings and the universality of being, at the level of reality and concept alike. Yet at the same time, Aquinas is adamant that "our intellect does not know singulars."[33] Thomas seems to suggest that, by contrast with God's uncreated mind, the created human mind lacks knowledge of things *qua* singulars. If this were so, the Angelic Doctor would struggle to explain how and why the link

32. *"perfectio hominis consistat in coniunctione ad deum"* (*In Boeth. de Trin.* q. 2, a. 1, resp.).

33. *". . . intellectus noster singularia non cognoscens"* (*De veritate* q. 2, a. 4, ad 1; cf. *SCG* I.65.9). Cf. George Klubertanz, "St. Thomas and the Knowledge of the Singular," *New Scholasticism* 26 (1952): 135-66.

between Creator and creation is rationally intelligible. Suddenly, theological realism and intellectualism appear less compelling than the rival positions of nominalism and voluntarism later defended by Scotus and Ockham. Likewise, the idea of illumined reason seems less persuasive than the fideistic alternative of Damiani and Porreta.

In the present and the following section of this chapter, I will argue that Aquinas builds on the Christian Neo-Platonism of Gregory, Augustine, Boethius, and Dionysius in order to defend a realist and intellectualist theology that outwits in advance both the nominalist-voluntarist synthesis and the false binary opposition between rationalism and fideism. By correcting both Augustinian illumination and Aristotelian abstraction, Thomas develops a theological epistemology that accentuates the mediating role of the common sense *(sensus communis)*, judgment, and the imagination. The common sense binds together the cognitive import of diverse sensory impressions and alerts us to the presence of common being in particular things, though we can only obtain cognition of universality through intellectual abstraction and separation. Judgment enables us to apprehend the fittingness *(convenientia)* of individuals in relation to other immanent individuals and transcendent forms, though we can only obtain cognition of singulars with the help of the imagination.

A. Being and Knowledge

In the tradition of Neo-Platonism, Aquinas defends an epistemological realism and intellectualism according to which both material and immaterial reality is within the remit of analogical being and as such can be known by the mind. In the words of Thomas, "every reality is essentially a being"[34] and "knowledge has only being for its object," as I have already mentioned.[35] As a result, knowledge is not concerned with a priori mental structures that we can simply name and project onto the world in order to make sense of confused and contradictory sensory experience. Instead, the noetic structure of intellection reflects the metaphysical structure of reality: knowledge is knowledge of both material and immaterial things that share in the act of being that endows everything with form, as

---

34. *"quaelibet natura est essentialiter ens"* (*De veritate* q. 1, a. 1, corp.).
35. See, *supra*, note 26.

Thomas insists as early as in his 1255 treatise *De principiis naturae* (I.2; IV.3). There is an 'appropriate' correspondence or fittingness *(convenientia)* between material things and immaterial ideas.[36] Even though reality precedes our knowledge of it, being and knowing are nevertheless coterminous (e.g., *De veritate* q. 1, a. 1, resp.) because in the created order intelligent beings perfect their God-given form through knowledge of their own creatureliness and the createdness of all that is. Like Augustine, Aquinas combines the theme of cosmic harmony (common to scriptural and philosophical reflections on measure, number, and weight) with the question of virtue and perfectibility. His Iamblichean-Proclean emphasis on theurgic elevation rather than the Aristotelian focus on abstractive contemplation is key, as I will show in the course of the present chapter.

Instead of a specific number of categories or purely causal accounts, Thomas privileges the more (Neo-)Platonist language of the creative, self-giving Good and universal forms in which things participate relationally. This retrieval of Plato — and not just Aristotle — also explains the accentuation of teleology and questions about 'why' things are the way they are — not just 'how' they might be so. Aquinas puts this as follows:

> [T]he problem of *why* something is so is related to the problem of *whether* it is so, in the same way that an inquiry as to *what* something is stands in regard to an inquiry as to *whether it exists*. For the question *why* looks for a means to demonstrate *that* something is so . . . likewise, the question *what is it* seeks a means to demonstrate *that something exists*, according to the traditional teaching in *Posterior Analytics* II, 1; 89b 22. Now, we observe that those who see *that something is so* naturally desire to know *why*. So too, those acquainted with the fact that *something exists* naturally desire to know what this thing is, and this is to understand its substance.[37]

---

36. This is what underpins Aquinas's adequation theory of truth, as outlined already in *De veritate* q. 1, a. 1, corp. Cf. John Milbank and Catherine Pickstock, *Truth in Aquinas* (London and New York: Routledge, 2001), ch. 1.

37. *"Sicut se habet quaestio propter quid ad quaestionem quia, ita se habet quaestio quid est ad quaestionem an est: nam quaestio propter quid quaerit medium ad demonstrandum quia est aliquid, puta quod luna eclipsatur; et similiter quaestio quid est quaerit medium ad demonstrandum an est, secundum doctrinam traditam in II posteriorum. Videmus autem quod videntes quia est aliquid, naturaliter scire desiderant propter quid. Ergo et cognoscentes an est aliquid, naturaliter scire desiderant quid est ipsum, quod est intelligere eius substantiam"* (*SCG* III.50.4; my italics).

Since we are endowed with a natural desire for knowing first principles and ultimate finalities (*In I Met.* lec. 1, nos. 1-4), we seek to discover not just whether things are and in what sense they are individual but also how and why this might be so (*In Boeth. de Trin.* q. 6, a. 3, resp.). By analogy with the link between *an Deus sit* and *quid sit Deus,* the created order can be understood only in terms of the relation between existence and essence, which both flow from the goodness of its Creator in whom all transcendentals are fully convertible (*De veritate* q. 21, a. 1, resp. and ad 5.; *ST* I, q. 5, a. 1, resp.). As I will demonstrate in greater detail below, 'individuality' is linked to transcendental unity in such a way that God himself is supremely singular. Therefore, it is not the case that general being somehow creates particular being. Rather, God's infinite mode of united 'definiteness' (*yliatim* in Aquinas's commentary on the *Liber de Causis*) imparts a share of its singular unity to created beings according to a finite mode. For this reason, individual things mirror and intimate divine singularity, and everything within creation is individuated in union with its Creator through contemplative knowledge of singularity, theurgic practices, and praise for the divine. Just as 'ontological' individuation marks the actualization and perfection of particular beings by the divine act of being, so 'epistemological' individuation describes the actualization and perfection of universal form in particular things through divinely illumined knowledge. As such, God's creative power of being provides both the original meta-physical act of self-giving and the meta-epistemic principle of intelligibility of all that is.

Before I can further explore Thomas's account of individuation, I will briefly return to the question of being, knowledge, and the human desire for divinely illumined truth. Aquinas explores the 'Meno paradox' of why we desire that which we do not as yet know by extending the Platonist insistence on the ecstatic outflow of the Good with the Aristotelian language of act and potency in the direction of creation *ex nihilo* and Trinitarian relationality. Divine goodness is that which endows us with the natural desire for the supernatural Good in God. Here Thomas positions *divina scientia* within the shared metaphysical tradition stretching from Plato via Aristotle and Plotinus to Dionysius: "'the good is that which all things desire.'"[38] Paradoxically, this natural desire for the supernatural good discloses the divinely infused self-transcendence of all things:

---

38. Quoted by Aquinas in *In de Div. Nom.* IV.7.10; *In Eth.* I.1.9; *ST* I, q. 5, a. 1, resp.; the reference in Aristotle is *Ethics* I 1, 1094ª3.

"[E]verything primarily and of itself seeks its own completion, which is 'the good' of each one and is always proportioned to what can be completed, and in this regard has a similitude with respect to it [the thing completed]."[39] Beyond Aristotle and Porphyry, Aquinas situates the Good within the orbit of being and associates the natural orientation to the supernatural truth in God with the desire to be in act: "[A]ll things, each according to its mode, desire to be in act; this is clear from the fact that each thing according to its nature resists corruption. To be in act, therefore, constitutes the nature of the good."[40] Pure actuality is not simply the final cause that provides the ultimate lure for things in this world. Instead, it is God's ecstatic self-giving which offers everything a share in the act of being and in so doing endows it with actual goodness. This is why being and the good are coterminous and the actuality of being enjoys absolute primacy over the potency of nonbeing. The latter also accounts for Aquinas's insistence that true knowledge is knowledge of the 'adequation' between the knowing mind and the known object. To say that "all things desire to be" is to say that "everything loves its own being and desires its preservation, an indication of which is the fact that every thing resists its own dissolution."[41]

Moreover, knowledge and being are not just coextensive but also mutually reinforcing. If things have being in virtue of form (*De prin.* I.2; IV.3), then knowledge of being is itself ontologically constitutive of reality: to know a thing is to make that thing's spiritual and material form more intensely present in the mind and in the world because a thing's potency and *telos* include its cognoscibility (or potency to be known, as Boethius remarks), which is actualized in the act of knowing. If things make themselves known to the mind via the senses and if things have first principles and final ends (*In I Met.* lec. 2, nos. 45-46), then coming to know a thing makes a difference to the known thing and the knowing mind — there is a harmonious correspondence *(convenientia)* between a thing's *telos* to be known and the mind's desire to know. The act of know-

39. "... *unumquodque primo et per se appetit suam perfectionem quae est bonum uniuscuiusque et est semper proportionata perfectibili et secundum hoc habet similitudinem ad ipsum"* (*In Boeth. de Hebd.* 2, 279-81).

40. "*Omnia autem appetunt esse actu secundum suum modum: quod patet ex hoc quod unumquodque secundum naturam suam repugnat corruptioni. Esse igitur actu boni rationem constituit"* (*SCG* I.37.4; cf. *SCG* III.3.4; *De veritate* q. 21, a. 2, resp.).

41. "*esse namque suum unumquodque amat et conservari appetit; signum autem est, quia contra pugnat unumquodque suae corruptioni"* (*SCG* II.41.5).

ing actualizes the potency to be known and in so doing brings a thing's being and the mind's being more intensely into actuality.

Epistemologically, the primacy of being over knowing translates into the priority of sense perception over abstraction. Aquinas develops Aristotle's imperative that "'all our knowledge begins with the senses'"[42] in a more theological direction by linking divine revelation to the disclosure of God's creative activity in created things. First of all, he argues that "a thing makes itself known in the soul by its exterior appearance, since our cognition takes its beginning from sense, whose direct object is sensible qualities."[43] Since they are brought into actuality by God's act of being, things are not merely passive entities that are 'just there.' Instead, everything *in actu* appeals to our senses and activates sense perception: "[A] sense cannot perceive unless it is stimulated by a sensible object,"[44] for there is a priority of being over knowing. Here Thomas's epistemology builds on Boethius' demonstration that universals are manifest in particulars and that the actuality of beings actualizes the potency to be and to know. *Pace* Gilbert, individuality describes not a thing's pure formal essence but rather the unique union of form and matter that differentiates *this* from *that*.

Second, Aquinas's epistemological realism has attracted derision from modern and contemporary critics who accuse him either of essentialism or of existentialism. Since he is guilty of neither, Thomas outwits all his deriders. Contrary to Descartes's circular and inward self-evidence of *cogito ergo sum,* Thomas inverts the primacy of the thinking mind and reestablishes the ontological primacy of object over subject. Like judgment and the imagination, the senses have a mediating function between the mind and the world. Sensory perception, far from inducing confusion and deception, constitutes a self-exteriorizing movement: to perceive anything at all is primarily to understand that both the

---

42. "*omnis nostra cognitio a sensu ortum habet,*'"in Aquinas, *In Boeth. de Trin.* q. 1, a. 3, s.c. 3. Crucially, in *Post. Anal.* II, 19, 100ᵃ14–ᵇ5, Aristotle argues that "for though one perceives the particular, perception is of the universal . . . for perception too instils in this way." Cf. *SCG* I.30.3. Cf. Cornelio Fabro, "Il Problema della Percezione Sensoriale," *Bollettino Filosofico* 4 (1938): 5-62.

43. "*res enim notitiam sui facit in anima per ea quae de ipsa exterius apparent, quia cognitio nostra a sensu initium sumit, cui per se obiectum sunt sensibiles qualitates*" (*De veritate* q. 1, a. 10, resp.).

44. "*sensus non sentit, nisi moveatur a sensibili*" (*In Boeth. de Trin.* q. 1, a. 1, resp.; cf. *SCG* II.57.8).

subject and the object exist rather than to become aware of the thinking self: "For one perceives that he has a soul, that he lives, and that *he exists, because he perceives that he senses*."[45] The centrality of sense perception requires a separate discussion, which I now turn to.

B. Knowledge and Sense Perception

In a rejoinder to a debate between Sheldon Cohen and John Haldane about Aquinas's theory of perception, Paul Hoffman dismisses Haldane's interpretation and seeks to reconcile Cohen's rereading with a more traditional understanding of sense cognition in Thomist philosophy.[46] In what follows, I shall argue that Hoffman is right about Cohen and Haldane, but wrong about Aquinas. Without sense power, Hoffman reduces perception to the passive reception of sensible form and fails to recognize the active apprehension of actual form-matter compounds. I revisit the triangular debate between Cohen, Haldane, and Hoffman before I outline my own account of sense power and perception in Thomas's metaphysics.

Cohen advances a physicalist reading of perception and ascribes special importance to Aquinas's distinction between the natural and spiritual reception of sensible forms. He takes issue with the interpretation defended by Étienne Gilson and D. W. Hamlyn, who argue that sensation involves a nonphysical reception of a sensible form which ultimately leads to a mental image or, in Aquinas's terminology, *phantasma*.[47] Cohen's contention is that both natural and spiritual reception is always a 'physical event' that results in a physical likeness rather than an intellectual representation.[48] As such, he attributes to Aquinas a uni-

---

45. *"In hoc enim aliquis percipit se animam habere, et vivere, et esse, quod percipit se sentire et intelligere"* (*De veritate* q. 10, a. 8, resp.; my italics).

46. Sheldon M. Cohen, "St. Thomas Aquinas on the Immaterial Reception of Sensible Forms," *Philosophical Review* 91 (1982): 193-209; John Haldane, "Aquinas on Sense Perception," *Philosophical Review* 92 (1983): 233-39; Paul Hoffman, "St. Thomas Aquinas on the Halfway State of Sensible Being," *Philosophical Review* 99 (1990): 73-92.

47. Étienne Gilson, *Le Thomisme. Introduction à la philosophie de St. Thomas d'Aquin*, 5th ed. (Paris: Vrin, 1948), English translation: *The Christian Philosophy of St. Thomas Aquinas*, trans. L. K. Shook (Notre Dame: University of Notre Dame Press, 1956), pp. 203-4; D. W. Hamlyn, *Sensation and Perception* (London: Routledge & Kegan Paul, 1961), p. 46 *passim*.

48. Cohen, "St. Thomas Aquinas on the Immaterial Reception of Sensible Forms," pp. 194-95.

tary theory of sensation whereby sensation is a power of the body-soul compound (not of the soul alone), which involves the natural *and* the spiritual reception of sensible forms as a physical event (not as a physical *and* a mental event). In other words, a sensible object effects a change at the level of the sense organ, but not at the level of the soul. For this reason, the likeness in the sense organ is physical insofar as it is a material reflection by receiving the material disposition of the sensible object without acquiring that particular material disposition. For instance, a mirror can receive the color 'red' without either turning red itself or ceasing to reflect other colors.

However, Cohen's monism disguises a more fundamental dualism in his interpretation between unconscious perception and conscious sensation — or perceptual and cognitive reception. He wrongly asserts that Aquinas separates the perceptual reception of sensible forms, which is passive and limited to the sense organ, from the cognitive reception of sensible forms, which is active and encompasses appetites, desires, and awareness.[49] Thomas rejects this separation, arguing instead that "intellectively, cognizing is like sensing: what they share is passion, being affected."[50] A purely physicalist reading like Cohen's, which focuses on the passive registration of a sensible form by a sense organ, misses the spiritual transformation involved in perception: "A change is spiritual when the form causing the change is received in the thing being changed according to a spiritual mode of being, as the form of color in the pupil, which is not made colored by this."[51] So in perceiving actual sensible things, the sense organ itself undergoes both a physical and a spiritual change.

This is crucial because it challenges the purported dualism in Aquinas between physical reception and spiritual change and, more fundamentally, between matter and form. Since composite substances constitute a single, unique matter-form compound (rather than the juxtaposition of

---

49. Cohen, "St. Thomas Aquinas on the Immaterial Reception of Sensible Forms," pp. 207-9.

50. "*Ex hoc autem sequitur quod, cum sentire sit quoddam pati a sensibili, aut aliquid simile passioni, quod intelligere sit vel pati aliquid ab intelligibili, vel aliquid alterum huiusmodi, simile scilicet passioni*" (*In De anima* lib. III, lec. 7, n. 5, commenting on *De anima* III 4, 429^{a}13-18).

51. "*spiritualis autem secundum quod forma immutantis recipitur in immutato secundum esse spirituale, ut forma coloris in pupilla, quae non fit per hoc colorata*" (*ST* I, q. 78, a. 3, resp.)

material potency and formal actuality),[52] individuation is not confined to essences and encompasses both the unity of each actual thing and its differentiation from other actual things, as I have already suggested. Likewise, perception is not limited to the 'physical event' of receiving sensible form, as Cohen maintains, but also entails the spiritual transformation of the knowing mind, the known thing, and the senses that mediate between them. Indeed, the realism of Thomas's metaphysics emphasizes that all cognition transforms both the knowing subject and the known object and that perception is a form of prereflexive cognition of singularity:

> A sense is a power in a corporeal organ; the intellect is an immaterial power that is not the act of any corporeal organ. . . . [T]he sense must corporeally receive a likeness of the thing being sensed. Intellect incorporeally and immaterially receives a likeness of what it cognizes. . . . A thing's likeness, received in the senses, represents that thing as it is singular. A likeness received in intellect represents that thing as the defining character of a universal nature. This is why the senses have cognition of singular things, whereas intellect has cognition of universals.[53]

Here Aquinas goes further than simply restoring Boethius' distinction between sensory cognition of singularity and intellective cognition of

52. Indeed, the essence of a composite substance is neither form itself nor the relation between form and matter but the matter-form compound itself: "[E]ssence embraces both matter and form . . . essence does not signify the relation between matter and form or something added to them *(essentia comprehendit materiam et formam . . . non potest dici quod essentia significet relationem quae est inter materiam et formam uel aliquid superadditum)" (De ente* c. 2, 1-2).

53. The full quote in Latin is as follows: *"sensus est virtus in organo corporali; intellectus vero est virtus immaterialis, quae non est actus alicuius organi corporalis. Unumquodque autem recipitur in aliquo per modum sui. Cognitio autem omnis fit per hoc, quod cognitum est aliquo modo in cognoscente, scilicet secundum similitudinem. Nam cognoscens in actu, est ipsum cognitum in actu. Oportet igitur quod sensus corporaliter et materialiter recipiat similitudinem rei quae sentitur. Intellectus autem recipit similitudinem eius quod intelligitur, incorporaliter et immaterialiter. Individuatio autem naturae communis in rebus corporalibus et materialibus, est ex materia corporali, sub determinatis dimensionibus contenta: universale autem est per abstractionem ab huiusmodi materia, et materialibus conditionibus individuantibus. Manifestum est igitur, quod similitudo rei recepta in sensu repraesentat rem secundum quod est singularis; recepta autem in intellectu, repraesentat rem secundum rationem universalis naturae: et inde est, quod sensus cognoscit singularia, intellectus vero universalia"* (In De anima lib. II, lec. 12, n. 5, commenting on *De anima* 417[b]19-29: 71-94).

universality. Since "sense and intellect are similar,"[54] perception is conceptually informed, just as intellection is always also perceptual. Indeed, in the *Summa contra Gentiles,* Thomas argues that sensation *(sentire)* is a joint operation of the soul and the body.[55] Cohen's physicalism ignores that sensation blends passivity and activity because sensation is both reception and mediation — immaterial reception of sensible form and mediation of sensible reality to the mind (*De veritate* q. 10, a. 11, resp.).

Why does this matter for the question of individuation? Knowledge of singularity perfects both the knowing subject and the known object, as I have already argued. Aquinas's metaphysics of analogy and participation builds on the patristic Neo-Platonist concepts of perfectibility and degrees of being and goodness (in the work of figures such as Gregory and Dionysius) in order to emphasize the idea of anagogy or elevation to union with God. The 'similarity' of the senses and the intellect that Thomas identifies is an integral part of his theological epistemology, such that one can speak of a hierarchical mediation of species from the senses via the intellect back to the senses and the imagination. Indeed, species are both sensible and intelligible, and in this way perception and intellective cognition are symmetrical: "We have actual sensation or actual knowledge because our intellect or our senses are informed by the species or likeness of the sensible or intelligible object."[56] Species are not neutral intermediate instances between sensible reality and the intellective soul. On the contrary, they represent the object to the senses and the mind in an appropriate or proportionate fashion — hence the importance of *convenientia* or 'adequation' in Aquinas's account of truth, as Gilbert Narcisse has shown.[57] Since true knowing is the product of "the assimilation of the knower to the thing known" (*De veritate* q. 1, a. 1, resp.), sensible species cannot be either mere pictorial images or proper objects of intellectual knowledge. Instead, they acti-

---

54. Aristotle, *De anima* III 2, 427ª9, quoted by Aquinas in his *De sen.* c. 18, 449ª17-18.

55. "*sunt tamen aliquae operationes communes sibi et corpori, ut timere et irasci et sentire et huiusmodi: haec enim accidunt secundum aliquam transmutationem alicuius determinatae partis corporis, ex quo patet quod simul sunt animae et corporis operationes. Oportet igitur ex anima et corpore unum fieri, et quod non sint secundum esse diversa*" (*SCG* II.57.6).

56. *ST* I, q. 14, a. 2, resp.

57. Gilbert Narcisse, *Les raisons de Dieu: Arguments de convenance et esthétique théologique selon St. Thomas d'Aquin et Hans Urs von Balthasar* (Fribourg: Éditions Universitaires Fribourg Suisse, 1997).

vate the power of sense organs and in so doing mediate the form of a sensible object to the senses and the mind alike. Leen Spruit summarizes this well:

> [The species] represents that characteristic feature of sensible things, which grounds the act of sense perception: it is an effect of the thing communicating itself according to its formal structure. This general view entails that the species in sensation is an instrumental principle rather than the perceptual object itself. Once received in our soul, it enables us to construct a sensory image or representation, that is, the phantasm.[58]

If the species is an "instrumental principle rather than the perceptual object itself," it follows for Aquinas that the senses perceive sensible reality itself — not a world of mere phenomena from which the mind must abstract in order to construct the world of noumena, as Kant would later assert.

C. Two Modes of Being

At this juncture it is instructive to consider Haldane's intervention in the debate with Cohen and Hoffman. Haldane characterizes Aquinas's definition of the nature of sensible being as a 'halfway state' between materiality and immateriality. Based on Thomas's distinction between two modes of being (*esse naturale* and *esse intentionale*), he suggests that form can exist according to two modes: in a particular composite substance, the form 'humanity' is instantiated 'naturally,' and in the senses, the same form is present 'intentionally.' He supports this argument by quoting from Aquinas's commentary of Aristotle's *De anima*: "And it is thus that a sense receives form without matter, the form having, in the sense, a different mode of being from that which it has in the object sensed. In the latter it has a material mode of being *(esse naturale)* but in the sense, a cognitional and spiritual mode *(esse intentionale)*."[59] This dis-

---

58. Leen Spruit, *Species Intelligibilis: From Perception to Knowledge* (Leiden: E. J. Brill, 1994), vol. 1, p. 163.

59. *"Et per hunc modum, sensus recipit formam sine materia, quia alterius modi esse habet forma in sensu, et in re sensibili. Nam in re sensibili habet esse naturale, in sensu autem habet esse intentionale et spirituale"* (*In de Anima* lib. II, lec. 24, n. 3).

tinction is important in three ways. First, Thomas contends that both the senses and the intellect cognize sensible objects according to the form of their materiality, in relation to material embodiment or by abstracting from it. In so doing, the senses and the mind receive being spiritually or intentionally. Intentionality signifies things themselves (first intention) or concepts (second intention), in such a way that knowledge of forms perfects the knowing mind as well as the known thing and enables intellectual beings to preserve and enhance their own unique singular form and that of other things in creation. The importance of intentionality for Aquinas's account of individuation is evinced by his fusion of the particularity of individual things with the universality of common concepts like 'individual,' as Thomas makes clear in the following passage:

> [T]he individual can be signified in a twofold way, either by a noun of the second intention, like the noun 'individual' or 'singular,' which does not signify the singular thing but the intention of singularity; or by a noun of the first intention, which signifies the thing to which the intention of particularity belongs.[60]

The distinction between first and second intention is instrumental to the notion of *demonstratio* in Aquinas's epistemology, i.e., a rationally intelligible account of being, as Joseph Owens has rightly remarked. In the case of a second-intention predicate, 'individual' refers to an instance of a species and in this sense is not unique, as there are other individuals with the same specific nature. Only according to the first intention does the notion of individuality limit the signification to the one unique actual thing.[61] In the following section, I provide a detailed account of the metaphysical meaning of individuality.

Second, the distinction between natural and intentional being confirms that perception is always already cognitive. If this is so, then

---

60. "*. . . individuum dupliciter potest significari vel per nomen secundae intentionis, sicut hoc nomen 'individuum' vel 'singulare', quod non significat rem singularem, sed intentionem singularitatis; vel per nomen primae intentionis, quod significat rem, cui convenit intentio particularitatis*" (*In I Sent.* d. 23, q. 1, a. 3, resp.). Cf. *In I Sent.* d. 26, q. 1, a. 1, ad 3m; *In III Sent.* d. 6, q. 1, a. 1, resp.

61. Joseph Owens, "Thomas Aquinas (b. ca. 1225; d. 1274)," in *Individuation in Scholasticism: The Later Middle Ages and the Counter-Reformation 1150-1650*, ed. Jorge J. E. Gracia (Albany: State University of New York Press, 1994), pp. 173-94 (179).

Haldane is wrong to allege that Aquinas's theory of universals in particulars is incoherent. He is also mistaken in following D. W. Hamlyn's point that *phantasmata* are mental products of sense stimulation which "fill a gap in a causal theory of perception . . . a link . . . between the stimulation of the sense organ and the final judgement about those objects."[62] In a synthesis of Plato and Aristotle, Aquinas argues instead that form is universal and singular, common, and particular, in the sense that humanity is indeed instantiated individually in each human being. Yet at the same time, the act of being, which brings things into existence and actualizes their form, is common to all beings, as I showed in section 2 of the present chapter. Equally, *phantasmata* do not have to fill any gap because there is no such gap: the symmetry between sense perception and intellectual cognition implies that species are present in the sense and in the mind according to the same cognitional or spiritual mode of being. *Phantasmata* do not bridge an otherwise unbridgeable gap because perception and cognition are always already related to each other in analogous and hierarchical ways, without any need to appeal to a tertiary instance.

Aquinas's distinction between a natural and a cognitional (or spiritual) mode of being is important in a third way. It shows that in the senses, species are immaterial yet individuated and received physically by the sense organ:

> There is the perfect immateriality of intelligible being; for in the intellect things exist not only without matter, but even without their individuating material conditions, and also apart from any material organ. Then there is the half-way state of sensible being. For as things exist in sensation they are free indeed from matter, but are not without their individuating material conditions, nor apart from a bodily organ.[63]

On this point, Hoffman's contribution to the debate with Cohen and Haldane is crucial. Hoffman states what he takes to be Aquinas's two guiding metaphysical principles in connection with individual sensible being:

---

62. Hamlyn, *Sensation and Perception*, p. 49, quoted by Haldane, "Aquinas on Sense Perception," p. 238.

63. *"Nam quoddam est penitus immateriale, scilicet esse intelligibile. In intellectu enim res habent esse, et sine materia, et sine conditionibus materialibus individuantibus, et etiam absque organo corporali. Esse autem sensibile est medium inter utrumque. Nam in sensu res habet esse sine materia, non tamen absque conditionibus materialibus individuantibus, neque absque organo corporali"* (*In De anima* lib. II, lec. 5, n. 6).

first of all, what is received is received according to the mode of the recipient and, second, the principle that individuates things is matter. Senses receive species corporeally and materially, while the intellect receives them incorporeally and immaterially. But since perception is always already cognitive, senses also somehow receive species incorporeally and immaterially, though not in the same way as the intellect. This is what Aquinas describes as the 'half-way' state of sensible being, which he conceptualizes in terms of degree of materiality and immateriality.[64] What does this mean and what are the implications? As Hoffman shows, the idea of degrees is paramount because it enables Thomas to argue that forms are present in the senses according to both modes. For this reason, Aquinas distinguishes between the reception by the senses, which is corporeal and material (Cohen's 'physical event'), and the apprehension by the senses, which is incorporeal and immaterial: "It must be said, as I have already said, that passion properly is found where there is corporeal change. This indeed is found in the acts of the sensitive appetite: there is not only spiritual change, as there is in sensitive apprehension, but also natural change."[65] Hoffman is also right to argue that corporeal or material reception is not the same as natural (as opposed to spiritual) change. For reception of sensible form always involves a recipient — the senses — but does not necessarily involve reception of matter: insofar as agents act by their form, every patient receives form without matter.[66] Aquinas addresses the question of whether changes are natural or spiritual and whether spiritual change requires a soul in terms of the material disposition of the patient and the agent vis-à-vis the form. If that disposition is identical, then forms are not received without matter (e.g., air acted on by fire). Applied to sensible being, the implication is that the immaterial reception of sensible species is material because it takes place in sense organs and it is immaterial because sensitive apprehension (or perception) is cognitive.

Why and how is this relevant to the question of individuation? So far we have seen that sensual perception is the double locus of material and immaterial reception and natural and spiritual change. Given that the intellect cognizes universal form abstracted from matter and without any sense organ, it is the senses that enable us to cognize particular

---

64. Hoffman, "St. Thomas Aquinas on the Halfway State of Sensible Being," pp. 83-85.

65. *"Respondeo dicendum quod, sicut iam dictum est, passio proprie invenitur ubi est transmutatio corporalis. Quae quidem invenitur in actibus appetitus sensitivi; et non solum spiritualis, sicut est in apprehensione sensitiva, sed etiam naturalis"* (*ST* I-II, q. 22, a. 3, resp.).

66. Hoffman quotes in support *In De anima* lib. II, c. 12, lec. 24: 551.

form. For this reason, sense perception is indispensable to the cognition of individuals. This is exactly what Thomas concludes in the *De veritate:*

> [O]ur mind is notably directed to know singulars, for we know singulars directly through our sensitive powers which receive forms from things into a bodily organ. In this way, our senses receive them under determined dimensions and as a source of knowledge of the material singular. For, just as a universal form leads to the knowledge of matter in general, so an individual form leads to the knowledge of designated matter, which is the principle of individuation.[67]

But Hoffman fails to address two questions that arise from this argument and are central to Aquinas's theory of individuation. First, how do we perceive sensible species? Second, what do we perceive when a species is present to our senses according to both the cognitional and the spiritual mode? In what follows, I will show that Thomas's answer to the first question is sense power and his answer to the second question is common being instantiated in individual beings.

D. Sense Power

In this subsection I outline Thomas's account of sense power by drawing primarily on his commentary of Aristotle's *On sense and what is sensed* (1267-69) but also on some key questions in the *Summa Theologiae.* Aquinas follows both biblical teaching and Greek metaphysics on the priority of being vis-à-vis knowing in order to show that it is actual objects that activate the senses: "'sensation occurs as a result of one's being moved by external objects of sense' [Aristotle, *De anima* II.5]. Hence, man cannot sense without an external sensible object, any more than a thing can be moved without a mover."[68] In other words, the actuality of sensible ob-

---

67. "*Unde patet quod mens nostra directe singulare cognoscere non potest; sed directe cognoscitur a nobis singulare per virtutes sensitivas, quae recipiunt formas a rebus in organo corporali: et sic recipiunt eas sub determinatis dimensionibus, et secundum quod ducunt in cognitionem materiae singularis. Sicut enim forma universalis ducit in cognitionem materiae universalis, ita forma individualis ducit in cognitionem materiae signatae, quae est individuationis principium*" (*De veritate* q. 10, a. 5, resp.).

68. "'*sentire accidit in ipso moveri a sensibilibus exterioribus*'. Unde non potest homo sentire absque exteriori sensibili: sicut non potest aliquid moveri absque movente" (*SCG* II.57.8).

jects actualizes the potency of our sense organs, such that our potential to see becomes actual seeing and what was visible is now seen (*De sen.* c. 5, 439ª12-18). In this process, which is both physical and spiritual, there is an adequation *(convenientia)* between seeing and what is seen. The bond that binds them together is the actuality of God's act of being, which (and here I anticipate my argument) we can dimly apprehend when we perceive actual sensible things. The faculty that enables us to do so is sense power. First of all, sense power is not limited to the body but also concerns the soul: "[S]ense-power is common to soul and body, for sensing pertains to the soul through the body."[69] For this reason, Hoffman is right to emphasize the physical and the spiritual dimension of sensation in Aquinas's epistemology. But here one can go further than this and relate sense power not only to the vegetative and appetitive part of the soul but also to the cognitive or intellective part and ultimately to the essence of an intelligent being. If sensing is necessary to knowing and if knowing is the proper act of the intellective part of the soul, then sensing is indispensable to the operation of the soul. If a substance's essence is related to that substance's specific operation, which it is for Aquinas (already in the *De ente et essentia*), then sensing is an integral part of what it is to be an intelligent being.

Second, sense power is both material and immaterial because there are degrees of materiality and immateriality and therefore sensible being can be said to be in a halfway state, as Hoffman argues correctly against both Cohen and Haldane. Beyond Hoffman, it is important to link the idea of degrees of materiality to cognition of singulars. For Aquinas, only the senses (and the imagination) can know singulars *qua* singulars precisely because singularity involves matter, which is the principle of individuation[70] — as I will argue in detail. Building on Aristotle's argument in the *De anima* that the knowledge of individuals is the joint prod-

---

69. *"sensus autem communis est animae et corpori, sentire enim convenit animae per corpus"* (*De sen.* proem 436ª18).

70. "[T]he sensitive power that is in animals is certainly open to what is outside, but only in the singular. Hence it also has an immateriality inasmuch as it is receptive of forms of sensible things without matter, but it has the lowest immateriality in the order of knowers, inasmuch as it can receive these forms only in a bodily organ *(Virtus autem sensitiva, quae inest animalibus, est quidem capax extrinsecorum, sed in singulari tantum: unde et quamdam immaterialitatem habet, inquantum est susceptiva specierum sensibilium sine materia; infimam tamen in ordine cognoscentium, inquantum huiusmodi species recipere non potest nisi in organo corporali)"* (*De sen.* c. 1, 436ᵇ10).

uct of the senses and the intellect but originates in the senses and requires sense power, Aquinas makes the crucial point that sense power gives us access to singularity:

> If [the object] is apprehended as an individual — e.g. when I see something coloured I perceive this human being or this animal — then this sort of apprehension in a human being is produced through the cogitative power. This is also called particular reason, because it joins individual intentions in the way that universal reason joins universal concept. But all the same, this power is in the soul's sensory part. For the sensory power, at its highest level, participates somewhat in the intellective power in a human being, in whom sense is connected to intellect. . . . The cogitative power apprehends an individual as existing under a common nature. It can do this insofar as it is united to the intellective power in the same subject. Thus it cognises this human being as it is this human being.[71]

Aquinas's argument is that sense power is *in* the sense organs but not *of* the sense organs, insofar as it is both physical and spiritual, both material and immaterial. The physicality and materiality of sense power derives from the activation by sensible objects, which are themselves material. The spirituality and immateriality of sense power follows from the idea that the sensible species are perceived immaterially yet in relation to their material individuating conditions. The difference between sense cognition and intellective cognition is precisely that the former relates sensible species to their embodiment while the latter abstracts from it.

More precisely, sense power is at an intermediary station between sensible objects and sense organs on the one hand and intelligible form and abstraction on the other hand: "[S]eeing itself is not located in the appearance of this form in the eye, but in what is doing the seeing, that

71. "*Si vero apprehendatur in singulari, utpute cum video coloratum, percipio hunc hominem vel hoc animal, huiusmodi quidem apprehensio in homine fit per vim cogitativam, quae dicitur etiam ratio particularis, eo quod est collativa intentionum individualium, sicut ratio universalis est collativa rationum universalium. Nihilominus tamen haec vis est in parte sensitiva; quia vis sensitiva in sui supremo participat aliquid de vi intellectiva in homine, in quo sensus intellectui coniungitur. . . . Nam cogitativa apprehendit individuum, ut existens sub natura communi; quod contingit ei, inquantum unitur intellectivae in eodem subiecto; unde cognoscit hunc hominem prout est hic homo*" (*In De anima* lib. II, lec. 13, nn. 14-16, commenting on *De anima* 417^{b}19-29: 191-222).

is, in what has the power of sight: for the eye is a seeing thing not because it is smooth, but because it has the power of sight."[72] In the *Summa contra Gentiles,* Aquinas refers to Aristotle in describing sense power as a "certain form of an organ,"[73] which indicates not just the blending of the material and the immaterial and the physical and the spiritual but also emphasizes the link with the intellect, insofar as sense power is capable of apprehending the *actuality* of sensible forms. As will by now be clear, Aquinas makes this astonishing claim by fusing Plato's metaphysics of relational participation with Aristotle's conceptuality of act and potency. Here it is important to clarify Thomas's precise use of Aristotle. To describe sensing as a power *(virtus)* is to say, first of all, that it is a disposition that stands in potency to the actuality of sensible objects. Indeed, he takes from Aristotle's *De anima* the idea that sensibles are sensed through sense organs because sensibles actualize sense power. For instance, color (or sound or odor) is sensed by sight (or hearing or smell) because color is actual (as opposed to purely potential) and as such actualizes sense power by activating and altering a sense organ: "[A] sense-power is a sensible object in potentiality and . . . sensible objects make a sense-power be in actuality."[74] For this reason, Aquinas effectively argues that to perceive an object is to sense its actuality. In other words, to perceive something is to perceive that *that thing* is in act.

The second use of Aristotle relates to sense power that functions as an agent in respect of the potential intellect. Aquinas explains this in terms of the Platonist idea of participation of the sense power in something higher than itself: "[T]he sensory power [*vis sensitiva*], at its highest level, participates somewhat in the intellective power in a human being, in whom sense is connected to intellect."[75] Knowledge of singulars is more than knowledge of individuals *qua* individuals — it is knowledge of something that exceeds separate, apparently self-sufficient individual entities. For each thing is relationally positioned and as such discloses

72. *"Et ita patet quod ipsum videre non consistit in hoc quod est apparere talem formam in oculo; sed consistit in vidente, idest in habente virtutem visivam: non enim oculus est videns propter hoc quod est laevis, sed propter hoc quod est virtutis visivae"* (*De Sen.* c. 3, 438ᵃ5).

73. *"de sensu dicit Aristoteles, in II de anima, quod est quaedam ratio organi"* (*SCG* II.69.9).

74. *"quod sensus est potentia sensibile, et quod sensibilia faciunt sensum esse in actu"* (*De Sen.* c. 5, 439ᵃ6).

75. See, *supra,* note 71.

other things as well as the shared transcendent source. As Haldane re-marks, Thomas writes in *De veritate* that truth as 'adequation' *(convenientia)* "is the perfection of a knower *qua* knower, for something is known by a knower only in so far as the known is somehow in the knower . . . in which way it is possible for the totality of the whole uni-verse to exist in one thing."[76] Here Aquinas extends the Christian Neo-Platonist idea we have already encountered in Augustine, that particu-larity intimates the universality it participates in, just as the microcosm of the household reflects the macrocosm of the universe which never-theless always exceeds it.[77] Emphatically, Thomas's metaphysics of rela-tional participation outwits in advance Suárez's dualist transcendental-ism which separates 'pure nature' from the supernatural and Spinoza's monist immanentism which equates God with substantiality, as I will show in chapters 7 and 8. For now, I will conclude the long *excursus* on Aquinas's theological epistemology by examining how sense perception relates to the apprehension of actuality.

5. Apprehending Actuality

A. Transcendental Thomism

The question of apprehending individual beings and common being has been at the heart of Thomist scholarship since the revival of Thomism in the wake of Pope Leon XIII's encyclical *Æterni Patris* (1880).[78] While there is agreement amongst different schools of interpretation on the impor-tance of judgment in apprehension, there is disagreement on the status of judgment in relation to the senses and the intellect.[79] According to 'tran-

---

76. *"haec est perfectio cognoscentis in quantum est cognoscens, quia secundum hoc a cognoscente aliquid cognoscitur quod ipsum cognitum est aliquo modo apud cognoscentem [. . .] Et secundum hunc modum possibile est ut in una re totius universi perfectio existat"* (*De veritate* q. 2, a. 2, resp.).

77. See, *supra,* chapter 2, section 7, where I mention Augustine's image of the "effigy of the whole universe."

78. On the transcendentalist, the participationist, and the analogical reading of Thomas, see Douglas C. Hall, *The Trinity: An Analysis of St. Thomas Aquinas' Expositio of the* De Trinitate *of Boethius* (Leiden: E. J. Brill, 1992), pp. 3-9.

79. A concise summary of this debate can be found in Joseph Owens, "Aquinas on Knowing Existence," *The Review of Metaphysics* 29 (1976): 670-90.

scendental Thomism' (a designation first coined by J. Donceel),[80] there is in the mind an a priori structure that cognizes intelligible essence and apprehends sensible existence. According to Karl Rahner, "[T]he formal structure of this judgement [sense judgment of existence] — and with more reason the structure and the content of universal judgements and especially of metaphysical judgements — cannot be grounded in the evidence of sense perception."[81] In other words, 'transcendental Thomists' assert that sense cognition requires supplementation by objective judgment not only to produce a universal form but also to ascertain the existence of universal form outside the mind in things.[82]

At the same time, 'transcendental Thomism' recognizes that knowledge of the actual existence of universal form outside the mind requires knowledge of sensible singulars and their relation to universal forms. Beyond Kant, this interpretation acknowledges that knowing universals is dynamic and tends towards infinite being *(esse)*, which is the a priori condition of possibility for judgment of both essence and existence. 'Transcendental Thomism' also takes into account Plato and Aristotle's shared insight that all cognition begins with the senses, but Karl Rahner insists that "in the line of Aristotle, Kant and Hegel, he [Aquinas] sees it [the a priori] in a formal a priori of the spontaneous spirit itself . . . its basis, speaking in the manner of St. Thomas, is the light of the intelligence itself, which informs, objectifies, conceptualizes and judges the data from sense cognition."[83] 'Transcendental Thomists' correctly view judgment as the epistemic operation through which the mind obtains knowledge of existence. Likewise, immanence is rightly construed as participatory rather than self-sufficient. However, the origin of the notion 'existence' is thought to be purely noetic and it is the mind that projects it onto sense perception.[84] In so doing, the formality of a priori objective judgment supplants the reality of sensation; the mind can only move to

---

80. J. Donceel, "Transcendental Thomism," *The Monist* 58 (1974): 67-85.

81. Karl Rahner, "Aquinas: The Nature of Truth," *Continuum* 2 (1964): 65.

82. See, *inter alia,* Joseph Maréchal, *Le point de départ de la métaphysique. Leçons sur le développement historique et théorique du problème de la connaissance,* 5 vols. (Paris: Desclée, 1944-1949); Karl Rahner, *Geist in Welt. Zur Metaphysik der endlichen Erkenntnis bei Thomas von Aquin,* 2nd rev. ed. (Munich: Kösel-Verlag, 1957); trans. Dych, *Spirit in the World* (New York: Herder & Herder, 1968); Bernard Lonergan, *Verbum: World and Idea in Aquinas* (New York: Philosophical Library, 1957).

83. Rahner, "Aquinas: The Nature of Truth," p. 65.

84. Donceel, "Transcendental Thomism," pp. 76-77.

the infinity of *esse* if judgment verifies that sensible singulars embody the universal forms which the mind fashions in its own image. For this reason, the *actus essendi* of 'transcendental Thomism' is neither in the eye of the beholder nor in the object of sensation but a product of the mind alone.

Such and similar readings of Aquinas are wrong on at least two accounts. First, they do not accord with Thomas's conception of the potential intellect, which is activated by sense perception (e.g., *De anima* III.4, 429^b30–430^a2). As early as in his commentary on Boethius' *De Trinitate* (c. 1256-59), Aquinas argues that both the possible intellect and the agent intellect are not separate substances (and thereby the same for all souls), but instead proper to each and every soul and conjointly capable of apprehending the truth: "[B]oth an active and a passive power are ascribed to the soul in its intellectual activity. . . . So, just as the other natural active powers, joined to their passive counterparts, suffice for natural activities, so also the soul, endowed with an active and passive power, is adequate for the perception of truth."[85] It is true to say that for Thomas, the efficacy of the active intellect extends to knowledge of natural principles and finalities. On the basis of sense perception, the intellect forms universals with which to cognize principles and *teloi*. But like Augustine and other patristic Neo-Platonists, Aquinas argues that divine activity is necessary to bring everything, including the intellect, into being, to make it what it is and to direct it to its specific end.

If this is true, then 'transcendental Thomism' is mistaken on a second account. To elevate the formality of *ens* as concept over above the reality of *ens* as being ignores Aquinas's emphasis on the ontological priority of being *(esse)* vis-à-vis both that which is (*ens* or *id quod est*) and essence *(essentia)*.[86] The origin of the notion 'existence' or 'act of being' cannot be exclusively noetic: "God is constantly at work in the mind, endowing it with its natural light and giving it direction. So the mind, as it goes about its work, does not lack the activity of the first cause."[87] The ex-

---

85. "... *in anima ponitur respectu intelligibilis operationis, quae est cognitio veritatis, et potentia passiva et potentia activa. Unde sicut aliae potentiae activae naturales suis passivis coniunctae sufficiunt ad naturales operationes, ita etiam anima habens in se potentiam activam et passivam sufficit ad perceptionem veritatis"* (*In Boeth. de Trin.* q. 1, a. 1, resp.).

86. *In I Sent.* d. 8, q. 1, a. 3, resp.; *De ente* prol. and c. 1, 1-2.

87. "*In hoc ergo continue Deus operatur in mente, quod in ipsa lumen naturale causat et ipsum dirigit, et sic mens non sine operatione causae primae in operationem suam procedit"* (*In Boeth. de Trin.* q. 1, a. 1, ad. 6).

tension of Augustine's theory of divine illumination operated by Aquinas reinforces the real presence of the divine act of being in beings. Moreover, the potential intellect is not activated by the agent intellect but by sensation. What the senses mediate to the intellect is always already in actuality and is sensed as an actuality or as an event, "something that occurs to the intellect by the mode of actuality, absolutely so."[88] Thus, the intellect neither passes judgment on mere existence nor has cognition of essence alone, by abstraction, or by division and composition. Instead, for Aquinas the mind conceptualizes that which the senses apprehend and mediate — the act of being in beings-in-act.

B. Thomist Existentialism

Both Jacques Maritain and Étienne Gilson, albeit for different reasons, reject transcendental Thomism and defend what they call a form of 'Thomist existentialism.' Against the Cartesian opposition of intelligence and mystery, Maritain follows Aquinas's theory of subalternation in order to describe the object of intellection as an inexhaustible, 'transobjective' reality, which he likens to an intelligible mystery that marks the terminus of the intellectual act.[89] As such, reality has two aspects — essence and existence — with two corresponding intellectual operations. The first operation consists in forming concepts of essences and the second operation concerns the attainment of the perfective end of things, i.e., their actuality.[90] Maritain draws on the late scholastic theologian Thomas de Vio (1469-1534), also known as Cardinal Cajetan, to equate the latter operation with judgment:

> [I]t is in the second operation of the mind, in judgement, in the composition and division, that the speculative intelligence grasps being not only from the point of view of essence but from the point of view of

88. "... *aliud quod cadit in intellectu per modum actualitatis absolute*" (*In I Peri Herm.* lec. 5, no. 73 [16ᵇ23]).

89. Jacques Maritain, *Distinguer pour unir: Ou, les degrés du savoir* (Paris: Desclée, 1932); J. Maritain, *Sept Leçons sur l'Être et les premiers principes de la raison spéculative* (Paris: Pierre Téqui, 1934), pp. 8-9, quoting Aquinas, "*non terminatur ad enuntiabile, sed ad rem*" (*ST* II-II, q. 1, a. 2, ad 2).

90. Maritain, *Sept Leçons sur l'Être et les premiers principes de la raison spéculative*, pp. 24-25.

existence itself, actual or possible, — existence thus grasped *ut exercita* (as exercised by a subject, not only presented to the mind as with the simple concept of existence, but as held possibly or actually by the subject). . . . [I]t is in the judgement that knowledge is completed and fulfilled.[91]

In short, judgment pertains to actual or possible existence, not to the concept of existence. For this reason, judgment must return to sensation because to judge is to apprehend the existential condition of essences.[92]

If, as Maritain claims, judgment corresponds to the second operation of the intellection, then the question is: What corresponds to the first operation? For Aquinas, the first operation of the intellect consists in abstracting the essence from a concrete being *(ens concretum quidditati sensibili)* or, as Maritain correctly defines it, a particular quiddity and being in general bound together in concrete things.[93] Being thus defined is the first object of the intellect. To this first object corresponds the common sense. According to Maritain, general being gives rise to what Thomists such as Cajetan or John of St. Thomas (1589-1644) termed *abstractio totalis* or extensive abstraction,[94] i.e., a pre- or infra-scientific abstraction of general being from the diversity of sensible, individual beings. As such, general being grounds the logical relations of generality and is an intermediary station between the diversity of sensible individual beings, on the one hand, and the unity of abstract being *qua* being, on the other hand. The latter is the object of intuition, which

91. "C'est dans la seconde opération de l'esprit, dans le jugement, dans la composition et la division, que l'intelligence spéculative tient l'être non seulement au point de vue de l'essence mais au point de vue de l'existence elle-même, actuelle ou possible, — existence saisie alors *ut exercita* (en tant qu'exercée par un sujet, en tant même que détenue, non pas seulement en tant que présentée à l'esprit comme il arrive dans le simple concept d'existence, mais en tant même que détenue possiblement ou actuellement par un sujet) . . . Or c'est dans le jugement que se complète et s'achève la connaissance," in Maritain, *Sept Leçons sur l'Être et les premiers principes de la raison spéculative*, p. 26.

92. Maritain, *Sept Leçons sur l'Être et les premiers principes de la raison speculative*, pp. 28-31.

93. Maritain, *Sept Leçons sur l'Être et les premiers principes de la raison speculative*, p. 24. Cf. Aimé Forest, *La structure métaphysique du concret selon Saint Thomas d'Aquin* (Paris: Vrin, 1956).

94. Maritain, *Sept Leçons sur l'Être et les premiers principes de la raison speculative*, pp. 36-40.

Maritain explicitly refers to as metaphysical intuition.[95] So if judgment is concerned with the actuality of sensible quiddities, then judgment is preceded by the common sense and by metaphysical intuition.

In later works, Maritain speaks of the intuition of being *(l'intuition de l'être)* as a unique judicative act. This differs from all predicative and other judgments, and it precedes and structures all ideas and concepts of existence. By defining the intuition of being as that which is produced *"in and through* an affirmative judgement of existing,"[96] Maritain makes it dependent on an a priori metaphysical framework and therefore restricts it to an extraordinary judgment. Indeed, he goes as far as saying that the intuition of being is absent from "the conversations of everyday life."[97] In short, Maritain reduces the apprehension of actuality to the metaphysical intuition of being, which is an extraordinary judgment and as such escapes the common sense.

However, this does not accord with Aquinas's argument, which I have already cited, that the senses mediate to the mind "something that occurs to the intellect by the mode of actuality, absolutely so."[98] Maritain is right to state that all intellection starts with the perception of sensible particular beings and returns to sensation in order to grasp the existential condition of the essence known. For this reason, physics or natural philosophy is not separate from metaphysics or *divina scientia* in Thomas's pyramidal ordering of the sciences, as Maritain himself suggests.[99] But Maritain is wrong to maintain that Thomas equates sensation of things with discernment of the self. Likewise, he is mistaken in restricting the intuition of being to the third act of intellection — metaphysical intuition.[100] Instead, Aquinas combines Augustine's account of the cosmically embedded self with Aristotle's insight that sensation of actual sensible things in the world precedes consciousness of the self in the mind.

---

95. Maritain, *Sept Leçons sur l'Être et les premiers principes de la raison speculative,* pp. 51-70.

96. *"dans et par un jugement* affirmatif de l'exister," in Jacques Maritain, "Réflexions sur la nature blessée et sur l'intuition de l'être," *Revue thomiste* 68 (1968): 5-41 (17) (original italics).

97. Maritain, "Réflexions sur la nature blessée et sur l'intuition de l'être," p. 20.

98. See, *supra,* note 88.

99. Maritain, *Sept Leçons sur l'Être et les premiers principes de la raison spéculative,* pp. 29-40.

100. Maritain, "Réflexions sur la nature blessée et sur l'intuition de l'être," pp. 20-23.

The Philosopher says: "We sense that we sense, and we understand that we understand, and because we sense this, we understand that we exist." [*Ethics* IX.] But one perceives that he understands only from the fact that he understands something. For to understand something is prior to understanding that one understands. Therefore, through that which it understands or senses the soul arrives at actual perception of the fact that it exists.[101]

According to Thomas, sensation is sensation of being in actuality. This kind of apprehension of being is not restricted to extraordinary metaphysical intuition of being, as Maritain claims. Instead, it is part of common, 'everyday' experience, which he wrongly regards as devoid of any apprehension of being in actuality.

Gilson, by contrast, argues that there is no strict equivalence between ideas or concepts of existence on the one hand and actual being on the other hand, for the latter precedes and exceeds the former. Gilson also contends that we intuit individual things in act, not a thing called 'existence.' Nor does intuition give us full cognition of God's pure act of being. No concept can ever grasp self-subsistent being in and of itself. Rather, human intellection can apprehend the act of being *(actus essendi)* in being *(ens)*, which is the first object of natural knowledge and to which corresponds the first in the order of sciences — metaphysics. Gilson describes this as follows:

> Since the existing *(l'exister)* proper to each being *(être)* is beyond any concept, we have to content ourselves to apprehend it in being, which is the first and most immediate determination of the act of being. This is why *ens* [sic] is the supreme concept and the first principle of our knowledge.... If we had a pure intellectual intuition of the sensible, we would have a science of existing, and our metaphysics would be that very science.[102]

---

101. *"unde dicit philosophus in IX Ethicorum: sentimus autem quoniam sentimus; et intelligimus quoniam intelligimus; et quia hoc sentimus, intelligimus quoniam sumus. Nullus autem percipit se intelligere nisi ex hoc quod aliquid intelligit: quia prius est intelligere aliquid quam intelligere se intelligere; et ideo anima pervenit ad actualiter percipiendum se esse, per illud quod intelligit, vel sentit"* (*De veritate* q. 10, a. 8, resp.).

102. Gilson, *Le Thomisme*, pp. 120-21. Gilson quotes *In IV Met.* lec. 6, n. 605 in support of his understanding of *ens*.

According to this interpretation, Aquinas denies sensation, intuition, and abstraction any cognition of the act of being. Only judgment can attain the act of existing and, as such, attain the truth of beings.[103] Against Maritain, Gilson maintains that Aquinas distinguishes the intuition of first principles from the apprehension of being in beings *(étants)*. So while we can have a sense intuition of really existing things — the common sense perceives sensibles that are — we cannot have an intellectual intuition of the act of existing.[104]

Not unlike Maritain, Gilson fails to think through the link Thomas establishes between perception and actuality. If that which the senses mediate to the intellect is always already in actuality and is intuited "by mode of actuality, absolutely so,"[105] then perception of a being *(ens)* is in some sense perception of being *(esse)*. How so? In perceiving that which is *(id quod est)*, we intuit being *(esse)* and not merely the 'fact' that something has existence. Whereas sense organs perceive the real existence of individual sensibles in their singularity but do not grasp actuality in itself or as such, the common sense extends beyond individual sensitive operations such as sight to the unity that underlies the multiplicity of sensibles. As a result, we apprehend the act of being in beings-in-act through the common sense, even though the common sense does not know it as such, for only the intellective power of the mind can cognize being as an act. Both Maritain and Gilson ignore Thomas's insight that sensation of sensibles is sensation of being.

C. Aquinas's Metaphysics beyond Participationist Thomism

Cornelio Fabro and Louis-Bertrand Geiger reject both transcendental Thomism and Thomist existentialism in favor of a 'participationist' reading of Aquinas's metaphysics. Fabro is correct to argue that the act of being *(actus essendi)* describes not so much the state of existence but rather the act of things — being in order to be in act *(esse ut actus)*. This is why things can be said to participate in the pure actuality of being or God.[106] He is

103. Gilson, *Le Thomisme*, pp. 122-23.

104. Gilson, *The Christian Philosophy of St. Thomas Aquinas*, pp. 204-5; Étienne Gilson, "Propos sur l'être et sa notion," in *San Tommaso e il pensiero moderno*, ed. Pontificia Accademia di S. Tommaso (Rome: Città Nuova Editrice, 1974), pp. 7-17.

105. See, *supra*, note 88.

106. Cornelio Fabro, *La nozione metafisica di partecipazione secondo S. Tommaso*

equally right to emphasize the primacy of the ontological *ens* (*id quo est* or *quod habet esse*) vis-à-vis the epistemological *ens* (*quod primo intellectus intelligit).*[107] Yet at the same time, Fabro maintains that *ens* grounds both the concrete and the abstract and as such differs from ancient formalism and modern existentialism.[108] But to view the Thomist *ens* as a transcendental is precisely to privilege formality over actuality, a late scholastic fallacy that gave rise to modern transcendentalism.[109] Indeed, Fabro contends that the notion of being *(notio entis)* precedes the notion of existence and essence as objects of the intellect because, through a combined act of judgment and conceptualization, we know the formality of essence before we conceptualize the factuality of existence.[110] However, this does not accord with Aquinas's distinction of judgment and conceptualization and his insistence that in apprehending beings, we apprehend the actuality of being — the act of being in beings-in-act.

For his part, Geiger denies that sense apprehension according to Thomas enables cognition of transcendent being. Instead, the mind can only cognize transcendent being by separating it from movement and matter. As such, "*separatio* is a judgement that is passed on the immateriality of being *in rerum natura.*"[111] Put differently, the mental act of separation is not a form of abstraction but instead a cognitive judgment. But in order to be able to pass an objective judgment, Geiger asserts that the mind must somehow be able to have a priori knowledge of immaterial being, the object of metaphysics. While he is right to say that physics is

d'Aquino (Turin: Marietti, 1950), pp. 200 *passim.* C. Fabro, *Partecipazione e causalità secondo S. Tommaso d'Aquino* (Turin: Marietti, 1960), pp. 20-50, 212-44; C. Fabro, *Dall' essere all' esistente,* 2nd ed. (Brescia: Morcelliana, 1965), pp. 40-60. On Fabro's reading of Aquinas, see Carlo Giacon, "S. Tommaso e l'esistenza come atto," *Mediœvo* 1 (1975): 1-28, esp. pp. 23-27.

107. Cornelio Fabro, "Die Wiederaufnahme des Thomistischen 'Esse' und der Grund der Metaphysik," *Tijdschrift voor Filosofie* 43 (1981): 90-116, esp. pp. 91-94.

108. Fabro, "Die Wiederaufnahme des Thomistischen 'Esse' und der Grund der Metaphysik," pp. 103-8.

109. See Adrian Pabst, "Wisdom and the Art of Politics," in *Encounter between Radical Orthodoxy and Eastern Orthodoxy: Transfiguring the World through the Word,* ed. Adrian Pabst and Christoph Schneider (Aldershot, UK: Ashgate, 2009), pp. 109-37.

110. Cornelio Fabro, "The Intensive Hermeneutics of Thomistic Philosophy: The Notion of Participation," *Review of Metaphysics* 27 (1974): 449-91, esp. p. 470.

111. "la *separatio* est un jugement qui se prononce sur l'immatérialité de l'être *in rerum natura,*" in Geiger, "Abstraction et séparation d'après s. Thomas *In De Trinitate,* q. 5, a. 3," p. 24.

an incomplete science that requires metaphysical supplementation, he is wrong to suggest that the mind cognizes transcendent being through judgment that is founded in the a priori metaphysical knowledge of immaterial being. To maintain this is to ignore Aquinas's argument that perception of sensible, material composites *(entia)* is to perceive neither mere existence or pure essence nor being *qua* being but instead *esse* in *ens* — something like the advent or unfolding of being-in-act. In the remainder of this section, I will set out Thomas's account of how the common sense apprehends the divine act of being.

Aquinas himself makes the point about apprehending actuality. Once more he fuses Plato's emphasis on relational participation with Aristotle's accentuation of act, potency, and sense perception. Drawing on *De Anima,* he writes in *De Senso* that the sense organs perceive and mediate to the mind the actuality of sensibles: "[W]hat each of them [the sensibles] is according to actuality — that is according as colour, flavour or any other sensible object, is in actuality perceived by sense — as has been said in *On the Soul.*"[112] For this reason, the actuality of sensibles, which inhere in particular things and participate in the divine act of being, actualizes the potency of sense powers which inhere in sense organs and participate in cognitive power. There is thus a hierarchical 'adequation' or *convenientia* between being and knowing: "[T]he visible in actuality is the same as seeing in actuality."[113] According to Aquinas, to perceive a particular thing is to see the actuality that envelops it. This is mediated by the common sense, which synthesizes the perceptual and cognitive power of all the senses. Indeed, many different sensible objects within one genus — say, the visible — are sensed in virtue of one sense-power — in this case, seeing. Moreover, many different sensible objects across different genera — the visible or the audible — are sensed by one and the same indivisible 'organ' — the sensitive part of the soul (*De Sen.* c. 18, 449ª2-10). In turn, the proper senses — seeing or hearing — are bound together by the common sense *(sensus communis),* which "perceives by means of sight, and by means of hearing, and by means of other proper senses, which are different potential parts of the soul, and not . . . like different parts of a continuum."[114] Thomas also describes the com-

112. "*Quid autem sit unumquodque eorum secundum actum, idest secundum quod est color actu perceptus a sensu, aut sapor vel quodcumque aliud sensibile, dictum est in libro de anima*" (*De Sen.* c. 5, 439ª12-18).

113. "*videlicet visibile in actu est idem visioni in actu*" (*De Sen.* c. 5, 439ª12-18).

114. "*sensus communis sentit per visum et per auditum, et alios sensus proprios, qui sunt*

mon sense as the first and common principle that underlies the operations of the proper senses: "[S]ince the operations of the proper senses are referred to the common sense as their first and common principle, the common sense is related to the proper senses and their operations in the way that one point is related to different lines that meet in it."[115] The common sense is the sense power that informs all sense organs and unifies the mediations it receives.

Indeed, the actuality we perceive is in fact the common being that enfolds and upholds all sensibles. Thomas develops this crucial argument in four stages. First of all, he distinguishes between proper sensible objects and common sensibles (*De Sen.* c. 5, 439ᵃ6). Sensible objects are perceived in relation to each sensitive part or individual sense organ: color, sound, odor in relation to sight, hearing, and smell. Second, common sensibles are aspects of sensibles that are common to different genera of sensibles like movement, number, figure, magnitude, unity, time, etc.[116] Within different genera of different sensible things, there are common features, e.g., color with respect to all visible things. Color has two principles: a material principle — the transparent — and a formal principle — light itself. The transparent is not a property of different bodies but rather a 'common nature,' "that is, a natural property found in many things — one that he [Aristotle] also calls a 'power' inasmuch as it is a principle of vision."[117] Third, this 'common nature' is not separate, but instantiated in sensible objects to varying degrees. Light, the formal principle of color, shines forth in all bodies and is therefore the actuality within the genus of the visible. Equally, the transparent, the material principle of color, is that which is receptive of light and is therefore the potentiality within the genus of the visible. Conjointly, the act of light and the potency of the transparent produce the visibility of sensible ob-

---

diversae partes potentiales animae; non autem diversae partes sunt alicuius continui" (*De Sen.* c. 18, 449a9).

115. *"operationes sensuum propriorum referantur ad sensum communem, sicut ad primum et commune principium, hoc modo se habet sensus communis ad sensus proprios et operationes eorum, sicut unum punctum ad diversas lineas, quae in ipsum concurrunt"* (*De Sen.* c. 18, 449a10-12).

116. Bernard J. Muller-Thym, "The Common Sense, Perfection of the Order of Pure Sensibility," *The Thomist* 2 (1940): 315-43, esp. p. 321.

117. *"[natura communis], quae in multis corporibus invenitur; scilicet quaedam naturalis proprietas in multis inventa, quam etiam virtutem nominat, inquantum est quoddam principium visionis"* (*De Sen.* c. 5, 439a21).

jects. Perception concerns the interplay of the act of form and the potency of matter. Fourth, Aquinas argues that to perceive an individual sensible object is in fact to perceive a commonality that binds together apparently separate, discrete entities. Since the senses mediate species form in its material embodiment and its transcendently received actuality, the common sense dimly apprehends God's act of being which underpins all things.

But two questions arise that cast doubt on my argument. First, since contrary sensibles like whiteness and blackness do not coincide in natural bodies and therefore cannot be sensed simultaneously, how can the common sense be a unitary principle? Second, how can Aquinas move from common sensation to apprehension of common being without leaping from sensitive to intellective cognition, which conflates the nonreflexivity of the sense with the self-reflexivity of the intellect? Indeed, does Thomas himself not write that "the sense knows neither itself nor its operation; for instance, sight neither sees itself nor sees that it sees. This self-reflexive power belongs to a higher faculty, as is proved in *De anima* [III.2]"?[118] The key to unlock Aquinas's complex reflections on apprehending actuality is a double analogy. Just as the multiplicity of the proper senses paradoxically points to the unity of sensitive operations which is the common sense, so the multiplicity of sensible objects paradoxically intimates the unity of sensibles and the underlying principle which is common being. Since "sense and intellect are similar" (Aristotle, *De anima* III.2, 427ᵃ9), Thomas concludes that

> sense and intellect receive the forms of things spiritually and immaterially according to an *intentional being*, in such a way that they have no contrariety. Hence sense and intellect can simultaneously receive species of contrary sensible objects . . . sense and intellect not only receive the forms of things, but also make a judgement about them. Now judgement about contraries is not itself contrary, but something one and the same, because by one of the contraries a judgement is taken about the other.[119]

118. "*Nullus sensus seipsum cognoscit, nec suam operationem: visus enim non videt seipsum, nec videt se videre, sed hoc superioris potentiae est, ut probatur in libro de anima*" (*SCG* II.66.5).

119. "*sed sensus et intellectus recipiunt formas rerum spiritualiter et immaterialiter secundum esse quoddam intentionale prout non habent contrarietatem. Unde sensus et intellectus simul potest recipere species sensibilium contrariorum. . . . sensus et intellectus*

So far, I have argued that perception as the immaterial reception of sensible form constitutes according to Aquinas a physical event that affects the sense organs and a spiritual transformation that affects the sensitive part of the soul. The latter is passive and active, in that the sensitive part of the soul is both the patient and the agent of sense power, which is activated by sensible objects and in turn activates the mind. As such, perception is in some sense sensitive as well as intellective. Conversely, intellection is in some sense reflexive as well as perceptual. As Thomas explains, judgment is not concerned either with separate discrete entities or with contraries but instead with the relational positioning of particular things — the noetic correspondence to the ontological reality of common being which enfolds all things. However, the accentuation of common being and the common sense seems to be at odds with Aquinas's double distinction between physical and spiritual change and between natural and intentional being. In turn, this brings into sharp focus the question of whether there is a single unitary or double binary principle of individuation. I briefly explore this problem in the following subsection.

D. Perception, Individuation, and Common Being

Since there are two modes of being (natural and spiritual or intentional), it would seem that there are also two principles of individuation — matter and spirit (or the intellect). The former constitutes the first principle that individuates forms which are received according to the natural mode of being. The latter is the second principle that individuates forms which are received according to the spiritual or intentional mode of being. Anthony Kenny defends this thesis of two principles of individuation against Peter Geach, who contends that there is only one principle of individuation and that Aquinas posits the important difference between form and *esse*.[120] Kenny is correct to highlight Thomas's distinction of substantial from accidental form. The senses grasp the latter (e.g., the

---

non solum recipiunt formas rerum, sed etiam habent iudicare: iudicium autem quod faciunt de contrariis non est contrarium, sed unum et idem, quia per unum contrariorum sumitur iudicium de altero" (*De Sen.* c. 18, 449ᵃ17-18; my italics).

120. Anthony Kenny, "Intentionality: Aquinas and Wittgenstein," in *Thomas Aquinas: Contemporary Philosophical Perspectives,* ed. Brian Davies (Oxford: Oxford University Press, 2002), pp. 243-56; Peter T. Geach, "Form and Existence," *Proceedings of the Aristotelian Society* 54 (1954-55): 250-76.

redness of *this rose*), whereas the intellect grasps the former (e.g., the form of rose or 'roseness'). However, Kenny ignores Aquinas's further distinction between internal proper accidents 'created' from the principles of their subjects (e.g., passions which are particular to species or individual accidents which are not present in every member of the same species)[121] and external accidents 'received' by a subject from without. Since nothing except God has either form or existence by itself, there must be a difference between form and *esse*, as Geach rightly insists. Indeed, proper accidental forms are created by their subject insofar as the subject is in act *(actu)*, and substantial form is received by that subject insofar as the subject is in potency *(in potentia)* to the act of being, as Aquinas writes in the *Summa Theologiae* (*ST* I, q. 77, a. 6, resp.). And since substantial form is in act to the potency of matter and in potency to the act of being, form intimates the source which brings it into actuality. John Wippel comments on this question in *Summa* as follows:

> [I]nsofar as the soul is in potency in some way, he [Aquinas] has remarked, it can be the subject or receiving principle for those accidents which reside in it . . . as the form or act principle of a human essence, the human soul is still in potency with respect to the act of being which it receives and communicates to its correlative matter. This, apparently, is enough for it to be in potency in a second way as well, as the receiving principle of its accident. And if we wonder why the soul is in act (and therefore productive of its proper accidents), this must ultimately follow from the fact that it is actualised by its corresponding act of being.[122]

In perceiving sensible objects, we perceive the 'double act of being' which actualizes the substantial form or soul and produces its proper accidents. Aquinas however is no hylomorphist. The individuation of composite substances is not determined by form alone. Material embodiment, far from being accidental or arbitrary, defines the particularity of things that receive their particular form according a specific mode

---

121. As Wippel attests, in his *Commentary on the Sentences* Aquinas uses *'creantur'* as an equivalent for *'causantur'* to describe the relation between substantial subjects and their accidents (*In I Sent.* d. 17, q. 1, a. 2, ad 2). See John F. Wippel, *The Metaphysical Thought of Thomas Aquinas. From Finite Being to Uncreated Being* (Washington, DC: Catholic University of America Press, 2000), p. 266.

122. Wippel, *The Metaphysical Thought of Thomas Aquinas*, p. 272.

of being: "[T]he principle of that mode of existence, namely the principle of individuation, is not common, but differs in each individual: for this particular thing is individualised by this matter, and that one by that matter."[123] For this reason, the principle of individuation is matter, but the 'cause' of individuation is the act of being, as I will demonstrate in the remainder of this chapter.

6. The 'Relativity' of Individuals

In this and the following section, I will explore Aquinas's account of individuality and the link he establishes between the 'relativity' of individuals and the self-diffusive Good of God which individuates all things relationally. Individuality is not confined to God and separate substances but extends to the material universe. In composite material substances, individuality encompasses three aspects: first of all, the unity of composites, i.e., that which unifies matter and form and makes it into *this* rather than *that* compound; second, the plurality of numerically distinct forms within a single species. As early as his commentary on the Sentences, Aquinas writes that "[t]wo features belong to the notion of an individual, namely that it be actually existent either in itself or in something else; and that it be divided from other things that are or can be in the same species, existing undivided in itself."[124] To say that something is individual is to say that *that* thing is in itself undivided and differentiated from other things in the same species.

In other texts, Thomas emphasizes a third feature of individual entities to highlight the connection with other individual entities. In *De veritate,* he describes the order of things in relation to one another (*secundum ordinem unius ad alterum, De veritate* q. 1, a. 1, corp.) and distinguishes between oneness or 'undividedness' *(unum),* 'otherness' *(aliquid),* and relation *(ad aliud).* These distinctions are not merely logical properties but concern the metaphysical structure of the world and all things therein. Just as Augustine speaks of the beauty of individual mate-

123. *"sed principium talis modi existendi quod est principium individuationis, non est commune; sed aliud est in isto, et aliud in illo; hoc enim singulare individuatur per hanc materiam, et illud per illam"* (*De potentia* q. 9, a. 2, ad 1).

124. *". . . de ratione individui duo sunt: scilicet quod sit ens actu vel in se vel in alio; et quod sit divisum ab aliis quae sunt vel possunt esse in eadem specie, in se indivisum existens"* (*In IV Sent.* d. 12, q. 1, a. 1, ad 3m).

rial forms and the harmony that pertains between them, so Aquinas characterizes the relation of an individual thing to other such things in terms of *convenientia* (*alio modo secundum convenientiam unius entis ad aliud, De veritate* q. 1, a. 1, corp.). As Gilbert Narcisse has documented, *convenientia* is for Thomas an aesthetic term that is intimately connected with notions such as *analogia, proportio, harmonia,* and *ordinatio.*[125] As such, it conveys the aesthetic nature of relations and describes the harmonious proportions between individual things. So beyond the postmodern dichotomy of identity and difference (or *différance*), Thomas posits relation as a third dimension of being that mediates between 'undividedness' and differentiation. To be is to be 'relative' *(ad aliud)* to that which is, and 'being relative' is coextensive with being individual.[126]

So defined, an individual thing's 'relativity' describes the horizontal relations that pertain between beings. 'Relativity' is not merely an accidental property or an external factor like the location of one thing compared to another. Nor is 'relativity' the same as Aristotle's category, which is subordinate to substance. For Aquinas as for Plato, the 'relativity' of individuals is metaphysical because its foundation is being *(esse),* for being is that in which all concur fittingly (*omnia in esse conveniunt, SCG* I.42.16). Individuals are 'relative' and interrelated (rather than absolute and isolated) because they all share in one and the same cause — common being — which is created, as I have already documented. For precisely this reason, there is a second form of relation that is vertical and describes the link between being and God who gives being to all things (*dans esse rebus, In II Sent.* d. 1, q. 1, a. 4, corp.; cf. *ST* I^a, q. 105, a. 5, corp.). In the words of Thomas, "[f]or creation is not a change, but that dependence of created being on its source whence it is set forth. And so it [creation] is of the category of relation."[127] Like Boethius and other Christian Neo-Platonists who had knowledge of Aristotle's categorial 'theo-ontology,' Aquinas reconfigures the preeminence of substance in the direction of the primacy of relation.

Since God as *esse ipsum subsistens* is in no way affected by the rela-

125. Narcisse, *Les raisons de Dieu,* esp. pp. 184-92.

126. For a detailed exposition, see the brilliant book by Philipp W. Rosemann, *Omne ens est aliquid. Introduction à la lecture du "système" philosophique de saint Thomas d'Aquin* (Louvain-Paris: Ed. Peeters, 1996), pp. 48-71.

127. *"Non enim est creatio mutatio, sed ipsa dependentia esse creati ad principium a quo statuitur. Et sic est de genere relationis"* (*SCG* II.18.2); cf. *Comp. theol.* I.99; *In V Met.* lec. 17, no. 1004.

tion of creation, Aquinas views its relation as nonmutual and asymmetrical. For the Creator is wholly outside the genus of created being (*De potentia* q. 7, a. 10, corp.).[128] As a result, all things are relational to God as the universal origin and end of everything. Even though there is no textual equivalent in Thomas's works, the term 'relationality' is conceptually more accurate than the notion of 'relation' because the former highlights not only the asymmetry and nonmutuality but also the absence of any univocal foundation and instead an emphasis on the analogy of being.[129] Relationality is dynamic and describes God's act of being which brings everything into actuality, makes it what it is, and sustains it in being. Just as God is the source of all being and as such lacks any shared basis with everything else, so common being is not an independent station in the cosmic order against which the Creator and creation are measured. Rather, common being is the initial created effect of the first cause:

> The first of all effects is being itself, which is presupposed to all other effects, and does not presuppose any other effect.
>
> [B]eing is the most common first effect and more intimate than all other effects: wherefore it is an effect which it belongs to God alone to produce by His own power.[130]

For Aquinas, the relationality of beings to God is the gift of being which he bestows upon creation. The horizontal and the vertical models of relationality in Thomas are intimately connected. Through God's creative action, beings can share in the ecstatic relationality of the Trinity and thereby perfect relations with other beings, not by becoming identical with the one and only triune God, but by manifesting his utter plenitude, goodness, and love.

To say that relationality or relativity *(ad aliud)* is integral to individuality has important implications for Aquinas's account of individuation. The reason why something is individuated cannot be purely formal be-

---

128. A. Krempel, *La doctrine de la relation chez saint Thomas* (Paris: Vrin, 1952), pp. 554-62; Mark G. Henninger, *Relations: Medieval Theories 1250-1325* (Oxford: Clarendon Press, 1989), pp. 13-39.

129. Krempel, *La doctrine de la relation chez saint Thomas*, pp. 174-79.

130. *"primus autem effectus est ipsum esse, quod omnibus aliis effectibus praesupponitur, et ipsum non praesupponit aliquem alium effectum;" "ipsum esse enim est communissimus effectus primus et intimior omnibus aliis effectibus; et ideo soli Deo competit secundum virtutem propriam talis effectus"* (*De potentia* q. 3, a. 4, resp., and a. 7, resp.).

cause members of the same species are formally identical but numerically different. Numerical difference suggests that matter explains how things are undivided in themselves and differentiated from other things of the same species. Indeed, Aquinas argued that matter is a necessary condition for differentiating specifically or formally identical individuals (*In II Sent.* d. 3, q. 1, a. 4, sol.; *In IV Sent.* d. 44, q. 2, a. 2, sol. 2). However, the reason why things are individuated cannot be exclusively material because matter does not explain unity (or 'undividedness'). So it would seem as if the confluence of form and matter individuates composites. Since neither individual forms nor particular bodies exist by themselves, neither form nor matter can explain why *this* individual form coalesces with *that* particular body (*SCG* II.81). Both depend on higher causes and ultimately on the first cause for their existence.

For this reason, the double mark of Aquinas's account of individuation is the emphasis on the act of being (which brings everything into existence) and on the distinction between the cause and the principle of individuation. Contrary to Porreta's logic, which begins with God's *essentia* and moves down via forms *('quo ests')* to all things that are *('quod ests')*, Aquinas eschews this grammatical and formalist Platonism in favor of a more metaphysical and realist Platonism, which he inherits in part from figures such as Gregory, Augustine, Boethius, and Dionysius. Since being makes itself known to the mind via the senses, knowledge starts with the supernaturally infused finite actuality of that which is (Boethius' *id quod est* or *ens*) rather than the naturally limited infinite possibility of essence (Porreta's *'quo ests'*). Joseph Owens puts this succinctly:

> From the existence that comes and goes in sensible things, existence that is accidental even though it is the basic actuality of those existents, one can reason to existence that is a nature [*In I Sent.* d. 8, q. 1, a. 2, sol.; d. 26, q. 1, a. 2, ad 1m; *Quodl.* VIII.1c]. . . . It contains and unites everything within its own unity. It is the existence of all things and all things have their primary existence in it. It necessarily individualizes itself. Subsistent existence is its own individuation.[131]

The nature of the first cause of existence leads Aquinas to draw the distinction between the cause and the principle of individuation. Unity is convertible with, and follows from, being. That which has being has

---

131. Owens, "Thomas Aquinas (b. ca. 1225; d. 1274)," pp. 173-94 (174-75).

unity and to have unity is to be an individual. For this reason, actualization and individuation are coextensive. This is why "everything in accordance with the way it has existence has unity and individuation."[132] In the metaphysical order, being is the 'cause of individuation' *(causa individuationis)*, and it applies to separate substances and matter-form compounds alike. Crucially, it does so analogously and specifically, not univocally: "As existents, however, they differ, for a horse's existence is not a man's, and this man's existence is not that man's."[133] For this reason, being *(esse)*, in bringing all things into actuality, individuates each and every existent. As such, being is the universal cause of individuation — it creates everything out of nothing into particular 'somethings.' To be individuated is to be unique, for individuated beings are *not* copies of a uniform exemplar that are merely differentiated by accidents. Instead, all individual beings are unique particulars or singulars.

In other words, Aquinas makes the astonishing claim that the most universal is also that which particularizes things. How and why might this possibly be true and rationally intelligible? For Thomas, universal or common being is received diversely in particular beings: "[E]verything is received in something else according to the mode of the recipient."[134] This is why there is not only a cause but also a principle of individuation, designated matter *(materia signata)* — that which receives being. In the remainder of this chapter, I examine the implications of Aquinas's conception of the cause and the principle of individuation. In the following chapter, I compare and contrast Thomas's position with that of Scotus, Ockham, and Buridan.

7. *Bonum Diffusivum Sui* and the Hierarchy of Relations

In the preceding section, I showed that individuation is for Aquinas a philosophical problem because it concerns the metaphysical structure of the world, in particular the simultaneous occurrence of unity and di-

---

132. ". . . *unumquodque enim secundum quod esse habet, habet unitatem at individuationem*" *(Responsio ad Fr. Joannem Vercellensem de articulis XLII* q. 108, in *Op. theol.* I, no. 935 [240]).

133. ". . . *differunt autem secundum esse; non enim idem est esse hominis et equi, nec huius hominis et illius hominis)*" *(ST* I[a], q. 3, a. 5).

134. "*unumquodque recipitur in altero per modum recipientis*" *(De potentia* q. 7, a. 7, ad 10).

versity in material things. In this section, I show that the primary cause which individuates matter-form compounds is the ultimate source of all being — divine love and goodness (*In II Sent.* d. 1, q. 1, a. 4, corp.; *SCG* III.24; *ST* I^a, q. 105, a. 5, corp.). Indeed, in his commentary on the *Liber de causis* Thomas writes that the Good is itself individual and infuses all things with pure goodness:

> But if someone should say: the first cause must have *yliatim,* we will say: its *yliatim* is infinite being and its individuality is the pure goodness that infuses the intelligences with all goodness and, with the mediation of the intelligence, [also infuses] the rest of things.[135]

In other words, divine creation is that event by which the infinity of united 'definiteness' is converted into the finitude of composite 'definiteness.' As such, individual things reflect in particular and diverse ways the universal triunity of their Creator whose goodness individuates all beings relationally. For God's ecstatic self-subsistence brings everything into being and makes it in the image and likeness of the relational Godhead.

Here one can distinguish three kinds or levels of relation in Aquinas: first, the horizontal relation amongst beings that all share in common being (e.g., *ST* I^a-II^a, q. 29, a. 1, ad 1; *ST* III^a, q. 1, a. 2, resp.); second, the vertical asymmetric relationality of created being to God upon which the horizontal relation depends (e.g., *De veritate* q. 2, a. 11, corp.; *Comp. theol.* I.67); third, the absolutely symmetric relationality between the Trinitarian persons, which provides the ultimate source for the relational individuation of the whole of creation (e.g., *De potentia* q. 8, a. 2, ad 1; *ST* I^a, q. 28, a. 2, corp.).[136] In the present subsection, I detail these three dimensions of Thomas's account of relationality.

---

135. "*Quod si dixerit aliquis: necesse est ut sit abens* yliatim, *dicemus:* yliatim *id est suum esse infinitum, et individuum suum est bonitas pura, effluens super intelligentiam omnes bonitates et super reliquas res mediante intelligentia*" (*In de causis* prop. 9^a [65/57]). On the meaning of *yliatim* in Aquinas, see Jan A. Aertsen, *Medieval Philosophy and the Transcendentals: The Case of Thomas Aquinas* (Leiden: E. J. Brill, 1996), esp. p. 260; Andreas Speer, "'*Yliathin quod est principium individuandi*' — Zur Diskussion um das Individuationsprinzip im Anschluß an prop. 8[9] des 'Liber de causis' bei Johannes de Nova Domo, Albertus Magnus und Thomas von Aquin," in *Individuum und Individualität im Mittelalter,* ed. Jan A. Aertsen and Andreas Speer (Berlin and New York: De Gruyter, 1996), pp. 266-86, esp. 282-86.

136. Krempel, *La doctrine de la relation chez saint Thomas,* esp. pp. 170-79.

I have already highlighted the influence of both Christian and pagan Neo-Platonism on the metaphysics of Aquinas.[137] Thomas's hierarchy of relations is a particular case in point. The Good, whose individuality is pure goodness, infuses all things with goodness. This is because the Good communicates itself (*bonum diffusivum sui, De veritate* q. 24, a. 3, corp.; *SCG* I.37; *ST* I^a, q. 19, a. 2, corp.).[138] As such, the Good is manifest in all that is because each and every existent thing shares in goodness by virtue of participating in common being. Goodness in beings is intelligible, for the good is convertible with being (*ens et bonum convertuntur, In I Sent.* d. 44, q. 1, a. 1, corp.), and being is naturally oriented towards the Good (e.g., *In I Sent.* d. 44, q. 1, a. 2, corp.; *In Boeth. de Trin.* 4). Likewise, the intellect seeks the truth of things because intelligent nature is always already instilled with a natural desire for knowledge and the Good:

> The essence of goodness consists in this, that it is in some way desirable. Hence the Philosopher says (*Ethic.* i): "Goodness is what all desire." Now it is clear that a thing is desirable only in so far as it is perfect; for all desire their own perfection. But everything is perfect so far as it is actual.[139]

---

137. Against the strongly Aristotelian interpretation of Étienne Gilson and A. C. Pegis, other Thomist scholars have documented the importance of Platonism and Neo-Platonism. In addition to L.-B. Geiger and C. Fabro, see, *inter alia*, André Hayen, *L'intentionnel dans la philosophie de Saint Thomas* (Paris: Vrin, 1942); Joseph de Finance, *Être et Agir dans la Philosophie de Saint Thomas* (Paris: Vrin, 1945); Louis de Raeymaeker, *Philosophie de l'être. Essai de synthèse métaphysique,* 2nd ed. (Louvain: Editions Nauwelaerts, 1947); William Norris Clarke, "The Limitation of Act by Potency in St. Thomas: Aristotelianism or Neo-Platonism?" *New Scholasticism* 26 (1952): 167-94; W. N. Clarke, "The Meaning of Participation in St. Thomas," *Proceedings of the American Catholic Philosophical Association* 26 (1952): 147-57; W. N. Clarke, "The Platonic Heritage of Thomism," *Review of Metaphysics* 8 (1954): 105-24; W. N. Clarke, "The Problem of the Reality and Multiplicity of Divine Ideas in Christian Neoplatonism," in *Neoplatonism and Christian Thought,* ed. Dominic J. O'Meara (Albany: State University of New York Press, 1982), pp. 109-27; cf. Mark D. Jordan, *The Alleged Aristotelianism of Thomas Aquinas* (Toronto: Pontifical Institute of Mediaeval Studies, 1992); O'Rourke, *Pseudo-Dionysius and the Metaphysics of Aquinas;* and te Velde, *Participation and Substantiality in Thomas Aquinas.* For a concise overview of this (ongoing) debate, see Fergus Kerr, *After Aquinas: Versions of Thomism* (Oxford: Blackwell, 2002), esp. pp. 9-10, 48-50, 70-71.

138. W. N. Clarke, SJ, "Person, Being, and St. Thomas," *Communio* 19 (Winter 1992): 601-18; W. N. Clarke, SJ, *Explorations in Metaphysics: Being, God, Person* (Notre Dame: University of Notre Dame Press, 1994), pp. 102-22, "To Be Is to Be Substance-in-Relation."

139. "*Ratio enim boni in hoc consistit, quod aliquid sit appetibile: unde Philosophus, in* I

Here Aquinas's mention of actuality is crucial. A thing is good and desires the good of its own perfection insofar as it actually exists (*ST* I^a, q. 5, a. 1). Only that which is can be truly desired (*sic nihil est appetibile nisi ens, ST* I^a, q. 5, a. 2, ad 4). All of which underscores Thomas's hierarchical conception of being.

Paradoxically, this metaphysical hierarchy reinforces relationality between God and the world and also within the created order. Beyond Boethius' synthesis, Thomas combines Plato's emphasis on the Good which individuates all things relationally with the shared Platonist and Aristotelian focus on the desirability of goodness and the perfectibility of being. Since being and the good are coterminous in the Creator, all things that are brought out of nothing into actuality share in the plenitudinous reality of their creative source. For this reason, to desire the good is a sign of creation and a means of preserving and perfecting one's unique form within God's relational economy: "[A]ll things, each according to its mode, desire to be in act; this is clear from the fact that each thing according to its nature resists corruption. To be in act, therefore, constitutes the nature of the good."[140] Indeed, like Plato (and to some extent Aristotle), Aquinas views the Good as that which propels all intelligent substances to perfect their own form by pursuing goodness intellectually and practically. All activities, speculative and practical, that are governed by the Good enhance the actuality of beings by fulfilling the unique forms of each thing. Since the form of created things is 'relative' or relational, to act in accordance with intimations of divine goodness is to promote both individual and communal relationality by diffusing and distributing being and goodness to other things:

> The communication of being and goodness arises from goodness. This is evident from the very nature and definition of the good. By nature, the good of each thing is its act and perfection. Now each thing acts in so far as it is in act, and in acting it diffuses being and good-

---

Ethic., *dicit quod bonum est 'quod omnia appetunt.' Manifestum est autem quod unumquodque est appetibile secundum quod est perfectum: nam omnia appetunt suam perfectionem. Intantum est autem perfectum unumquodque, inquantum est actu"* (*ST* I^a, q. 5, a. 1).

140. *"Omnia autem appetunt esse actu secundum suum modum: quod patet ex hoc quod unumquodque secundum naturam suam repugnat corruptioni. Esse igitur actu boni rationem constituit"* (*SCG* I.37.4).

ness to other things. Hence, it is a sign of a being's perfection that it 'can produce its like,' as may be seen from the Philosopher in *Meteorologica* IV.[141]

This passage highlights Aquinas's conception of horizontal relationality among created things, which are not isolated self-contained entities but instead relational beings. He emphasizes the perfectibility of beings-in-act and the dynamic nature of the Good which is coextensive with being and action. *Pace* Norman Kretzmann, who has alleged that the self-diffusive good is subordinate to the good as final cause,[142] it is clear that Thomas associates both final and efficient causality with the Good: "Now, the nature of the good comes from its being something appetible. This is the end, which also moves the agent to act. That is why it is said that the good is 'diffusive of itself and of being.'"[143] Thus there is a key difference with Aristotle, which is that Aquinas does not limit the Good to the status of final cause but extends it to formal and efficient causality. More in line with Plato and Christian Neo-Platonism, Thomas connects the formal actuality of the Good with the actuality of creation.

So configured, the Good acts as both a final and as a formal-efficient cause of particular sensible things and explains not just *how* but also *why* intelligent beings pursue being and goodness by seeking ever more intense actualization. At the first horizontal level — the creaturely station in the metaphysical order — being *(esse)* is relational in the sense that actuality pours over into action which is not confined to the individual self but extends to other beings too, establishing relations amongst them. The self-diffusiveness of created *esse* implies that all things are always already relational because to be in act is to act upon other beings at the

141. "*Communicatio esse et bonitatis ex bonitate procedit. Quod quidem patet et ex ipsa natura boni, et ex eius ratione. Naturaliter enim bonum uniuscuiusque est actus et perfectio eius. Unumquodque autem ex hoc agit quod actu est. Agendo autem esse et bonitatem in alia diffundit. Unde et signum perfectionis est alicuius quod 'simile possit producere,' ut patet per Philosophum in IV Meteororum*" (*SCG* I.37.4).

142. Norman Kretzmann, "A General Problem of Creation: Why Would God Create Anything at All?" in *Being and Goodness: The Concept of the Good in Metaphysics and Philosophical Theology,* ed. Scott MacDonald (Ithaca, NY: Cornell University Press, 1991), pp. 208-29, esp. 219-23; N. Kretzmann, *The Metaphysics of Theism: Aquinas' Natural Theology in Summa Contra Gentiles I* (Oxford: Oxford University Press, 1996), pp. 223-25.

143. "*Ratio vero boni est ex hoc quod est appetibile. Quod est finis. Qui etiam movet agentem ad agendum. Propter quod dicitur bonum esse 'diffusivum sui et esse'*" (*SCG* I.37.4; cf. *De veritate* q. 21, a. 2, resp.).

same time as being acted upon by them. Properly understood, metaphysical relationality constitutes the source for the interconnectedness throughout the *cosmos* and translates into practicing relations that establish human association at all levels, from the family and the household via communities to a common polity.[144] Even though these have different ends, they are all hierarchically ordered and governed by the supreme common good.[145]

An important point that emerges from Thomas's metaphysics of creation and individuation is a certain vision of politics that is centered upon the common good in which all beings share. Aquinas's conception of the common good has received widely and wildly different interpretations, ranging from Jacques Maritain's existentialist defense to Michael Novak's liberal cooptation.[146] However, both positions fail to recognize that participation in the common good requires participation in common being because being and the good are coextensive. Crucially, to partake of common being presupposes relationality to the self-subsistent being *(ipsum esse subsistens),* for only God's gift of being enables participation. There can only be relationality among created beings if they are relationally constituted by the Creator (*In II Sent.* d. 1, q. 1, a. 2, ad 4; *De potentia* q. 3, a. 3, ad 2; *ST* I^a, q. 45, a. 3, ad 1): "[C]reation is really nothing other than a relation with God with the newness of being."[147]

Here the point needs to be made emphatically that Aquinas is more Platonist than Aristotelian. Thomas's account of God focuses on Trinitarian relationality rather than either on Aristotle's substance alone (as

---

144. Jan A. Aertsen, "Thomas Aquinas on the Good: The Relation between Metaphysics and Ethics," in *Aquinas's Moral Theory: Essays in Honor of Norman Kretzmann*, ed. Scott MacDonald and Elenore Stump (Ithaca, NY: Cornell University Press, 1999), pp. 235-53; M. S. Kempshall, *The Common Good in Late Medieval Political Thought* (Oxford: Clarendon Press, 1999); Bernhard Blankenhorn, "The Good as Self-Diffusive in Thomas Aquinas," *Angelicum* 79 (2002): 803-37, esp. p. 810.

145. *ST* I^a, q. 65, a. 2; I^a-II*ae*, q. 113, a. 9, ad 2; II^a-II*ae*, q. 39, a. 2, ad 2; II^a-II*ae*, q. 47, a. 11, resp.; *De regno* I.1. On horizontal relationality in Aquinas, see Philipp W. Rosemann, *Omne ens agit sibi simile: A "Repetition" of Scholastic Metaphysics* (Leuven: Leuven University Press, 1996), esp. pp. 279-305. On second- and third-act causality and the link to intra-Trinitarian relations, see Milbank and Pickstock, *Truth in Aquinas*, esp. pp. 19-59.

146. Jacques Maritain, *The Person and the Common Good* (Notre Dame: University of Notre Dame Press, 1947); Michael Novak, *Free Persons and the Common Good* (Lanham, MD: Madison Books, 1989).

147. *"creatio nihil est aliud realiter quam relatio quaedam ad Deum cum novitate essendi"* (*De potentia* q. 3, a. 3, corp.).

John Zizioulas wrongly ascribes to Western theology from Augustine on) or on a Platonized dyad of substance-in-relation (as William Norris Clarke falsely associates with Thomist 'ontology').[148] Zizioulas is right to contrast the Trinitarian personalism of the Greek Fathers with the essentialism of some Latin theologians (though not Augustine, Boethius, or Aquinas, as I have shown), but he is wrong to claim that the unity of God's substance or being is somehow grounded in the freedom of the three divine persons. Nor is it correct to suggest that Thomas supplements Aristotelian substantiality with a greater Platonist emphasis on relationality, as Clarke argues — even though his accentation of Aquinas's indebtedness to Platonism is crucial. Rather, God reveals himself as both substance and relation, as Thomas maintains in all his works.[149] On a basic level, substance secures the unity of divine being whereas relation ensures the diversity and distinctness of the three Trinitarian persons. But more fundamentally, God is beyond any genus (*De potentia* q. 7, a. 3, ad 7; q. 8, a. 2, ad 1) and exceeds all languages and concepts. Here the influence of Neo-Platonist negative theology in general and Dionysius' mystical metaphysics in particular is key, as both Fran O'Rourke and Rudi te Velde have shown. Beyond the binary link of the One and the Many in both Plato and Plotinus, Aquinas shifts the focus to Trinitarian relations of the Godhead and the triadic ordering of creation. More so than his patristic Neo-Platonist forebears, he shows how the only concept that applies to God is relation (*In I Sent.* d. 33, q. 1, a. 1, ad 5). In God there cannot be any categorial relations that depend on substance. Instead, the three divine persons are subsistent relations (*ST* I^a, q. 29, a. 4). Only subsistence secures 'real' distinction (*In I Sent.* d. 26, q. 2, a. 1 *contra; ST* I^a, q. 36, a. 2) without undermining essential substantial unity (*In I Sent.* d. 8, q. 4, a. 1, ad 4; *De potentia* q. 9, a. 5, ad 3). Since "in God relation and essence do not differ from each other, but are one and the same,"[150] God is the only fully relational substance or substantial relation. As such,

---

148. See John Zizioulas, *Being as Communion* (Crestwood, NY: St. Vladimir's Seminary Press, 1985), pp. 16-49; William Norris Clarke, "To Be Is to Be Substance-in-Relation," pp. 102-22. For a useful summary of their positions, see Matthew Webb Levering, *Scripture and Metaphysics: Aquinas and the Renewal of Trinitarian Theology* (Oxford: Wiley-Blackwell, 2004), pp. 197-251.

149. See, *inter alia, In 1 Sent.* d. 2, q. 1, a. 3; d. 22, q. 1, a. 3, ad 2; *De potentia* q. 10, a. 5; *ST* I^a, q. 28, a. 2, ad 1.

150. *"in Deo non est aliud esse relationis et esse essentiae, sed unum et idem"* (*ST* I^a, q. 28, a. 2, corp.).

Thomas develops Augustine's argument (*De Trin.* V.v) that "whatever is in God is His substance"[151] in the direction of divine, pure, unreserved, absolute, and self-subsistent relationality, which is revealed to us in the triple Book of Scripture, Nature, and History.

The common good is created by God's love and self-diffusive good, which individuates individuals relationally. It is the supreme good in God which all beings are ordered to and which is mediated through the *cosmos* and the city. The implications for politics and for individuation within a common polity are significant. Unlike Maritain's and Novak's Aristotelian separation of the material and the spiritual or the contemplative and the practical,[152] Aquinas — although he indeed makes such and similar distinctions — emphasizes that all levels and dimensions are equally ordered towards the one and only common good in God (*ST* I^a-II*ae*, q. 113, a. 9, ad 2). And it is this more Platonist metaphysics of relationality that distinguishes Aquinas most clearly from Aristotle. The main difference with Plato is that Aquinas (building on Augustine and Boethius) accounted for the relationality of being itself in terms of the substantial relations of the Trinity and of the relationality of created in terms of God's outpouring love.[153]

The self-diffusiveness of the Good and the outpouring of divine love is the reason why God creates everything out of nothing and individuates all things relationally. Aquinas makes this argument by linking individuation, communication, and relation. Everything is what it is not through itself but in relation to other things by receiving them and by giving itself to them, as Philipp Rosemann has argued.[154] The mode of communication and relation amongst created things is perhaps best described as a dynamic of gift-reception and return. This dynamic is sustained by God's original and continuous gift of being. That is why the di-

---

151. *"Quidquid est in Deo, Deus est"* (*De potentia* q. 8, a. 2, corp.), where Aquinas mentions Augustine's *De Trinitate; "Quidquid est in Deo, est eius substantia"* (*De potentia* q. 8, a. 2, corp.).

152. Maritain, *The Person and the Common Good*, pp. 15-30.

153. Cf. Clarke, "The Limitation of Act by Potency in St. Thomas: Aristotelianism or Neo-Platonism?" esp. pp. 190-94. I agree with Clarke that Aquinas reconfigured Neo-Platonism and produced an original synthesis that cannot be described as dominantly Aristotelian. Beyond Clarke, I argue that the novelty of Thomist metaphysics consists in developing the three dimensions of relationality (amongst created beings, between creation and the Creator, and within the Godhead) and showing how the triadic structure of the world discloses the Trinitarian relations of the three divine persons.

154. Rosemann, *Omne ens est aliquid*, pp. 13-47.

vine act of being is the ultimate source of individuation, the first cause and final end of creation.

8. Prime Matter and Substantial Form

In this section, I analyze Aquinas's account of the link between matter and form. The reason why Aquinas posits not just a cause but also a principle of individuation is that the divine act of being cannot itself account for the diverse reception of form into materiality. Unlike Porreta's 'grammatical Platonism' and his essentialist ontology, which focus on individuating forms, Thomas follows the metaphysical Platonism and relational realism of his Christian Neo-Platonist forebears and transforms Aristotle's conception of matter as pure potency in the direction of created matter that reflects the singularity of its transcendent source.

If prime matter is pure potentiality (*De princ. nat.* c. 2, 7), then matter cannot individuate anything at all because pure potency is free of all determinations and therefore unable to differentiate formally or specifically identical particulars, e.g., members of the same species (*In I Sent.* d. 8, q. 5, a. 2). The problem that this argument raises is how universal form and the act of being that actualizes it can be limited by the pure potency of matter. As William Norris Clarke has argued, Aquinas solves this problem by providing a new synthesis of Aristotle's metaphysics of act and potency and the (Neo-)Platonist framework of participation. Thomas's solution is to show that "act is not limited except by reception in a distinct potency."[155] This solution is the result of two fundamental transformations of the philosophical tradition he inherited. Aquinas replaces the Neo-Platonic procession of universal concepts with the plenitudinous pure act which is self-diffusive and infuses all things with being and goodness. He also disengages Aristotle's act and potency from its hitherto exclusive attachment to the phenomenon of substantial change and emphasizes the limitations placed upon plenitude by the participation of recipient beings in pure actuality.

The implications for matter as the principle of individuation are far-

155. Clarke, "The Limitation of Act by Potency in St. Thomas: Aristotelianism or Neo-Platonism?" p. 190. In support of this formula, Clarke cites the following textual references: *SCG* I.43; II.52-54; *De potentia* q. 1, a. 2; q. 7, a. 2, ad 9; *In De Div. Nom.* c. 5, lect. 1; *ST* I^a, q. 7, a. 1-2; q. 50, a. 2, ad 4; q. 75, a. 5, ad 1 et 4; *De spir. creat.* 1; *De subst. sep.* c. 3 and 6; *In VIII Phys.* c. 10, lect. 21; *Quodl.* III.8.20; *Comp. theol.* 18-21.

reaching. First, just as Plato introduces a conceptual difference between relationality and participation (acquiring and possessing form), so Aquinas distinguishes the self-diffusion of goodness and love through divine creation from the participation in God's plenitude through human agency. God's creative action provides the metaphysical ground for participating in the relational life of the Trinitarian Godhead, a foretaste of the beatific vision in this life (*ST* I^a, q. 12) which deifies us here and now.[156] Second, Aquinas develops Greek conceptions of causality to their theological conclusion by arguing that nothing comes from nothing and that for this reason prime matter cannot preexist form. Beyond both Plato and Aristotle, he insists that prime matter has God as its first cause (*SCG* II.16; *ST* I^a, q. 15, a. 3, ad 3, which mentions Plato). This is not simply an application of the doctrine of creation *ex nihilo* to cosmogony but follows from the very nature of the universe. If there is an ultimate source of reality and if this source is being itself, then that which receives being must have the capacity to do so. For this reason, pure potency cannot exist by itself but only in relation to pure act. The essence of prime matter, which is unable to actualize itself and cannot be ordered to any operation (*In I Sent.* d. 3, q. 4, a. 2, ad 4), is neither utter nothingness nor self-generation but instead the capacity to receive actuality from the pure act of being (*In I Phys.* lect. 15). Since prime matter and form stand in potency to God's pure self-subsistent being, both receive actuality from the divine act of being. Moreover, in created reality there is no pure matter without form. As a result, prime matter is not created alone or by itself *(per se)*, but under its appropriate form (*sub forma, De potentia* q. 3, a. 5, ad 3; cf. *ST* I^a, q. 44, a. 2, ad 3).

This conception of matter raises questions about the nature of the relation between prime matter and substantial form. This relation is not categorical, for otherwise it would be a property superadded to the

---

156. On the beatific vision and deification in Aquinas, see the contrasting accounts by Étienne Gilson, "Sur la problématique thomiste de la vision béatifique," *Archives d'histoire doctrinale et littéraire au Moyen-Âge* 31 (1964): 67-88; Maritain, "Réflexions sur la nature blessée et sur l'intuition de l'être," pp. 5-41; and, more recently, Olivier Boulnois, "Les deux fins de l'homme. L'impossible anthropologie et le repli de la théologie," *Les Études Philosophiques* 9 (1995): 205-22; Anna N. Williams, "Mystical Theology Redux: The Patterns of Aquinas's *Summa Theologiae*," *Modern Theology* 13 (1997): 53-74; A. N. Williams, "Deification in the *Summa Theologiae*: A Structural Interpretation of the *prima pars*," *The Thomist* 61 (1997): 219-55; A. N. Williams, *The Ground of Union: Deification in Aquinas and Palamas* (Oxford: Oxford University Press, 1999), esp. pp. 34-101.

essence of matter (*In I Phys.* lec. 15). In this case, matter could not be part of the essence of composite substances (*De ente* c. 2). Nor is this relation transcendental (as has been argued by Thomists such as Louis de Raeymaeker) or logical (as has been contended by A. Krempel).[157] For the relation of prime matter to substantial form is objective and extramental, and therefore perhaps best described as metaphysical. The essence of matter as pure potency is its ordering to form, for matter cannot exist apart from or outside its relation with form.[158] This is already contained in the divine idea of matter (*In I Sent.* d. 36, q. 2, a. 3, ad 2). If God is pure actuality, then there cannot be a perfect divine idea of prime matter void of any being. Indeed, particular sensible things have their proper ideas in God (*In I Sent.* d. 36, q. 2, a. 3, ad 3). For this reason, individuation is a function of divine ideas and the act of being which brings matter into actuality. John Wippel puts this well: "There is one divine idea for the composite whole, and it serves as a productive principle for the entire composite, including both its matter and its form."[159] Only in the sense of similitude can there be a divine idea of prime matter, which can be considered distinctly without existing separately (*De veritate* q. 3, a. 5, ad 3).

This is to suggest that matter has in some sense form, in that matter has the capacity to receive actuality. The 'form' of matter is the potency to be actualized. In reality there is no such thing as pure matter divorced from form or existence. To say that prime matter is pure potency is to say that it only exists by participating in the act of being. For this reason, the act which is participated in by matter gives form to matter and is thereby limited (*Quodl.* III, q. 1, a. 1). As Aquinas makes clear, this does not indicate a deficiency in divine power. On the contrary, the limit of the act of pure form by the potency of prime matter describes the (onto-)logic of creation: to receive the pure act of being is to be brought out of nothing

---

157. See de Raeymaeker, *Philosophie de l'être,* and Krempel, *La doctrine de la relation chez saint Thomas,* esp. pp. 174-79, 361-68, 583-96.

158. Influential Franciscan theologians at the time of Aquinas and not long after his death held that God's absolute power is able to bring and keep matter in actuality apart from any corresponding form. Among them were, *inter alia,* John Peckham, John Duns Scotus, and William of Ockham. See Allan B. Wolter, "The Ockhamist Critique," in *The Concept of Matter in Greek and Medieval Philosophy,* ed. Ernan McMullin (Notre Dame: University of Notre Dame Press, 1963), pp. 124-46; Wippel, *The Metaphysical Thought of Thomas Aquinas,* pp. 312-13. See, *infra,* chapter 6.

159. Wippel, *The Metaphysical Thought of Thomas Aquinas,* p. 322.

into actuality. The utter potency of prime matter somehow 'echoes' the nothing 'out of which' creation is made.

The question that arises from this account is how we know the relation of matter to form. In his commentary on Boethius' *De Trinitate* (which, as I argued in chapter 3, is indebted to Augustine), Thomas argues that relationality is what the actuality of particular composite substance manifests to the senses and to the intellect:

> For, since everything is intelligible insofar as it is in act, as the *Metaphysics* says, we must understand the nature itself or quiddity of a thing either inasmuch as it is a certain act (as happens in the case of forms themselves or simple substances); or through that which is its act (as we know composite substances through their forms), or through that which takes the place of act in it *(as we know prime matter through its relation to form).*[160]

According to this passage, the human mind can know matter through its relation to form. The idea of relation recurs in Aquinas's treatment of matter when he speaks of human knowledge of matter by analogy or proportion (*De princ. nat.* c. 2; *In Boeth. de Trin.* q. 4, a. 2). Before linking this relation to individuation, I will first discuss the nature of substantial form and the relation with prime matter. Generally, form in Aquinas is taken to mean that which causes or gives being to matter *(forma dat esse).* Yet at the same time, Thomas insists throughout his works that the essence of composite substance is not only form, but rather the composition of matter and form (*De ente* c. 2; *In VII Met.* c. 10, lec. 9, no. 1467; *Comp. theol.* c. 154). If form is part of essence, it cannot be the act of being which actualizes the composite as a whole. Therefore, Aquinas posits two distinct relations between matter and form at the level of composite substances. First, prime matter stands in potency to form, which serves as its act of being *(esse).* Second, the composite's essence (composed of matter and form) stands in potency to the act of being *(actus essendi),* which actualizes the entire composite (*De spir. creat.* q. 1, a. 1, resp.). In

---

160. "*Cum enim unaquaeque res sit intelligibilis secundum quod est in actu, ut dicitur in IX Metaphysicae, oportet quod ipsa natura sive quidditas rei intelligatur vel secundum quod est actus quidam, sicut accidit de ipsis formis et substantiis simplicibus, vel secundum id quod est actus eius, sicut substantiae compositae per suas formas, vel secundum id quod est ei loco actus, sicut materia prima per habitudinem ad formam*" (*In Boeth. de Trin.* q. 5, a. 3; my italics [35-36]).

Thomas's own words, "[A] thing composed of matter and form partici-pates in its act of being from God through its own form according to its proper mode."[161]

This double relation leads Aquinas to reject Porreta's thesis of the mul-tiplicity of forms in favor of the unicity of substantial form.[162] If substantial form communicates the act of being to prime matter and if a composite's unity follows from being (*De veritate* q. 1, a. 1; *De Boeth. de Trin.* q. 4, a. 1; *SCG* II.58), then composite substance can only have a single form. Otherwise there would be more than one act of being and more than one source of unity. The unicity of substantial form is central to the question of individu-ation because it modifies the Augustinian notion of 'seminal reasons' (*In II Sent.* d. 18, q. 1, a. 2) by specifying that prime matter receives a single indi-vidual substantial form (not a generic form) and that every subsequent form is accidental. So prime matter has being *(esse)* from form, and the matter-form compound as a whole has being from the act of being *(actus essendi)*. This raises questions about how the being of form and the act of being are linked. Since Thomas excludes a plurality of substantial forms in composites and any intermediary form between prime matter and its unique individual substantial form, the form *of* the composite is God's act of being as it is received diversely *in* different particular composites. As such, the actuality of universal form is particularized in relation to the po-tency of prime matter. In common being form is universal, whereas in indi-vidual things substantial form is unique to each particular thing. Individ-ual substantial form derives from the act of being, which cannot be reduced to any individual instance of being. As I show in the following sec-tion, the confluence of substantial form and prime matter explains the in-dividuation of concrete composite substances.

9. *Materia Signata* and the 'Relationality' of Creation

If prime matter limits God's infinite actuality through reception of the act of being, then prime matter ceases to be pure potency and becomes actualized. The form that actualized matter takes is corporeity. Indeed, the first substantial form that prime matter receives is corporeity, and

161. *"res composita ex materia et forma per suam formam fit participativa ipsius esse a Deo secundum quendam proprium modum"* (*De subst. sep.* c. 6).

162. Wippel, *The Metaphysical Thought of Thomas Aquinas,* pp. 327-51.

corporeity informs the whole of matter (*In I Sent.* d. 8, q. 5, a. 2). What follows from the same substantial form of corporeity is quantitative dimensionality, i.e., the extendedness of matter, which implies nonidentical locations in space and therefore the ability to receive different forms.[163] As such, in addition to the act of being and prime matter, there is according to Aquinas a third factor that helps explain individuation — quantity or quantitative dimension. However, this raises a fundamental problem: Do accidents such as quantity differentiate different specifically identical substances and thereby account for their identity? Is quantity the ultimate explanation of individuation?

Before examining Aquinas's solution to this problem, I will discuss his account of dimension in relation to matter. Drawing on Boethius' *De Trinitate,* Thomas explains that forms are not individuated by being received in prime matter or corporeity but only insofar as they are received in *this* matter, which is distinct from *that* matter and determined to the 'here and now.' So configured, matter is particular only through quantity because it is divided into parts and subjected to spatial and temporal determination. As such, quantity is self-individuating and individuates matter, which in turn individuates form. However, what is it about quantity that renders it determined in this way? Aquinas specifies the status of dimensionality as follows. Dimension can either be terminate, in which case it cannot explain the individuation of material substances because the particular dimensions of individuals change over time. Or dimension is indeterminate, in which case it makes matter *this* rather than *that* — individual and designated. Properly understood, dimension can account for individuation and numerical plurality within the same species while also remaining constant over time and therefore not undermining individual identity (*In Boeth. de Trin.* q. 4, a. 2).

However, to distinguish dimensionality in this manner leaves open the question about how an accident (quantity) can individuate a substance. Indeterminate dimensions must be presupposed in matter for it to be individuated and then to individuate form. But this might imply that dimensions precede the substantial form which gives being both to

163. Joseph Bobik, "La doctrine de saint Thomas sur l'individuation des substances corporelles," *Revue Philosophique de Louvain* 51 (February 1953): 5-41; J. Bobik, "Dimensions in the Individuation of Bodily Substances," *Philosophical Studies* 4 (1954): 60-79; J. Bobik, "Matter and Individuation," in McMullin, ed., *The Concept of Matter in Greek and Medieval Philosophy,* pp. 281-92; Joseph Owens, "Thomas Aquinas: Dimensive Quantity as Individuating Principle," *Mediaeval Studies* 50 (1988): 279-310.

matter and to accidents. In his early work (including the programmatic treatise *De ente et essentia*),[164] Aquinas's solution is that dimension can only be thought of as indeterminate. In reality, dimensions exist subject to a certain kind of measure and proportion. But it is not clear in what way this indeterminate dimension specifies matter and individuates it prior to the reception of form. The account of individuation that Thomas elaborates on this basis is so complex and open to misconception that he abandons it in favor of a different terminology that marks a fundamental shift. In later texts such as the *De veritate*, he adopts the vocabulary of designated matter *(materia signata)*, which can be defined in the following way: "matter insofar as it is considered with a determination of its dimensions, i.e. with these or those given dimensions."[165] In other words, whether in thought or in real existence, matter is always already determined to dimensions because divine ideas of concrete material composites encompass ideas about particularized matter. For example, it is impossible to think of human beings independently of embodiment. There is no idea or existence of a human body apart from a soul. So dimensions in matter are part of the idea and the reality of matter, which is already constituted by its individual substantial form.

It is this 'designated form' of matter which is the principle of individuation and from which the mind needs to abstract in order to cognize universals rather than perceive singulars (*De veritate* q. 2, a. 6; q. 10, a. 5). Coupled with dimensive quantity, which is self-individuating and thus constitutes the ultimate foundation for numerical diversity within the same species, designated matter is Aquinas's principle of individuation because matter considered under dimensions is always already particular and therefore individuates the form that it receives (*SCG* IV.65; *De potentia* q. 9, a. 1, a. 2, ad 1; *ST* Iᵃ, q. 75, a. 4; q. 119, a. 1). Compared with Porreta, what is significant about this account is not only the focus on matter rather than exclusively on form but also the retrieval and extension of the patristic Neo-Platonist metaphysics of relationality. In the

---

164. Martin Grabmann, "Die Schrift 'De ente et essentia' und die Seinsmetaphysik des heiligen Thomas von Aquin," in *Mittelalterliches Geistesleben* 1 (1926); Étienne Gilson, "La preuve du De ente et essentia," in *Acta III Congressus Thomistici Internationalis: Doctor Communis* (Turin: Marietti, 1950), vol. 3, pp. 257-60; Joseph Owens, "Aquinas' Distinction at *De Ente et Essentia* 4.119-123," *Mediaeval Studies* 48 (1986): 264-87; Alain de Libera and Cyrille Michon, eds., *L'être et l'essence. Le vocabulaire médiéval de l'ontologie: Deux traités De ente et essentia de Thomas d'Aquin et Dietrich de Freiberg* (Paris: Éditions du Seuil, 1996).

165. Wippel, *The Metaphysical Thought of Thomas Aquinas*, p. 367.

present chapter, I have argued that for Aquinas everything is in some fundamental sense relational. God is self-subsistent unreserved Trinitarian relationality. Angelic forms are in relation to the act of being and in this sense are composites (form-being compounds). Material things are likewise composites in this sense too: they are being-form compounds as well as form-matter compounds. The crux is that matter only exists in relation to form and that substantial form is always received in matter. Contrary to Porreta's theory, which begins with God and derives all other forms from God's absolute power (as I suggested in the previous chapter), Aquinas's account begins with the nature of particular sensible things and on this basis demonstrates both the existence and (in some way) the essence of the one triune God, in the sense that the relations amongst creatures reflect approximately and imperfectly the relations within the Trinity (even though this can never be fully grasped by reason alone).

As already mentioned, Rudi te Velde has shown how in Thomist metaphysics the existence of God cannot be divorced from his essence: *an sit* and *quid sit* are distinct yet related questions because to know that God exists is also to know in some sense what he is — self-subsistent being *(ipsum esse subsistens)* and pure actuality *(actus purus).*[166] If particulars are relational and are created by divine being itself and if the effects are in some way similar to the cause, then the first cause or self-subsistent being is also in some sense relational. Since the cause exceeds and encompasses its effects, the relationality of the cause surpasses that of the effect. This is how Thomas explicates the doctrine of creation in the image and likeness of God and provides an account of creation *ex nihilo* that is amenable to natural reason.

Matter as the principle of individuation highlights the nature of relationality in particular sensible things. Matter itself is relational in the sense that dimensive quantity which individuates prime matter constitutes a categorical real relation, as opposed to a relation of reason: "[O]ther genera, as quantity and quality, in their strict and proper meaning, signify something inherent in a subject."[167] Thomas also describes categorial real relations in terms of *esse in,* existing only in an actual subject that gives it being. In the case of matter, there can only be dimensive

---

166. Te Velde, "'The First Thing to Know about God': Kretzmann and Aquinas on the Meaning and Necessity of Arguments for the Existence of God," pp. 251-67.

167. *"quantitas et qualitas, secundum propriam rationem significant aliquid alicui inhaerens" (ST* I[a], q. 28, a. 1, corp.).

quantity because the individual substantial form gives being to prime matter. Likewise, form is relational, in the sense that it is received into particular matter and as such stands in relation to it as well as to the act of being. For this reason, form can only be the form of a particular because universal form, which is individual (though not particular), is limited by the potency of matter. Just as particular matter cannot exist apart from form to which it is ordered as potency is ordered to act, so too individual substantial form cannot exist separately from matter by which it is limited, as act is limited by potency. Both matter and form are really relational.

Moreover, the relation between matter and form is neither accidental nor logical nor transcendental. Rather, it is real because it is objective and extra-mental, and it is metaphysical because it intimates a real relation with transcendent forms, as I have already indicated. Matter is the principle of individuation in the sense that it is always already designated, i.e., determined to dimensions and thus capable of receiving and individuating form. Why? Because the divine idea of materiality ordains matter to actuality received from form (*SCG* II.81). Put differently, prime matter, which is pure potency, becomes designated by a divine idea of a particular thing. The dimensionality of matter is not a function of the substantial form but instead is the result of the creation by the divine mind. Only once matter is designated can it then receive form. For example, God creates particular matter in the form of bodies which are relational to souls. Individuation is therefore conceived in terms of relationality:

> For just as it is competent to the human soul in respect of its species to be united to a body of a particular species, so this particular soul differs only numerically from that one through having a habitude to a numerically different body. Thus human souls are individualized — and consequently the possible intellect also which is a power of the soul — in relation to the bodies, and not as though their individuality were caused by their bodies.[168]

One point that emerges from this passage is that bodies *per se* cannot individuate souls because this would presuppose the capacity to receive

168. *"Sicut enim animae humanae secundum suam speciem competit quod tali corpori secundum speciem uniatur, ita haec anima differt ab illa numero solo ex hoc quod ad aliud numero corpus habitudinem habet. Et sic individuantur animae humanae, et per consequens intellectus possibilis, qui est potentia animae, secundum corpora, non quasi individuatione a corporibus causata"* (*SCG* II.75.6).

souls. This capacity is given by God's idea of a particular body. Another point in this passage is that both matter and form individuate the composite matter by limiting the act of form which is ordered to a particular body in virtue of a relation *(habitudo).*[169] Just as matter only exists in relation to form, so form only has numerical unity through its ordering to matter. The nature of this relation is real in the sense that it is not a relation of reason but has an objective extra-mental reality. Likewise, the nature of this relation is 'essential' in the sense that it is not accidental (like quantity in the case of matter) but constitutive of both designated matter and individual substantial form.[170]

For Aquinas, the relationality of components and the composite as a whole discloses the relationality of the universe and its author. Particular sensible things are both substantial and relational, as "in all things a double perfection is found: one by which it subsists in itself and another by which it is ordered to other things."[171] Elsewhere he defines such an ordering as real relationality.[172] Like Augustine and Boethius, Thomas argued that a particular thing is not constituted and individuated by substance and accident alone but that relations with other individuals are part of what it is to be a properly individuated being:

> [T]he perfection and good which are in extra-mental things follow not only upon something inhering in things absolutely, but also upon the order of one thing toward another, as also the good of an army consists in the order of the parts of the army, for to this order the Philosopher compares the order of the universe. Therefore it is necessary that in those [extra-mental] things there be a certain order; but this order is a certain relation. So it is necessary that in those [extra-mental]

169. Robert A. O'Donnell, "Individuation: An Example of the Development in the Thought of St. Thomas Aquinas," *New Scholasticism* 33 (1959): 49-67, esp. pp. 57-67.

170. Henninger, *Relations*, pp. 13-39.

171. *"in rebus omnibus duplex perfectio invenitur; una qua in se subsistit; alia qua ad res alias ordinatur"* (*In III Sent.* d. 27, q. 1, a. 4, corp.). Cf. *ST* I^a, q. 22, a. 1, resp.

172. "Relation in its own proper meaning signifies only what refers to another. Such regard to another exists sometimes in the nature of things, as in those things which by their own very nature are ordered to each other, and have a mutual inclination; and such relations are necessarily real relations [*Ea vero quae dicuntur ad aliquid, significant secundum propriam rationem solum respectum ad aliud. Qui quidem respectus aliquando est in ipsa natura rerum; utpote quando aliquae res secundum suam naturam ad invicem ordinatae sunt, et invicem inclinationem habent. Et huiusmodi relationes oportet esse reales*]" (*ST* I^a, q. 28, a. 1, resp.).

things there be certain relations, according to which one [thing] is or-der to another.[173]

Thomas's account of relation is both realist and conceptualist, in the sense that the reality of particular relations in material beings is the source of abstract concepts of universal relation in the immaterial intellect.

Aquinas's metaphysics of pure actuality leads him to argue that the relation between the universe and its author is real but that the relation between God and creation is only one of reason. By transforming Aristotle's account of categorial relation in the direction of the individuating Good in God, he shows that the relation between Creator and creation is nonmutual because God "is altogether outside the genus of created being by which the creature is really referred to God."[174] In God the act of existence and essence coincide — *ipsum esse subsistens* and *esse per essentiam*. But in beings the act of existence is received from God and limited by essence — *esse creatum* and *esse participatum*. Creation marks God's gift of being that brings everything out of nothing and imparts a share of goodness and common being in which beings participate. Individuation marks the reception of the universal act of being in created beings in accordance with their particular modes, so that they may be what they are intended by the Creator — to be and to abide in union with God.

10. Conclusion: Aquinas's Theological Metaphysics

In this chapter, I have argued that for Aquinas individual beings in act are neither incommensurably different nor variations of the same; instead, individual beings in act combine the unity of being with the di-

---

173. *"perfectio et bonum quae sunt in rebus extra animam, non solum attenditur secundum aliquid absolute inhaerens rebus, sed etiam secundum ordinem unius rei ad aliam, sicut etiam in ordine partium exercitus, bonum exercitus consistit: huic enim ordini comparat philosophus ordinem universi. Oportet ergo in ipsis rebus ordinem quemdam esse; hic autem ordo relatio quaedam est. Unde oportet in rebus ipsis relationes quasdam esse, secundum quas unum ad alterum ordinatur"* (*De potentia* q. 7, a. 9, resp.). Cf. *In I Sent.* d. 26, q. 2, a. 1, corp.

174. *"est omnino extra genus esse creati, per quod creatura refertur ad Deum"* (*De potentia* q. 7 a. 10 corp.). Cf. *De potentia* q. 7, a. 8, ad 3; *ST* Iᵃ, q. 13, a. 7, corp.

versity of beings: "[B]eing is diverse in different beings."[175] In synthesizing and extending Platonist and Aristotelian metaphysics, Thomas argues that things-in-act tend naturally towards being (rather than nonbeing [*De princ. nat.* c. 3, 8]), which is the actuality of supernatural being in God (*ST* I[a], q. 5, a. 1). To be in act is to stand in potency to the act of being which actualizes beings whose essence or form is *to be:* "[E]verything is made in order that it may be, for making is the way to being. It befits every caused thing to be made, even as it befits it to be."[176] Individuation marks the reception of the universal act of being in each and every being according to its particular mode of being, so that it may be what it is — to be and to abide in the act of being. Being is good, for it testifies to God's gift of being in which all beings can participate (*In II Sent.* d. 1, q. 1, a. 4, corp.; cf. *ST* I[a], q. 105, a. 5, corp.). For Aquinas all beings are relational because being itself is unreservedly relational. Unlike the static deity of substantialist metaphysics, the Thomist God is self-subsistent being and pure act, utter and self-ecstatic plenitude, and self-diffusive goodness. God is fully relational *ad intra* and *ad extra,* between the Trinitarian persons and in relation to creation.

To be made in the image and likeness of God is therefore to be constituted by the creative relation of God with the world and to be perfected by participating in the infinite goodness of the pure act of being. Man as the highest being in the created material order (*ST* I[a], q. 29, a. 3) shares in the self-communicating love of God and participates in God's "everlasting bliss shared with the blessed"[177] and in God's Trinitarian economy. As such, man is both substantial and relational, both a person in the Boethian sense of an "individual substance of a rational nature"[178] and a created being constituted relationally by the act of being. To be relational is to be naturally oriented towards other relational beings through friendship and community. To seek to perfect one's own finite relationality is to partake of God's infinite Trinitarian relationality and therefore to restore and enhance the relational order of creation.

---

175. *"esse est diversum in diversibus"* (*De ente* c. 5, 1).

176. *"Omne quod fit, ad hoc fit quod sit: est enim fieri via in esse. Sic igitur unicuique causato convenit fieri sicut sibi convenit esse"* (*SCG* II.43.4). Cf. *"creatrix essentia"* (*In de Div. Nom.* c. 5, 2).

177. Kerr, *After Aquinas*, p. 157.

178. *"naturae rationalis individua substantia,"* Boethius, *Contra Eut.* III.1-5, quoted in *ST* I[a], q. 29, a. 2.

Interestingly, Aquinas's first and his final major treatises provide a summary statement of his account of individuation. Already in the *De ente et essentia,* Thomas shifts the Avicennian focus on essence to the divine act of being which is the ultimate cause of individuation. In his *Compendium Theologiae* (probably written about a year prior to his death in 1274), he insists that God is in a meta-sense supremely individual and yet contains all differences, for divine being is neither contained under any genus nor a genus itself nor a species that is predicable of any individuals (*Comp. theol.* 13-15). It is this divine act of being and not matter which individuates all things. For matter itself does not preexist God's creation of everything out of nothing and as such cannot individuate universal form. And since the diversity and unity of things depend on their existence, matter cannot be the cause of individuation through actualization:

> Again, the plurality or unity of things is dependent on their existence. For, to the extent that anything is a being, it is also one. But forms do not possess existence on account of matter; on the contrary, matter receives existence from form. For act is more excellent than potency; and that which is the reason for a thing's existence must be the more excellent component. Consequently forms are not diverse in order that they may befit various types of matter, but matter is diversified that it may befit various forms. (*Comp. theol.* 71)

In the following section of the *Compendium,* Aquinas states more clearly than perhaps anywhere else in the Thomistic corpus that being is the ultimate cause of individuation: "If the unity and multiplicity of things are governed by their being, and if the entire being of things depends on God, as has been shown to be the case, the cause of plurality in things must be sought in God" (*Comp. theol.* 72). In this manner, Thomas explains that things *qua* individuals most resemble God, whose plenitude is best reflected in this world by a multitude of diverse and uniquely distinct individualities, for no single finite thing could ever be equal to God or contain the divine ecstatic overflow of creative being and goodness (here Aquinas's indebtedness to Dionysius is once more in clear evidence).[179]

---

179. In the *Summa Contra Gentiles,* he puts this as follows: "There would not be a perfect likeness of God in the universe if all things were of one grade of being. For this reason, then, is there distinction among created things: that, by being many, they may receive God's likeness more perfectly than by being one" (*SCG* II.45.3; cf. SCG III.97.2).

Furthermore when in the *Compendium* Aquinas gives a *précis* of what he thinks, a Trinitarian metaphysics of relationality comes to the fore. Everything is in terms of divinely created motion and a hierarchy of more and more intimate procession. A metaphysics of three acts is also foregrounded: first of all, substance is in some way in itself; second, substance is realized in the divine act of being; third, substance-in-act is always already towards another substance as communicated and related. These three acts are ultimately the Augustinian conceptual triad of being, intellect, and will in man imaging the Trinity. Essence as such is seen as communicating, which is how and why we can know — up to some point — that the divine essence is Trinitarian. Following Augustine, the idea of numerical series is also central, to which Aquinas adds that all specific difference must be hierarchical (here following Dionysius). Finally, there is barely any mention at all of the clear distinction, let alone separation, of *divina scientia* and *sacra doctrina*. The one triune God known to pagans is also the God of the Creed, while inversely the arguments for the Trinity are of a highly cosmic kind — with intimations and reflections in the natural, material world. In short, Aquinas defends a relational, Trinitarian, and hierarchical metaphysics that avoids the modern dualisms opposing substance to property/accidents (or cause to effect), Christology to Trinitarianism, and transcendence to immanence, as I suggest in the remaining chapters of this book.

CHAPTER 6

The Invention of the Individual

1. Introduction: After the Thomist Synthesis

In the present chapter, I examine the link between creation and individuation in the works of John Duns Scotus, William Ockham, and Jean Buridan. I compare and contrast their accounts with that of Thomas Aquinas because they associate individuation with formal principles rather than transcendent causes. Such principles are located in beings and lack any metaphysical relation with God's creative activity. As a result, individuation becomes unhinged from creation, and the operation of the natural world is cut off from transcendence. This shifts the onus of individuation upon individual entities themselves and reinforces the separation of *potentia Dei ordinata* and *potentia Dei absoluta* that was already incipient in Porreta's twelfth-century theory of individuation.

I begin by sketching the conceptual context in which Scotus, Ockham, and Buridan address the question of individuation, in particular the aftermath of the condemnations of 7 March 1277 at the University of Paris.[1] I then discuss the relation between creation and individuation in some key texts before examining the growing importance of the concept of *potentia Dei absoluta* for their conceptions of metaphysics and politics. I conclude by arguing that Scotus, Ockham, and Buridan radicalize Porreta's formalism and thereby undermine the realism that pa-

---

1. For a general overview of the condemnations, see Roland Hissette, *Enquête sur les 219 articles condamnés à Paris le 7 mars 1277* (Louvain: Publications Universitaires de Louvain, 1977), and David Piché, ed., *La condamnation parisienne de 1277. Texte latin, traduction, introduction et commentaire* (Paris: Vrin, 1999).

tristic and medieval theology had inherited from Plato and transformed in the direction of Trinitarian relationality.

2. The 1277 Condemnations and the Implications for Metaphysics

St. Bonaventure notes in Book II of his commentary on the *Sententiae* that the question of individuation caused "a dispute between philosophical men" *(contentio inter philosophicos viros).*[2] At his time, some commentators argued that matter individuates substances, while others contended that individuation is a function of form. The shift from matter to form as the principle of individuation preceded the works of John Duns Scotus, as Rega Wood has documented. Already in the 1230s, Richard Rufus of Cornwall composed a tractate titled 'On the cause of individuation' *(De causa individuationis),* in which he spoke of a "clamorous dispute of philosophers" over the question of individuation and attributed the cause that individuates substances to individual forms.[3] In chapter 4, I argued that form had already played a key role in twelfth-century theories of individuation, especially Porreta's conception of 'total property' composed of a collection of *'quo ests'* or *formae nativae.* In this chapter, I show how, after Aquinas, matter as the principle of individuation was abandoned in favor of form. This shift, which intervened in the wake of the 1277 condemnations, marked a radicalization of the earlier twelfth-century formalism. Porreta's formalist account of the individual influenced Scotus's, Ockham's, and Buridan's conception of individuality in the late thirteenth and early fourteenth century.[4]

Before I examine the main difference between Aquinas's and subsequent theories of individuation, I briefly analyze the general change of the philosophical and theological context that underlies this shift, above

---

2. St. Bonaventure, *In II Sent.* d. 3, q. 2, a. 3.

3. Rega Wood, "Individual Forms: Richard Rufus and John Duns Scotus," in *John Duns Scotus: Metaphysics and Ethics,* ed. Ludgar Honnefelder, Rega Wood, and Mechthild Dreyer (Leiden: E. J. Brill, 1996), pp. 251-72.

4. Étienne Gilson, *La philosophie au Moyen Âge. Des origines patristiques à la fin du XIVe siècle,* 2nd rev. ed. (Paris: Ed. Payot & Rivages, 1999 [1922]), p. 266; Alain de Libera, *La querelle des universaux. De Platon à la fin du moyen âge* (Paris: Éditions du Seuil, 1996), p. 414; Grzegorz Stolarski, *La possibilité et l'être. Un essai sur la détermination du fondement ontologique de la possibilité dans la pensée de Thomas d'Aquin* (Fribourg: Éditions Universitaires, 2001), pp. 204-5.

all the 1277 condemnations. On 7 March 1277 the Bishop of Paris Étienne Tempier condemned 219 theses that had been taught in the Arts faculties of the University. As both Stephen Brown and Jan Aertsen have shown,[5] at least three theses directly concerned the question of individuation:

> Thesis 81: That, because intelligences do not contain matter, God could not produce many intelligences belonging to the same species.
>
> Thesis 96: That God cannot multiply many individuals in any given species without matter.
>
> Thesis 191: That forms do not admit division except by reason of matter.[6]

The theory of individuation that is censured by the 1277 condemnations is the Aristotelian account, which focuses on matter. The last of the three condemned theses concerns the general application of the material principle to spiritual substances. According to the censors, the first two theses pose a threat to the creative power of God. As I argue below, the reconfiguration of the relation between *potentia Dei absoluta* and *potentia Dei ordinata* by Scotus, Ockham, and Buridan had a significant impact on late-thirteenth- and fourteenth-century metaphysics and politics and favored the rise of modern philosophy and ethics.

The importance of the 1277 condemnations has attracted extensive scholarly interest and debate in the last thirty years or so. The principal contention relates to the impact on the relations between theology and philosophy in general and the teachings of Aquinas in particular. Pierre Duhem's argument that the condemnation of Aristotelian philosophy precipitated the development of modern science has been disputed.[7]

---

5. Stephen F. Brown, "Henry of Ghent (b. ca. 1217; d. 1293)," in *Individuation in Scholasticism: The Later Middle Ages and the Counter-Reformation 1150-1650*, ed. Jorge J. E. Gracia (Albany: State University of New York Press, 1994), pp. 195-219, esp. 195-96; Jan A. Aertsen, "Die Thesen zur Individuation in der Verurteilung von 1277, Heinrich von Gent und Thomas von Aquin," in *Individuum und Individualität im Mittelalter*, ed. Jan A. Aertsen and Andreas Speer (Berlin and New York: De Gruyter, 1996), pp. 249-65, esp. 250-52.

6. "*Quod, quia intelligentiae non habent materiam, Deus non posset plures eiusdem speciei facere — Error*"; "*Quod Deus non possit multiplicare plura individua sub una specie sine materia — Error*"; "*Quod formae non recipiunt divisionem nisi secundum materiam — Error*" (quoted in Henry of Ghent, *Quodlibet* II, q. 8).

7. See Pierre Duhem, *Études sur Léonardo de Vinci*, vol. 13: *Jean Buridan (de Béthune) et*

Alain de Libera, Luca Bianchi, and David Piché contend that the 1277 censure introduced an irreversible split between theology and philosophy and inaugurated the rise of modern philosophy in the West.[8] Despite important differences, these two interpretations are not necessarily opposed or mutually exclusive: the separation of theology from philosophy reinforced the idea of 'pure nature' separate from the supernatural and thereby sundered physics from metaphysics and theology. In any case, there can be little doubt about the initial impact of the 1277 condemnations. Less than twenty years after their publication, Godfrey of Fontaines discussed in Book XII of his *Quodlibet* whether the then Bishop of Paris ought to correct some of the condemned articles, especially regarding the question of individuation.[9] Following some general remarks on the need to have *disputationes* and foster theological debate, Godfrey argues that the above-cited theses 81 and 96 are defendable *(opinabilis)* because Catholic ecclesial and lay authorities *(auctoritates)* had advocated them in their teachings and writings, including Thomas Aquinas whom Godfrey mentioned explicitly. This alone is indicative of the effect of the condemnations on the status of philosophy in the Arts faculties. It also highlights the extent to which the censored articles were associated with the work of Aquinas, providing the advocates of 1277 with a set of reasons to dismiss his theological metaphysics.[10]

Léonard de Vinci (Paris: A. Hermann, 1909); J. E. Murdoch, "Piere Duhem and the History of Late Medieval Science and Philosophy in the Latin West," in *Gli studi di filosofia medievale fra Otto e Novecento: Contributo a un bilancio storiografico. Atti del convegno internazionale, Roma 21-23 settembre 1989*, ed. Rudi Imbach and A. Maierù (Rome: Edizioni di Storia e Letteratura, 1991), pp. 253-302; J. E. Murdoch, "1277 and Late Medieval Natural Philosophy," in *Was ist Philosophie im Mittelalter?* ed. Jan A. Aertsen and Andreas Speer (Berlin and New York: De Gruyter, 1998), pp. 111-21.

8. See Alain de Libera, "Philosophie et censure. Remarques sur la crise universitaire parisienne de 1270-1277," in Aertsen and Speer, eds., *Was ist Philosophie im Mittelalter?* pp. 71-89; Luca Bianchi, "1277: A Turning Point in Medieval Philosophy?" in Aertsen and Speer, eds., *Was ist Philosophie im Mittelalter?*, pp. 90-110; Piché, *La condamnation parisienne de 1277*, pp. 159-288. For alternative accounts, see Jan A. Aertsen, Kent Emery, Jr., and Andreas Speer, eds., *After the Condemnation of 1277: Philosophy and Theology at the University of Paris in the Last Quarter of the Thirteenth Century* (Berlin: De Gruyter, 2001).

9. Aertsen, "Die Thesen zur Individuation in der Verurteilung von 1277, Heinrich von Gent und Thomas von Aquin," esp. pp. 251-52.

10. On Aquinas, see John F. Wippel, "Thomas Aquinas and the Condemnations of 1277," *The Modern Schoolman* 72 (1995): 233-72; J. F. Wippel, "Bishop Stephen Tempier and Thomas Aquinas: A Separate Process against Aquinas?" *Freiburger Zeitschrift für*

Concerning the impact of the 1277 condemnation, it is also instructive to refer to Henry of Ghent (c. 1217-1293), who was one of the sixteen theologians on the commission that examined the positions subsequently censored by Bishop Tempier.[11] In the same year as the condemnations — at Christmas 1277 — Henry discussed the question of individuation in his second *disputatio de quolibet* and dismissed matter as either cause or principle that individuates composites. His critique of both matter and quantity is certainly directed at Aristotle but also applies to Aquinas. Referring to the divine power of creation, he argues that individual substantial form could by itself have several individual instantiations, were it not for the limits of matter. Compared with Aquinas, Henry emphasizes God's absolute power at the expense of perfect divine ideas of particular things (*not* ideal-types with multiple instantiations, as Porreta seems to suggest). So not unlike Gilbert, Henry reasons from abstract possibility to concrete actuality: logically speaking, there could be multiple individuals with an identical form in the absence of materiality. Matter imposes limits, which is of course not the same as saying that matter individuates form through its divinely intended dimensionality, as Thomas held.

Henry of Ghent also claims that the essence of created being is such that it can be multiplied in many substrates or *supposita,* including without matter. In other words, matter is no longer an integral part of the individuation of corporeal substances. This is why he argues that "matter and quantity cannot be called the exact reason or cause of the individuation and distinction of individuals belonging to the same species."[12] What is questionable about Henry's conception of created beings is that they contain in themselves unrealizable possibilities. Yet for Aristotle and Aquinas, in nature nothing is in vain because everything is

---

Philosophie und Theologie 44 (1997): 117-36; H. Thijssen, "1277 Revisited," *Vivarium* 35 (1997): 72-101. See also criticisms of Wippel's interpretation by Roland Hissette, "Thomas d'Aquin directement visé par la censure du 7 mars 1277? Réponse à John F. Wippel," in *Roma, Magistra mundi. Itineraria cultura medievalis,* ed. J. Hamesse (Louvain-la-Neuve: Mélanges L. E. Boyle — FIDEM, 1998), pp. 425-37; R. Wielockx, "A Separate Process against Aquinas: A Response to John F. Wippel," in Hamesse, ed., *Roma, Magistra mundi,* pp. 1009-30; R. Wielockx, "Procédures contre Gilles de Rome et Thomas d'Aquin," *Revue des Sciences Philosophiques et Théologiques* 83 (1999): 293-313.

11. Brown, "Henry of Ghent (b. ca. 1217; d. 1293)," esp. p. 195.

12. *"materia et quantitas non possunt dici praecisa ratio et causa individuationis et distinctionis individuorum eiusdem speciei"* (Henry of Ghent, *Quodlibet* II, q. 8).

oriented towards being and the good, as I showed in chapters 1 and 5. The consequence of the primacy of possibility over actuality means that individuation is no longer a primarily metaphysical problem but rather becomes a question of modal logic. Having ruled out matter as the principle of individuation and actualization as its cause, Henry concludes that God's absolute power is the first cause and also the efficient cause that brings things into being and makes them what they are. There is no mention of the act of being which is common to all beings yet received diversely and as such the cause that individuates substances relationally, as Thomas had already demonstrated. The shift that occurred since the time of Aquinas and that Henry's position tends to consolidate can be stated as follows: like Damiani and Porreta before him, Ghent abandons the interaction of transcendent causes and immanent principles in favor of the transcendentality of God's absolute power which overrides everything else. This prefigures the separation of philosophy and theology and the emphasis on the self-individuation of composite substances in the works of Scotus, Ockham, and Buridan to which I now turn.

3. Metaphysics and Formalism in Duns Scotus

"At the heart of the real, in Thomas Aquinas, there is the act of being; in Duns Scotus, one finds haecceity."[13] Gilson's concise summary of the difference between Aquinas's and Scotus's metaphysics highlights a fundamental shift in high and late medieval theories of individuation. Whereas the Angelic Doctor attributes individuation to God's pure actuality, the Subtle Doctor situates it within each particular thing. Indeed, *haecceitas* refers to the *hoc aliquid* (or Aristotle's τόδε τι), the 'thisness' of things. In this and the following section, I trace the Scotist account of individuation. Compared with Thomas, Scotus identifies a formal principle that abstracts from the actuality of things. As a result, individuation becomes unhinged from actualization and is severed from God's creative action.

Coupled with the univocity of being and the formal distinction of ex-

---

13. "Au coeur du réel, chez Thomas d'Aquin, se trouve l'acte d'être; chez Duns Scot on y trouve l'haeccéité," in Étienne Gilson, *Jean Duns Scot. Introduction à Ses Positions Fondamentales* (Paris: Vrin, 1952 [orig. pub. 1922]), p. 466.

istence and essence,[14] Scotus reconfigures theological realism and locates a certain kind of formalism at the center of metaphysics by elevating the formality of essence over and above the actuality of existence.
This move paves the way for the modern separation of philosophy from
theology and the self-individuation of particular things independently
from God's act of being.[15] As such, it is a metaphysical change that underpins the long and uneven transition from the Middle Ages to modernity, as I already suggested in chapter 4.

Allan Wolter has documented that Scotus's position on individuation did not undergo any significant change in the course of his academic life.[16] Already in the *Lectura* (his commentary on the Sentences),
Scotus provides a comprehensive statement of his theory and adds only
minor qualifications in the *Ordinatio*. I therefore focus on the text in the
Lectura. One salient feature of Scotus's account is that he gives the 1277

14. On Scotus's 'double destruction' of analogy and the real distinction, see Olivier
Boulnois, "Analogie et univocité selon Duns Scot: La double destruction," *Les Études
Philosophiques* 3 (juillet-décembre 1989): 347-69; O. Boulnois, *Être et représentation. Une
généalogie de la métaphysique moderne à l'époque de Duns Scot (XIIIe-XIVe siècle)* (Paris:
Presses Universitaires de France, 1999); Catherine Pickstock, *After Writing: On the Liturgical Consummation of Philosophy* (Oxford: Blackwell, 1998), pp. 122-31. For a recent debate
on Scotus's metaphysics, see a special issue of *Modern Theology* 21, no. 4 (October 2005)
with contributions by the following: Catherine Pickstock, "Duns Scotus: His Historical
and Contemporary Significance," pp. 543-74; Thomas Williams, "The Doctrine of
Univocity Is True and Salutary," pp. 575-85; Matthew Webb Levering, "Participation and
Exegesis: Response to Catherine Pickstock," pp. 587-601; Olivier Boulnois, "Reading Duns
Scotus: From History to Philosophy," pp. 603-8; Mary Beth Ingham, "Re-situating Scotist
Thought," pp. 609-18; and Emmanuel Perrier, OP, "Duns Scotus Facing Reality: Between
Absolute Contingency and Unquestionable Consistency," pp. 619-43.

15. On Scotus and the rise of modern philosophy, see Gilson, *La philosophie au
Moyen-Âge*, esp. p. 600; Ludgar Honnefelder, *Ens inquantum ens. Der Begriff des Seienden
als solchen als Gegenstand der Metaphysik nach der Lehre des Johannes Duns Scotus*
(Münster: Aschendorff, 1979); L. Honnefelder, *Scientia transcendens. Die formale
Bestimmung der Seiendheit und Realität in der Metaphysik des Mittelalters und der Neuzeit
(Duns Scot, Suarez, Kant, Peirce)* (Hamburg: F. Meiner, 1990); Jean-François Courtine,
Suarez et le système de la métaphysique (Paris: Presses Universitaires de France, 1990), esp.
pp. 137-54; Eric Alliez, *Les Temps Capitaux. Tome 1: Récits de la conquête du temps* (Paris:
Éditions Cerf, 1991), pp. 269-322; Louis Dupré, *Passage to Modernity: An Essay in the Herme-
neutics of Nature and Culture* (New Haven and London: Yale University Press, 1993), esp. ch.
1; Olivier Boulnois, "Théologie, métaphysique et représentation de l'être selon Duns Scot,"
Revue de théologie et de philosophie 21 (1999): 83-102.

16. Allan B. Wolter, "John Duns Scotus (b. ca. 1265; d. 1308)," in Gracia, ed., *Individuation in Scholasticism*, pp. 271-98, esp. 271-72.

condemnations universal doctrinal authority, beyond their limited canonical applicability to the diocese of Paris.[17] As I show below in greater
detail, he tends to accept Bishop Tempier's dismissal of Aristotle's theory
of individuation in general and Aquinas's emphasis on matter and quantity in particular. This critique leads him to develop an alternative principle, centered on the notion of haecceity *(haecceitas).*

The context in which Scotus addresses the question of individuation
throughout his work is primarily philosophical and focuses on the principle that individuates material substances. Divergences about this principle lead to different treatments of angelic individuation (*Lect. II Sent.* d.
3, pars 1, q. 1, n. 1). In other words, concerning the problem of individuation philosophy has absolute priority over theology. This priority is different from the autonomy of metaphysics in Aquinas because in Scotus,
there is no subordination of philosophy to *Scientia Dei.* In Aquinas,
metaphysics refers its subject matter (being) to a higher cause (God) and
the Science of God, as I showed in the previous chapter. By contrast, in
Scotus metaphysics (both its subject matter and its operation) is independent of *Scientia Dei.* For this reason, metaphysics becomes detached
from cosmology and nature, and physics is elevated into a quidditative
science that is no longer confined to change and motion.[18] As the science of the quiddity of mobility, physics imitates the metaphysical focus
on quiddities and thus becomes more autonomous from metaphysics. In
part, the shift away from a hierarchical subordination of the sciences towards an increasing degree of autonomy of physics and metaphysics
from theology inaugurated modern science and the emergence of physics divorced from both metaphysics and revealed theology.[19]

The origin of this turn can be traced to the centrality and nature of
knowledge in Scotist metaphysics. Scotus distinguishes between common notions and universals. The former denote general aspects of objects whereas the latter are forms in the mind. If intellectual cognition is
by definition abstract and grasps some common or general aspect of the
objects it apprehends, then it is not concerned with that which makes ob-

---

17. Olivier Boulnois, *Duns Scot. La Rigueur de la charité* (Paris: Éditions Cerf, 1998),
ch. 1.

18. Olivier Boulnois, "Au-delà de la physique?" in *Duns Scot à Paris, 1302-2002: Actes du
colloque de Paris, 2-4 septembre 2002,* ed. Olivier Boulnois, Elisabeth Karger, Jean-Luc
Solère, and Gérard Sondag (Paris: Éditions Brepols, 2004), pp. 219-54, esp. 245-54.

19. Amos Funkenstein, *Theology and the Scientific Imagination from the Middle Ages to
the Seventeenth Century* (Princeton: Princeton University Press, 1986), esp. pp. 25-63.

jects individual or singular. What the intellect grasps is *'natura communis,'* which can be described as something in an object that is isomorphic with the sort of thing we think it to be. In other words, the 'common nature' is some common feature, characteristic, or property that it shares with other similar objects. In this sense, *natura communis* provides the metaphysical ground for being and knowledge. Put differently, nothing can be or be known without *natura communis* because everything shares a substantial likeness with other things that belong to the same species. Cognition of commonality which abstracts *natura communis* from material singularity wields supreme sway. Sense perception of the actuality of things has no cognitive import at all in relation to cognition of haecceity (*Rep. par.* II, d. 3, q. 3, n. 15; d. 12, q. 8, n. 10; *In Metaph.* VII, q. 13, n. 26). As a result, singularity cannot be known by either sense perception (because it delivers only confused images) or intellection (because it abstracts from individual things altogether). In our present condition *(pro statu isto),* the human intellect only has an approximate grasp of individuality through intuitive knowledge *(notitia intuitiva)* — the immediate intuition of things themselves *(in se),* that is, both their objectity and their proper existence and presence (*Ord.* II, d. 3, q. 6, n. 16; III, d. 14, q. 3, n. 14; *Quodlib.* q. 6, a. 1; q. 7, a. 2; q. 13, a. 2).[20]

This position contrasts with the natural priority of *ens* or *entia* in Avicenna and Aquinas, i.e., individual beings which constitute the first objects of the senses and the intellect. The difference lies with Scotus's formalism, which is halfway between Aquinas's realism and Ockham's nominalism. Scotus defends a variant of realism against contemporary nominalists such as Roger Marston and Peter de Falco. He rightly rejects the claim that existence must be reduced to particularity and that universality is purely mental or nominal. Nor is singularity by or of itself, for otherwise a thing's unity would be merely numerical, not qualitative (*Lect. II Sent.* d. 3, pars 1, q. 1, nn. 28-30). Moreover, Scotus's *natura communis* is not a nominalist concept, because it is founded upon a real similarity among individual beings that enables the knowing mind to discern a substantial likeness in the known object.

However, Scotus's realism is qualified by the nature of this similarity.

---

20. Cf. John F. Boler, "Intuitive and Abstract Cognition," in *The Cambridge History of Later Medieval Philosophy: From the Rediscovery of Aristotle to the Disintegration of Scholasticism,* ed. Norman Kretzmann, Anthony Kenny, and Jan Pinborg (Cambridge: Cambridge University Press, 1982), pp. 460-78, esp. 463-75.

His account of similarity is formal, in the sense that it is indifferent of itself to existence in things or existence in the intellect. So conceived, similarity is neither one nor many, neither singular nor universal. As a result, the identity of each thing and the difference with other things is formal rather than actual because it is limited to essence and does not encompass the actuality of existent things. Not unlike Porreta's 'dividuality,' which is neither individual nor universal (and based on his own distinction of universals from common notions), Scotus defines the source of unity of things and their differentiation from one another as neither universal nor singular: "I understand 'it is not of itself one' of numerical unity, and 'it is not several' of the plurality opposed to that unity; and that it is actually 'universal' (viz. in the sense that, as an object of the intellect, something is universal), nor is it of itself 'singular.'"[21]

Following Porreta's concept of 'dividual,' Scotus also views the similarity between things as prior to actual individual things. For this peculiarly nontheological reason, he privileges essence over existence in the analysis of what individuates material composite substances. The above-cited quotation continues as follows:

> For though it is never in reality without some one of these features, of itself it is not any one of them, but it is something naturally prior to all of these — and according to this natural priority the "what it is" is the *per se* object of the intellect, and as such it is considered by the metaphysician and is expressed by an [essential] definition.[22]

This nature is of itself indifferent to existence as a universal or as a particular because it is indifferent to being in things or in the intellect. Unlike patristic and medieval Christian Neo-Platonism, Scotus separates the reality of likeness from the actuality of its manifestation.

The concept of this nature is neither universal because it is grounded in an extra-mental reality nor particular because it is always already common to more than one thing. The indifference to existence is

---

21. *"Unde sicut apud intellectum non est tantum singulare nec tantum universale, sic nec natura extra intellectum de se est una nec multa; unde nec includit natura de se hanc unitatem numeralem nec illam"* (*Lect. II Sent.* d. 3, pars 1, q. 1, n. 31).

22. *"sic in exsistentia extra animam nec est primo una numero nec multa numero, sed habet unitatem propriam sibi, quae minor est unitate quae convenit illi singulari: et illud est 'esse' quiditativum lapidis et rei universaliter, secundum quod 'esse' datur de re definitio"* (*Lect. II Sent.* d. 3, pars 1, q. 1, n. 32).

explained by the argument that the real unity of individual things "lies within the essential notion of the nature (for 'equinity is only equinity,' according to Avicenna, *V Metaphysics*)" (*Lect. II Sent.* d. 3, pars 1, q. 1, n. 34). So Scotus's metaphysics is realist in the sense that the commonality is in things rather than exclusively in the mind or in names. Yet at the same time, his metaphysics tends towards formalism in that *natura communis* concerns the essence or form of things, not their existence. Therefore it abstracts from actuality and is unrelated to the universal act of being. It is this formalism in Scotus's metaphysics and epistemology that underlies his theory of individuation, as I will suggest in the following section.

4. The Principle of *Haecceitas*

Scotus sets out his critique of existing accounts of individuation (including Aquinas's) before elaborating his concept of haecceity. His critique centers upon the status of existence, quantity, and matter. Against existence as a principle that individuates particulars, he argues that existence is common and as such cannot differentiate anything. The unicity and difference of all particulars implies that each must have its own proper principle of individuation (*Lect. II Sent.* d. 3, pars 1, q. 1, nn. 55-57; cf. *Ord.* II, d. 3, pars 1, q. 1, nn. 61-62). Against quantity, he repeats his claim that each thing has its unique principle of individuation because all things have their own proper 'this-ness' *(haecceitas),* which is *per se* and as such requires explanation. He then invokes God's absolute power and maintains that God can make substances exist without the initially individuating quantity because individual form can be separated from materiality (*Lect. II Sent.* d. 3, pars 1, q. 1, nn. 73-76; cf. *Ord.* II, d. 3, pars 1, q. 1, nn. 77-80). Moreover, quantity as an accident cannot account for an essential feature, that which makes something *this* unique thing rather than *that* equally unique thing. Finally, quantity *qua* quantity is general and not this singular quantity. As such, quantity cannot explain how or why something is a 'this' because it lacks specification.

Against matter, Scotus contends that the individuating principle must be diverse and nonidentical. Just as the form 'humanity' can be abstracted from *this* man and *that* man, so materiality can be abstracted from *this* matter and *that* matter. If this is true, then matter does not capture what is specific about individuals (*Lect. II Sent.* d. 3, pars 1, q. 1, n. 133). Rather than explaining singularity, matter raises the question of how and why materiality itself can be individuated. The only aspect on which material substances can be compared is their relation to the common nature and to God. For two individuated things or 'haecceities,' the relation to common nature differs and therefore provides an element of differentiation. However, Scotus insists that relation is not an integral part of the nature of particular sensible things. For this reason, relation does not individuate individuals. This is also true for the link between composite substances and God. Aquinas's position is described as follows: a thing's relation to God is real because composites are dependent on God, but God is not really related to things because he is simply and lacks nothing (*Ord.* I, d. 30, q. 2, nn. 49-51). Insofar as this relation of God with creatures is identical for all created things, it cannot differentiate them from one another. On this basis, Scotus dismisses Thomas's argument that the divine act of being is the cause of individuation and divinely created matter its principle. This rejection of Aquinas's proposed solution to the problem of what individuates different species within a genus means that for the Subtle Doctor, the metaphysical link between God and creation is irrelevant for the individuation of material substances.

This conclusion follows from Scotus's formal distinction between the foundation of things and their relation to God, their existence, and their essence, as Catherine Pickstock has demonstrated. Indeed, the formality of this distinction relativizes the ontological link between creatures and their Creator to the point where actuality is devalued in favor of possibility and the real actualization of individuated things subordinated to the logical possibility of their existence. Scotus does stress the real dependence of all things on God (*Ord.* II, d. 1, q. 5, n. 257 and *textus interpolatus*).[23] But contrary to the metaphysical realism of Christian Neo-Platonists like Gregory, Augustine, Boethius, Dionysius, or Aquinas, he excludes the option that something can be both substantial and relational (*Ord.* II, d. 1, q. 5, *textus interpolatus*). Creatures are formally absolute (purely substantial) and not relational (*Ord.* II, d. 1, q. 5, nn. 189, 276-50) because the relation to God does not enter into the essential definition of a creature. Nor does it add any perfection to it. This rejection of relationality seeks to preserve the absolute character of a creature (even

---

23. Mark G. Henninger, *Relations: Medieval Theories 1250-1325* (Oxford: Clarendon Press, 1989), pp. 68-97.

though it is really identical with its dependence on God): "[T]he foundation [of a creature] is not only the relation (which it contains through
identity), but is as absolute as if the relation had been added to it or it
had no relation altogether."[24] Moreover, the focus on essence at the expense of existence entails a further devaluation of actuality and a separation of the essential relation of a thing to God from the existential relation. Because of divine infinity, God's presence is effectively removed
from the actuality of finite things.

Taken together, the critique of existence, quantity, and matter and
the rejection of existential relation constitute the metaphysical basis for
the Scotist theory of individuation in terms of *haecceitas*. The question
that frames this theory is the following: "Is a material substance individual through something positive determining the nature to be just this individual substance?"[25] First, Scotus rejects Godfrey of Fontaines' attempted solution, which is that quantity is not the formal reason for the
unity of material substances, but that it is a dispositional cause for their
divisibility. For Scotus, this could mean one of two things. Either that "the
same material substance undivided and indistinct in itself is informed by
many quantities, and for this reason there are many individuals of that
species,"[26] in which case quantity (or dimensionality) itself individuates
things. Or that quantity is a necessary but insufficient condition and that
nature itself becomes several singularities by receiving this or that quantity (*Lect. II Sent.* d. 3, pars 1, q. 1, n. 153). Scotus then rejects both possible
interpretations: the first on grounds of an extreme unwarranted realism
and the second because material substance may be divisible by nature
without being actually divided before receiving quantity.

This objection already indicates Scotus's proposed alternative,
which does not appeal to accidents (e.g., quantity) but to the substantial
nature itself. Even though originally it is not divided, it is divisible *qua*
nature, in virtue of an individuating difference *(haecceitas)* which is a
positive entity in itself and intrinsic to a substantial nature (*Lect. II Sent.*
d. 3, pars 1, q. 1, n. 162). This individuating difference is formally distinct
from the nature of the quiddity of an individual thing. Rather than being

24. *"fundamentum non est tantum relatio (quam continet per identitatem), sed est ita
absolutum sicut si relatio esset sibi addita, vel omnino nullam haberet relationem"* (*Ord.* II, d.
1, q. 5, n. 275).

25. *"utrum substantia materialis sit individua per entitatem positivam determinantem
naturam ad essendum hanc substantiam individualem"* (*Lect. II Sent.* d. 3, pars 1, q. 6, n. 139).

26. Wolter, "John Duns Scotus (b. ca. 1265; d. 1308)," p. 285.

accidental to the individual, it forms a *per se* unity with it (*Lect. II Sent.* d. 3, pars 1, q. 1, n. 166). Moreover, this difference must be different in each individual, otherwise it would be formally identical (like a quiddity) and therefore unable to account for the real diversity of specifically equal individuals — that which makes an individual a *'this'* and another one a *'that'* (*Lect. II Sent.* d. 3, pars 1, q. 1, n. 166; cf. *Ord.* II, d. 3, pars 1, q. 1, n. 170).

The mark of Scotus's *haecceitas* is that it is a reality which is formally distinct from a thing's quiddity. In the *Ordinatio,* he defines haecceity as that which

> is not matter or form or the composite insofar as each of these is a "nature," but it is the ultimate reality of the being which is matter or form or which is the composite; so that wherever something is common and nevertheless determinable, even though it involves one real thing, we can still distinguish further several formally distinct realities, of which this formally is not that; and this is formally the entity of singularity and that is formally the entity of a nature. Nor can these two realities ever be two distinct real things, in the way the two realities might be that from which the genus is taken (from which two realities the specific reality is taken), but in the same real thing there are always formally distinct realities (be they in the same real part of the same real whole).[27]

In short, haecceity or the individuating difference is a positive entity that is formally distinct from, but really identical with, the specific quiddity of a material substance. As such, the entity is self-individuating because as a 'formal reality' *haecceitas* is not part of the act of being which actualizes such substances. Instead, it is closer to essence, with which it forms a real unity (though according to Scotus essence is and always remains indivisible). In some sense, it constitutes the intrinsic mode of being of

---

27. "*non est igitur 'ista entitas' materia vel forma vel compositum, in quantum quodlibet istorum est 'natura,' sed est ultima realitas entis quod est materia vel quod est forma vel quod est compositum; ita quod quodcumque commune, et tamen determinabile, adhic potest distingui (quantumcumque sit una res) in plures realitates formaliter distinctas, quarum haec formaliter non est illa: et haec est formaliter entitas singularitatis, et illa est entitas naturae formaliter. Nec possunt istae duae realitates esse res et res, sicut possunt esse realitas unde accipitur genus et realitas unde accipitur differentia (ex quibus realitas specifica accipitur), sed semper in eodem (sive in parte sive in toto) sunt realitates eiusdem rei, formaliter distinctae*" (*Ord.* II, d. 3, pars 1, q. 6, n. 188).

essences, the individual distinct particular way one essence is a *'this'* and another essence is a *'that,'* as I have indicated in the present chapter. For this reason, haecceity is unintelligible to the human mind because in our present state the intellect has knowledge of universals but not of singulars.

In summary, the key difference with Aquinas's account of individuation is that Scotus abstracts from the actuality of particular sensible things and focuses almost exclusively on the formality of haecceity. In so doing, he ignores the reality of the individuating act of being which brings everything from nothing into actuality and makes it what it is, as Aquinas had already demonstrated.[28] As a result of this fundamental difference, the onus of individuation shifts from the interaction between God's transcendent cause of being and the immanent principle of designated matter towards the self-individuation of essences independently of their actual materiality. This reinforces the primacy of formal essence over actual existence and deepens the divide between metaphysics and theology. Both these conceptions constitute a marked departure from Aquinas's Neo-Platonist synthesis and a return to more radically Aristotelian tendencies that were already incipient in Porreta and Avicenna, as I showed in chapters 4 and 5.

5. Nominalism and Absolute Singularity in Ockham

Strictly speaking, William of Ockham rejects the very concept of individuation because everything outside the mind is always already a 'this' and owes its individuality to nothing but its own proper self. Individuality is an essential property that belongs to a thing immediately and intrinsically, not in virtue of any relation with anything else. There are no essences or natures that are both common to many individuals and also diversified in each. Since individuals do not have natures or essences distinct from themselves, Ockham opposes realist, formalist, and conceptualist accounts of the relation between universals and particulars (*Ord.* I, d. 2, q. 7). In reality, everything is radically individual, and outside of names *(nomina),* nothing is common or universal.[29] As a result, he

---

28. Étienne Gilson, *Jean Duns Scot. Introduction à Ses Positions Fondamentales*, p. 110.

29. Ockham, *Ordinatio*, I, d. 2, q. 6, in *Guillelmi de Ockham. Opera Theologica*, ed. Gedeon Gál et al. (St. Bonaventure, NY: Franciscan Institute, 1967-1984), vol. 7, p. 350. On

reconfigures individuation in terms of the extrinsic and intrinsic causes that determine a thing's existence — efficient and final causes, as well as form and matter. Given the absolute singularity of each and every individual thing, the question is not what individuates matter or form but how we can speak of the four Aristotelian causes as common or universal (*Ord.* I, d. 2, q. 6).

Even though Ockham's treatment of individuals covers most of his philosophical works (including his *Summa Logicae, Quodlibets,* and *Questions on Aristotle's Physics*), the most comprehensive account is in the first book of his commentary on the *Sententiae* known as the *Ordinatio* (d. 2, q. 4-8).[30] This discussion of universals is divided into a critique of variants of realism and the presentation of Ockham's nonrealist alternative, upon which I will focus. The first position that Ockham dismisses maintains that universals are univocal things *(res)* that exist outside the mind in every individual and belong to its essence. So conceived, every universal is really distinct from individuals and from all other universals. Accordingly, universals are uniform and in no way diversified or multiplied in different individuals (*Ord.* I, d. 2, q. 4). What is instructive about Ockham's critique of this extreme form of realism is his emphasis on divine omnipotence and language. He argues that by his absolute power God could create universals void of individual instantiation and individuals independently of their participation in universals. Moreover, to predicate humanity of Socrates is merely to substitute a term or name for the individual man Socrates himself and to posit a real distinction at the heart of his essence (*Ord.* I, d. 2, q. 4). These objections indicate Ockham's own position, to which I turn after outlining his critique of further variants of realism.

The second position on universals that Ockham attacks is that of Gilbert Porreta (even though Ockham does not mention him explicitly). While agreeing with the previous position that universals have an extramental reality and are really distinct from individuals, this position views universals as being composed with the individual and being contracted by an individuating difference that individuates things. Ockham recognizes

---

singularity in Ockham, see Pierre Alféri, *Guillaume d'Ockham. Le Singulier* (Paris: Minuit, 1989), pp. 15-146. For a different account, see Marilyn M. Adams, *William of Ockham* (Notre Dame: University of Notre Dame Press, 1987), vol. 1, pp. 3-141.

30. Armand Maurer, "William of Ockham (b. ca. 1285; d. 1347)," in Gracia, ed., *Individuation in Scholasticism*, pp. 373-96, esp. p. 374 n. 6.

that this is not Duns Scotus's position because the latter posits a formal distinction. However, Ockham repeats his point that the real distinction between individuals and universals is open to the possibility that divine absolute power can separate individuals from universals and keep both in existence separately from one another (*Ord.* I, d. 2, q. 5). As Maurer notes, this second critique foreshadows Ockham's alternative: "The humanities of Socrates and Plato, being really distinct, could exist in separation from their individuating differences. They would then be really distinct by themselves *(seipsis)* and not through individual differences really distinct from them. This is the position Ockham himself will defend."[31]

The third position that he opposes is Scotus's formalist realism, in particular the claim that the individuating difference is really identical with, but formally distinct from, the nature or essence of material substances. The universal is real in that it exists outside the mind, but its extra-mental existence is incompletely universal as a result of its composition and contraction with the individual thing. This position is identified with "the opinion of the Subtle Doctor [i.e., Duns Scotus] who surpassed the others in keenness of judgement."[32] Ockham's main objection concerns the indifference of the Scotist *natura communis,* which oscillates ambiguously between the physical reality of a real thing *(res realis)* and the mental reality of a being of reason *(res rationis).* According to the logic of Ockham's 'Razor,' it is a superfluous entity that is not essential to individuals or universals.[33] Against Scotus's argument that an essence is universal in the mind and particular in reality, he contends that a definition is a concept and all concepts denote individuals. Humanity refers to all particular human beings, not to some shared common ground or nature. The difference is not predicative but suppositional, as 'universal humanity' is a simple supposition, while 'particular humanity' is a personal supposition (*Ord.* I, d. 2, q. 6). The semantic logic of supposition replaces the onto-logic of Thomist real difference. Maurer puts this well: "Thus, with an adroit use of his theory of *suppositio,* Ockham banishes common natures from the real world."[34] Ockham also rejects the Scotist formal dis-

31. Maurer, "William of Ockham (b. ca. 1285; d. 1347)," p. 377.

32. *"ista opinio est, ut credo, opinio Subtilis Doctoris, qui alios in subtilitate iudicii excellebat"* (*Ord.* I, d. 2, q. 6).

33. Armand Maurer, "Method in Ockham's Nominalism," *Monist* 61 (1978): 426-43, esp. pp. 427-31; A. Maurer, "Ockham's Razor and Chatton's Anti-Razor," *Mediaeval Studies* 46 (1984): 463-75; Adams, *William of Ockham,* esp. pp. 156-61.

34. Maurer, "William of Ockham (b. ca. 1285; d. 1347)," p. 378.

tinction between nature and *haecceitas* by arguing that there are only three types of distinctions (*Ord.* I, d. 2, q. 6) — a real distinction between things *(res)*, mental distinctions between beings of reason *(ens rationis)*, and as yet unspecified distinctions between a real thing *(ens reale)* and a being of reason *(ens rationis)*.

Finally, in question seven of the second distinction in Book One of the *Ordinatio*, Ockham considers further variants of realism and attacks an account that is identified with that of Aquinas or one of his disciples.[35] Ockham's main charge is that this variant of realism defends a doctrine of multiple being *(multiplex esse)*. Natures or essences do not have being or unity by themselves. Rather, through actualization they can acquire the universality of mental existence and the particularity of real existence (*Ord.* I, d. 2, q. 7). Against this conception, Ockham contends that everything that is thought can become universal without actually being universal, e.g., Plato as an object of thought can be universal and thus common to Aristotle. Moreover, universality cannot be added extrinsically through the act of existence to an individual nature. So, similarly to Scotus, Ockham dismisses the Thomist argument that actuality has individuating effects. Instead, he holds that existence and essence are merely nominal distinctions, for otherwise *potentia Dei absoluta* could maintain both of them separately in being. As the noun and the verb of the same thing, *res* and *esse* have identical signification. The whole of reality is radically singular and as such cannot communicate anything at all: "There is nothing in [any two individuals] that is one and the same: whatever is in one simply and absolutely of itself is not something that exists in another."[36] Both the creator and his creation have being, but for Ockham this warrants neither Augustine's definition of God as the highest being in which all other beings share nor Aquinas's divine act of being that brings all things into existence and makes them what they are. Instead, Ockham's ontology posits a strict duality between the one sovereign omnipotent God and the individual many.

This critique paves the way for Ockham's nominalism, which is an application of his metaphysics of singularity to the question of the universality of concepts and words. He begins, however, by rejecting Roscelin of Compiègne's claim that universals are but a *flatus vocis*, for

35. Maurer, "William of Ockham (b. ca. 1285; d. 1347)," p. 382.

36. ". . . *nihil est unum et idem in utroque, sed quidquid est in uno simpliciter et absolute de se non est aliquid quod est in alio*" (*Ord.* I, d. 2, q. 6, in *Opera Theologica*, vol. 7, p. 350).

genera and species are natural rather than merely linguistic conventions (the universality of genus and species is natural in the sense of a generalizing likeness). Words are universal in the sense that they signify many different individual things, but this does not mean that things are universal too. Universals are not real beings that exist either actually or potentially in the world. They are acts of knowing, i.e., particular concepts whose object is one individual (*Quodl.* IV.35; *Qu. in Phys.* I.6). There are also general acts of knowing, i.e., universal concepts whose object is a number of individuals with some similarity. But unlike Aquinas's *ens commune* in which all beings share and which is diversely distributed in them, for Ockham similarity so configured lacks any correlate in reality.

The negation of any ontological commonality is at the origin of Ockham's metaphysics of singularity: "[W]hatever is universal is a singular thing."[37] Universals are mental, spoken, or written names. As mental names *(nomina mentalia)* they constitute the mark of Ockham's nominalism. In some sense, to speak of a 'singular thing' is a tautology because each thing is by definition and by nature singular. There are no nonsingular things and everything, including each and every nature, is singular in and of itself *(de se haec)*. Ockham rejects the very possibility of a cause or principle of individuation because all things are always already radically singular, and unreservedly so (*Ord.* I, d. 2, q. 6).

Compared with Aquinas, the main difference is that relations between individual things are severed from relations with God. Things entertain real (extra-mental) relations between one another, not in virtue of a common source to which they are ordered, but on the basis of an intrinsic similarity. This similarity is so general that the reality of such relations is very weak. The degree of likeness determines whether a generic or specific concept best captures this similarity (humanity in the case of human beings and animate substances in the case of animals and plants). But likeness does not in this way intimate a real relation with a transcendent instance. The absolute primacy of the singular and the denial of real universality shifted the focus from God's free gift of being onto God's absolute power and the divine prerogative to keep all singulars in existence separately, not bound together by the act of existence.

---

37. *"quodlibet universale est una res singularis"* (*SL* I.3). Cf. Gérard Sondag, *Duns Scot: La métaphysique de la singularité* (Paris: Vrin, 2005), pp. 77-164.

6. The Ontology of Political Sovereignty

By denying the reality of transcendent universals in immanent things, Ockham restricts human knowledge of divine self-revelation in the world to uncertain intuition and experience. And by subordinating divine intellect to divine will, he also separates God's volition from the incarnate *Logos* and natural law. The combined result of univocal being and the unreality of universals is to introduce a split between creator and creation and to privilege divine intervention in the world through God's omnipotent will at the expense of nature infused by divine grace and wisdom (as for much of patristic and medieval theology). Ockham's nominalist and voluntarist theology is of special significance for the genesis of the dominant modern model of sovereign power because it establishes the primacy of the individual over the universal and posits a radical separation between the infinite eternal and the finite temporal 'realm,' which provides the foundation for state supremacy vis-à-vis the church and all other institutions within the temporal-spatial realm of the *saeculum.*

First, Ockham abandons the Neo-Platonist emphasis on God's free gift of being and the divine act of being binding together all individual things in favor of God's absolute, unmediated power *(potentia Dei absoluta)* that keeps all beings in separate existence, without any unifying bond of being,[38] as I have already indicated. Based on this ontological priority of the individual, Ockham denies the reality of universals in things and limits universality to concepts in the mind alone. Universals are mental names of concepts and not real 'things' in actually existing beings.[39] Individuality is an essential property that belongs to a thing immediately and intrinsically — not in virtue of any relation with anything else.

The reason for this 'ontological individualism' is of course theological. Ockham contends that after the Fall there can be no metaphysical link between God and the world. This absence of real relations extends to all beings within creation. Different beings can be called animals, not because they participate in a really existing universal called 'animality' or 'animal-ness,' but because their individual essences exhibit a certain

---

38. William Courtenay, *Capacity and Volition: A History of the Distinction of Absolute and Ordained Power* (Bergamo: Pierluigi Lubrina Editore, 1990), pp. 119-26.

39. William of Ockham, *Ordinatio* I, d. 2, q. 6, in *Opera Theologica,* vol. 7, p. 350.

similarity that can be described by the mind as a universal. This similarity is generic (for all animals) or specific (for all humans), but in either case no real, ontological relation pertains between individual beings. Besides the individuality of each and every thing, there is only the overriding absolute power of God's arbitrary will. In the postlapsarian world, God grants humans two powers: to designate those who rule and to appropriate only individual (rather than also communal) property.[40] In this way, he lays the theological and philosophical foundations for the primacy of the individual over the universal in which all can participate. Any form of commonality is now based on individual power and not on a shared divine gift of being.

Second, Ockham's political thought largely mirrors his ontology. Secular authority comes from God via the people. As such, he combines elements of hieronic sovereignty (with power descending from above) with elements of popular sovereignty (with power ascending from below). Nevertheless Ockham, like his fellow secularists and their papalist opponents, argues for the unity of governmental rule. A single monarchy is the most appropriate regime because it combines the unity of 'the sovereign one' with the freedom of 'the many' who are born individual and who are invested with the power of designating their ruler. In principle, secular sovereignty is not absolute, as the monarch can be legitimately corrected or deposed.[41] Likewise, the empire is not a unitary state but instead accommodates kingdoms, dukedoms, and autonomous groups. However, in practice, the emperor rules over the entire temporal sphere, and the common good which he has the obligation to defend tends to serve the interests of the state against the transnational papacy and the national church. The reason is that for Ockham, church authority comes from Christ and his apostles, who all refused to have any civil jurisdiction or political power. As such, the church has no legitimate temporal power in her own right. Ockham, like Marsilius of Padua (c. 1270-1342), argues that whenever the Pope or the clergy exercise temporal jurisdiction, they can only do so by the will of the people.[42] In effect, it is the

40. William of Ockham, *Breviloquium de principatu tyrannico* [*On Tyrannical Rule*], in *Wilhelm von Ockham als politischer Denker,* ed. R. Scholz (Leipzig: SRADG, 1952), III.13, p. 113.

41. Ockham, *Breviloq.,* III.7-8, 14-15 and IV.8, in *Wilhelm von Ockham als politischer Denker und sein Breviloquium de principatu tyrannico,* pp. 125-28, 136-40, 153-58; Ockham, *Dialogus de imperio et pontificia potestate,* III.2.3; III.2.5-10.

42. Ockham, *Dialogus de imperio et pontificia potestate,* III.2.3.vi. On Marsilius, see

monarch's God-given duty to defend the independence of the temporal realm vis-à-vis the papacy and the church. By contrast, Aquinas develops a more mediated account of papal *plenitudo potestatis* in the political sphere. Ockham equates the temporal sphere with coercive jurisdiction, which is a monopoly of the state. In consequence, ecclesiastical sentences based on papal and clerical authority have no legal force without the sanction of the secular authorities.

In the name of individual freedom and monarchical sovereign power, ecclesiastical power is subordinated to the state and the authority of the papacy is curtailed.[43] (On Ockham's advice, King Louis of Bavaria used this argument to limit the imperial jurisdiction of the papacy in his dispute with Pope John XXII.)[44] As a result, state sovereignty is no longer framed by the church, and religious limits on secular power are progressively loosened. As Janet Coleman concludes, the consequence is that

> secular politics not only has its own process of self-correction, but that it is independent of ecclesial power. . . . Because the temporal sphere is imperfect, he [Ockham] argued that secular sovereignty, once established, could be legitimate even when 'absolute,' in that there need not be regular participation of the people in government, nor need there be institutions to restrain the power of kings.[45]

Ockham's political philosophy is therefore governed by the unilateral link between 'the sovereign one' and 'the many,' as reflected in the primacy of the individual over the universal and the supremacy of the state over the church. These ideas tend to remove religious limits on secular politics and to legitimate the *de facto* absolute power of monarchs. Since

---

Alan Gewirth, *Marsilius of Padua and Medieval Political Philosophy* (New York: Columbia University Press, 1951), pp. 237-48.

43. Alain Boureau, *La Religion de l'État. La construction de la République étatique dans le discours théologique de l'Occident médiéval, 1250-1350* (Paris: Les Belles Lettres, 2006), pp. 111-77. On the long debate in relation to the separation of church and state that preceded the fourteenth century, see Brian Tierney, *The Crisis of Church and State, 1050-1300* (Englewood Cliffs, NJ: Prentice Hall, 1964).

44. A. S. McGrade, *The Political Thought of William of Ockham* (Cambridge: Cambridge University Press, 1974), pp. 78-172, 197-206.

45. Janet Coleman, "Ockham's Right Reason and the Genesis of the Political as 'Absolutist,'" *History of Political Thought* 20 (1999): 35-64 (48, 50).

the temporal realm is monopolized by the state at the expense of the church and other intermediary institutions that mediate the vision of a substantive common good as partaking of the highest good in God, Ockham's account of popular sovereignty cannot prevent monarchical absolutism. As I will show in chapter 7, this strand of thought was reinforced by Francisco Suárez (1548-1616), who prioritized popular sovereignty over the *corpus mysticum* and in so doing eliminated from the polity both the Eucharist as the manifestation of God's reconciliation with the world and the church as universal community.

7. Semantics and Universal Individuality in Buridan

Like Ockham, Jean Buridan maintains that individuation does not constitute a metaphysical problem because things are individual in and of themselves and do not require any cause or principle that individuates them. Individuality is an *a priori datum* which is self-explanatory because it is self-founded. Everything that exists in its own right or as a constituent *of* a thing *in* a thing is individual. In reality there simply are no nonindividual entities at all. The specificity of Buridan's position is the priority of semantics over ontology. Instead of treating the question of individuality as a metaphysical problem, he recast the related issues formally and located them exclusively in semantics. Since all entities are presupposed to be singular, the challenge is to explain how expressions can be universal and yet identify individuals *qua* individuals. My contention is that Buridan's account of individuals and universals seals the late medieval exit from the metaphysics of relationality and participation insofar as his semantic theory frames ontology and makes mental language more fundamental than actual particular sensible beings.[46]

As Peter King has argued, Buridan's semantic framework dictates his ontology in general and his account of individuality in particular.[47] Buridan distinguishes between mental, written, and spoken language and holds that written and spoken terms ultimately signify that which is conceived by the concept. Put differently, inscriptions and utterances

---

46. *Pace* Lambertus M. de Rijk, "John Buridan on Universals," *Revue de Métaphysique et de Morale* 97 (1992): 35-59.

47. Peter O. King, "Jean Buridan (b. ca. 1295/1300; d. after 1358)," in Gracia, ed., *Individuation in Scholasticism*, pp. 397-430, esp. 407-13. Cf. P. King, *Jean Buridan's Logic* (Dordrecht: D. Reidel, 1985).

signify particular things more immediately than concepts (*Tract. Sup.* III.ii.8). However, unlike spoken and written language, only mental language is natural (not conventional) and universal (applicable to all thinking beings except God). As such, mental language frames written and spoken language: "[I]t is the vehicle through which written and spoken language are 'given meaning' or have an ultimate signification, in the last analysis due to the ways in which a concept may signify that of which it is a concept."[48] In extending Ockham's theory of *suppositio*, Buridan also distinguishes between signification and supposition and argues that supposition denotes the actual use of terms in order to refer to significates (as opposed to signification, which merely correlates terms with their significates).[49] The difference between reference and correlation is that reference links words to things, whereas correlation establishes linguistic conventions and therefore helps constitute a language. Crucially, Buridan's theory of meaning and reference structures his ontology. For example, only individual absolute terms of mental language involve ontological commitments because only concepts relate to actually existing individual entities (*Tract. Sup.* I.iv.1, 8; V.i.1; V.ii.5; *Sophism.* I, th. 6). Buridan's semantic approach to metaphysics is evinced by his definition of singularity:

> The name 'singular' is opposed to the name 'plural,' according to grammar, but this is not relevant for us; rather, we shall take it as opposed to the name 'common' or 'universal,' and then it seems to me that according to the logician these terms 'singular' and 'individual' are taken as synonymous terms to which [these terms] 'common' and 'universal' are opposed. These are all names of second intention, suppositing for significative terms: 'singular' and 'individual' supposit for discrete terms, and 'universal' suppoits for common terms.[50]

---

48. King, "Jean Buridan (b. ca. 1295/1300; d. after 1358)," p. 398.

49. Cf. Joel Biard, *Logique et théorie du signe au XIVe siècle* (Paris: Vrin, 1989).

50. *"Dico quod hoc nomen 'singulare' secundum grammaticam opponitur huic nomini 'plurale,' sed de hoc nihil ad nos; immo capiamus ipsum prout opponitur huic nomini 'commune' vel 'universale,' et tunc videtur mihi quod apud logicum isti termini 'singulare' et 'individuum' verificantur pro terminis synonymis quibus opponitur 'commune' vel 'universale.' Et sunt haec omnia nomina secundarum intentionum supponentia pro terminis significativis: 'singulare' enim et 'individuum' supponunt pro terminis discretis, et 'universale' supponit pro terminis communibus"* (*Qu. Met.* VII, q. 19).

In this passage, Buridan argues that the singular and the individual are terms of second intention, which signify other terms, not things. Such terms are also described as discrete terms that are "predicable of only one," e.g., a statement of identity such as 'this is Plato' (*Tract. Sup.* III.iii.1). As a result, he conceives singularity and individuality primarily as properties of terms before they are properties of things.

As properties of things, they describe the indivisibility of a thing and its differentiation from other things (*Qu. Met.* IV, q. 7; VII, q. 17, q. 19). Buridan is particularly interested in the numerical unity of things, and he stresses that things which can exist by themselves (e.g., substances as opposed to accidents) cannot be divided either "into beings [specifically] similar to themselves" or "into subjective parts" (*Qu. Met.* VII, q. 19). In other words, individuality in the sense of indivisibility excludes anything like Aquinas's *ens commune* and relations among things in virtue of their collective sharing in the same source of being.

The differentiation of individuals from other individuals leads him to emphasize the semantic rather than metaphysical nature of difference between species and sameness within species. Not only do individuals from different species have different substantial forms (as Aquinas and Scotus also held), but individuals of the same species also differ in terms of their forms. The only way to group them together as members of the same species exhibiting a certain similarity is by way of a general term or supposit, not a metaphysical principle that is diversely received by different particulars (*Qu. Met.* VII, q. 17).

Radicalizing Ockham's absolute singularity, Buridan excludes all forms of universality and commonality: "Every thing exists as singular such that it is diverse from any other thing, since it is never possible that a term suppositing precisely for one thing be truly affirmed of a term suppositing precisely for another [thing]" (*Qu. Phys.* I, q. 7). Since they are always already individual in and of themselves, things do not require a cause or principle of individuation. Individuality is a fundamental mark of reality as a whole. Everything is individual, substances as well as accidents, material as well as immaterial beings. Individuality is irreducible and indicates the unicity of each and every thing. Yet at the same time, Buridan denies any common source or origin of individuality. He replaces Ockham's metaphysics of singularity with a semantics and logic of individual terms. As King argues, "Concepts, even general concepts, are individual acts of understanding in individual intellects, spoken and written language of so many individual utterances or inscriptions."[51] This account of the world rules out the existence of any entities that might not be self-individuating or any metaphysical links between individual things.

The primacy of individuality brings Buridan into engagement with the medieval question of the reality of universals and the nature of the distinction between universals and particulars. He attributes the position that defends a real distinction to Plato and dismisses it as "completely absurd" (*Qu. Met.* VII, q. 15). He also claims that the separation of 'Plato' and 'man' undermines the unity of the man Plato, and that the universality of man in Plato and Aristotle entails an identity of the man Plato and the man Aristotle. Either unaware or unconvinced of the Platonist framework of participation, Buridan reduces this problem to a set of semantic questions and rejects the very possibility that forms may be separate: "Something is not intrinsically a being by a thing separate [from it]; yet nothing is a being except intrinsically by its entity; therefore, if the entity of this [individual] were separate from it, it would not be a being."[52] This position seeks to secure the coherence of identity and characterized as nonsensical any idea that there might be universals. However, this critique of the real distinction between singular things and universal forms fails to explain how and why individuals that are different from one another are nevertheless like other individuals. Why is there an immediately perceptible likeness amongst diverse things? Buridan's refusal to address this kind of question explains his rejection of both Thomist designated matter and Scotist *haecceitas* as universal principles of individuation (*Qu. Met.* VII, q. 16).

His de-ontologized semantics and logic propel him to read Aristotle in an entirely nonmetaphysical way. In his discussion of the distinction between essence and being, he posits at the outset that essences are by definition singular and that there is no ontological difference between a thing's essence and its *esse*. Essences are denied universality, for "I understand by 'essence' the thing itself" (*Qu. Met.* IV, q. 8). Likewise, *esse* is stripped of any commonality or universality, as each individual is both its essence and its being. The difference that pertains between them is purely mental, in the sense that these two terms involve distinct conno-

---

51. King, "Jean Buridan (b. ca. 1295/1300; d. after 1358)," p. 402.

52. *"Aliquid non est ens intrinsice per rem separatam, et tamen nihil est ens nisi per suam entitatem intrinsice; ergo si entitas huius esset ab isto separata non esset ens"* (*Qu. Met.* VII, q. 15).

tations that are unrelated to differences in supposition.[53] The result is that Buridan locates universality exclusively at the semantic level and denies universals any reality. The question this anti-metaphysical move raises is how and why knowledge of things can be said to be universal. Buridan's solution is to say that intelligible species deliver a likeness that applies to more than a single individual. However, this likeness is a product *of* the mind *in* the mind *for* the mind. Beyond intellective generality, the human mind can cognize a thing's singularity by way of intuitive cognition (*Qu. Met.* VII, q. 20), which circumvents both the confusion of sense perception and the abstraction of intellection. True knowledge of the world is immediate intuition of singulars, and therefore to intuit singulars is to intuit the coincidence of their essence and their being.

Compared with Aquinas's account of God's act of being which brings everything into actuality and makes it what it is, Buridan excludes divine creative activity from individual existence. Instead, he attributes the existence of individual entities either to themselves or to the absolute power of God. Self-subsisting substances do not require any cause or principle in order to be. Prime matter, which is a being in itself, can exist *per se* by God's power: "[Prime] matter is in act, and it would be in act even if it were to exist without either substantial or accidental form inhering [in it]"; the natural composition of matter with forms makes matter nonindividual, "unless God were to conserve it without them" (*Qu. Phys.* I, q. 20).

The exit from metaphysics and relationality is sealed when Buridan severs all ties between the Aristotelian categories and ontology, including ontological relation.[54] Only individuals exist, and any properties they might exhibit are merely semantic. Nothing reflects in any way more than its own proper singular self. Individuation is a purely semantic question that is severed from metaphysics because, contrary to Aquinas, Buridan asserts that particular sensible things do not intimate God's creative and individuating action. As such, Buridan is instrumental in the invention of the individual.

53. King, "Jean Buridan (b. ca. 1295/1300; d. after 1358)," p. 406.

54. Cf. Rolf Schönberger, *Relation als Vergleich: Die Relationstheorie des Johannes Buridan im Kontext seines Denken und der Scholastik* (Leiden: E. J. Brill, 1994).

8. *Potentia Dei Absoluta* and Individuation

An important theory that Scotus, Ockham, and Buridan draw on for their respective accounts of individuation is *potentia Dei ordinata*. The context in which they deploy the concept of divine absolute power in relation to the question of actualization was framed by previous interpretations and the 1277 condemnations. Thirteenth-century theology tended to distinguish between ordained and absolute power: "*[P]otentia ordinata* was equated with the total pre-ordained, providential will of God, while *potentia absoluta* was divine power without considering the divine will or the created order."[55] The 1277 condemnations did not fundamentally alter this theological distinction, but what changed was the growing emphasis on the possibility of immediate, direct, and preordained divine action which suspends or even violates the laws of nature. More importantly, the distinction between ordained and absolute power was henceforth applied to the analogy of divine and human will, in particular the question of the sovereignty of individuals and communities.

Scotus favors the canonical concept of free choice between *de facto* (ordained) and *de iure* (absolute) action over the theological distinction between ordained and absolute power. As a result of the univocity of being, free choice applies univocally to God and to man. Moreover, *potentia absoluta* does not define the realm of possibility whence God chooses to create one of many possible worlds. Instead it is the power to act outside of an already established order (*Ord.* I, d. 44). Scotus's canonical interpretation shifts the focus towards a real distinction of divine power and a formal distinction between divine action and divine will. The use of *potentia absoluta* is now above the law *(supra legem)*.[56] Ockham reacts against this distinction and reasserts the unity of divine power. Since in God, being and activity are one, divine power and divine essence must be united. At the same time, Ockham's conception of the analogy between divine and human freedom leads him to separate the temporal from the spiritual realm and to assert the independence and sovereignty of human law-making,[57] independently of natural law (*Breviloq.* III.7-8, 14-15; IV.8; *Dial.* III.2.3; III.2.5-10). Individuals have inalienable rights given to them by God directly, but the exercise of this power is not mediated by

55. Courtenay, *Capacity and Volition*, p. 87.
56. Courtenay, *Capacity and Volition*, pp. 87-113.
57. Courtenay, *Capacity and Volition*, pp. 115-71.

any community, whether the temporal political community of the state or the spiritual community of the church.

In this way, Ockham lays the theological foundations for the primacy of the individual over the collective. All forms of commonality are based on individual power. In the name of individual autonomy, the power of the papacy over the temporal sphere is limited. This primacy also underlies the creation of the state. States emerge as a result of individuals freely consenting to specific ordinances that govern their individual and collective behavior. However, once this consent has taken place, the transfer of power from individuals to the state is irreversible, as the state is the absolute sovereign that rules unopposed over its constituents. That is why Janet Coleman is right to describe Ockham's politics in general and his conception of royal power in particular as absolutist, as I have already indicated.

The reason why Ockham's theory of sovereignty licensed absolute secular power is that he severed the ties between God's continuous creative activity and the operation of the natural world. God's action is divided into the original act of creation which bestows inalienable rights on the individual and the extraordinary act which suspends the natural order. By eliminating God from the dispensation of political power, Ockham grants the secular sphere unprecedented *de iure* autonomy and *de facto* independence. Relations amongst individuals are dictated by the individual will alone, not the common sharing in God's continuous creative act. Likewise, relations between the world and God are confined to the initial act of creation. The operation of the natural order is autonomous and independent from divine activity. Ockham's account not only denied God any import in the individuation of created beings but also eliminated politics from the formation of individuals. Individuality is an *a priori datum,* a static condition, not a dynamic process. As such, it marks a rupture with the Christian Neo-Platonist metaphysics of relationality.

9. Conclusion: Rationalism and Fideism

In the previous and the present chapter, I compared and contrasted different medieval accounts of the link between creation and individuation. Aquinas connects actualization and individuation to God's creative action and in so doing argues that the divine gift of being is the gift of relationality. Everything is constituted relationally, in God's likeness and image. Thus, relations amongst created beings intimate in some sense, approximately and imperfectly, divine relationality within the Trinity. This is not to say that for Aquinas Trinitarian relations could be known in any other way than by the supernatural gift of faith. Duns Scotus defends a variant of realism but introduced a formal distinction between the foundation of things and their relation to God. The formality of this distinction relativizes the ontological link between creatures and the Creator. The dependence of all created things on God is real, but (contrary to Augustine, Boethius, and Aquinas) creatures are purely substantial and not relational. This is so because the relation to God does not enter into the essential definition of a creature. Nor does it add any perfection to it. This rejection of relationality seeks to preserve the absolute character of a creature (even though it is really identical with its dependence on God).

Ockham denies the real presence of universals in particulars and argues that singularity is the most fundamental mark of reality. This removes any kind of commonality and relationality among created beings. Likewise, the ontological link between God's creative action and the individuation of composites becomes unhinged. The absolute primacy of the singular and the denial of real universality shifted the focus away from God's free gift of being onto God's absolute power and the divine prerogative to keep all singulars in existence separately. So configured, individuals do not share in common being. They have nothing real in common because they are not bound together by God's act of being. There are thus no real relations amongst created beings or between the world and God. Buridan radicalizes this turn by elevating semantics over ontology. Like Ockham, he argues that only individuals exist. Universal properties such as humanity are purely semantic, not real. Things subsist either by themselves or in virtue of God's absolute power. Every existing thing represents nothing more than its own singular self. Individuation is a purely semantic question that is disconnected from ontology because contrary to Augustine, Boethius, and Aquinas, Buridan asserts that particular sensible things do not in any way intimate God's creative action. There are no causes or principles of individuation because individuality is an *a priori datum* and as such cannot be explained.

As will by now be clear, the alternative to modernity is not simply to return to ancient philosophy but rather to retrieve and develop the fusion of reason and revelation and to bind together faith and works in a new compact. The shape of such a synthesis in both the Islamic and the Christian tradition will have to be pursued elsewhere. But we can say that this will have to involve a recovery of Neo-Platonic philosophical and mystical theology that was at different moments at the heart of Christianity and also central to Islam. In the Christian case, this vision runs from St. Paul and Augustine via Dionysius and Eriugena to Aquinas, Eckhart, and Cusa. From Leo XIII's encyclical *Æterni Patris* via John Paul II's *Fides et Ratio* to Benedict XVI's Regensburg lecture, successive pontiffs have not so much opposed modernity as a whole but rather rejected the secular outlook of modern thought that has destroyed the union between biblical revelation and ancient philosophy. Neither the secularization of Christianity by liberal Christians nor the fundamentalist hijacking by evangelical-pentecostal sects will be mitigated or reversed without a profound theological renewal of the old mainstream traditional faith in all the episcopally based churches.

In the Islamic case, figures such as Al-Arabī and (with some qualifications) Mullā Sadrā view existence as primary and real and essence as embodied in actual beings, as I suggested in chapter 4. In consequence, they endorse a theological metaphysics that combines an illuminationist account of knowledge with an ontological realism centered on the presence of universals in the human mind and in particular things. By viewing truth as that which descends from God and induces a desire for wisdom and salvation, they fuse philosophy *(falsafa)* with mysticism. Crucially, this combination of spiritual contemplation and transformative practices mitigates the emphasis on absolute divine unity in Islamic theology *(kalām)* in the direction of diverse divine mediations and deification. This stretches from nonliteral readings of the Qur'an to the teaching of social and political virtues, making man theomorphic while preserving God's ineffability. A revival of mystic Sufism would not just mark a renaissance of Islamic Neo-Platonism but also contain Islamic fundamentalism and deprive extremists of their primary motivating principle — that they alone know the will of God totally and are therefore justified in enforcing it absolutely upon the earth.

Pope Benedict's Regensburg address combines a critique of violence in religion (both Islam and Christianity, albeit for different reasons) with a call to integrate faith with reason in new ways so that the world's religious cultures could once more debate their rival claims to universality. What this requires is nothing less than a postsecular nonliberal vision of politics, the economy, and society. The kind of liberal interfaith dialogue that has been prevalent for the past half century or so has done little to promote genuine mutual understanding except to reinforce simplistic ideas about the shared essence of different creeds and belief in the same God.[58] As a number of religious authorities have remarked, we can no longer ignore the fundamental differences that distinguish diverse faiths. The best hope for real peace and tolerance between world religions is to have a proper theological engagement about the nature of God and the meaning of peace and justice.

Of course, this does not preclude pragmatic cooperation between the faiths on issues and problems of common concern such as aggressive secularism, militant atheism, and perhaps most importantly, violence in religion. But the fundamentalists on all sides will be intellectually defeated and politically marginalized only by reasoned belief and rational argument. Faith can play a positive role in debates between religions and cultures only if it expands rather than reduces the scope of rational cognition and promotes the 'grandeur of reason.'

---

58. For a critique of recent initiatives such as "A Common Word between Us and You," see Adrian Pabst, "We Need a Real Debate, Not More Dialogue," *International Herald Tribune,* 15 November 2007.

PART III

Transcendence and Immanence

If one is to believe much of contemporary philosophy, modern metaphysics is constitutively and irreducibly onto-theological. As such, the only genuine alternative is a postmodern, pure philosophy of immanence stripped of all traces of theological transcendence. But if 'postmodernity' is in the end an intensification of certain modern ideas rather than a new phase of history, perhaps it is then also the case that modern onto-theology and postmodern philosophy are not diametrically opposed to each other but instead part of the same tradition which inaugurated modernity and underpinned neo-scholasticism as well as the (English, French, and German) Enlightenment. That tradition is the mixed Scotist-Cartesian-Kantian legacy which combines a metaphysics and epistemology of representation either with a transcendental priority of infinity over finitude or a critical limitation of knowledge to the finite.[1]

Nor is this profound continuity between the modern and the postmodern confined to ontology (Husserl and Heidegger), metaphysics (Levinas and Badiou), or some pure phenomenology (Marion). The insistence on a sphere of pure immanence is correlated with a conception of theology as an exclusively regional science (here uncritically following Heidegger) and also with the idea that the supernatural virtue of faith is disconnected from the natural virtues governing societies. Linked to this is a bizarre failure on the part of many (phenomenological) philosophers

---

1. See, *inter alia,* André de Muralt, "Kant, le dernier occamien. Une nouvelle définition de la philosophie moderne," *Revue de Métaphysique et de Morale* 80 (1975): 32-53; Olivier Boulnois, *Être et représentation. Une généalogie de la métaphysique moderne à l'époque de Duns Scot (XIIIe-XIVe siècle)* (Paris: Presses Universitaires de France, 1999).

to recognize that religion was never eliminated from the public realm or that it has already reverted to political significance. More fundamentally, the notion of sheer givenness without either gift or giver seems to preclude any way in which asymmetrical gift-exchange can subvert and transform the dominant modern logic of social contract and monetary exchange that accompanies the modern biopolitical fusion of constitutional democracy with market capitalism, as I have argued elsewhere.[2]

The apolitical and aneconomic stance in much of contemporary phenomenology betrays a strange, ahistorical view of phenomenal disclosure that in turn is based on the modern separation of transcendent infinite eternity from immanent finite temporality. All of which suggests that the 'theological turn of French phenomenology' centered on God without being (as in the work of Marion) is mired in irreconcilable tensions between philosophy and theology and perhaps best described as an attempt to engineer a 'phenomenological turn of theology.'[3] For these reasons, the most significant work in this trajectory is by those scholars who refuse a clear and distinct separation of theology and philosophy and who are open to the Neo-Platonic framework (like Jean-Louis Chrétien), which avoids in advance the modern idolatry of onto-theology.[4]

Other influential contemporary philosophers such as Jacques Derrida, Gilles Deleuze, and Alain Badiou also look back to early modernity, notably Duns Scotus's reduction of the infinite and the finite to univocal being as well as Spinoza's deconstruction of analogical being in favor of univocal substance. But once more there are profound continuities between the 'early modern' thought of Scotus and Spinoza and the 'late scholasticism' of Descartes (who stands between the two) and Kant, notably the turn to subjectivity and the separation of transcendence from immanence which also can be traced in part to Baroque scholasticism.

That is why the third and final part of this essay turns to early mod-

2. Adrian Pabst, "Modern Sovereignty in Question: Theology, Democracy and Capitalism," *Modern Theology* 26, no. 4 (October 2010): 570-602.

3. Dominique Janicaud, *Le tournant théologique de la phénoménologie française* (Paris: Éditions de l'Éclat, 1991), English translation: *Phenomenology and the "Theological Turn": The French Debate* (New York: Fordham University Press, 2001). Cf. Jean Greisch, "Un tournant phénoménologique de la théologie?" *Transversalités* 63 (1997): 75-97.

4. In terms of alternatives to Husserl, Heidegger, and Marion, I am thinking of elements in the work of Maurice Blondel, Maurice Merleau-Ponty, Michel Henry, Jean-Yves Lacoste, and above all Jean-Louis Chrétien (as well as the recent publications by Emmanuel Falque). See, *infra,* chapter 9.

ern philosophy and theology. Chapters 7 and 8 explore the works of Francisco Suárez (1548-1617) and Benedict (Baruch de) Spinoza (1632-1677). In the wake of Porreta, Scotus, Ockham, and Buridan, Suárez completes the exit from the patristic and medieval metaphysics of relational participation by severing the links between individuation and creation. The primacy of metaphysics in his scholastic system, aimed at securing a rational space within which theology investigates the main articles of faith concerning the Trinity and the Christological doctrines, has implications for the relation between philosophy and theology and between reason and faith. Revealed theology is divorced from nature and relegated to a separate realm that is disconnected from the natural drive towards the supernatural. Likewise, reason no longer requires faith, and faith no longer intensifies reason. Instead, just as the order of nature and that of revelation become independent from one another, so the order of reason precedes the order of faith and grounds all knowledge (*Dis. Met.* prol.; *De Fide* III, intro.).

The consecration of metaphysics as an overarching system completes the late scholastic turn from patristic and medieval theology to early modern philosophy. In consequence, the idea of individuating relations between a transcendent God and his creation is abandoned in favor of an alternative theory of individuation that revolves around two tenets of early modern philosophy: first, the transcendental dependence of effects upon their cause and the self-individuation of entities (Suárez); second, the immanent generation of individual beings and their individuation in a perpetual rivalry with other groups of individual beings (Spinoza).

In the final chapter, I argue that much of modern metaphysics is in fact little more than the post-Scotist and post-Suárezian ontological science of being *qua* being which erases the ontological difference between divine and created *esse* and in the end collapses into the transcendental science of what can be known about univocal being. By contrast, the metaphysical science of *ens commune* preserves the 'analogical difference' between Creator and creation; it also binds together kenotic, cataphatic descent with apophatic ascent, which perfects degrees of being and goodness through mystical elevation and union with God. As such, the alternative to modern transcendentalism (and the mirror image of positivism) is not some postmetaphysical phenomenological or analytic philosophy but rather a revivified theological metaphysics that overcomes ancient and modern monism or dualism (as well as postmodern pluralism) in the direction of Trinitarian relationality.

CHAPTER 7

Transcendental Individuation

1. Introduction: On Scholastic Transcendentalism

In this chapter, I trace the genealogical links between high medieval theology and early modern philosophy. In the wake of John Scotus and William of Ockham, Francisco Suárez (1548-1617) embraces and reinforces the separation of revealed theology from metaphysics and the incipient dualism of reason and faith as well as nature and grace.[1] Without a theology that can secure analogical being and relational participation, the autonomy of metaphysics gives rise to a scholastic transcendentalism that makes reason primary to faith and grace extrinsic to nature. As such, post-Scotist and post-Ockhamist scholasticism consolidates the 'passage to modernity' (Louis Dupré), above all the erasure of God from the world and the consecration of the human mind as the ultimate arbiter of meaning and value. In some sense, this shift marks a metaphysical elaboration of the early Renaissance idea of man as the measure of all things.[2] By contrast with Porreta and Buridan however, Suárez challenges the primacy of logic and semantics over metaphysics. He does so by recovering elements of Thomist realism against the formalism of Scotus's *haecceitas* and the nominalism of Ockham's singularity. More-

---

1. John Montag, SJ, "Revelation: The False Legacy of Suárez," in *Radical Orthodoxy: A New Theology,* ed. John Milbank, Catherine Pickstock, and Graham Ward (London and New York: Routledge, 1999), pp. 38-63.

2. Louis Dupré, *Passage to Modernity: An Essay in the Hermeneutics of Nature and Culture* (New Haven and London: Yale University Press, 1993), pp. 15-90.

over, he strongly qualifies late medieval nominalism with a stronger emphasis on the divine intellect and the human mind. However, Suárez's scholastic transcendentalism subordinates both the physical and the theological dimension of individuality to a metaphysics of transcendental individuation that is paradoxically rationalist and fideist, as I will suggest in this chapter.

In defending a purely metaphysical theory of individuation, Suárez makes the questionable claim that theology has nothing to say about the nature of individuality and that creation cannot account for why things are individual and what the *telos* of individuation might be. Indeed, individuality is for Suárez and those who follow him an undemonstrated *datum*. It is part of the *posita* of metaphysics, that is to say, one of the presuppositions that form its subject-matter, which is posited beyond doubt and secured prior to the investigation of actual objects.[3] By contrast, for patristic and medieval Christian Neo-Platonists the subject of each science is not an a priori *positum* but is defined by an a posteriori demonstration that constitutes the foundation of scientific inquiry.[4] Suárez's division of the sciences and his definition of metaphysics separate the subject of a science *(subiectum)* from the objects it explores *(quaesitum)*. Paradoxically, since individuality is inscribed in the subject of metaphysics, it eludes metaphysical investigation.

Following Scotus, Suárez founds theology upon metaphysics, making 'metaphysical doctrine' an absolute prerequisite for all theological knowledge: "As it is impossible for one to become a good theologian without having first been established on the solid foundations of metaphysics, thus I always believed it important, Christian reader, to offer you previously this work [the *Disputationes Metaphysicae*] . . . in order to grant — or better to restore — to *metaphysical doctrine* the place that belonged to it."[5] The priority of metaphysics over theology reverses Porreta's and Buridan's primacy of logic and semantics and restores the idea that individuality is real *(esse in re)* and that individuation is metaphysical. Yet at the same time, the formalization of metaphysics and the

---

3. Jean-François Courtine, *Suarez et le système de la métaphysique* (Paris: Presses Universitaires de France, 1990), pp. 13-19.

4. Rudi te Velde, "'The First Thing to Know about God': Kretzmann and Aquinas on the Meaning and Necessity of Arguments for the Existence of God," *Religious Studies* 39 (2003): 251-67, esp. pp. 254-59.

5. Suárez, *Dis. Met.*, "*Ratio et discursus totius operis: ad lectorem*," quoted by Montag, "Revelation: The False Legacy of Suárez," p. 53 (my italics).

predominance of abstraction over sense perception and judgment abandon the patristic and medieval Christian Neo-Platonist quest for a rationally intelligible account of why entities are individual and to what end they 'desire' to be individuated. Coupled with the emergence of modern skepticism, Suárezian metaphysics threatens the status of theology as the queen of sciences by predefining the space within which *sacra doctrina* can operate.[6] In this manner, his theological realism is more akin to the philosophical formalism of Porreta with which it shares the separation of existence from essence and the exclusion of God's act of being from the operation of the created order.

2. Early Modern Scholasticism

The work of Suárez on creation and individuation was instrumental to the emergence of early modern metaphysics. First, he systematized the modern epistemological project inaugurated by Ockham and developed by Buridan, in particular the idea that with the help of God's absolute power *(potentia Dei absoluta)* the mind either could or in some instances actually does cognize things independently of their actualization. Second, he built on Duns Scotus in order to reestablish the primacy of metaphysics over all other sciences, in particular theology (Aquinas), logic (Porreta), and semantics (Buridan), as I argued in Part II of this essay. Metaphysics as defined by Suárez is grounded in a priori objective concepts such as the individuality and singularity of all actually existing things (*Dis. Met.* V.i.4). Likewise, metaphysics is reconfigured as the foundation for revealed theology in the sense of defining the realm in which *sacra doctrina* operates. Since only metaphysics provides a rationally intelligible account of the most general principles, it must foreground all other sciences.

The significance of Suárez's system is that individuality applies univocally to all actual beings, including God. Because everything that exists is always already individual (*Dis. Met.* V.i.4), individuation is not a function of the relation between God and creation but is internal to each and every individual thing. According to Suárez, entities are in fact self-individuating (*Dis. Met.* V.i.2). In turn, this conception reflects and confirms fundamental changes in late medieval and early modern theories of causation. For Aquinas and faithful Thomists, the first cause or God

6. Cf. Montag, "Revelation: The False Legacy of Suárez," esp. pp. 55-58.

gives being, whereas secondary created causes specify beings. By contrast, for Scotus, Ockham, and their numerous disciples, God's creative action as the first cause exercises a general influence *(influentia generalis)* from which a specific influence is largely disconnected, as I indicated in chapters 5 and 6.[7] In Suárez's metaphysical system, secondary causes are sufficient and provide the foundation of the state of nature, which is upheld by the concurrence of the primary cause but operates independently of God's creative action *(Dis. Met.* XXII.iv).

Compared with his nominalist and voluntarist predecessors, Suárez's innovation is to make the general influence or concurrence purely extrinsic and superadded to the state of nature. God's concurrent causal activity is thus consonant with naturalism. The separation of general from specific influence and the sufficiency of secondary causes give rise to two orders, one natural and the other supernatural. As such, it foreshadows the thesis of 'pure natural capacity' *(ex puris naturalibus)* and 'pure nature' *(pura natura),* as Henri de Lubac described it in his seminal work *Surnaturel.*[8] Coupled with the primacy of metaphysics over theology, Suárez's emphasis on the causation and operation of things independently of their dependence on the Creator God leads him to discard the patristic and medieval Christian Neo-Platonist metaphysics of relationality and participation.

More specifically, he questions Aquinas's *esse commune* and the Thomist conception of human beings as in some way through their very humanity already oriented towards grace.[9] Compared with Thomas, Suárez's post-Scotist and post-Ockhamist dualism of will and intelligence entails a demotion of the will to a mere faculty, rather than an integral part of humanity and its natural desire for the beatific vision.[10] Therefore, the natural desire for the supernatural is no longer intrinsi-

7. For a more detailed account of this shift, see André de Muralt, *L'Enjeu de la philosophie médiévale. Études thomistes, scotistes, occamiennes et grégoriennes* (Leiden: E. J. Brill, 1991), pp. 331-51; A. de Muralt, "La causalité aristotélicienne et la structure de pensée scotiste," *Dialectica* 47 (1993): 121-41; Jacob Schmutz, "La doctrine médiévale des causes et la théologie de la nature pure (XIIIᵉ-XVIIᵉ siècles)," *Revue thomiste* 101 (2001): 217-64.

8. Henri de Lubac, *Surnaturel. Études historiques* (Paris: Aubier-Montaigne, 1946), pp. 261-321.

9. De Lubac, *Surnaturel,* pp. 231-60.

10. Olivier Boulnois, "Les deux fins de l'homme. L'impossible anthropologie et le repli de la théologie," *Les Études Philosophiques* 9 (1995): 205-22; O. Boulnois, "Surnaturel," in *Dictionnaire critique de théologie,* ed. Jean-Yves Lacoste (Paris: Presses Universitaires de France, 1998), pp. 980-95; John Milbank, *The Suspended Middle: Henri de Lubac and the Debate concerning the Supernatural* (Grand Rapids: Eerdmans, 2005), esp. pp. 20-28.

cally present in human nature but instead is now elicited extrinsically. This removes the orientation towards the beatific vision from the realm of being and locates it exclusively in the realm of knowing (as either innate or radically contingent and superadded).[11] In either case, this metaphysics runs counter to the scripturally and naturally revealed presence of creation *in* the Creator and the manifold intimations of the supernatural in the natural.

Moreover, Suárez embraces the concept of univocal being and edges closer to the idea of 'pure nature' *(pura natura)* drained of any phenomenally visible trace of God.[12] He brackets out everything that exceeds nature itself in order to attain natural man *per se* (*De Ult. Fin.* XV.ii). André de Muralt has traced a genealogical account of intentionality in which Suárez is the central late scholastic figure. His bracketing of the supernatural is effectively the early modern metaphysical precursor of Edmund Husserl's late-modern epistemological *epoche*.[13] Suárez's tendency towards *pura natura* severs natural beings from supernatural goods and thereby consolidates the transition towards the modern separation of nature from grace and reason from faith. In consequence, he consigns the human natural orientation towards the beatific vision entirely to the special realm of theology and adopts a rival anthropology centered on the metaphysical nature of man *(natura metaphysica hominis),* which is cognoscible in itself and as such.[14] Conjointly, erasing the transcendent presence of God from nature and immanentizing the principle of individuation mark the consecration of modern thought: "For Suárez," as Alasdair MacIntyre notes, "both in his preoccupations and in his methods, was already a distinctively modern thinker, perhaps more authentically than Descartes the founder of modern philosophy."[15]

11. On the difference of the relation between nature and grace in Aquinas and Suárez, see Montag, "Revelation: The False Legacy of Suárez," pp. 38-63, and Milbank, *The Suspended Middle,* esp. pp. 15-32.

12. For an account that situates Suárez in the genesis and evolution of the term *pura natura,* see de Lubac, *Surnaturel,* pp. 101-27, 129-55.

13. Cf. André de Muralt, *La métaphysique du phénomène: Les origines médiévales et l'élaboration de la pensée phénoménologique* (Paris: Vrin, 1985).

14. For a systematic comparison of Aquinas and Suárez on the beatific vision and the ultimate finality of man, see Jean-François Courtine, *Nature et Empire de la Loi. Études suaréziennes* (Paris: Vrin, 1999), pp. 45-67.

15. Alasdair MacIntyre, *Three Rival Versions of Moral Enquiry: Encyclopaedia, Genealogy, and Tradition* (London: Duckworth, 1990), p. 73. Cf. José Ferrater Mora, "Suárez and Modern Philosophy," *Journal of the History of Ideas* 14 (1953): 528-47.

In the following section, I examine Suárez's contribution to early modern epistemology and metaphysics before I provide a critical reading of his account of creation and individuation.

3. Singularity without Actuality

Influenced by Petrus Damianus's *Letter on Divine Omnipotence* (c. 1060), much of medieval theology explored the nature and modality of God's power and its relation to human intellection, as I discussed in chapter 4. Among the most important stages in the evolution of this and cognate themes were, first of all, the systematic treatment of power and possibility in the *Sentences* of Peter Lombard (c. 1105-1164); second, the distinction of *potentia absoluta* and *potentia ordinata,* which was first conceptualized by Hugo of St. Cher (c. 1200-1263); third, the idea of a plurality of worlds, which was first articulated by Augustinus Triumphus of Ancona (c. 1243-1328).[16] Following the 1277 condemnations, the growing emphasis on divine power and possibility led to the abandonment of Aquinas's real distinction between existence and essence and the emergence of Scotus's formalist and Ockham's nominalist alternative, as I indicated in chapters 5 and 6. Coupled with the continued impact of Avicenna and Porreta on Christian theology since the twelfth and the thirteenth century (as detailed in chapter 4), essence *(essentia)* and singular being *(ens)* — rather than being itself *(esse ipsum)* and common being *(ens commune)* — became the focus of both epistemology and metaphysics.

Central to the rise of early modern philosophy was Petrus Aureoli (c. 1280-1322), a forerunner of Ockham who radicalized Scotus's theory of intuitive knowledge *(notitia intuitiva)* or the immediate intuition of things themselves *(in se)* — that is to say, both their objectity and their proper existence and presence.[17] Aureoli's theory goes beyond Scotus's by positing that intuition provides something absolute *(aliquid abso-*

16. See Olivier Boulnois, ed., *La puissance et son ombre. De Pierre Lombard à Luther* (Paris: Aubier, 1992), pp. 71-78, 131-34, 253-56.

17. Cf. André de Muralt, "La doctrine médiévale des distinctions et l'intelligibilité de la philosophie moderne (I) et (II)," *Revue de théologie et de philosophie* 112 (1980): 113-32, 217-40; John F. Boler, "Intuitive and Abstract Cognition," in *The Cambridge History of Later Medieval Philosophy: From the Rediscovery of Aristotle to the Disintegration of Scholasticism,* ed. Norman Kretzmann, Anthony Kenny, and Jan Pinborg (Cambridge: Cambridge University Press, 1982), pp. 460-78.

lutum), which can be described as the sole foundation *(fundamentum)* upon which all knowledge is built.[18] For this reason, immediate intuition does not require a thing's existence and/or its presence *(existentia et praesentia rei)* because they are no longer indispensable to cognition. Instead of the self-manifestation of things that reflects and intimates God's revelation to his creation, it is henceforth the mind and God's absolute power that are determinative of what is and can be known.

In the wake of Al-Fārābī's theory of abstraction, late medieval and early modern accounts of cognition focus increasingly on the relation between the intellect and things outside the soul *(extra animam)* and between concepts and words (including mental language). Key to these accounts is the distinction between objects of cognition and intentions.[19] If the object is *extra animam,* then the intention is a first intention. If, by contrast, the object is itself an intention, then the intention is a second intention. Aureoli's innovation is to separate predication from acts of cognition and claim that predication concerns the objective concept of the thing, i.e., the conceptual content that is immediately present to the intellect, not the thing as it appears to the senses and is mediated to the mind. His theory shifts knowledge towards the "objective content of the first-order concept that is formed"[20] by the intellect (*In Sententias* I, d. 23, a. 2). Second intentions are no longer founded upon the primary cognition of beings themselves but rather on intentional being *(esse intentionale)*. Intentional being is an objective or represented being *(esse obiective sive repraesentatum)*, i.e., being abstracted from actual existence and present to the senses and the imagination.[21]

Intentional being is paramount in Suárez's epistemology, in particular his understanding of 'objective reality' *(realitas obiectiva)*. For it is as 'objective or represented being' that things are 'presented' to the mind, in the form of objective concepts which are predicable but not present in the

18. *Peter Aureoli Scriptum super Primum Sententiarum, Proemium,* sect. II, art. 3, no. 93, quoted by Courtine, *Suarez et le système de la métaphysique,* p. 164.

19. Christian Knudsen, "Intentions and Impositions," in Kretzmann et al., eds., *The Cambridge History of Later Medieval Philosophy,* pp. 479-95. I am indebted to Knudsen for some arguments in this paragraph.

20. Knudsen, "Intentions and Impositions," p. 490.

21. Timothy J. Cronin, *Objective Being in Descartes and Suarez* (Rome: Gregorian University Press, 1966), pp. 77-89; Robert Pasnau, *Theories of Cognition in the Later Middle Ages* (Cambridge: Cambridge University Press, 1997), pp. 161-294.

very things themselves.[22] For this reason, 'objective and represented being' can be cognized immediately, in itself and as such. Concepts are no longer that with which the mind has knowledge of reality (as for Boethius) but become themselves the objects of knowledge, a theory that Suárez pushes further to the point where the very act of intellection comes to possess its own reality, *realitas obiectiva* (as I will show in the present chapter). Incidentally, Aureoli's account helps inaugurate Ockham's nominalism, in particular the immediate cognition of singulars and the independence of the intellect from the light of faith *(lumen fidei)*.

After Ockham, essence is separated from existence and actuality is devalued in favor of possibility, as I argued in chapter 6. Indeed, the human intellect can be set in motion by divine will rather than by actually present and existing things *(in actu)*. The absoluteness of God's power *(potentia Dei absoluta)* and divine volition presents the mind with objects of knowledge that can *not be*.[23] In turn, this requires a mental ability to cognize things without sense perception, judgment, or the imagination. By contrast with Christian Neo-Platonist relationality, this account privileges individual singular things as the ultimate foundation of concepts and knowledge. Singulars *extra animam* are the primary cause for all concepts and the first object of cognition. However, concepts encompass essences that neither exist nor bear any relation to things in the world. As such, Ockham transforms concepts of objects into "objective concepts without actual present objects."[24]

The epistemology that underpins Ockham's account of divine omnipotence provides the basis for Suárez's system. First of all, this system is based on rejecting the patristic and medieval convertibility of being and knowing and the aesthetic judgment involved in cognition, including Aquinas's idea that in God being is fully intellectual and beings can come to cognize it as such in the beatific vision. Second, the system also

---

22. See Jan Pinborg, "Zum Begriff der Intentio Secunda — Radulphus Brito, Harvaeus Natalis und Petrus Aureoli in Diskussion," *Cahiers de l'Institut du Moyen-Age grec et latin* 13 (1974): 49-59.

23. The separation of *potentia dei ordinata* and *potentia dei absoluta* can be traced to Damianus and was reinforced by Ockham's account of the nature of creation. Cf. Alain de Muralt, "Epoché — Malin Génie — Théologie de la toute puissance divine: Le concept objectif sans objet, recherche d'une structure de pensée," *Studia Philosophica* 26 (1966): 159-91.

24. De Muralt, "Epoché — Malin Génie — Théologie de la toute puissance divine," pp. 180-81.

consecrates the reign of a rival account of knowledge centered upon immediate intuition of objectity and mediate abstraction from actuality (intuitive knowledge being the direct cause of abstractive knowledge). Most importantly, the object of cognition is no longer the relation among individual beings *(ens)* through their sharing in common being *(esse commune)* as well as their relationality to self-subsistent being *(ipsum esse subsistens)*. Instead, the first object of knowledge is singular being in itself and as such. For universality and commonality are *of* the mind *in* the mind, not grounded in the actuality of things.

4. The Reality of Singular Essence and the Possibility of Universal Existence

For all the reasons adduced above, this epistemological shift is important for the relation between being and knowing. Building in part on Scotus and Ockham, Suárez posits a new doctrine of objective knowledge independently of any actual objects. His epistemology extends the idea of pure nature *(pura natura)* and develops a conception of possibility according to which essences are real in the sense of existing in logically possible worlds and capable of existing in the real, actual world *(Dis. Met.* II.iv.9). Since essences can be without actually existing, existence is subordinated to essence. The reality of beings is abstracted from their actual presence and consequently becomes unhinged from their effective manifestation.[25] As a result, nature *(natura)* is cleared of all traces of transcendence and being *(esse)* is drained of any mysterious profundity. Beings no longer intimate their transcendent source which brings them into actuality. The distinction between existence and essence is neither real (Aquinas) nor formal (Scotus) but instead purely mental *(tantum ratione).*[26] Even though the distinction between a thing's existence and its essence is ultimately grounded in *that* thing *(distinctio rationis cum fundamento in re),*[27] it is the mind that alone can ascertain it. Since objectivity is determined by the mind, there is no objectively real difference between the reality of essence and the actuality of existence. Therefore, what counts as a being is primarily determined by the intellect and its concepts, not by the actual reality of being itself.

25. Courtine, *Suarez et le système de la métaphysique,* pp. 157-94.
26. *Dis. Met.* XXXI.i.13 (English translation, pp. 225, 231).
27. *Dis. Met.* XXXI.vi.23 (English translation, p. 250).

Suárez's claim that objectivity — or perhaps more accurately objectity[28] — is primarily in the mind and that things outside the mind are objective in a secondary sense also builds on Ockham's idea of an intuition of nonexistence, by which the latter meant that we can apprehend the reality of things abstracted from their existence.[29] One key difference between the Platonist metaphysics of Gregory, Augustine, Boethius, Dionysus, and Aquinas, on the one hand, and the Aristotelianized ontology of Gilbert, Scotus, Ockham, Buridan, and Suárez, on the other hand, is the nature of the relation of mind to world. For the former thinkers, things make themselves known to the mind in virtue of their beauty and harmony that intimates God and discloses his ongoing creative activity to us, which we can apprehend via sense perception, judgment, and the imagination (as I showed in relation to Aquinas in chapter 5). By contrast, for the latter thinkers it is the mind's intentionality that with the help of divine absolute power discerns a thing's essence and objective reality independently of its actual existence and manifestation.

Suárez's distinct contribution to the rise of modern epistemology is his idea of 'real essence' *(essentia realis)*, i.e., "actually existing essence" *(Dis. Met.* XXXI.i.13). If essences can exist independently of any act of being or existing, then the distinction between essence and existence is mental because the real foundation *(fundamentum in re)* is intelligible only to the intellect, not to sense perception, judgment, or the imagination. Suárez's account is indebted, first of all, to Henry of Ghent's conception of being, in which the notion *(intellectus)* of being is prior to God and to creatures, and second, to Ghent's concept of the being of essence *qua* essence *(esse essentiae)*, which is the being proper to a thing's singular essence. Indeed, Suárez embraces Henry's redefinition of singular being as a 'real thing' *(res)*, rather than a being-in-act *(ens in actu)*. The being of real things *(esse reale)* constitutes the content of what is presented to the mind, i.e., a being abstracted from any reality outside the intellect *(extra*

28. Intentionality and objectity are of course central concepts in modern and contemporary phenomenology, starting with Husserl. See, for instance, Edmund Husserl, *Prolegomena zur reinen Logik* (Tübingen: Max Niemeyer Verlag, 1900), §3. Cf. de Muralt, *La métaphysique du phénomène*, pp. 161-77; Jean-Luc Marion, *Réduction et donation. Recherches sur Husserl, Heidegger et la phénoménologie* (Paris: Presses Universitaires de France, 1989), pp. 11-118.

29. William of Ockham, *Ordinatio sive Scriptum in librum primum Sententiarum*, prol., q. 1, cor. 1. Cf. Pierre Alféri, *Guillaume d'Ockham. Le Singulier* (Paris: Éditions Minuit, 1989), pp. 169-85.

intellectum). As such, *esse reale* is more objective than *esse in actu* because it is reduced to the being of pure essence *(esse essentiae),* freed from the constricting shackles of actuality.

Thus, from Henry to Suárez a twofold change occurs: first of all, identifying *esse essentiae* with *esse reale* and, second, equating *esse reale* with *esse obiectivum.* The significance of this double shift is that the being of essence is the true objective reality of things — a thing's genuine objectity. Jean-François Courtine summarizes this well: "Suárez operates the reduction of a thing to its reality and then from the reality to the objectity."[30] Since concepts derive from particular things *(entia),* 'real essence' is singular, not universal. After Scotus and Ockham, knowledge of being no longer concerns cognition of universals *in re* but instead the formation of concepts of singularity and the quest for principles that individuate things in the first place.

To say that Suárez reinforces the modern turn away from a theological metaphysics towards a formalized ontology and epistemology is not to say that within his system logic and semantics determine metaphysics and theology. Rather, in his *Disputationes Metaphysicae* Suárez appears to embrace Aquinas's theory of subordination of metaphysics and theology to *Scientia Dei (Dis. Met.* proem.). However, such is Suárez's belief in the foundational nature of the highest natural principles proper to metaphysics or first philosophy *(prima philosophia),* that they also secure and confirm the principles of all other sciences, including *sacra doctrina (Dis. Met.* proem.; *Dis. Met.* I.v.15). Moreover, the object of metaphysics encompasses all that falls under the univocity of *ens,* not least God and all separate substances:

> We have shown that the adequate object of this science [metaphysics] must include God and other immaterial substances, but not only those. It must also include not just substances but real accidents too, and not beings of reason and those which are exclusively by accident; however, no object can be such if it is not *ens ut sic;* it is therefore this which constitutes the adequate object.[31]

30. Courtine, *Suarez et le système de la métaphysique,* p. 194.

31. "*Ostentum est enim, obiectum adequatum huius scientiae debere comprehendere Deum, et alias substantias immateriales, non tamen solas illas. Item debere comprehendere non tantum substantias, sed etiam entia realia, non tamen entia rationis, et omnino per accidens; sed huiusmodi obiectum nullum aliud esse potest praeter ens ut sic; ergo illud est obiectum adequatum*" (*Dis. Met.* I.i.26).

The guiding principle of metaphysics is formal reason *(ratio formalis sub qua)*, according to which all the various investigations of *ens* are systematically ordered towards the unity of being. So from Aquinas's theory of subalternation via Scotus's univocity of being, Suárez's definition of the adequate object of metaphysics extends the autonomy of first philosophy from theology and its subsequent primacy over all sciences, all in the name of the univocity and unity of being which precede the analogy and the plurality of beings. Since God is granted the status of 'principal object' *(obiectum praecipuum)*, which signifies the special object (that which has more of which everything else has less — the power of possibility), metaphysics so configured "subjects God to the realm of this science."[32]

Moreover, Suárez specifies the adequate object of metaphysics as *ens in quantum ens reale,* i.e., being insofar as it is real being, defined as "that which has a real essence,"[33] independently of its manifestation and abstracted from actuality. This confirms the break with the patristic and medieval account of beings in relation with God who can be participated in. On the basis of 'real essence' and 'real being,' Suárez develops a metaphysics that exceeds Scotus's elevation of univocal being above God by positing a common subject-matter (univocal *ens reale*) and a common 'reason' both to metaphysics and to theology. In response to the separation and increasing autonomy of natural and revealed theology since Scotus and Ockham, the rationale for Suárez is to include God and all that is created under one and the same logic of investigation (*Dis. Met.* I.i.11 and 13). The significance of the redefinition of the object of philosophy and theology is that abstraction from the actuality of existence and the reduction of reality to objectity are (epistemo-)logical preconditions for all sciences, including theology (*Dis. Met.* I.i.21).

Having thus expanded the boundary of metaphysics to include theology, Suárez completes the crucial modern turn of Baroque scholasticism by identifying the subject of metaphysics with its proper object. Since substantiality is the ultimate ground or foundation for all entities, including accidents (*Dis. Met.* I.i.21), the subject of metaphysics is the substance insofar as it is substance. As cited above, the 'adequate object' of metaphysics, which must include all substances, is being as such *(ens*

---

32. "*. . . ergo absolute Deus cadit sub obiectum huius scientiae [. . .]*" (*Dis. Met.* I.i.19).

33. "*quod sit habens essentiam realem*" (*Dis. Met.* II.iv.5). See Courtine, *Suarez et le système de la métaphysique,* pp. 243-76.

ut sic).[34] This is why Suárez follows Buridan in arguing that the proper object of metaphysics is substance *qua* substance, freed from all determinations, materiality and immateriality, infinity and finitude, actuality and possibility.[35] So Suárez equates substantiality with beingness *(étantité)* or being as such *(ens ut sic)*. For both are absolutely indeterminate and thereby encompass God who has neither first principles nor final ends. The only concept that is common to all substances and all beings *qua* beings is the 'objective concept of being' *(conceptus obiectivus entis, Dis. Met.* I.i.21), obtained by the reduction of a thing's actuality to its reality and from its reality to its objectity.

The reason why for Suárez the actuality of existent things does not disclose anything about their singularity is that a thing's 'real essence' is always already singular. Curiously, essences do not need to be actualized in order to be individuated. Since essences are endowed with their own being *(esse essentiae)* and in this sense are real *(Dis. Met.* II.iv.9), essences do not call forth actualization. In fact, being in itself and as such *(ens ut sic)* is 'real being' *(ens reale)* and has a higher reality than actual beings precisely because it is "that which has a real essence."[36] Contrary to the Christian Neo-Platonism discussed in this essay, Suárez's real being is not a being in act — *id quod est* or *ens*, i.e., an existence-essence compound that is brought into being by *ipsum esse*. But instead the Suárezian real being is the substratum for singularity, an existent that is at the service of a singular essence. As I argue in the following section, existence makes no difference to the singularity of 'real essences.' That is how individuation becomes unhinged from divine creation and actualization.

5. Singularity as Transcendental Precondition

Suárez outlines his account of individuation in Part V of his *Disputationes Metaphysicae*, which are composed of fifty-four disputations and were first published in Salamanca in 1597.[37] As Gracia indicates, the fact

---

34. See, *supra*, note 31.

35. Suárez writes that *"Sexta opinio, quae Buridani esse dicitur, est obiectum adaequatum huius scientiae esse substantiam, quatenus substantia est, id est, ut abstrahit a materiali et immateriali, finita et infinita"* (*Dis. Met.* I.i.21). The reference to Buridan is *Qu. Met.* VII, q. 1.

36. See, *supra*, note 33.

37. Francisco Suárez, *De unitate individuali eiusque principio*, English translation:

that Suárez discusses individuation in the fifth disputation highlights the importance he attaches to this question.[38] Only four other questions precede it: the nature of metaphysics, the essential nature or concept of being, the transcendental attributes of being (unity, truth, and goodness), and transcendental unity. The discussion of individuation or individual unity is followed by that of formal and universal unity (in the sixth and the seventh disputation). The order of the disputations is significant because it reflects the order within Suárez's metaphysical system. Just as unity is prior to truth and goodness in Suárez's metaphysical system, so individuality is prior to universality. Before I discuss this double priority, I will set out the structure of Suárez's discussion of individuality in the fifth disputation.

His discussion is divided into nine sections. The first two sections concern the metaphysical determination of the unity of individuals, in particular the definition and the formal delimitation of the 'individual difference' *(differentia individualis)* in terms of the link between the specific difference and the genus. Sections 4, 5, and 6 focus on the physical determination of the unity of individuals, namely the physical real foundation of the individual (or individuating) difference. Sections 7, 8, and 9 address the principle of individuation of accidents. The metaphysical determination as set out in sections 1 and 2 frames Suárez's entire account of individuation. Section 1 raises the question of the nature and the extent of individuality in things that exist or can exist. This question concerns the relation between simplicity and plurality. Suárez argues that this problematic is common to the metaphysics of the one and the many and the theology of creation (*Dis. Met.* V.i.1). Likewise, he posits in the same section 1 the following assumption which underlies his entire metaphysical treatment of individuation: "[A]ll things that are actual beings or that exist or can exist immediately, are singular and individual."[39] For Suárez, individuality is a *positum,* not a *quaesitum,* and it is ultimately an a priori claim, not an object of investigation. For a thing's individuality always already is and as such provides the foundation for indi-

---

Suárez on individuation: Metaphysical disputation V, Individual Unity and Its Principle, trans. and ed. J. J. E. Gracia (Milwaukee: Marquette University Press, 1982).

38. Jorge J. E. Gracia, "Francis Suárez (b. 1548; d. 1617)," in Gracia, ed., *Individuation in Scholasticism: The Later Middle Ages and the Counter-Reformation 1150-1650* (Albany: State University of New York Press, 1994), pp. 476-77.

39. *"res omnes quae sunt actualia entia, seu quatenus existunt, vel existere possunt immediate, esse singulares ac individuas"* (*Dis. Met.* V.i.4).

viduation. Entities are self-individuating in virtue of the individual unity that constitutes them. In this way, Suárez immanentizes the principle of individuation and thereby excludes divine creation as an account of why things are individual and to what end they desire to be individuated.

Suárez's definition of individuality in terms of unity derives from his treatment of transcendental unity in the fourth disputation. In line with the scholastic idea of the convertibility of the transcendentals which was systematized by Thomas Aquinas (as I discussed in chapter 5),[40] Suárez defines transcendental unity as the unity that is 'convertible with being.' Since everything that is one is a being and everything that is a being is one, being *(ens)* and the one *(unum)* are coterminous. As such, unity is not accidental to being; it is essential to being. However, the disagreement among scholastics is about whether unity adds anything to being and, if so, what the nature of this addition might be — real or conceptual. For Suárez, who invokes Aristotle, Aquinas, and Cajetan, unity does not add anything at all to being: "Unity and being are one and the same nature, because unity does not express any positive notion other than the notion of being."[41]

However, unity and being are not identical because they are distinguished by nominal as well as formal and objective differences: "not only because it [unity] is one of its attributes, but because the names ['one' and 'being'] are not synonymous, and to them correspond diverse *formal and objective concepts in the mind*."[42] As I argued in the previous section, the objective concept of being *(conceptus obiectivus entis)* is more objective than an actually existing thing because it captures a thing's real singular essence. So just as there is an objective concept of being in the mind that is more real than beings in actuality because it abstracts essence from existence, so there is an objective concept of unity that is also more real in the mind than in the actual beings in act because it abstracts from individual unity. The implication is that the actuality of indi-

---

40. *ST* I[a], q. 11, a. 1. Cf. Jan A. Aertsen, "Die Transzendentalienlehre bei Thomas von Aquin in ihren historischen Hintergründen und philosophischen Motiven," in Albert Zimmermann, ed., *Thomas von Aquin. Werk und Wirkung im Licht neuer Forschung* (Berlin and New York: De Gruyter, 1988), pp. 82-102.

41. *"unum et esse unam ac eamdem naturam, quia nimirum nullam rationem positivam dicit praeter rationem entis"* (*Dis. Met.* V.i.6).

42. *"unum aliquo modo distingui ab ente, quia et est passio eius et illa nomina non sunt synonyma, sed diversi conceptus formales et obiectivi illis in mente respondent"* (*Dis. Met.* V.i.12; my italics).

vidual beings does not disclose anything about their unity. Instead, a priori transcendental unity is an absolute precondition for things being known as unified and individuated. Likewise, the a priori transcendental unity of univocal being is an absolute precondition for things to be unified and individuated.

Suárez's variant of the convertibility of being and the one implies that transcendental and individual unity are coextensive, i.e., transcendental unity as an attribute of 'real being' applies univocally to being as such and to individual beings. Put differently, transcendental unity can be and is instantiated in actual individual existing things. What is new in Suárez is the idea that objects without any actual existing equivalents also embody transcendental unity. Unity is both univocal and transcendental. Unity applies univocally to the Creator and his creation. Transcendental unity cannot be discerned on the basis of the unity of individual things. Instead, the intellect needs to abstract from actually existing individuals and form an objective concept of unity before it can cognize the unity of beings. Even though individual unity has a *fundamentum in re*,[43] Suárez discards Aquinas's aesthetic judgment in the discernment of *convenientia* between transcendentals in favor of a conceptualism based on reason alone.

In fact, Suárez rejects two different positions: first of all, Scotus's idea that there can be two kinds of unity in a thing (the unity of the nature and the unity of the individual); second, Aquinas's idea that unity is proportional and analogous to an individual's station in the hierarchical order of being — God's unity is different from that of angels whose unity is different from that of humans. Suárez's conception of unity in terms of a univocal transcendental category destroys not only the incipient dualism in Scotus's idea of a double unity but also and above all Aquinas's analogy between the transcendent Creator and his creation. Unity as a transcendental prepares the modern path towards Descartes's 'objective reality' of ideas independently of the object represented by them as well as Kant's transcendental a priori and the conditions of possibility of knowledge outside the direct relation between subject and object,[44] as I will suggest in chapter 9.

43. See, *supra*, note 27.
44. For a concise genealogical account from Scotus and Ockham via Suárez and Descartes to Kant, see de Muralt, "Kant, le dernier occamien. Une nouvelle définition de la philosophie moderne," *Revue de Métaphysique et de Morales* 80 (1975): 32-53; de Muralt, *L'unité de la philosophie politique. De Scot, Occam et Suarez au libéralisme contemporain* (Paris: Vrin, 2002), pp. 17-28.

The emphasis on reason at the expense of sense perception and judgment has important consequences for Suárez's metaphysics of individuality. The priority of unity over other attributes like truth and goodness implies that unity precedes all forms of distinction and diversity. In this way, he seeks to safeguard God's oneness and simplicity against the multiplicity and plurality of creation (*Dis. Met.* IV.i.16). This amounted to a devaluation of particular sensible things. Rather than being a diverse reflection of the single self-diffusive Good, particulars manifest nothing but their singular self. Likewise, the preeminence of transcendental unity betrays the primacy of metaphysics over all other sciences and the univocity of *ens reale* vis-à-vis both God and his creation. Metaphysics as first philosophy conditions theology and subordinates the theo-onto-logic of creation to the heno-logic of the one.

This account has far-reaching implications for the question of individuation. Individual unity is transcendentally determined and thus constitutes an a priori assumption rather than an object of metaphysical investigation that can be demonstrated. If a thing's individuality is its real singular essence, then individuation is 'situated' exclusively within things themselves. Indeed, in paragraph 2 of section 1 of the fifth disputation on individual unity, Suárez defines individuality in terms that suggest individuals are self-individuating rather than being individuated through relations with other individuals or with God — as Augustine, Boethius, Aquinas, and other Christian Neo-Platonists argued:

> That is called 'common' or 'universal' which is communicated to many entities or is found in many entities according to one single nature. On the other hand, that is called 'one in number' or 'singular' or 'individual' which is one being in such a way that, according to that nature of being through which it is called 'one,' it is not communicable to many entities. For example, to those that are lower to or placed below it, or to those that are many under that nature. . . .[45]

Suárez agrees with Aquinas that to be individual is not to be able to communicate oneself to any other entity because an individual cannot be di-

45. *"Commune enim seu universale dicitur quod secundum unam aliquam rationem multis communicatur seu in multis reperitur; unum autem numero seu singulare ac individuum dicitur quod ita est unum ens, ut secundum eam entis rationem, qua unum dicitur, non sit communicabile multis, ut inferioribus et sibi subiectis, aut quae in illa ratione multa sint"* (*Dis. Met.* V.i.2).

vided into entities without being destroyed as an individual. Nor can it be participated in. The contrast that Suárez draws is between individuals and universals. The latter are communicable because they are divisible and participable.[46] The incommunicability of individuals paradoxically implies their 'self'-communication. All individual self-communicative things are entities that express nothing but their own individual unity, secured by the transcendental unity of univocal being.[47]

However, Suárez disagrees with Aquinas on why individuality is incommunicable. Unlike Aquinas, for whom individuality and relationality are coextensive and thus individuation and differentiation are simultaneous, unity for Suárez precedes individuality and individuation. The incommunicability of individuality follows not only from Suárez's emphasis on the unity of individuals but also from the concomitant subordination of differentiation and multiplicity. He argues that to be an individual precedes being differentiated from other individuals and being numerically multiplied within the same species (*Dis. Met.* V.i.7; V.iii.12). For Suárez then, unity and self-identity ground individuality and determine individuation.

Moreover, Suárez makes individuality in God and in all creatures identical and thereby denies that individuality (and also universality) is analogous rather than univocal. He also argues that all actual beings are individual because individuality is intrinsic to individuals, prior to and independent of any relations with other individuals (*Dis. Met.* V.ii.28). Individuality belongs to everything that exists immediately (*Dis. Met.* V.i.4).[48] For there is only one kind of individuality in the entire *cosmos,* grounded in the reality of transcendental unity. Since unity is convertible with being, everything that is actual exhibits necessarily the unity of individuality. Actual beings (including spiritual beings, composite beings, material beings, and all their properties) are individual. By contrast, forms, universals, and natures such as humanity are not — they have a purely conceptual unity which is not individual. If all actually existing things are individual because they derive from the individuality of tran-

---

46. See Courtine, *Nature et Empire de la Loi,* pp. 69-90, esp. pp. 74-81.

47. Courtine, *Nature et Empire de la Loi,* pp. 81-90. However, on the question of 'expression' Courtine omits Spinoza from his account of Suárez's legacy. Suárez's conception of individual unity as an instantiation of transcendental unity marks a move that foreshadows Spinoza's understanding of all finite individuals as expressions of the unique infinite substance. See, *infra,* chapter 8, section 6.

48. See, *supra,* note 39.

scendental unity which is a priori, then this raises questions of how individuals can be individuated and why.

6. The Self-Individuation of Entities

Suárez's own account of individuation attempts to chart an alternative beyond the realism of Aquinas's idea of designated matter, the formalism of Scotus's *haecceitas,* and the nominalism of Ockham's singularity (*Dis. Met.* V.ii.2-6). This alternative consists of four elements. First of all, Suárez argues that the individual adds something real to common nature (not as the concept in the mind but as it is found in real things) because individuality gives the common nature an individual unity that is real because the one and being are convertible: "I say, first, that the individual adds something real to the common nature, by reason of which it is such individual and there comes to it the negation of divisibility into many [individuals] similar [to itself]."[49] Individuality is not a mere name or concept but is in a thing because it is only in virtue of individuality that something is *this* rather than *that.*

However, second, individual unity — that which is added to the common nature — is not really or modally different from it because the common nature is not real independently of the individual: "I say, second, that the individual as such does not add anything distinct *ex natura rei* from the specific nature."[50] After Scotus and Ockham, a reversal occurs in the order of universality and individuality. Whereas for Aquinas the question is how the particular can entertain a relation with the universal, for Scotus, Ockham, and Suárez the question is how the common or the universal can be in the singular. For humanity per se is not real in the same way as an individual. Humanity is only real in Plato, in Aristotle, etc. There is no composition of humanity and individuality. There is identity because, transcendentally secured, individual unity is indivisible. And since the objective concept of being is the ultimate arbiter of what can be known, the difference between individual unity and the common nature is conceptual: "I say, third, that the individual adds to

49. "*Dico primo: individuum aliquid reale addit praeter naturam communem, ratione cuius tale individuum est et ei convenit illa negatio divisibilitatis in plura similia*" (*Dis. Met.* V.ii.8).

50. "*Dico secundo: individuum, ut sic, non addit aliquid ex natura rei distinctum a natura specifica*" (*Dis. Met.* V.ii.9).

the common nature something conceptually distinct from it, belonging to the same category and metaphysically composing the individual as an individual difference which contracts the species and constitutes the individual."[51]

But what does 'conceptual' difference mean? According to Gracia, "conceptual distinctions do not hold between mental entities: they are grounded in reality."[52] Without sense perception and judgment, there is no way for the mind to ascertain the reality of things upon which this conceptual distinction is founded — other than by way of abstract concepts that the mind somehow projects onto the world. For Suárez, all knowledge is knowledge by abstraction and through concepts that refer to singular essences (*Dis. Met.* V.i.4). So while he insists that individuality is not confined to the concept of individual unity but extends to real things, only mental abstraction of singular essences from a thing's existence gives the mind access to *that* thing's individuality, not its phenomenal manifestation and sensory apprehension or judgment. Unlike Augustine, Boethius, and Aquinas, Suárez sees the mind as the final arbiter of what individual unity is. Indeed, the devaluation of phenomenality in favor of the conceptualism of reason is evinced by the application of individual unity to material and immaterial beings alike: "I say, fourth, that the individual adds something conceptually distinct to the species not only in material things and accidents, but also in created and finite immaterial substances."[53] Therefore, against Thomas's idea of matter-form compounds, Suárez denies that in things there is composition and real difference between the essence and the act of being which brings things into actuality.

To deny composition and real difference is to exclude existence (or the act of being) as the cause of individuation. Suárez's exclusively conceptual approach to actuality and possibility reinforces his rejection of this Thomist account. But his approach can be questioned. At the level of objective concept, there is no difference between the individuality of

51. *"Dico tertio: individuum addere supra naturam communem aliquid ratione distinctum ab illa, ad idem praedicamentum pertinens, et individuum componens metaphysicae, tamquam differentia individualis contrahens speciem et individuum constituens"* (*Dis. Met.* V.ii.16).

52. Gracia, "Francis Suárez (b. 1548; d. 1617)," p. 493.

53. *"Dico quarto: individuum non solum in rebus materialibus et accidentibus, sed etiam in substantiis immaterialibus creatis et finitis addit aliquid ratione distinctum supra speciem"* (*Dis. Met.* V.ii.21).

an existing actual and a nonexisting possible individual. However, at the level of reality, there is a genuine difference. As I argued in chapter 5, for Thomas nothing other than God can bring itself into existence. Likewise, everything except God stands in potency to the actuality of being which causes all things to be and makes them what they are. As such, each being *(ens)* exhibits a *real* difference between its actuality and its potency and by extension between existence and essence. For form instantiated in body (or form joined to being in the case of angels) is not fully actualized but instead desires perfection. This is what individuation is — the ever more intense formation of individuals. On the contrary, for Suárez who 'locates' objective reality at the level of the intellect and its concepts, the difference between actuality and potency and between existence and essence is exclusively conceptual. Actuality adds nothing to individuality and so, according to Suárez, existence (Aquinas's act of being) cannot possibly individuate beings.

Having dismissed individuation by matter, form, and existence, the logic that underpins Suárez's conceptualism leads him to develop the idea that the principle of individuation is entity *(entitas)*. This claim is that entities are self-individuating: "[I]t seems that every singular substance is singular in itself, that is, by its entity, and needs no other principle of individuation in addition to its entity, or in addition to the intrinsic principles that constitute its entity."[54] The entity that constitutes an individual thing is nothing but "the essence as it exists" (*Dis. Met.* VII.i.12 and 19). So Suárez argues that individuals self-individuate because individuality is the nature of the existence of essences — individuality *is* how essences exist. Since the essence of individual finite things is the compound of form and matter, he concludes his fifth disputation by stating that "the adequate principle of individuation is this matter and this form in union. The form alone is the sufficient and chief principle so that the composite, as an individual thing of a certain species, can be considered numerically one and the same thing."[55] This signifies that the actually existing essence is its own immanent principle of individuation because it does not require a transcendent act of being in order to be brought into

---

54. *"omnem substantiam singularem* [*se ipsa, seu per entitatem suam, esse singularem*] *neque alio indigere individuationis principio praeter suam entitatem, vel praeter principia intrinseca quibus eius entitas constat"* (*Dis. Met.* V.vi.1).

55. *". . . adequatum individuationis principium esse hanc materiam et hanc formam inter se unitas, inter quae praecipuum principium est forma, quae sola sufficit, ut hoc compositum, quatenus est individuum talis speciei, idem numero censeatur"* (*Dis. Met.* V.vi.15).

existence. A real essence always already exists because it is endowed with its own being *(esse essentiae).* So configured, individuation becomes unhinged from creation, as Suárez locates the principle of individuation within individual things and limits God's creative action to efficient causality, which the following section shows.

7. Creation as Efficient Causality

In the *Disputationes Metaphysicae* XX-XXII, Suárez argues that creation *ex nihilo* is amenable to human reason and that it explains the coming into being and the preservation of material substances, as well as their concurrence with divine action.[56] But unlike the patristic and medieval metaphysics of relationality and participation, Suárez's system redirects the focus away from the actuality of effects that intimate the first cause towards the univocity of being and a priori transcendental unity. All things are created by God in the sense of being brought into existence and sustained in being. However, the reality of essences precedes the actuality of existence, which signifies that a thing's actual phenomenal appearance does not disclose any relation with God, first principle, and final end. The subordination of existence to essence implies that the createdness (or creatureliness) of things is purely conceptual and lacks any phenomenality. Creation provides a general framework that explains the causation of things, but it cannot account for their singularity.

Indeed, just as Suárez proceeds from the transcendental *ens reale* to the concrete reality of an individual thing, so he moves from creation in general to the specific causation of particulars (*Dis. Met.* XX.ii.24-26).[57] As a result, he maintains that entities are principally created by God but some specific things may not be: "[A] power that corresponds adequately to a certain sort of creation, rather than to creation as such, need not be absolutely universal; therefore, it is not necessary that such a power should be proper to the First Cause."[58] Moreover, his emphasis on

56. Translated by Alfred J. Freddoso in "Introduction: Suárez on Metaphysical Inquiry, Efficient Causality, and Divine Action," in Francisco Suárez, *On Creation, Conservation, and Concurrence: Metaphysical Disputations 20, 21, and 22,* trans. and ed. Alfred J. Freddoso (South Bend, IN: St. Augustine's Press, 2002), pp. xi-cxxiii.

57. Schmutz, "La doctrine médiévale des causes et la théologie de la nature pure (XIIIe-XVIIe siècles)," pp. 217-64.

58. *"potentia quae non respicit adequate creationem ut sic, sed talem creationem, sit*

abstraction at the expense of sense perception and judgment leads him to privilege the probability of a general theory of creation rather than the certainty of demonstration based on the 'created' shape of actual things and the phenomenal visibility of creative action: "I believe that on the basis of the things that have been made it can be shown with a very high degree of probability that an absolutely infinite power is required for the creation of any entity whatsoever."[59]

Ultimately, Suárez cuts the links between creation and final causes and identifies God's creative action with efficient causality alone. For the exclusion of actuality from metaphysics and the shift towards immanent self-individuation eliminated the relation between the actualization of things and their *telos*. Ever more intense existing (or participation in the act of being) is no longer crucial to a thing's fulfillment of its God-given form because existence does not matter to essence. Since entities self-individuate, independently of God's creative action, creation explains how something is produced, but not to what end. Suárez's identification of creation with efficient causality deprives his metaphysics of the ability to explain *why* all things desire to be individuated and how God's creativity is fundamental to the individuation of entities that are created individual. His commitment to conceptualism — the claim that 'objective reality' is more real than the actuality of things — rules out any account of the difference that actualization makes and why things, as it were, desire to be brought into being and to be actualized further.

As I argue in the following chapter, Spinoza attempts precisely to answer these two questions. First, what difference does actuality make to individuality (and actualization to individuation)? Second, why do entities 'wish' to be individuated? Before I can give an account of Spinoza's theory of individuation, I will conclude on Suárez. In this section I have argued that his negotiation of the relation between metaphysics and theology and his theory of the self-individuation of entities identifies God's creative action with efficient causality. Suárez excludes God's creativity from final and formal causality and therefore could not explain why individuals desire ever more intense individuation, an idea that Augustine, Boethius, and Aquinas call the perfectibility of form and the perfection

---

universalissimae potentia, ergo non oportet sit propria primae causae" (*Dis. Met.* XX.ii.26 [English translation, p. 761]).

59. *"censeo ex rebus factis probabilissime ostendi ad cuiusvis rei creationem requiri potentiam simpliciter infinitam"* (*Dis. Met.* XX.ii.40 [English translation, p. 766]).

of individuality. Suárez's conception of creation in terms of efficient causality and his account of pure nature and expression prepare the way for Spinoza's system. Instrumental to this transition is Suárez's transformation of the natural law tradition. In the following section, I discuss Suárez's account of natural law and analyze the link between the metaphysical and political dimension of individuation.

8. Natural Law and Transcendental Politics? Sovereignty and Alienation

Suárez's metaphysics of individuality has a decisive impact on his understanding of natural law theory and on the natural law tradition as a whole. In line with his shift from the actuality of existence in the world to the reality of essence in the mind, his account of law and ethics moves the precept of natural law away from a phenomenally visible order in external nature to an order that is internal to the intellect. He accomplishes this modern turn of the natural law tradition by grounding the natural law both in the will and in reason. Unlike *lumen naturale* and *synderesis* in Aquinas, Suárez maintains that will is essential to law because law is "an act of a just and right will by which a superior wills to oblige his inferiors to do this or that."[60]

At the same time, natural law requires reason, in the sense that only reason (and not faith) can ascertain whether an obligation is integral to the demands of nature. In other words, Suárez attempts to conjoin late medieval rationalism which we owe to Scotus's separation of reason from faith with late medieval voluntarism which we owe to Ockham's separation of *potentia Dei absoluta* from *potentia Dei ordinata*.[61] The voluntarist dimension of Suárez's conception of natural law prevails over the rationalist dimension because will has a normative function while reason makes normativity intelligible but does not decree it: "For the intellect is able merely to point out a necessity existing in the object itself, and if such necessity does not exist, the intellect cannot impart it; whereas the will endows the object with a necessity which did not for-

---

60. ". . . *actum voluntatis iustae et rectae, quo superior vult inferiorem obligare ad hoc, vel illud faciendum*" (*De Leg.* I.v.24 [English translation, p. 82]).

61. William Courtenay, *Capacity and Volition: A History of the Distinction of Absolute and Ordained Power* (Bergamo: Pierluigi Lubrina Editore, 1990), esp. pp. 119-26.

merly characterize it."[62] According to Suárez, law is binding, not because reason validates it but because the lawgiver confers onto law its obligatory quality. This is why neither nature nor reason is sufficient to secure natural law:

> Although the rational nature is the foundation of the objective goodness of the moral actions of human beings, it may not for that reason be termed law; and, by the same token, that nature may be spoken of as a standard, yet it is not correct to conclude on that ground that it is law, for 'standard' is a term of wider application than is 'law.'[63]

This passage highlights Suárez's departure from the shared theological realism of Christian Neo-Platonism and his embrace of Porreta's and Scotus's formalism and Ockham's nominalism, insofar as nature or the world no longer discloses God's will or intentionality and as such does not provide a source for objective knowledge of natural law. This moves knowledge from the reality of actual particular sensible things to the mind and the will. Sense perception and judgment are subordinate to abstraction and volition. For individual judgment has a directive rather than a legislative function: it orients the rationality of the mind towards the necessity of the law "but it does not sanction it as law."[64] Human will is the key determinant of natural law.

The prominence of voluntarism and rationalism in natural law theory is not new in seventeenth-century scholastic Spain but can in fact be traced back to the first half of the fourteenth century when a number of nominalist theologians, chief of all Ockham, provided a theological justification for the divine right of kings in general and the absolutist rule of King Louis of Bavaria in particular.[65] Suárez is part of this tradition of natural law theory to the extent that he espouses the primacy of will over judgment and the devaluation of the divine *cosmos* in favor of the rationality of the intellect.

However, he diverges from this legacy in two related ways that have direct consequences for his theory of individuation. First, he rejects Ockham's idea that God's will is unintelligible to the human mind. In-

---

62. *De Leg.* I.v.15 (English translation, p. 66).
63. *De Leg.* II.v.6 (English translation, p. 181).
64. Dupré, *Passage to Modernity,* p. 137.
65. Coleman, "Ockham's Right Reason and the Genesis of the Political as 'Absolutist,'" *History of Political Thought* 20 (1999): 35-64.

stead, he seeks to tie divine volition to nature by arguing that God's will can in fact be rationally known and God wills what is good in the nature of things (*De Leg.* II.vi.11). As such, knowledge of the divine will enables knowledge of what is good in beings as they are. This constitutes a reaction against the attempt of nominalism to erase God from nature and to replace the relation of creation with a model of arbitrary divine intervention.

Following Aquinas on this point, Suárez views the good as real insofar as things that actually exist are good in the sense of actualizing their form. Not unlike the Christian Neo-Platonist idea of the natural desire of the supernatural good in God, goodness in actually existing beings can also be for Suárez an inclination or capacity for the good because the good adds agreeability to being (*Dis. Met.* X.i.12). And what is agreeable is rightly desired. There is then between a thing that is good and a being that is inclined towards goodness a real relation (*Dis. Met.* XLVII), a configuration that opposes in advance Descartes's dualism between the knowing subject and the known object. This real relation individuates the subject insofar as it actualizes the subject's potency to know and fulfills the subject's desire for the good.

However, as I indicated in the previous section, Suárez's natural law theory differs from the Thomist tradition in terms of the metaphysical and theological status of nature. The turn away from self-transcendent to pure nature and the concomitant separation of nature and grace (and reason and faith) undermine the relational dimension of individuation. For the ultimate cause that individuates corporeal substances is no longer the real relation between creatures and their Creator God but instead is the nature of individual entities themselves, i.e., their real essences, cognoscible in themselves and as such. Equally, from the hypothesis of pure nature follows a profoundly abstract conception of natural law that separates knowledge of legal entitlements and obligations from actual political practices. This fundamental change is evinced by three distinct yet connected moves: first of all, Suárez's conception of reason sundered from faith; second, his separation of the will from the faculty of judgment; third, the bestowal of individual rights independently of shared political structures.

This abstractness introduces a formality into the natural law tradition which threatens the reality of actually practicing relations between members of living communities. Rather than relating natural law to the operation of the created universe, Suárez grounds natural rights and duties solely in the will and thereby separates knowledge and exercise of the law from any collective discernment and joint practices, thereby undermining the social and communal nature of the individual. This opens up an autonomous space for individual rights independently of shared political institutions and mutual practices. Accordingly, human beings are individuated by exercising their sovereign will rather than by participating in a common polity.

The second way in which Suárez departs from the thirteenth- and fourteenth-century natural law tradition is by challenging the absoluteness of monarchical power which purports to be divinely sanctioned. He does so in the name of reason and revelation and by founding sovereignty upon human community, rather than the monarchy or the individual.[66] Indeed, imperial decrees are only binding insofar as they correspond to the exigencies of reason and the truth of revelation. Likewise, sovereignty emanates from the people:

> [T]his [legislative] power, viewed solely according to the nature of things, resides not in any individual man but rather in the whole body of mankind. . . . In the nature of things all men are born free; so that, consequently, no person has political jurisdiction over another person, even as no person has dominion over another; nor is there any reason why such power should [simply] in the nature of things, be attributed to certain persons over certain other persons, rather than *vice versa*.[67]

Neither reason nor revelation warrants the primacy of the individual over the collective or of the sovereign all-powerful monarchy over the people. Instead, sovereignty is grounded in the social and political body composed of all men who are born free and equal. As André de Muralt has documented, Suárez's *Defensio fidei* is an attack on the doctrine of the divine right of kings championed by James VI of Scotland (James I of England).[68] The aim is to reconfigure the relation between the absolute sovereignty of the people and the absolute sovereignty of the king who does not invoke the divine authority directly in order to establish his power and righteousness. The main innovation is to say that the original

---

66. De Muralt, *L'unité de la philosophie politique,* pp. 115-22.
67. *De Leg.* III.ii.3 (English translation, p. 374).
68. De Muralt, *L'unité de la philosophie politique,* pp. 115-56.

organic unity of the body politic is neither the result of divine volition nor the product of a social contract. Rather, in virtue of God's creation of human nature, this unity is both divine and natural and its constitution is an equal function of divine and natural law (*Def. fidei* III.i.7). For creation marks the immediate investment of the people with the power that is from God (*potestas a deo*). The power of the prince is grounded exclusively in the absolute sovereignty of the people (*Def. fidei* III.iv.1).

What distinguishes Aquinas's medieval account of metaphysical and political power from Suárez's early modern alternative is the nonhierarchical nature of popular unity. Unlike the patristic and medieval Christian Neo-Platonist idea of different degrees of being and goodness that characterize the created order, Suárez's formalism (bequeathed by Porreta and Scotus, as I have already indicated) flattens the whole of creation by eliminating any hierarchical differentiations amongst individuals. The natural state of created being in general and humanity in particular is an original democracy, the rule of entire people without any real distinction, for all humans share a natural desire for natural blessedness: "[T]he finality of civilian power is the natural felicity of the perfect human community."[69] It is the unity of this natural desire that constitutes the people as a 'single mystical body' (*unum corpus mysticum*).

So to describe the organic social and political community as primary is to secularize the patristic and medieval vision of the *corpus mysticum* as the highest community on earth, the profound and permanent spiritual union within the church in the reciprocal love of the Holy Spirit, in the words of Saint Paul. This constitutes a fundamental difference between Suárez's and Aquinas's account of politics. Whereas the *Doctor Angelicus* draws a real distinction between the theological community of the *corpus mysticum* and the secular realm of political governance,[70] the *Doctor Eximius* posits a formal distinction within a real identity. As such, the theological body is conflated with the secular body and the mystical body now denotes primarily the population — not the ecclesial community. What generates and sustains the unity of mankind is not God's creative and concurrent action coupled with human agency.

---

69. *"[Potestatis civilis] finem esse felicitatem naturalem communitatis humanae perfectae"* (*De Leg.* III.xi.7 [English translation, p. 456]).

70. Henri de Lubac, *Corpus mysticum. L'Eucharistie et l'Église au moyen âge* (Paris: Aubier-Montaigne, 1949), pp. 123-52.

Instead, Suárez's embrace of Porretan and Scotist formalism prizes apart matter and form and by extension (as a result of the metaphysical foundation of politics) divorces the human embodied community from its immaterial form.

In consequence, the natural organic unity of the social body precedes the supernatural spiritual unity of the theological body. Thus, the operation of the *corpus mysticum* is severed from divine creative activity. This rupture has two implications. First, the mystical community as a primarily political entity is cut off from divine creative action. For the operation of the human secular sphere is now thought to be independent of God's creativity. Second, the political community is not unified and sustained by any collective 'drive' to the supernatural as there is in Aquinas's account of *corpus mysticum*.[71] For grace is now conceived of as being so extrinsic that the communal dimension of the mystical community is completely naturalized. The state of nature is in some sense independent of human creatureliness and defines the space within which the God-given desire for the supernatural operates. According to Suárez, nature is not infused with this desire by God's supernatural grace, as it is for Aquinas.

Likewise, the priority of the organic body over the political body implies that the state of nature is somehow apolitical — a radical break away from the ancient, patristic, and medieval tradition of man as a political animal and the irreducibly political dimension of the created order. In consequence, the constitution of political communities and a common polity is in some fundamental sense counter-natural and as such causes alienation. Suárez accounts for this claim as follows. First, his emphasis on will leads him to relate community not to God's act of creation and the renewed covenant in Christ but to the sovereign "will of all who were assembled therein [in the community]."[72] This would suggest that will is after all collective and as such provides a safeguard against the incipient individualism of an anarchic democracy based on the equal rights of all men. Indeed, for Suárez what is required in order to form a political union is a

> special volition or common assent, by which they [men] are gathered together into one political body through one bond of fellowship and

71. De Lubac, *Corpus mysticum,* pp. 123-52.
72. *De Leg.* III.ii.3 (English translation, p. 374).

for the purpose of aiding one another in the attainment of a single political end. Thus viewed, they form a single mystical body which, morally speaking, may be termed essentially a unity; and that body accordingly needs a single head.[73]

However, collective will and common assent are only exercised in two instances: when forming the *corpus mysticum* (conceived as the population that gives rise to the political community) and when transferring sovereignty from the people to the ruler. Both instances are unique, irreversible, and caused the abandonment *(largitio)* of power, rather than the revocable delegation (*De Leg.* III.iv.11). Suárez argues that the transfer of power amounts to something like alienation *(quasi alienatio)* and he likens it to slavery (*De Leg.* III.iv.6). As a result of a 'special volition,' the community submits itself to the unrestrained power of the sovereign who reigns unopposed. Paradoxically, by exercising will, the collectivity surrenders any free communal discernment of the natural order to the power of the sovereign. Obedience and alienation replace freedom and individuation. Suárez seeks to defend the social and collective nature of man, yet at the same time deprives human beings of regular common discernment. As subjects of absolute monarchy, they are members of a body that is subjugated to the discipline of the head.

The parallel emphasis on the inalienable rights of individuals and the supreme power of the ruler prefigures secular theories of the social contract and the substitution of empires for absolute monarchies and the state model they embody. This is not to say that Suárez formulates a wholly secular political philosophy of the modern state.[74] As is the case with his metaphysics, Suárez's politics is neither exclusively scholastic nor purely modern nor merely intermediary. Rather, he provides the metaphysical foundations for later modern secular political philosophies. In contrast to Hobbes, Suárez rejects the idea of a violent state of nature that is prepolitical and governed by perpetual war of all against all. Instead, power is invested in the people as a whole and as such nature is always already political. The *corpus mysticum* exceeds both the natural rights and duties and those imposed and policed by the state. In consequence, the political dimension of individuation is not confined to

73. *De Leg.* III.ii.4 (English translation, p. 375).
74. Benno Teschke, *The Myth of 1648: Class, Geopolitics and the Making of Modern International Relations* (London: Verso, 2003), esp. pp. 151-96.

the state but extends to the mystical community which is prior to state-hood. Individuals cannot perfect their particular form unless they are part of such communities that are political because they acknowledge the social nature of human beings and frame their lives in cooperative association with one another.

However, Suárez's variant of the natural law tradition does not consti-tute a genuine alternative to theories of the social contract in Hobbes, Locke, and Rousseau because Suárez shares the presupposition that indi-viduality precedes and grounds communality.[75] By contrast, the Christian Neo-Platonists discussed in this essay view the individual and the com-munal as coextensive with one another. The conjunction of transcenden-tal unity and self-individuating entities entails a reconfiguration of sover-eignty: Suárez's understanding of sovereignty as popular power uniquely bestowed by God (not continuously so) and uniquely transferred to the prince amounts to a theological defense of political power that helps pro-duce the secular logic of the modern state and its monopoly power over the entire citizenry. The transfer of sovereignty from the people to the prince is irreversible. As such, the constitution of a political community embodies the permanent alienation of its constituents: "Even though the king has received his authority from the people by donation or contract, the people is no longer entitled to strip the king of it nor to reclaim its freedom,"[76] for this would be an illegitimate usurpation.

What this signifies is the permanent elimination of God's creative action from the activity of politics and the operation of the state. Instead of the more orthodox distinction between the church as *corpus mysticum* and the state as body politic, Suárez's conception of the population as the 'single mystical body' constitutes a turn away from the superiority of the ecclesial community towards the supremacy of the state over the people. Even though Suárez rightly rejects the divine right of kings and

---

75. William T. Cavanaugh, "'A Fire Strong Enough to Consume the House': The Wars of Religion and the Rise of the State," *Modern Theology* 11 (1995): 397-420; Thomas Ertman, *Birth of the Leviathan: Building States and Regimes in Medieval and Early Modern Europe* (Cambridge: Cambridge University Press, 1997); W. T. Cavanaugh, "The City: Beyond Secu-lar Parodies," in Milbank, Pickstock, and Ward, eds., *Radical Orthodoxy*, pp. 182-200; W. T. Cavanaugh, "Killing for the Telephone Company: Why the Nation-State Is Not the Keeper of the Common Good," *Modern Theology* 20 (April 2004): 243-74.

76. *"Ergo quamvis rex habuerit a populo illud dominium per donationem vel contractum, non ideo licebit populo dominium regis auferre libertatem suam iterum"* (*Def. Fidei* III.iii.2).

sketches the contours of a natural democracy,[77] he emphasizes absolute state sovereignty and the primacy of the governing king. As Courtine has documented, this provides the conceptual basis for the dangerous sacralization of the state.[78] Coupled with an increasingly centralized church and state, the unprecedented focus on sovereignty follows from replacing God's creative activity at the heart of the world with human agency founded on the will.[79] The erasure of God from nature paved the way for a separation of the transcendental realm from the immanent dominion. Suárez, in rejecting the divine right of kings, invests the people with power, yet at the same time sanctifies total state sovereignty and the absolute rule of the monarch. Politics and power are severed from the relationality of the world to God. This shift was part of a tendency towards the modern dualism between the temporal and the eternal, the finite and the infinite, the individual and the communal, the transcendent and the immanent. As I argue in the final chapter, Spinoza dismissed the monotheist theology of transcendence altogether and attempted to replace it with a philosophy of immanence.

9. Conclusion: Abstract Individuality and the Rise of the Modern State

In this chapter, I have shown that Suárez develops an account of individuation that inaugurates modern philosophy and politics. All particular

77. De Muralt, *L'unité de la philosophie politique,* pp. 115-39.

78. For some genealogical elements, see Courtine, *Nature et Empire de la Loi,* pp. 8-43. It has also been argued that the supreme sovereignty of the modern state is modeled on the quasi-theocratic turn of the papacy since Petrus Damianus's eleventh-century separation of *potentia Dei absoluta* and *potentia Dei ordinata.* As the *vicarius Christi,* the Pope was given absolute power in the temporal realm. The rise of a Roman 'theocracy' was part of the secularization within the church and provided the path towards state sacralization. See Ernst H. Kantorowicz, *The King's Two Bodies: A Study of Political Theology in the Middle Ages* (Princeton: Princeton University Press, 1957), chs. 4-5; Dupré, *Passage to Modernity,* chs. 2-3.

79. See, *inter alia,* John Neville Figgis, *Studies of Political Thought from Gerson to Grotius, 1414-1625* (Cambridge: Cambridge University Press, 1916), pp. 1-30, esp. 11-15; Otto F. von Gierke, *Das deutsche Genossenschaftsrecht,* 4 vols. (Berlin: Weidmann, 1868-1913), trans. of four subsections as *Natural Law and the Theory of Society, 1500-1800,* trans. and intro. Ernest Barker (Cambridge: Cambridge University Press, 1934); Joseph R. Strayer, *On the Medieval Origins of the Modern State* (Princeton: Princeton University Press, 1970), esp. pp. 15-27; Robert I. Moore, *The Formation of a Persecuting Society: Power and Deviance in Western Europe, 950-1250* (Oxford: Blackwell, 1990), esp. pp. 101-53.

material things self-individuate and as such do not require God's creative activity for their individuality. This leads Suárez to equate creation with efficient causality and to exclude both formal and final causality from divine creativity. If the cause and principle of individuation is no longer transcendent but immanent, then God is also eliminated from relations between individuals and the operation of the *polis*. Indeed, Suárez's metaphysics views relations as the product of the will and the intellect, which is disconnected from divine creativity and in no way reflects divine relationality. Likewise, his politics replaces divine agency with human agency. His critique of the divine right of kings entails a defense of popular power that lapses into alienation because the transfer of sovereignty from the people to the king is irreversible.

As such, Suárez's attempt to establish a natural democracy prepared the rise of the modern secular absolutist state. This was reinforced by his account of the mystical body as a political body that is prior to that of the *ecclesia* and grants the state primacy over the church. Individuation was thus rendered immanent and made subordinate to the secular logic of state power and sovereignty. This move was mirrored by the emphasis on the transcendental nature of unity and the relegation of God to a separate realm that is disconnected from the natural drive towards the supernatural.

CHAPTER 8

The Creation of Immanence

1. Introduction: 'True Politics Is Metaphysics'

In this chapter, I argue that Benedictus (Baruch) de Spinoza (1632-1677) develops an account of individuation that is both indebted to late scholastic theology and shapes modern (and postmodern) philosophy. As such, it marks a significant moment in the history of the concept of individuality, which has been neglected by philosophical and theological genealogies of (post)modernity alike.[1] This omission is all the more surprising since in contemporary thought, Spinoza has been widely credited with providing an original philosophy that rejects both Jewish and Christian understandings of the nature of creation and refutes both

---

1. Spinoza is largely absent from a number of prominent philosophical and theological genealogies, including Hans Blumenberg, *Die Legitimität der Neuzeit* (Frankfurt am Main: Suhrkamp, 1996 [orig. pub. 1966)]; Michael J. Buckley, *At the Origins of Modern Atheism* (New Haven and London: Yale University Press, 1987); Charles Taylor, *Sources of the Self: The Making of Modern Identity* (Cambridge, MA: Harvard University Press, 1989), and, more recently, Jerrold E. Seigel, *The Idea of the Self: Thought and Experience in Western Europe since the Seventeenth Century* (Cambridge: Cambridge University Press, 2005). On the centrality of Spinoza in the genesis of modernity, see Louis Dupré, *Passage to Modernity: An Essay in the Hermeneutics of Nature and Culture* (New Haven and London: Yale University Press, 1993); Jonathan I. Israel, *Radical Enlightenment: Philosophy and the Making of Modernity 1650-1750* (Oxford: Oxford University Press, 2001); J. I. Israel, *Enlightenment Contested: Philosophy, Modernity, and the Emancipation of Man 1670-1752* (Oxford: Oxford University Press, 2006). On the importance of Spinoza in the history of the concept of individuation, see Don Garrett, "Spinoza's *Conatus* Argument," in *Spinoza: Metaphysical Themes*, ed. Olli Koistinen and John Biro (Oxford: Oxford University Press, 2002), pp. 127-58, esp. 150-52.

Greek and Christian conceptions of the relation between universals and particulars. He is acclaimed by leading contemporary philosophers such as Gilles Deleuze for inventing a radical ontology and politics that blend individuality with commonality.[2]

This interpretation has led a number of commentators to assert that Spinoza's 'true politics is his metaphysics' (Antonio Negri) and that his system liberates the individual from the repressive forces of the divinely sanctioned absolute monarchy and the feudal society alike, while also resisting the alienation of capitalist production.[3] Thus, Spinoza's conception of politics is thought to constitute an alternative to the (proto-) Enlightenment liberalism of Locke (1632-1704), Rousseau (1712-1778), and Kant (1724-1804). Spinoza's vision is also said to foreshadow the philosophy of life that has been attributed to Schopenhauer (1788-1860), Marx (1818-1883), and Nietzsche (1844-1900).[4]

2. References to Deleuze's work on Spinoza can be found throughout this chapter. Alexandre Matheron's much-vaunted book *Individu et communauté chez Spinoza* (Paris: Éditions de Minuit, 1988 [orig. pub. 1969]), is perhaps the best statement of this reading of Spinoza. See chs. 1-4, pp. 9-78. The predominant accounts of individuation in Spinoza agree with Matheron's main thesis that Spinoza blends the individual with the common. See Lee C. Rice, "Spinoza on Individuation," *The Monist* 55 (1971): 640-59; William J. Edgar, "Continuity and the Individuation of Modes in Spinoza's Physics," in *Spinoza's Metaphysics: Essays in Critical Appreciation,* ed. James B. Wilbur (Assen: Van Gorcum & Co, 1976), pp. 85-132; Frederick Ablondi and Steven Barbone, "Individual Identity in Descartes and Spinoza," *Studiana Spinozana* 10 (1994): 69-92; Don Garrett, "Spinoza's Theory of Metaphysical Individuation," in *Individuation and Identity in Early Modern Philosophy: Descartes to Kant,* ed. Kenneth F. Barber and Jorge J. E. Gracia (Albany: State University of New York Press, 1994), pp. 73-101; Genevieve Lloyd, *Part of Nature: Self-knowledge in Spinoza's* Ethics (Ithaca, NY: Cornell University Press, 1994); Charles Ramond, *Quantité et qualité dans la philosophie de Spinoza* (Paris: Presses Universitaires de France, 1995); and Steven Barbone, "What Counts as an Individual for Spinoza?" in Koistinen and Biro, eds., *Spinoza: Metaphysical Themes,* pp. 89-112. In the present chapter, I contend that Spinoza's metaphysics posits rather than demonstrates individuality and that it defends commonality for essentially negative reasons.

3. Cf. Étienne Balibar, *Spinoza et la politique* (Paris: Presses Universitaires de France, 1990), English translation: *Spinoza and Politics,* trans. and ed. Peter Snowdon (London: Verso, 1998); Steven Barbone and Lee C. Rice, "La naissance d'une nouvelle politique," in *Architectures de la raison. Mélanges offerts à Alexandre Matheron,* ed. Pierre-François Moreau (Fontenay-aux-Roses: ENS Éditions, 1996), pp. 47-61.

4. Antonio Negri's book *The Savage Anomaly* is a comprehensive account of this sort of reading of Spinoza's project. See A. Negri, *L'anomalia selvaggia. Saggio su potere e potenza in Baruch Spinoza* (Milan: Feltrinelli, 1981), English translation: *The Savage Anomaly: The Power of Spinoza's Metaphysics and Politics,* trans. and ed. Michael Hardt (Minne-

Other commentators have contended that Spinoza defended an account of the state that limits the authority of those in power and ties *lex* (command) to *ius* (law), which explains his advocacy of democratic forms of government. In so doing, his politics secures both individual freedom of expression and the well-being of the commonwealth as a whole. The reason why one of the protagonists of nineteenth-century liberal thought, T. H. Green (1836-1882), viewed Spinoza (rather than Hobbes) as the historical precursor of liberalism is *not* in virtue of his metaphysical or meta-ethical conceptions. Rather, it is because his political theory defended liberal values.[5]

However, I argue that such and similar readings of Spinoza are questionable premises and claims because they tend uncritically to accept a number of assumptions and assertions, chief of all Spinoza's own contention to demonstrate the following three claims. First, that everything has two parallel aspects, the ideal and the material, which pertain to separate attributes or orders, Extension and Thought; concomitantly, ideas *(ideae)* and their objects *(ideata)* do not interact because the two orders are wholly unrelated. Second, that every phenomenon is irreducibly individual, while also being inexorably interconnected with other phenomena within each of the two orders. Third, that essence, existence, and act are all caused by the one and only all-encompassing substance or God, that is to say, nature (*Deus sive natura, Ethica* IV, pref.). Yet at the same time, the principle of individuation is not God but the fixed laws of the eternal order (motion and rest in the order of Extension and common notions in the order of Thought), and the act of individuation is the natural striving for self-preservation (the *conatus*) that inheres in all things.

In what follows, I begin by questioning on Spinoza's own terms the

apolis: University of Minnesota Press, 1991), p. 257 for the quote "True politics is his metaphysics." See Konrad Hecker, *Gesellschaftliche Wirklichkeit und Vernunft. Untersuchungen über die immanente Systematik der Gesellschaftsphilosophie Spinozas im Zusammenhang seines philosophischen Gesamtwerks und zum Problem ihres ideologischen Sinngehalts* (Regensburg: Kommissionsverlag Buchhandung Pustet, 1975); Étienne Balibar, *"Jus — Pactum — Lex.* Sur la constitution du sujet dans le *Traité Théologico-Politique,"* *Studiana Spinozana* 1 (1985): 105-42; Alexandre Matheron, *Individu et communauté chez Spinoza.* On Negri and Hecker, see Manfred Walther, "Philosophy and Politics in Spinoza," *Studiana Spinozana* 9 (1993): 49-57. On Spinoza's philosophy of life and its influence on modern and late modern thinkers, see Sylvain Zac, *L'idée de vie dans la philosophie de Spinoza* (Paris: Presses Universitaires de France, 1963).

5. Douglas Den Uyl and Stuart D. Warner, "Liberalism and Hobbes and Spinoza," *Studiana Spinozana* 3 (1987): 261-317.

logic and coherence of the parallelism and noninteraction of the two orders. Interaction within the extensional and the ideational order (but not across them) is exclusively determined by the fixed laws of the eternal universe and the adequate common notions that correspond to them. There are two related reasons why this system runs into philosophical and theological problems. First, Spinoza envisages the union of the mind with the body and with the 'whole of Nature' (*Tract. de Intel. Em.* 13.4). This is significant for individuality and individuation because mind-body compounds constitute single individuals. Likewise, only the union of the mind with the 'whole of Nature' can provide knowledge of the oneness of the unique substance. Yet at the same time, he maintains that ideas and their *ideata* do not interact, since they are parallel. The question then is how the coincidence yet separation of the order of ideas and the order of things (*Ethica* II, P7) is compatible with the real union of minds and bodies and with knowledge of the universe based on bodily affections of the soul.

The second reason for questioning the noninteraction between the extensional and the ideational is Spinoza's conception of the infinite and the finite. This problem concerns the link between the infinite substance, its attributes (each of which constitutes the essence of the substance) and its modes (affections of the substance, which are divided into infinite immediate, infinite mediate, and finite modes). On the one hand, the infinite and the finite are separate, as the finite modes cannot be determined to exist or to act by the infinite substance (*Ethica* I, P28). On the other hand, the substance is in everything as the immanent (not transitive) cause (*Ethica* I, P18) and everything (including finite modes) is in the substance as its effects: "[A]ll things that are, are in God, and depend on God in such a way that they can neither be nor be conceived without him."[6] Moreover, infinite and finite modes alike belong to *Natura naturata* (*Ethica* I, P29, Schol.) and as such follow from the necessity of God's nature, that is to say, the modes of God's attributes which are in God and can neither be nor be conceived without God. Not unlike Duns Scotus and Descartes, Spinoza posits the priority of the infinite over the finite. But he cannot explain how and why the infinity of the substance involves the finitude of modes. In the absence of such an account, his system begs the question as to why there are any finite modes at all in

---

6. "*omnia quae sunt in Deo sunt et a Deo ita dependent, ut sine ipso nec esse, nec concipi possint*" (*Ethica* I, P28, Schol.).

the substance. How can finite modes be self-individuating or individuating each other (in virtue of the *conatus*) while also depending on the substance for their existence and their essence?

Therefore I question Spinoza's system on account of the undemonstrated formality of the parallelism between the ideational and the extensional and the equally undemonstrated formality of the separation of the infinite and the finite. In turn, this parallelism and this separation raise a third problem. How can Spinoza's parallelism square the eternity in the order of Thought (e.g., the sharing of singular essences in the eternity of the substance) with the transience in the order of Extension (the mortality of finite material things)? Without an account of how mind-body compounds are individual things whose dual aspects do not interact, individuality and commonality are little more than undemonstrated claims.

2. Parallel Order and Common Notions

Broadly speaking, there are two rival interpretations of Spinoza's method. The first interpretation claims that Spinoza's work marks the apogee of seventeenth-century rationalism, notably the self-evidence of a priori premises from which the main parameters of the all-encompassing system can be deduced.[7] By contrast, the second interpretation suggests that Spinoza's philosophy is part of empiricism and combines an analytic approach to a posteriori data (given by sense-perception) with a synthetic approach that discovers the system and makes all its components intelligible.[8] However, I contend that both empiricism and rationalism underpin his entire *œuvre*. This is one reason for the parallelism of the ideal and the material — the correspondence of a priori ideas in the order of Thought and a posteriori material contingencies in the order of Extension.

Spinoza develops some of the constitutive elements of the doctrine of parallelism already in the treatise on the intellect, one of his earlier

---

7. Richard H. Popkin, *The History of Skepticism from Erasmus to Spinoza* (Berkeley: University of California Press, 1979), pp. 229-48, esp. p. 233 n. 24; Bernard A. O. Williams, "Descartes's Use of Skepticism," in *The Skeptical Tradition,* ed. Myles Burnyeat (Berkeley: University of California Press, 1983), pp. 337-52.

8. Edwin M. Curley, *Spinoza's Metaphysics: An Essay in Interpretation* (Cambridge, MA: Harvard University Press, 1969); Isaac Franck, "Spinoza's Logic of Enquiry: Rationalist or Experientialist?" in *The Philosophy of Baruch Spinoza,* ed. Richard Kennington (Washington, DC: Catholic University of America Press, 1980), pp. 247-72.

writings.[9] In the first part of this treatise, he argues that all finite mutable things are determined by the eternal infinite order of fixed natural laws. Happiness depends on the nature of the object of love and "love towards a thing eternal and infinite feeds the mind wholly with joy."[10] As a result, the highest good *(summum bonum)* is knowledge of the eternal order and fixed laws of nature (*aeternum ordinem et secundum certas naturae leges, Tract. de Intel. Em.* 12.3). Human nature per se is capable of attaining such knowledge, which fosters a 'stable character,' "that is, the knowledge of the union existing between the mind and the whole of nature."[11] Even though the multitude and general customs prove to be a hindrance in acquiring such a 'character,' "all our actions and thoughts must be directed to this one end."[12] Thus, in the name of the mind's longing for certainty, Spinoza posits the primacy of the eternal and infinite order of stability over the ephemeral and finite chaos of disorder.

Another constitutive element of Spinoza's parallelism between the ideational and the extensional is the claim that we can only know "the union between the mind and the whole of nature" on the basis of sensation, which is the effect of the union of the mind with the body (*Tract. de Intel. Em.* 21.1; *Ethica* II, P21). In order to overcome the dualism between mind and body and mind and world in Descartes, Spinoza argues that we infer the cause (the body-mind union) from the effect (sensing a certain body). This is not to say that the body affects the mind. Rather, bodily affections that we can sense have a mental correlate. Since body and mind are united yet pertain to attributes that share nothing in common (Extension and Thought),[13] there is, as Spinoza writes in the *Ethics,*

9. On this point I disagree with Matheron, who asserts that the doctrine of parallelism "was entirely unavailable to him [Spinoza] in the TIE [*Tractatus de Intellectus Emendatione*]." See Alexandre Matheron, "Ideas of Ideas and Certainty in the *Tractatus de Intellectus Emendatione* and the *Ethics,*" in *Spinoza on Knowledge and the Human Mind: Papers Presented at the Second Jerusalem Conference (Ethica* II), ed. Yirmiyahu Yovel (Leiden: E. J. Brill, 1994), pp. 83-91 (91).

10. *"amor erga rem aeternam et infinitam sola laetitia pascit animum"* (*Tract. de Intel. Em.* 10.1).

11. *"cognitionem unionis, quam mens cum tota natura habet"* (*Tract. de Intel. Em.* 13.4).

12. *"omnes nostrae operationes simul et cogitationes ad hunc sunt dirigendae finem"* (*Tract. de Intel. Em.* 16.3).

13. Spinoza stipulates the noncommonality of attributes already in the *Short Treatise:* "Things that have different attributes, as well as those that belong to different attributes, have nothing in themselves the one from the other [i.e., nothing in common with one another]" (*Kor. Verh.* App. I, Ax. 4). Cf. *Ethica* I, P10 and P11.

"no common measure between the will and motion . . . no comparison between the powers or strength of the Mind and the Body."[14] Thus, there is in everything the coincidence yet nonidentity of the extensional and the ideational. He defines this in terms of complete noncausal correspondence of body, such that "the Mind and the Body . . . are one and the same thing which, when considered under the attribute of Thought and explicated through Thought, we call decision, and when considered under the Attribute of Extension and deduced from the laws of motion-and-rest, we call a physical state."[15]

As a result of this configuration, everything is both intellectual and real, both ideal and material. Concerning the mind, Spinoza wrote in the *Ethics* that "the first thing which constitutes the actual being of the human mind is nothing other than an idea of some single thing actually existing."[16] Concerning material things, he argues that for every mutable individual existent there is always already an eternal singular essence in the divine mind. Thus, Spinoza embraces the early modern skepticism concerning the cognitive inadequacy of sense perception, judgment, and the imagination. In response, he claims that an empirically framed rational method can enable the finite intellect to cognize the infinite substance and all it encompasses, thereby attaining the certain knowledge of the eternal order of fixed natural laws.

Such knowledge is knowledge of the parallel order of the ideational and the extensional. The intellectual unfolding of ideal possibilities marks the real unfolding of material actualities. It is therefore in virtue of the parallelism between the ideational and the extensional that finite minds can cognize their utter dependence on the infinite substance. If this account of the parallelism in Spinoza is correct, then three connected questions arise. First of all, how and why does the infinite substance express itself in an infinity of attributes that divide in parallel from the outset? Second, how and why do the finite modes of the infinite

---

14. *"nulla detur ratio voluntatis ad motum, nulla etiam datur comparatio inter mentis et corporis potentiam seu vires"* (*Ethica* V, pref.).

15. *". . . unam eandemque rem, quam, quando sub cogitationis attributo consideratur et per ipsum explicatur, decretum appellamus, et quando sub extensionis attributo consideratur et ex legibus motus et quietis deducitur, determinationem vocamus"* (*Ethica* III, P2, Schol.). Cf. Roger S. Woolhouse, *Descartes, Spinoza, Leibniz: The Concept of Substance in Seventeenth Century Metaphysics* (London: Routledge, 1993), pp. 170-73.

16. *"Primum, quod actuale mentis humanae esse constituit, nihil aliud est, quam idea rei alicuius singularis actu existentis"* (*Ethica* II, P11).

substance constitute distinct individuals, while at the same time being composed of ideality and materiality, which never interact? Third, if sensation is at the origin of cognizing the mind-body union and its dependence on 'the whole of nature,' how does Spinoza negotiate sense perception and intellection? I will now address these questions, beginning with the third.

Since neither sensory experience nor intellectual cognition is self-sufficient, Spinoza's method is both empiricist and rationalist. Without sense perception, there can be no intellection because physical affections produce sensory imprints *(imagines)* on the body and reflexive correlates in the mind *(ideae)*. Affection is always already sensory and intellectual. By itself, the mind cannot think anything at all; there is no pure self-reflexivity, thought thinking nothing but itself. Reflexivity is the product of mental and bodily affectiveness on the basis of sensation. The mind's self-consciousness is primarily an approximate idea of material modification, "not — *pace* Descartes — a monadic mental event that can occur even without a body."[17] True knowledge is knowledge of adequate ideas. Just as ideality has a perceptible material correlate because each adequate idea has a real object for its *ideatum,* so materiality has an intellective ideal correlate because there is a true adequate idea of each thing.

Equally, without intellection sense perception leads to error because the ideas of impressions are confused, since they correspond neither to the perceived objects nor to the affected body. By itself, sense perception does not know anything at all because it sees things in isolation from 'the whole of nature' and solely from a limited perspective, the single location that the body happens to occupy within the extended universe.[18] As a result, things appear as locally related parts and seem to be confined to a finite spatiotemporal position. So sensory perception gives rise to the first kind of knowledge, the *experientia vaga* of the memory and the imagination, a confused discernment of things in terms of the 'common order of nature' (*Ep.* XXXII) which contrasts sharply with nature as a whole — the parallel order and connection of things and of

17. Yirmiyahu Yovel, "The Second Kind of Knowledge and the Removal of Error," in Yovel, ed., *Spinoza on Knowledge and the Human Mind,* pp. 93-110 (95).

18. In a letter to Oldenburg, Spinoza describes this perspective in terms of a worm in a bloodstream, mistaking each particle of blood for a whole instead of a part (*Ep.* XXXII, esp. pp. 210-11). Cf. William Sacksteder, "Spinoza on Part and Whole: The Worm's Eye View," in *Spinoza: New Perspectives,* ed. Robert W. Shahan and John I. Biro (Norman: University of Oklahoma, 1978), pp. 139-59.

ideas (*Ethica* II, P7). As I argue below, this confusion leads Spinoza to distinguish between the sages and the ignorant, which affects his account of democracy.

Cognition of adequate ideas is therefore required to correct the errors of sense perception and to reconnect *ideae* with their specific *ideata*. In this process, the mind first acquires reason *(ratio)*, the second kind of knowledge. Ultimately, cognition attains *scientia intuitiva* — the third kind of knowledge which marks the intellection of things solely through their essences. The mind does so via the formation of common notions *(notiones communes)*. Common notions are "the foundations of our reasoning *(fundamenta rationis)*" (*Ethica* II, P40, Schol. 1; cf. *Ethica* II, P44, Cor. 2, D). Even though common notions are a priori, Spinoza's method is not purely rationalist because both sensation and common notions are grounded in the inherence of the mind-body union in the extended and ideated order of nature. Indeed, just as sensation is the mind's self-consciousness of its union with the body, so common notions are notions of things that have existence in virtue of being modes of the substance whose essence it is to exist. Unlike Descartes's unfettered *cogito* — disembodied and worldless — Spinoza's intellect is firmly inscribed into the ordered structure of nature.

Moreover, common notions themselves have both an a priori and an a posteriori dimension. They are inborn clear and distinct ideas which the mind discovers in itself, independently of all experience. Yet at the same time, cognition of the self and of nature as a whole via common notions is refined by contact with actually existing things that constitute the true objects of ideas in the mind: ". . . the mind apprehends itself better in proportion as it understands a greater number of natural objects . . . the more things the mind knows, the better does it understand its own strength and the order of nature."[19] The mind can form a priori common notions because this is what the nature of reflexivity and intellection is. These innate intellectual instruments constitute not only tools for further inquiry but also and above all a kind of knowledge, reflective knowledge, which he defines as "the idea of an idea" and which "has for its objective the most perfect being" (*Tract. de Intel. Em.* 38.1-3; 31.3; 69.1-2; 71.4).

---

19. ". . . *quomodo mens plura intelligendo alia simul acquirat instrumenta, quibus facilius pergat intelligere . . . quo plura mens novit, eo melius et suas vires et ordinem naturae intelligit*" (*Treat. de Intel. Em.* 39-40).

Before I discuss what the mind knows when it grasps common notions, it is important to relate common notions to Spinoza's division of sciences. Since common notions constitute the foundations of reasoning, they provide the basis for logic and geometry. And since they have a correlate in nature, they also ground physics. As such, there is no separation of the formal from the empirical sciences. Instead, all sciences are concerned with the substance, its attributes and modes. As Yovel remarks, "Logic, too, is not abstract, but describes uniform patterns in which all physical and mental things in the universe act and exist. No science is 'formal' in the sense of 'not being about the world,' since all true ideas have reality as their *ideata*."[20] Common notions are the most proper exercise of reason, purely immanent and unaided by the divine illumination of transcendent revelation. In this sense, Spinoza exceeds Descartes's skepticism regarding both natural and revealed theology. He also excludes the supernatural light of faith from the natural light of reason: "[C]ommon notions are the foundations of Philosophy and should be drawn from nature alone."[21]

As such, common notions are the axioms and first principles of all branches of rational knowledge, including logic, mathematics, physics, psychology, and politics. They give the mind immediate access to God: "For we cannot imagine God, but we can indeed conceive him" (*Ep.* LVI). In this way, rational inquiry corresponds more closely to empirical nature: in the *Ethica,* Spinoza speaks of the proper order of philosophical inquiry according to which the divine nature is prior in cognition and in Nature (*Ethica* II, P10, Schol.). This is why common notions structure philosophical investigation and pertain to metaphysics. On this basis metaphysics is concerned with the eternal order of nature and the fixed laws that govern all that is in the substance. Metaphysics is therefore the queen of sciences and has the exclusive claim to universal rationality. Theology is stripped of the status of science, separated from philosophy and relegated to the realm of faith, itself confined to Scripture and no longer amenable to natural reason.[22]

Thus liberated from any constricting shackles of transcendence, reason enables the mind to grasp the eternal laws of nature directly in virtue

20. Yovel, "The Second Kind of Knowledge and the Removal of Error," p. 100.
21. *Tract. Theol.-Pol* XIV, *fine.*
22. Alan Donagan, "Spinoza's Theology," in *The Cambridge Companion to Spinoza,* ed. Don Garrett (Cambridge: Cambridge University Press, 1996), pp. 343-82.

of the intellect's inscription into the immanent cosmic order. According to the parallel order that structures Spinoza's entire system, the ideated correlate of the laws of extended nature is the set of common notions, cognized immediately without any induction or abstraction. As a result, knowledge of common notions is knowledge of the causes and operation of nature beyond the particular spatiotemporal location of an individual body that is affected by other individual bodies. In perceiving particular modes of the universal substance, we perceive immutable ideas or notions that "are equally in the part and in the whole."[23]

Indeed, common notions give the mind access to the universe as a whole. The mind sees that it is determined by the one and only universal law of the divine intellect and not by laws that govern proximate causes. In this way, Spinoza substitutes substantive universals (the fixed laws of the eternal order) which are characteristic of modern "mechanical principles of philosophy" (*Ep.* XIII; *Prin. Phil. Cart.*) for universals embodied in particulars which are the mark of patristic and medieval metaphysics. As a result, common notions are ideas of those things "in which all bodies agree" (*Ethica* II, P40, Schol. 1). The things in which all bodies agree are, first of all, that they have the same attribute of extension and, second, that "they are capable of motion and rest, and of motion at one time quicker and at one time slower."[24] In Spinoza's system, motion and rest are therefore the principle of individuation for bodies.

For this reason, the common notion or idea of motion and rest is instrumental to the cognition of a body as individuated or singular. Coupled with the primacy of metaphysics over theology, the method of inquiry which is grounded in common notions is significant for the question of individuation because knowledge of the substantive universals ('the fixed laws of the eternal order') is not confined to the general patterns of the universe but extends to individual things in virtue of their share in the infinite substance. This is why Spinoza asserts that "[e]very idea of any body or particular thing existing in actuality necessarily involves the eternal and infinite essence of God."[25] Reason is capable of knowing God or substance and the dependence of all that is in the universe on it because rea-

23. The full citation is as follows: *"illa, quae omnibus communia, quaeque aeque in parte ac in toto sunt"* (*Ethica* II, P38).

24. *"quod iam tardius, iam celerius, et absolute iam moveri, iam quiescere possunt"* (*Ethica* II, P13, L2, D).

25. *"Unaquaeque cuiuscumque corporis, vel rei singularis actu existentis idea Dei aeternam et infinitam essentiam necessario involvit"* (*Ethica* II, P45).

son itself is constituted by the common notions. As such, "[i]t is in the nature of reason to perceive things in the light of eternity."[26] Thus, reason views things as necessary rather than contingent and since the essence of the infinite substance is to exist, "this necessity is the very necessity of God's eternal nature."[27] Through reason, common notions enable the mind to see the nomological link between individual things and 'the whole of nature.' So if we grasp common notions such as motion and rest, then we can know the particular station of each thing in the universal order.

Finally, common notions equip the mind not only with the activity of reasoning (the second kind of knowledge) but also lay the ground for intuition of essences by themselves (the third kind of knowledge). For it is from cognition of things *sub specie aeternitatis* that the mind can deduce their utter dependence on the infinite substance whose essence is necessarily to exist. In so doing, the mind can intuit their station in the eternal order of nature according to the fixed laws of the universe (*Ethica* II, P47, Schol.). In this sense, Spinoza produces an immanentized version of Parmenides' metaphysics of the one and the many.[28] He dismisses the patristic and medieval account of relationality and develops the idea of nomological links between the modes and the substance in order to demonstrate that things are individual by natural necessity and individuated by the fixed ratio of motion and rest. In the following section, I examine the status of individuality in Spinoza's metaphysics and politics and his conception of individuation.

3. A Hierarchy of Relative Individuality

The importance of individuality and singularity in Spinoza emerges in the light of the two constituent elements of his system, metaphysics and politics. First of all, a metaphysics that is grounded in the clarity of the geometric method *(more geometrico)* and seeks to overcome the dualism of both late scholastic theology and early modern philosophy. Second, a politics that is founded upon the rationality of argument and debate and

26. *"De natura rationis est res sub quadam aeternitatis specie percipere"* (*Ethica* II, P44, Cor. 2).

27. *"haec rerum necessitas est ipsa Dei aeternae naturae necessitas"* (*Ethica* II, P44, Proof).

28. Edgar, "Continuity and the Individuation of Modes in Spinoza's Physics," esp. pp. 87-88.

seeks to protect the individual and the commonwealth against the obscurantism of absolutist regimes. The overriding objective of his metaphysics and politics is to free the mind from mysticism and superstition, to liberate individuals from the constricting shackles of despotism, and to enable citizens to maximize their particular well-being within a universal commonwealth that defends freedom of judgment and the unconstrained exercise of any religion.[29] Since he maintains that both nature and society are composed of individuals with singular essences that are all in God (*Ethica* II, P45, Schol.), individuality and singularity are central to Spinoza's metaphysics and politics.

Individual things *(individua)* are modes of the single unique infinite substance and modes conjoin in order to form a single thing *(res singularis),* as everything is composed of lower-order individual parts and is itself a component in a higher-order whole (*Prin. Phil. Cart.* II, P5, Dem.; *Ethica* II, D7). Equally, the universal commonwealth is constituted by a collection of particular citizens, and their well-being depends on the preservation and perfection of their individuality and their commonality (*Ethica* IV, P37, Schol. 2). Individuation is at once metaphysical and political in the sense that individuality is perfected by preserving and enhancing the self-identity of each individual phenomenon and the shared belonging of all phenomena in the common order of nature and society.

For Spinoza, individuality is ultimately grounded in the oneness and indivisibility of the all-encompassing substance which is absolute and infinite. This claim is summarized in propositions 13-16 of Part One of the *Ethics:*

Prop. 13: Absolutely infinite substance is indivisible.

Prop. 14: There can be, or be conceived, no other substance but God.

Prop. 15: Whatever is, is in God, and nothing can be or be conceived without God.

Prop. 16: From the necessity of the divine nature there must follow infinite things in infinite ways (i.e., everything that can come within the scope of infinite intellect).[30]

29. *Tract. de Intel. Em.* 7.3; *Kor. Verh.* I.1; *Cog. Met.* I.1-2; *Ethica* I, App.; *Tract. Theo.-Pol.* pref.; *Tract. Pol.* ch. 1.

30. *"Substantia absolute infinita est indivisibilis; Praeter Deum nulla dari neque concipi potest substantia; Quicquid est in Deo est, et nihil sine Deo esse neque concipi potest; Ex necessitate divinae naturae infinita infinitis modis (hoc est, omnia, quae sub intellectum infinitum cadere possunt) sequi debent"* (*Ethica* I, P13, 14, 15, 16).

To say that there is only one substance and that this substance is God is to say that substance is in some fundamental sense single (not dual) and individual (not multiple). Moreover, to say that everything which exists *is in God* is to say that all individual things are modes of the one unique substance rather than substances or attributes in their own right: "Particular things are nothing but affections of the attribute of God, that is, modes wherein the attributes of God find expression in a definite and determinate way."[31]

However, this "doctrine of the uniqueness of substance"[32] casts doubt on the self-identity of individual things and raises questions about how and why the single infinite substance gives rise to a multiplicity of individual finite things. Since everything is a mode of the substance, it expresses the substance's individuality. The individuality of modes is therefore relative to that of the substance. According to Spinoza, a thing can be said to be individual if it constitutes a whole composed of distinct parts. However, he does not identify parts with atoms because atoms are indivisible entities, whereas each thing is extensional and as such divisible. In his *Principles of Cartesian Philosophy*, Spinoza dismisses atomism by arguing that everything is always both a part of a greater whole and itself a composition of smaller components:

> because the nature of matter consists in extension (Prop. 2 Part 2), which by its own nature is divisible, however small it be (Ax. 9 and Def. 7); therefore however small a part of matter may be, it is by its own nature divisible. That is, there are no atoms, or parts of matter that are by their own nature indivisible. Q.E.D.[33]

In this passage, Spinoza argues that nothing is indivisible because every part is constituted by yet smaller parts and in turn constitutes a component in a larger entity. This critique of atomism derives from his argument that everything is a part of 'the whole of Nature' because everything is produced by the one and only substance and only persists in existence in virtue of being in some sense in the substance.

Ultimately, individuality is not an absolute mark of something that

---

31. "*Res particulares nihil sunt nisi Dei attributorum affectiones, sive modi, quibus Dei attributa certo et determinato modo exprimuntur*" (*Ethica* I, P25, Cor.).

32. Lloyd, *Part of Nature*, p. 5.

33. *Prin. Phil. Cart.* II, P5, Dem.

follows from *that* thing's singular essences. On the contrary, to be an individual is a relative quality that indicates a certain degree of individuality and is itself a function of the complexity of the composition of individual parts:

> When a number of bodies of the same or different magnitude form close contact with one another through the pressure of other bodies upon them, or if they are moving at the same or different rates of speed so as to preserve an unvarying relation of movement among themselves, these bodies are said to be united with one another and all together form one body or individual thing, which is distinguished from other things through this union of bodies.[34]

Spinoza deploys the term 'body' to emphasize that entities are both composed of smaller parts and constitute elements of a larger individual. Since to be an individual is to entertain a certain link with other individual entities that have different sizes determined by the complexity of their composition, it follows that individuality is relative. This notion of relativity is fundamentally different from the Christian Neo-Platonist concept of relationality, as the latter requires a theological account of transcendent creation rather than immanent production. By contrast, the whole universe *(facies totius universi)* is for Spinoza an infinite series of relative individuals, a hierarchical ordering from the one and only absolute infinite substance to infinitesimally small things that it encompasses (*Ep.* LXIV). All entities are in some important sense individual. This applies not only to simple bodies (*corpora simplissima, Ethica* II, P13) but also to composites (*Ethica* II, P12, Lem. 3, A2 Dem.) and to groups of individual things that form a singular thing (*Ethica* II, D7). In the *Ethics*, he describes his conception of relative individuality as follows:

> We thus see how a composite individual can be affected in many ways yet preserve its nature. Now previously we have conceived an individual thing composed solely of bodies distinguished from one another

---

34. "*Cum corpora aliquot eiusdem aut diversae magnitudinis a reliquis ita coercentur, ut invicem incumbant, vel si eodem aut diversis celeritatis gradibus moventur, ut motus suos invicem certa quadam ratione communicent, illa corpora invicem unita dicemus, et omnia simul unum corpus, sive individuum componere, quod a reliquis per hanc corporum unionem distinguitur*" (*Ethica* II, P13, Lem. 3, Ax. 2, Def.). Cf. Étienne Balibar, "Individualité et transindividualité chez Spinoza," in Moreau, ed., *Architectures de la raison*, pp. 35-46.

only by motion-and-rest and speed of movement; that is, an individual thing composed of the simplest bodies. If we now conceive another individual thing composed of several individual things of different natures, we shall find that this can be affected in many other ways while still preserving its nature. . . . *If we thus continue to infinity, we shall readily conceive the whole of Nature as one individual whose parts — that is, all the constituent bodies — vary in infinite ways without any change in the individual as a whole.*[35]

Thus configured, the individuality of the infinite substance is the sum of its parts whereas the Christian Neo-Platonist Creator God is pure excess which is both more immanent and more transcendent than the self-expression of Spinoza's productive substance. Within 'the individual as a whole,' there are infinite ways in which the 'constituent bodies' can entertain different links. Individuality is relative because all things are always already connected with other things and with the entire universe. Nothing is individual in isolation from other individuals because everything is a body, not in a material sense but in the sense of being composed of parts. Spinoza identifies the link between individual bodies with 'motion-and-rest and speed of movement' and conceives this link as the principle of individuation of bodies. I now turn to the problem of individuation in his system.

4. The Problem of Individuation in Spinoza's System

The hierarchy of relative individuality that I sketched in the previous section raises three problems. First of all, why does the oneness of the substance divide into the duality of Thought and Extension? This question follows from Spinoza's understanding of identity and noninteraction of

---

35. "*His itaque videmus, qua ratione individuum compositum possit multis modis affici, eius nihilominus natura servata. Atque hucusque individuum concepimus, quod non, nisi ex corporibus, quae solo motu et quiete, celeritate et tarditate inter se distinguuntur, hoc est, quod ex corporibus simplicissimis componitur. Quod si iam aliud concipiamus ex pluribus diversae naturae individuis compositum, idem pluribus aliis modis posse affici reperiemus, ipsius nihilominus natura servata. . . . Et si sic porro in infinitum pergamus, facile concipiemus, totam naturam unum esse individuum, cuius partes, hoc est, omnia corpora infinitis modis variant absque ulla totius individui mutatione*" (*Ethica* II, P13, Lem. 7, Schol.; my italics).

individual ideas and their corresponding individual objects. To say that both immaterial ideas and material things are individual is not to say that ideas are individual because they are the ideas *of* individual things or that things are individual because they are the product *of* individual ideas in God's intellect. Indeed, Spinoza denies any relations between ideas and things and instead posits two separate yet somehow identical orders, the ideational-extensional parallelism: "The order and connection of ideas is the same as the order and connection of things."[36] Rather than envisioning any relation between materiality and ideality, he insists on the radical singularity of both things and ideas and the interaction within each order, not across them.

The second problem relates to the question as to how an immaterial substance produces material things that are modes of that same substance and whose essences are in that same substance. This question follows from an apparent paradox in Spinoza's metaphysics and his politics. On the one hand, he argues that unity and plurality are merely modes of thinking that do not add anything real to the things to which they apply:

> [U]nity is in no way distinct from the thing itself or additional to being and is merely a mode of thinking whereby we separate a thing from other things that are similar to it or agree with it in some respect. . . . [P]lurality . . . likewise obviously adds nothing to things, nor is it anything but a mode of thinking.[37]

This conception might suggest that Spinoza's system is nominalist, in the sense that unity and plurality are solely in the mind and not in things. Correspondingly, concepts like humanity or society are nothing but collective nouns that point to a complex set of interconnections.[38] On the other hand, Spinoza is adamant that for each mode of thought there is a corresponding mode of extension and that everything is grounded in Nature, which consists of two identical yet somehow distinct orders, the order of things and the order of ideas. This paradox, which can perhaps be described as a form of 'nominalist naturalism,' raises the question of how singular essences in God's immaterial intellect relate to individual material things in nature.

---

36. "*Ordo et connexio idearum idem est, ac ordo et connexio rerum*" (*Ethica* II, P7).
37. *Cog. Met.* I.6.
38. Robert J. McShea, "Spinoza on Power," *Inquiry* 1 (Spring 1969): 133-43.

The third problem is how and why the infinite substance and the infinity of attributes that express the essence of the substance are modified by finite modes. This question arises in relation to Spinoza's paradoxical claim that the substance is the immanent and proximate (not transitive and remote) cause of *all* things (*Ethica* I, P18 and P28, Schol.). Yet at the same time, the finite individual modes are actualized and individuated by other such finite individual modes, and not by the substance itself (*Ethica* I, P28).

These three questions can be summarized as the division of the substance, the production of materiality, and the passage from infinity to finitude. Taken together, they raise the problem of why things are individual and how they are individuated. Nowhere does Spinoza give a coherent account of why and how finite individual material modes are caused by the infinite immaterial substance, yet at the same time are neither actualized nor individuated by it. There are two competing interpretations of Spinoza's attempted resolution. Either the substance is the immanent cause of all things (*Ethica* I, P18), in which case it causes both the finite modes themselves and the fixed laws of the eternal order (motion and rest) that individuate them (*Ethica* II, P13, Lem. 1, Lem. 3, Dem., Lem. 7, Schol.). In this case, Spinoza's principle of individuation is motion and rest, which determine the exact proportions of individual things in themselves and in relation to other things. If so, then the substance causes not simply the essence and the coming into existence (*secundum fieri*, *Ethica* II, P10, Schol.) of finite modes, but also their preservation in being and their perfection of virtue.[39]

Or else the infinite substance is the remote cause of finite modes (*Ethica* I, P28, Schol.), in which case the finite modes are produced through the medium of primary things (immediate and mediate infinite modes). In this case, Spinoza's principle of individuation is *this* motion and *this* rest (motion and rest proper to each and every individual). If so, then finite modes are actualized and individuated by themselves and by other modes in a perpetual struggle against other groups of finite modes. Why? Because Spinoza's conception of finitude is such that different groups of finite modes are rival, for each mode requires a group of other modes in order to be brought into existence and to remain in being. For things cannot exist individually. Everything exists communally.

39. Steven Barbone, "Virtue and Sociality in Spinoza," *Iyuun* 42 (1993): 383-95.

But paradoxically it is the mode of their communal existence that is itself conflictual. Since modes do not exist in, of, or by themselves, they do not come into actuality unconditionally. They are only actualized on the condition that related modes are actualized simultaneously as well. If not, then they remain virtual. If they are actualized, then their duration is limited because they depend on the other modes of their group in order to remain in being. The actualization of a hitherto nonexisting group of finite modes requires the elimination of an already-existing group of finite modes. Thus, groups of modes are rival. As a result, the individuation of such modes is the self-preservation of individual beings by their own power, the *conatus* (*Ethica* III, P6). The power of self-preservation is both metaphysical and political because it constitutes the essence of finite modes (*Ethica* III, P7) and the foundation of their natural right (*Ethica* IV, P22).

Spinoza attempts to square this circle by arguing that the causation, actualization, and individuation of finite modes depend on the substance but are not fully determined by it. The all-encompassing substance enfolds all things and causes the infinite immediate modes (motion and rest) but somehow does not determine the fixed proportions of motion and rest that pertain both between separate individual bodies and among the single parts that constitute a collective body (*Ethica* II, P13, Lem. 7, Schol.). Instead, these proportions are determined by finite modes themselves. Motion-and-rest is the principle that individuates all bodies, and the fixed proportions of motion and rest are maintained by the power of self-preservation *(conatus)* which inheres in each thing.

These claims are arbitrary because they represent assertions and rely on presuppositions that are part of Spinoza's method and as such remain no more than undemonstrated assumptions. His argument that only infinite modes (and not finite modes) are caused by the infinite substance derives from his undemonstrated separation of the infinite and the finite — a claim that follows from his equally undemonstrated parallelism of the ideational and the extensional. In order to substantiate my argument, I will therefore briefly examine his account of the connection between the substance and its attributes and modes. In the following section, I focus on the causation of modes. In the section thereafter, I discuss the implications for his theory of causal laws as the principle of individuation.

5. Substance and Attributes:
Monism, Dualism, and the 'Reality' of the Natural Order

The two constitutive elements of Spinoza's metaphysics are the 'doctrine of the uniqueness of substance'[40] and the 'doctrine of the infinity of attributes.'[41] Spinoza also emphasizes the unity of the infinite substance and the union of finite modes like body-mind compounds (*Kor. Verh.* I.2; *Tract. de Intel. Em.* 13.4, 21.1; *Ethica* II, P13, Dem. and Cor.). The infinite substance does not coincide with, or correspond to, the extended corporeal world but encompasses infinite modes and the eternal essences of the 'ideated world': "Nothing, then, can happen in Nature to contravene her own universal laws [N.B. Here, by Nature, I do not mean simply matter and its modifications, but infinite other things besides matter]."[42] Indeed, the *positum* that the infinite substance is the most real being *(ens realissimum)* and enfolds all things that exist — ideas as well as their objects (*Kor. Verh.* I.2; *Cog. Met.* II.2) — is one compelling reason for the thesis that Spinoza does not defend pantheism but instead pan*en*theism, a term coined by Karl Christian Friedrich Krause (1781-1832) who argues that, while the material world is embedded in God, God nonetheless exceeds nature and cannot be equated with it.[43]

For Spinoza to be real is to be in the substance, *Deus sive natura,* even though God surpasses nature. Reality is the natural order, which is equally ideational and extensional. There is God and the idea of God, and for God to exist is for God to act (*Ethica* I, P34-35): God's being is his

---

40. Lloyd, *Part of Nature,* p. 5.

41. As Roger Woolhouse has documented, these two claims distinguish Spinoza from the other two eminent seventeenth-century metaphysical systems founded upon substance and attribute, that of Descartes and that of Leibniz. See Woolhouse, *Descartes, Spinoza, Leibniz,* pp. 28-53.

42. *Tract. Theol.-Polit.* ch. 6. Cf. ". . . I [Spinoza] believe that I have shown clearly enough . . . that matter is by Descartes badly defined in terms of extension; whereas it must necessarily be explained in terms of an attribute which expresses an eternal and infinite essence" (*Ep.* LXXXIII).

43. On Krause, see Keith Ward, *God: A Guide for the Perplexed* (Oxford: Oneworld, 2002), p. 161; cf. Friedrich Bülow, "Einführung," *Die Ethik,* 7th ed. (Stuttgart: Alfred Kröner Verlag, 1976), pp. vii-xxx. See also Michael P. Levine, *Pantheism: A Non-Theistic Concept of Deity* (New York and London: Routledge, 1994), p. 21; Richard V. Mason, *The God of Spinoza: A Philosophical Study* (Cambridge: Cambridge University Press, 1997), p. 32; Douglas Hedley, "Pantheism, Trinitarian Theism and the Idea of Unity: Reflections on the Christian Concept of God," *Religious Studies* 32 (1996): 61-77.

self-expression and his production, as Gilles Deleuze has rightly argued.[44] Since God expresses himself in both and both are in God, ideas in Thought and things in Extension, it follows for Spinoza that there are ideas and their objects and that both are equally real.[45] The attribute parallelism mirrors the parallelism between the being of God and the idea of God. Just as God's necessary existence (which is his essence) is the cause of God's production (which is his self-expression), so the necessary idea of God (which is the idea of his essence) is the cause of all other ideas (which express his essence).

This double parallelism implies that reality is not confined to the being of God and to the order of Extension but also encompasses the idea of God and the order of Thought. As such, reality is above and beyond materiality and physicality. Indeed, Spinoza expands the orbit of the real to include all essences. For this reason, essences *qua* essences are real in the sense that they exist independently of their corresponding objects (*Ethica* I, P8, Schol. 2; II, P8 and Cor.). Deleuze also argues that Spinoza's pure ontology demonstrates the existence of all essences insofar as they are essences, not because essences are *causa sui,* but because essences require their own cause of existence which differs from the cause of existence of existents (*Ethica* I, P24 and Dem.). Essences are therefore neither logical possibilities nor mathematical structures nor metaphysical entities. Instead, essences are themselves physical realities *(res physicae).* This represents an extension not only of Scotus's formal distinction, as Deleuze notes,[46] but also of Suárez's 'objective reality,' as I explained in the previous chapter. Spinoza shares with both the priority of essence over existence and the concomitant devaluation of actuality. By contrast, the Christian Neo-Platonist metaphysics of Augustine, Boethius, Aquinas, and others establishes the epistemological priority of existence and the metaphysical primacy of the highest being or pure act of God.

On the philosophical status of essences, Deleuze's reading must however be questioned. Essences cannot be equated with his notion of 'physi-

44. Gilles Deleuze, *Spinoza et le problème de l'expression* (Paris: Éditions de Minuit, 1968), pp. 87-113. Cf. G. Deleuze, *Spinoza. Philosophie pratique* (Paris: Éditions de Minuit, 1981).

45. As Deleuze has documented, the unity between the oneness of the infinite substance and the plurality of finite objects and their singular essences is secured by the univocity of the attribute parallelism. For attributes are forms that are common to the substance and its modes. Deleuze, *Spinoza et le problème de l'expression*, pp. 33-43.

46. Deleuze, *Spinoza et le problème de l'expression,* pp. 173-96.

cal realities' because they can be in God without being in actuality (*Ethica* II, A1): to be in God is to be essentially (or virtually), not existentially. This follows from my earlier argument that for Spinoza the actualization of individual finite modes depends on the actualization of other finite modes. Since modes are modifications of the substance's attributes, modes in some sense disclose the nature of God and the coincidence of essence and existence *of* God *in* God: God who includes both existents and non-existents and who is constituted by Extension and Thought exceeds 'physical reality' and real actuality. Since God is both *causa sui* (*Kor. Verh.* I.1) and the efficient cause of all essences and existences (*Ethica* I, P25) including all immaterial ideas and material things, the 'reality' of the infinite substance — *Deus sive natura* — is best described as eternally present possibility and not actuality. Woolhouse puts this well:

> The reality of Spinoza's single substance is . . . in no way that of existent instantiation. It is, rather, a reality of a kind which makes it possible for there to be actual instantiations of extension, actual extended modes. . . . When he [Spinoza] says 'God exists' or 'extended substance exists', he means it 'essentially' rather than 'existentially'. It would not, however, be quite correct to say that Spinoza's extended substance or God is actually a nature or essence. It is rather . . . that it is what supports natures or essence, or where they are located.[47]

Spinoza equates God with possibility, which contrasts not only with the act of Aristotle's Prime Mover but also and above all with the pure act and self-diffusive goodness of God according to Aquinas. As such, to be in God is to be in the highest possibility, which is virtual, not actual. The actualization of finite modes is not integral to their being because higher than actuality stands reality. Nor is God's possibility utter transcendence which exceeds our grasp. On the contrary, *Deus sive natura* marks the identity of immanence with possibility, an idea that recurs in modern and contemporary phenomenology, in particular in the works of Martin Heidegger and Jean-Luc Marion, as I will briefly discuss in the following chapter.

47. Woolhouse, *Descartes, Spinoza, Leibniz*, pp. 45, 49. Matheron argues that attributes cannot produce all the finite modes at the same time, so that the essences of some modes are in God's mind before they exist. Matheron, *Individu et communauté chez Spinoza*, p. 20.

If the reality of the whole natural order is possibility and not actuality, then there are far-reaching implications for Spinoza's entire system and his theory of individuation, above all the unresolved passage from the infinity of God to the finitude of individual modes that do not necessarily exist. It is as if Spinoza's formal distinction between the order of ideas and the order of things had 'real' consequences — if the ideational were identical with the infinite immaterial and the extensional identical with the finite material. This requires a brief discussion of the connection between attributes and modes and existence and essence.

6. Attributes and Modes: Existence or Essence?

For Spinoza, only in God do essence and existence coincide and are one (*Ethica* I, P20). The uniqueness or unicity of God's eternal and infinite essence is necessarily to exist and to consist of an infinity of attributes, each of which expresses the divine eternal and infinite essence (*Ethica* I, P11). All modes are affections of the substance and are both extensional and ideational. Infinite *immediate* modes always already exist because they follow directly from the absolute nature of the substance. So do infinite *mediate* modes because they are caused through the medium of the primary modes (*Ethica* I, P28, Dem.). But finite modes are not automatically brought into existence: each finite mode has a singular essence *(essentia singularis),* which is in God's intellect but does not necessarily exist (*Kor. Verh.* App. I, P4; *Ethica* II, A1). Finite modes are actualized, not by the transcendence of divine will, but by the immanent self-caused activity of the substance which expresses itself in and through attributes and modes. The connection between the substance and its modes is provided by the attributes, which are common univocal forms that constitute the essence of the substance and encompass the essence of the modes. The community of forms between the substance and its modes ensures the dual inherence of God in all things and of all things in God (*Ethica* I, P28, Schol.). Likewise, the univocity of the attributes guarantees the essential difference between the necessary existence of God and the possible (though not contingent) existence of finite modes (*Ethica* IV, D4).[48]

Another way of explaining the distinction of essence in the sub-

---

48. Deleuze, *Spinoza et le problème de l'expression,* pp. 33-43, 87-98.

stance and in the modes is to highlight the two key differences between attributes and modes. First of all, attributes express the essence of the substance formally or qualitatively, whereas modes express the substance modally or quantitatively. As such, attributes are infinite, whereas modes can be both infinite and finite because quantity is divisible into infinitesimally small parts, including finite modes that express the substance in a "definite and determinate way" (*Ethica* I, P28, Dem.). Second, attributes not only express God's essence but also constitute God's existence (*Ethica* I, P20, Dem.). This does not apply to modes because their essence is distinct from their existence. The essence of modes expresses God intensively and the existence of modes expresses God extensively, but the modes do not constitute or modify the essence of God at all (*Kor. Verh.* I.2).

However, the nature of the link between the substance and its modes raises fundamental questions about Spinoza's theory of individuation. Univocity is not confined to the attributes (which are forms common to substance and modes) but also extends to causes, as God is both *causa sui* and the immanent and proximate cause of all things (*Kor. Verh.* I.3; *Ethica* I, P18, P28, Schol.), though not the transitive and remote cause. Coupled with the formal distinction between the essence of the substance and the essence of modes, this double univocity severs the metaphysical relation between God and all finite things. For finite modes are actualized and individuated by other modes which are themselves finite and have a "determinate existence" (*Ethica* I, P28, Dem. and Schol.), not by God. This does not mean that God is wholly erased from finitude. Spinoza's embrace of the mechanical principles of early modern philosophy (*Ep.* XIII) implies that God is the cause of all things and that all things depend on him for their reality and their conception.[49] But the actualization and the individuation of finite modes are cut off from God's causative productive action, as I have already indicated in the previous section.

This implication also emerges from Spinoza's understanding of finite modes: "A body in motion or at rest must have been determined to motion or rest by another body, which likewise has been determined to motion or rest by another body, and that body by another, and so *back to*

---

49. "All things which are, are in God, and depend on God, in such a way that they can neither be nor be conceived without him *(At omnia quae sunt in Deo sunt et a Deo ita dependent, ut sine ipso nec esse, nec concipi possint)*" (*Ethica* I, P28, Schol.).

infinity.[50] As David Rappaport Lachterman has argued, this conception of modality eliminates God from actualization and individuation because finite modifications do not and cannot emanate directly from God.[51] There is then in Spinoza's metaphysical system an unresolved question concerning the deduction of the finite from the infinite. Ultimately, it is not clear *why* the infinite substance would generate finite things and *how* it would cause infinite immediate modes which in turn actualize and individuate finite modes. Spinoza's claim that finite modes exist necessarily and do so in a definite and determinate manner is not an explanation of why the *infinite* substance expresses itself in *finite* modes.

Even if we accept Spinoza's distinction between the existence of singular things in God's attributes as ideas (*Ethica* II, P8, Cor.) and their existence in reality as objects (*Ethica* V, P29, Schol.),[52] we are faced with the non-correspondence of the two parallel orders because ideas are infinite and eternal, whereas objects are finite and temporal. This raises the question of why the essences of singular things are at all instantiated in finite materiality. Equally, to say that God acts because he is and because his essence is power (*Ethica* I, P34) fails to give an account of *why* God would express himself in finite rather than in infinite modes. Divine self-expression explains multiplicity, but not finitude: Spinoza asserts that "[p]articular things are nothing but affections of the attributes of God, that is, modes wherein the attributes of God find expression in a definite and determinate way."[53] But he fails to demonstrate *why* the 'definite and determinate' self-expression of the infinite requires material instantiation and *how* the difference between the finite and the infinite does not undermine the perfect parallelism and formal identity of Extension and Thought. Without an

50. *"Corpus motum vel quiescens ad motum vel quietem determinari debuit ab alio corpore, quod etiam ad motum vel quietem determinatum fuit ab alio, et illud iterum ab alio, et sic in infinitum"* (*Ethica* II, P13, Lem. 3). Here I follow the translation in Woolhouse, *Descartes, Spinoza, Leibniz*, p. 89.

51. David R. Lachterman, "The Physics of Spinoza's *Ethics*," in Shahan and Biro, eds., *Spinoza: New Perspectives*, pp. 71-111, esp. pp. 88-90.

52. Emilia Giancotti, "On the Problem of Infinite Modes," in *God and Nature: Spinoza's Metaphysics. Papers Presented at the First Jerusalem Conference (Ethica I)*, ed. Yirmiyahu Yovel (Leiden: E. J. Brill, 1991), pp. 97-118, esp. 108-13. Cf. John Carriero, "On the Relationship between Mode and Substance in Spinoza's Metaphysics," *Journal of the History of Philosophy* 33 (1995): 245-73.

53. *"Res particulares nihil sunt nisi Dei attributorum affectiones, sive modi, quibus Dei attributa certo et determinato modo exprimuntur"* (*Ethica* I, P25, Cor.).

account of the relation between the finite and the infinite, Spinoza's metaphysical system in general and his theory of individuation in particular are incomplete and incoherent. To say that these two orders coincide or correspond to the two constitutive aspects of reality (or 'the whole of Nature') is an assertion, not a demonstration. As such, it fails to address the real difference between the finite material and the infinite ideal.

In this and the previous section, I have argued that the distinction of the parallel orders is formal but also involves the tendency to identify the infinite with the ideational and the finite with the extensional, such that the doctrine of parallelism is paradoxically founded upon the separation of the finite from the infinite (as for Duns Scotus and Descartes). Since motion-and-rest is the principle that individuates finite modes and is part of the infinite immediate modes, this separation has consequences for Spinoza's theory of individuation and requires a discussion of his conception of modality, which is the focus of the next section.

7. The Causal Laws of Nature and the Nature of Causal Laws

Substance exceeds and enfolds the extended world because the latter is a mode of the substance, in this instance an infinite mediate mode that pertains to *natura naturata* rather than *natura naturans*.[54] In Part One of the *Ethics,* Spinoza defines modes as "the affections of substance, that is, that which is in something else and is conceived through something else."[55] This definition is developed into a complex three-tiered structure: infinite immediate modes, infinite mediate modes, and finite modes. The first two are eternal and infinite (*Ethica* I, P21-23). Infinite immediate modes derive absolutely and directly from one of God's attributes (*Kor. Verh.* I.8-9; *Ethica* I, P21 and Dem.), whereas infinite mediate modes derive from the divine attributes indirectly and "through the mediation of some modification which follows from the absolute nature of the attribute."[56] The third group can be described as finite modes,

---

54. *Natura naturans* is defined as "that which is in itself and is conceived through itself; that is, the attributes of substance that express eternal and infinite essence" (*Ethica* I, P29. Schol.). For an earlier account of this distinction, see *Kor. Verh.* I.8-9.

55. *"Per modum intelligo substantiae affectiones, sive id quod in alio est, per quod etiam concipitur"* (*Ethica* I, D5).

56. *"mediante aliqua modificatione, quae ex eius absoluta natura sequitur"* (*Ethica* I, P23, Dem.).

each of which "is finite and has a determinate existence" and follows from other such modes, not from God absolutely and directly. As a result, finite modes are from "God or one of his attributes insofar as it was modified by a modification which is finite and has a determinate existence."[57]

Examples of infinite immediate modes are 'absolutely infinite understanding' and 'motion and rest,' which are modes of the attribute of Thought and of Extension respectively (*Ep.* LXIV). The "body of the whole universe" *(facies totius universi)* is one of the few examples of infinite mediate modes within Spinoza's system, and it should be seen in relation to his definition of 'the whole of Nature' as one individual.[58] Most importantly for the purposes of my argument, finite modes are also described as singular things *(res singulares)*. Indeed, already in the *Short Treatise,* Spinoza excludes substance from the definition of individual things and instead associated motion and rest with individuality: "[E]xtension contains no other mode than motion and rest, and . . . every particular material thing is nothing else than a certain proportion of motion and rest."[59] This definition is repeated in the *Ethics,* where Spinoza writes that "[b]odies are distinguished from one another in respect of motion-and-rest, quickness and slowness, and not in respect of substance."[60]

It is however doubtful whether motion and rest can account for the individuation of bodies and whether the fixed proportions (or ratios) of motion and rest adequately capture the singularity of each and every body. Based on Jonathan Bennett's idea of Spinoza's 'field metaphysics,' Don Garrett maintains that Spinoza's conception of motion and rest as the principle of individuation is coherent. This is so because in his *Principles of Cartesian Philosophy,* Spinoza argues that the principle of motion and rest denotes not only a single pervasive feature of the universe in virtue of being an infinite immediate mode but also a double force — the quantity of motion and the quantity of rest. This double force, according to Garrett, explains the local motion and rest of particular bodies because the correlation between the quantity of force and the quan-

---

57. *"finita est et determinatam habet existentiam . . . a Deo, vel aliquo eius attributo, quatenus modificatum est modificatione, quae finita est et determinatam habet existentiam"* (*Ethica* I, P28 and Dem.).

58. Cited, *supra,* note 11. Cf. Giancotti, "On the Problem of Infinite Modes," p. 102.

59. *Kor. Verh.* App. II.

60. *"Corpora ratione motus et quietis, celeritatis et tarditatis, et non ratione substantiae ab invicem distinguuntur"* (*Ethica* II, P13, Lem. 1).

tity of rest constitutes singular things. As such, motion and rest can differentiate *qualitatively* between bodies and therefore explain what individuates bodies over time and across space.[61]

However, this account rests on the questionable assumption that Spinoza's complex three-tiered structure of modes in the *Ethics,* according to which motion-and-rest is an infinite immediate mode, is qualified by an earlier argument about local motion in the *Principles.* The point is that motion is not just universal or general but also particular and local. As such, it is the principle that individuates *this* and *that* finite mode, whereas motion-and-rest is the universal cause of individuation. But this is all the more questionable since Spinoza does not seem to refer to the concept of local motion and local rest in his account of finite modes in the *Ethics.* His core argument is instead that there is a fixed ratio of motion and rest for individual bodies 'back to infinity' and thus for Nature as a whole (*Ethica* II, P13, Lem. 3 and Lem. 7, Schol.). To say that universal motion-and-rest somehow individuates particular things begs the question.

Philosophically, Spinoza denies any relation between the particular (local motion and rest) and the universal (the infinite immediate mode of motion and rest) because he rejects the idea of relationality and instead posits the priority of the nomological infinite over the determinate finite — a claim that rests on the veracity of the mechanical laws which are said to govern the entire universe. These laws are the extended correlate of the 'ideated' common notion, as I suggested in section 2. My objection to this account is twofold. First of all, Spinoza himself wonders whether the human mind has the capacity to cognize these laws as universal. In the *Theological-Political Treatise,* composed after Part One and Two of *Ethics,* he writes:

> [W]e ought to define and explain things through their proximate causes; generalisations about fate and the interconnection of causes can be of no service to us in forming and ordering our thoughts concerning particular things. Furthermore, *we plainly have no knowledge as to the actual co-ordination and interconnection of things* — i.e. the

61. Garrett, "Spinoza's Theory of Metaphysical Individuation," esp. pp. 79-82. The reference to Spinoza is *Prin. Phil. Cart.* II, D8 and P21-22. Jonathan Bennett's term 'field metaphysics' can be found in Jonathan Bennett, *A Study of Spinoza's Ethics* (Indianapolis: Hackett, 1984), ch. 4.

way in which things are in actual fact ordered and connected — so that for practical purposes it is better, indeed, it is essential to consider things as contingent.[62]

Our effective inability to know "the actual coordination and interconnection of things" not only casts doubt on Spinoza's metaphysical system but has far-reaching implications for his politics, in particular his negative defense of democracy as the regime best suited to deal with the consequences of a lack of understanding the substance, its attributes and modes. Indeed, democracy is about diffusing power in order to prevent the formation of oligarchies and to cancel out conflicting narrow self-interest as a result of the failure to grasp one's own true station within the universe.

My second objection is that Spinoza fails to explain how motion, which follows immediately from extension, can be deduced a priori from the conception of extension on the basis of common notions that the mind cognizes without induction or abstraction. Ultimately, this problem is the result of Spinoza's failure to account for how and why matter is first set in motion, which he himself admits he has not solved.[63] In the following section I argue that Spinoza's identification of creation with efficient causality strips his metaphysical system of a conception of causality that would be in a position to account for the setting into motion of matter.

I will conclude this section by briefly examining Spinoza's account of the fixed proportions. In line with his doctrine of the parallel orders, Spinoza suggests that each and every thing is individual in virtue of having a certain determinate quantity of motion and rest (*Kor. Verh.* II, pref., app. II; *Ethica* II, P13). This quantity remains constant as a result of a fixed pattern or proportion *(ratio),* which is ultimately determined by the fixed laws of the eternal universe (*Ethica* II, P13, Lem. 7, Schol.; *Ep.* LXII). The actual quantity of motion and rest pertains to Extension, while the ratio and the laws pertain to Thought. In defense of Spinoza, Don Garrett claims that these conditions are less restrictive than they might seem.[64] As a result, Spinoza's idea of a certain kind of pattern, which describes the interrelation between the parts of a body, consti-

---

62. *Tract. Theol.-Polit.* chap. 4, 2 (my italics).
63. Cf. his last letter to Tschirnhaus of 15 July 1676 (*Ep.* LXXXIII [p. 365]).
64. Garrett, "Spinoza's Theory of Metaphysical Individuation," p. 86.

tutes — so Garrett's argument goes — a reasonable and coherent theory of individuation.

However, such and similar interpretations fail to recognize that the specificity of Spinoza's conception is to eliminate God from the process of individuation altogether and to shift the onus onto the individual itself and its tendency towards self-preservation vis-à-vis other individuals. (The *conatus,* which I discuss below, provides the link between Spinoza's metaphysics and his politics.) As Étienne Balibar has noted, the formulation "there is preserved in all together, that is in the whole universe, the same proportion of motion and rest"[65] derives from Descartes (cf. *Prin. Phil. Cart.* II.36).[66] But the crucial difference is that conservation is no longer attributed to the constant action of God's omnipotence but to an even closer union of each part with its whole. Given that individual bodies are "determined to exist and to act by another cause which is also finite and has a determinate existence,"[67] divine creative action is limited to efficient causality and has no import in the actualization and individuation of finite modes. While motion and rest at the cosmic level follow directly and absolutely from God, the fixed proportion at the level of the finite individual is determined by other finite individuals. This leads us to a discussion of Spinoza's understanding of creation.

8. Naturalized Creation

In this section, I argue that Spinoza's understanding of creation is philosophically and theologically questionable. This is significant for the question of individuation because his identification of God's creative action with efficient causality has the paradoxical effect of both immanentizing God and denying God any import in the production and individuation of singular things. I first summarize Spinoza's critique of creation *ex nihilo* before examining his theory of God's creative action. Spinoza dismisses the monotheistic conception of creation *ex nihilo* on three related

65. *Ep.* XXXII (p. 211).

66. Étienne Balibar, "Individualité, Causalité, Substance. Réflexions sur l'ontologie de Spinoza," in *Spinoza: Issues and Directions. The Proceedings of the Chicago Spinoza Conference,* ed. Edwin M. Curley and Pierre-François Moreau (Leiden: E. J. Brill, 1990), pp. 58-76 (61).

67. *"ad existendum et operandum determinetur ab alia causa, quae etiam finita est et determinatam habet existentiam"* (*Ethica* I, P28).

accounts. First, "something cannot come from nothing," and the theological claim that nothing is real is philosophically untenable (*Kor. Verh.* I.2; *Cog. Met.* II.7, 10). Second, creation implies that there is a finality that is external to God and acts upon him (*Cog. Met.* II.10; *Ethica* I, App.). Third, the theological idea of preserving beings in being in virtue of God's continuous creation is incompatible with the theological assertion of the free will. Philosophically, to say that God produces and sustains all beings is to say that nothing except God has free will because everything is and acts necessarily and in a divinely determined way (*Kor. Verh.* II.16; *Ethica* I, P16, P21-23, P26-27).

However, Spinoza wrongly claims that creation *ex nihilo* grants nothingness the same metaphysical station as reality. This is clearly not true for the Christian Neo-Platonism of Gregory of Nyssa, Augustine, Boethius, Dionysius, and Aquinas, who all maintain that 'nothing' *(nihil)* does not have the same metaphysical status as 'something.' For nothingness is privation of being. Spinoza himself recognizes that creation does in fact mean bringing things into being from nothingness:

> [B]ecause God has created all things wholly, not generating them from something else, and because the act of creation acknowledges no other cause but the efficient cause (for this is how I define 'creation'), which is God, it follows that before their creation things were nothing at all, and therefore God was also the cause of their essence.[68]

In this passage, Spinoza emphasizes the difference between creation and generation. Like the Christian Neo-Platonists analyzed in this essay, he argues that before being created, a being is nothing at all. But unlike them, he insists that creation must be equated with efficient causation: "We say that creation is an operation in which no causes concur beyond the efficient cause or that a created thing is that which presupposes nothing except God for its existence" (*Cog. Met.* II.10). As a result, God's creative action does not encompass material, formal, and final causality. The reality of the substance does not create directly and immediately the materiality of the modes; instead, the three types of modes follow from

---

68. *Prin. Phil. Cart.* I, P12, Cor. 2, Dem. Elsewhere Spinoza equates being with perfection and nonbeing with imperfection: "In a created thing, it is a perfection to exist and to have been produced by God, for the greatest imperfection of all is not being" (*Kor. Verh.* I.4).

the infinity of the attributes. Moreover, the substance does not determine the form of things: "The being of substance does not pertain to the essence of man, i.e., substance does not constitute the form of man."[69]

Finally, in the *Ethics,* he excludes final causation from creation and insists that philosophy must be purged of all forms of teleology: "[A]ll final causes are but figments of the human imagination."[70] Finality cannot apply to creation because nothing can be outside the all-encompassing substance. For the substance lacks nothing at all and is always already all that is and can be. God is not only the efficient operation that brings things into actual existence but also the condition of possibility for essences to be. For existence and act are coextensive in God: to exist is to act and to act is to exist (*Ethica* IV, preface). To reduce formal causality to efficient causality means that if an absolute infinite substance exists, which according to Spinoza it does necessarily, then the substance must give rise to an infinity of individual things.[71] Thus to identify creative action with efficient causality is to say that creation is God's self-expression. As such, creation is necessary, not free. But theologically, this proposition is incompatible with God's absolute freedom and omnipotence as well as with the freedom and autonomy of creation.

The second respect in which creation is philosophically and theologically problematic concerns the question of God's existence. In order to constitute the formal ground for existence for all things, God himself must of course exist. At first, this appears to be a rigorous (onto)-logical proof of the existence of God because it can be rationally derived from the existence of finite things that are knowable (Spinoza's a posteriori

---

69. *"Ad essentiam hominis non pertinet esse substantiae, sive substantia formam hominis non constituit"* (*Ethica* II, P10).

70. *"omnes causas finales nihil nisi humana esse figmenta"* (*Ethica* I, App.). The philosophical rationale for Spinoza is that the doctrine of final causes turns Nature upside down, "for it regards as an effect that which is in fact a cause, and vice-versa. And it makes that which is by nature first to be last" (*Ethica* I, App.). Cf. Don Garrett, "Teleology in Spinoza and Early Modern Rationalism," in *New Essays on the Rationalists,* ed. Rocco J. Gennaro and Charles Huenemann (New York: Oxford University Press, 1999), pp. 310-35.

71. In Spinoza's own words, "From the necessity of the divine nature there must follow infinite things in infinite ways (i.e. everything that can come within the scope of infinite intellect)" (*Ethica* I, P16). "From God's supreme power or infinite nature an infinity of things in infinite ways — i.e. everything — has necessarily flowed or is always following from that same necessity, just as from the nature of a triangle.... Therefore God's omnipotence has from eternity been actual and will remain for eternity in the same actuality" (*Ethica,* I, P17, Schol.).

proof in the *Short Treatise* I.1). Conjointly, the reality of the one substance and the formality of the attribute parallelism imply that each thing is both idea and object and that each idea and each object require a first idea and a first object that coincide. However, on closer inspection, the structure of Spinoza's metaphysics subjects God to an (onto-)logic of possibility which is above and prior to actuality. Indeed, drawing on Descartes's definition of God as *causa sui*,[72] Spinoza specifies that "[b]y that which is self-caused I mean that whose essence involves existence; or that whose nature can be conceived only as existing."[73] This definition of *causa sui* implies one of two things. Either God's effective existence is formally deduced from his a priori essence — but Spinoza excludes this by arguing that in God essence and existence are coterminous.[74] Or God exists necessarily because there is no reason to suppose why he would not: "[E]ither nothing exists, or an absolutely infinite Entity necessarily exists, too. But we do exist, either in ourselves, or in something else which necessarily exists. Therefore, an absolutely infinite Entity — that is, God, necessarily exists."[75]

This kind of reasoning subjects God to an (onto-)logic of abstract possibility. God necessarily exists because there is no *logical* reason for his nonexistence,[76] even though ontologically there could be: "For every thing a cause or reason must be assigned either for its existence or its

72. On Descartes's account of God as *causa sui*, see Jean-Luc Marion, *Sur le prisme métaphysique de Descartes. Constitution et limites de l'onto-théo-logie dans la pensée cartésienne* (Paris: Presses Universitaires de France, 1986), esp. §7, pp. 88-111. On the difference and similarities between Spinoza and Descartes concerning *causa sui*, see Vincent Carraud, *Causa sive ratio. La raison de la cause, de Suarez à Leibniz* (Paris: Presses Universitaires de France, 2002), pp. 295-341. I am indebted to Carraud for some of the arguments in this and the following paragraph.

73. *"Per causam sui intelligo id, cuius essentia involvit existentiam, sive id, cuius natura non potest concipi, nisi existens"* (*Ethica* I, D1). Subsequently in the *Ethics*, Spinoza of course writes that "existence belongs to the nature of substance" and that "substance cannot be produced by anything else and is therefore its own cause" (*Ethica* I, P7 and proof).

74. *Kor. Verh.* App. I, P4; *Cog. Met.* I.2.

75. *"vel nihil existit, vel ens absolute infinitum necessario etiam existit. Atqui nos, vel in nobis, vel in alio, quod necessario existit, existimus. Ergo ens absolute infinitum, hoc est, Deus necessario existit"* (*Ethica* I, P11, Dem. 3).

76. In the words of Spinoza, "If there can be no reason or cause which prevents God from existing or which annuls his existence, we are bound to conclude that he necessarily exists [*Si itaque nulla ratio, nec causa dari possit, quae impedit, quominus Deus existat, vel quae eius existentiam tollat, omnino concluendum est, eundem necessario existere*]" (*Ethica* I, P11, second proof).

non-existence."[77] Put differently, God exists not only because he is his own cause but also and above all because ultimately there is no reason or cause why he would not exist.[78] Paradoxically, nonexistence is the condition of logical possibility for God's necessary a priori existence.

The implication for creation and individuation is that the actuality of individual finite modes does not disclose anything about God because God's self-expression is complete in the infinity of attributes. Matheron would reject this interpretation on the ground that for Spinoza, "everything does indeed end up existing."[79] However, the unresolved passage from the infinite to the finite shifts the onus of actualization of the finite modes away from the directly creative action of the substance onto the infinite immediate and mediate modes.[80] As a result, the actualization of finite modes is severed from creation.

The third respect in which Spinoza's account of creation is philosophically and theologically dubious stems from the priority of essential possibility over existential actuality and the nature of actualization. Since God is at the same time *causa sui* and cause of all phenomena (their singular essences as well as their individual existences),[81] it follows that formal causality is univocal for the substance as well as for its modifications. This is because both the substance and all its modifications require a cause or a (principle of) sufficient reason *(causa seu ratio)*[82] in order to be. So not unlike Duns Scotus's development of a theory of univocity of being, Spinoza defends the idea of a univocity of cause for the Creator and for creatures alike. As I have indicated, God exists because there is no reason for him not to exist. But for all things other than the substance, essence does not involve existence — as essences, entities can be in God's intellect without their actually existing objective correlates. Yet at the same time, God's necessary existence is his equally nec-

77. *Ethica* I, P11, second proof.

78. This sort of reasoning calls forth arguments about theodicy, as was indeed the case with Leibniz.

79. Alexandre Matheron, "Essence, Existence and Power in *Ethics* I: The Foundations of Proposition 16," in Yirmiyahu Yovel, ed., *God and Nature: Spinoza's Metaphysics* (Leiden: E. J. Brill, 1991), pp. 23-34 (29).

80. As I argue in the following section, this configuration shifts the onus of individuation onto the finite modes themselves, i.e., the *conatus*, which inheres in each and every one of all the modes.

81. *Ethica* I, P25, Schol. and II, P10, Schol.

82. *Inter alia, Ethica* IV, App.

essary creative activity. So the actuality of individual modes is either accidental or arbitrary. This conclusion emerges from Spinoza's own
definition of existence in relation to essence:

> [F]ormal essence is not self-generated nor again is it created — for
> both these would presuppose that it is a thing existing in actuality —
> but it depends on the divine essence alone, in which all things are con-
> tained. And so in this sense we agree with those who say that the es-
> sences of things are eternal.[83]

So the formal difference of the infinite and the finite and the ideational
and the extensional amounts to a real primacy of the eternity of essences
in God's mind over the finitude of existences that unfold. For God does
not create all possible actualities at once.

Most importantly Spinoza, by rejecting creation *ex nihilo,* also dismisses two key concepts: first of all, the patristic and medieval idea that
God is beyond substance and, second, the idea of a real difference and
real relations between ideas and objects and ultimately between the substance and its modes.[84] Instead, Spinoza reconfigures Aristotelian metaphysics in the direction of an asymmetric inherence of the substance in
the modes and of the modes in the substance by positing God's self-
expression as the cause of creative inherence and dependency as the
cause of created inherence. Spinoza's variant of metaphysics cannot
demonstrate why God creates and why he creates individual things. To
say, as Spinoza does, that individual phenomena and 'the whole of Nature' (the sum total of the infinity of individual phenomena) exist because they are the self-expression of God is not to enquire into the question of why God would wish to express himself and why his self-
expression takes the form of individuals. His account of creation and individuation is therefore philosophically and theologically problematic.
In the following section, I relate this to Spinoza's theory of the individual
power of self-preservation — the *conatus.*

---

83. *Cog. Met.* I.2. In chapter 3 of the same text, Spinoza writes that "if it is in the divine
decree that a thing should exist, it will necessarily exist" (*Cog. Met.* I.3).

84. *Kor. Verh.* I.8; I.10. Cf. Marcelo Dascal, "Unfolding the One: 'Abstract Relations' in
Spinoza's Theory of Knowledge," in Yovel, ed., *Spinoza on Knowledge and the Human Mind,*
pp. 171-85.

9. *Conatus* or the Ethics of Self-Individuation and the Politics of Democracy

In the previous sections, I argued that in Spinoza's system creation becomes unhinged from actualization and individuation. Paradoxically, the onus shifts away from the one infinite substance to the infinite immediate and infinite mediate modes, which are the direct mediation through which finite modes are generated. Likewise, finite modes are individuals as a result of a certain ratio (or proportion) of motion and rest, determined by the fixed laws of the eternal order which are part of the infinite immediate and the infinite mediate modes respectively. In this section, I argue that individuation is for Spinoza the endeavor for self-preservation of all things. Self-preservation is a function of the natural power that inheres in each and every thing, or Spinoza's idea of the *conatus* (*Ethica* III, P6).

The *conatus* marks the coincidence of metaphysics, ethics, and politics on three related accounts. First of all, the striving towards self-preservation applies to animate and inanimate beings alike (*Ethica* III, P7). Second, the activity involved in this striving defines the nature and the scope of each thing's natural right (*Ethica* IV, D8; *Tract. Pol.* II.3). Third, the power of this striving defines each person's virtue (*Ethica* IV, D8). As a result, actualization and individuation are metaphysical, ethical, and political. Before I highlight the ethical and political dimension, I will briefly outline Spinoza's argument for the *conatus* and the underpinning theory in relation to his metaphysical system, notably his conception of inherence.

Part One of the *Ethics* on God lays the foundation of Spinoza's theory of the *conatus,* in particular the necessary coincidence of essence and existence in the one substance which is the immanent and proximate (not transitive and remote) cause of "the whole of Nature" and all that is in it. God is in all things and all things are in God (*Ethica* I, P28, Schol.). As such, each individual thing depends on God for its essence, existence, and sustenance in being. All singular things are modes that express in a certain and determinate way God's essence, i.e., the power by which God is and acts (*Ethica* I, P25, Cor., and I, P34). In Parts Two and Three, Spinoza extends this metaphysical system by arguing that "nothing can be destroyed except by an external cause" (*Ethica* III, P4, Dem.) because there is nothing in a thing's essence that can destroy that thing. Conversely, "every thing, insofar as it is in itself, strives to persevere in its being," a universal endeavor that Spinoza describes elsewhere as the *conatus*.[85] In virtue of the *conatus*, each thing resists that which can take its existence away (*Ethica* III, P6, Dem.). As such, the *conatus* is the actual essence of all things (*Ethica* III, P7).

Spinoza argues that the power of persevering in one's being is a function of the extent of being in oneself. In consequence, one key question this definition raises is the meaning of being in itself (*in se est*). If, as he maintains, all modes, including singular finite modes, are modes of God (*Ethica* I, D5; I, P25, Cor.) and must therefore be *in* God (*Ethica* I, P28, Schol.), then how can they also be partly in themselves? According to Don Garrett, Spinoza's argument is coherent because there are infinitely many "ways of being in God" and being partly in oneself is just one such way: "[W]hatever is to any extent *in* a singular thing is *in* God as well, *in* God *through* being *in* one of his finite modes."[86] Garrett describes this position as Spinoza's metaphysics of inherence. But the problem that Spinoza fails to resolve is how all things are to some extent in themselves (*in se*), while also lacking any freedom because they exist necessarily and are utterly dependent on the one substance. The question then is whether Spinoza's metaphysical system can conjoin the absolute power of the substance with the relative autonomy of the finite modes.

Spinoza's own answer is that finite modes and their striving for self-preservation are an expression of God's eminent being and his omnipotence. However, it is not clear in what manner the infinite substance, which alone sustains everything in being, can be squared with a self-preserving power that is proper to finite modes. To say that finite modes are endowed with their own endeavor for preservation as well as a share in God's infinite power fails to explain how there can be anything in addition to the infinity of divine power. Either the *conatus* is part of God's self-expression, in which case finite modes cannot be partly in themselves because they depend absolutely on God and only are in virtue of being in God. Or else the *conatus* is distinct from God's self-expression, in which case there appears to be something beyond the substance, something for which the causal productive action of the substance cannot account. Since modes are not directly caused by God, yet at the same time nothing is outside the all-encompassing substance, neither configuration is compatible with the tenets of Spinoza's own metaphysical system.

---

85. "*Unaquaeque res, quantum in se est, in suo esse perseverare conatur*" (*Ethica* III, P6).
86. Garrett, "Spinoza's *Conatus* Argument," p. 140 (original italics).

The unresolved connection between God's productive power and the finite power of self-preservation can be traced back to the equally unresolved link between the single substance and the dual attributes and between the infinite and the finite. For the formality of these two distinctions precludes any real difference and therefore any real relation between the finite modes and the substance. There is a marked contrast with the patristic and medieval Christian Neo-Platonist vision of relationality. Instead of the metaphysics that describes how the whole of creation is constituted by its relation to God, which testifies to the utter ecstatic plenitude of God's goodness and love, Spinoza advocates a meta-logic that merely asserts the coincidence and nonidentity of a productive God and the whole of Nature, which constitutes nothing but divine self-expression.

This shift from the patristic and medieval metaphysics of relationality, which centers on the ontological difference and participation, has significant consequences for individuation. Both actualization and individuation are situated at the level of the three-tiered structure of modes, as I argued in the previous section. The actualization of hitherto nonexisting modes (i.e., the coming into actual existence of eternal essences) requires the displacement of already existing modes. Each thing has its ascribed place, which is determined by the fixed laws of the *cosmos,* as I suggested in section 6. Coupled with Spinoza's mechanistic principle that there is a constant quantum of motion and rest (or energy) in the universe, the consequence is that the advent of a new set of modes involves the destruction of an established group of modes.

Thus, at the heart of Spinoza's account of the creation (or production) of modes, there is a necessary and inevitable competition and rivalry among different groups of modes. This shaped his theory of individuation, as individuals *qua* individuals are limited in their knowledge of the 'whole of Nature' and therefore ignore their particular station therein. As a result, there is potential conflict between individual finite modes. Moreover, only those individuals who can attain the third kind of knowledge (the immediate grasp of essences) can transcend their own finitude and individuality and rise to the point where they are able to cognize the commonality of the substance in which all modes inhere. The aporia in Spinoza's system is that individuality is at once a necessary reality and a contingent illusion: necessary and real because the substance is individual and everything is *of* the substance; contingent and illusory because nothing is by itself and individuals exist as part of groups

378

of modes. In Spinoza's system, true knowledge of one's simultaneous individuality and commonality is in some crucial sense a privilege granted only to the sages. Among those who do not attain the third kind of knowledge there is conflict because illusions about individuality collide.

In fact, individual knowledge is governed by the confusion of the particular environment with the universal order. Individuals, not unlike the worm in the bloodstream (*Ep.* XXXII),[87] tend to ignore the fixed laws of the eternal order and thereby fail to recognize their true station therein. The ensuing transgression requires a democratic regime, which represents the best attempt to conjoin majority rule with the protection of individual natural rights in order to strike a balance between conflicting interest and legitimate power. Both commonality and democracy constitute responses to a metaphysics that posits the violence of opposition and an inherently conflictual state of nature (in the absence of third knowledge). This contrasts with the shared Christian Neo-Platonist vision of a created order whose relationality intimates the peace of reconciliation and a harmonious mediation of difference.

This account has significant implications for ethics and politics, in particular the metaphysical foundations of commonality and democracy. First of all, the parallelism of the extensional and the ideational signifies that there is coincidence yet noninteraction between being and knowing. Just as commonality follows from the nature of individual being, so democracy follows from the nature of individual knowledge. Individual being is dictated by the struggle for self-preservation against rival groups of individuals, such that commonality is the result of causally determined relations that ascribe fixed stations in the hierarchical order of the universe. Commonality marks the attempt, first, to enforce hierarchy according to the particular share in the absolute power of infinite substance, second, to secure equality by granting each and every thing a natural right to exist and to act and, third, to proscribe transgressions of this order by denying freedom of the will.

Indeed, Spinoza's vision of politics follows from his metaphysics and is a complex mixture of the hierarchical and the egalitarian. Just as metaphysics and politics are coextensive, so the "existential contract" (Alexandre Matheron) between the finite modes and the substance is the basis for the social contract and natural law. This fundamental egalitarianism is qualified by an equally fundamental hierarchy of power. Finite

---

87. Sacksteder, "Spinoza on Part and Whole: The Worm's Eye View," pp. 139-59.

modes act according to their naturally given power and each strives for self-preservation and a station in the natural order according to power thus distributed. Only the sages are apt to rule over others because only they are in a position to attain the third kind of knowledge. Not unlike Aristotle's aristocracy, Spinoza posits absolute divisions between those who are able to engage in contemplative activity and those who are confined to nonintellectual work. This is markedly different from Plato's idea of the Good, which infuses all things with goodness and thus enables all things to have some knowledge of it.

The second implication for Spinoza's ethics and politics is that commonality and democracy are embodied by a politics that seeks to regulate the rivalry and competition between individual finite modes that follows from his metaphysics, instead of aiming at real reconciliation and genuine peace. Commonality is a necessary consequence of the nature of individual being, i.e., the hierarchy of relative individuals where each individual is at once composed of lower-order individual parts and itself a component of a higher-order individual. This hierarchy is potentially violent because it is grounded in the idea that beings are distinguished by their power to destroy other beings: "There is in Nature no individual thing that is not surpassed in strength and power by some other thing. Whatsoever thing there is, there is another more powerful by which the said thing can be destroyed."[88] The pursuit of self-preservation involves exclusion and elimination and therefore men are naturally enemies (*Tract. Pol.* VIII.12). As a result, all beings are always already inscribed in causally determined relations with other beings. But these relations are absolutely necessary and serve nothing but survival. Indeed, the formation of communities occurs because men cannot lead an isolated solitary existence, and the sustenance of life requires mutual assistance (*Ethica* IV, App. 12).

Equally, democracy is a necessary consequence of the nature of individual knowledge, i.e., the limits on human understanding according to which each individual (by analogy with the worm in the bloodstream [*Ep.* XXXII]) mistakes its environment for the whole world and fails to grasp the universal fixed laws of the eternal universe. As a result, individuals confound their own self-interest with the common interest. In order to avoid the formation and consolidation of oligarchic clusters of power,

---

88. *"Nulla res singularis in rerum natura datur, qua potentior et fortior non detur alia. Sed quacumque data datur alia potentior, a qua illa data potest destrui"* (*Ethica* IV, Ax.).

what is required is a democratic regime that tends to diffuse power and to cancel out conflicting self-interest. So configured, democracy seeks to regulate the opposition and ensuing conflict between natural enemies. Yet at the same time, the very logic of democracy — policing rival interests — does not overcome the violence of rivalry and competition and foreshadows the path towards two ideologies — the libertarianism of J. S. Mill and the organicism of Marx. As such, Spinoza's metaphysics inaugurates the modern (and postmodern) dualism and opposition between two false alternatives — liberalism and communism. This conflict mirrors the nature of finite modality, which is at once a necessary reality and a contingent illusion. Only the sages transcend this aporetic condition and can grasp the commonality of the substance below and beyond the individuality of finite modes. Neither free nor individuated, Spinoza's vision of politics oscillates between a *de facto* autocracy of the wise and a *de iure* democracy of the ignorant.

10. Conclusion: Ontology of Production

In this chapter, I have argued that Spinoza's rejection of ancient and medieval philosophy and theology leads him to discard both transcendent causes of individuality and transcendent principles of individuation. Things are not individual because they are particular substances but by virtue of being finite modes of the single infinite substance. Likewise, things are not actualized by the substance but by the infinite immediate and the infinite mediate modes. Finally, things are not individuated by matter or form but by the power of preservation and perfection (the *conatus*), which is immanent to each and every mode. Moreover, Spinoza's dismissal of the idea of creation *ex nihilo* redefines creation in terms of efficient causality and to accomplish the late scholastic turn that had been inaugurated by Scotus and extended by Suárez. This turn establishes the absolute primacy of metaphysics over theology. I have also shown that in reducing formal to efficient causality Spinoza makes divine creative action utterly necessary.

Spinoza's claim about the necessity of all existing things raises the problem of how to combine individuality and commonality. If everything is a mode of the one substance and if, as such, everything is an integral part of the universe which exists necessarily because the essence of the all-encompassing substance is to exist and to express itself in an infinity of modes, then all singular modes require a community in order to exist. Yet at the same time, since attributes cannot produce all modes at the same time, groups of modes compete with each other over their place in the universe.

Spinoza attempts to blend the particular and the communal by arguing that there is no rivalry between the *conatus* of singular modes because each individual has a certain power of perseverance, which determines its proportionate participation in the all-inclusive substance. Just as the *conatus* grounds the natural right of all individuals, so democracy secures both individuality and commonality. However, I contend that the basis for community and democracy is the need to overcome the conflict that arises from a lack of knowledge and understanding. There is competition because individuals fail to grasp their own station within the natural order. While the rule of the sages is the ideal form of government, the rule of the many is the best of all actually available forms. The tension between self-preservation and the commonweal can be traced to Spinoza's metaphysics of necessary self-production and marks a significant contrast with the Christian Neo-Platonist metaphysics of free creation.

Ultimately, my argument is that Spinoza cannot give an account of *how* and *why* nature at once individuates and enfolds all phenomena. Why would the one and only absolute infinite indivisible substance express itself in finite material divisible things? Why — in the absence of any final causes — would individual finite things want to be individuated (*Ethica* I, App.)? How would they be so by their connection with a substance that does not need them and is not their proximate cause (*Kor. Verh.* I.3)? I therefore conclude that his account of individuation fails on its own terms because it is unable to demonstrate its specific claims about the individuality and interconnection of particular phenomena and 'the whole of Nature.'

CHAPTER 9

Ontology or Metaphysics?

1. Introduction: The Modern End of Metaphysics

In this final chapter, I argue that modernity radicalizes the late medieval, scholastic redefinition of metaphysics as the transcendental science of ontology and the concomitant relegation of theology to the sole sphere of the supernatural. Late modern critics from Nietzsche to Heidegger to Jacques Derrida to Jean-Luc Marion are wrong to dismiss the whole western tradition of metaphysics since Plato as onto-theological. Rather, the dominant traditions of modern thinking are founded upon a more Aristotelian 'categorial ontology' and 'causal theology' that rejected the Christian Neo-Platonist metaphysics of creation. In fact, the rise of modernity is linked to the development of a mechanistic natural theology (based on efficient causality) and an atomistic ontology (grounded in univocal being and radical singularity) that supplanted the symphonic — albeit imperfect — synthesis of metaphysical theology, teleological cosmology, and relational anthropology in the tradition of Christian Neo-Platonism, as I have argued in the preceding chapters. The present chapter goes further and suggests that 'the modern' collapses divine being and created being into a single univocity and singularity whose virtual formality is transcendentally prior even to the possibility of essence and the actuality of existence. By contrast, Neo-Platonist theology defends the idea of a metaphysical reality of God's transcendent creative act of being in which all immanent beings participate. In this sense, modern philosophy is correlated with a transcendental science of ontology that displaces and ultimately destroys metaphysics.

It follows that the real alternative to the transcendental science of ontology is neither an ontology purged of all theology (Husserl and Heidegger) nor a pure phenomenology without being (Marion), nor even an 'ontological' metaphysics beyond the phenomenological and analytic divide (Levinas and Badiou). Instead, the only genuine alternative that will be proposed in the present chapter is a revivified theological metaphysics that develops Plato's notion of relational participation in the direction of Trinitarian relationality, which upholds the 'ontological difference' between Creator and creation through analogical relation and anagogical union with God. This account — which can be traced to the plural tradition of patristic and medieval Christian Neo-Platonism from Gregory of Nyssa, Augustine, and Dionysius via Boethius and Aquinas to Meister Eckhart and Nicholas of Cusa — finds its modern expressions in a variety of distinct yet converging strands. First of all, the metaphysical theology of Renaissance Italian civic humanism and the Neapolitan Enlightenment (Marsilio Ficino, Pico della Mirandola, Leonardo Bruni, Paolo Mattia Doria, Gianbattista Vico, Antonio Genovesi, and Pietro Verri).[1] Second, the Cambridge Platonism of Shaftesbury and Cudworth (and, to a lesser extent, the Scottish Enlightenment of Hume and Smith via Hutcheson).[2] Third, nineteenth- and early-twentieth-century Russian sophiology. Fourth, *nouvelle théologie* and its contemporary developments in Europe and North America. It is the unrealized potential of this rival tradition of Renaissance and Enlightenment philosophy and theology which offers a path towards an alternative modernity that is far more theologically orthodox and politically radical than the dubious attempts to rehabilitate the mainstream English, French, German, or American enlightenments championed by Anglo-Saxon and continental European thinkers of the left or the right.[3]

1. On the Platonist civic humanism of the Italian Renaissance and Enlightenment, see Eugenio Garin, *L'umanesimo italiano* (Bari: G. Laterza, 1958), English translation: *Italian Humanism: Philosophy and Civic Life in the Renaissance,* trans. Peter Munz (Oxford: Blackwell, 1965); Henri de Lubac, *Pic de la Mirandole. Études et discussions* (Paris: Aubier-Montaigne, 1974); John Milbank, *The Religious Dimension in the Thought of Giambattista Vico, 1668-1744,* 2 vols. (Lampeter, UK: Edwin Mellen Press, 1991); James Hankins, *Plato in the Italian Renaissance,* 2 vols., rev. ed. (Leiden: E. J. Brill, 1994).

2. On the shared intellectual foundations of the Italian and the Scottish Enlightenment, which combine key aspects of Christian Neo-Platonist metaphysics with Epicurean and Stoic elements, see John Robertson, *The Case for the Enlightenment: Scotland and Naples 1680-1760* (Cambridge: Cambridge University Press, 2005), pp. 201-405.

3. See, *inter alia,* Jürgen Habermas, *Der gespaltene Westen* (Frankfurt am Main:

A detailed discussion of the main theories of individuation in modernity is beyond the scope of this chapter. Instead, I will relate the late medieval and early modern shifts within theology to modern accounts of individuation. As in previous chapters, the focus will be on theological alternatives to purely philosophical conceptions, in this case the new science of transcendental ontology and the concomitant idea that individuality is grounded in immanent things themselves rather than linked to the transcendent source of being in which all things participate.

2. Modern Metaphysics as Transcendental Ontology

This section of the chapter challenges the dominant terms of debate framing the relation between philosophy and theology. Traditionally modernity has been equated with metaphysics and 'postmodernity' with postmetaphysics, whether a phenomenological science of pure appearing without being or an analytic philosophy of language and logic prior to being. However, this foundational distinction relies on a questionable reading of the origins and the nature of the 'modern' and the 'postmodern.' Here one can say with the French philosopher of science Bruno Latour that "we have never been modern," for there was never any absolute, irreversible break in history that gave rise to a coherent system of ideas and institutions which we commonly call 'modernity.'[4] Rather, there are profound continuities between the late Middle Ages and the modern era that continue to shape our contemporary 'postmodern condition' (Jean-François Lyotard).[5] Indeed, both modern philosophy and theology emerged from the confluence of three significant shifts within

Suhrkamp, 2004), English translation: *The Divided West,* ed. Ciaran Cronin (Cambridge: Polity Press, 2006), pp. 113-93; Gertrude Himmelfarb, *The Roads to Modernity: The British, French, and American Enlightenments* (New York: Random House, 2004); Jonathan I. Israel, *Radical Enlightenment: Philosophy and the Making of Modernity, 1650-1750* (Oxford: Oxford University Press, 2001), and *Enlightenment Contested: Philosophy, Modernity, and the Emancipation of Man 1670-1752* (Oxford: Oxford University Press, 2006).

4. Bruno Latour, *Nous n'avons jamais été modernes. Essai d'anthropologie symétrique* (Paris: Éditions la Découverte, 1991), English translation: *We Have Never Been Modern,* trans. Catherine Porter (New York and London: Harvester Wheatsheaf, 1993).

5. Jean-François Lyotard, *La condition post-moderne. Rapport sur le savoir* (Paris: Éditions de Minuit, 1979), English translation: *The Postmodern Condition: A Report on Knowledge,* trans. Geoff Bennington and Brian Massumi (Manchester: Manchester University Press, 1984).

the 'Western' traditions of late medieval scholasticism: first of all, the Avicennian primacy of essence over existence (chapter 4); second, the Scotist destruction of (what would later be validly described as) Thomist *analogia entis* in favor of the univocity of being (chapters 5 and 6); and third, the Suárezian priority of metaphysics as the science of general being over theology as the science of revelation and the concomitant separation of 'pure nature' from the supernatural (chapter 7).[6]

Taken together, these shifts amount to the substitution of transcendental ontology for metaphysics. Following Scotist univocity and Suárezian general metaphysics, the German thinker Johannes Clauberg or Clauvergius (1622-1665) replaced the term 'metaphysics' with *'ontosophia'* or 'ontology' in order to describe the science of being *qua* being[7] — a science that theorizes the common nature or degree of being that is both in God and in creatures. In turn, this conception underpins three traditions that have dominated philosophy ever since: first, the rationalist or idealist transcendentalism of Descartes, Hobbes, Wolff, and Kant; second, the empiricist or vitalist immanentism of Spinoza, Locke, Smith, and Bergson; third, the residually transcendental science of ontology masquerading as an atheological, pure philosophy (from Husserl and Heidegger via Sartre to Deleuze and, perhaps to a lesser extent, Marion). Moreover, much of postmodern philosophy (especially in its phenomenological guise) retrieves and extends the late medieval, onto-theological scholasticism that inaugurated the modern era, as the work of John Milbank and Catherine Pickstock has shown.[8] So if 'postmodernity' is in the end an intensification of certain modern trends rather than a new phase of history, perhaps it is then also the case that

---

6. As the previous chapters indicate, this argument is based on the pioneering work of Étienne Gilson and Henri de Lubac's *nouvelle théologie* in the first half of the twentieth century, which was subsequently refined and developed by scholars as varied as André de Muralt, Jean-Luc Marion, Jean-François Courtine, Olivier Boulnois, Ludger Honnefelder, and Louis Dupré (amongst others).

7. Johannes Clauberg, *Elementa philosophiae sive ontosophiae* (Groningen: Joannis Nicolai, 1647). See Étienne Gilson, *L'Être et l'Essence*, 2nd ed. (Paris: Vrin, 1972), pp. 144-86; Jean-François Courtine, *Suarez et le système de la métaphysique* (Paris: Presses Universitaires de France, 1990), pp. 246-92, 436-57.

8. For a summary statement of this thesis, see the two complementary articles by Catherine Pickstock, "Postmodern Scholasticism: Critique of Postmodern Univocity," *Telos* 126 (2003): 3-24, and "Modernity and Scholasticism: A Critique of Recent Invocations of Univocity," *Antonianum* 78 (2003): 3-46.

the modern is in fact synonymous with transcendental ontology and not after all with metaphysics.

How so? First of all, much of modern philosophy — and theology — rejects the metaphysical realism that views being and God as the transcendental reality in which everything participates. Since the important scholarship of Jean-Luc Marion, we know that René Descartes's 'mechanistic metaphysics' is not reducible to an epistemological project predicated on early modern skepticism but instead seeks to renew and surpass Aristotle's 'first philosophy' by grounding knowledge of the self and God's existence in a 'gray ontology' and a 'white theology.'[9] Here one can go beyond Marion's proto-phenomenological reading and argue that Descartes operates a double substitution. First, he replaces the metaphysics of participation with an onto-theology of representation, and second, he replaces the politics of transcendently ordered objectivity governed by the good with a politics of transcendentally secured immanent subjectivity ruled by God's absolute power. Both representation and subjectivity derive from two Cartesian claims that are diametrically opposed to the Neo-Platonist metaphysics of creation: first, Descartes's undemonstrated separation of the infinite from the finite; second, fusing God's arbitrary will (beyond even Ockham's voluntarism) and divine *causa sui* (beyond even Aristotle's theo-ontology) in order to explain the ultimate ground of being. Accordingly, the finite *ego* cogitates the foundationalism of *deus infinitus* based on clear and distinct, divinely caused eternal ideas which are innate in the human mind — an account that is at odds with Augustine's theological epistemology of divine illumination and his 'musical metaphysics' (as detailed in chapter 2).

Empiricism, like rationalism, is similarly founded upon the destruction of the Neo-Platonist vision of analogical relation between the finite things of creation that participate in the infinite plenitudinous actuality of the Creator. For example, Descartes's empiricist critic John Locke attacks the idea of creation's sharing in intra-Trinitarian relations on the basis of his dogmatic commitment to ontological atomism and posses-

---

9. Jean-Luc Marion, *Sur l'ontologie grise de Descartes: Science cartésienne et savoir aristotélicien dans les Regulae*, 2nd ed. (Paris: Vrin, 1981); J.-L. Marion, *Sur la théologie blanche de Descartes: Analogie, création des vérités éternelles et fondement* (Paris: Presses Universitaires de France, 1981); J.-L. Marion, "Descartes et l'Onto-théologie," *Bulletin de la Société Française de Philosophie* 76 (1982): 117-71; J.-L. Marion, *Sur le prisme métaphysique de Descartes. Constitution et limites de l'onto-théo-logie dans la pensée cartésienne* (Paris: Presses Universitaires de France, 1986).

sive individualism, as I will argue later in this chapter. Beyond rationalism and empiricism, Kant seeks to ground his metaphysics of morals in a critically bounded rationality, which in his late work mutates into a reason reaching infinity (rather like Spinoza) and a transcendental ontology combining subjective immanence with objective transcendence.[10] But more fundamentally, Kant's critique replaces the metaphysically given natural desire for the supernatural (central to Christian Neo-Platonism) with an onto-theological positing of auto-volition as the highest and most general cause. Even the attempt of speculative idealists like Fichte, Schelling, and Hegel to eschew the modern transcendental science of onto-theology does in the end privilege subjectivity[11] and immanence at the expense of a more mediated metaphysic. Such a metaphysic links the subject and the immanent to cosmic objectivity and divine transcendence by cutting across the false divide between existence and essence, actuality and possibility, or finitude and infinity bequeathed by Avicenna, Scotus, and Descartes.

Contemporary philosophy is perhaps even more transcendental and certainly no less anti-metaphysical. Since Nietzsche and Heidegger, virtually the whole of ancient thought and Christian metaphysics has been wrongly identified with the absolutism of the will to power and the idolatry of onto-theology. Following Foucault and Derrida, western philosophy in its entirety has been falsely associated with Plato's alleged (phal-)logo-centrism and the rationalist God of classical theism. As such, both premodern and modern metaphysics is simply and simplistically equated with the illusion of clear and distinct foundations and the forgetting of the 'ontological difference.' In part, that's why the pure and unadulterated philosophy proposed by phenomenological philosophers (chief of all Heidegger and Marion) promised a new dawn — liberated from the constricting shackles of God, faith, and theology.[12]

10. Alberto Toscano, *The Theatre of Production: Philosophy and Individuation Between Kant and Deleuze* (London: Palgrave Macmillan, 2006), pp. 19-106.

11. Cf. Robert Pippin, *Persistence of Subjectivity: On the Kantian Aftermath* (Cambridge: Cambridge University Press, 2005).

12. On Heidegger's reduction of theology to a regional science, see Martin Heidegger, "Phänomenologie und Theologie," in *Gesamtausgabe* (Frankfurt am Main: V. Klostermann, 1976), vol. 9, pp. 45-78. On Marion's genealogy of metaphysics and ontology, see Jean-Luc Marion, "Une époque de la métaphysique," in *Jean Duns Scot ou la révolution subtile*, ed. C. Goëmé (Paris: FAC Éditions Radio-France, 1982), pp. 87-95. Cf. Jean-Luc Marion, *Réduction et donation. Recherches sur Husserl, Heidegger et la phénoménologie* (Paris:

The second set of reasons why late modernity marks the destruction of metaphysics is that both phenomenology and analytic philosophy remain caught within the modern logic of absolute immanence that imposes arbitrary limits on both divine and human reason. The rationality of God's *Logos* is subordinated to divine volition, which is as unintelligible as it is fideistic — a blending of nominalism and voluntarism first proposed by Ockham. And since neither self-willing nor pure intentionality without transcendent teleology can adequately account for the excess of infinite reason which envelopes finite reason, it is also the case that neither Kant's practical reason nor Husserl's transcendental I outside being nor even Marion's reduction of phenomenality to sheer givenness without gift or giver can escape modern dualisms. None of these three 'solutions' can either break the circle of infinitized finitude of immanence or else account for the paradox of transcendence at the heart of immanence, "more interior to me than I to myself," as St. Augustine writes in the *Confessions*.[13]

Likewise, much of recent and current theology has embraced the triple Baroque scholastic separation of nature from grace, reason from faith, and metaphysics from revealed theology — including Barthian neo-orthodoxy and Catholic neo-scholasticism. As such, both contemporary philosophers and theologians are secretly complicit in bracketing the natural desire for the supernatural, the participatory nature of all beings, the Trinitarian 'shape' of all that is given by the divine *donum*, and

---

Presses Universitaires de France, 1989); J.-L. Marion, *Étant donné. Essai de phénoménologie de la donation*, rev. ed. (Paris: Presses Universitaires de France, 1997); J.-L. Marion, *De surcroît. Études sur les phénomènes saturés* (Paris: Presses Universitaires de France, 2001); J.-L. Marion, *Le phénomène érotique* (Paris: LGF, 2004); J.-L. Marion, *Le visible et le révélé* (Paris: Éditions Cerf, 2005). For a compelling critique of the multiple tensions between Marion's phenomenological ontology and his theology (which are ultimately irreconcilable on Marion's own terms), see Emmanuel Falque, "*Larvatus pro Deo* — Phénoménologie et théologie chez J.-L. Marion," *Gregorianum* 86 (2005): 45-62.

13. Marion's claim in his recent book *Au lieu de soi. L'approche de Saint Augustin* (Paris: Presses Universitaires de France, 2008) that Augustine's theology is nonmetaphysical and free of any debt to Christian Neo-Platonism is textually and historically unpersuasive, as chapter 2 of the present essay suggests. Rather than providing a better understanding of Augustine, this sort of approach seeks to legitimate Marion's own phenomenological method and his theologically questionable concepts of saturated phenomena and the I as *'adonné.'* For a longer statement of my critique of Marion, see Adrian Pabst, "Jean-Luc Marion," in *Introduction à la phénoménologie contemporaine*, ed. Philippe Cabestan (Paris: Éditions Ellipses, 2005), pp. 83-96.

the transformative dimension of culture and all forms of human making. The metaphysics of relational participation is beyond the division between philosophy and theology, as if the former could really be supremely autonomous or the latter merely regional. Rather, the idea and reality of relationality and participatory being is always already part of a wider economy that encompasses donation, excess, deification *(theosis),* and theurgy — as articulated in the works of Russian sophiology, *nouvelle théologie* and Radical Orthodoxy.[14]

Thirdly and for the reasons adduced above, 'postmodern' philosophy and theology fail to distinguish between the science of transcendental ontology and the Christian Neo-Platonist metaphysics of creation. Transcendental ontology is not attributable to Aristotle or Boethius but can be traced to the confluence of Avicennian and Porretan essentialism which paved the way for the acceptance of Duns Scotus's destruction of *analogia entis,* as I argued in chapters 4 and 6. Similarly, onto-theological metaphysics did not start with Plato, Augustine, or Aquinas. Instead, it was inaugurated by Duns Scotus's conflation of the highest being in God with the most common being in beings.[15] This new account was further developed by Suárez's conception of metaphysics as a general science that foregrounds all other sciences and predefines the realm in which revealed theology operates, as I suggested in chapter 7. As the work of the Swiss philosopher André de Muralt attests, there is a clear genealogy that links the priority of possibility over actuality in Scotus, the primacy of the will over the intellect and the denial of universals in things in Ockham, and the transcendental status of being qua being in Suárez to Descartes, Wolff, Kant, and their contemporary liberal successors such as John Rawls.[16]

14. On the enduring importance of *nouvelle théologie,* see John Milbank, *The Suspended Middle: Henri de Lubac and the Debate Concerning the Supernatural* (Grand Rapids: Eerdmans, 2005). For an account of how Russian sophiology echoes and surpasses the metaphysical idealism of Schelling, see J. Milbank, "Sophiology and Theurgy: The New Theological Horizon," in *Encounter between Eastern Orthodoxy and Radical Orthodoxy: Transfiguration of the World through the Word,* ed. Adrian Pabst and Christoph Schneider (Aldershot, UK: Ashgate, 2009), pp. 45-85. On the importance of Vladimir Solovyov's metaphysical critique of positivism, see my chapter in the same collection, "Wisdom and the Art of Politics," pp. 109-37.

15. Olivier Boulnois, "Quand commence l'ontothéologie? Aristote, Thomas d'Aquin et Duns Scot," *Revue thomiste* 95 (1995): 85-108.

16. See, *inter alia,* André de Muralt, "Kant, le dernier occamien. Une nouvelle définition de la philosophie moderne," *Revue de Métaphysique et de Morale* 80 (1975): 32-53;

By contrast, the Neo-Platonic metaphysics of participation stretches not only from Plato to Aquinas but also underpins the alternative, properly theological 'modernity' envisioned by figures as diverse as Meister Eckhart, Nicholas of Cusa, the Cambridge Platonists, the nineteenth-century Russian sophiologists, and the protagonists of *nouvelle théologie,* as I have already indicated. The problem with the dominant traditions of (post)modern philosophy is that they all seek in different ways to replace a theologically mediated metaphysic with a certain ontology. That ontology oscillates between the transcendental category of being that encompasses God and absolute divine volition, on the one hand, and quasi-positivist notions of human will or cognition that are severed from divinely infused grace and the natural desire for the supernatural Good in God, on the other hand. Thus, the idea that transcendental ontology has *not* been the dominant modern philosophy is just as misguided as the idea that a theological metaphysic that upholds the 'ontological difference' in terms of *analogia entis* ever fell into total oblivion. Likewise, the notion that metaphysics is constitutively onto-theological and needs to be overcome in the direction of a philosophy of pure appearance or pure language/logic is just as erroneous as the notion that it cannot return to the heart of philosophy and restore a theological ordering of all the sciences.

In the remainder of this chapter, I will argue that the twin thematic of individuation in philosophy and individuality in politics is central to the modern passage from metaphysics to ontology. Connected with this is a series of theoretical shifts and practical transformations that brought about modernity — first of all, a growing focus on individual substance instead of real relations; second, the primacy of individual will, social contract, and commercial exchange at the expense of social sympathy and charity which are integral to a theologically ordered economy of mutuality, reciprocity, and gift-exchange.

3. Transcendental Ontology as a Science of the Individual

No single shift within the Western Latin tradition of scholasticism can account for the passage from the patristic and medieval Christian Neo-

A. de Muralt, *L'Enjeu de la philosophie médiévale. Études thomistes, scotistes, occamiennes et grégoriennes* (Leiden: E. J. Brill, 1991); A. de Muralt, *L'unité de la philosophie politique. De Scot, Occam et Suarez au libéralisme contemporain* (Paris: Vrin, 2002).

Platonist metaphysics of creation to the modern transcendental science of ontology. However, rival accounts of individuation encapsulate the conceptual change which both reflected and reinforced practical transformations that led to the primacy of abstract, formal individuality over real relations embodied in liturgical, political, and socioeconomic practices. What binds together all the aforementioned shifts is the idea shared by Scotus, Ockham, Suárez, and Spinoza that in some important sense things self-individuate, a claim that is central to the genesis and evolution of modern ontology.

Indeed, Scotus inverts the former scholastic sequence of studying the problem of universals before exploring the principle of individuation. By arguing that the ultimate source of individuation of all things is in fact an entity's *haecceitas,* Scotus posits individuality as

> a fundamental and primitive component of reality. . . . For Scotus, individuality, that is *haecceitas,* was not subject to further analysis; indeed it was not even subject to definition. And Ockham was not far from this position when he maintained that individual things are individual essentially, for, if individuality is a matter of essence, it cannot be subject to analysis. Thus Scotus explained individuation in terms of a primitive and unanalyzable principle, and Ockham indicated that individuality needs no explanation because everything is individual by itself.[17]

Here one can go further than Gracia and link Scotus's substitution of an ontology of representation for a metaphysics of participation to Ockham's ontology of individuality without individuation. For the conceptual key that reconciles the apparent opposition between Scotist realism and Ockhamist nominalism is the shift away from both analogical being and the divine act to the idea of univocal being and this-ness *(haecceitas)* or singularity. Paradoxically, Scotus's defense of common nature is compatible with Ockham's denial of the real presence of universals in particular things because *natura communis* describes the essence of a thing, which is indifferent to that thing's really existent instantiation and embodiment. As such, both Scotus and Ockham — in an attempt to tie to-

17. Jorge J. E. Gracia, "Epilogue: Individuation in Scholasticism," in *Individuation in Scholasticism: The Later Middle Ages and the Counter-Reformation 1150-1650,* ed. J. J. E. Gracia (New York: State University of New York Press, 1994), pp. 543-50 (548).

gether individual, empirical reality with universal, conceptual intelligibility — conclude that the source of individuality is the thing itself rather than its creative source in God. The transcendental ontology that supplants the Neo-Platonist metaphysics of creation is in this sense a science of the individual that nonetheless leaves individuality unexplained.

On this both Scotus's and Ockham's onto-theologies are much closer to Aristotle's theo-ontology than Plato's metaphysical theology. The Stagirite separates all composite substances in the sublunary world from the efficient causality of the Prime Mover, which merely acts as final cause. By contrast, Plato views things as existing through the participation in the forms and the Good as the form of all forms which is described as the author of all things — a conception that arguably implies both efficient and final causality as well as the idea of a gift of being whereby particulars have neither existence nor essence outside their relations to forms and to other particulars.

This fundamental difference between Aristotle and Plato was already glossed over by early Neo-Platonists such as Porphyry, who in his *Isagoge* — the standard introduction to Aristotle's *Categories* for many centuries — wrongly attributes to Plato an ontology and epistemology of essentially individual things. Writing that individuals "which are predicated of one alone . . . are infinite," Porphyry adds that "[t]his is why Plato exhorts us to stop going down from the most general to the most specific, to go down through the intermediary levels and to divide by differences. He tells us to leave the infinite [individuals] alone. For there is no knowledge of them."[18] While it is true that Plato rules out absolute knowledge of individuals *qua* individuals, he argues that things are individuated and known as such in relation to the Good which endows them with goodness. For this reason, Plato balances the metaphysical and the epistemic modality of individuation. By contrast, Aristotle privileges the epistemic modality because he shifts the onus from relation to substance and from the relational individuation of the Good to the unity of individual substance and proximate matter, as I argued in chapter 1.

The link between Aristotle and Scotus is the twin thematic of being and intelligibility. On the question of individuation, Bruno Pinchard has made the point that Aristotle's science of generation and corruption is over-determined by his science of abstraction and predication in such a

---

18. Quoted in Paul Vincent Spade, ed., *Five Texts on the Medieval Problem of Universals: Porphyry, Boethius, Abelard, Duns Scotus, Ockham* (Indianapolis: Hackett, 1994), pp. 5-6.

way that unintelligible matter is paradoxically the main epistemic (and genetic) principle of individuation.[19] Leaving aside problems with Pinchard's interpretation, it is instructive to consider Alberto Toscano's argument (based on Pinchard) that "[t]he determination of what is proper to thought — the binding of thought to the question of universality — generates an impasse in the interrogation of the relationship between being and individuality. This relationship becomes explicitly thematized only within medieval scholasticism, and specifically in the work of Duns Scotus."[20] Aquinas (and others before him) had already conceptualized the convertibility of being and unity, so beyond Toscano one can suggest that both Scotus and Ockham eschew a metaphysics of creation in favor of an abstract ontology of self-individuation — an account that is clearly more Aristotelian than Neo-Platonist.

Even though Suárez rejects some key aspects of the Scotist and Ockhamist account of individuation, he does accept their argument that the Aristotelian category of individual substance is a superior explanation of reality compared to the Platonist notion that participable universals are instantiated in participating particulars. This break with the Neo-Platonist metaphysics of relationality is reflected in Suárez's discussion in his *Disputationes metaphysicae* of individuality as a fundamental kind of unity that precedes formal unity and underpins universality. Likewise, Spinoza's insistence on *conatus* as the self-individuating power of finite, immediate modes confirms and radicalizes the disjunction between the individuality of particular things and the universality of the infinite substance, for substantial infinity cannot explain why there would be modal finitude.

Common to these accounts is the assumption that individuality *qua* individuality is more fundamental than any link that might pertain between universals and particulars. This ontological claim is correlated with a shift away from the patristic and medieval theological argument (made by Origen, the Cappadocians, and Cyril of Alexandria, and later developed by Aquinas) that the event of the Incarnation marks the fusion of the divine and the human in Christ through whom we ascend to union with God. Thus, Christological and Trinitarian theology is inextricably bound up with a theological metaphysics of creation and individuation.

19. Bruno Pinchard, "Le principe d'individuation dans la tradition aristotélicienne," in *Le problème de l'individuation*, ed. Pierre-Noël Mayaud (Paris: Vrin, 1991), pp. 27-50.
20. Toscano, *The Theatre of Production*, pp. 6-7.

For the manifestation of the Son in the created order reveals the Trinitarian economy in which we can participate through him and in this manner perfect our own unique form as well as the whole of creation.

Crucially, the transcendental science of ontology reinforces the early modern notion that the ancient, patristic, and medieval problem of individuation has been resolved and that the question of individuality no longer requires detailed analysis, as evinced by the absence of any significant discussion in Descartes' *Meditationes,* which were written a mere forty-four years after Suárez had devoted more than 150 pages in his *Disputationes metaphysicae* in 1597.[21] Although Descartes himself rectifies this lacuna elsewhere in his *oeuvre,* much of early modern philosophy viewed all things as irreducibly and somehow unexplainably individual. Empiricist philosophers from Locke via Berkeley to Hume go even a step further and treat individuality as an a priori given that is coextensive with the existence of all things: "All Things, that exist, being particulars . . ."; "But it is a universally received maxim, that every thing which exists, is particular"; ". . . this a principle generally receiv'd in philosophy, that every thing in nature is individual."[22] As such, the perennial problem of the causes and principles of individuation mutates into the modern maxim of fixed individual identity in space and time. Coupled with the idea of pure nature (which was a modern theological invention linked to Duns Scotus's substitution of univocal being for analogical being and Suárez's theory of general and specific metaphysics),[23] the concept of individual substances as self-individuating entities in Descartes, Spinoza, and Leibniz is integral to the foundation of modern philosophy.

In the following sections, I will trace the connections between late medieval and modern conceptions of individuation in greater detail, notably in Kant's ontology. My argument is that a theological metaphys-

21. Jorge J. E. Gracia, "The Centrality of the Individual in the Philosophy of the Fourteenth Century," *History of Philosophy Quarterly* 8 (1991): 225-51.

22. John Locke, *An Essay Concerning Human Understanding,* III.3.i, III.27.iii, ed. P. H. Nidditch and intro. Pauline Phemister (Oxford: Oxford University Press, 2008), p. 409; George Berkeley, *Three Dialogues Between Hylas and Philonous,* 2:192, in *The Works of George Berkeley,* ed. A. Luce and T. E. Jessop (London: Thomas Nelson & Sons, 1948); David Hume, *A Treatise of Human Nature,* I.i.7, ed. L. A. Selby-Bigge (Oxford: Oxford University Press, 1958), p. 19.

23. For an overview and important extension of this argument, see Jacob Schmutz, "La doctrine médiévale des causes et la théologie de la nature pure (XIIIe-XVIIe siècles)," *Revue thomiste* 101 (2001): 217-64.

ics of relational participation outflanks the modern dichotomy between autonomous, self-organizing modalities of individuation (Suárez and Spinoza) and heteronomous, mechanistic modalities of individuation (Descartes and Leibniz) by inscribing human agency and natural laws into the ecstatic excess of divine creativity which underpins all natural motion and social activity. The emphasis on relational being and triadic structures in the world also outwits in advance the later modern opposition between transcendentalism (Wolff and Kant) and positivism (Comte and Bentham).

4. Being Transcendentalized (Descartes and Leibniz)

In this and the following section, I will relate modern ontology as a science of the individual and the transcendental status of being *(ens)* to the primacy of abstract individuality over primary real relations in modern political thought. The conceptual link is the ontological replacement of analogical being with univocal being and the epistemological reduction of actual things to abstract entities.

A. The Transcendental Status of Being (ens)

As Alberto Toscano has rightly argued, the wider implications of Scotus's thesis of univocity for the new science of ontology can only be fully appreciated in relation to his account of individuation.[24] Indeed, Scotus's claim that the indifferent essence of a being (its *natura communis*) and its this-ness (or *haecceitas*) are both real and intelligible as such is key to his closely connected claim that being is neither analogical nor equivocal but instead univocal. Furthermore, Scotus surpasses the divide in Aristotle's theo-ontology between the conceptual intelligibility of universals (arrived at by abstraction) and the empirical reality of particulars (apprehended by sensory perception) by suggesting that both being and individuality (not unity) are coterminous.

By contrast, Aquinas had defended the thesis that being and unity are transcendentally convertible and that individuality in the created order dimly reflects the Creator's meta-individual nature — in a similar way that

24. Toscano, *The Theatre of Production*, pp. 7-11.

analogical common being does not exist by itself but instead *is* by sharing in God's pure act (as I showed in chapter 5). Taken together, the Scotist univocity of being as well as the coextension of what is *(ens)* and what is individual imply that being insofar as it is being *(ens qua ens)* can now be investigated by metaphysics independently of either theology or physics.[25]

The absolute unity of the object of metaphysics — which encompasses being *(ens)*, thing *(res)*, and something *(aliquid)* — means that being and individuality are collapsed into a single category that must be univocal and transcendental so that it contains all the equivocal meanings of being *(esse)* and unity *(unitas)*. For this reason, the status of metaphysics shifts from being inscribed in a theological ordering of sciences (as for Aquinas) towards a new science of transcendental ontology whereby being is now seen as a spatialized object and entity abstracted from its constitutive relations with other things which can be known by reason alone. On the contrary, Aquinas argues that being *(ens)* is more like a mysterious reality that involves trust and faith but can nevertheless be apprehended by the senses (always physical as well as spiritual) and the imagination (as detailed in chapter 5).

Crucially, just as Aristotle's theo-ontology over-determines the epistemic modality over the genetic modality of the process of individuation, so Scotus's onto-theology privileges the epistemological dimension over the metaphysical dimension of theories of individuation. The reason for this parallel has to do with their shared emphasis on the foundations of individuality in beings themselves (rather than in the source of being, which brings all things into actuality). In either case, this reduces real beings either to effects that are ordered towards God in virtue of final causality (Aristotle) or to an abstract concept that conflates being and individuality — secured by the transcendental form of unity that characterizes both the *natura communis* and *haecceitas* of all things (Scotus).

By contrast with the Angelic Doctor's theological metaphysics of transcendent individuation, the Subtle Doctor's transcendental ontology of immanent self-individuation goes beyond Aristotle's theory by superimposing "being and thought in the transcendental unity of a concept of the *ens* within a unified science of ontology."[26] Moreover, univocal being elimi-

---

25. See the detailed exposition in Ludgar Honnefelder, *Ens inquantum ens. Der Begriff des Seienden als solchen als Gegenstand der Metaphysik nach der Lehre des Johannes Duns Scotus* (Münster: Aschendorff, 1979).

26. Toscano, *The Theatre of Production*, p. 9.

nates the real difference between existence and essence and therefore prioritizes the formality of a thing's essence over the reality of its actual instantiation and embodiment. In this manner, Scotus reduces things inscribed in cosmic space and time to spatialized objects and even to abstract entities or mere 'somethings' *(aliquid)*, as Eric Alliez has documented.[27] This shift is central to the emergence and evolution of modern ontology, for it abstracts beings from the metaphysical relations that constitute them as unique, particular, individuated, real things. As set out in chapter 7, Petrus Aureoli builds on Scotus's epistemologically overdetermined ontology of representation and reconfigures intentional being *(esse intentionale)* as an objective or represented being *(esse obiective sive repraesentatum)*, which is the objective content of the first-order concept formed by intellective abstraction from a thing's actual instantiation. On the contrary, Aquinas defines *esse intentionale* as a spiritual mode of cognition whereby the senses mediate to the mind the species form of composites or form in relation to material embodiment (chapter 5). Like Scotus, Aureoli devalues real actuality in favor of formal possibility by focusing on form or essence fully abstracted from material existentiality.

In turn, Suárez inverts the patristic and medieval Neo-Platonist priority of being over knowledge by making the 'objective reality' of represented being the focus of knowing — rather than beings in their full actuality.[28] In this way, concepts are no longer that with which the mind has knowledge of reality (as for Boethius or Aquinas) but become themselves the objects of knowledge. Linked to this is the shift in emphasis from the virtuality of Scotus's formal possibility to the reality of existent essence, a shift that marks a return to Thomist realism in name alone. In fact, Suárez reinforces the earlier Scotist displacement of actuality by equating a being's reality with the objectity of its real essence *(essentia realis)*. Since the adequate object of metaphysics is *ens in quantum ens reale* (defined as that which has a real essence), being *(ens)* is drained of its metaphysical reality and reduced to an entity of abstraction. As shown in chapter 7, this is why he follows Buridan in defining the proper object of metaphysics as substance *qua* substance — freed from all determinations, materiality and immateriality, infinity and finitude, actual-

---

27. Eric Alliez, *Les Temps Capitaux*, 2/1: *L'état des choses* (Paris: Éditions Cerf, 2000), pp. 49-70.

28. Timothy J. Cronin, *Objective Being in Descartes and Suarez* (Rome: Gregorian University Press, 1966), pp. 77-89. Cf. Courtine, *Suarez et le système de la métaphysique*, p. 194.

ity and possibility.[29] Compared with Aristotle, substance as real essence is not just extracted from the union with proximate matter but also stripped of any teleological links with God's actuality. In part, it is this scholastic legacy that underpins both Descartes's and Leibniz's theory of individuation, to which I briefly turn now.

B. On Descartes's Spiritual Monism

Broadly speaking, the post-scholastic metaphysics of substance seeks to explain the individuality of things and their continuity over time in space by focusing on fixed laws and ratios of motion. These laws eschew the shared Platonist and Aristotelian teleological ordering of things to their final end in favor of self-individuating substances that either constitute a Cartesian/Malebranchian system or represent something like Lockean atoms and Leibnizian monads. As a result, Aristotelian primary substances, which had previously been the essence of things, are reduced to secondary substances. Specifically, Descartes was first to radicalize Aristotle's causal theology in the direction of divine *causa sui*, which is the foundation for essentially arbitrary ratios and laws of motion (here surpassing even Ockham's voluntarism). Understood primarily in terms of effectivity, God's causal activity is severed from divine love and the infusion of everything with shares of goodness. As such, the individuating actualization of things is mechanistic (rather than creative) and immanent (rather than connected with intra-Trinitarian relations). In what follows, I also suggest that the Cartesian dualism between *res cogitans* and *res extensa* is secured by an equally questionable monism of the Spirit as consciousness into which both God and souls are collapsed.

Descartes's *Principles* set out his theory of individuation in terms of a thing's spatiality as well as the underlying geometric and kinematic principles. I will discuss these two principles in turn. First of all, unlike the patristic and medieval Neo-Platonist idea of particular beings as microcosms that reflect in some limited and imperfect manner the macrocosm of the universe, the Cartesian view emphasizes the identity of a thing's substance and its internal space:

> Nor in fact does space, or internal place, differ from the corporeal substance contained in it, except in the way in which we are accustomed

29. See *supra*, chapter 7, n. 33, p. 319.

to conceive of them. For in fact the extension in length, breadth, and depth which constitutes the space occupied by a body, is exactly the same as that which constitutes the body.[30]

Descartes's assumption is that the nonrelational spatiality intrinsic to each thing is absolutely independent from its extrinsic spatial relations. Except for causality and space, there is thus no ontological link between the modulations of the universe (as Augustine would put it) and all the individual things therein.

This focus on internal space at the expense of cosmic place is based on Descartes's claim that the spatial features of a composite substance are essential, not accidental properties, and that extension is coterminous with essence. In turn, properties such as color are particular to a composite and cognizable through the essence alone.[31] Here it is important to point out that Descartes views substance and extension as being so intimately intertwined that abstraction from materiality renders notions of extension incomplete. So rather like Aristotle, he insists on the link between form and matter (e.g., the 'substantial union' of body and soul), but rather like Scotus and Suárez he emphasizes essence instead of existence. Since the relation between species and individuals is collapsed into the relation between species and genus, both are treated as relations of abstraction between concepts. For this reason, the conception of an object's individuality is now twice removed from particular beings themselves: first of all, the concept of an extended thing abstracts from the actuality of the thing (e.g., abstracting from a cubic thing to the concept of cube) and, second, the objective reality of the idea of a represented thing is a further abstraction from the entity of *that* thing (abstracting from the concept of cube to the concept of polyhedron). In the words of Descartes, "by the objective reality of an idea I mean that in respect of which the thing represented in the idea is an entity,"[32] a conception that strongly echoes Scotus's and Suárez's shared accentuation of

30. René Descartes, *Principles of Philosophy,* ed. V. R. Miller and R. P. Miller (Dordrecht: D. Reidel, 1983), pp. 43-44.

31. Emily Grosholz, "Descartes and the Individuation of Physical Objects," in *Individuation and Identity in Early Modern Philosophy: Descartes to Kant,* ed. Kenneth F. Barber and Jorge J. E. Gracia (Albany: State University of New York Press, 1994), pp. 41-58. Some arguments in this section are based on Grosholz's interpretation.

32. René Descartes, *Oeuvres,* ed. C. Adam and P. Tannery (Paris: Éditions Cerf, 1897-1910), vol. 7, p. 161.

representation (not participation) and 'objectity' (not actuality). At the same time, knowledge of individuals *qua* individuals requires the reverse of abstraction whereby we apply ideas of things in a series of instantiations until we have knowledge of something that has no further instance.

However, this process is grounded in prior cognition of the I or *ego* as an isolated and immanent, finite thinking substance and of God as a self-caused and transcendent, infinite 'other'. As such, ideas are not universals in things (as for Plato and Christian Neo-Platonism) but rather representations of entities already abstracted from their real actualization. Knowledge of individuals involves projecting ideas back onto reality until we encounter noninstantiable things, as I have already indicated. Moreover, this process of reverse abstraction runs into intractable problems, notably a discrepancy between the shape or 'internal space' of an object and its positioning within temporality and spatiality. For example, even if the concept of cube were to include position and location in an indeterminate way, it is still not clear how this relates to position and location in material reality. Nor is the move from genus to species the same as the move from species to individual, physical instantiation. Here Descartes's ontology of individuality is framed by the a priori knowledge of mathematical entities which precedes and determines any encounter with the material world, as the Fifth Meditation makes clear.[33] Mathematics and physics predefine the space within which ontology and theology operate — a striking resemblance with the work of Porreta, as set out in chapter 4.

In addition to geometric principles, the *Principles* (sections 23-53 of Part II) also set out the kinematic dimension of individuation. Descartes describes the motion that is divinely injected into matter and operates between contiguous bodies as the transference of a particular body whose parts move together. So configured, transference — a term that also occurs in the work of Porreta (even though Descartes does not seem to have had any knowledge of this) — and the laws of impact must be added to geometric shape and metric location as co-principles that individuate substances. In this manner, Descartes links divine causal activity to the individuation of things, though the reason for this link is arbitrary and not governed by God's *Logos* of love and goodness (as in Christian Neo-Platonism). Rather, Descartes appeals to divine necessary existence

---

33. On the non-correspondence between mathematical and physical space, see Grosholz, "Descartes and the Individuation of Physical Objects," pp. 44-49.

as the extrinsic source of motion that provides the conditions of possibility for the formal unity of things that exist as individuals (bodies whose parts move together):

> For I can well enough recognize that that idea [of a perfect body] has been put together by my mind uniting together all corporeal perfections, because it can equally well be affirmed and denied of them. Nay, because when I examine this idea of body I see in it no force by means of which it may produce or preserve itself, I rightly conclude that necessary existence [a term that resonates with Avicenna and Scotus], which alone is here in question, does not belong to the nature of a body.[34]

Descartes can only appeal to his doctrine of continuous creation in order to account for this extrinsic source of motion. This conception confirms that his theologically independent physics is paradoxically overdetermined by his causal theology.

However, it would be misguided to conclude that Descartes's theory of individuation runs into the same problems as the dualism between *res cogitans* and *res extensa*. As I have already suggested, knowledge of material things presupposes and requires knowledge of the self and God, both of which are cognized as nonmaterial entities (the self as a thinking thing and God as separate from divine physical creation). Since mathematical concepts provide knowledge of physical things only from the perspective of generality (not particularity), both the knowing subject and the known object must be embodied, and the intellect necessitates the testimony of the senses as well as confirmation of the imagination. It is only because ideas in the mind are infinite that the human intellect can see the self and God as transcendent objects of knowledge exceeding determinate concepts, a vision that is spiritual as much as intellectual. But Descartes denies the objects of physics this kind of natural transcendence and views them as complex machines that somehow stand behind the collision of simple bits of matter that are not fully individuated. For this reason, his epistemology reinforces the — otherwise undemonstrated — onto-theological gulf between Creator and creation and restricts proper individuation to the finite, imperfect individuality of the

---

34. Quoted in *The Philosophical Works of Descartes,* ed. E. S. Haldane and G. R. T. Ross (Cambridge: Cambridge University Press, 1912), vol. 2, p. 21.

self and the infinite, perfect individuality of God. Here the finitude of the self is absolutely separate from divine infinity and at the same time qualified by the permanent intrusion of God's seemingly arbitrary volition which transgresses the dualism of *res extensa* and *res cogitans*.

Moreover, mathematical and geometrical ideas — which are not individual but instead general — cannot explain how the disembodied intellect of the thinking self can come to know the individuality of extended physical objects. It is not enough to object that these ideas introduce stability and structure into the volatile and uncertain flux of sensory experience. For this does not explain where they are located, as Emily Grosholz has rightly remarked. Extension cannot be discovered in the unextended *ego* thinking nothing but itself. Nor can such an idea be embodied in nature, which can after all be undone by God's overriding, absolute will. And since the immaterial God is not an instance of extension, the only remaining locus is the divine mind which thinks eternal essences. If this is the case, then the Fifth Meditation describes the self's encounter of God's necessary existence (and divine essence) as an encounter with eternal ideas in the divine intellect, which transgresses both the autonomy and self-certainty of the *ego*.

The Cartesian system, by radicalizing Scotus's representational epistemology and Suárez's transcendental ontology, transcendentalizes both knowing and being. In this manner, Descartes rules out any possibility of a real, ontological difference and an analogical relation between Creator and creation that would secure both the integrity of the latter and its participation in the former. Without the unity of form and matter as well as their shared relationality vis-à-vis the divine source of being, both God and souls "tend to collapse back into an undifferentiated spiritual oneness. . . . Spirit, as consciousness, is always one; thinking that thinks thinking is just more thinking. But undifferentiated spirit is no more an individual than undifferentiated matter."[35] As such, behind the ontologically questionable Cartesian dualism of *res cogitans* and *res extensa* lurks a theologically dubious monism that negates materiality and shifts the onus of individuation onto the generality of geometric/kinematic principles and ideas in God's mind, which the human intellect somehow cognizes intuitively rather than through the illumination of divine grace (as for Augustine).

---

35. Grosholz, "Descartes and the Individuation of Physical Objects," pp. 55-56.

C. On Leibniz's Mental Monism

Leibniz's theory of individuation is widely associated with his conception of substantial entities and nonmaterial monads, which are self-individuating and therefore require neither the divine act of being (as in Aquinas) nor the confluence of common nature and haecceity (as in Scotus). However, in what follows I argue that Leibniz's account requires some kind of mental monism in order to see things as really distinct in nature but somehow common in the mind. Not unlike Descartes's fusion of dualism with monism, Leibniz's conception of individuation oscillates between the real individuality of things and the mental unity of the world.

Contrary to many other modern philosophers, Leibniz accords a central place to the question of individuation. The nature of individuality is discussed extensively not just in his *Disputatio metaphysica de principio individui* of 1663 but also in his *Discourse de métaphysique* (1686), the *Nouveux essais sur l'entendement humain* (1704), the *Monadologie* (1714), and *The Principles of Nature and of Grace, Based on Reason* (1714). Common to all these texts is the idea that the source of individuation is a real, physical principle that is founded in actual things and "serves as the foundation for the formal notion in the mind of 'individual,' understood as individuation or numerical difference."[36] So configured, the ontological principle that individuates substances is different from the epistemological principle that enables us to know the logical sense of individuality based on predication.

Here the philosophical and theological status of substance is crucial. Whereas Descartes's account of individuation is closer to Scotus's substitution of representation for participation, Leibniz's theory is in fact more indebted to Ockham's denial (*contra* the Subtle Doctor) of the presence of real universals in actual things and also to Suárez's emphasis on self-individuating substances. Indeed, Leibniz rejects what he calls the extreme realism of the Scotists and instead combines Ockham's nominalism with Suárez's transcendentalism to argue that there is no common nature in things and no formal distinction.[37] Rather, any ratio that might

---

36. Gottfried Wilhelm Leibniz, *Disputatio metaphysica de principio individui,* in G. W. Leibniz, *Sämtliche Schriften und Briefe,* 6th ed. (Darmstadt: Otto Reich Verlag, 1930), vol. 1, p. 11.

37. Laurence B. McCullough, *Leibniz on Individuals and Individuation: The Persistence of Premodern Ideas in Modern Philosophy* (Dordrecht: Kluwer Academic, 1996), ch. 3.

apply to individuals is an *ens rationis* in the mind and not a shared *fundamentum in re*. As such, substantiality in things is always already individual, not universal. In this manner, he argues that substances somehow self-individuate in virtue of their whole entity *(entitas tota)*, consisting of individuated 'natures' (and, in the case of composites, also of individuated 'matters').[38]

Compared with Suárez and Descartes, Leibniz shifts the focus even more from Aristotelian substance to the late scholastic and early modern idea of entity, stripped of any constitutive relationality. In this way, the mind can abstract a single concept that represents a thing's form — independently from its actual embodiment in matter and its positioning in relations with other beings and the source of being in God. In turn, this allows Leibniz to reject the Scotist formal distinction between existence and essence in favor of a monist account according to which existence and essence coincide and are really identical. Since existence is always existence of some kind, it follows for Leibniz that all that exists is always ordered to individual existence, which presupposes individuation and therefore cannot be its principle.[39] But Leibniz — like Scotus, Suárez, and Descartes before him — fails to recognize that the divine act of being which brings something into actuality (as in Aquinas) avoids both the formalism of the Scotist theory and the monism of Leibniz's proposed solution.

Indeed, in his mature work Leibniz replaces the language of whole entities with a grammar of monads. What underpins the latter is the undemonstrated claim that individual, nonmaterial substances subsist in themselves and have an intrinsic principle of action — centers of activity or monads consisting of appetition and perception. Not unlike Descartes's system, Leibniz's ontology posits a quasi-cosmic consciousness located in each mind which can apprehend the rest of the world in a single act of perception. Since each perception contains all of its predecessors and successors (and therefore forms an indivisible whole) and since perception is coextensive with individual monads, perception is self-individuated. Similarly, appetition as the principle of activity underlying the generation of perceptions secures the unity of each monad and thus

---

38. That is why Leibniz argues that *"omne individuum sua tota entitate individuatur."*

39. Laurence B. McCullough, "Leibniz's Principle of Individuation in His *Disputatio metaphysica de principio individui* of 1663," in Barber and Gracia, eds., *Individuation and Identity in Early Modern Philosophy*, pp. 201-17.

distinguishes it from all other monads. As such, appetition is self-individuated. Like 'natures' and 'matters' in the earlier works, perception and appetition are always already individuated and ensure that the individuation of monads is an intrinsic principle that does not require the divine act of being.

As a result, Leibniz is forced to posit some kind of mental universalism that enables the human intellect to know at the same time each monad in its radical singularity and the unity of the world as a whole. Here he inverts the Augustinian idea of microcosms reflecting the macrocosm by suggesting that each individual monad fully contains all other monads, thereby collapsing transcendence into immanence. In turn, this explains why in his treatise on theodicy he equates the actuality at any one time with the highest possibility available. As I will suggest later in this chapter, this leads to the modern transcendentalization of the immanent. Before I can discuss this, I turn to the twin thematic of creation and individuation in the work of Hobbes and Locke.

5. Being Atomized (Hobbes and Locke)

In this section, I show how both Thomas Hobbes (1588-1679) and John Locke (1632-1704) are deeply indebted to the voluntarism and nominalism of Ockham. This is significant, for it underscores the continuity between late scholasticism and (early) modern thought, notably in relation to the tradition of social contract. Ockham's theology is central to the emergence of modern political philosophy for at least two reasons. First, the erasure of God from the perceptible universe negates the patristic and medieval idea that even after the Fall the biblical primacy of divinely created peace over human violence is dimly reflected in the structures of the natural and the social realm.[40] Second, it establishes the primacy of God's absolute power (which is fideistically believed) over the divine ordering of the universe (which is mediated through natural law).

40. The medieval argument is that the Incarnation restored the 'visibility' of the primacy of peace over violence in Christ and that the living, apostolic tradition of the church transmits this mediated revelation. As such, the tradition binds together the distinct — though complementary — accounts of divine revelation in the Book of Scripture, the Book of Nature, and the Book of History. See Henri de Lubac, *Exégèse médiévale. Les Quatre Sens de l'Écriture* (Paris: Aubier-Montaigne, 1964), première partie, ch. I, 2 and 5, pp. 56-74, 100-118; ch. III, pp. 171-220; ch. V, pp. 305-72.

A. On Hobbes

That the thought of Hobbes is deeply indebted to late medieval nominalism and voluntarism is clear from his emphasis in the *Leviathan* on will and artifice rather than reason and nature as the foundational categories of political philosophy. Moreover, Hobbes's epistemological skepticism leads him to argue that human reasoning cannot provide natural knowledge of supernatural ends in God. Instead, the nominalist denial of real universals in particulars and the voluntarist account of both divine and human nature — taken together — imply that individuality is more fundamental than communality. These two philosophical commitments also underpin his claim that modern, centralized authority of the 'sovereign one' is more clearly compatible with the individual freedom of 'the many' than the ancient, patristic, and medieval idea of the rule by 'the few' (Plato's Guardians or virtuous elites) who have knowledge of the Good.[41]

Even more clearly than Ockham and Suárez, Hobbes links *potentia Dei absoluta* to sovereignty. First of all, the denial of real universals means that both God and the created structures of the world remain hidden from human cognition. We cannot know the world as it really is. All that we experience are the effects of the world upon our passions and our intellect. In line with certain strands of Calvinist theology, Hobbes believes that the postlapsarian condition is one of permanent violence. In the 'state of nature,' life is "solitary, poor, nasty, brutish, and short" because "man is a wolf to man" *(homo homini lupus)* and there is a "war of all against all" *(bellum omnium contra omnes).*[42] Even if this original threat of violent death does not describe an epoch in history but instead constitutes a principle that is internal to the state (evident only at the hypothetical moment of its dissolution), it remains the case that Hobbes's acceptance of a nominalist ontology leads him to posit violence as more fundamental to life than peace.

Second, linked to this is the modern *aporia* between unalterable nature and human artifice, as reflected in Hobbes's conception of the human body as a machine and the commonwealth as an artificial human

---

41. Thomas Hobbes, *Leviathan or the Matter, Forme and Power of a Commonwealth Ecclesiasticall and Civil* (1651), ed. and intro. Michael Oakeshott (Oxford: Blackwell, 1960), I.xi, xiii-xiv; II.xxi, xxviii, and xxxii.

42. Thomas Hobbes, *De Cive*, reprint of 1651 edition (Whitefish, MT: Kessinger Publishing, 1994), I.xii and xiii, pp. 17-18; Hobbes, *Leviathan* I.xiii, p. 82.

being. His distinct contribution to early modern thought is to fuse mechanism, materialism, and nominalism: since human emotions, thoughts, and reasoning are the sole product of mechanical interactions, the Christian Neo-Platonist idea of an immaterial Creator God whose spirit permeates material creation and ordains all things to the highest Good is ruled out. The political order does not mirror either the city, the universe, or the Body of Christ; instead, it is constructed based on a priori first principles and a fixed material world characterized by the 'state of nature.' Crucially, Hobbes's commitment to a nominalist ontology is illustrated by the absence of any naturally given moral ties or social bonds: in *De Cive*, the state of nature is described in terms of "looking at men as if they had just emerged from the earth like mushrooms and grown up without any obligation to each other" (*De Cive* viii.1).

Here it is important to stress that Hobbes, unlike Locke after him, is opposed to extreme versions of ontological atomism precisely because of the mechanical structure of all material reality, which is not the same as a crude determinism. Rather, it allows for the centrality of human experiment — a conception that Hobbes shares in part with Boyle.[43] This is confirmed by his critique of the Aristotelian focus on separate essences in the *De corpore* where Hobbes insists that intelligent beings are thinking bodies and that bodies or their properties are never separated from each other.[44] What binds all matter together is a set of mechanical links. At the same time, Hobbes's indebtedness to late scholasticism is nowhere more visible than in his endorsement of nominalism and the mechanization of Aristotelian ontology, as Cornelius Leijenhorst has ex-

---

43. Steven Shapin and Simon Schaffer, *Leviathan and the Air-Pump: Hobbes, Boyle, and the Experimental Life* (Princeton: Princeton University Press, 1985).

44. In the word of Hobbes, "But the abuse consists in this, that when some men see that the increases and decreases of quantity, heat, and other accidents can be considered, that is, submitted to reasons, as we say, without consideration of bodies or their subjects (which is called "abstraction" or "existence apart from them"), they talk about accidents as if they could be separated from every body. The gross errors of certain metaphysicians take their origin from this; for from the fact that it is possible to consider thinking without considering body, they infer that there is no need for a thinking body; and from the fact that it is possible to consider quantity without considering body, they also think that quantity can exist without body and body without quantity, so that a quantitative body is made only after quantity has been added to a body. These meaningless vocal sounds, 'abstract substances,' 'separated essence,' and other similar ones, spring from the same fountain" (Thomas Hobbes, *De corpore* III.4, ed. Karl Schuhmann [Paris: Vrin, 1999], p. 34 [orig. Latin], English trans. and ed. William Molesworth [London: J. Bohn, 1839-45]).

tensively documented.[45] In short, Hobbes's metaphysics rejects Cartesian dualism in favor of a material monism in which beings are linked by mechanistic interactions alone. By stripping things of any other links, he unwittingly paves the way for the atomism of Locke (which will be discussed in the next subsection).

Third, this ontology has important political ramifications. Since he assumes a natural state of disorder that cannot be overcome (because no other knowledge of the world is available to us), Hobbes can only imagine the imposition of an artificial order. This takes the form of the commonwealth, which merely regulates the violence of life. By contrast, Christian Neo-Platonists like Augustine and Aquinas do not think of human fallibility and the penultimacy of politics in fatalistic terms but instead see them as part of our efforts to resolve violence through peace by way of the creative perfection of a more fundamental natural, created order. Even though Hobbes distinguishes the commonwealth by free, contractual institution from the commonwealth by forceful, violent acquisition, in either case the sovereign has supreme power to 'give life' or to withdraw it from his subjects. Similarly, obedience to the sovereign is always for fear of a violent death.[46]

Fourth, since man is driven by fear of violent death and self-interested self-preservation, peace (or rather the absence of open conflict) can only be enforced through the absolute authority of the Leviathan. Beyond Ockham and Suárez, Hobbes's commonwealth does not just elevate the state over the church but also subjects the multiplicity of the people to a uniform social contract that purports to represent their single will:

> A multitude of men, are made *one* person, when they are by one man, or one person, represented; so that it be done with the consent of every one of that multitude in particular. For it is the *unity* of representer, not the *unity* of the represented, that maketh the person *one.*[47]

As such, the 'sovereign one' embodies and enforces the unity of 'the many,' without however offering a genuine body politic that upholds its members *qua* members of a transcendent whole.

---

45. Cornelius H. Leijenhorst, *The Mechanisation of Aristotelianism: The Late Aristotelian Setting of Thomas Hobbes' Natural Philosophy* (Leiden: E. J. Brill, 2002).

46. Hobbes, *Leviathan* II.xvii-xx, pp. 109-36.

47. Hobbes, *Leviathan* I.xvi, p. 107 (editor's italics).

Fifth, because we cannot know any alternative natural order either through reason or faith, human beings are compelled to submit obediently to the supreme sovereignty of the Leviathan. Once more, it is divine omnipotence that legitimates this arrangement and sanctifies the extension of central power to all realms of life and to the preservation or extinction of individual existences. Here we can clearly see the modern 'biopolitical' imperative, as I have argued in greater detail elsewhere.[48]

Finally, the absence of a proper body politic also explains how Hobbes's nominalist ontology (and anthropology) leads him to view man as nothing but an owner of himself, an individual who does not stand in relations of mutuality or reciprocity with fellow human beings. As a result, Hobbes tends to define social relations in proprietary terms, largely independent of communal bonds governed by substantive values of peace and justice.[49] Such values are unavailable to Hobbes because his nominalist denial of real universals in the world commits him to rely on fear and domination in order to impose an artificial order on mutually distrustful citizens.

In summary, without an account of a transcendent Good that orders all immanent things, Hobbes can only appeal to the unitary power of the Leviathan who exercises absolute control through fear and submission. Justice no longer denotes the harmonious ordering of real relations amongst members of the body politic (as it does for Augustine and Aquinas), but is reduced to contractual obligation. As such, the omnipotent Leviathan and 'sovereign market relations' enforce the coexistence of individuals as rival 'self-proprietors.' In Hobbes, the modern model of state and market sovereignty begins to converge and to form the nominalist horizon that encompasses the modern dialectic between 'the one' and 'the many.' It is within this nominalist horizon that politics becomes 'biopolitics' and sovereign power is redefined as dominion over life.[50]

48. Adrian Pabst, "Modern Sovereignty in Question: Theology, Democracy and Capitalism," *Modern Theology* 26, no. 4 (October 2010): 570-602.

49. Even if some of C. B. MacPherson's textual analysis is questionable, his argument in respect of modern political and economic thought is broadly correct, in particular the centrality of 'market relations' in the work of Hobbes and Locke. C. B. MacPherson, *The Political Theory of Possessive Individualism: Hobbes to Locke* (Oxford: Clarendon, 1962), pp. 34-95.

50. Giorgio Agamben, *Homo Sacer: Sovereign Power and Bare Life*, trans. Daniel Heller-Roazen (Stanford, CA: Stanford University Press, 1998), pp. 30-38, 104-15; John Milbank, "Paul against Biopolitics," *Theory, Culture & Society* 25 (2008): 125-72.

B. On Locke

In what follows, I argue that Locke radicalizes Ockham's nominalist and voluntarist ontology as well as Hobbes's mechanistic materialism in the direction of metaphysical and political atomism. Since we do not know the real essences of things, all that is available to us according to Locke is to infer from the sense perception of properties that these inhere in substances which act as their substrata — a relation of inherence that we know a priori (not unlike Aristotle). In turn, we can ascertain that real essences exist in substances because the former act as causes for the latter — a relation of causation (or necessary connection) that we also know a priori (unlike Plato or Augustine). Given Locke's critique of innate ideas and his skepticism about the reliance on perceptual experience, he locates the source of our knowledge in volition. It is the exercise of the human will that enables us to know the existence of necessary connections between things. As such, nominalism and voluntarism combine to produce an ontological atomism in the work of Locke, according to which the world is a set of observable regularities that are grounded in the necessity of causal links — not bound together and governed by the creative act of God.

As the work of Fred Wilson attests,[51] Locke's theory of individuation of composites departs from the tradition of substance metaphysics stretching back to Aristotle in a number of ways. First of all, he distinguishes man in terms of rationality and (not unlike Boethius) defines person as "a thinking intelligent being."[52] Locke links the rationality of man to consciousness, which implies self-consciousness. This includes past actions (as for Leibniz) and raises the issue of identity over time. Here the crucial difference with both the Neo-Platonist metaphysics of relational participation and the more Aristotelian (theo-)ontology of substance is that Locke questions the unity of individual substance by pointing to the separateness of events in a person's past experience that neither reason nor memory can unify (e.g., *Essay* II.i.14-15, 18-19).

Second, memory is for Locke merely a contingent link and therefore it cannot secure certain knowledge of the necessary continuity of a sin-

---

51. Fred Wilson, "Substance and Self in Locke and Hume," in Barber and Gracia, eds., *Individuation and Identity in Early Modern Philosophy*, pp. 155-99.

52. John Locke, *Essay Concerning Human Understanding*, ed. P. H. Nidditch, intro. Pauline Phemister (Oxford: Oxford University Press, 2008), II.xxvii.9, p. 208 (henceforth *Essay*).

gle substance. Since responsibility and consciousness do not coincide (e.g., drunkenness), the principle of responsibility cannot provide a connection between past and present events of experience either. And since Locke rejects both the Augustinian-Thomist option of God's transcendent act of being and the Cartesian transcendental *ego*, he is left with appealing to a seeming endless series of events contingently linked in time. The self is either reduced to merely causal relations cognized by reason or else dissolved in an unintelligible flux of experience. As a result, the Lockean theory of individuation oscillates between a residual rationalism more akin to the substance tradition and an impoverished empiricism that lacks key elements such as social sympathy and reciprocity (as in Vico, Genovesi, or Hume).

Third, Locke's position is close to Ockham and Buridan in the sense that he shares their denial of the reality of universals in things. In the *Essay* he writes that

> . . . *General and Universal,* belong not to the real existence of Things; but *are the Inventions and Creatures of the Understanding,* made by it for its own use, *and concern only Signs,* whether Words, or *Ideas.* Words are general, as has been said, when used for Signs of general *Ideas;* and so are applicable indifferently to many particular Things; And Ideas are general, when they are set up, as the Representatives of many particular Things: but universality belongs not to things themselves, which are all of them particular in their Existence, even those Words, and *Ideas,* which in their signification, are general. The signification they have, is nothing but a relation, that by the mind of Man is added to them.[53]

This indebtedness to late scholastic nominalism moves Locke's account away from the realist idea of primary, metaphysical relations between particulars participating in universals towards a more mechanistic conception focusing on spatiotemporal ratios. The difference with Descartes's mechanistic metaphysics is a greater emphasis on a corpuscular kind of mechanism, which Locke, like Hobbes, takes in part from Boyle (cf. *Essay* IV.iii.16). This perspective views material things as aggregates of corpuscles, each of which has an identity of its own and is constituted by atomic particles of matter.

53. Locke, *Essay* III.iii.11, p. 263 (original italics).

Here Locke's atomism is perhaps most clearly visible. Like other atomists, he attempts to avoid the problem of infinite regress by arguing that all material things form bodies, defined in the *Essay* as a "Particle of Matter, to which no Addition or Subtraction of Matter [is] made." However, Locke applies the notion of 'body' not simply to aggregates of particles but also individual atomic particles and living organisms. As such, the term 'body' cuts across the conceptual distinction affirmed elsewhere in the *Essay* between individual things and general kinds. It is true that the further distinction between simple and compounded substances allows him to argue that these belong to different kinds and can therefore exist in the same place at the same time. But the smallest identifiable entity remains the atom, defined as "a continued body under one immutable superficies."[54] So configured, each atom is always already individual and the basis for the self-individuation of things. The further distinction between simple and compounded substances does not modify the atomic foundation of individuality. Indeed, Locke goes as far as suggesting that compounds are series of numerically different aggregations of material particles. As a result, compounded substances are individual because they are constituted by sequences of numerically different individual components that are somehow coordinated, without however relying on a transcendent first principle or final end in God. By extension, this also applies to persons and personal identity, grounded in self-consciousness. Indeed, the parts of human bodies are "vitally united to this same thinking conscious self, so that we feel when they are touch'd, and are affected by, and conscious of good or harm that happens to them, are a part of our *selves*."[55] So, like his corpuscularian predecessor Boyle, Locke fails to provide a philosophically compelling solution to the question of how and why atomic particles conjoin to form bodies and in what way this rules out individuation by an act of divine creativity.

Fourth, Locke attempts to solve the problem of the identity of things over time and across space by appealing to spatial relations, a conception that qualifies the primacy of substance over relationality in the tradition from Aristotle via Scotus to Descartes and Suárez. Accordingly, bodies are individuated by their location in a unique place, and places are individu-

54. Quoted in Martha Brandt Bolton, "Locke on Identity: The Scheme of Simple and Compounded Things," in Barber and Gracia, eds., *Individuation and Identity in Early Modern Philosophy*, pp. 103-31 (114).

55. Quoted in Bolton, "Locke on Identity: The Scheme of Simple and Compounded Things," p. 117.

ated by distance relations to bodies — another circularity in Locke's theory. Moreover, it is unclear how Locke would account for these relations metaphysically, for there is a circularity at work: bodies are distinguished from each other by their mutual relations of distance in time, a process of individuation which is the result of a world composed of individual bodies always already separated by spatial distance (*Essay* II.xxvii.2).[56] Linked to this is the problem that Locke does not simply establish a dependency of modes and relations on substance but, crucially, that he makes them like substance, spatialized (e.g., *Essay* III.iii.1 and 6) and ending in substance: "All other things being but Modes or Relations ultimately terminated in Substances, the Identity and Diversity of each particular Existence of them too will be by the same way determined" (*Essay* II.xxvii.2). Following Leibniz and Spinoza, Locke posits the individuality of modes without ever demonstrating why this might be so or how relations ontologically qualify the substantiality of things.

Finally, in the case of persons there is a tension in Locke's theory between material atomism and his emphasis on immaterial consciousness. Either a person's thinking self is a unique set of immaterial, simple substances or else a single, immaterial simple substance. Even though Locke suggests that God's goodness ensures the nontransference of consciousness among different thinking substances, he does conceptualize the conscious activity of thinking in terms of different thinking substances — such that the unity of personhood is undermined and perhaps fatally compromised by the multiplicity of thinking agents. A further problem is that only an appeal to divine goodness can prevent the dissolution of personhood into series-beings, but in Locke's system of atomistic mechanism this appeal lacks any metaphysical reality and is ultimately fideistic. So beyond Descartes's spiritualist monism and Hobbes's material mechanism, Locke's accentuation of atomic particulars shifts ontology further in the direction of atomism.

6. Transcendental Immanence (Wolff and Kant)

In this section, I turn to the work of Christian Wolff (1679-1754) and Immanuel Kant (1724-1804). My argument is that Wolff's rationalist ontol-

---

56. On this point I disagree with Bolton, who speaks of a benign circularity. See her "Locke on Identity: The Scheme of Simple and Compounded Things," esp. pp. 103-9.

ogy posits as the principle of individuation the notion of complete determination which is internal to individual things. This line of argument is developed by Kant, who fuses the individuation of noumena centered on the objective reality of *ens realissimum* with the individuating principle of spatial relations for phenomena. In the *Opus Postumum,* however, Kant's account of individuation takes a radical turn towards the concept of moving forces of matter and foreshadows a transcendental materialism that nonetheless remains trapped in a representational mode predicated on an uncritical rejection of the Neo-Platonist theological metaphysics of creation.

A. On Wolff

There are at least three ways in which Wolff's theory of individuation is firmly inscribed in the tradition of transcendental ontology as I have outlined it. First of all, he equates 'first philosophy' *(philosophia prima)* with ontology *(ontologia),* like Clauberg or Clauvergius about seventy-five years before him. Published in 1729, Wolff's book *Philosophia prima sive ontologia* deals with the science of being in general whose object is being insofar as it is being *(ens inquantum ens).*[57] As argued at the beginning of the present chapter, the shift from metaphysics to ontology was never merely terminological but reflected the idea that being is univocal and transcendental rather than an analogical and transcendent, universal reality in which particular beings participate (as for Christian Neo-Platonism).

Second, Wolff — like Scotus and Suárez before him — grants the question of individuality greater prominence by discussing it prior to concepts such as universality, truth, or relation. Indeed, successive chapters of the aforementioned book address questions like identity, similarity, the singular, and the universal.

Third, epistemological and methodological issues come to the fore in Wolff, who (following Porreta, Aureoli, and Buridan) bases his investigation on principles such as noncontradiction and sufficient reason and deploys an axiomatic method that excludes the discussion of contrary views and responses to objections (as the *quaestio* method differently

---

57. Christian Wolff, *Philosophia prima sive ontologia,* ed. Jean Ecole (Hildesheim: Georg Olms, 1962).

developed by Porreta and Aquinas). In part as a result of privileging epistemology over ontology, Wolff fails to address key questions such as the ontological status of individuality in particular things.[58]

In accordance with the primacy of the mathematical method, Wolff makes the curious argument that to be individual is to be completely determinate (as opposed to universals in which not everything is determinate or which share determinations with other things). Moreover, to be individual means that the notion of individual can be affirmed of something. Since both determination and instantiation relate primarily to the cognoscibility of things, they represent conditions of individuality that are epistemological rather than ontological, as Jorge Gracia has rightly remarked.[59] Based on a mathematical definition of determination, Wolff posits the principle that a thing's full determination is the same thing as its individuality. By contrast, universals can never be completely determinate, for otherwise they could not be participated in by particulars. Based on this argument, Wolff concludes that universals cannot exist in the order of being — a conviction he shares with Ockham. The fact that for Wolff, universality as a concept denotes some similarity among things which the mind alone can discern, confirms his debt to nominalism. On the other hand, he also describes universality as that which individuals have in common, a position that comes closer to the 'formalist realism' of Duns Scotus. The sense that Wolff embraces the latter rather than the former is reinforced by his conception of the principle that individuates a thing as "the intrinsic sufficient reason of the individual" or this-ness *(haecceitas)*.[60]

However, Wolff does not follow Scotus in claiming that haecceity is primitive and unanalyzable. Since Wolff's account emphasizes the generic, specific, and numerical determination of individuals, it is also the case that his theory of individuation comes close to the idea of individuating determinations or bundles. Even though he does not express it in

58. Marco Paolinelli, "Metodo matematico e ontologia in Christian Wolff," *Rivista di Filosofia Neo-scholastica* 66 (1974): 3-39.

59. Jorge J. E. Gracia, "Christian Wolff on Individuation," in Barber and Gracia, eds., *Individuation and Identity in Early Modern Philosophy*, pp. 219-43. Cf. J. J. E. Gracia, *Individuality: An Essay on the Foundations of Metaphysics* (Albany: State University of New York Press, 1988).

60. Wolff, *Philosophia prima sive ontologia*, par. 228, p. 189: *"Per Principium individuationis intelligitur ratio sufficiens intrinseca individui. . . . Quamobrem per principium individuationis intelligitur, cur ens aliquod sit singulare."*

those terms in his book *Ontologia*, his text on logic makes the point unambiguously: "The principle of individuation includes all principles, whether numerical, specific or generic. It is the bundle of all the differences [constituting the individual]."[61] As such, Wolff eschews the Thomist account of the transcendent divine act of being in favor of immanent determinations combining Scotist with Ockhamist elements. Beyond Scotus, Wolff equates the numerical difference of an individual with a bundle of what the scholastics termed 'accidental properties' such as quantity, size, or color. These can be shared with other individuals and are neither dependent upon a thing's essence nor contrary to it. As such, an individual is *this* particular thing rather than *that* particular thing because of the unique combination of accidental properties that singularizes either a simple or a compounded substance.

The most fundamental problem with this theory of individuation is the denial that each thing has its own unique form, in the sense of divinely given particular shares in common created universal being and goodness. As I have already indicated, Wolff's account is ultimately based upon the claim that being is a transcendental foundation of all that is. The counterpart to this ontology is the affirmation that individuation can be reduced to unique combinations of accidental properties that are quasi-positivist. Since the concept of being includes both divine and created being, it is not surprising that the onus of individuation has shifted to individuals themselves and now seems to rule out any links with the first cause. As such, Wolff's theory can be described as a variant of precritical rationalism that qualifies the transcendentalism of Scotus and Suárez. As I suggest in the following subsection, Kant took this strand even further towards a transcendentalism that is paradoxically linked to finitized reason and immanentized individuation whereby spatiotemporal relations and rules of the mind individuate things.

B. On Kant's Meta-Ontology

Since the work of Étienne Gilson and *nouvelle théologie*, we know the extent to which Kant's philosophy is shaped by the legacy of late scholasti-

---

61. Christian Wolff, *Philosophia rationalis sive logica*, ed. Jean Ecole (Hildesheim: George Olms, 1983), part 1, sec. 1, ch. 2, par. 75: *"Principium autem individuationis complectitur differentias omnes, sive numericas fuerit, sive specificae, sive genericae. Est adeo omnium differentiarum complexus."*

cism, notably Ockham's nominalist and voluntarist theology. For this reason alone, it would be misguided to equate Kant's project with epistemology and cognate fields in philosophy. While he shares the priority of knowledge over being with Descartes (and arguably also with Scotus), Kant radicalizes the modern tradition of transcendental ontology by substituting the transcendental unity of the concept for the transcendental unity of *ens* and equating individuation with objectification.[62] Indeed, substance and other categories are not simply pure concepts of the understanding which are a priori rather than abstracted from a posteriori sense perceptions; they also denote the 'objective reality' that structures both phenomenal and noumenal substances. Since knowledge requires an intuitional grasp of things to which properties can be attached, the formal abstraction of the transcendental unity of the concept also raises the question of what lies beyond the concept (its dependence on intuition).

As such, Kant reconfigures 'substance' in ways that depart from an Aristotelian grammar of logical subject or metaphysical being towards a meta-ontological concept that lies beyond the old divide between the abstract intelligibility of universals and the concrete reality of particulars. Unsurprisingly therefore, the question of the individual is central to Kant's meta-ontology, for "science as such is only possible if the individual can be brought under the conceptual jurisdiction of the understanding in the form of an object of representation."[63] And since the self-organization of individuals cannot be such an object, ontology is not a science of the individual but rather a science that determines the conditions of possibility for the production of individuality — or ontogenesis, as Toscano is right to argue. The recognition that individuals self-organize does not just introduce teleological principles into a mechanistic system but, crucially, escapes the cognitive control underpinning Kant's own fusion of Newtonian physics with the Scotist onto-theology of representation. This marks an interruption that destabilizes the architectonics of the Kantian system, as evinced in the *Opus Postumum*.

This is not to say however that Kant comes closer to a Neo-Platonist account of individuality in terms of divine creative activity than he does to a more Aristotelian focus on form-matter union and causality. Rather, his redefinition of substance is a shift away from both precritical ratio-

---

62. Toscano, *The Theatre of Production*, pp. 19-43.
63. Toscano, *The Theatre of Production*, p. 11.

nalism and atomistic empiricism in ways that are nevertheless more akin to late scholastic Aristotelian ontology than to the Christian Neo-Platonist metaphysics of creation. Indeed, Kant's meta-ontology is based on his exposition of the substance concept as that which contains logical relations of subject and predicate as well as relations of cause and effect:

> [Substance is] something which can exist as subject and never as mere predicate.[64]

> Each substance (inasmuch as only in respect of its determinations can it be an effect) must therefore contain in itself the causality of certain determinations in the other substance, and at the same time the effects of the causality of that other. (*CPR* B259)

Crucially, essence or that which makes a substance a substance is intrinsic to things and does not depend on any transcendent cause or source of being: "As object of the pure understanding, every substance must have inner determinations and powers which pertain to its inner reality" (*CPR* B321).

Linked to this Wolffian notion of inner essential determination is Kant's argument about the relations of substances to space and relations of things themselves to appearances. Space is ideal — not real — and as such does not require any absolute foundation for spatial relations between things *(relata)*. As relations that are mental modify mental substance, spatial relations do not need absolute, nonrelational *relata,* as Michael Radner has shown.[65] Instead, the terms of spatial relations are themselves composed of relations that can be deconstructed into their constituent parts — substances separated by space. Unlike early modern accounts, the individuation of substances is for Kant not the product of spatial relations (or location within such relations). For such relations pertain to appearances, not things in themselves: "Everything in our knowledge which belongs to intuition . . . contains nothing but mere relations; namely of location in an intuition (extension), of change of loca-

---

64. Immanuel Kant, *Critique of Pure Reason* B149; cf. A246, B300, B288 (henceforth *CPR*).

65. Michael Radner, "Substance and Phenomenal Substance: Kant's Individuation of Things in Themselves and Appearances," in Barber and Gracia, eds., *Individuation and Identity in Early Modern Philosophy*, pp. 245-65.

tion (motion), and of laws according to which this change is determined (moving forces)" (*CPR* B66-67).

On this basis, Kant makes the argument that only appearances are relational and that knowing the relations which pertain between objects does not tell us anything about things in themselves: "Now a thing in itself cannot be known through mere relations; and we may therefore conclude that since outer sense gives us nothing but mere relations, this sense can contain in its representation only the relation of an object to the subject, and not the inner properties of the object in itself" (*CPR* B67). Because Kant is worried about the idea of things consisting wholly of relations (*CPR* B341), he subordinates all relations to a thing's substantiality in order to secure its independence. It is this accentuation of substance that lies behind the separation of appearances from genuine substances or essences. Since substances are simple and representable in terms of 'objective reality,' it follows that they are pure essences devoid of any link to prime matter. As such, Kant follows the Avicennian and Scotist emphasis on essence at the expense of the Thomist notion of the unity of essential form and prime matter in the divine act of being.

This is not to suggest that relations between things are eliminated altogether in Kant's meta-ontology. On the contrary, he is adamant that we only know appearances *qua* appearances in terms of the relations constituting them. In the Second Analogy, he applies the category of substance to physical objects in space and their causal relations, also described as *substantia phenomena* in space whose "inner determinations are nothing but relations; and it itself is entirely made up of mere relations" (*CPR* B321). As Radner indicates, Kant attributes the individuation of phenomenal substances to the form of appearance "which so determines the manifold of appearance that it allows of being ordered in certain relations" (*CPR* B34). Since space is for him ideal (and not material), it is best classified as a network of relations without *relata,* as I have already indicated. As such, the transcendental unity of infinite space precedes and grounds its finite parts — hence Kant's transcendental idealism. The infinity of space can be represented by ideas, which are modes or modifications of mental substance (their ontological function) and make something known besides themselves (their epistemological function). In this manner, the representation of transcendental 'objective reality' (rather than the participation of particular things in universal being) is the cornerstone of Kant's meta-ontology. Just as space is "the form of all appearances of outer sense" (*CPR* B42) and therefore the transcendental ground for the existence of individual substances arranged according to spatial relations, so space is also the condition of possibility of outer sensible intuition and therefore a representation that relates immediately to the object and is singular. Put differently, it is only because there always already is a network of spatial relations that we can know the world of outer sense.

As for things in themselves, Kant makes the point that both rationalist and empiricist philosophers have failed properly to distinguish sensibility from understanding. In a trenchant critique, he concludes that "[i]n a word, Leibniz *intellectualized* appearances, just as Locke . . . *sensualized* all concepts of the understanding, i.e., interpreted them as nothing more than empirical or abstracted concepts of reflection" (*CPR* B327, original italics). In some ways like Wolff before him, Kant argues that real substances (the essences of things in themselves) are the product of complete determination — a condition that surpasses identity and difference and could restrict essential properties to mere relations of inner determinations. Following Suárez, Kant deploys the notion of *ens realissimum* as the representation of the whole set of possible predicates, or "concept of an individual being. . . . Only in this one case is a concept of a thing — a concept which is in itself universal — completely determined in and through itself, and known as the representation of an individual" (*CPR* B604). Since the complete determination is a concept whose totality cannot be exhibited but whose conditions can be thought, there is here according to Kant an ontological and epistemological coincidence of the abstract intelligibility of universals and the concrete reality of particulars under the aegis of this meta-conceptual level which is correlated with being at its most general. Paradoxically, the individuation of things in themselves is for Kant synonymous with the objectification of singularity.

C. On Kant's Transcendental Materialism

Yet precisely at the point where all is subsumed under the meta-concept of the represented individual, the Kantian system is almost fatally undermined by the irruption of the organic — the self-organization of living individuals that evades the cognitive control of both concept and intuition, as Alberto Toscano's seminal book has shown. The way in which Kant attempts to recalibrate the transcendental ontology he inherited from late scholasticism is key here. The claim to truth of representation rests on "the agreement of knowledge with the object" (*CPR* B236), a formulation that mirrors the shared Aristotelian and Thomist idea of adequation or *convenientia*. But building on Scotus and Suárez, Kant replaces *res* and *intellectus* with 'object' and 'concept,' whose relation must be "in conformity with a rule" (*CPR* B238), i.e., some necessary link establishing some particular mode of connection of the object to the manifold. Put differently, without necessity objects would be indistinguishable from the endless series of appearances and there would be no synthesis of apprehensions. It is this onto-logic of necessity that removes the possibility of a metaphysic of creation, as Kant himself makes clear. The idea of object as an event in terms of an interruption of temporality out of 'empty time' is inadmissible: "For if coming to be out of nothing [creation *ex nihilo*] is regarded as effect of a foreign cause, it has to be entitled creation, and that cannot be admitted as an event among appearances, since its mere possibility would destroy the unity of experience" (*CPR* B251).

With divine creation excluded, Kant's transcendental ontology seeks to explain the singularity of things in terms of the twin logic of Newtonian laws of motion and Kantian rules of the mind. Since phenomena are assumed to be divorced from noumena and "since matter has absolutely no internal determinations and ground of determination,"[66] only natural laws of succession and mental rules structuring the flux of sensations can secure both the unity of experience and the singularity of each object-as-event in its unique time-position. As Toscano notes, Kant views the mechanical causation of matter as purely external. As such, he divides mechanistic from essential natures, with the former governed by efficient and the latter by final causality. This partition does not however account for the individuation of organic, self-organizing individuals, for the reality of self-organization escapes the formality of the individuating principle based on the correlation of transcendental subjectivity and transcendental objectivity.

Since organisms cannot be equated with abstract entities or objects, self-organizing individuals evade rule-bound cognition and their particularity cannot be captured by the formal principle of objective individuation. Real individuals are not subsumable under the concept of objectivity

---

66. Immanuel Kant, *Metaphysical Foundations of Natural Science*, in *Philosophy of Material Nature* (Indianapolis: Hackett, 1985), p. 453.

because for Kant himself we cannot ascertain whether the organic as object has objective reality.[67] For this reason, transcendental ontology is over-determined by the logic of representation and undermined by the irruption of reality of which all real things are part and which is not reducible to spatiotemporal relations determined by rules of the mind or laws of motion. Crucially, the latter two cannot account for the real unity beyond the causal chain of 'positionings' in space and time. As Toscano notes, organic self-organization for Kant involves a relational unity of parts, an integrated reciprocal causality and auto-production, none of which can be explained by the externality of both efficient and final causes.[68] That is why Kant seeks to develop an account of organic individuation beyond the modern opposition between transcendental foundation and empirical induction, an account that is nevertheless part of the modern science of transcendental onto-theology which is predicated on rejecting — though not refuting — the Christian Neo-Platonist metaphysics of creation.

Indeed, one can suggest with Toscano that Kant develops his theory of causation in the direction of a psycho-vitalist theism that postulates an immaterial principle termed 'intelligence' — analogous to a cognitive power of desire — that individuates matter. Why so? First of all, material inertia excludes the possibility of material self-individuation. Second, his argument that matter is divisible to infinity leads him to reject Lockean atomism. Third, given his opposition to the idea of creation *ex nihilo,* Kant also rules out souls in bodies or some world-soul corresponding to the aggregate of general matter. Fourth, the intelligence or life-force *(Lebenskraft)* allows Kant to separate life from matter (anti-hylozoism) and posit an immaterial ideality behind apparently self-organizing material phenomena. Far from reintroducing the efficient causality of a first mover, Kant stresses that life-force acts as an efficient cause "only on the analogy with an intelligence, that is, a cause which we can represent to ourselves in no other way."[69] So configured, efficient causality operates neither in terms of Neo-Platonist (including Aristotelian) transcendent final ends nor Cartesian iatromechanics but rather in terms of the purposive activity animating organic, material things. Ultimately, the disjunctive separation of life and matter ensures that Kant

67. Immanuel Kant, *Critique of Judgement* 396 (henceforth *CJ*).

68. Toscano, *The Theatre of Production,* pp. 32-36.

69. Immanuel Kant, *Opus Postumum,* ed. and trans. E. Förster (Cambridge: Cambridge University Press, 1993), Ak. 22: 506-7.

posits individuality as an irreducible, conceptual foundation that grounds the modalities of existence and the conditions of possibility for our understanding. Since Kant merely argues from the logical requirement of individuality to its ontological basis, his philosophy of individuation is in fact a philosophy of individuals grounded in a fundamentally and irreducibly representational logic that eliminates a priori the participation of immanent things in a transcending act of being.

My account parts company with Toscano's reading where the latter suggests that the introduction of the concept of 'ether' or 'caloric' marks a fundamental change in the trajectory of modern theories of individuation. Conceptualized as the unity of absolute matter which escapes experience but must be presupposed for the sake of evading the undifferentiated series of apprehensions, this concept undergirds all instances of mechanist causation and material self-organization. As Toscano concludes, that is

> where we see the workings of a veritable transcendental materialism, the attempt to think the non-empirical determinations of a single matter understood as the field of individuation for all the bodies that constitute the objects of our cognition, a cognition that cannot experience this matter as such but must postulate it indirectly.[70]

However, the problem with this variant of transcendental materialism is that it posits an entirely undemonstrated and unwarranted monism that nonetheless masks a dualism. If a 'single matter' is ultimate, then it must be self-causing and auto-generating. But what is the source of and 'reason' for this self-causation and auto-generation? Kant's dismissal of the metaphysical logic of creation *ex nihilo* robs him of the necessary conceptual resources fully to account, first of all, for the transcendental grounding of all immanent things in an individual, single instance (material or ideal) which is uncaused and nonrelational, and second, for reason's grasp of infinite immanence beyond the confines of finitude (in the *Opus Postumum*). Kant's material monism is deeply dualistic precisely because it drives an absolute wedge between the one and the many and excludes any kind of participatory mediation by ruling out the idea of divine creativity which brings everything out of nothing into actuality and sustains all beings in being.

70. Toscano, *The Theatre of Production*, p. 53.

Moreover, the critical destruction of the medieval metaphysics of creation did not of course bracket God altogether but instead replaced a personal and relational Creator with the arbitrary intervention of an anonymous and willful deity whose existence can be cognized but whose essence remains wholly unintelligible to human reason reaching to infinity. For otherwise how can Kant explain that there is such a primary, onto-(theo-)logical, hyper-individual instance which grounds all ontic individuals? In other words, Kant's post-rationalist and post-empiricist philosophy neither corrects nor overcomes the skeptical formalism/ nominalism and fideistic voluntarism bequeathed by Scotus and Ockham. Morever, Kant's account of individuation in terms of single matter radicalizes Scotus's transcendental ontology of representation and Ockham's politics of divine omnipotence in the direction of an onto-theology of auto-volition whereby divine will is the ultimate and arbitrary source of individuation whose origin remains wholly inscrutable by reason and accessible to blind faith alone.

7. The Transcendentalism and Positivism of Modern Ontology

If alternatively we substitute a kind of post-theistic virtuality for the act of a willful divinity — as the post-Kantian transcendental materialism of Gilbert Simondon and Gilles Deleuze stipulates[71] — then we are nonetheless faced with a similarly unresolved tension between the virtuality of the one and the reality of the many. This requires rather unconvincing appeals to a prior (vitalist) force or field of individuation that has a residually henological primacy over the actuality of ordinary individual beings. As Conor Cunningham has argued, this tension between the one and the many either plunges rational materialism into mystical nihilism (for the One itself is nothing and as such still *is*).[72] Or else it requires an account of mediation whereby the 'middle' neither represents a *tertium quid* between the one and the many nor is it ultimately obliterated by the one or the many but instead acts as a 'vanishing mediator.'[73] This con-

---

71. On Simondon and Deleuze, see — once more — Toscano, *The Theatre of Production*, pp. 109-201.

72. Conor Cunningham, *Genealogy of Nihilism: Philosophies of Nothing and the Difference of Theology* (London: Routledge, 2002).

73. Slavoj Žižek and John Milbank, *The Monstrosity of Christ: Paradox or Dialectic?* ed. Creston Davis (Cambridge, MA: MIT Press, 2009).

cept is championed by Slavoj Žižek and builds on the work of Frederic Jameson. It refers to the third moment of a dialectic whereby a concept charts a passage between two opposing concepts and in this mediating process disappears.[74]

Other materialist philosophers have advanced theories of mediation and *metaxu* in terms of the pan-psychic (Deleuze), the logic of appearances (Badiou), or the clone of the One (Laruelle). But none of them can actually uphold the integrity of immanence because the latter is equated either with the unity of the 'objective' exterior world or the multiplicity of 'subjective' interior experience — or somehow both at once.[75] By contrast with dialectical or transcendental materialism, the Christian Neo-Platonist idea of relational participation views the mediation of Plato's *metaxu* as that which infinitely sustains immanence by participating in the infinite reality of a God whose Trinitarian nature ensures the irreducible relationality of both Creator and creation in their analogical difference.

This points to a wider difference between theological metaphysics and modern ontology on the question of individuation. If the ultimate source or force of individuation is an immanent potency or virtuality, then we are left wondering how and why it actualizes finite things, as I already pointed out in relation to Spinoza in the previous chapter, but the same question a fortiori arises in the ontology of Deleuze. Or if it is a transcendent power or actuality, then we have to ask in what ways it ultimately differs from the transcendent act of God and divine grace, as Pickstock and Milbank's deconstruction of Badiou's ontology reveals.

Moreover, these variants of 'postmodern' immanentism perpetuate the modern ontological and political complicit collusion of the one and the many, for the monism of univocal being either dissolves into a hierarchical dualism whereby the sovereign one holds supreme sway over the disempowered many (*à la* Bodin and Hobbes) or into the mirror image of an inverted hierarchical dualism whereby the many are now superior to the one (*à la* Levinas, Badiou, or the politics of Hardt and

74. Frederic Jameson, *The Ideologies of Theory: Essays 1971-1986* (Minneapolis: University of Minnesota Press, 1988); Slavoj Žižek, *For They Know Not What They Do: Enjoyment as a Political Factor,* 2nd ed. (London: Verso, 2002).

75. John Milbank, "The Mystery of Reason," in *The Grandeur of Reason: Religion, Tradition and Universalism,* ed. Peter M. Candler Jr. and Conor Cunningham (London: SCM, 2010), ch. 4. I am indebted to conversations with John Milbank for a number of arguments in this section.

Negri).[76] In either case, the onto-theo-logic of representation and the nominalist poles of the individual and the collective supplanted and displaced the theological metaphysics of relational participation and the primary, real relations between creation and Creator.[77]

Here one can also make the point that (post)modern ontology and politics are trapped in a logic that oscillates between transcendentalism and positivism. This argument can be traced to the work of the Russian philosopher and theologian Vladimir Solovyov (1853-1900). Perhaps more so than any other nineteenth-century figure, he showed that the speculative philosophy of rationalism and the practical philosophy of empiricism share the same conceptual basis — an ontology that seals the exit from both theology and metaphysics and ultimately consecrates the triumph of both transcendentalism and positivism in all areas of theory and practice. This also applies to Kant's critical onto-theology as well as the postcritical analytic and phenomenological strands of philosophy and theology. Solovyov identifies nine key 'moments' in the long transition from late medieval scholasticism to late modern nihilism.[78] First of all, separating the rationality of individual thought and the authority of communal faith from their single source, divine wisdom (wrongly attributed to Eriugena but in reality developed by Franciscan theologians like St. Bonaventure and John Duns Scotus); second, elevating reason over faith and mind over nature (Ockham's late medieval nominalism); third, dissociating individual beings and their knowledge from the wholeness of reality and the divine wisdom that infuses the entire created universe (Descartes and Spinoza); fourth, bridging the gap between the internal unity of the knowing subject and the external unity of known reality through an ontology of representation (Leibniz, Bacon, Hobbes, Locke, Berkeley, and Hume); fifth, dividing phenomena from noumena and replacing realism, rationalism, and empiricism with transcendental idealism (Kant); sixth, rethinking the Kantian knowing subject in terms of

76. See the trilogy by Michael Hardt and Antonio Negri, *Empire* (Cambridge, MA: Harvard University Press, 2000); *Multitude: War and Democracy in the Age of Empire* (London: Penguin, 2005); and *Commonwealth* (Cambridge, MA: Harvard University Press, 2009).

77. See my "The Primacy of Relation over Substance and the Recovery of a Theological Metaphysics," *American Catholic Philosophical Quarterly* 81 (Fall 2007): 553-78, and "Modern Sovereignty in Question: Theology, Democracy and Capitalism," pp. 570-82.

78. Vladimir Solovyov, *The Crisis of Western Philosophy: Against the Positivists*, trans. and ed. Boris Jakim (Hudson, NY: Lindisfarne Press, 1996), pp. 11-69.

self-consciousness and the absolute subject and, concomitantly, developing critical philosophy in the direction of pure subjective idealism (Fichte and Schelling); seventh, redefining the absolute principle of all being as the very form of concept and overcoming the split between idealism and rationalism by way of absolute pan-logism (Hegel); eighth, positing a concept-independent reality and reconfiguring empirical philosophy in the direction of materialism (Marx); ninth, reducing matter to its atomic constituents and the human intellect to the physical brain, thereby equating consciousness with the sensory perception of external, material phenomena (Comte, Mill, and Spencer). As such, positivism constitutes the end-point of late medieval scholasticism and represents the triumph of 'positive science' (Comte) over metaphysical theology and theological philosophy[79] — a victory with profound consequences for religion, culture, and politics.[80]

Leaving aside the detail of his reading of history, Solovyov's argument that only philosophical theology and a theological metaphysic can guard against the separation of mind from world and the primacy of subject over object in modern philosophy outwits in advance Nietzsche's attack on Platonism as inherently dualist and Christianity as otherworldly. It also outwits Heidegger's charge that metaphysics is constitutively onto-theological, Derrida's accusation that the whole of western thought is coterminous with Plato's 'phallogocentrism' as well as Levinas's assertion that philosophy and theology are totalizing and must be overcome in the direction of an ontology and ethics of alterity.

The significance of Solovyov's argument becomes fully clear when seen in conjunction with his conclusion that positivism is valid exclusively in natural sciences because only "external relative phenomena as such must be studied in an external relative manner."[81] The implication is that the modern physical sciences, on account of their premises and their method, always already bracket God and exclude a cosmological metaphysics. The problem, as Solovyov already foresaw, is that positivism in the natural or the social sciences claims universal validity and arrogates for itself a monopoly on truth: the whole of reality can be reduced to external empirical phenomena that are scientifically knowable,

79. Solovyov, *The Crisis of Western Philosophy*, pp. 150-68.

80. Andrew Wernick, *Auguste Comte and the Religion of Humanity: The Post-Theistic Program of French Social Theory* (Cambridge: Cambridge University Press, 2001), pp. 1-21, 81-115, 186-220.

81. Solovyov, *The Crisis of Western Philosophy*, p. 167.

and it is the physical brain that alone can determine what is real and how it is structured. This impoverished view has led philosophers and natural scientists from Russell to Popper to Dennett and to Dawkins to propound an increasingly militant form of atheism that is scientifically questionable, philosophically dubious, and theologically illiterate.[82] Thus, the mark of positivism is to enthrone the immaterial mind as the sole source of knowledge — at the expense of material reality and the link that might pertain between them. But rather than annulling the possibility of religion and philosophy, this opens a space for the recovery of a theological metaphysics. For only theology can give an account of the relation between subjectivity and objectivity and the 'vanishing mediator' that binds them together in a higher unity.

That is what Solovyov explores in his book *The Critique of Abstract Principles* of 1880, where he develops a 'critique of critiques' of the entire tradition of post-scholastic philosophy by arguing that modern abstraction either separates the mind from the world or reduces reality to particular aspects and as such cannot encapsulate the 'unity-of-all' (*vseedinstvo,* literally the 'whole of things').[83] Whereas the rationalist philosophy of Descartes or Hegel is 'a system of concepts without any reality,' the empiricist philosophy of Comtean positivism is 'a system of facts without any inner connection.' In consequence, neither is equal to the unity of being.[84] Solovyov's critique is not limited to theoretical philosophy but extends to aesthetics and practical philosophy, including ethics, politics, economics, and other social sciences. Modern theories of aesthetics deny that beauty is objective and universal; instead, it is claimed that "beauty in things exists merely in the mind which contemplates them" (as David Hume wrote in his *Essays, Moral and Political* of 1742). Similarly, modern accounts of ethics absolutize one element of the social and political reality (like the law or utility) to the detriment of the rest.

---

82. For a compelling critique of militant atheism and a defense of Christianity, see Terry Eagleton, *Reason, Faith, and Revolution: Reflections on the God Debate* (New Haven: Yale University Press, 2009); David Bentley Hart, *Atheist Delusions: The Christian Revolution and Its Fashionable Enemies* (New Haven: Yale University Press, 2009); and Conor Cunningham, *Darwin's Pious Idea* (Grand Rapids: Eerdmans, 2010).

83. Vladimir Solovyov, *Critique of Abstract Principles,* pp. v-vi, quoted in Paul Valliere, *Modern Russian Theology: Bukharev, Soloviev, Bulgakov — Orthodox Theology in a New Key* (Edinburgh: T. & T. Clark, 2000), p. 121.

84. In the following section, I discuss some of the ways in which Solovyov surpasses Hegel.

The same problem applies to politics: the liberal defense of individual freedom and the socialist emphasis on collectivity represent two extremes that mirror each other and cannot meet 'the ideal of a free communality' *(svobodnaia obshchinnost)*.[85] By adopting the same positivistic approach as the natural sciences, the humanities and social sciences reject any import from metaphysics and are therefore unable to describe or conceptualize the integral nature of being.

Beyond Solovyov, we can also say that this is linked to the nominalist and voluntarist foundation of modern ontology and liberalism and the inability of postmodern philosophy and politics to provide an account of the one and the many that does not collapse either into monism or into dualism or both at once, as I have already indicated. Nor do these failures validate various theories of pluralism proffered by contemporary postliberal thinkers as varied as Isaiah Berlin, Joseph Raz, Richard Rorty, John Gray, or Peter Sloterdijk, who tend to view western claims to universality as absolutist and monolithic, a fundamental flaw that they variously trace to the Christian attempt to universalize the monotheistic revelation of Judaism. According to this sort of reading, the dominant forms of modern liberalism represent little more than a secular variant of revealed religion and remain trapped in the conceptuality of monotheism. As a result, the only alternative to absolutism is to break with all forms of universalism and envision a true pluralism that can secure a peaceful *modus vivendi* between rival and incommensurable values and belief systems.[86] For John Gray, both theist faiths and secular creeds reproduce in different ways the same religious myths about the salvific transformation of human life through apocalyptic violence. Both are hopelessly utopian and both have been dissolved by

85. Solovyov, *Critique of Abstract Principles,* p. 166, quoted in Valliere, *Modern Russian Theology,* p. 127.

86. See, *inter alia,* John Gray, *Enlightenment's Wake: Politics and Culture at the Close of the Modern Age* (London: Routledge, 1995), pp. 131-84; J. Gray, *False Dawn: The Delusions of Global Capitalism* (London: Granta, 1998), pp. 184-235. Gray attributes the modern ideal of a *modus vivendi* among people with incommensurate values to Hobbes and Hume and opposes this kind of inclusive, tolerant liberalism to Kant's and Locke's exclusive, hegemonic liberalism founded upon uniform principles and universal regimes. See John Gray, *Two Faces of Liberalism* (Cambridge: Polity Press, 2000), pp. 1-33. But this sort of reading subscribes uncritically to the distinctly modern assumption of a violent state of nature that requires the delegation of sovereignty to a single authority (from Suárez to Hobbes and Spinoza) and the state's monopoly on the use of systematic violence (from Kant to Weber and Schmitt).

their shared claim to universal foundations that lack any basis in humanity or the natural world. As a result, the delusion of (western) universalism must give way to a posthumanist pluralism that rejects the quest for universals and advocates the search for a peaceful coexistence of incommensurable values and rival ways of life. By viewing humans as essentially the same as animals, posthumanism purports to reinscribe man into nature.[87]

However, this sort of critique of the monism and dualism of modern philosophy is caught in the irreconcilable dialectic of positivism and transcendentalism. Posthumanist philosophies obliterate all essential differences among animate beings and assert that humans lack the sort of rational faculties to ascertain the categorical claims about salvation and progress in revealed religion and the natural sciences. This skepticism leads to similar categorical claims about the agonistic and agnostic nature of human beings. Humans, like nonrational animals, are presumed to be naturally locked into violent struggles for individual self-preservation. Likewise, human fallibility is thought to rule out the possibility of knowing a transcendent corrective Good that can direct everyone to a common *telos*. But far from refuting the monotheistic belief in human perfectibility and the natural desire for supernatural perfection, pluralist and pragmatist accounts are little more than a secularized version of certain Protestant and Calvinist views of the Fall and human corruption, except that there is no saving grace by faith — let alone the gift of divine love and goodness. For pragmatists and value-pluralists, the only way that man can be saved from himself and his fellow human beings is by recognizing the illusion of infinite progress based on human reason and freedom and by accepting the pragmatic necessity to pool power and sovereignty — without any appeal to overarching principles that are mediated through particular practices.

What remains wholly unexplained is the existence of universal desires such as individual and communal self-preservation, human civic association, or mutually extending peace. Postliberal thinkers like Gray correctly reject the twin delusion of violent millenarian salvation and peaceful secular progress,[88] but they dismiss it in the name of a hidden

87. John Gray, *Straw Dogs: Thoughts on Humans and Other Animals* (London: Granta, 2002).

88. John Gray, *Al Qaeda and What It Means to Be Modern* (London: Faber & Faber, 2003); J. Gray, *Heresies: Against Progress and Other Illusions* (London: Granta, 2004); J. Gray, *Black Mass: Apocalyptic Religion and the Death of Utopia* (London: Allen Lane, 2007).

universality which their ontological and epistemological skepticism has already ruled out — the shared human quest for a *modus vivendi* of coexistence and peace. If peace is something like the harmonious ordering of diversity for the sake of guaranteeing unity in difference, then peace must involve the universal natural desire for a supernatural common good in which all beings can participate equally according to their particular station in the order of being. For only a transcendent good of a personal God who is open to all can blend differences peacefully and thus preserve and extend equality without destroying identity and unicity.

In summary: by excluding any ontological hierarchy within the *cosmos*, postmodern pragmatism and postliberal pluralism deny humans natural knowledge of the supernatural universals they desire. And by ruling out the existence of a transcendent God who endows all beings with goodness and the capacity to desire the good, the underlying skepticism about the irredeemable corruption of human nature becomes a self-fulfilling prophecy. As a result, the defense of value-pluralism amounts to nothing more than a pragmatic search for peaceful coexistence in order to mitigate the consequences of an irreducibly violent state of nature. In this, postliberal pluralism and pragmatism merely repeat the logic that underlies the liberal attempt to assert its primacy over all other ideologies (albeit replacing liberal arrogance with posthumanist humility but in this process also ignoring the truth that something always rules). This sort of pluralism enshrines difference as the new absolute, which eliminates the universal that is embodied in particularity and as such reflects the unity binding us all together.

For these reasons, postmodern pluralism — like modern liberalism — is caught between a transcendentalism that is blind and a positivism that is empty: just as secular liberalism appeals to a nominalist and voluntarist mode of representation (e.g., Rousseau's *volonté générale*) which is transcendentally grounded in order to legitimate positivistic values like liberty, individual choice, or equality of opportunities, so too value-pluralism can only secure positivistic notions of diversity by appealing to difference or alterity, both of which are residually transcendental. As such, both pluralism and liberalism represent a false universalism that is, first of all, predicated on abstract and disembodied principles and categories and, second, denies the existence of a substantive transcendent Good which can order conflicting freedoms and direct the diversity of difference to the unity of common being in which all beings participate. So the more radical move is to view liberalism and pluralism as mirror images of each other and to reestablish theology as the only metaphysics and politics that can defend the universal ideals that both liberals and postliberals variously purport to offer but fail to deliver.

8. Theological Metaphysics and Political Theology

Ontological transcendentalism and positivism are correlated with political absolutism. Here the crucial nexus is between Ockham's nominalist-voluntarist theology and Machiavelli's new science of politics. Machiavelli fuses the late medieval nominalist-voluntarist account of autonomous secular authority with a neo-pagan conception of power as *virtù* (or heroic agonism). He radicalizes the early modern redefinition of *dominium* as power, private property, individual rights, and absolute sovereignty[89] by divorcing the exercise of legitimate authority from notions of moral goodness. In this way, his account inverts the primacy of good over evil (defined by St. Augustine as *privatio boni*) and defends a political anthropology that is predicated on violent conflict. This inversion goes back to Ockham's nominalist erasure of universal goodness from particular beings and anticipates the idea of a violent state of nature in the modern tradition of the social contract from Hobbes to Kant. Contrary to the metaphysics of participation that views the *civitas terrena* as ordered toward the hierarchical ends of the *civitas Dei* in which it partakes, transcendental 'political ontology' equates the kingdom and city-republic with a competition for survival, power, and wealth.

In *The Prince* (esp. chap. IX), it is the use of fear and force that ultimately regulates political and civic life, not the pursuit of peace or virtuous practice. Connected with this is the appeal to the myth of *fortuna*, an imagined existential threat to the political order that demands a violent response — based on redefining virtue in terms of the neo-pagan heroism that invests the leader with a secular sacrality.[90] Just as Scotus and Ockham secularize the political order, so Machiavelli and Suárez sacralize state power.

89. John Milbank, *Theology and Social Theory: Beyond Secular Reason*, 2nd ed. (Oxford: Wiley-Blackwell, 2006), pp. 7-25.

90. Niccolò Machiavelli, *The Prince*, ch. XXV, in idem, *The Chief Works and Others*, trans. A. Gilbert (Durham: Duke University Press, 1965), vol. 1, esp. pp. 90-92.

Divine will and *potentia Dei absoluta* are in some sense reflected in the monarch's will-to-power. Arguably, one can speak of political absolutism because power is now neither seen as a gift of divine grace that requires righteous rule nor constrained by substantive transcendent *telos* — whether an impersonal cosmic force such as Plato's Good and Aristotle's Prime Mover or the personal Creator God of the Judeo-Christian tradition. Machiavelli's purported realism turns out to be an extension of Ockham's nominalism and voluntarism that builds on Scotus's ontology of representation.

Taken together, the triple currents of possibilism, transcendentalism, and absolutism flow from Avicenna, Scotus, and Ockham through Machiavelli and Suárez to Hobbes, Locke, and Kant. The collective dimension of sovereign authority is reduced to an individualist mode of power, while at the same time the citizens and corporate groups that compose the common polity are subsumed under a collectivity whose continued assent is no longer required. Popular sovereignty is entirely compatible with the absolute, executive power of the sovereign. Authoritarian democracy — whether in its republican (Machiavelli) or its monarchical guise (Suárez) — is not so much a contradiction or an oxymoron as a paradox that links modern absolutism to modern liberalism.[91] Here one can already see the dialectic between the 'one' and the 'many' that is coextensive with the nominalist poles of left versus right, which govern both modern and postmodern politics.

Philosophically and politically, there are thus three fundamental continuities from the late Middle Ages through modernity to our late modern era. First of all, there is a twin accentuation on 'the rule of the one' and 'the rule of the many.' The former is the sovereign center that is either more autocratic or more plutocratic — or indeed both. The latter is the sovereign people who are either in contracted dispersion or in collective unity. The 'one' and 'the many' are dialectically related and collude at the expense of the mediating role of the 'the few,' a notion that for Plato, Aristotle, and Christian Neo-Platonists refers to virtuous elites who uphold principles and practices of reciprocity and mutuality such as the exercise of justice and charity.[92]

---

91. Cf. Milbank, *Theology and Social Theory*, p. 14.

92. Aristotle develops this line of argument in the direction of a constitutional system of 'mixed government' that combines 'monarchical,' 'aristocratic,' and 'democratic' elements, which blend hierarchy with equality (e.g., *Politics* IV, 1288^{b}10-1301^{a}15).

Second, linked to this configuration is the power of the central state and the free market. Both are constructed based on the myth of human artifice (such as the social contract) that brings about a peaceful natural order (beyond the violent state of nature). As such, state and market converge and subsume the intermediary institutions of local and global civil society under the hegemony of the international system of nation-states. The logic of abstraction that governs both bureaucratic control and commercial exchange does not just commodify labor and social relations but also subordinates the sanctity of life and land to the secular sacrality of the market-state.[93]

Third, the political 'right' and the political 'left' have defined themselves variously either in terms of the 'one' and the 'many' or in terms of the market and the state or in terms of the economic and the political — or indeed all at once. All these poles are dialectically positioned and converge around a shared liberalism that fuses Machiavelli's 'new science of politics' with the eighteenth-century invention of political economy.

Crucially, these three binary relations of the 'one' versus the 'many,' the market versus the state, and the 'right' versus 'the left' are all rational, spatial constructs that combine ontological nominalism with political voluntarism, as André de Muralt's genealogical account shows.[94] Taken together, these binary relations have redefined the nature and reality of civil society that in principle enjoys primacy over states and markets and embeds both abstract rights and formal contracts in real relations. Indeed, modern political ontology combines 'the sovereign one' associated with the right and 'the sovereign many' linked with the left that are variously more authoritarian-statist or more market-fundamentalist — or again both at once.

With this nominalist space, the primary real relations among persons — who cooperate for both self-interest and the common, public good — are superseded by abstract, formal links consisting of either constitutional-legal rights or economic-contractual ties. Those links favor activities for either commercial-market or state-administrative purposes and therefore are to the detriment of practices that are not purely instrumental but might pursue wider, social purposes. As a result, modern politics is little more than a social contract between the general will represented by the

---

93. Karl Polanyi, *The Great Transformation: The Political and Economic Origins of Our Time* (Boston: Beacon Press, 1944).

94. Muralt, *L'unité de la philosophie politique.*

state (e.g., Hobbes, Kant, Hegel, and, more recently, Norberto Bobbio), on the one hand, and the personal will asserted through inalienable individual rights (e.g., Bodin, Locke, J. S. Mill, and, more recently, John Rawls), on the other hand. The logic of representation is the same nominalist-voluntarist logic of transcendentalism and possibilism that underpins both modern absolutism and modern liberalism.

The extension of popular democracy and human rights since 1848 has in some measure curtailed the arbitrary power of the 'sovereign one' to the benefit of the 'sovereign many.' However, democratization and individual rights have not just weakened the participation of the 'few' but also subverted the ideal of representation. Democratic rule, especially in its secular liberal guise, views as legitimate only a vacuous generality such as abstract values that are drained of any substantive universal *telos* embodied in particular virtues. As such, liberal democracy privileges the spectacle of representing the general will over the concerns of the represented people. Tocqueville's observation that freedom of expression is perfectly compatible with the tyranny of mass general opinion could hardly be more prescient in today's 'society of spectacle' (Guy Debord).

Liberalism has not only extended the three currents of possibilism, transcendentalism, and absolutism but also fused them with the new doctrine of positivism. The liberal belief in boundless, linear progress was in large part founded on the scientific positivism of Comte and Spencer and shaped both Marxism and Fascism/Nazism.[95] Indeed, the twentieth century saw an apparent bifurcation between statisms on the far left or the far right, on the one hand, and economic-social ultra-liberalism, on the other hand. But both were grounded in the legal-positivist equation of 'is' with 'ought' that is nominalist-voluntarist. Moreover, both at the end of the nineteenth century and in the twilight of the twentieth century the collusion of the strong state with the free market has produced "a hidden mutual complicity and reinforcement between the voluntarism of the absolute state and the voluntarism of the self-governing, negatively choosing individual."[96] Connected with this is the claim that only liberalism provides pluralism and diversity of choice

95. Wernick, *Auguste Comte and the Religion of Humanity;* Gray, *Black Mass.*
96. John Milbank, "The Real Third Way," in *The Crisis of Global Capitalism: Pope Benedict XVI's Social Encyclical and the Future of Political Economy,* ed. Adrian Pabst (Eugene, OR: Cascade Books, 2011), p. 40.

— a 'possibilist' utopia that Michael Oakeshott poignantly called "the blank sheet of infinite possibility."[97] Yet at the same time, the liberal settlement is really an imposed, even coercive, consensus to ensure that no choice other than liberalism can ever be effectively exercised. As such, the notion of illiberal liberalism is increasingly warranted.

Much of postmodern thought seeks to overcome the transcendental foundationalism and liberal absolutism that characterize modern 'political ontology.' However, the shift in emphasis away from modern dialectics toward postmodern difference (however spelled) merely repeats and even reinforces the pan-modern logic of dualism. By enshrining difference as the new 'absolute,' much of postmodern philosophy and politics brackets the mediating relation between the unity of the 'sovereign one' and the diversity of the 'sovereign many.' As such, the postmodern reign of difference collapses into monism — whether a monism of the 'one' such as the Spinozism of Deleuze or a monism of the 'many' like the rule of the multiple according to Hardt and Negri.[98] The problem is that post-modern monism so configured risks lapsing back into absolutism or else hovers closely above nihilism. In either case, the securing of difference is of a piece with the celebration of neo-pagan *agōn* that is variously more tragic or more heroic. Thus, postmodern difference is ultimately reducible to modern dialectics, and both are part of the logic of dualism that privileges nominal connections grounded in the will — the power of the one substance or the multiple multitude to 'will' themselves into actuality.

If, as I have argued, the modern redefines metaphysics as the onto-theological sciences of transcendental ontology, then the post-modern marks not so much an alternative to this project as an aporetic extension of it. But there is an alternative modernity that builds on the metaphysical realism inaugurated by Plato and further developed by the Neo-Platonist Church Fathers and Doctors in both the Greek East and the Latin West. The triple current of participation, analogy, and universalism flows through the work of Meister Eckhart, Nicolas of Cusa, the Cambridge Platonists, and the Neapolitan and the Scottish Enlightenment to the post-secular metaphysics in the work of J. G. Hamann, Jacobi, and Schelling, who reach back beyond Kant and Hegel to renew

---

97. Michael Oakeshott, *Rationalism in Politics and Other Essays* (Indianapolis: Liberty Fund, 1991), p. 9.

98. Hardt and Negri, *Multitude: War and Democracy in the Age of Empire.*

the tradition of metaphysical realism.[99] Common to these and other modern metaphysicians is a refusal to accept absolute finite limits on the cognoscibility of the infinite — without however returning to the transcendentalism of Cartesian innate ideas in the mind and the dualistic separation of the knowing subject from the known object.

Knowing infinity is also a key theme of the contemporary revival of metaphysics associated with speculative materialism. Knowledge of the infinite is no longer confined to blind faith or pure reason but intelligible to both the senses and the mind because it is mediated in language and appearances. Linked to this move beyond the nineteenth-century secretly collusive opposition of rationalism and fideism (e.g., Kant) is an overcoming of twentieth-century agnosticism that had sought to chart a third way between naturalism and speculation.[100] Similarly, the renaissance of metaphysical and theological ethics shifts the focus from abstract, general being to the singularity of each person and the universality of truth beyond power or culture.[101] Truth so configured is perennially invariant and at the same time reflected in ephemeral, material things. As such, truth is both universal and particular, which coincide in the singular.

This account differs from Hegel's argument in the *Science of Logic* on "The Absolute Relation" (which is defined as the ultimate category and highest dialectical unity subsuming substantiality and accidentality) and in the earlier *Phenomenology of Spirit* (where cognition of the individual is described in terms of participating in the Absolute Knowing of the Spirit). For Hegel's conception gives rise to the idea of a self-related Absolute whose heterodox onto-logic of necessity has already replaced the orthodox theo-logic of gratuity and gift exchange. By contrast, the account advanced here is much closer to the paradox of faith first articulated in Kierkegaard's *Fear and Trembling* that the "single individual is higher than the universal," for "the single individual relates himself as

99. John Milbank, "Knowledge: The Theological Critique of Philosophy in Hamann and Jacobi," in *Radical Orthodoxy*, pp. 21-37; John R. Betz, *After Enlightenment: The Post-Secular Vision of J. G. Hamann* (Oxford: Wiley-Blackwell, 2009); John Laughland, *Schelling versus Hegel: From German Idealism to Christian Metaphysics* (Aldershot: Ashgate, 2007).

100. Quentin Meillassoux, *Après la finitude: Essai sur la nécessité de la contingence* (Paris: Seuil, 2006).

101. Robert Spaemann, *Personen: Versuche über den Unterschied zwischen 'etwas' und 'jemand'* (Stuttgart: Klett-Cotta, 1998); Alain Badiou, *Saint Paul: La fondation de l'universalisme* (Paris: Presses Universitaires de France, 1998).

the single individual absolutely to the absolute."[102] As such, the particular self is "a relation that relates itself to itself or . . . the relation's relating itself to itself in the relation; the self is not the relation but is the relation's relating itself to itself."[103] Taken together, the horizontal, symmetric relationality of the self to the self and the vertical, asymmetric relationality of the individual to the absolute overcome the modern dialectic of transcendentalism and positivism.

With Kierkegaard, one can also suggest that the natural desire of all human and cosmic reality to surpass itself in the direction of the absolute that is sheer and unreserved relationality is a sign that the absolute is always already related to the universe. Such an asymmetric relation calls forth a theological metaphysics because the freedom that is expressed in the act of self-transcendence can only be the gift of a supremely free God who did not need to create the world but chose to do so out of love and goodness. And we know the Creator God because he made himself known to us, as the living God of Israel and the incarnate God in Jesus of Nazareth. All of which points to the truth of Christian universalism.

Thus, common to Christian Neo-Platonism is the argument that theology offers a redescription of reality that reveals the Christic orientation of the human-cosmic realm and the triune structure of the whole of reality, divine and natural. First of all, Platonist metaphysics is key to Christian theology because it demonstrates how the divine infinite is intelligible to the finite human intellect. Instances of beauty and harmony in the world are not illusions of the mind but imperfect reflections of the perfect beauty and harmony that characterizes the divine Good which endows all things with the natural desire for knowledge and justice. The crucial contribution of biblical revelation is to show that the divine is a living personal God who established a covenant with the people of Israel. In this sense, Christianity is the fulfillment of all religions: Jesus Christ does not merely subsume and accomplish all preexisting notions of divinity; uniquely, he reveals himself as the Son of God, the divine humanity, the living incarnate truth, the *Logos* that sustains everything which has been created out of nothing.

102. Søren Kierkegaard, *Fear and Trembling*, ed. C. Stephen Evans and trans. Sylvia Walsh (Cambridge: Cambridge University Press, 2006), p. 61.
103. Søren Kierkegaard, *Sickness unto Death*, trans. Howard V. Hong and Edna H. Hong (Princeton: Princeton University Press, 1980), p. 13.

Second, the form of the human-cosmic order is indeed Christic. Solovyov argues that the history of humanity and the whole of reality are in some sense ordered towards the Christian God:

> Strictly speaking, the incarnation of Divinity is not something miraculous, that is, it is not alien to the general order of being. On the contrary, it is essentially connected with the whole history of the world and humankind. . . . This appearance of God in the human flesh is only a more complete, more perfect theophany in a series of other, imperfect, preparatory, and transformative theophanies. . . . Both these new and unprecedented appearances [the birth of the first and the second Adam] were prepared for in advance by all that had happened before; they constituted what the former life desired, what it strove and moved towards. All nature strove and gravitated towards humanity, while the whole history of humanity was moving toward Divine humanity.[104]

Unlike the logic of necessity that governs Hegel's rational idealism, the Neo-Platonism of Kierkegaard and Solovyov retrieves and extends an existential Christian realism that links free divine kenotic self-renunciation with cosmic and human self-transcendence of natural limits in the divine humanity of Christ. Thus, the real event of the Incarnation marks the ontological and historical coincidence of divine kenosis and human-cosmic anagogy. The former upholds the natural order, while the latter reveals the supernatural, transcendent outlook of all that is. The sacramental liturgy of the Church, which weaves together the Books of Nature, Scripture, and History, testifies to God's loving wisdom and divine grace that deify the whole of creation. As such, the Incarnation confirms and fulfills created nature, and nature discloses and describes God's manifestation in the world. In this sense, only Christian theology can give a rationally intelligible account of divine revelation because in and through Jesus Christ alone is God visible and able to be known as a personal Creator God.

Thus it is not so much the case that we are seeing a 'return of metaphysics,' as if the metaphysical had ever gone away. Much rather, the renewed concern with questions of truth and universality beyond mere empirical validity or logical coherence points toward a theological realism. Key to a revivified metaphysical theology is the notion of paradox.

---

104. Vladimir Solovyov, *Lectures on Divine Humanity,* trans. and ed. Boris Jakim (Hudson, NY: Lindisfarne Press, 1995), p. 157.

Philosophically, the logic of paradox concerns the realm of real relations and the transcendent good, which infuses all things with (a desire for) goodness in which all can share. In a quest for true knowledge that exceeds mere opinion *(doxa)*, Socrates opposes the sophists on the grounds that they reduce their speeches to commodities, which they sell to the highest bidder in the marketplace of ideas. By contrast, to uncover the paradoxical nature of speech is for Socrates to disclose the true reality that language mediates. The depth and mysteriousness of reality warrant the use of myths, metaphors, and analogies that go beyond the categories of logic. That is why Socrates eschews merely contradiction-free, coherent, and logically valid arguments in favor of paradox that fuses *logos* with *mythos*. The creedal theology of the Church Fathers and Doctors and modern Christian Neo-Platonists in both East and West have developed this vision in the direction of Christ's paradox of divine humanity and God's Trinitarian economy in which all can participate.

This is connected with the idea of a virtuous guiding elite — the guardians of the republic or the Church and the corporate bodies of civil society. The pursuit of wisdom in defense of a just political order balances the democratic demand for the equal right of all opinions with universal standards of truth and goodness. As such, the perennial realism of theological metaphysics from Plato to Aquinas to modern Christian Neo-Platonists rejects the empty universalism that underpins the liberal fusion of political absolutism with moral relativism under the guise of individual freedom of choice and the tyranny of mass opinion. Crucially, a metaphysical politics and ethics overcomes the abstract, vacuous generality of being, which is the mark of modern 'political ontology.'

Politically and economically, the metaphysical logic of paradox upholds real relations by accentuating social bonds of reciprocity and solidarity that are based on universal sympathy and are more mutualist in outlook (as in the modern philosophy of David Hume, Edmund Burke, or Pierre-Joseph Proudhon). Thus, the logic of paradox views groups and associations as more primary than the individual and the collective. Across different societies and cultures, social bonds and intermediary institutions have traditionally been more fundamental than either constitutional-legal rights or economic-contractual ties. The activities of autonomous and democratically self-governing groups and associations are for social purposes and reasons of mutual recognition that paradoxically can serve both private and public interests. In this manner, the intermediary institutions of civil society — whose autonomy is ultimately upheld by the Church that embodies the universal, mystical body of Jesus Christ — promote the 'good life' in which all can share.

Taken together, Augustine's distinction of the two cities and Solovyov's conception of a 'free theocracy' avoid the dualism and secularization of power that tend to be associated with the West and the monism and sacralization of power that tend to be associated with the East. Augustine's emphasis on the ecclesia as the only universal polity is preserved and extended by Solovyov's conception of a 'free theocracy' where all spheres of activity are framed and ordered by Christian principles and virtues of charity, solidarity, equality, and the pursuit of the common good.

9. Conclusion: Relation, Creation, and Trinity

In this chapter, I have shown that modern philosophy is best theorized as the science of ontology which collapses either into transcendentalism or into positivism (or both at once) and is trapped in a binary dialectic of the one and the many. By contrast, metaphysics — theologically reimagined — offers a different account of reality. If being and life are neither self-generated nor self-sustaining, then only something like a transcendent God can bring beings into actuality and preserve them in existence. If God creates all beings *ex nihilo* and actualizes them out of love and goodness (not necessity), then the being of beings is both substantial and relational — a substance that is in subsistence by virtue of being in relation to God. Just as the Creator is a mystery of substantive relations within the Trinitarian Godhead (as Augustine already demonstrated in the *De Trinitate*), so created individual things are relational substances that mirror their creative source in God. It is the transcendent Goodness of God that individuates all beings relationally. Since this is true for the source of being in God, it also holds analogously for relations among beings.

This vision is not confined to theology and metaphysics but extends to politics. How so? If we are created in the image and likeness of the triune God, then we participate in these relations and are ourselves in a certain way relational. The Trinitarian relations in God provide the basis for the Christian idea of justice in terms of civic equality and meritocratic hierarchy. Indeed, Christianity calls for a society that is radically egalitarian, beyond any divisions of race, class, or gender (1 Cor. 12:13). Christianity also calls for a society that promotes an ethos of excellence in all human activities, because perfection mirrors God's goodness more faithfully.

As such, the Christian conception of justice differs from contemporary politics. The 'right' reduces justice to equality of opportunity in the marketplace, whereas the 'left' views justice as the redistribution of income through central state taxation. By contrast, Christianity defends an idea of justice in terms of relations that maintain each person's uniqueness and promotes perfection within human communities. Substantive relations establish human association at different levels — from the family and the household via communities to a shared polity. Such relations pursue diverse ends but they are all governed by the unity of the common good and its manifold, diverse instantiations in different variants of the good life.

In fact, this Christian Neo-Platonist theology underpinned Christendom in both East and West — a shared vision that the *cosmos* is sacred, that virtues preserve and perfect natural law, and that all creatures stand in indissoluble relations with each other and with their Creator. Even though medieval Christendom was divided and ultimately lost, Christian Neo-Platonist theology was never refuted. The unrealized potential of this tradition contrasts with the crisis of liberalism in its secular or religious guise. The present essay has not further developed the theological metaphysics of Christian Neo-Platonism in close engagement with contemporary philosophy and theology. Nor has it explored the wider implications for ethics and politics. This will have to be pursued elsewhere. However, this essay argues for the futurity of the Neo-Platonist tradition. It was in fact this more orthodox tradition that led to a revival of theological metaphysics in the late nineteenth and the early twentieth century by both eastern and western theologians. Beginning with J. G. Hamann, F. H. Jacobi, and Søren Kierkegaard, Christian theologians such as Vladimir Solovyov, Sergei Bulgakov, Maurice Blondel, Henri de Lubac, and Joseph Ratzinger have deepened and broadened a vision that seeks to be universal and faithful to the true teachings of Jesus and the apostolic church. According to this vision, there are at the heart of immanence irreducible traces of transcendence, and nature is always already infused with divine grace. In spite of historical schisms that have separated the western and eastern churches, there is a shared theological legacy grounded in the discernment that nature and grace, reason and faith, and philosophy and theology are all complementary and mutually rein-forcing. This vision is framed by the recognition that the historical en-counter between the biblical revelation and Greco-Roman philosophy produced a unique synthesis that is genuinely catholic and Orthodox. That perennial synthesis gave rise to an ecumenical and political unity that has the potential to overcome the largely false theological divisions between the Latin 'West' and the Greek 'East.'

The heritage of Roman and Byzantine theology converges to produce a vision that is metaphysical, political, and cultural. Metaphysically, it binds together the one and the many and blends differences harmoni-ously and peacefully. Politically, it opposes both absolutist theocracy and arbitrary secularism in the name of an integral model that distinguishes state and church without divorcing religion from politics. Culturally, it re-jects postmodern celebrations of relativism and nihilism in favor of a vi-brant civic culture based around "free associations" and their interrela-tions, thus giving expression to the fundamentally relational nature of man created in the image and likeness of the one and triune God. Insofar as orthodox catholicity mediates the universal in manifold particular ways, this vision contains the prolegomena to a truly global Christendom. There is thus a long tradition of Christian Platonism that opposes both modern positivism and transcendentalism without however embracing postmodern pragmatism and pure ontology in its analytic or phenomen-ological guise. The hallmark of the Neo-Platonist tradition is that meta-physics is central to politics and that a properly restored metaphysics re-veals its theological nature and discloses the transcendent outlook of all that is.

The New Imperative of Relationality

This essay has argued that only a theological metaphysic can overcome the perennial problem of individuation — *what* it is that *makes* an individual an individual — bequeathed by antiquity and left unresolved by modernity. By refusing the binary opposition between the one and the many, Christian Neo-Platonist theology provides an account that mediates between unity and multiplicity by locating being in the realm of the 'between' (Plato's *metaxu*) which is itself positioned within the relational hierarchy of the Trinitarian Creator God.

To begin with Plato is paramount, as it subverts from the outset the predominantly Aristotelian 'categorial' grammar of ancient and modern theories of individuation. Indeed, most accounts deal with the problem of what individuates composite things in purely philosophical terms and within the realm of strict immanence. As a result, such treatments locate the source of individuation in the individuality of substances or in the links between their constituent elements — either matter or form or both at once (as Aristotle himself does). Since the Stagirite removes the First Mover or God from the actualization of the sublunary world and all things therein, we can trace a genealogy to late medieval scholasticism, early modern philosophy, and even postmodern ontologies of pure immanence. For all of these perspectives insist that individuals are ultimately generated by other individuals and that individuality is somehow constitutive of both being and knowing. Thus, the main dividing line of rival solutions to the problem of individuation is between those who provide an account in terms of a transcendent source and those who limit it to an immanent source — even if they do so for transcendent reasons.

As I argued in chapter 1, Aristotle's priority of substance over relation

445

foregrounds the severing of the Prime Mover's actuality from the generation and evolution of all individual substances. The separation of transcendent principles and ends from immanent causes and effects has
both metaphysical and political implications. Metaphysically, it assumes
the preexistence of matter and does not explain why the form-matter
realm comes into existence or why it is sustained in being. Aristotle simply presupposes a kind of drive of material potentiality towards the final
telos for which his idea of matter as pure potency offers no rationale. Politically, this account divorces action or activity, which is the prime mode
of perfecting one's particular form, from the actuality of the final cause.
The ultimate *telos* is therefore eliminated from the goods that are proper
and internal to specific practical activities. Such a conception shifts the
emphasis from relation and participation to auto-generation and autonomy. This is why Aristotle celebrates self-sufficiency and sovereignty,
both at the level of the *polis* and the individual. Notwithstanding the perpetual risk of anachronism, Aristotle's theo-ontology foreshadows the
late medieval shift from metaphysics to onto-theology and in this sense
anticipates much of philosophic modernity.

Indeed, Aristotle's original rejection of Plato's ideas on relationality,
participation, and mediation — coupled with other shifts within theology that displace Aristotle's metaphysical language of act and potency —
reinforces the passage from a metaphysics of creation and individuation
to ontologies of generation and individuality. Here Avicenna and Gilbert
Porreta are pivotal, as chapter 4 suggests. Avicenna's onto-logic of necessity and Gilbert's 'mathematical Platonism' radicalize Porphyry's
logicized Aristotelianism in the direction of a primacy of logic and semantics and a more immanentist construal of individuation. Instead of
individual substances being seen as participating in the transcendental
unity of God's being and goodness, created being is now seen either as a
transcendentally necessary logical category or the product of divine volition — disconnected from inner divine reality and denied a limited
'share' of divine unity.

Duns Scotus, William of Ockham, and Jean Buridan — followed by
Francisco Suárez and Benedict Spinoza — elaborate variations on these
twin themes (as detailed in chapters 6-8). Once creation is no longer
seen as participation in the relational hierarchy of the Trinity, it is gradually reduced to efficient causality, which means that particularity is regarded as either a simple result of a divine *fiat* or as something brought
about by an individual thing itself under a transcendental compulsion

(or both at the same time). So either individuation is intelligible to blind faith alone or else it is coterminous with being and knowing and thus ultimately inexplicable, because it is simply assumed that this is how transcendentally everything exists and is known. Following Suárez, the object of metaphysics is being insofar as it is, i.e., an individual 'thing' that is in itself prior to any relations with other individual 'things.' Whether or not it is caused by God, individuality is now seen as pertaining to essence and not itself participating in the unity of the divine transcendent source of being. Paradoxically, it was a series of theological shifts that brought about the more 'secular' accounts of individuation, stretching from (elements in) Aristotle, Porphyry through Gilbert, to the formalist-fideistic onto-theology of Duns Scotus and the nominalist-voluntarist variant of Ockham. Since these accounts rest on dubious metaphysical arguments, the theological approaches to individuation from late Antiquity to early modern scholasticism can be questioned on objective philosophical grounds.

The same applies to later theories. Erasing God from the internal constitution of the world opens up a gap between the transcendent and the immanent that continues to govern modern and postmodern ontologies. Spinoza is first to abandon the idea of creation *ex nihilo* altogether and invent a realm of pure immanence where the oneness of the substance determines the diversity of finite modes. In the natural order all finite modes are equal and there is no hierarchy. But both his ontology of single substance and his politics of plural democracy are defined on essentially negative grounds. The single substance is infinite and autoproductive, but this begs the question of why it would choose to express itself in finite modes. Likewise, democracy is a necessary consequence of the nature of individual knowledge — the limits on human understanding according to which individuals ignore their own particular station in the communal order and fail to grasp the universal fixed laws of the eternal universe. The result is that individuals confound their own self-interest with the common sharing in the substance. In order to avoid the formation and consolidation of oligarchic clusters of power, only a democratic regime can diffuse power and cancel out conflicting egotism. Democracy so configured seeks to regulate the opposition and conflict between 'natural enemies' (Spinoza). This conflict mirrors the nature of finite modality, which is at once a necessary reality and a contingent illusion. Only the sages transcend this aporetic condition and can understand the commonality of the substance below and beyond the individu-

447

ality of finite modes. Neither free nor good, Spinoza's vision of politics oscillates between a *de facto* autocracy of the wise and a *de iure* democracy of the ignorant.

Other modern theories of individuation are similarly trapped in the aporia of the one and the many and the dilemma of monism and dualism. Monist and dualist elements are present in all the proposed solutions by Descartes, Leibniz, Hobbes, Locke, Wolff, and Kant — none of them can escape the transcendentalism and positivism which in the final instance collapse into one another, as I argue in chapter 9. The shift away from a transcendent Creator God towards an immanent absolute principle marks the final exit from metaphysics and the rise of the modern science of transcendental ontology. However, once any objective limits are removed on ontological and political individuality, relations amongst particular things are governed exclusively by sovereign volition (divine or human) or sheer, unmediated power — or a sinister combination of both, as in the case of the modern (not medieval) absolutism of the divine right of kings.[1] Without any transcendent objectivity that orders individuals and situates them in mutual relations, there is in the end only Nietzsche's will-to-power.

In response, the 'postmodern' flight into an infinite flux promises to unsettle the fixed foundations of rationalism, empiricism, and transcendentalism. However, now that the 'death of God' and the 'end of metaphysics' have so conspicuously failed to secure emancipation and universal prosperity, radical ontologies of pure immanence are once again in question. The 'postmodern' fixation upon the 'totally other' is but the mirror image of the modern turn to the solipsistic self. Thus, contemporary culture hovers between a subjectivity that is absolute and an objectivity that is arbitrary. Instead of pursuing the common good, politics serves little more than the power of the market-state and private self-gratification. Fundamentally, my argument is that the individual, understood as a constitutive category in both philosophy and politics, is a modern invention that can only be understood as a shift within theology that eschewed the patristic and medieval vision of relationality in favor of abstract individuality.

By contrast, Plato construes the 'individuality' of a thing metaphysically as its positioning in relation to other things, mirroring the mutual

1. See John Neville Figgis, *The Theory of the Divine Right of Kings* (Cambridge: Cambridge University Press, 1896).

interlinks of forms and the Good as the form of all forms. And since the Good is the author of all things in whose ecstatic 'self-giving' everything participates, there are in Plato's metaphysics adumbrations of horizontal and vertical relationality, as the second half of chapter 1 argues. This priority of relation within Platonism is the single most fundamental reason why — as Pope Benedict has also argued in the widely misunderstood and misrepresented Regensburg address — the hellenization of Christianity was never a distortion of biblical revelation but instead a development of Jewish and early Christian ideas on creation and the Trinity (partially intimated in the Hellenized Judaism of Jesus and the Apostles). Indeed, the doctrine of the Trinity tends to accentuate the priority of relation over substance, as evinced by the work of Latin and Greek Fathers such as Gregory of Nyssa, Augustine, Boethius, or Dionysius the Areopagite (discussed in chapters 2 and 3). Creation *ex nihilo* newly brings matter itself within the scope of originating asymmetrical relationality, while the supremacy of relation over substance in the case of the Godhead itself is demonstrated by Augustine in the *De Trinitate* and further developed by Boethius.

Other Platonist elements are also present in the theology of the Church Doctors, notably Aquinas, as chapter 5 documents in detail. For example, 'individuality' is linked to transcendental unity, such that God himself is hyper-individual in such a way that God himself is supremely singular. Therefore, it is not the case that general being somehow creates particular being. Instead, God's infinite mode of united 'definiteness' (*yliatim* for Aquinas in his commentary on the *Liber de Causis*) imparts a share of its singular unity to created being according to a finite mode. Here the theological metaphysic of Christian Neo-Platonism outflanks both monism and 'postmodern' pluralism based on a certain mediation between the one and the many — already present in Plato as the interplay between the One and the Dyad. Moreover, the world of things reflects both the 'horizontal' participation among forms and their 'vertical' sharing in the Good that positions everything relationally. Far from being exclusively metaphysical, Greek and Latin Neo-Platonist theology also offered a political vision that gave rise to Christendom in both East and West — a shared vision that the *cosmos* is sacred, that virtues preserve and perfect natural law, and that all creatures stand in indissoluble relations with each other and with their Creator within the relational and hierarchical order of God's creation.

Even though the ecclesial and political edifice of Christendom eventually dissolved, it is argued in this essay that Christian Neo-Platonist theology was never refuted.[2] On the contrary, it has provided an alternative not only to the late medieval and early modern proto-secular structures of thought and practice but also to the questionable use of theological categories in contemporary phenomenology and political thought. As such, the Christian theological vision of relationality outwits in advance the modern and late modern oscillation between the one and the many in both philosophy and politics.

While the primary object of this inquiry is the metaphysical problem of individuation, the essay has also suggested some of the political implications of the shift from a theological metaphysics of creation and individuation to a pure ontology of generation and individuation. The removal of God from the political sphere is itself grounded in the metaphysical removal of God from creation as such. Thus from Aristotle through to Suárez, I have shown how the individual substance prior to primary, embodied relation generates a politics of either individual or collective autonomy, deficient in any true sense of a sharing in a common good. Only the primacy of a specific set of relations and reciprocal duties over individual rights can prevent institutions and actors from descending into a formalistic, procedural, and managerial mode whose abstractness is empty and blind. A polity not acknowledging its relation to God (in receptivity and gratitude) will prove a polity without true human relations, bound either to disintegrate or else to submit to an enforced tyrannical unity (in a more or less democratic guise).[3] Even in the case of Spinoza, a democracy of the many is but a desperate and second-best device designed to make the competitions of ignorant individuals balance each other out, as I have already indicated. In various ways, this can be extended to the Cartesian city of abstract individuals, Locke's apology for commercial market relations, and Kant's case for a liberal *cosmopolis*

---

2. As indicated in chapter 1, my argument differs from David Bradshaw's in his very important book *Aristotle East and West: Metaphysics and the Division of Christendom* (Cambridge: Cambridge University Press, 2004).

3. In addition to recent work on biopolitics (already cited), there is also a growing literature on illiberal liberalism and authoritarian democracy. See, *inter alia*, Colin Crouch, *Post-Democracy* (Cambridge: Polity Press, 2004), pp. 1-69; Sheldon S. Wolin, *Democracy Incorporated: Managed Democracy and the Specter of Inverted Totalitarianism* (Princeton: Princeton University Press, 2008); Emmanuel Todd, *Après la démocratie* (Paris: Gallimard, 2008). Cf. my "The Crisis of Capitalist Democracy," *Telos* 152 (Winter 2010): 44-67.

where there is an unresolved tension between individual rights, national sovereignty, and the *ius gentium*.[4]

These arguments extend into the arena of contemporary political theology, particularly with respect to the post-Schmittian theory of sovereignty and debates on democracy and capitalism. Given that secular liberal democracy and unbridled 'free-market' capitalism have so clearly failed to deliver universal freedom and prosperity, it is perhaps no longer surprising — though no less significant — that Pope Benedict XVI's argument on the impasse of modern secularism and the Enlightenment is changing the terms of debate. This is most clearly evinced by his dialogue with Jürgen Habermas,[5] in which the latter recognizes that we have in some sense moved into a postsecular phase of history when religious traditions should no longer be confined to the private sphere but instead be able to intervene in the public square. For Habermas, however, the norms that govern public, political engagement between religious and nonreligious traditions must remain strictly secular and liberal (procedural and majoritarian).[6] The Pope contends that secularism brackets the substantive common good out of the picture, which perpetuates the late scholastic separation of pure nature from the supernatural — bequeathed by Suárez and enthusiastically embraced by neo-liberal/neo-conservative Catholics such as Michael Novak and George Weigel. This logic is wedded to early modern rationalism and fideism which can be opposed on objective metaphysical grounds. Joseph Ratzinger, who further develops *nouvelle théologie,* argues for a new form of constitutional corporatism against modern liberalism, which is closely connected with the fundamental metaphysical relationality of all beings and the indelible role of basic social units above the level of the individual. Benedict's paradoxical argument is that a post-secular politics requires a pre-secular metaphysics. Linked to this is a recovery of the mediating role of the 'few', a notion

---

4. Cf. Carl Schmitt, *The Nomos of the Earth in the International Law of the Jus Publicum Europaeum,* trans. Gary L. Ulmen (New York: Telos Press Publishing, 2003).

5. Jürgen Habermas and Joseph Ratzinger, *Dialektik der Säkularisierung. Über Vernunft und Religion* (Freiburg: Herder, 2004), English translation: *The Dialectics of Secularization: On Reason and Religion* (San Francisco: Ignatius Press, 2007).

6. Habermas's distinction between procedural and substantive democracy ignores the ontological problem of elevating representation over above participation. It also posits the normative primacy of modern, abstract secular values like tolerance or the will of the majority over nonmodern virtues embodied in civic practices such as justice governed by notions of the good rather than merely fairness.

that for Plato, Aristotle, and Christian Neo-Platonists refers to virtuous elites who strive to uphold standards of excellence and promote notions of truth as a more important principle of politics than the sovereign power of the 'one' or the democratic will of the 'many' or both at once.

Historically, the political 'right' and the political 'left' have defined themselves variously either in terms of the 'sovereign ruler' versus the 'sovereign people' or the market versus the state or the economic versus the political — or indeed all at once. These and other binary relations are rationalist, spatial constructs that fuse ontological nominalism with political voluntarism. The realism of Neo-Platonist metaphysics and politics rejects the empty universalism that underpins the liberal blending of political absolutism with moral relativism under the guise of individual freedom of choice and the tyranny of mass opinion. A theological politics of paradox is concerned with real, primary relations by emphasizing social bonds of reciprocity and fraternity that are based on universal sympathy and mutualist in outlook.

Thus, this essay raises the question whether our politics of 'right and left' remains caught within shared secular, liberal axioms — axioms that are *also* those of theocratic fundamentalisms since they too deal in a politics of the indifferent will, inherited — as is equally the case in the end for liberalism — from the theological voluntarism of the late Middle Ages. This is not at all to search for a new political center; on the contrary, it is to search for a way that cannot be charted on our current conceptual map. It is to investigate again notions of fundamental relationality, of the common good and economic reciprocity, and of principles that can determine appropriate 'mixtures' of government as between the one, the few, and the many; the center and localities; political government and prepolitical society; international community and nations; education in time and government in space; absolute right and free decision; economic freedom and just distribution; and finally, secular and religious authorities. In short, it is to explore whether we are seeing the emergence of a politics of paradox beyond modern, secular liberal norms.

In summary, the tradition of Christian Neo-Platonism described in this essay retrieves and extends the legacy of theological realism and intellectualism developed by the Church Fathers and Doctors and defended by Aquinas against the nominalism and voluntarism of radical Aristotelians in the twelfth and early thirteenth centuries. The emphasis on a hierarchical and relational ordering of transcendence and immanence eschews both transcendentalism (in both materialist and idealist variants) and immanentism. In this manner, the theological metaphysic this essay defends gestures towards a pluralist universalism that avoids the enduring metaphysical dilemma of either monism or dualism and the similarly enduring ethical temptation of either absolutism or relativism.

Finally, the focus on relationality has a strongly contemporary dimension. Both the natural sciences and humanities are seeing the emergence of different relational paradigms attempting to theorize the widespread recognition that reality cannot be reduced to self-generating, individual beings, and that the outcome of interactions between various entities is more than the sum of parts (whether these be more atomistic or more collectivist). For instance, in particle physics it has been suggested that there are 'things' such as quarks (subatomic particles) that cannot be measured individually because they are confined by force fields and only exist inside certain particles (hadrons) that are themselves bound together by strong 'substantial' interplay with other hadrons.[7]

Likewise, recent evidence from research in fields such as evolutionary biology and neuroscience shows that modern ontological atomism and the spontaneous spirit of possessive acquisitiveness are at odds with more holistic models of human nature. Indeed, the human brain is in some important organic sense connected to the world and responds unconsciously to the social environment within which it is embedded. Such an account of selfhood contrasts sharply with the dominant modern conception that the self is a separate, self-standing agent that makes conscious, rational decisions based on individual volition.[8] Linked to the naturally given social embeddedness of the self is the argument (substantiated by findings from a comprehensive, global survey) that fundamental moral distinctions are somehow 'hard-wired' in human beings and that virtuous habits such as cooperative trust or mutual sympathy

---

7. This goes back to nineteenth-century 'field theorists' such as Michael Faraday and James Clerk Maxwell, whose research shaped Einstein's theory of relativity. See Albert Einstein, *Relativity: The Special and General Theory* (New York: Crown, 1961), Appendix V. Cf. Einstein's "The Mechanics of Newton," in *Ideas and Opinions* (New York: Bonanza, 1954).

8. Mark Hauser, *Moral Minds: How Nature Designed Our Universal Sense of Right and Wrong* (London: Ecco, 2006). This needs to be complemented by the argument that a proper ethics surpasses the classically modern dichotomy between 'right' and 'wrong' in the direction of an outlook towards the virtue of justice and the transcendent reality of goodness. Such an outlook is a fusion of natural desire and supernaturally infused habit, as Christian Neo-Platonists in East and West have tended to argue.

precede the exercise of instrumental reason or the interplay of senti-mental emotions.[9]

Relational patterns and structures are also moving to the fore in a growing number of disciplines in the humanities and social sciences. For example, in anthropology it is argued that the idea of a purely self-interested *homo oeconomicus* in pursuit of material wealth (central to Adam Smith's *Wealth of Nations*) reduces the natural desire for goodness to a series of vague, prerational moral feelings (as set out in his *Theory of Moral Sentiments*). As such, it marks a radical departure from older ideas of 'political animals' in search for mutual social recognition through the exercise of virtues embodied in practices and the exchange of gifts — in-stead of a mechanical application of abstract values and the trading of pure commodities.[10] For these (and other) reasons, individuals cannot be properly understood as separate from the relations that bring them into existence and sustain them in being. Instead, individuals are best conceived in terms of personhood, defined as the plural and composite locus of relationships and the confluence of different microcosms.

Similarly, in sociology, cultural studies, and cognate fields, the past decade or so has seen a growing body of research on human coopera-tion, creativity, and connectedness framed by the concept of relation-ality.[11] Closely connected with these themes is a renewed interest in rival conceptions of ontology. Here the focus on social relationality in the so-cial sciences coincides with a growing focus on metaphysical rela-tionality in philosophy and theology. In turn, this is linked to a fresh con-cern with a theological metaphysics that rejects the late medieval and modern primacy of individual substance over ontological relation.[12]

9. In this context, Matt Ridley's claim in his influential book *The Origins of Virtue* (Lon-don: Penguin, 1996) that human virtue is driven by self-interest and closely connected to the division of labor uncritically accepts the modern dualism of egoism and altruism and also the premise that morality is grounded in a purely immanent account of human nature.

10. Karl Polanyi, *The Great Transformation: The Political and Economic Origins of Our Time* (Boston: Beacon Press, 2000; orig. pub. 1944), pp. 45-70; Marcel Hénaff, *Le prix de la vérité. Le don, l'argent, la philosophie* (Paris: Éditions du Seuil, 2002), pp. 351-80. See my "The Paradoxical Nature of the Good: Relationality, Sympathy, and Mutuality in Rival Traditions of Civil Economy," in *The Crisis of Global Capitalism: Pope Benedict XVI's Social Encyclical and the Future of Political Economy*, ed. Adrian Pabst (Eugene, OR: Cascade Books, 2011), pp. 173-206.

11. Pierpaolo Donati, *Relational Sociology: A New Paradigm for the Social Sciences* (London: Routledge, 2010).

12. E.g., F. LeRon Shults, *Reforming Theological Anthropology: After the Philosophical*

As part of this growing literature on relational paradigms, this essay seeks to make a metaphysical intervention that moves notions of relationality to the center of debates in philosophy and politics. The real, true account of the human person is not about unbridled freedom in the marketplace or about our obedient dependence on the state, but about our social bonds which discipline us and make us the unique persons we all are, as David Hume and Antonio Genovesi argued in the late eighteenth century and as Pope Benedict has recently reaffirmed in his social encyclical *Caritas in veritate*. At their best, the social bonds of family, neighborhood, local community, professional associations, nation, and faith help instill civic virtues and a shared sense of purpose. Concretely, this means solidarity and a commitment to the common good in which all can participate — from a viable ecology via universal education and healthcare to a wider distribution of assets and other means to pursue true happiness beyond pleasure and power. Christian conceptions of God stress the relations between the three divine persons of the Holy Trinity. Therefore, the belief that we are all made in the image and likeness of a personal, 'relational' Creator God translates into an emphasis on the strong bonds of mutual help and reciprocal giving. For true Christians, charity is never about handing out alms to the poor and feeling better about oneself. Rather, it is about an economy of gift-exchange where people assist each other — not based on economic utility or legal obligation but in a spirit of free self-giving, receiving, and returning by members of a social body greater than its parts, grounded as it is ultimately in the mystical union of the divine and the human in Jesus Christ.

Turn to Relationality (Grand Rapids: Eerdmans, 2003); William Desmond, *God and the Between* (Oxford: Wiley-Blackwell, 2007).

Sources

Abbreviations

ANF   *Ante-Nicene Fathers*
CSEL   *Corpus Scriptorum Ecclesiasticorum Latinorum*
Leon.   *Sancti Thomae de Aquino. Opera omnia iussu Leonis XIII P. M.*
               edita
PL   *Patrologia Latina*

I. Pre-Socratic Poets and Philosophers

Hesiod: Theogony, trans. S. Lombardo. Indianapolis: Hackett Publishing Company, 1993.

Xenophanes of Colophon: Fragments, trans. James H. Lesher. Toronto: University of Toronto Press, 1992.

Heraclitus: Fragments, trans. T. M. Robinson. Toronto: University of Toronto Press, 1991.

Parmenides of Elea: Fragments, trans. David Galop. Toronto: University of Toronto Press, 1991.

II. Plato (c. 429-347 BC)

Crat.   *Cratylus*
               (trans. Jowett 1937, Vol. I, pp. 171-229)
Euthy.   *Euthyphro*
               (trans. Jowett 1937, Vol. I, pp. 381-98)
Euthyd.   *Euthydemus*
               (trans. Jowett 1937, Vol. I, pp. 131-70)

456

Hipp. Maj.	*Hippias Major*
	(trans. Woodruff 1982, pp. 1-31)
Leg.	*Laws*
	(trans. Jowett 1937, Vol. II, pp. 405-703)
Men.	*Meno*
	(trans. Jowett 1937, Vol. I, pp. 349-80)
Parm.	*Parmenides*
	(trans. Jowett 1937, Vol. II, pp. 85-140)
Phae.	*Phaedo*
	(trans. Jowett 1937, Vol. I, pp. 439-501)
Phaedr.	*Phaedrus*
	(trans. Jowett 1937, Vol. I, pp. 231-82)
Phileb.	*Philebus*
	(trans. Jowett 1937, Vol. II, pp. 341-403)
Polit.	*Politicus*
	(trans. Jowett 1937, Vol. II, pp. 281-340)
Rep.	*The Republic*
	(trans. Jowett 1937, Vol. I, pp. 589-879)
Soph.	*The Sophist*
	(trans. Jowett 1937, Vol. II, pp. 219-80)
Symp.	*Symposium*
	(trans. Jowett 1937, Vol. I, pp. 299-345)
Theaet.	*Theaetetus*
	(trans. Jowett 1937, Vol. II, pp. 141-217)
Tim.	*Timaeus*
	(trans. Jowett 1937, Vol. II, pp. 1-68)

III. Aristotle (c. 384-322 BC)

Cat.	*Categories*
	(trans. J. L. Ackrill, in Barnes, ed., 1984, Vol. I, pp. 3-24)
De An.	*De Anima*
	(trans. J. A. Smith, in Barnes, ed., 1984, Vol. I, pp. 641-92)
De Caelo	*On the Heavens*
	(trans. J. L. Stocks, in Barnes, ed., 1984, Vol. I, pp. 447-511)
De Gen. An.	*Generation of Animals*
	(trans. A. Platt, in Barnes, ed., 1984, Vol. I, pp. 1111-1218)
De Gen. et Corr.	*On Generation and Corruption*
	(trans. H. H. Joachim, in Barnes, ed., 1984, Vol. I, pp. 512-54)
De Part. An.	*Parts of Animals*
	(trans. W. Ogle, in Barnes, ed., 1984, Vol. I, pp. 994-1086)
Eud. Eth.	*Eudemian Ethics*
	(trans. J. Solomon, in Barnes, ed., 1984, Vol. II, pp. 1922-1981)

Met.	*Metaphysics*
	(trans. W. D. Ross, in Barnes, ed., 1984, Vol. II, pp. 1552-1728)
Nic. Eth.	*Nicomachean Ethics*
	(trans. W. D. Ross, in Barnes, ed., 1984, Vol. II, pp. 1729-1867)
Peri Herm.	*Peri Hermeneias*
	(trans. J. L. Ackrill, in Barnes, ed., 1984, Vol. I, pp. 25-38)
Phys.	*Physics*
	(trans. R. P. Hardie and R. K. Gaye, in Barnes, ed., 1984, Vol. I, pp. 315-446)
Pol.	*Politics*
	(trans. B. Jowett, in Barnes, ed., 1984, Vol. II, pp. 1986-2129)
Post. An.	*Posterior Analytics*
	(trans. J. Barnes, in Barnes, ed., 1984, Vol. I, pp. 114-66)
Top.	*Topics*
	(trans. W. A. Pickard-Cambridge, in Barnes, ed., 1984, Vol. II, pp. 167-277)

IV. Saint Augustine of Hippo (354-430)

An. et Orig.	*De Anima et Eius Origine* (c. 419)
	(ed. Migne, in *PL* 44)
Beat. Vit.	*De Beata Vita* (c. 386)
	(ed. Migne, in *PL* 32)
Civ. Dei	*De Civitate Dei* (c. 413-25/6)
	(ed. Migne, in *PL* 41)
Conf.	*Confessiones* (c. 390)
	(ed. Migne, in *PL* 32; trans. Boulding, in Rotelle, ed., 1997)
Cont. Acad.	*Contra Academicos* (c. 386)
	(ed. Migne, in *PL* 32)
De Mag.	*De Magistro* (c. 389)
	(ed. Migne, in *PL* 32)
De Mus.	*De Musica* (c. 390/1)
	(ed. Migne, in *PL* 32)
De Ord.	*De Ordine* (c. 386)
	(ed. Migne, in *PL* 32)
De Trin.	*De Trinitate* (c. 404-20+)
	(ed. Migne, in *PL* 42; trans. Hill, in Rotelle, ed., 1991)
Div. Quest.	*De Diversis Quaestionibus LXXXIII* (c. 388-96)
	(ed. Migne, in *PL* 40)
Doc. Christ.	*De Doctrina Christiana* (c. 396)
	(ed. Migne, in *PL* 34)
Enchir.	*Enchiridion de Fide, Spe et Caritate* (c. 421-23)
	(ed. Migne, in *PL* 40)

En Ps.	*Enarrationes in Psalmos*
	(ed. Migne, in *PL* 36)
Epist.	*Epistulae*
	(ed. Migne, in *PL* 33)
Fid. et Oper.	*De Fide et Operibus* (c. 412/13)
	(ed. Migne, in *PL* 40)
Fid. Rer.	*De Fide Rerum Quae Non Videntur* (c. 400)
	(ed. Migne, in *PL* 40)
Gen. ad Lit.	*De Genesi ad Litteram* (c. 405-15)
	(ed. Migne, in *PL* 34; trans. Hill, in Rotelle, ed., 2002, pp. 168-506)
Gen. ad Lit. Imp.	*Opus Imperfectum* (c. 393/4)
	(ed. Migne, in *PL* 34; trans. Hill, in Rotelle, ed., 2002, pp. 114-51)
Gen. c. Man.	*De Genesi contra Manichaeos* (c. 388/9)
	(ed. Migne, in *PL* 34; trans. Hill, in Rotelle, ed., 2002, pp. 39-102)
Grat. et Lib.	*De Gratia et Libero Arbitrio* (c. 426-27)
	(ed. Migne, in *PL* 44)
Immort. An.	*De Immortalitate Animae* (c. 387)
	(ed. Migne, in *PL* 32)
Ion. Ev.	*In Ioannis Evangelium Tractatus*
	(ed. Migne, in *PL* 35)
Lib. Arb.	*De Libero Arbitrio Voluntatis* (c. 388-96)
	(ed. Migne, in *PL* 32)
Mor. Eccl.	*De Moribus Ecclesiae Catholicae* (c. 388-90)
	(ed. Migne, in *PL* 32)
Nat. Bon.	*De Natura Boni* (c. 399)
	(ed. Migne, in *PL* 42)
Nat. et Grat.	*De Natura et Gratia* (c. 415)
	(ed. Migne, in *PL* 44)
Pul. et Apt.	*De Pulchro et Apto* (c. 380-81)
	(lost)
Quant. An.	*De Quantitate Animae* (c. 387-88)
	(ed. Migne, in *PL* 32)
Retrac.	*Retractationes* (c. 426/7)
	(ed. Migne, in *PL* 32)
Solil.	*Soliloquia* (c. 387)
	(ed. Migne, in *PL* 32)
Util. Cred.	*De Utilitate Credendi* (c. 391-92)
	(ed. Migne, in *PL* 42)
Ver. Relig.	*De Vera Religione* (c. 390)
	(ed. Migne, in *PL* 34)

V. Anicius Manlius Severinus Boethius (c. 480-525)

Contra Eut.	*Contra Eutychen* (Stewart et al. 1973 Latin edition with facing English translation, pp. 72-129)
De Consol.	*Philosophiae Consolationis* (Stewart et al. 1973 Latin edition with facing English translation, pp. 130-435)
De Fide Cath.	*De Fide Catholica* (Stewart et al. 1973 Latin edition with facing English translation, pp. 52-71)
De Hebdom.	*Quomodo Substantiae in eo quod Sint Bonae Sint cum non Sint Substantialia Bona* (Stewart et al. 1973 Latin edition with facing English translation, pp. 38-51)
De Trinitate	*Trinitas Unus Deus ac Non Tres Dii* (Stewart et al. 1973 Latin edition with facing English translation, pp. 2-31)
In Cat.	*In Categorias Aristotelis* (ed. Migne 1847, pp. 159-278)
In Isag.	*In Isagogen Porphyrii Commenta* (ed. Brandt 1906)
In Periherm.	*In librum Aristotelis Peri Hermeneias* (ed. Meiser 1880)
Utrum Pater	*Utrum Pater et Filius et Spiritus Sanctus de Divinitate Substantialiter praedicentur* (Stewart et al. 1973 Latin edition with facing English translation, pp. 32-37)

VI. Islamic Philosophers and Theologians

Al-Fārābī	*Philosophy of Plato and Aristotle* (in Al-Fārābī 2001)
Al-Kindī	*On First Philosophy* (in Ivry 1974)
Ibn Sīnā	*Metaphysics* (in Avicenna 1973)
Ibn Sīnā	*Isagoge* (in Avicenna 1974)
Ibn Sīnā	*Opera* (in Avicenna 1508)

VII. Gilbert Porreta (c. 1085-1154)

In Contra Eut.	*Expositio in Boecii librum contra Euticen et Nestorium* (ed. Häring 1966, pp. 233-364)
In de Hebdom.	*Expositio in Boecii librum de bonorum ebdomade* (ed. Häring 1966, pp. 183-230)
In de Trin.	*Expositio in Boecii librum de Trinitate* (ed. Häring 1966, pp. 53-180)

VIII. Saint Thomas Aquinas (c. 1225-1274)

Comp. theol.	*Compendium Theologiae* (c. 1273) (ed. Leon. Vol. 42, 1979, pp. 5-191)
De anima	*Quaestio Disputata de Anima* (1266-68) (ed. Leon. Vol. 24/1, 1996)
De ente	*De Ente et Essentia* (c. 1254-56) (ed. Leon. Vol. 43, 1976, pp. 315-81)
ˋ *De potentia*	*Quaestiones Disputatae de Potentia Dei* (c. 1265-67) (ed. Pession 1965, t. 2, pp. 1-276)
De princ. nat.	*De Principiis Naturae* (c. 1255) (ed. Leon. Vol. 43, 1976, pp. 1-47)
De reg.	*De Regno ad Regem Cypri* (c. 1267) (ed. Leon. Vol. 42, 1979, pp. 417-71)
De sensu	*Sentencia Libri de Sensu et Sensate* (1267-69) (ed. Leon. Vol. 45/2, 1984)
De spir. creat.	*Quaestio Disputata de Spiritualibus Creaturis* (1266-68) (ed. Leon. Vol. 24/2, 2000)
De subst. sep.	*De Substantiis Separatis* (c. 1272-73) (ed. Leon. Vol. 40, 1969)
De unit.	*De Unitate Intellectus contra Averroistas* (c. 1270) (ed. Leon. Vol. 43, 1976, pp. 243-314)
De veritate	*Quaestiones Disputatae de Veritate* (c. 1256-59) (ed. Leon. Vol. 22, 1970-76)
In Boeth. de Hebd.	*In Librum Boethii de Hebdomadibus Expositio* (c. 1256-59) (ed. Leon. Vol. 50, 1992, pp. 231-97)
In Boeth. de Trin.	*In Librum Boethii de Trinitate Expositio* (c. 1256-59) (ed. Leon. Vol. 50, 1992, pp. 1-230)
In de Caelo	*In Libros Aristotelis de Caelo et Mundo Expositio* (c. 1272-73) (ed. Leon. Vol. 3, 1886, pp. 1-257)
In de Causis	*In Librum de Causis Expositio* (c. 1272) (ed. Saffrey 1954)
In de Div. Nom.	*In Librum Beati Dionysii de Divinis Nominibus Expositio* (c. 1256-59) (ed. Pera et al. 1950)

In Met.	*In Duodecim Libros Metaphysicorum Aristotelis* (c. 1269-71/72) (ed. Cathala et al. 1971)
In Peri Herm.	*In Libros Peri Hermeneias Aristotelis Expositio* (c. 1269-1272) (ed. Leon. Vol. 1/1, 1989)
In Phys.	*In Aristotelis Librum de Physica Expositio* (c. 1267-1268) (ed. Leon. Vol. 2, 1884)
In Post. An.	*In Libros Posteriorum Analyticorum Aristotelis Expositio* (c. 1270) (ed. Leon. Vol. 1/2, 1989)
In Sent.	*Scriptum super Libros Sententiarum Magistri Petri Lombardi* (c. 1252-56) (*In I Sent.* and *In II Sent.* ed. Mandonnet 1929; *In III Sent.* and *IV Sent.* d. 1-22, ed. Moos 1947-1956; *In IV Sent.* d. 23-50, ed. Fiaccadorus 1858)
Op. theol.	*Opuscula Theologica* (ed. Verado 1954)
Quodl.	*Quaestiones de quodlibet* (c. 1256-59 and 1269-72) (ed. Leon. Vols. 25/1 and 25/2, 1996)
SCG	*Liber de Veritate Catholicae Fidei contra Errores Infidelium seu Summa contra Gentiles* (c. 1259-1264) (ed. Marc et al. 1961)
Sent. de Anima	*Sentencia Libri de Anima* (c. 1267-1268) (ed. Leon. Vol. 45/1, 1984)
ST	*Summa Theologiae* (c. 1265-1272) (ed. Leon. Vols. 4-12, 1888-1906)

IX. John Duns Scotus (c. 1265/66-1308)

In Metaph.	*Quaestiones Subtilissimae super Libros Metaphysicorum Aristotelis* (ed. Etzkorn and Wolter 1997-1998)
Lec.	*Lectura* (basis for the *Ordinatio*) (ed. Balic 1950-1982, Vols. 16-18)
Ord.	*Ordinatio (Opus oxoniense)* (ed. Balic 1950-1982, Vols. 1-6)
Quodlib.	*Quodlibet* (ed. Alluntis and Wolter 1975)
Rep. par.	*Reportata Pariensia* (ed. Wolter and Bychkov 2004)

Sources

X. William of Ockham (c. 1288/89-1349)

Breviloq.   *Breviloquium de principatu tyrannico*
             (ed. Scholz 1952)
Dial.   *Dialogus*
             (ed. Goldast 1614)
Ord.   *Ordinatio sive Scriptum in Libros Sententiarum*
             (ed. Gál et al. 1967-1984)
Qu. in Phys. *Quaestiones in Libros Physicorum*
             (ed. Brown 1974)
Quodl.   *Quodlibeta*
             (ed. Wey 1980)
SL   *Summa Logicae*
             (ed. Boehner et al. 1974)

XI. Jean Buridan (c. 1300-1360)

Qu. Met.   *Quaestiones in Metaphysicam Aristotelis*
             (ed. Dullaert 1964*b*)
Qu. Phys.   *Quaestiones Subtilissimae super octo Physicorum Libros*
             Aristotelis
             (ed. Dullaert 1964)
Sophism.   *Sophismata*
             (ed. Scott 1977)
Tract. Sup. *Tractatus de Suppositionibus*
             (ed. Reina 1959)

XII. Francisco Suárez (1548-1616)

De Fide   *De Triplici Virtute Theologica, Fide, Spe et Caritate* (c. 1614-15)
             (ed. André 1856-1878)
Def. Fidei   *Defensio Fidei* (c. 1613)
             (ed. André 1856-1878)
De Leg.   *De Legibus ac Deo Legislatore* (1612)
             (ed. André 1856-1878)
De Ult. Fin. *De Ultimo Fine Hominis*
             (ed. André 1856-1878)
Dis. Met.   *Disputationes Metaphysicae* (1597)
             (ed. André 1856-1878)

XIII. Benedict (Baruch de) Spinoza (1632-1677)

Cog. Met.	*Cogitata Metaphysica* (1663) (ed. Gebhardt 1972-1987, Vol. I, pp. 231-81; trans. Shirley in Morgan, ed., 2002, pp. 177-212)
Ep.	*Epistolae* (ed. Gebhardt 1972-1987, Vol. IV, pp. 3-336; trans. Wolf in Wolf, ed., 1928, pp. 73-366)
Ethica	*Ethica Ordine Geometrico Demonstrata* (1661-74) (ed. Gebhardt 1972-1987, Vol. II, pp. 43-308; trans. Shirley in Morgan, ed., 2002, pp. 213-382)
Kor. Verh.	*Korte Verhandeling van God de Mensch, en des zelfs Welstand* (c. 1660-62/3) (ed. Gebhardt 1972-1987, Vol. I, pp. 3-121; trans. Shirley in Morgan, ed., 2002, pp. 31-107)
Prin. Phil. Cart.	*Renati Des Cartes Principia Philosophiae* (1663) (ed. Gebhardt 1972-1987, Vol. I, pp. 127-230; trans. Shirley in Morgan, ed., 2002, pp. 108-89)
Tract. de Intel. Em.	*Tractatus de Intellectus Emendatione* (c. 1658-60) (ed. Gebhardt 1972-1987, Vol. II, pp. 3-40; trans. Shirley in Morgan, ed., 2002, pp. 1-32)
Tract. Pol.	*Tractatus Politicus* (c. 1675-77) (ed. Gebhardt 1972-1987, Vol. III, pp. 271-360; trans. Shirley in Morgan, ed., 2002, pp. 676-754)
Tract. Theol.-Pol.	*Tractatus Theologico-Politicus* (c. 1670) (ed. Gebhardt 1972-1987, Vol. II, pp. 3-267; trans. Shirley in Morgan, ed., 2002, pp. 383-572)

Bibliography

Abbreviations

AHDLMA	*Archives d'histoire doctrinale et littéraire au Moyen-Âge*
MM	*Miscellanea Medievalia*
MS	*Mediaeval Studies*
OSAP	*Oxford Studies in Ancient Philosophy*
RSPT	*Revue des Sciences Philosophiques et Théologiques*
St. Sp.	*Studiana Spinozana*

Works Cited

Ablondi, Frederick, and Steven Barbone. "Individual Identity in Descartes and Spinoza." *St. Sp.* 10 (1994): 69-92.

Ackrill, John L. *Aristotle on Eudaimonia*. London: Longwood, 1974.

Adams, Marilyn M. *William of Ockham*. 2 vols. Notre Dame: University of Notre Dame Press, 1987.

Aertsen, Jan A. *Nature and Creature: Thomas Aquinas's Way of Thought*. Translated by Herbert D. Morton. Leiden: E. J. Brill, 1988.

———. "Die Transzendentalienlehre bei Thomas von Aquin in ihren historischen Hintergründen und philosophischen Motiven," in Zimmermann, ed. (1988), pp. 82-102.

———. *Medieval Philosophy and the Transcendentals: The Case of Thomas Aquinas.* Leiden: E. J. Brill, 1996.

———. "Die Thesen zur Individuation in der Verurteilung von 1277, Heinrich von Gent und Thomas von Aquin," in Aertsen and Speer, eds. (1996), pp. 249-65.

———. "Thomas Aquinas on the Good: The Relation between Metaphysics and Ethics," in MacDonald and Stump, eds. (1999), pp. 235-53.

Aertsen, Jan A., and Andreas Speer, eds. *Individuum und Individualität im Mittelalter.* *MM,* vol. 18. Berlin and New York: De Gruyter, 1996.

————, eds. *Was ist Philosophie im Mittelalter? MM,* vol. 26. Berlin/New York: De Gruyter, 1998.

Aertsen, Jan A., and Gerhard Endress, eds. *Averroes and the Aristotelian Tradition: Sources, Constitution and Reception of the Philosophy of Ibn Rushd (1126-1198). Proceedings of the Fourth Symposium Averroicum.* Leiden: E. J. Brill, 1999.

Aertsen, Jan A., Kent Emery Jr., and Andreas Speer, eds. *After the Condemnation of 1277: Philosophy and Theology at the University of Paris in the Last Quarter of the Thirteenth Century. MM,* vol. 28. Berlin: De Gruyter, 2001.

Agamben, Giorgio. *Homo Sacer: Sovereign Power and Bare Life.* Translated by Daniel Heller-Roazen. Stanford, CA: Stanford University Press, 1998.

————. *Stato di eccezione.* Turin: Bollati Boringhieri, 2003; English translation: *State of Exception.* Translated by K. Attell. Chicago: University of Chicago Press, 2005.

Albritton, Rogers. "Forms of Particular Substances in Aristotle's *Metaphysics." Journal of Philosophy* 54 (1957): 699-708.

Al-Fārābī. *Philosophy of Plato and Aristotle.* Translated by Mushin Mahdi, rev. ed. Ithaca, NY: Cornell University Press, 2001.

Alféri, Pierre. *Guillaume d'Ockham: Le Singulier.* Paris: Éditions Minuit, 1989.

Allen, R. E. "Participation and Predication in Plato's Middle Dialogues." *Philosophical Review* 69 (1960): 147-64.

Alliez, Eric. *Les Temps Capitaux. Tome 1: Récits de la conquête du temps.* Paris: Éditions Cerf, 1991.

————. *Les Temps Capitaux,* vol. 2/1: *L'état des choses.* Paris: Éditions Cerf, 2000.

Alluntis, Felix, and Allan B. Wolter, eds. *God and Creatures: The quodlibetal Questions.* Translated with an introduction, notes, and glossary. Princeton: Princeton University Press, 1975.

d'Alverny, Marie-Thérèse. *Avicenne en Occident.* Paris: Vrin, 1993.

d'Ancona, Cristina. "Greek into Arabic: Neoplatonism in Translation," in *The Cambridge Companion to Arabic Philosophy.* Edited by Peter Adamson and Richard C. Taylor. Cambridge: Cambridge University Press, 2005, pp. 10-31.

André, Michel. *Franciscus Suarez: Opera omnia.* Paris: Vivès, 1856-1887.

Angelelli, Ignacio. "The Scholastic Background of Modern Philosophy: *Entitas* and Individuation in Leibniz," in Gracia, ed. (1994), pp. 535-42.

Annas, Julia. "Individuals in Aristotle's *'Categories':* Two Queries." *Phronesis* 19 (1974): 146-52.

————. "Forms and First Principles." *Phronesis* 19 (1974): 257-83.

————. "Aristotle on Inefficient Causes." *Philosophical Quarterly* 32 (1982): 311-26.

Anscombe, G. Elisabeth M. "Symposium: The Principle of Individuation II." *Aristotelian Society* suppl. 27 (1953): 83-96.

Antonelli, Teresa. "Elementi della metafisica di Pier Damiani — Il problema del possibile nel medio evo," in Wilpert, ed. (1963), pp. 161-64.

Armstrong, A. Hilary. *The Architecture of the Intelligible Universe in the Philosophy of*

Plotinus: An Analytical and Historical Study. Cambridge: Cambridge University Press, 1940.

————. "Form, Individual and Person in Plotinus." *Dionysius* 1 (1977): 49-68.

Armstrong, A. Hilary, and Robert A. Markus. *Christian Faith and Greek Philosophy.* London: Darton, Longman & Todd, 1960.

Armstrong, David M. *Universals and Scientific Realism.* 2 vols. Cambridge: Cambridge University Press, 1978.

Aubenque, Pierre, ed. *Études sur la Métaphysique d'Aristote.* Paris: Vrin, 1979.

————. *Le problème de l'être chez Aristote. Essai sur la problématique aristotélicienne.* Paris: Presses Universitaires de France, 1997 (orig. pub. 1962).

Avicenna. *Metaphysics.* Translated by P. Morewedge. Chicago: Chicago University Press, 1973.

————. *Isagoge,* in *Treatise on Logic.* Translated by F. Zabeeh. The Hague: Martinus Nijhoff, 1974.

————. *Opera.* Translated by Dominic Gundissalinus. Venice: Bonetus Locatellus for Octavianus Scotus, 1508.

Ayres, Lewis. "'Remember That You Are Catholic' (serm. 52.2): Augustine on the Unity of the Triune God." *Journal of Early Christian Studies* 8 (2000): 39-82.

————. *Nicaea and Its Legacy: An Approach to Fourth-Century Trinitarian Theology.* Oxford: Oxford University Press, 2004.

Ayres, Lewis, and Gareth Jones, eds. *Christian Origins: Theology, Rhetoric and Community.* London: Routledge, 1998.

Badiou, Alain. *Saint Paul. La Fondation de l'Universalisme.* Paris: Presses Universitaires de France, 1998.

Baker, Deane-Peter, and Patrick Maxwell, eds. *Explorations in Contemporary Continental Philosophy of Religion.* Amsterdam and New York: Editions Rodopi B. V., 2003.

Balibar, Étienne. "*Jus — Pactum — Lex.* Sur la constitution du sujet dans le *Traité Théologico-Politique.*" *St. Sp.* 1 (1985): 105-42.

————. *Spinoza et la politique.* Paris: Presses Universitaires de France, 1990; English translation: *Spinoza and Politics.* Translated and edited by Peter Snowdon. London: Verso, 1998.

————. "Individualité, Causalité, Substance. Réflexions sur l'ontologie de Spinoza," in Curley and Moreau, eds. (1990), pp. 58-76.

————. "Individualité et transindividualité chez Spinoza," in Moreau, ed. (1996), pp. 35-46.

Balic, C., ed. *Ioannis Duns Scoti O.F.M. Lectura.* Vatican City: Typis Polyglottis Vaticanis, 1950.

Balthasar, Hans Urs von. *The Glory of the Lord: A Theological Aesthetics.* Translated and edited by Joseph Fessio and John Kenneth Riches. Edinburgh: T. & T. Clark, 1989.

Bambrough, Renford, ed. *New Essays on Plato and Aristotle.* London: Routledge & Kegan Paul, 1965.

Barber, Kenneth F., and Jorge J. E. Gracia, eds. *Individuation and Identity in Early Mod-*

ern Philosophy: Descartes to Kant. Albany: State University of New York Press, 1994.

Barbone, Steven. "Virtue and Sociality in Spinoza." *Iyyun* 42 (1993): 383-95.

————. "What Counts as an Individual for Spinoza?" in Koistinen and Biro, eds. (2002), pp. 89-112.

Barbone, Steven, and Lee C. Rice. "La naissance d'une nouvelle politique," in Moreau, ed. (1996), pp. 47-61.

Barker, Andrew. *Greek Musical Writings.* Volume II: *Harmonic and Acoustic Theory.* Cambridge: Cambridge University Press, 1989.

Barnes, Jonathan. *The Presocratic Philosophers.* 2nd ed. London: Routledge & Kegan Paul, 1982.

————, ed. *The Complete Works of Aristotle: The Revised Oxford Translation.* Bollingen Series LXXI.2. Two volumes. Princeton: Princeton University Press, 1984.

Barnes, Jonathan, Malcolm Schofield, and Richard Sorabji, eds. *Articles on Aristotle.* 3 vols. London: Duckworth, 1975-1979.

Barnes, Michel René. "Augustine in Contemporary Trinitarian Theology." *Theological Studies* 56 (1995): 237-50.

————. "De Régnon Reconsidered." *Augustinian Studies* 26 (1995): 51-79.

————. "Rereading Augustine's Theology of the Trinity," in Davis et al., eds. (1999), pp. 145-76.

————. *The Power of God: Dunamis in Gregory of Nyssa's Trinitarian Theology.* Washington, DC: Catholic University of America Press, 2001.

————. "The Visible Christ and the Invisible Trinity: Mt. 5:8 in Augustine's Trinitarian Theology of 400." *Modern Theology* 19, no. 3 (July 2003): 329-55.

Bechler, Zev. *Aristotle's Theory of Actuality.* Albany: State University of New York Press, 1995.

Bennett, Jonathan. *A Study of Spinoza's Ethics.* Indianapolis: Hackett, 1984.

Berkeley, George. *Three Dialogues between Hylas and Philonous,* in *The Works of George Berkeley.* Edited by A. Luce and T. E. Jessop. London: Thomas Nelson & Sons, 1948.

Bernadete, Seth. "On Plato's Timaeus and Timaeus' Science Fiction." *Interpretation* 2 (1971): 21-63.

————. *Socrates' Second Sailing: On Plato's Republic.* Chicago: University of Chicago Press, 1989.

Berndt, R., M. Lutz-Bachmann, and R. M. W. Stammberger, eds. *"Scientia" and "Disciplina." Wissenstheorie und Wissenschaftspraxis im 12. und 13. Jahrhundert.* Berlin: Akademie Verlag, 2002.

Berthaud, Auguste. *Gilbert de la Porrée, évêque de Poitiers, et sa philosophie (1077-1154),* reprint of the original 1892 Poitiers edition. Frankfurt am Main: Minerva Verlag, 1985.

Berti, Enrico. "Multiplicity and Unity of Being in Aristotle." *Proceedings of the Aristotelian Society* 101 (2000): 185-207.

Betz, John R. *After Enlightenment: The Post-Secular Vision of J. G. Hamann.* Oxford: Wiley-Blackwell, 2009.

Bibliography

Bianchi, Luca. "1277: A Turning Point in Medieval Philosophy?" in Aertsen and Speer, eds. (1998), pp. 90-110.

Biard, Joël. *Logique et théorie du signe au XIVe siècle*. Paris: Vrin, 1989.

Blankenhorn, Bernhard. "The Good as Self-Diffusive in Thomas Aquinas." *Angelicum* 79 (2002): 803-37.

Blond, Phillip, ed. *Post-Secular Philosophy: Between Philosophy and Theology*. London and New York: Routledge, 1997.

Blumenberg, Hans. *Die Legitimität der Neuzeit*. Frankfurt am Main: Suhrkamp, 1996 (orig. pub. 1966).

Bobik, Joseph. "La doctrine de saint Thomas sur l'individuation des substances corporelles." *Revue Philosophique de Louvain* 51 (1953): 5-41.

―――. "Dimensions in the Individuation of Bodily Substances." *Philosophical Studies* 4 (1954): 60-79.

―――. "Matter and Individuation," in McMullin, ed. (1963), pp. 281-92.

Boehner, Philotheus, Gedeon Gál, and Stephen Brown, eds. *Guillelmi de Ockham. Summa Logicae*. St. Bonaventure, NY: Franciscan Institute, 1974, in *Opera Philosophica* I, pp. 47-67.

Boler, John F. "Intuitive and Abstract Cognition," in Kretzmann et al., eds. (1982), pp. 460-78.

Bolton, Martha Brandt. "Locke on Identity: The Scheme of Simple and Compounded Things," in Barber and Gracia, eds. (1994), pp. 103-31.

Booth, Edward. "St. Augustine's 'notitia sui' Related to Aristotle and the Early Neo-Platonists." *Augustiniana* 27 (1977): 70-132, 364-401.

―――. "St. Augustine's 'notitia sui' Related to Aristotle and the Early Neo-Platonists." *Augustiniana* 28 (1978): 183-221.

―――. "St. Augustine's 'notitia sui' Related to Aristotle and the Early Neo-Platonists." *Augustiniana* 29 (1979): 97-124.

―――. *Aristotelian Aporetic Ontology in Islamic and Christian Thinkers*. Cambridge: Cambridge University Press, 1983.

―――. *Saint Augustine and the Western Tradition of Self-Knowing: The St. Augustine Lecture 1986*. Villanova, PA: Villanova University Press, 1989.

Boulnois, Olivier. "Analogie et univocité selon Duns Scot. La double destruction." *Les Études Philosophiques* 3 (1989): 347-69.

―――, ed. *La puissance et son ombre. De Pierre Lombard à Luther*. Paris: Aubier, 1992.

―――. "Les deux fins de l'homme. L'impossible anthropologie et le repli de la théologie." *Les Études Philosophiques* 9 (1995): 205-22.

―――. "Quand commence l'ontothéologie? Aristote, Thomas d'Aquin et Duns Scot." *Revue thomiste* 95 (1995): 85-108.

―――. *Duns Scot. La Rigueur de la charité*. Paris: Éditions Cerf, 1998.

―――. "Surnaturel," in Lacoste, ed. (1998), pp. 980-95.

―――. *Être et représentation. Une généalogie de la métaphysique moderne à l'époque de Duns Scot (XIIIe-XIVe siècle)*. Paris: Presses Universitaires de France, 1999.

―――. "Théologie, métaphysique et représentation de l'être selon Duns Scot." *Revue de théologie et de philosophie* 21 (1999): 83-102.

————. "Au-delà de la physique?" in Boulnois et al., eds. (2004), pp. 219-54.

————. "Reading Duns Scotus: From History to Philosophy." *Modern Theology* 21 (2005): 603-8.

Boulnois, Olivier, Elisabeth Karger, Jean-Luc Solère, Gérard Sondag, eds. *Duns Scot à Paris, 1302-2002. Actes du colloque de Paris, 2-4 septembre 2002.* Paris: Éditions Brepols, 2004.

Boureau, Alain. *La Religion de l'État. La construction de la République étatique dans le discours théologique de l'Occident médiéval, 1250-1350.* Paris: Les Belles Lettres, 2006.

Bourke, Vernon J. *Augustine's View of Reality.* Villanova, PA: Villanova University Press, 1964.

Bradshaw, David. *Aristotle East and West: Metaphysics and the Division of Christendom.* Cambridge: Cambridge University Press, 2004.

Brague, Rémi. *Du temps chez Platon et Aristote. Quatre études.* Paris: Presses Universitaires de France, 1982.

Brandt, Samuel. *Anicii Manlii Severini Boethii in Isagogen Porphyrii Commenta.* Vienna/Leipzig: Tempsky/Freitag, 1906. *CSEL* vol. 48.

Broadie, Sarah. "Que fait le premier moteur d'Aristote?" *Revue philosophique* 183 (1993): 375-411.

Brosch, Hermann Josef. *Der Seinsbegriff bei Boethius. Mit besonderer Berücksichtigung der Beziehung von Sosein und Dasein.* Innsbruck: Verlag von Felizian Rauch, 1931.

Brown, David. "Trinitarian Personhood and Individuality," in Plantinga and Feenstra, eds. (1989), pp. 48-78.

Brown, Montague. "Augustine and Aristotle on Causality," in Lienhard et al., eds. (1993), pp. 465-76.

Brown, Stephen F. "Henry of Ghent (b. ca. 1217; d. 1293)," in Gracia, ed. (1994), pp. 195-219.

Brown, Stephen F., ed. *Guillelmi de Ockham. Quaestiones in libros Physicorum Aristotelis.* St. Bonaventure, NY: Franciscan Institute, 1974. In *Opera Philosophica* VI.

Brunning, Bernard, Mathijs Lamberigts, and Jozef van Houtem, eds. *Collectanea Augustiniana. Mélanges T. J. von Bavel.* Leuven: Leuven University Press, 1990.

Buchheim, Thomas, Corneille H. Kneepkens, and Kuno Lorenz, eds. *Potentialität und Possibilität. Modalaussagen in der Geschichte der Metaphysik.* Stuttgart: Frommann-Holzboog, 2001.

Buckley, Michael. *At the Origins of Modern Atheism.* New Haven and London: Yale University Press, 1987.

Bullimore, Matthew J. *Government by Transcendence: The Analogy of the Soul, the City and the Cosmos in Plato, Philo and St Paul.* University of Cambridge PhD thesis, 2007.

Bülow, Friedrich. "Einführung," in *Die Ethik.* 7th ed. Stuttgart: Alfred Kröner Verlag, 1976, pp. vii-xxx.

van Buren, John, ed. *Martin Heidegger: Supplements. From the Earliest Essays to Being and Time and Beyond.* Albany: State University of New York Press, 2002.

Burnyeat, Myles, ed. *The Skeptical Tradition.* Berkeley: University of California Press, 1983.

Burrell, David B. "Essence and Existence: Avicenna and Greek Philosophy." *Mélanges de l'Institut Dominicain des Études Orientales* 17 (1986): 53-66.

Camus, Albert. *Notebooks 1942-1951.* Translated by Justin O'Brien. New York: Paragon House, 1991.

————. *Christian Metaphysics and Neoplatonism.* Translated by Ronald D. Srigley. Columbia: University of Missouri Press, 2007.

Cantin, André, ed. *Pierre Damien. Disputatio super quaestione qua quaeritur, si deus omnipotens est, quomodo potest agere ut quae facta sunt facta non fuerint* (c. 1067). Translated and edited by A. Cantin. Sources chrétiennes, no. 191. Paris: Éditions Cerf, 1972.

Carey, Phillip. *Augustine's Invention of the Inner Self: The Legacy of a Christian Platonist.* Oxford: Oxford University Press, 2000.

Carraud, Vincent. *Causa sive ratio. La raison de la cause, de Suarez à Leibniz.* Paris: Presses Universitaires de France, 2002.

Carriero, John. "On the Relationship between Mode and Substance in Spinoza's Metaphysics." *Journal of the History of Philosophy* 33 (1995): 245-73.

Castañeda, Héctor-Neri. "Plato's Phaedo Theory of Relations." *Journal of Philosophical Logic* 1 (1972): 467-80.

Catan, John R., ed. *St. Thomas Aquinas on the Existence of God: The Collected Papers of Joseph Owens.* Albany: State University of New York Press, 1980.

Cathala, M. R., and R. M. Spiazzi, eds. *S. Thomae Aquinatis. In duodecim libros Metaphysicorum Aristotelis expositio.* 2nd ed. Rome: Marietti, 1971.

Cavanaugh, William T. "'A Fire Strong Enough to Consume the House': The Wars of Religion and the Rise of the State." *Modern Theology* 11 (1995): 397-420.

————. "The City: Beyond Secular Parodies," in Milbank et al., eds. (1999), pp. 182-200.

————. "Killing for the Telephone Company: Why the Nation-State Is Not the Keeper of the Common Good." *Modern Theology* 20 (2004): 243-74.

Chadwick, Henry. *The Early Church: Story of Emergent Christianity from the Apostolic Age to the Dividing of the Ways Between the Greek East and the Latin West.* London: Hodder & Stoughton, 1967.

————. *Boethius: The Consolations of Music, Logic, Theology, and Philosophy.* Oxford: Oxford University Press, 1981.

Charlton, William. "Aristotle and the Principle of Individuation." *Phronesis* 17 (1973): 239-49.

Chenu, Marie-Dominique. "Un essai de méthode théologique au XIIe siècle." *RSPT* 24 (1935): 258-67.

————. *La théologie comme science au XIIIe siècle.* 3rd ed. Paris: Vrin, 1969.

————. *La théologie au douzième siècle.* 3rd ed. Paris: Vrin, 1976.

————. *Introduction à l'étude de Saint Thomas d'Aquin.* Paris: Vrin, 1993.

Cherniss, Harold F. *Aristotle's Criticism of Plato and the Academy.* Baltimore: Johns Hopkins University Press, 1944.

Chrétien, Jean-Louis. *L'inoubliable et l'inespéré*. Paris: Desclée de Brouwer, 1991.

Clarke, William Norris. "The Limitation of Act by Potency in St. Thomas: Aristotelianism or Neo-Platonism?" *New Scholasticism* 26 (1952): 167-94.

————. "The Meaning of Participation in St. Thomas." *Proceedings of the American Catholic Philosophical Association* 26 (1952): 147-57.

————. "The Platonic Heritage of Thomism." *Review of Metaphysics* 8 (1954): 105-24.

————. "The Problem of the Reality and Multiplicity of Divine Ideas in Christian Neoplatonism," in O'Meara, ed. (1982), pp. 109-27.

————. "Person, Being, and St. Thomas." *Communio* 19 (Winter 1992): 601-18.

————. "To Be Is to Be Substance-in-Relation," in *Explorations in Metaphysics: Being, God, Person*. Notre Dame: University of Notre Dame Press, 1994, pp. 102-22.

————. *The One and the Many: A Contemporary Thomistic Metaphysics*. Notre Dame: University of Notre Dame Press, 2001.

Clauberg, Johannes. *Elementa philosophiae sive ontosophiae*. Gröningen: Joannis Nicolai, 1647.

Clement of Alexandria. *Stromata*, in *ANF*. Edited by Alexander Robertson, James Donaldson, and Arthur Cleveland Coxe. New York: Cosimo, 2007 (orig. pub. 1885), Vol. II: *Fathers of the Second Century*, pp. 299-568.

Cohen, S. Marc. "Aristotle and Individuation," in Pelletier and King-Farlow, eds. (1984), pp. 41-65.

Cohen, Sheldon M. "St. Thomas Aquinas on the Immaterial Reception of Sensible Forms." *Philosophical Review* 91 (April 1982): 193-209.

Coleman, Janet. "Ockham's Right Reason and the Genesis of the Political as 'Absolutist.'" *History of Political Thought* 20 (1999): 35-64.

Courcelle, Pierre. *La Consolation de Philosophie dans la tradition littéraire. Antécédents et postérité de Boèc*. Paris: Études Augustiniennes, 1967.

————. *Late Latin Writers and Their Greek Sources*. Cambridge, MA: Harvard University Press, 1969.

Courtenay, William. *Capacity and Volition: A History of the Distinction of Absolute and Ordained Power*. Bergamo: Pierluigi Lubrina Editore, 1990.

Courtine, Jean-François. *Suarez et le système de la métaphysique*. Paris: Presses Universitaires de France, 1990.

————. *Nature et Empire de la Loi. Études suaréziennes*. Paris: Vrin, 1999.

Cousin, D. R. "Aristotle's Doctrine of Substance." *Mind* 42 (1933): 319-37.

————. "Aristotle's Doctrine of Substance (II)." *Mind* 44 (1935): 168-85.

Cronin, Timothy J. *Objective Being in Descartes and Suarez*. Rome: Gregorian University Press, 1966.

Crouch, Colin. *Post-Democracy*. Cambridge: Polity Press, 2004.

Crouse, Robert. "The Doctrine of Creation in Boethius: The *'De hebdomadibus'* and the *Consolatio*," in Livingstone, ed. (1979), Part 1, pp. 417-21.

————. "*Semina Rationum:* St. Augustine and Boethius." *Dionysius* 4 (December 1980): 75-86.

————. "*Paucis Mutatis Verbis:* St. Augustine's Neoplatonism," in Dodaro and Lawless, eds. (2000), pp. 37-50.

Cunningham, Conor. *Genealogy of Nihilism: Philosophies of Nothing and the Difference of Theology.* London and New York: Routledge, 2002.

———. *Darwin's Pious Idea.* Grand Rapids: Eerdmans, 2010.

Curd, Patricia. *The Legacy of Parmenides: Eleatic Monism and Later Presocratic Thought.* Princeton: Princeton University Press, 1998.

Curley, Edwin M. *Spinoza's Metaphysics: An Essay in Interpretation.* Cambridge, MA: Harvard University Press, 1969.

Curley, Edwin M., and Pierre-François Moreau, eds. *Spinoza: Issues and Directions. The Proceedings of the Chicago Spinoza Conference.* Leiden: E. J. Brill, 1990.

D'Ancona, Cristina. "Greek into Arabic: Neoplatonism in Translation," in *The Cambridge Companion to Arabic Philosophy.* Edited by Peter Adamson and Richard C. Taylor. Cambridge: Cambridge University Press, 2005, pp. 10-31.

Daniélou, Jean. *Message Evangélique et Culture Hellénistique.* Tournai: Desclée & Cie, 1961.

Dascal, Marcelo. "Unfolding the One: 'Abstract Relations' in Spinoza's Theory of Knowledge," in Yovel, ed. (1994), pp. 171-85.

Davies, Brian, ed. *Thomas Aquinas: Contemporary Philosophical Perspectives.* Oxford: Oxford University Press, 2002.

Davis, Stephen T., David Kendall, and Gerald O'Collins, eds. *The Trinity: An Interdisciplinary Symposium on the Trinity.* Oxford: Oxford University Press, 1999.

Decker, Bruno. *Sancti Thomae de Aquino. Expositio super librum Boethii de Trinitate.* Rev. ed. Leiden: E. J. Brill, 1965.

Deleuze, Gilles. *Spinoza et le problème de l'expression.* Paris: Éditions de Minuit, 1968.

———. *Spinoza. Philosophie pratique.* Paris: Éditions de Minuit, 1981.

Den Uyl, Douglas, and Stuart D. Warner. "Liberalism and Hobbes and Spinoza." *St. Sp.* 3 (1987): 261-317.

Descartes, René. *Oeuvres.* Edited by C. Adam and P. Tannery. Paris: Éditions Cerf, 1897-1910.

———. *The Philosophical Works of Descartes.* Edited by E. S. Haldane and G. R. T. Ross. Cambridge: Cambridge University Press, 1912.

———. *Principles of Philosophy.* Edited by V. R. Miller and R. P. Miller. Dordrecht: D. Reidel, 1983.

Desmond, William. *God and the Between.* Oxford: Wiley-Blackwell, 2007.

Dillon, John. "Iamblichus' Defence of Theurgy: Some Reflections." *The International Journal of the Platonic Tradition* 1 (2007): 30-41.

Dix, Dom Gregory. *The 'Hellenization' of the Gospel.* Uppsala: Almqvist & Wiksell, 1953.

Dodaro, Robert, and George Lawless, eds. *Augustine and His Critics: Essays in Honour of Gerald Bonner.* London: Routledge, 2000.

Dodds, Michael J. "Ultimacy and Intimacy: Aquinas on the Relation between God and the World," in Pinto de Oliveira, ed. (1993), pp. 211-27.

Donagan, Alan. "Spinoza's Theology," in Garrett, ed. (1996), pp. 343-82.

Donati, Pierpaolo. *Relational Sociology: A New Paradigm for the Social Sciences.* London: Routledge, 2010.

Donceel, J. "Transcendental Thomism." *The Monist* 58 (1974): 67-85.

Dronke, Peter, ed. *A History of Twelfth-Century Western Philosophy.* Cambridge: Cambridge University Press, 1988.

Druart, Thérèse-Anne. "Metaphysics," in *The Cambridge Companion to Arabic Philosophy.* Edited by Peter Adamson and Richard C. Taylor. Cambridge: Cambridge University Press, 2005, pp. 327-48.

Dubarle, Dominique. *Dieu avec l'être. Traité d'ontologie théologale.* Paris: Éditions Cerf, 1986.

Duhem, Pierre. *Études sur Léonardo de Vinci.* Paris: A. Hermann, 1909, vol. 13: *Jean Buridan (de Béthune) et Léonard de Vinci.*

――――. *Le système du monde. Histoire des doctrines cosmologiques de Platon à Copernic.* Paris: Vrin, 1965, vol. 5.

Dullaert, Johannes. *Johannes Buridanus. Questiones super octo Physicorum libros Aristotelis.* Reprinted Frankfurt am Main: Minerva, 1964 (orig. pub. 1509).

――――. *Johannes Buridanus. Questiones in Metaphysicen Aristotelis.* Reprinted Frankfurt am Main: Minerva, 1964 (orig. pub. 1518).

Dumont, Louis. *Essais sur l'individualisme. Une perspective anthropologique sur l'idéologie moderne.* Paris: Éditions du Seuil, 1983.

Dupré, Louis. *Passage to Modernity: An Essay in the Hermeneutics of Nature and Culture.* New Haven: Yale University Press, 1993.

Düring, Ingemar, and Gwilym E. L. Owen, eds. *Aristotle and Plato in the Mid-Fourth Century: Papers of the Symposium Aristotelicum held at Oxford in August 1957.* Göttingen, Stockholm, and Uppsala: Elanders, 1960.

Eagleton, Terry. *Reason, Faith, and Revolution: Reflections on the God Debate.* New Haven: Yale University Press, 2009.

Easterling, H. J. "The Unmoved Mover in Early Aristotle." *Phronesis* 21 (1976): 252-65.

Ebbesen, Sten. "Boethius as an Aristotelian Commentator," in Sorabji, ed. (1990), pp. 373-91.

Edgar, William J. "Continuity and the Individuation of Modes in Spinoza's Physics," in Wilbur, ed. (1976), pp. 85-132.

Edwards, Mark J. "Christ or Plato? Origen on Revelation and Anthropology," in Ayres and Jones, eds. (1998), pp. 11-25.

――――. *Origen against Plato.* Aldershot, UK: Ashgate, 2002.

Einstein, Albert. "The Mechanics of Newton," in *Ideas and Opinions.* New York: Bonanza, 1954.

――――. *Relativity: The Special and General Theory.* New York: Crown, 1961.

Elders, Leo J. *Aristotle's Theology: A Commentary on Book Λ of the Metaphysics.* Assen: Van Gorcum, 1972.

van Elswijk, H. C. *Gilbert Porreta. Sa vie, son œuvre, sa pensée.* Louvain: Publications Universitaires de Louvain, 1966.

Ertman, Thomas. *Birth of the Leviathan: Building States and Regimes in Medieval and Early Modern Europe.* Cambridge: Cambridge University Press, 1997.

Eslick, Leonard J. "The Material Substrate," in McMullin, ed. (1963), pp. 39-54.

Etzkorn, Girard J., and Allan B. Wolter, eds. *Questions on the Metaphysics of Aristotle by John Duns Scotus.* Translated in two volumes. St. Bonaventure, NY: Franciscan Institute Publications, 1997-1998.

Evans, Gillian R. "*More geometrico:* The Place of the Axiomatic Method in the Twelfth-Century Commentaries on Boethius' *Opuscula sacra.*" *Archives internationales d'histoire des sciences* 27 (1977): 207-21.

————, ed. *The Medieval Theologians: An Introduction to Theology in the Medieval Period.* Oxford: Blackwell, 2001.

Fabro, Cornelio. "Il Problema della Percezione Sensoriale." *Bollettino Filosofico* 4 (1938): 5-62.

————. *La nozione metafisica di partecipazione secondo S. Tommaso d'Aquino.* Turin: Marietti, 1950.

————. *Partecipazione e causalità secondo S. Tommaso d'Aquino.* Turin: Marietti, 1960; French translation: *Participation et causalité selon S. Thomas d'Aquin.* Louvain: Publications Universitaires de Louvain, 1961.

————. *Dall' essere all' esistente.* 2nd ed. Brescia: Morcelliana, 1965.

————. "The Intensive Hermeneutics of Thomistic Philosophy: The Notion of Participation." *Review of Metaphysics* 27 (1974): 449-91.

————. "Die Wiederaufnahme des Thomistischen 'Esse' und der Grund der Metaphysik." *Tijdschrift voor Filosofie* 43 (1981): 90-116.

Falque, Emmanuel. "Saint Augustin ou comment Dieu entre en théologie. Lecture critique des Livres V-VII du '*De Trinitate.*'" *Nouvelle Revue Théologique* 117 (1995): 84-111.

————. "*Larvatus pro Deo* — Phénoménologie et théologie chez J.-L. Marion." *Gregorianum* 86 (2005): 45-62.

Fedwick, Paul J., ed. *Basil of Caesarea: Christian, Humanist, Ascetic. A Sixteen-Hundredth Anniversary Symposium.* Toronto: Pontifical Institute of Mediaeval Studies, 1981.

Ferrater Mora, José. "Suárez and Modern Philosophy." *Journal of the History of Ideas* 14 (1953): 528-47.

Figgis, John Neville. *The Theory of the Divine Right of Kings.* Cambridge: Cambridge University Press, 1896.

————. *Studies of Political Thought from Gerson to Grotius, 1414-1625.* Cambridge: Cambridge University Press, 1916.

De Finance, Joseph. *Être et Agir dans la Philosophie de Saint Thomas.* Paris: Vrin, 1945.

Fine, Gail. "The One over Many." *Philosophical Review* 89 (1980): 197-240.

————. "Relational Entities." *Archiv für Geschichte der Philosophie* 65 (1983): 225-49 (reprinted in Fine [2003], pp. 326-49).

————. "Plato and Aristotle on Form and Substance." *Proceedings of the Cambridge Philological Society* 209 (1983): 23-47 (reprinted in Fine [2003], pp. 397-425).

————. "Separation." *OSAP* 2 (1984): 31-87 (reprinted in Fine [2003], pp. 252-300).

————. "Truth and Necessity in *De interpretatione* 9." *History of Philosophy Quarterly* 1 (1984): 23-47.

————. "Immanence." *OSAP* 4 (1986): 71-97 (reprinted in Fine [2003], pp. 301-25).

————. "Forms as Causes: Plato and Aristotle," in Graeser, ed. (1987), pp. 69-112.

————. *On Ideas: Aristotle's Criticism of Plato's Theory of Form.* Oxford: Clarendon, 1993.

————. *Plato on Knowledge and Form: Selected Essays.* Oxford: Oxford University Press, 2003.

FitzGerald, John J. "'Matter' in Nature and Knowledge of Nature: Aristotle and the Aristotelian Tradition," in McMullin, ed. (1963), pp. 59-78.

Forest, Aimé. "Le réalisme de Gilbert de la Porrée dans le commentaire du 'De Hebdomadibus.'" *Revue Néoscolastique de Philosophie* 36 (1934): 101-10.

————. *La structure métaphysique du concret selon Saint Thomas d'Aquin.* Paris: Vrin, 1956.

Franck, Isaac. "Spinoza's Logic of Enquiry: Rationalist or Experientialist?" in Kennington, ed. (1980), pp. 247-72.

Frank, Jill. *A Democracy of Distinction: Aristotle and the Work of Politics.* Chicago: University of Chicago Press, 2005.

Freddoso, Alfred J. "Introduction: Suárez on Metaphysical Inquiry, Efficient Causality, and Divine Action," in Francisco Suárez, *On Creation, Conservation, and Concurrence. Metaphysical Disputations 20, 21, and 22,* translated and edited by Alfred J. Freddoso. South Bend, IN: St. Augustine's Press, 2002, pp. xi-cxxiii.

Frede, Michael. *Essays in Ancient Philosophy.* Oxford: Clarendon Press, 1987.

Funkenstein, Amos. *Theology and the Scientific Imagination from the Middle Ages to the Seventeenth Century.* Princeton: Princeton University Press, 1986.

Gadamer, Hans-Georg. *Die Idee des Guten zwischen Plato und Aristoteles.* Heidelberg: Winter, 1978; English translation: *The Idea of the Good in Platonic-Aristotelian Philosophy.* Translated and introduced by P. Christopher Smith. New Haven: Yale University Press, 1986.

Gál, Gedeon, Stephen Brown, Gerard Etzkorn, Francis Kelley, Rega Wood, and R. Green, eds. *Guillelmi de Ockham. Scriptum in libris Sententiarum. Ordinatio.* St. Bonaventure, NY: Franciscan Institute, 1967-84. In *Opera Theologica,* vols. 1-7.

Garin, Eugenio. *L'umanesimo italiano.* Bari: G. Laterza, 1958; English translation: *Italian Humanism: Philosophy and Civic Life in the Renaissance.* Translated by Peter Munz. Oxford: Blackwell, 1965.

Garrett, Don. "Spinoza's Theory of Metaphysical Individuation," in Barber and Gracia, eds. (1994), pp. 73-101.

————, ed. *The Cambridge Companion to Spinoza.* Cambridge: Cambridge University Press, 1996.

————. "Teleology in Spinoza and Early Modern Rationalism," in Gennaro and Huenemann, eds. (1999), pp. 310-35.

————. "Spinoza's *Conatus* Argument," in Koistinen and Biro, eds. (2002), pp. 127-58.

Gasper, Giles E. M. *Anselm of Canterbury and His Theological Inheritance.* Aldershot, UK: Ashgate, 2004.

Geach, Peter T. "Form and Existence." *Proceedings of the Aristotelian Society* 54 (1954-55): 250-76.

————. "The Third Man Again." *Philosophical Review* 65 (1956): 72-82.

————. *God and the Soul.* London: Routledge & Kegan Paul, 1969.

Gebhardt, Carl. *Benedictus de Spinoza. Opera.* Heidelberg: Winter, 1972-1987 (orig. pub. 1925).

Geiger, Louis-Bertrand. "Abstraction et séparation d'après s. Thomas *In De Trinitate,* q. 5, a. 3." *RSPT* 31 (1947): 3-40.

―――. *La participation dans la philosophie de saint Thomas d'Aquin.* 2nd ed. Montréal: Institut d'Études Médiévales, 1952 (orig. pub. 1942).

Gennaro, Rocco J., and Charles Huenemann, eds. *New Essays on the Rationalists.* New York: Oxford University Press, 1999.

Gersh, Stephen. *Middle Platonism and Neoplatonism: The Latin Tradition,* vol. 2. Notre Dame: University of Notre Dame Press, 1986.

Gerson, Lloyd P. *God and Greek Philosophy: Studies in the Early History of Natural Theology.* London: Routledge, 1990.

―――, ed. *The Cambridge Companion to Plotinus.* Cambridge: Cambridge University Press, 1996.

―――. *Knowing Persons: A Study in Plato.* Oxford: Oxford University Press, 2003.

Gewirth, Alan. *Marsilius of Padua and Medieval Political Philosophy.* New York: Columbia University Press, 1951.

Giacon, Carlo. "S. Tommaso e l'esistenza come atto." *Mediœvo* 1 (1975): 1-28.

Giancotti, Emilia. "On the Problem of Infinite Modes," in Yovel, ed. (1991), pp. 97-118.

Gibson, Margaret, ed. *Boethius: His Life, Thought and Influence.* Oxford: Blackwell, 1981.

―――. "The *Opuscula Sacra* in the Middle Ages," in Gibson, ed. (1981), pp. 214-34.

Von Gierke, Otto F. *Das deutsche Genossenschaftsrecht.* 4 vols. Berlin: Weidmann, 1868-1913, translation of four subsections as *Natural Law and the Theory of Society, 1500-1800.* Translation and introduction by Ernest Barker. Cambridge: Cambridge University Press, 1934.

Gill, Mary L. *Aristotle on Substance: The Paradox of Unity.* Princeton: Princeton University Press, 1989.

―――. "Individuals and Individuation," in Scaltsas et al., eds. (1994), pp. 55-71.

―――. "Perceptible Substances in *Metaphysics* H 1-5," in Rapp, ed. (1996), pp. 209-28.

―――. "Aristotle's Attack on Universals." *OSAP* 20 (2001): 235-60.

Gilson, Étienne. *Jean Duns Scot: Introduction à ses Positions Fondamentales.* Paris: Vrin, 1922.

―――. *La philosophie au Moyen-Âge: Des origines patristiques à la fin du XIV* siècle.* 2nd rev. ed. Paris: Ed. Payot & Rivages, 1999 (orig. pub. 1922).

―――. "Pourquoi saint Thomas a critiqué saint Augustin." *AHDLMA* 2 (1926): 5-127.

―――. "Avicenne et le point de départ de Duns Scot." *AHDLMA* 2 (1927): 89-149.

―――. "Les sources gréco-arabes de l'augustianisme avicennisant." *AHDLMA* 4 (1929): 5-107.

―――. *Introduction à l'étude de Saint Augustin.* Paris: Vrin, 1941.

―――. "Note sur les noms de la matière chez Gilbert de la Porrée." *Revue du moyen âge latin* 2 (1946): 173-76.

―――. *L'être et l'essence.* 2nd ed. Paris: Vrin, 1948.

————. *Le Thomisme: Introduction à la philosophie de St. Thomas d'Aquin.* 5th ed. Paris: Vrin, 1948.

————. *Being and Some Philosophers.* Toronto: Pontifical Institute of Mediaeval Studies, 1949.

————. "La preuve du De ente et essentia," in *Acta III Congressus Thomistici Internationalis: Doctor Communis.* Turin: Marietti, 1950, vol. 3, pp. 257-60.

————. *The Christian Philosophy of St. Thomas Aquinas.* Translated by L. K. Shook. Notre Dame: University of Notre Dame Press, 1956.

————. "Sur la problématique thomiste de la vision béatifique." *AHDLMA* 31 (1964): 67-88.

————. "Avicenne en Occident au Moyen Âge." *AHDLMA* 39 (1969): 89-121.

————. "Propos sur l'être et sa notion," in *San Tommaso e il pensiero moderno.* Edited by Pontificia Accademia di S. Tommaso. Rome: Città Nuova Editrice, 1974, pp. 7-17.

Goëmé, C., ed. *Jean Duns Scot ou la révolution subtile.* Paris: FAC Éditions Radio-France, 1982.

Goichon, Amélie-Marie. *La distinction de l'essence et de l'existence d'après Ibn Sīnā (Avicenne).* Paris: Desclée de Brouwer, 1937.

————. *La philosophie d'Avicenne et son influence en Europe médiévale.* 2nd rev. ed. Paris: Adrien-Maisonneuve, 1951.

Goldast, Melchior, ed. *Monarchia Sancti Romani Imperii.* Graz: Verlagsanstalt, 1960 (orig. pub. 1614).

Gouguenheim, Sylvain. *Aristote au Mont Saint-Michel: Les racines grecques de l'Europe chrétienne.* Paris: Éditions du Seuil, 2008.

Grabmann, Martin. *Die Geschichte der scholastischen Methode.* Freiburg im Breisgau: Herdersche Verlagshandlung, 1911, vol. 2.

————. "Die Schrift 'De ente et essentia' und die Seinsmetaphysik des heiligen Thomas von Aquin," in *Mittelalterliches Geistesleben* 1 (1926).

————. *Die theologische Erkenntnis- und Einleitungslehre des heiligen Thomas von Aquin auf Grund seiner Schrift "In Boethium de Trinitate" im Zusammenhang der Scholastik des 13. und beginnenden 14. Jahrhunderts dargestellt.* Freiburg in der Schweiz: Paulusverlag, 1948.

Gracia, Jorge J. E. "Boethius and the Problem of Individuation in the *Commentaries on the 'Isagoge,'*" in Obertello, ed. (1981), pp. 169-82.

————, ed. *Suárez on Individuation: Metaphysical Disputation V, Individual Unity and Its Principle (De unitate individuali eiusque principio).* Translated and edited by J. J. E. Gracia. Milwaukee: Marquette University Press, 1982.

————. *Introduction to the Problem of Individuation in the Early Middle Ages.* Munich: Philosophia Verlag, 1984.

————. *Individuality: An Essay on the Foundations of Metaphysics.* Albany: State University of New York Press, 1988.

————. "The Centrality of the Individual in the Philosophy of the Fourteenth Century." *History of Philosophy Quarterly* 8 (1991): 225-51.

————, ed. *Individuation in Scholasticism: The Later Middle Ages and the Counter-Reformation 1150-1650*. Albany: State University of New York Press, 1994.

————. "The Legacy of the Early Middle Ages," in Gracia, ed. (1994), pp. 21-38.

————. "Francis Suárez (b. 1548; d. 1617)," in Gracia, ed. (1994), pp. 475-510.

————. "Epilogue: Individuation in Scholasticism," in Gracia, ed. (1994), pp. 543-50.

————. "Christian Wolff on Individuation," in Barber and Gracia, eds. (1994), pp. 219-43.

Graeser, Andreas, ed. *Mathematics and Metaphysics in Aristotle/Mathematik und Metaphysik bei Aristoteles*. Bern: Haupt, 1987.

Gray, John. *Enlightenment's Wake: Politics and Culture at the Close of the Modern Age*. London: Routledge, 1995.

————. *False Dawn: The Delusions of Global Capitalism*. London: Granta, 1998.

————. *Two Faces of Liberalism*. Cambridge: Polity Press, 2000.

————. *Straw Dogs: Thoughts on Humans and Other Animals*. London: Granta, 2002.

————. *Al Qaeda and What It Means to Be Modern*. London: Faber & Faber, 2003.

————. *Heresies: Against Progress and Other Illusions*. London: Granta, 2004.

————. *Black Mass: Apocalyptic Religion and the Death of Utopia*. London: Allen Lane, 2007.

Gregory of Nyssa. "Ad Petrum," in *Saint Basil: The Letters*. Translated by Roy J. Deferrari. The Loeb Classical Library. London: Heinemann, 1961, pp. 197-227.

Gregory Thaumaturgus. *In Origenem oratio*, in *St. Gregory Thaumaturgus, Life and Works*, translated by Michael Slusser. The Fathers of the Church. Washington, DC: Catholic University of America Press, 1998, pp. 91-126.

Greisch, Jean. "Un tournant phénoménologique de la théologie?" *Transversalités* 63 (1997): 75-97.

Grillmeier, Alois. *Mit ihm und in ihm. Christologische Forschungen und Perspektiven*. Freiburg: Herder, 1975.

Grosholz, Emily. "Descartes and the Individuation of Physical Objects," in Barber and Gracia, eds. (1994), pp. 41-58.

Guardini, Romano. *Das End der Neuzeit*. Würzburg: Werkbund-Verlag, 1950.

Gunton, Colin E. *Enlightenment and Alienation: An Essay towards a Trinitarian Theology*. Basingstoke, UK: Marshall, Morgan & Scott, 1985.

————. *The Promise of Trinitarian Theology*. Edinburgh: T. & T. Clark, 1991.

Guthrie, W. K. C. *A History of Greek Philosophy*. Cambridge: Cambridge University Press, 1965.

Habermas, Jürgen. *Der gespaltene Westen*. Frankfurt am Main: Suhrkamp, 2004; English translation: *The Divided West*, ed. Ciaran Cronin. Cambridge: Polity Press, 2006.

Habermas, Jürgen, and Joseph Ratzinger. *Dialektik der Säkularisierung. Über Vernunft und Religion*. Freiburg: Herder, 2004; English translation: *The Dialectics of Secularization: On Reason and Religion*. San Francisco: Ignatius Press, 2007.

Hadot, Pierre. "Fragments d'un commentaire de Porphyre sur le Parménide." *Revue des Études Grecques* 74 (1961): 410-38.

————. "La distinction de l'être et de l'étant dans le *'De hebdomadibus'* de Boèce," in Wilpert, ed. (1963), pp. 147-53.

————. *"Forma essendi:* Interprétation philologique et interprétation philosophique d'une formule de Boèce." *Les Études Classiques* 38 (1970): 143-56.

————. "L'être et l'étant dans le néoplatonisme." *Études néoplatoniciennes* (1973): 27-41.

Haldane, John, "Aquinas on Sense Perception." *Philosophical Review* 92 (1983): 233-39.

Hall, Douglas C. *The Trinity: An Analysis of St. Thomas Aquinas' Expositio of the De Trinitate of Boethius.* Leiden: E. J. Brill, 1992.

Hall, Stuart G. *Doctrine and Practice in the Early Church.* London: SPCK, 1991.

Hamesse, J., ed. *Roma, Magistra mundi. Itineraria cultura medievalis.* Louvain-la-Neuve: Mélanges L. E. Boyle — FIDEM, 1998.

Hamyln, D. W. *Sensation and Perception.* London: Routledge & Kegan Paul, 1961.

Hanby, Michael. "Desire: Augustine beyond Western Subjectivity," in Milbank et al., eds. (1999), pp. 109-26.

————. "Augustine and Descartes: An Overlooked Chapter in the Story of Modern Origins." *Modern Theology* 19, no. 4 (October 2003): 455-82.

————. *Augustine and Modernity.* London: Routledge, 2003.

Hankey, Wayne J. "Between and Beyond Augustine and Descartes: More Than a Source of the Self." *Augustinian Studies* 32 (2001): 65-88.

————. "Misrepresenting Neoplatonism in Contemporary Christian Dionysian Polemic: Eriugena and Nicholas of Cusa versus Vladimir Lossky and Jean-Luc Marion." *American Catholic Philosophical Quarterly* 82 (2008): 683-703.

Hankins, James. *Plato in the Italian Renaissance.* 2 vols. Rev. ed. Leiden: E. J. Brill, 1994.

Hardt, Michael, and Antonio Negri. *Empire.* Cambridge, MA: Harvard University Press, 2000.

————. *Multitude: War and Democracy in the Age of Empire.* London: Penguin, 2005.

————. *Commonwealth.* Cambridge, MA: Harvard University Press, 2009.

Häring, Nikolaus M. "The Case of Gilbert de la Porrée Bishop of Poitiers (1142-1154)." *MS* 13 (1951): 1-40.

————. "Sprachlogische und philosophische Vorraussetzungen zum Verständnis der Christologie Gilberts von Poitiers." *Scholastik* 32 (1957): 373-98.

————, ed. *The Commentaries on Boethius by Gilbert of Poitiers.* Toronto: The Pontifical Institute of Mediaeval Studies, 1966.

von Harnack, Adolf. *History of Dogma.* 3rd ed. Translated by Neil Buchanan. London: Williams & Norgate, 1897.

Harrison, C. "Measure, Number and Weight in Saint Augustine's Aesthetics." *Augustinianum* 28, no. 3 (1988): 591-602.

Hart, David Bentley. *Atheist Delusions: The Christian Revolution and Its Fashionable Enemies.* New Haven: Yale University Press, 2009.

Hart, James G., and John C. Maraldo, eds. *The Piety of Thinking: Essays by Martin Heidegger.* Bloomington: Indiana University Press, 1976.

Hathaway, Ronald F. *Hierarchy and the Definition of Order in the Letters of Pseudo-*

Dionysius: A Study in the Form and Meaning of the Pseudo-Dionysian Writings.
The Hague: Nijhoff, 1969.

Hauser, Mark. *Moral Minds: How Nature Designed Our Universal Sense of Right and Wrong.* London: Ecco, 2006.

Hayen, André. "Le Concile de Reims et l'Erreur Théologique de Gilbert de la Porrée."
AHDLMA 10 (1935): 29-102.

————. *L'intentionnel dans la philosophie de Saint Thomas.* Paris: Vrin, 1942.

————. "La théologie aux XIIe, XIIIe et XXe siècles." *Nouvelle Revue Théologique* 79
(1957): 1009-28 and 80 (1958): 113-32.

Hecker, Konrad. *Gesellschaftliche Wirklichkeit und Vernunft: Untersuchungen über die immanente Systematik der Gesellschaftsphilosophie Spinozas im Zusammenhang seines philosophischen Gesamtwerks und zum Problem ihres ideologischen Sinngehalts.* Regensburg: Kommissionsverlag Buchhandung Pustet, 1975.

Hedley, Douglas. "Pantheism, Trinitarian Theism and the Idea of Unity: Reflections on the Christian Concept of God." *Religious Studies* 32 (1996): 61-77.

Heidegger, Martin. "Phänomenologische Interpretationen zu Aristoteles. Anzeige der hermeneutischen Situation." *Dilthey-Jahrbruch für Philosophie und Geschichte der Geisteswissenschaften* 6 (1922): 237-74 (trans. in van Buren [2002]).

————. "Phänomenologie und Theologie," in *Gesamtausgabe.* Frankfurt am Main:
V. Klostermann, 1976, vol. 9, pp. 45-78 (trans. "Phenomenology and Theology," in Hart and Maraldo [1976]).

Helmig, Christoph. "What Is the Systematic Place of Abstraction and Concept Formation in Plato's Philosophy? Ancient and Modern Readings of *Phaedrus* 249 b-c," in *Platonic Ideas and Concept Formation in Ancient and Medieval Thought.* Edited by Gerd Van Riel and Caroline Macé. Leuven: Leuven University Press, 2004, pp. 83-97.

Hénaff, Marcel. *Le prix de la vérité. Le don, l'argent, la philosophie.* Paris: Éditions du Seuil, 2002.

Hengel, Martin. *Jews, Juden, Griechen und Barbaren. Aspekte der Hellenisierung des Judentums in vorchristlicher Zeit.* Stuttgarter Bibelstudien 76. Stuttgart: Katholisches Bibelwerk, 1976; English translation: *Greeks and Barbarians: Aspects of the Hellenization of Judaism in the Pre-Christian Period.* Translated by John Bowden. Philadelphia: Fortress, 1980.

————. *The 'Hellenization' of Judea in the First Century after Christ.* Translated by John Bowden. Philadelphia: Trinity, 1989.

Henninger, Mark G. *Relations: Medieval Theories 1250-1325.* Oxford: Clarendon Press, 1989.

Himmelfarb, Gertrude. *The Roads to Modernity: The British, French, and American Enlightenments.* New York: Random House, 2004.

Hissette, Roland. *Enquête sur les 219 articles condamnés à Paris le 7 mars 1277.* Louvain: Publications Universitaires de Louvain, 1977.

————. "Thomas d'Aquin directement visé par la censure du 7 mars 1277? Réponse à John F. Wippel," in Hamesse, ed. (1998), pp. 425-37.

Hobbes, Thomas. *De Corpore* (1650). Latin editor Karl Schuhmann. Paris: Vrin, 1999. English translator and editor William Molesworth. London: J. Bohn, 1839-45.

———. *De Cive* (1651). Whitefish, MT: Kessinger Publishing, 1994.

———. *Leviathan or the Matter, Forme and Power of a Commonwealth Ecclesiasticall and Civil* (1651). Edited and introduced by Michael Oakeshott. Oxford: Basil Blackwell, 1960.

Hoffman, Paul. "St. Thomas Aquinas on the Halfway State of Sensible Being." *Philosophical Review* 99 (January 1990): 73-92.

Holte, Ragner. "*Logos Spermatikos:* Christianity and Ancient Philosophy according to St. Justin's Apologies." *Studia Theologica* 12 (1958): 109-68.

Honnefelder, Ludgar. *Ens inquantum ens. Der Begriff des Seienden als solchen als Gegenstand der Metaphysik nach der Lehre des Johannes Duns Scotus.* Münster: Aschendorff, 1979.

———. *Scientia transcendens. Die formale Bestimmung der Seiendheit und Realität in der Metaphysik des Mittelalters und der Neuzeit (Duns Scot, Suarez, Kant, Peirce).* Hamburg: F. Meiner, 1990.

———. "Der zweite Anfang der Metaphysik. Vorraussetzungen, Ansätze und Folgen der Wiederbegründung der Metaphysik im 13./14. Jahrhundert," in *Philosophie im Mittelalter. Entwicklungslinien und Paradigmen.* Edited by J.-P. Beckmann and Wolfgang Kluxen. Hamburg: F. Meiner, 1987, pp. 165-86.

Honnefelder, Ludgar, Rega Wood, and Mechthild Dreyer, eds. *John Duns Scotus: Metaphysics and Ethics.* Leiden: E. J. Brill, 1996.

Hübner, Reinhard. "Gregor von Nyssa als Verfasser des Sog. *Ep. 38* des Basilius," in *Epektasis: Mélanges patristiques offerts au Cardinal Daniélou.* Edited by Jacques Fontaine and Charles Kannengiesser. Paris: Beauchesne, 1972, pp. 463-90.

Hume, David. *A Treatise of Human Nature.* Edited by L. A. Selby-Bigge. Oxford: Oxford University Press, 1958.

Husserl, Edmund. *Introduction to the Prolegomena.* Tübingen: Max Niemeyer, 1900.

Imbach, Rudi, and A. Maierù, eds. *Gli studi di filosofia medievale fra Otto e Novecento. Contributo a un bilancio storiografico. Atti del convegno internazionale, Roma 21-23 settembre 1989.* Rome: Edizioni di storia e letteratura, 1991.

Ingham, Mary Beth. "Re-situating Scotist Thought." *Modern Theology* 21 (2005): 609-18.

Iskandar, A. Z. "Hunayn Ibn Ishāq," in *The Dictionary of Scientific Biography.* Edited by Charles Coulston Gillispie. New York: Charles Scribner's Sons, 1978, vol. XV (suppl. I), pp. 230-49.

Israel, Jonathan I. *Radical Enlightenment: Philosophy and the Making of Modernity, 1650-1750.* Oxford: Oxford University Press, 2001.

———. *Enlightenment Contested: Philosophy, Modernity, and the Emancipation of Man, 1670-1752.* Oxford: Oxford University Press, 2006.

Ivry, Alfred L. *Al-Kindī's Metaphysics.* Albany: State University of New York Press, 1974.

Jacobi, Klaus. "Natürliches Sprechen — Theoriesprache — Theologische Rede. Die Wissenschaftslehre des Gilbert von Poitiers (ca. 1085-1154)." *Zeitschrift für Philosophische Forschung* 49 (1995): 511-28.

————. "Einzelnes — Individuum — Person. Gilbert von Poitiers' Philosophie des Individuellen," in Aertsen and Speer, eds. (1996), pp. 3-22.

————. "Philosophische und theologische Weisheit. Gilbert von Poitiers' Interpretation der 'Regeln' des Boethius *(De hebdomadibus)*," in Berndt et al., eds. (2002), pp. 71-77.

Jameson, Frederic. *The Ideologies of Theory: Essays 1971-1986.* Minneapolis: University of Minnesota Press, 1988.

Janicaud, Dominique. *Le tournant théologique de la phénoménologie française.* Paris: Éditions de l'Éclat, 1991; English translation: *Phenomenology and the "Theological Turn": The French Debate.* New York: Fordham University Press, 2001.

Jolivet, Jean. "Rhétorique et théologie dans une page de Gilbert de Poitiers," in Jolivet and de Libera, eds. (1987), pp. 183-97.

————. *Aspects de la pensée médiévale: Abélard. Doctrines du langage.* Paris: Vrin, 1987.

————. "Trois variations médiévales sur l'universel et l'individu: Roscelin, Abélard, Gilbert de la Porrée." *Revue de métaphysique et de morale* 97 (1992): 111-55.

Jolivet, Jean, and Alain de Libera, eds. *Gilbert de Poitiers et ses contemporains. Aux origins de la logica modernorum.* Naples: Bibliopolis, 1987.

Jordan, Mark D. *Ordering Wisdom: The Hierarchy of Philosophical Discourses in Aquinas.* Notre Dame: University of Notre Dame Press, 1986.

————. *The Alleged Aristotelianism of Thomas Aquinas.* Toronto: Pontifical Institute of Mediaeval Studies, 1992.

Jowett, Benjamin. *The Dialogues of Plato.* Translated by B. Jowett in two vols. New York: Random House, 1937.

Jung, Carl G. *Memories, Dreams, Reflections.* Rev. ed. Edited by C. Winston and translated by R. Winston. New York: Random House, 1989.

Justin Martyr. *First Apology,* in *ANF.* Edited by Alexander Robertson, James Donaldson, and Arthur Cleveland Coxe. New York: Cosimo, 2007 (orig. pub. 1885), Vol. I: *The Apostolic Fathers with Justin Martyr and Irenaeus,* pp. 159-87.

————. *First Apology,* in *ANF.* Edited by Alexander Robertson, James Donaldson, and Arthur Cleveland Coxe. New York: Cosimo, 2007 (orig. pub. 1885), Vol. I: *The Apostolic Fathers with Justin Martyr and Irenaeus,* pp. 188-93.

————. *Dialogue with Trypho,* in *ANF.* Edited by Alexander Robertson, James Donaldson, and Arthur Cleveland Coxe. New York: Cosimo, 2007 (orig. pub. 1885), Vol. I: *The Apostolic Fathers with Justin Martyr and Irenaeus,* pp. 194-270.

Kant, Immanuel. *Kritik der reinen Vernunft,* in *Werke.* Edited by Wilhelm Weischedel. Frankfurt am Main: Insel-Verlag, 1964, vol. 2; English translation: *Critique of Pure Reason.* Edited by P. Guyer and A. W. Wood. Cambridge: Cambridge University Press, 2000.

————. *Kritik der Urteilskraft,* in *Werke.* Edited by Wilhelm Weischedel. Frankfurt am Main: Insel-Verlag, 1964, vol. 5, pp. 173-620; English translation: *Critique of Judgement.* Translated by W. Pluhar. Indianapolis: Hackett, 1987.

————. *Metaphysische Anfangsgründe der Naturwissenschaften,* in *Werke.* Edited by Wilhelm Weischedel. Frankfurt am Main: Insel-Verlag, 1964, vol. 5, pp. 11-135; English translation: *Metaphysical Foundations of Natural Science*, in *Philosophy of Material Nature*. Indianapolis: Hackett, 1985.

————. *Opus Postumum*. Translated and edited by E. Förster. Cambridge: Cambridge University Press, 1993.

Kantorowicz, Ernst H. *The King's Two Bodies: A Study of Political Theology in the Middles Ages*. Princeton: Princeton University Press, 1957.

Kardaun, Maria, and Joke Spruyt, eds. *The Winged Chariot: Collected Essays on Plato and Platonism in Honour of L. M. de Rijk*. Leiden: E. J. Brill, 2000.

Katô, Takeshi. "Melodia interior — Sur le traité *De pulchro et apto*." *Revue des études augustiniennes* 12 (1966): 229-40.

Kelly, C. J. "Abstraction and Existence: A Study on St. Thomas, *In Boethii De Trinitate* q. 5, a. 3." *Laval théologique et philosophique* 21 (1965): 17-42.

Kelly, J. N. D. *Early Christian Doctrines*. 4th ed. London: Adam & Charles Black, 1968.

Kempshall, M. S. *The Common Good in Late Medieval Political Thought*. Oxford: Clarendon Press, 1999.

Kennington, Richard, ed. *The Philosophy of Baruch Spinoza*. Washington, DC: Catholic University of America Press, 1980.

Kenny, Anthony. "Intentionality: Aquinas and Wittgenstein," in Davies, ed. (2002), pp. 243-56.

Kerr, Fergus. *After Aquinas: Versions of Thomism*. Oxford: Blackwell, 2002.

Kierkegaard, Søren. *Fear and Trembling* (1843). Edited by C. Stephen Evans and translated by Sylvia Walsh. Cambridge: Cambridge University Press, 2006.

————. *The Sickness unto Death* (1849). Translated by Howard V. Hong and Edna H. Hong. Princeton: Princeton University Press, 1980.

King, Peter O. *Jean Buridan's Logic*. Dordrecht: D. Reidel, 1985.

————. "Jean Buridan (b. ca. 1295/1300; d. after 1358)," in Gracia, ed. (1994), pp. 397-430.

Klinger, Ingbert. *Das Prinzip der Individuation bei Thomas von Aquin. Versuch einer Interpretation und Vergleich mit zwei umstrittenen Opuscula*. Münsterschwarzach: Vier-Türme-Verlag, 1964.

Klingner, F. *De Boethii Consolatione Philosophiae*. Zurich: Weidmann, 1921.

Klocker, Harry R. *William of Ockham and the Divine Freedom*. Milwaukee: Marquette University Press, 1992.

Klubertanz, George. "St. Thomas and the Knowledge of the Singular." *New Scholasticism* 26 (1952): 135-66.

Knudsen, Christian. "Intentions and Impositions," in Kretzmann et al., eds. (1982), pp. 479-95.

Knuuttila, Simo. "Possibility and Necessity in Gilbert of Poitiers," in Jolivet and de Libera, eds. (1987), pp. 199-218.

————, ed. *Modern Modalities: Studies of the History of Modal Theories from Medieval Nominalism to Logical Positivism*. Dordrecht: Kluwer, 1988.

————. *Modalities in Medieval Philosophy*. London and New York: Routledge, 1993.

————. "On the History of Theory of Modality as Alternativeness," in Buchheim et al., eds. (2001), pp. 219-36.

Knuuttila, Simo, and Lilli Alanen. "The Foundations of Modality and Conceivability in Descartes and His Predecessors," in Knuuttila, ed. (1988), pp. 1-69.

Koistinen, Olli, and John Biro, eds. *Spinoza: Metaphysical Themes*. Oxford: Oxford University Press, 2002.

De Koninck, Thomas. "La 'Pensée de la Pensée' chez Aristote," in *La question de Dieu chez Aristote et Hegel*, ed. Thomas De Koninck. Paris: Presses Universitaires de France, 1991, pp. 69-151.

Krämer, Hans-Joachim. *Plato and the Foundations of Metaphysics*. Translated by John R. Caton. Albany: State University of New York Press, 1990.

Kraut, Richard, ed. *The Cambridge Companion to Plato*. Cambridge: Cambridge University Press, 1992.

Krempel, A. *La doctrine de la relation chez saint Thomas*. Paris: Vrin, 1952.

Kretzmann, Norman. "A General Problem of Creation: Why Would God Create Anything at All?" in MacDonald, ed. (1991), pp. 208-29.

———. *The Metaphysics of Theism: Aquinas' Natural Theology in Summa Contra Gentiles I*. Oxford: Oxford University Press, 1996.

Kretzmann, Norman, ed. *Meaning and Inference in Medieval Philosophy*. Amsterdam: Kluwer, 1988.

Kretzmann, Norman, Anthony Kenny, and Jan Pinborg, eds. *The Cambridge History of Later Medieval Philosophy: From the Rediscovery of Aristotle to the Disintegration of Scholasticism*. Cambridge: Cambridge University Press, 1982.

LaCugna, Catherine M. *God for Us: The Trinity and Christian Life*. San Francisco: Harper, 1991.

Lacey, A. R. "Οὐσία and Form in Aristotle." *Phronesis* 10 (1965): 54-69.

Lachterman, David R. "The Physics of Spinoza's *Ethics*," in Shahan and Biro, eds. (1978), pp. 71-111.

———. *The Ethics of Geometry: A Genealogy of Modernity*. New York and London: Routledge, 1989.

Lacoste, Jean-Yves, ed. *Dictionnaire critique de théologie*. Paris: Presses Universitaires de France, 1998.

Ladrière, Jean. "Préface: Individu et individuation," in Mayaud, ed. (1991), pp. 9-36.

Lancaster, Sarah Heaner. "Three-Personed Substance: The Relational Essence of the Triune God in Augustine's *De Trinitate*." *The Thomist* 60 (1996): 123-39.

Latour, Bruno. *Nous n'avons jamais été modernes: Essai d'anthropologie symétrique*. Paris: Éditions La Découverte, 1991; English translation: *We Have Never Been Modern*. Translated by Catherine Porter. New York and London: Harvester Wheatsheaf, 1993.

Laughland, John. *Schelling versus Hegel: From German Idealism to Christian Metaphysics*. Aldershot, UK: Ashgate, 2007.

Layman, Stephen C. "Tritheism and the Trinity." *Faith and Philosophy* 5 (1988): 291-98.

Le Blond, Jean Marie. *Logique et méthode chez Aristote. Étude sur la recherche des principes dans la physique aristotélicienne*. Paris: Vrin, 1939.

Lee, E. N. "On the Metaphysics of the Image in Plato's *Timaeus*." *The Monist* 49 (1966): 341-68.

Leibniz, Gottfried Wilhelm. *Sämtliche Schriften und Briefe.* 6th ed. Darmstadt: Otto Reich Verlag, 1930.

Leijenhorst, Cornelius H. *The Mechanisation of Aristotelianism: The Late Aristotelian Setting of Thomas Hobbes' Natural Philosophy.* Leiden: E. J. Brill, 2002.

Lesher, James H. *Xenophanes of Colophon: Fragments.* Toronto: University of Toronto Press, 1992.

Levering, Matthew W. *Scripture and Metaphysics: Aquinas and the Renewal of Trinitarian Theology.* Oxford: Blackwell, 2004.

————. "Participation and Exegesis: Response to Catherine Pickstock." *Modern Theology* 21 (2005): 587-601.

Levine, Michael P. *Pantheism: A Non-Theistic Concept of Deity.* New York and London: Routledge, 1994.

Lewry, Osmund. "Boethian Logic in the Medieval West," in Gibson, ed. (1981), pp. 90-134.

de Libera, Alain. *La querelle des universaux. De Platon à la fin du moyen âge.* Paris: Éditions du Seuil, 1996.

————. "Philosophie et censure. Remarques sur la crise universitaire parisienne de 1270-1277," in Aertsen and Speer, eds. (1998), pp. 71-89.

————. *L'art des généralités. Théories de l'abstraction.* Paris: Aubier, 1999.

————. *La philosophie médiévale.* 3rd ed. Paris: Presses Universitaires de France, 2001.

Libera, Alain de, and Cyrille Michon, eds. *L'être et l'essence. Le vocabulaire médiéval de l'ontologie. Deux traités De ente et essentia de Thomas d'Aquin et Dietrich de Freiberg.* Paris: Éditions du Seuil, 1996.

Lienhard, Joseph T., Earl C. Muller, and Roland J. Teske, eds. *Collectanea Augustiniana. Augustine: presbyter factus sum.* New York: Peter Lang, 1993.

Livingstone, E. A., ed. *Studia Patristica: Eighth International Conference on Patristic Studies.* Oxford: Pergamon Press, 1979.

Lloyd, Antony C. "Aristotle's Principle of Individuation." *Mind* 79 (1970): 519-29.

Lloyd, Genevieve. *Part of Nature: Self-knowledge in Spinoza's Ethics.* Ithaca, NY: Cornell University Press, 1994.

Locke, John. *An Essay Concerning Human Understanding.* Edited by P. H. Nidditch. Introduction by Pauline Phemister. Oxford: Oxford University Press, 2008.

Lonergan, Bernard. *Verbum: World and Idea in Aquinas.* New York: Philosophical Library, 1957.

Lossky, Vladimir. "Le sens des 'analogies' chez Denys le Pseudo-Aréopagite." *AHDLMA* 5 (1930): 279-309.

————. *Essai sur la Théologie Mystique de L'Église d'Orient.* Paris: Éditions Cerf, 2005 (orig. pub. 1944); English translation: *The Mystical Theology of the Eastern Church.* Crestwood, NY: St. Vladimir's Seminary Press, 1997 (orig. trans. and pub. 1957).

Louth, Andrew. *Denys the Areopagite.* Wilton, CT: Morehouse-Barlow, 1989.

Loux, Michael J. *Substance and Attribute: A Study in Ontology.* Dordrecht: Reidel, 1978.

de Lubac, Henri. *Surnaturel. Études historiques.* Paris: Aubier-Montaigne, 1946.

————. *Corpus mysticum. L'Eucharistie et l'Église au moyen âge.* Paris: Aubier-Montaigne, 1949.

————. *Exégèse médiévale. Les Quatre Sens de l'Écriture.* 4 vols. Paris: Aubier-Montaigne, 1959-1961.

————. *Pic de la Mirandole. Études et discussions.* Paris: Aubier-Montaigne, 1974.

Lukasiewicz, Jan. "Symposium: The Principle of Individuation I." *Aristotelian Society* suppl. 27 (1953): 69-82.

Lutz-Bachmann, Matthias. "Die Einteilung der Wissenschaften bei Thomas von Aquin. Ein Beitrag zur Rekonstruktion der Epistemologie in Quaestio 5, Artikel 1 des 'Kommentars' von Thomas zum Trinitätstraktat des Boethius," in Berndt et al., eds. (2002), pp. 235-47.

Luyten, Norbert. "Matter as Potency," in McMullin, ed. (1963), pp. 102-23.

Lyotard, Jean-François. *La condition post-moderne. Rapport sur le savoir.* Paris: Éditions de Minuit, 1979; English translation: *The Postmodern Condition: A Report on Knowledge.* Translated by Geoff Bennington and Brian Massumi. Manchester: Manchester University Press, 1984.

MacDonald, Scott. "Augustine's Christian-Platonist Account of Goodness." *The New Scholasticism* 63 (1989): 485-509.

————, ed. *Being and Goodness: The Concept of the Good in Metaphysics and Philosophical Theology.* Ithaca, NY: Cornell University Press, 1991.

MacDonald, Scott, and Eleonore Stump, eds. *Aquinas's Moral Theory: Essays in Honor of Norman Kretzmann.* Ithaca, NY: Cornell University Press, 1999.

Macfarlane, Alan. *The Origins of English Individualism: The Family, Property and Social Transition.* Oxford: Blackwell, 1978.

Machiavelli, Niccolò. *The Prince*, ch. XXV, in idem, *The Chief Works and Others.* Translated by A. Gilbert. Durham, NC: Duke University Press, 1965.

MacIntyre, Alasdair. *After Virtue: A Study in Moral Theory.* 2nd ed. London: Duckworth, 1985.

————. *Whose Justice? Which Rationality?* London: Duckworth, 1988.

————. *Three Rival Versions of Moral Enquiry: Encyclopaedia, Genealogy, and Tradition.* London: Duckworth, 1990.

————. *Dependent Rational Animals: Why Human Beings Need the Virtues.* London: Duckworth, 1999.

MacKinnon, Donald M. "Aristotle's Conception of Substance," in Bambrough, ed. (1965), pp. 97-119.

MacPherson, C. B. *The Political Theory of Possessive Individualism: Hobbes to Locke.* Oxford: Clarendon, 1962.

Madec, Goulven. *Saint Augustin et la Philosophie: Notes Critiques.* Paris: Institut d'Études Augustiniennes, 1996.

Magee, John. *Boethius on Signification and Mind.* Leiden: E. J. Brill, 1989.

Mahdi, Muhsin S. *Alfarabi and the Foundation of Islamic Political Philosophy: Essays in Interpretation.* Chicago: University of Chicago Press, 2001.

Mandonnet, Pierre, ed. *S. Thomae Aquinatis. Scriptum super Sententiis magistri Petri Lombardi.* Paris: Lethielleux, 1929.

Marc, P., C. Pera, and P. Caramello, eds. *S. Thomae Aquinatis. Liber de veritate catholicae Fidei contra errores infidelium seu Summa contra Gentiles.* Rome: Marietti, 1961.

Maréchal, Joseph. *Le point de départ de la métaphysique. Leçons sur le développement historique et théorique du problème de la connaissance.* 5 vols. Paris: Desclée, 1944-1949.

Marenbon, John. *From the Circle of Alcuin to the School of Auxerre: Logic, Theology and Philosophy in the Early Middle Ages.* Cambridge: Cambridge University Press, 1981.

————. "Gilbert of Poitiers," in Dronke, ed. (1988), pp. 328-52 (reprinted in Marenbon [2000], ch. 15).

————. "Boethius: From Antiquity to the Middle Ages," in *Medieval History: Routledge History of Philosophy.* London: Routledge, 1998, vol. 3, ch. 1, pp. 11-28.

————. *Aristotelian Logic, Platonism, and the Context of Early Medieval Philosophy in the West.* Aldershot, UK: Ashgate, 2000.

————. "Gilbert of Poitiers and the Porretans on Mathematics in the Division of Sciences," in Berndt et al., eds. (2002), pp. 37-69.

————. *Boethius.* Oxford: Oxford University Press, 2003.

Maritain, Jacques. *Distinguer pour unir. Ou, Les degrés du savoir.* Paris: Desclée, 1932.

————. *Sept Leçons sur l'Être et les premiers principes de la raison spéculative.* Paris: Pierre Téqui, 1934.

————. *The Person and the Common Good.* Notre Dame: University of Notre Dame Press, 1947.

————. "Réflexions sur la nature blessée et sur l'intuition de l'être." *Revue thomiste* 68 (1968): 5-41.

Marion, Jean-Luc. *Sur l'ontologie grise de Descartes: Science cartésienne et savoir aristotélicien dans les Regulae.* 2nd ed. Paris: Vrin, 1981.

————. *Sur la théologie blanche de Descartes. Analogie, création des vérités éternelles et fondement.* Paris: Presses Universitaires de France, 1981.

————. "Descartes et l'Onto-théologie." *Bulletin de la Société Française de Philosophie* 76 (1982): 117-71; English translation: "Descartes and Onto-Theology." Translated by Bettina Bergo, in Blond, ed. (1997), pp. 66-107.

————. "Une époque de la métaphysique," in Goëmé, ed. (1982), pp. 87-95.

————. *Sur le prisme métaphysique de Descartes. Constitution et limites de l'onto-théologie dans la pensée cartésienne.* Paris: Presses Universitaires de France, 1986.

————. *Réduction et donation. Recherches sur Husserl, Heidegger et la phénoménologie.* Paris: Presses Universitaires de France, 1989.

————. *L'idole et la distance. Cinq études.* 3rd ed. Paris: Biblio-Essais, 1991 (orig. pub. Paris: Éditions Grasset & Fasquelle, 1977).

————. *Dieu sans l'être.* 2nd ed. Paris: Presses Universitaires de France, collec. 'Quadrige,' 1991 (orig. pub. Paris: Éditions Fayard, 1982).

————. "Saint Thomas et l'onto-théo-logie." *Revue thomiste* 95 (1995): 31-66.

————. *Étant donné. Essai de phénoménologie de la donation.* Rev. ed. Paris: Presses Universitaires de France, 1997.

————. *De surcroît. Études sur les phénomènes saturés.* Paris: Presses Universitaires de France, 2001.

————. *Le phénomène érotique.* Paris: LGF, 2004.

————. *Le visible et le révélé.* Paris: Éditions Cerf, 2005.

————. *Au lieu de soi. L'approche de Saint Augustin.* Paris: Presses Universitaires de France, 2008.

Markus, Robert A. *Christianity in the Roman World.* London: Thames & Hudson, 1974.

————. *Saeculum: History and Society in the Theology of St Augustine.* Rev. ed. Cambridge: Cambridge University Press, 1988 (orig. pub. 1970).

Mason, Richard V. *The God of Spinoza: A Philosophical Study.* Cambridge: Cambridge University Press, 1997.

Matheron, Alexandre. *Individu et communauté chez Spinoza.* Le sens commun. Paris: Les Éditions de Minuit, 1988 (orig. pub. 1969).

————. "Essence, Existence and Power in *Ethics* I: The Foundations of Proposition 16," in Yovel, ed. (1991), pp. 23-34.

————. "Ideas of Ideas and Certainty in the *Tractatus de Intellectus Emendatione* and the *Ethics*," in Yovel, ed. (1994), pp. 83-91.

Matthews, Gareth B. *Thought's Ego in Augustine and Descartes.* Ithaca, NY: Cornell University Press, 1992.

Matthews, Gareth B., and S. Marc Cohen. "The One and the Many." *Review of Metaphysics* 21 (1967-68): 630-55.

Maurer, Armand. *St. Thomas Aquinas: The Division and Methods of the Sciences. Questions V and VI of His Commentary on the* De Trinitate *of Boethius.* 3rd rev. ed. Translated with introduction and notes. Toronto: The Pontifical Institute of Mediaeval Studies, 1963.

————. *Saint Thomas Aquinas: On Being and Essence.* Translated with introduction and notes. 2nd rev. ed. Toronto: The Pontifical Institute of Mediaeval Studies, 1968.

————. "Method in Ockham's Nominalism." *Monist* 61 (1978): 426-43.

————. "Ockham's Razor and Chatton's Anti-Razor." *MS* 46 (1984): 463-75.

————. *St. Thomas Aquinas: Faith, Reason and Theology. Questions I-IV of His Commentary on the* De Trinitate *of Boethius.* Translated with introduction and notes. Toronto: The Pontifical Institute of Mediaeval Studies, 1987.

————. "William of Ockham (b. ca. 1285; d. 1347)," in Gracia, ed. (1994), pp. 373-96.

Mayaud, Pierre-Noël, ed. *Le problème de l'individuation.* Paris: Vrin, 1991.

McCabe, Mary M. *Plato's Individuals.* Princeton: Princeton University Press, 1994.

McCullough, Laurence B. "Leibniz's Principle of Individuation in His *Disputatio metaphysica de principio individui* of 1663," in Barber and Gracia, eds. (1994), pp. 201-17.

————. *Leibniz on Individuals and Individuation: The Persistence of Premodern Ideas in Modern Philosophy.* Dordrecht: Kluwer Academic, 1996.

McGrade, A. S. *The Political Thought of William of Ockham.* Cambridge: Cambridge University Press, 1974.

McInerny, Ralph. *Being and Predication: Thomistic Interpretations*. Washington, DC: Catholic University of America Press, 1986.

———. *Aquinas and Analogy.* Washington, DC: Catholic University of America Press, 1996.

McMullin, Ernan, ed. *The Concept of Matter in Greek and Medieval Philosophy.* Notre Dame: University of Notre Dame Press, 1963.

McShea, Robert J. "Spinoza on Power." *Inquiry* 1 (1969): 133-43.

Meillassoux, Quentin. *Après la finitude: essai sur la nécessité de la contingence.* Paris: Seuil, 2006.

Meiser, Karl. *Ancii Manlii Severini Boetii in librum Aristotelis Peri Hermeneias.* Leipzig: B. G. Teubner, 1880.

Menn, Stephen P. *Descartes and Augustine.* Cambridge: Cambridge University Press, 1998.

Merlan, P. "Abstraction and Metaphysics in St. Thomas' Summa." *Journal of the History of Ideas* 14 (1953): 284-91.

———. *From Platonism to Neoplatonism.* 3rd ed. The Hague: Nijhoff, 1968.

Mews, Constant J. "Nominalism and Theology before Abaelard: New Light on Roscelin of Compiègne." *Vivarium* 30 (1992): 4-33.

Migne, Jean-Paul. *Santi Aurelii Augustini opera omnia.* Paris: Montrouge, 1841. *PL* 32-45.

———. *Manlii Severini Boetii opera omnia.* Paris: Montrouge, 1847. *PL* 64.

Milbank, John. *Theology and Social Theory: Beyond Secular Reason.* Oxford: Blackwell, 1990.

———. *The Religious Dimension in the Thought of Giambattista Vico, 1668-1744.* 2 vols. Lampeter, UK: Edwin Mellen Press, 1991.

———. "Sacred Triads: Augustine and the Indo-European Soul." *Modern Theology* 13 (1997): 451-74.

———. *The Word Made Strange: Theology, Language, Culture.* Oxford: Blackwell, 1997.

———. *The Suspended Middle: Henri de Lubac and the Debate concerning the Supernatural.* Grand Rapids: Eerdmans, 2005.

———. "Only Theology Saves Metaphysics: On the Modalities of Terror," in *Belief and Metaphysics.* Edited by Conor Cunningham and Peter M. Candler Jr. London: SCM, 2007, pp. 452-500.

———. "Paul against Biopolitics." *Theory, Culture & Society* 25 (2008): 125-72.

———. "Sophiology and Theurgy: The New Theological Horizon," in *Encounter between Eastern Orthodoxy and Radical Orthodoxy: Transfiguring the World through the Word.* Edited by Adrian Pabst and Christoph Schneider. Aldershot, UK: Ashgate, 2009, pp. 45-85.

———. "The New Divide: Romantic versus Classical Orthodoxy." *Modern Theology* 26 (2010): 26-38.

———. "The Mystery of Reason," in *The Grandeur of Reason: Religion, Tradition and Universalism.* Edited by Peter M. Candler Jr. and Conor Cunningham. London: SCM, 2010, ch. 4

———. "The Real Third Way." In *The Crisis of Global Capitalism: Pope Benedict XVI's*

Social Encyclical and the Future of Political Economy. Edited by Adrian Pabst. Eugene, OR: Cascade Books, 2011, pp. 27-70.

Milbank, John, Catherine Pickstock, and Graham Ward, eds. *Radical Orthodoxy: A New Theology.* London: Routledge, 1999.

Milbank, John, and Catherine Pickstock. *Truth in Aquinas.* London and New York: Routledge, 2001.

Montag, John, SJ. "Revelation: The False Legacy of Suárez," in Milbank et al., eds. (1999), pp. 38-63.

Moore, Robert I. *The Formation of a Persecuting Society: Power and Deviance in Western Europe, 950-1250.* Oxford: Blackwell, 1990.

Moos, M. F. ed. *Scriptum super Sententiis magistri petri Lombardi,* vols. 3 and 4. Paris: Lethielleux, 1956.

Moran, Dermot. *Introduction to Phenomenology.* London: Routledge, 2000.

Moreau, Pierre-François, ed. *Architectures de la raison: Mélanges offerts à Alexandre Matheron.* Fontenay-aux-Roses: ENS Éditions, 1996.

Muller-Thym, Bernard J. "The Common Sense, Perfection of the Order of Pure Sensibility." *The Thomist* 2 (1940): 315-43.

de Muralt, André. "Epoché — Malin Génie — Théologie de la toute puissance divine. Le concept objectif sans objet, recherche d'une structure de pensée." *Studia Philosophica* 26 (1966): 159-91.

———. "Kant, le dernier occamien. Une nouvelle définition de la philosophie moderne." *Revue de Métaphysique et de Morale* 80 (1975): 32-53.

———. "La structure de la philosophie politique moderne." *Souveraineté et pouvoir. Cahiers de la Revue de Théologie et de Philosophie* 2 (1978): 3-84.

———. "La doctrine médiévale des distinctions et l'intelligibilité de la philosophie moderne (I) et (II)." *Revue de théologie et de philosophie* 112 (1980): 113-32, 217-40.

———. *La métaphysique du phénomène. Les origines médiévales et l'élaboration de la pensée phénoménologique.* Paris: Vrin, 1985.

———. *L'Enjeu de la philosophie médiévale. Études thomistes, scotistes, occamiennes et grégoriennes.* Leiden: E. J. Brill, 1991.

———. "La causalité aristotélicienne et la structure de pensée scotiste." *Dialectica* 47 (1993): 121-41.

———. *Néoplatonisme et aristotélisme dans la métaphysique médiévale. Analogie, causalité, participation.* Paris: Vrin, 1995.

———. *L'unité de la philosophie politique. De Scot, Occam et Suarez au liberalisme contemporain.* Paris: Vrin, 2002.

Murdoch, J. E. "Piere Duhem and the History of Late Medieval Science and Philosophy in the Latin West," in Imbach and Maierù, eds. (1991), pp. 253-302.

———. "1277 and Late Medieval Natural Philosophy," in Aertsen and Speer, eds. (1998), pp. 111-21.

Narcisse, Gilbert. *Les raisons de Dieu. Arguments de convenance et esthétique théologique selon St. Thomas d'Aquin et Hans Urs von Balthasar.* Fribourg: Éditions Universitaires Fribourg Suisse, 1997.

Negri, Antonio. *L'anomalia selvaggia. Saggio su potere e potenza in Baruch Spinoza.*

Milan: Feltrinelli, 1981; English translation: *The Savage Anomaly: The Power of Spinoza's Metaphysics and Politics*. Translated and edited by Michael Hardt. Minneapolis: University of Minnesota Press, 1991.

Nehamas, Alexander. "Participation and Predication in Plato's Late Dialogues." *Review of Metaphysics* 32 (1982): 343-74.

Neumann, Siegfried. *Gegenstand und Methode der theoretischen Wissenschaften nach Thomas von Aquin aufgrund der* Expositio super librum Boethii De Trinitate. Münster/Westfalen: Aschendorfsche Verlagsbuchhandlung, 1965.

Nielsen, Lauge Olaf. "On the Doctrine of Logic and Language of Gilbert Porreta and His Followers." *Cahiers de l'Institut du Moyen Âge Grec et Latin* 17 (1976): 40-69.

———. *Philosophy and Theology in the Twelfth Century: A Study of Gilbert Porreta's Thinking and the Theological Expositions of the Doctrine of the Incarnation during the Period 1130-1180*. Leiden: E. J. Brill, 1982.

———. "Peter Abelard and Gilbert of Poitiers," in Evans, ed. (2001), pp. 102-28.

Nietzsche, Friedrich. *On the Genealogy of Morals*. Translated by Douglas Smith. Oxford: Oxford University Press, 1996.

———. *The Twilight of the Idols*. Translated by Duncan Large. Oxford: Oxford University Press, 1998.

———. *The Antichrist*. Translated by Thomas Common. Mineola, NY: Dover Publications, 2004.

Novak, Michael. *Free Persons and the Common Good*. Lanham, MD: Madison Books, 1989.

Nussbaum, Martha C. "Nature, Function, and Capability: Aristotle on Political Distribution." *OSAP* Suppl. (1988): 144-84.

———. *The Fragility of Goodness: Luck and Ethics in Greek Tragedy and Philosophy*. Cambridge: Cambridge University Press, 1991.

———. "Human Functioning and Social Justice: In Defence of Aristotelian Essentialism." *Political Theory* 20 (1992): 202-46.

Oakeshott, Michael. *Rationalism in Politics and Other Essays*. Indianapolis: Liberty Fund, 1991.

Obertello, Luca, ed. *Atti di Congresso Internazionale di Studi Boeziani*. Rome: Herder, 1981.

O'Collins, Gerald. *Christology: A Biblical, Historical and Systematic Study of Jesus Christ*. Oxford: Oxford University Press, 1995.

O'Connell, Robert J. *St. Augustine's Early Theory of Man, AD 386-391*. Cambridge, MA: Belknap Press of Harvard University Press, 1968.

———. *Saint Augustine's Platonism*. Villanova, PA: Villanova University Press, 1984.

O'Donnell, Robert A. "Individuation: An Example of the Development in the Thought of St. Thomas Aquinas." *New Scholasticism* 33 (1959): 49-67.

O'Meara, Dominic J., ed. *Neoplatonism and Christian Thought*. Albany: State University of New York Press, 1982.

———. *Platonopolis: Platonic Political Philosophy in Late Antiquity*. Oxford: Clarendon Press, 2003.

O'Meara, John J. "The Neoplatonism of Saint Augustine," in O'Meara, ed. (1982), pp. 34-41.

O'Rourke, Fran. *Pseudo-Dionysius and the Metaphysics of Aquinas*. Leiden: E. J. Brill, 1992.

Owen, Gwilym E. L. "Logic and Metaphysics in Some Early Works of Aristotle," in Düring and Owen, eds. (1960), pp. 162-90.

————. "Eleatic Questions." *The Classical Quarterly*, n.s. 10 (1960): 84-102.

Owens, Joseph. *St. Thomas Aquinas and the Future of Metaphysics*. Milwaukee: Marquette University Press, 1957.

————. "Thomistic Common Nature and Platonic Idea." *MS* 21 (1959): 211-23.

————. "Matter and Predication in Aristotle," in McMullin, ed. (1963), pp. 79-101.

————. "Aquinas on Knowing Existence." *Review of Metaphysics* 29 (1976): 670-90 (reprinted in Catan, ed. [1980], pp. 20-33).

————. "The Relation of God to the World in the *Metaphysics*," in Aubenque, ed. (1979), pp. 207-28.

————. "Aquinas' Distinction at *De Ente et Essentia* 4.119-123." *MS* 48 (1986): 264-87.

————. "Thomas Aquinas: Dimensive Quantity as Individuating Principle." *MS* 50 (1988): 279-310.

————. "Thomas Aquinas (b. ca. 1225; d. 1274)," in Gracia, ed. (1994), pp. 173-94.

Ozilou, Marc. "Introduction générale," in *Saint Bonaventure: Les Sentences, Questions sur Dieu, Commentaire du premier livre des sentences de Pierre Lombard*. Edited by M. Ozilou. Paris: Presses Universitaires de France, 2002.

Pabst, Adrian. "De la chrétienté à la modernité. Une lecture critique des thèses de *Radical Orthodoxy* sur la rupture scotiste et ockhamienne et sur le renouveau de la théologie de Saint Thomas." *Revue des Sciences Philosophiques et Théologiques* 86 (2002): 561-99.

————. "Jean-Luc Marion," in *Introduction à la phénoménologie contemporaine*. Edited by Philippe Cabestan. Paris: Éditions Ellipses, 2005, pp. 83-96.

————. "The Primacy of Relation over Substance and the Recovery of a Theological Metaphysics." *American Catholic Philosophical Quarterly* 81 (Fall 2007): 553-78.

————. "On the Theological Origins of the Secular Market State," in *The Migration of Ideas*. Edited by Roberto Scazzieri and Raffaella Simili. Sagamore Beach, MA: Watson International Publishing, 2008, pp. 99-122.

————. "Wisdom and the Art of Politics," in *Encounter between Eastern Orthodoxy and Radical Orthodoxy: Transfiguring the World through the Word*. Edited by Adrian Pabst and Christoph Schneider. Aldershot, UK: Ashgate, 2009, pp. 109-37.

————. "Sovereign Reason Unbound," in *The Grandeur of Reason: Religion, Tradition and Universalism*. Edited by Peter M. Candler Jr. and Conor Cunningham. London: SCM, 2010, pp. 135-66.

————. "Modern Sovereignty in Question: Theology, Democracy and Capitalism." *Modern Theology* 26 (October 2010): 570-602.

————. "The Crisis of Capitalist Democracy." *Telos* 152 (Winter 2010): 44-67.

————. "The Paradoxical Nature of the Good: Relationality, Sympathy, and Mutuality in Rival Traditions of Civil Economy," in *The Crisis of Global Capitalism: Pope*

Benedict XVI's Social Encyclical and the Future of Political Economy. Edited by Adrian Pabst. Eugene, OR: Cascade Books, 2011, pp. 173-206.

Paolinelli, Marco. "Metodo matematico e ontologia in Christian Wolff." *Rivista di Filosofia Neo-scholastica* 66 (1974): 3-39.

Pasnau, Robert. *Theories of Cognition in the Later Middle Ages*. Cambridge: Cambridge University Press, 1997.

Patzig, Günther. "Theology and Ontology in Aristotle's Metaphysics," in *Articles on Aristotle*. Edited by Jonathan Barnes, Malcolm Schofield, and Richard Sorabji. London: Duckworth, 1979, vol. 3, pp. 33-49.

Peck, A. L. "Plato versus Parmenides." *Philosophical Review* 71 (1962): 159-84.

Pelletier, Francis J., and John King-Farlow, eds. *New Essays on Aristotle*. Calgary, AB: University of Calgary Press, 1984.

Pera, C., P. Caramello, and C. Mazzantini, eds. *S. Thomae Aquinatis. In librum Beati Dionysii De divinis nominibus expositio*. Rome: Marietti, 1950.

Perczel, Istvân. "Pseudo-Dionysius and the Platonic Theology: A Preliminary Study," in *Proclus et la Théologie Platonicienne*. Edited by A. Ph. Segonds and C. Steel. Leuven: Leuven University Press, 2000, pp. 492-530.

Perl, Eric D. *Theophany: The Neoplatonic Philosophy of Dionysius the Areopagite*. Albany: State University of New York Press, 2007.

Perrier, Emmanuel, OP. "Duns Scotus Facing Reality: Between Absolute Contingency and Unquestionable Consistency." *Modern Theology* 21 (2005): 619-43.

Pession, P. M., ed. *S. Thomae Aquinatis. Quaestiones disputatae de potentia*. 10th ed. Rome: Marietti, 1965.

Piché, David, ed. *La condamnation parisienne de 1277. Texte latin, traduction, introduction et commentaire*. Paris: Vrin, 1999.

Pickstock, Catherine. *After Writing: On the Liturgical Consummation of Philosophy*. Oxford: Blackwell, 1998.

———. "Music: Soul, City and Cosmos after Augustine," in Milbank et al., eds. (1999), pp. 243-77.

———. "Justice and Prudence: Principles of Order in the Platonic City." *Telos* 119 (2001): 3-17.

———. "The Soul in Plato," in *Explorations in Contemporary Continental Philosophy of Religion*. Edited by Deane-Peter Baker and Patrick Maxwell. Amsterdam and New York: Editions Rodopi B. V., 2003, pp. 115-26.

———. "Modernity and Scholasticism: A Critique of Recent Invocations of Univocity." *Antonianum* 78 (2003): 3-46.

———. "Postmodern Scholasticism: Critique of Postmodern Univocity." *Telos* 126 (2003): 3-24.

———. "Duns Scotus: His Historical and Contemporary Significance." *Modern Theology* 21 (2005): 543-74.

———. *Theory, Religion and Idiom in Platonic Philosophy*. Oxford: Blackwell, forthcoming.

Pinborg, Jan. "Zum Begriff der Intentio Secunda — Radulphus Brito, Harvaeus

Natalis und Petrus Aureoli in Diskussion." *Cahiers de l'Institut du Moyen-Age grec et latin* 13 (1974): 49-59.

Pinchard, Bruno. "Le principe d'individuation dans la tradition aristotélicienne," in Mayaud, ed. (1991), pp. 27-50.

Pinto de Oliveira, Carlos-Josaphat, ed. *Ordo Sapientiae et Amoris. Image et message de saint Thomas d'Aquin à travers les récentes études historiques, herméneutiques et doctrinales. Hommage au Professeur Jean-Pierre Torrell, OP.* Fribourg: Éditions Universitaires, 1993.

Pippin, Robert. *Persistence of Subjectivity: On the Kantian Aftermath.* Cambridge: Cambridge University Press, 2005.

Planinc, Zdravko. *Plato's Political Philosophy: Prudence in the* Republic *and the* Laws. Columbia: University of Missouri Press, 1991.

Plantinga, Cornelius. "Gregory of Nyssa and the Social Analogy of the Trinity." *The Thomist* 50 (1986): 325-52.

————. "Social Trinity and Tritheism," in Plantinga and Feenstra, eds. (1989), pp. 21-47.

Plantinga, Cornelius, and Ronald Feenstra, eds. *Trinity, Incarnation and Atonement: Philosophical and Theological Essays.* Notre Dame: University of Notre Dame Press, 1989.

Polanyi, Karl. *The Great Transformation: The Political and Economic Origins of Our Time.* Boston: Beacon Press, 2000 (orig. pub. 1944).

Popkin, Richard H. *The History of Skepticism from Erasmus to Spinoza.* Berkeley: University of California Press, 1979.

Popper, Karl. "Symposium: The Principle of Individuation III." *Aristotelian Society* suppl. 27 (1953): 97-120.

Radner, Michael. "Substance and Phenomenal Substance: Kant's Individuation of Things in Themselves and Appearances," in Barber and Gracia, eds. (1994), pp. 245-65.

Raeymaeker, Louis de. *Philosophie de l'être. Essai de synthèse métaphysique.* 2nd ed. Louvain: Editions Nauwelaerts, 1947.

Rahner, Karl. *Geist in Welt. Zur Metaphysik der endlichen Erkenntnis bei Thomas von Aquin.* 2nd ed. rev. Munich: Kösel-Verlag, 1957; English translation: *Spirit in the World.* Translated by A. Dych. New York: Herder & Herder, 1968.

————. "Aquinas: The Nature of Truth." *Continuum* 2 (1964): 60-72.

Ramond, Charles. *Quantité et qualité dans la philosophie de Spinoza.* Paris: Presses Universitaires de France, 1995.

Rapp, Christof, ed. *Aristoteles, Metaphysik, die Substanzbücher* ([*Zeta*], [*Eta*], [*Theta*]). Berlin: Akademie Verlag, 1996.

Ratzinger, Joseph/Pope Benedict XVI. *Introduction to Christianity.* New York: Herder & Herder, 1970.

————. "Concerning the Person in Theology." *Communio* 17 (1990): 438-54.

————. *Glaube und Vernunft. Die Regensburger Vorlesung.* Freiburg: Herder, 2006; English translation: *The Regensburg Lecture.* Translated by James V. Schall, SJ. Chicago: St. Augustine's Press, 2007.

Reeve, C. D. C. *Substantial Knowledge: Aristotle's Metaphysics.* Indianapolis: Hackett, 2000.

Reisman, David C. "Al-Fārābī and the Philosophical Curriculum," in *The Cambridge Companion to Arabic Philosophy.* Edited by Peter Adamson and Richard C. Taylor. Cambridge: Cambridge University Press, 2005, pp. 52-71.

Rice, Lee C. "Spinoza on Individuation." *The Monist* 55 (1971): 640-59.

Riches, Aaron. "After Chalcedon: The Oneness of Christ and the Dyothelite Mediation of His Theandric Unity." *Modern Theology* 24 (2008): 199-224.

————. *Christ: The End of Humanism.* Grand Rapids: Eerdmans, forthcoming.

Ridley, Matt. *The Origins of Virtue.* London: Penguin, 1996.

Rijk, Lambertus M. de. "Boèce logicien et philosophe. Ses positions sémantiques et sa métaphysique de l'être," in Obertello, ed. (1981), pp. 141-56.

————. "Gilbert de Poitiers, ses vues métaphysiques et sémantiques," in Jolivet and de Libera, eds. (1987), pp. 147-71.

————. "On Boethius' Notion of Being: A Chapter on Boethian Semantics," in Kretzmann, ed. (1988), pp. 1-29.

————. "Semantics and Metaphysics in Gilbert of Poitiers: A Chapter of Twelfth-Century Platonism (1)." *Vivarium* 26 (1988): 73-122.

————. "Semantics and Metaphysics in Gilbert of Poitiers: A Chapter of Twelfth-Century Platonism (2)." *Vivarium* 27 (1989): 1-35.

————. "John Buridan on Universals." *Revue de Métaphysique et de Morale* 97 (1992): 35-59.

Rist, John M. *Eros and Psyche: Studies in Plato, Plotinus, and Origen.* Toronto: University of Toronto Press, 1964.

————. "The Immanence and Transcendence of the Platonic Form." *Philologus* 108 (1964): 217-32.

————. *Plotinus: The Road to Reality.* Cambridge: Cambridge University Press, 1967.

————. "The One of Plotinus and the God of Aristotle." *Review of Metaphysics* 27 (1973): 75-87 (reprinted in Rist [1985], ch. 9).

————. "Basil's 'Neoplatonism': Its Background and Nature," in Fedwick, ed. (1981), pp. 137-220 (reprinted in Rist [1985], ch. 12).

————. *Platonism and Its Christian Heritage.* London: Variorum, 1985.

————. "Plotinus and Christian Philosophy," in Gerson, ed. (1996), pp. 386-413.

Robertson, John. *The Case for the Enlightenment: Scotland and Naples 1680-1760.* Cambridge: Cambridge University Press, 2005.

Roche, W. J. "Measure, Number and Weight in Saint Augustine." *The New Scholasticism* 15 (1941): 350-76.

Roques, René. *L'univers dionysien. Structure hiérarchique du monde selon le Pseudo-Denys.* Paris: Éditions Cerf, 1983.

Rorty, Richard. "Genus as Matter: A Reading of *Metaphysics* Z-H." *Phronesis* suppl. 1 (1973): 393-420.

Rosemann, Philipp W. *Omne ens est aliquid: Introduction à la lecture du "système" philosophique de saint Thomas d'Aquin.* Louvain and Paris: Ed. Peeters, 1996.

————. *Omne ens agit sibi simile: A "Repetition" of Scholastic Metaphysics.* Leuven: Leuven University Press, 1996.

Rotelle, John E., ed. *Saint Augustine: The Trinity.* Introduction, translation, and notes by Edmund Hill. The Works of Saint Augustine: A Translation for the 21st Century, part 1, vol. 5. New York: New City Press, 1991.

————. *Saint Augustine: The Confessions.* Introduction, translation, and notes by Maria Boulding. London: Hodder & Stoughton, 1997.

————. *Saint Augustine: On Genesis.* Introduction, translation, and notes by Edmund Hill. The Works of Saint Augustine: A Translation for the 21st Century, part 1, vol. 13. New York: New City Press, 2002.

Rowe, William V. "Adolf von Harnack and the Concept of Hellenization," in *Hellenization Revisited.* Edited by Wendy Hellman. Lanham, MD: University Press of America, 1994, pp. 69-98.

Russell, Bertrand. *A History of Western Philosophy.* London: Routledge, 2004 (orig. pub. 1945).

Sacksteder, William. "Spinoza on Part and Whole: The Worm's Eye View," in Shahan and Biro, eds. (1978), pp. 139-59.

Saffrey, Henri D., ed. *Thomas d'Aquin. Super librum de causis expositio.* Paris: Vrin, 1954.

Sayre, Kenneth M. *Plato's Late Ontology: A Riddle Resolved.* Princeton: Princeton University Press, 1983.

Scaltsas, Theodore, David Charles, and Mary Louise Gill, eds. *Unity, Identity, and Explanation in Aristotle's Metaphysics.* Oxford: Clarendon Press, 1994.

Schmidt, Martin A. *Gottheit und Trinität nach dem Kommentar des Gilbert Porreta zu Boethius De Trinitate.* Basel: Philosophische Gesellschaft, 1956.

Schmitt, Carl. *The Nomos of the Earth in the International Law of the Jus Publicum Europaeum.* Translated by Gary L. Ulmen. New York: Telos Press Publishing, 2003.

Schmitt, F. S. *Anselmi Opera Omnia.* Rome and Edinburgh, 1938-1968.

Schmutz, Jacob. "La doctrine médiévale des causes et la théologie de la nature pure (XIIIe-XVIIe siècles)." *Revue thomiste* 101 (2001): 217-64.

Schnaubelt, Joseph C., and Frederick van Fleteren, eds. *Collectanea Augustiniana. Augustine: "Second Founder of the Faith."* New York: Peter Lang, 1990.

Scholz, Richard. *Wilhelm von Ockham als politischer Denker und sein Breviloquium de principatu tyrannico.* Stuttgart: Hiersemann, 1952.

Schönberger, Rolf. *Relation als Vergleich. Die Relationstheorie des Johannes Buridan im Kontext seines Denken und der Scholastik.* Leiden: E. J. Brill, 1994.

Schultz, Janice L., and Edward A. Synan. *Saint Thomas Aquinas: An Exposition of the "On the Hebdomads" of Boethius.* Washington, DC: Catholic University of America Press, 2001.

Schumacher, Lydia. *Divine Illumination: The History and Future of Augustine's Theory of Knowledge.* Oxford: Wiley-Blackwell, 2011.

Scott, T. K. *Johannes Buridanus. Sophismata.* Stuttgart: Frommann-Holzboog, 1977.

Seigel, Jerrold E. *The Idea of the Self: Thought and Experience in Western Europe Since the Seventeenth Century.* Cambridge: Cambridge University Press, 2005.

Sellars, Wilfrid. "Vlastos and the Third Man." *Philosophical Review* 64 (1955): 405-37.

————. "Substance and Form in Aristotle." *Journal of Philosophy* 54, no. 22 (1957): 688-99.

Shahan, Robert W., and John I. Biro, eds. *Spinoza: New Perspectives.* Norman: University of Oklahoma, 1978.

Shapin, Steven, and Simon Schaffer. *Leviathan and the Air-Pump: Hobbes, Boyle, and the Experimental Life.* Princeton: Princeton University Press, 1985.

Shaw, Gregory. *Theurgy and the Soul: The Neoplatonism of Iamblichus.* University Park: Pennsylvania State University Press, 1995.

Shults, F. LeRon. *Reforming Theological Anthropology: After the Philosophical Turn to Relationality.* Grand Rapids: Eerdmans, 2003.

Simondon, Gilbert. *L'individu et sa genèse physico-biologique (l'individuation à la lumière des notions de forme et d'information).* Paris: Presses Universitaires de France, 1964.

Solovyov, Vladimir. *The Crisis of Western Philosophy* (1873). *Against the Positivists.* Translated and edited by Boris Jakim. Hudson, NY: Lindisfarne Press, 1996.

————. *Lectures on Divine Humanity* (1880). Translated and edited by Boris Jakim. Hudson, NY: Lindisfarne Press, 1995.

Sondag, Gérard. *Duns Scot. La métaphysique de la singularité.* Paris: Vrin, 2005.

Sorabji, Richard, ed. *Aristotle Transformed: The Ancient Commentators and Their Influence.* London: Duckworth, 1990.

Spade, Paul Vincent. *Five Texts on the Medieval Problem of Universals: Porphyry, Boethius, Abelard, Duns Scotus, Ockham.* Indianapolis: Hackett, 1994.

————. "Degrees of Being, Degrees of Goodness: Aquinas on Levels of Reality," in MacDonald and Stump, eds. (1999), pp. 254-75.

Spaemann, Robert. *Personen: Versuche über den Unterschied zwischen 'etwas' und 'jemand.'* Stuttgart: Klett-Cotta, 1998.

Speer, Andreas. "'Yliathin quod est principium individuandi' — Zur Diskussion um das Individuationsprinzip im Anschluß an prop. 8[9] des 'Liber de causis' bei Johannes de Nova Domo, Albertus Magnus und Thomas von Aquin," in Aertsen and Speer, eds. (1996), pp. 266-86.

Spruit, Leen. *Species Intelligibilis: From Perception to Knowledge.* Leiden: E. J. Brill, 1994, vol. 1.

————. *Species Intelligibilis: From Perception to Knowledge.* Leiden: E. J. Brill, 1995, vol. 2.

Spruyt, Joke. "Gilbert of Poitiers on the Application of Language to the Transcendent and Sublunary Domains," in Kardaun and Spruyt, eds. (2000), pp. 205-35.

Stalnaker, Robert. "Anti-Essentialism." *Midwest Studies in Philosophy* 4 (1979): 343-55.

Steenberghen, Fernand van. *Thomas Aquinas and Radical Aristotelianism.* Washington, DC: Catholic University of America Press, 1980.

Stewart, H. F., E. K. Rand, and S. J. Tester, eds. *Boethius: The Theological Tractates.* Cambridge, MA: Harvard University Press, 1973.

Stokes, Michael C. *One and Many in Pre-Socratic Philosophy.* Cambridge: Harvard University Press, 1972.

Stolarski, Grzegorz. *La possibilité et l'être: Un essai sur la détermination du fondement ontologique de la possibilité dans la pensée de Thomas d'Aquin.* Fribourg: Éditions Universitaires, 2001.

Stone Haring, Ellen. "Substantial Form in Aristotle's *Metaphysics Z.*" *Review of Metaphysics* 10 (1956-57): 308-32, 482-501, 698-713.

Strayer, Joseph R. *On the Medieval Origins of the Modern State.* Princeton: Princeton University Press, 1970.

Studer, Basil. *Trinity and Incarnation: The Faith of the Early Church.* Edinburgh: T. & T. Clark, 1993.

Swinburne, Richard. *The Christian God.* Oxford: Oxford University Press, 1994.

Taylor, Charles. *Sources of the Self: The Making of Modern Identity.* Cambridge, MA: Harvard University Press, 1989.

————. *A Secular Age.* Cambridge, MA: Harvard University Press, 2007.

Tertullian. *"De praescriptione haereticorum,"* in *ANF,* ed. Alexander Robertson, James Donaldson, and Arthur Cleveland Coxe. New York: Cosimo, 2007 (orig. pub. 1885), Vol. III: *Latin Christianity,* pp. 243-65.

Teschke, Benno. *The Myth of 1648: Class, Geopolitics and the Making of Modern International Relations.* London: Verso, 2003.

Théry, G. "L'Augustinisme médiéval et le problème de l'unité de la forme substantielle," in *Acta Hebdomadae Augustinianae-Thomisticae* (Rome, 1931).

Thijssen, H. "1277 Revisited." *Vivarium* 35 (1997): 72-101.

Tierney, Brian. *The Crisis of Church and State, 1050-1300.* Englewood Cliffs, NJ: Prentice Hall, 1964.

Todd, Emmanuel. *Après la démocratie.* Paris: Gallimard, 2008.

Toscano, Alberto. *The Theatre of Production: Philosophy and Individuation Between Kant and Deleuze.* London: Palgrave Macmillan, 2006.

Turcescu, Lucian. "The Concept of Divine Persons in Gregory of Nyssa's *To His Brother Peter, On the Difference between Ousia and Hypostasis.*" *Greek Orthodox Theological Review* 42 (1997): 63-82.

————. *Gregory of Nyssa and the Concept of Divine Persons.* Oxford: Oxford University Press, 2005.

Turner, Denys. *The Darkness of God: Negativity in Christian Mysticism.* Cambridge: Cambridge University Press, 1995.

————. *Eros and Allegory.* Kalamazoo, MI: Cistercian Publications, 1995.

————. *Faith, Reason and the Existence of God.* Cambridge: Cambridge University Press, 2004.

Valliere, Paul. *Modern Russian Theology: Bukharev, Soloviev, Bulgakov — Orthodox Theology in a New Key.* Edinburgh: T. & T. Clark, 2000.

Van Fleteren, Frederick, Joseph C. Schnaubelt, and Joseph Reino, eds. *Collectanea Augustiniana. Augustine: Mystic and Mystagogue.* New York: Peter Lang, 1994.

Velde, Rudi A. te. *Participation and Substantiality in Thomas Aquinas.* Leiden: E. J. Brill, 1995.

————. "'The First Thing to Know about God': Kretzmann and Aquinas on the Meaning and Necessity of Arguments for the Existence of God." *Religious Studies* 39 (2003): 251-67.

Verdenius, W. J. "Traditional and Personal Elements in Aristotle's Religion." *Phronesis* 5 (1960): 56-70.

Vernet, François. "Gilbert de Poitiers," in *Dictionnaire de théologie catholique*. Paris: Librarie Letouzey et Ané, 1915, vol. 6, col. 1350-58.

Vicaire, M. H. "Les Porrétains et l'avicennisme avant 1215." *RSPT* 26 (1937): 449-82.

Vlastos, Gregory. "The Third Man Argument in the Parmenides." *Philosophical Review* 63 (1954): 319-49.

————. "Addenda to the TMA: Reply to Professor Sellars." *Philosophical Review* 64 (1955): 438-48.

————. "Postscript to the TMA: Reply to Professor Geach." *Philosophical Review* 65 (1956): 83-94.

————. "Plato's 'Third Man' Argument (*Parm.* 132A1-B2): Text and Logic." *Philosophical Quarterly* 19 (1969): 289-301.

————. "Reasons and Causes in the *Phaedo*." *Philosophical Review* 78 (1969): 291-325 (reprinted in Vlastos [1981], pp. 76-110).

————. *Platonic Studies: Collected Papers*. Princeton: Princeton University Press, 1981.

Vries, Josef de. "Das '*esse commune*' bei Thomas von Aquin." *Scholastik* 39 (1964): 163-77.

Walther, Manfred. "Philosophy and Politics in Spinoza." *St. Sp.* 9 (1993): 49-57.

Ward, Keith. *God: A Guide for the Perplexed*. Oxford: Oneworld, 2002.

Wéber, Édouard-Henri. "Eckhart et l'ontothéologisme: Histoire et conditions d'une rupture," in Zum Brunn et al., eds. (1984), pp. 13-83.

Weinandy, Thomas. *Does God Change?* Still River, MA: St. Bede's Publications, 1985.

————. *Does God Suffer?* Notre Dame: University of Notre Dame Press, 2000.

Weisheipl, James A. "Classification of the Sciences in Medieval Thought." *MS* 27 (1965): 54-90.

Wernick, Andrew. *Auguste Comte and the Religion of Humanity: The Post-Theistic Program of French Social Theory*. Cambridge: Cambridge University Press, 2001.

Westley, Richard J. "A Philosophy of the Concreted and the Concrete: The Construction of the Creatures according to Gilbert de la Porrée." *The Modern Schoolman* 37 (1960): 257-86.

Wey, Joseph C., ed. *Guillelmi de Ockham. Quodlibeta Septem*. St. Bonaventure, NY: Franciscan Institute, 1980. In *Opera Theologica*, vol. IX.

White, Nicolas P. "Aristotle on Sameness and Oneness." *Philosophical Review* 80 (1971): 177-97.

————. "Plato's Metaphysical Epistemology," in *The Cambridge Companion to Plato*. Edited by Richard Kraut. Cambridge: Cambridge University Press, 1992, pp. 277-310.

Whiting, Jennifer E. "Form and Individuation in Aristotle." *History of Philosophy Quarterly* 3 (1986): 359-77.

Wielockx, R. "A Separate Process against Aquinas: A Response to John F. Wippel," in Hamesse, ed. (1998), pp. 1009-30.

———. "Procédures contre Gilles de Rome et Thomas d'Aquin." *RSPT* 83 (1999): 293-313.

Wilbur, James B., ed. *Spinoza's Metaphysics: Essays in Critical Appreciation.* Assen: Van Gorcum & Co., 1976.

Williams, Anna N. "Mystical Theology Redux: The Patterns of Aquinas's *Summa Theologiae.*" *Modern Theology* 13 (1997): 53-74.

———. "Deification in the *Summa Theologiae:* A Structural Interpretation of the *prima pars.*" *The Thomist* 61 (1997): 219-55.

———. *The Ground of Union: Deification in Aquinas and Palamas.* Oxford: Oxford University Press, 1999.

Williams, Bernard A. O. "Descartes's Use of Skepticism," in Burnyeat, ed. (1983), pp. 337-52.

Williams, Michael E. "The Teaching of Gilbert Porreta on the Trinity as Found in His Commentaries on Boethius." *Analecta Gregoriana* 41 (1955), section B, pp. 1-130.

Williams, Rowan. "Politics and the Soul: A Reading of the City of God." *Milltown Studies* 19/20 (1987): 55-72.

———. "*Sapientia* and the Trinity: Reflections on the *De Trinitate,*" in Brunning et al., eds. (1990), pp. 317-32.

———. "The Paradoxes of Self-Knowledge in the *De Trinitate,*" in Lienhard et al., eds. (1993), pp. 121-34.

Williams, Thomas. "The Doctrine of Univocity Is True and Salutary." *Modern Theology* 21 (2005): 575-85.

Wilpert, Peter, ed. *Die Metaphysik im Mittelalter. Ihr Ursprung und ihre Bedeutung. MM,* vol. 2, Berlin: De Gruyter, 1963.

Wippel, John F. "Thomas Aquinas and the Condemnations of 1277." *The Modern Schoolman* 72 (1995): 233-72.

———. "Bishop Stephen Tempier and Thomas Aquinas: A Separate Process against Aquinas?" *Freiburger Zeitschrift für Philosophie und Theologie* 44 (1997): 117-36.

———. *The Metaphysical Thought of Thomas Aquinas: From Finite Being to Uncreated Being.* Washington, DC: Catholic University of America Press, 2000.

Wisnovsky, Robert. *Avicenna's Metaphysics in Context.* Ithaca, NY: Cornell University Press, 2003.

———. "Avicenna and the Avicennian Tradition," in *The Cambridge Companion to Arabic Philosophy.* Edited by Peter Adamson and Richard C. Taylor. Cambridge: Cambridge University Press, 2005, pp. 105-13.

Wolf, A., ed. *Correspondence of Spinoza.* Translated and edited with introduction and annotations by A. Wolf. London: Allen & Unwin, 1928.

Wolff, Christian. *Philosophia prima sive ontologia.* Edited by Jean Ecole. Hildesheim: Georg Olms, 1962.

———. *Philosophia rationalis sive logica.* Edited by Jean Ecole. Hildesheim: George Olms, 1983.

Wolfson, Harry A. *The Philosophy of the Church Fathers.* 3rd ed. Cambridge, MA: Harvard University Press, 1970.

Wolin, Sheldon S. *Democracy Incorporated: Managed Democracy and the Specter of Inverted Totalitarianism.* Princeton: Princeton University Press, 2008.

Wolter, Allan B. "The Ockhamist Critique," in McMullin, ed. (1963), pp. 124-46.

————. "John Duns Scotus (b. ca. 1265; d. 1308)," in Gracia, ed. (1994), pp. 271-98.

Wolter, Allan B., and Oleg Bychkov, eds. *Opus parisiense: The Examined Report of the Paris Lecture.* Latin text and English translation. St. Bonaventure, NY: Franciscan Institute, St. Bonaventure University, 2004.

Wood, Rega. "Individual Forms: Richard Rufus and John Duns Scotus," in Honnefelder et al., eds. (1996), pp. 251-72.

Woodruff, Paul. *Plato: Hippias Major.* Indianapolis: Hackett, 1982.

Woolhouse, Roger S. *Descartes, Spinoza, Leibniz: The Concept of Substance in Seventeenth Century Metaphysics.* London: Routledge, 1993.

Wulf, Maurice De. *Histoire de la philosophie médiévale.* 6th ed. Louvain: Institut Supérieur de Philosophie, 1924, vol. 1.

Yovel, Yirmiyahu, ed. *God and Nature: Spinoza's Metaphysics. Papers Presented at the First Jerusalem Conference (Ethica I).* Leiden: E. J. Brill, 1991.

————, ed. *Spinoza on Knowledge and the Human Mind. Papers Presented at the Second Jerusalem Conference (Ethica II).* Leiden: E. J. Brill, 1994.

————. "The Second Kind of Knowledge and the Removal of Error," in Yovel, ed. (1994), pp. 93-110.

————, ed. *Desire and Affect: Spinoza as Psychologist. Papers Presented at the Third Jerusalem Conference (Ethica III).* New York: Little Room, 1999.

Zac, Sylvain. *L'idée de vie dans la philosophie de Spinoza.* Paris: Presses Universitaires de France, 1963.

Zachhuber, Johannes. *Human Nature in Gregory of Nyssa: Philosophical Background and Theological Significance.* Leiden: E. J. Brill, 2000.

Zimmermann, Albert, ed. *Thomas von Aquin. Werk und Wirkung im Licht neuer Forschung. MM,* vol. 19. Berlin and New York: De Gruyter, 1988.

Žižek, Slavoj. *For They Know Not What They Do: Enjoyment as a Political Factor.* 2nd ed. London: Verso, 2002 (orig. pub. 1991).

Žižek, Slavoj, and John Milbank. *The Monstrosity of Christ: Paradox or Dialectic?* Edited by Creston Davis. Cambridge, MA: MIT Press, 2009.

Zizioulas, John D. *Being as Communion: Studies in Personhood and the Church.* Crestwood, NY: St. Vladimir's Seminary Press, 1985.

Zum Brunn, Emilie, Zénon Kaluza, Alain de Libera, Paul Vignaux, and Edouard-Henri Wéber, eds. *Maître Eckhart à Paris. Une critique médiévale de l'ontothéologie.* Les questions parisiennes no. 1 et no. 2 d'Eckhart. Paris: Presses Universitaires de France, 1984.

Index